SECURITY AND LAW

SECURITY AND LAW

Legal and Ethical Aspects of Public Security, Cyber Security and Critical Infrastructure Security

Anton VEDDER
Jessica SCHROERS
Charlotte DUCUING
Peggy VALCKE
(eds.)

intersentia
Cambridge – Antwerp – Chicago

KU LEUVEN CITIP
CENTRE FOR IT & IP LAW

Intersentia Ltd
Sheraton House | Castle Park
Cambridge | CB3 0AX | United Kingdom
Tel.: +44 1223 370 170 | Fax: +44 1223 370 169
Email: mail@intersentia.co.uk
www.intersentia.com | www.intersentia.co.uk

Distribution for the UK and Ireland:
NBN International
Airport Business Centre, 10 Thornbury Road
Plymouth, PL6 7 PP
United Kingdom
Tel.: +44 1752 202 301 | Fax: +44 1752 202 331
Email: orders@nbninternational.com

Distribution for Europe and all other countries:
Intersentia Publishing nv
Groenstraat 31
2640 Mortsel
Belgium
Tel.: +32 3 680 15 50 | Fax: +32 3 658 71 21
Email: mail@intersentia.be

Distribution for the USA and Canada:
Independent Publishers Group
Order Department
814 North Franklin Street
Chicago, IL60610
USA
Tel.: +1 800 888 4741 (toll free) | Fax: +1312 337 5985
Email: orders@ipgbook.com

Security and Law. Legal and Ethical Aspects of Public Security, Cyber Security and Critical Infrastructure Security

Cover image: Thatsaphon Saengnarongrat / Alamy Stock Photo

ISBN 978-1-78068-889-3
ISBN 978-1-78068-890-9 (PDF)
D/2019/7849/110
NUR 827

GPRC
Guaranteed
Peer Reviewed
Content

British Library Cataloguing in Publication Data. A catalogue record for this book is available from the British Library.

CONTENTS

LIST OF CONTRIBUTORS

All contributors are affiliated to the KU Leuven Centre for IT and IP law (CiTiP) and members of CiTiP's security research team.

Daniela Brešić completed her legal clerkship in the district of the Higher Regional Court Munich, after graduating from Ludwig-Maximilians-University Munich, Germany. She also obtained an LL.M. degree in Law and Technology from Tilburg University, the Netherlands.

Alessandro Bruni is focusing his research activities primarily on communication law and legal challenges related to new technologies such as Artificial Intelligence and blockchain. He obtained his degrees in Law at the University of Siena and at Tilburg University. He was affiliated to a civil society organisation on specific EU digital dossiers involving fundamental rights, to a consultancy group, dealing with cybersecurity matters, and to a European telecom operator as a Regulatory Officer.

Pierre Dewitte mainly focuses his research on Data Protection by Design, privacy engineering, smart cities and algorithmic transparency issues.

Charlotte Ducuing holds a master's degree in law with specialisation in European law, a master's degree in political sciences from the University Lille (Institut d'Etudes Politiques de Lille) and an LL.M. Intellectual Property and ICT Law from KU Leuven. As a PhD fellow, her main research interests extend to the regulation of emerging digital infrastructure in network industries.

Ivo Emanuilov is a PhD fellow in public international law working on the (in) adequacy of the concept of control in risk-based international law. His research is centered around problems of (shared) international responsibility, non-state actors, due diligence, risk analysis and new technologies in international humanitarian law, air and space law and cyber law. Ivo has degrees in international and EU law, English law, ICT law, and software engineering. He is a visiting lecturer on legal and ethical aspects of artificial intelligence at the University of Sofia and biometrics and privacy law at the Swiss Distance Learning University (UniDistance), Switzerland.

Stefano Fantin joined CITIP in 2017 after previous public sector and e-Government experiences. His research now covers various aspects of cybersecurity and accountability in the counter-terrorism and national security governance domains, as well as critical infrastructures protection and cyber defense policies. He is also an affiliated guest researcher at the Center for EU Policy Studies (CEPS).

Thomas Marquenie obtained his master's degree of Laws from the University of Leuven in 2015 and specialised in Criminal, International and European Law. In 2016, he obtained an Advanced Master's (LL.M.) in Intellectual Property Rights & ICT Law at the University of Leuven. At CiTiP, his research focuses on human rights and data protection as well as the legal aspects of Artificial Intelligence, security and law enforcement. He has contributed to several European Commission projects on the development and implementation of innovative police technologies, such as FP7 VALCRI and the ongoing H2020 MAGNETO, and is currently preparing a PhD project regarding fairness and accountability in law enforcement AI.

Yuliya Miadzvetskaya joined CiTiP in 2019, after having worked as an academic assistant at the College of Europe in Bruges. She also was trainee in the Legal Service of the European Parliament in Brussels and at the United Nations offices in Minsk.

Laurens Naudts is a doctoral researcher. His research focuses on the interrelationship between artificial intelligence, ethics, justice, fairness and the law. Laurens' doctoral research reconsiders the concepts of equality and data protection within the context of machine learning and algorithmically guided decision-making. Laurens has also been involved in several national and EU funded research projects, including amongst others iLINC and Preemptive, and, currently, VICTORIA (Video Analysis for Investigation of Criminal and Terrorist Activities). Laurens was formerly appointed as a researcher at the European University Institute (Centre for Media Pluralism and Media Freedom).

Domenico Orlando is currently involved in two projects about smart grids development (ROLECS and SNIPPET). He graduated in Business and Competition law at the Bocconi University and has an LL.M. in ICT law from the University of Oslo. He is interested in themes such as Security and Data Protection by Design and he focuses on data protection, cybersecurity and energy.

Danaja Fabčič Povše focuses her research activities on legal and ethical aspects of data security, data protection and privacy within organisations and in design processes.

Katherine Quezada is mainly working on the MAGNETO project within CiTiP. Her educational background includes an LL.B. from Universidad Autónoma de Santo Domingo (2013, homologated to the Spanish equivalent in 2017), a master's degree of Criminology and Criminal Justice from Universidad Camilo José Cela (2015) and an LL.M. in IP and ICT law from KU Leuven (2018–2020).

Jessica Schroers is a doctoral researcher at CiTiP. Her research focuses on data protection law and the legal issues related to identity management. She writes her doctoral thesis on the responsibility for electronic identity. Originally from Germany, she studied in the Netherlands at the University of Tilburg, where she obtained a bachelor's degree in Law and Management and Master's degrees in International Business Law and in Law and Technology. In 2009 she was an Erasmus exchange student at the University of Helsinki. Before joining CiTiP in 2013, Jessica completed an internship at a Dutch law firm where she focused on IT and intellectual property law.

Peggy Valcke is professor of technology and law at KU Leuven, CiTiP, and principal investigator at the Security & Privacy Group at imec (previously iMinds). She is also member of Leuven.AI (the Leuven Centre for Artificial Intelligence) and LICT (Leuven Centre on ICT). In previous years, she has taken up part-time or visiting professorships at Bocconi University in Milan; the European University Institute in Florence; Tilburg University; and Central European University in Budapest. Peggy has been assessor (member of the deciding body) of the Belgian Competition Authority and member of the General Chamber of the Flemish Media Regulator since 2008. She was a member of Google's Advisory Council on the Right to be Forgotten and of Digital Minds for Belgium, and also sits on the Scientific Committee of AI4People, the first global forum in Europe on the Social Impacts of Artificial Intelligence set up by Atomium-European Institute for Science, Media and Democracy.

Anton Vedder is a professor of IT Law at CiTiP. He is especially interested in the interplay of technological developments and the articulation of basic moral and legal concepts. Recent publications include articles and books on trust in e-health, innovative technologies, care, enhancement, and justice, privacy, data protection and profiling, ethics of artificial intelligence in a big data environment, and privacy versus public security. He is the academic director of KU Leuven's LL.M. program of IP and IT Law and a member of KU Leuven's Ethics Committee on Dual Use, Military Use and Misuse of Research.

Plixavra Vogiatzoglou is a doctoral researcher at CiTiP and a certified lawyer in Greece. Her main interests revolve around surveillance and criminal analytics, and their effects on fundamental rights, in particular privacy and data protection. Before joining CiTiP in January 2017, Plixavra obtained an LL.M. in Intellectual Property and ICT law from the Faculty of Law of KU Leuven and an LL.M. in International Studies from the Faculty of Law of Aristotle University of Thessaloniki.

CHAPTER 1

INTRODUCTION: SECURITY AND LAW IN A DIGITIZING WORLD

Charlotte DUCUING, Jessica SCHROERS and Anton VEDDER

Few people would doubt the importance of security of a state, society, its organizations and institutions, and individuals as an unconditional basis for personal and societal flourishing. Equally few people would deny being concerned by the often-occurring conflicts between security and other values and fundamental freedoms and rights, such as individual autonomy or privacy to name but a few. While the search for a balance between these public values is far from new, ICT and data-driven technologies have undoubtedly given it a new impulse. These technologies have a complicated and multifarious relationship with security.

Based on their knowledge discovery capacity – e.g. in the form of big data analysis – they are powerful tools in the hands of public authorities in charge of public and national security. In other words, they can have an instrumental function to security. Protection of citizens and individuals from abuses committed by public authorities having a monopoly of legitimate violence is far from new and has been a major task of the law, especially at national and EU levels. By significantly reinforcing the security public authorities, these new technologies may affect the balance of power to the detriment of citizens in many ways. There is a need for reconsidering the balance between the pursuit of public and national security, on the one hand, and the legitimate interests and fundamental rights of citizens, on the other.

Moreover, these new technologies have pervaded our daily environment to the point that they have become critical to the functioning of the economy and of society at large. Against this background, they themselves are increasingly perceived as requiring security, for example when they lie at the core of essential societal services such as healthcare, energy, education or mobility. Safeguarding the security of ICT and data-driven technologies is, however, a challenging endeavour. Amongst others, one has to deal with their inherent connectedness, which makes them liable to the 'least secured link of the chain' risk. The anonymity and global scale of the internet multiplies their risk exposure. Furthermore, while security is pursued to the benefit of all, who is or should be made responsible for achieving it remains a highly debated question. The public good features of security therefore require the law to regulate and allocate responsibilities. Simultaneously, however, the task of the law-maker is made difficult by four aspects of the nature of technologies: the often specialized expertise required to understand them, their fast pace of development, their border-crossing character, and the fact that they are mostly run and managed by private entities altogether. As a result, there is a need for reflection on the regulatory means which can be leveraged by the law-maker and the entities exactly to be made responsible for security, as well as the levels of organizations at which such obligations can best promote security.

The protection of ICT and data-driven technologies has been given various names and 'cybersecurity' seems to be the best-established. This term illustrates another connection between these technologies and security. 'Cybersecurity' would at first glance seem to point quite simply to security of 'cyber' assets and/or security in the cyber environment. Yet, cybersecurity appears to reach beyond 'security' strictly speaking. Cybersecurity was often found to lie at the crossroads of security and safety. The delineation of these two concepts has never been entirely clear, but the reliance of safety-critical products and services on ICT technologies has been bringing them even closer to each other. For instance, the reliance of transport means on ICT technologies simultaneously affects their sensitivity to external attacks on the one hand and can make them hazardous for users on the other hand. This calls for a more comprehensive management of risks and consequently has important legal consequences, such as the choice of the right regulatory instrument.

It is against the backdrop of this three-dimensional impact of ICT and big data technologies on security that this book discusses security and the law. In the midst of the on-going debates on security, the book combines theoretical discussion of the concepts at stake and case studies following the development of the technologies.

Part I sets the scene, by looking at the definition of security. On the one hand, security must be distinguished from neighbouring concepts. On the other hand, security itself is subject to sub-categories which, while they are of paramount importance to delineate the reach of the law, appear to be difficult to ascertain in practice such as the distinction between public and national security.

With the aim to define security in a technological environment, **part I** begins with "Safety, security, and ethics" (chapter 2), where **Anton Vedder** sets out to clarify definitions of security and safety and to analyse these notions as normative concepts. According to him, many recent authors on safety and security seem to agree – albeit often tacitly – that safety is primarily concerned with the adverse effects an entity might have on (the integrity of) the entities surrounding it, while security primarily is the unimpairedness of the integrity of the entity as such. Many authors, furthermore, distinguish between safety as controlling events caused by system malfunctions versus security as dealing with mitigating attacks by malicious agents. With the blending of the physical and virtual world through the Internet of Things, the notions of security and safety come to be used more and more interchangeably. This chapter thus informs the more sector-focused considerations on the increasing overlap of safety and security aspects in cybersecurity law, which can then be found in chapters 8 and 13 (introduced further below), respectively focusing on connected and autonomous road vehicles and aviation. Concerning security and safety as normative notions, Vedder claims that articulations and justifications of security and safety as value notions can build on objectivist need-consequentialist considerations. Security and safety policies and arrangements provide for the satisfaction of basic, social, and functional needs. Some protect life, health and shelter; some protect our institutions, some protect the facilities that make our lives comfortable. The benefits and burdens of policies and other arrangements for the protection of security and safety are not automatically distributed equally. This raises questions of distributive justice. The issues of distributive justice can overlap with the delicate fundamental issues of moral conflict in which the realization of a (proposed) policy or measure of security or safety protection collides with liberties or rights of individuals or specific groups. This chapter ends with the discussion of two alternative ways of approaching the resulting dilemmas.

The notion of 'security' is further discussed in chapter 3, where **Plixavra Vogiatzoglou** and **Stefano Fantin** focus on the delineation between national and public security ("National and public security within and beyond the Law Enforcement Directive"). During the drafting of Directive (EU) 2016/680 (so-called 'Data Protection Law Enforcement Directive' or in short 'DPLE Directive'), the major European data protection supervisory bodies raised their concerns as regards the scope of the Directive, and in particular the purpose of safeguarding public security. The Directive does not further define the notion of public security, while explicitly juxtaposing the concept with national security, as the latter is excluded from the scope of application of EU legislation. Several months after the official deadline for the national transposition of the Directive, this question has not been given any more thought. This chapter seeks to clarify the scope of the directive and the meaning of public security, first through the confrontation with the concept of national security, and then through the definition of competent authorities, as formulated in the text of the Directive and transposed into national law.

Part II questions whether and to what extent the law has been able to regulate the use of ICT and data-driven technologies *as a means to maintain, create or protect* *security* in search of a balance between security and other public values, such as privacy and equality. These technologies may be used by public authorities in charge of security. Interestingly, they may also be used by citizens as a means to 'fire back' and secure themselves from (perceived) intrusions and insecurity stemming from third parties or from the State (e.g. encryption). Both chapters 4 and 5 discuss under which legal conditions public authorities in charge of security may use these technologies, while keeping a balance with other public values. In chapter 4 "Criminal Profiling and Non-Discrimination: on firm grounds for the digital era?", **Laurens Naudts** focusses on the value of equality. He discusses the regulation of criminal profiling practices. He explains how, from a legal perspective, new forms of differentiation generated by data-driving analytics tools, might constitute illegal forms of discrimination. The DPLE Directive provides clear and concrete guidelines regarding the use of specific types of information in building profiles, indicating quite well when, and under what conditions, profiling practices could be allowed. Moreover, the Directive includes equality-sensitive considerations, noting the potential discriminatory nature data-driven techniques might have. It does so in particular where special categories of data are involved. Nevertheless, considering the requirement that profiling practices should not be discriminatory, public bodies should still consider the fundamental right to equality and non-discrimination as it has been enshrined in the European Convention of Human Rights, and as it has been interpreted by the European Court of Human Rights. The Court's case law is at times both complex and confusing. Through the open-ended phrasing of article 14, the Convention's non-discrimination clause can, in principle, allow the Court to condemn new forms of discrimination. Yet, the case law shows that the Court's reasoning might be ill-equipped to tackle the risks new technologies pose. Perhaps, so Naudts argues, a heightened level of awareness across society regarding the dangers that profiling techniques pose to the fundamental principles of equality and non-discrimination, could become a common ground amongst Member States and in turn increase the level of protection afforded to citizens in the case of criminal profiling.

In chapter 5 entitled "Operationalization of information security through compliance with Directive 2016/680 in law enforcement technology and practice", **Thomas Marquenie** and **Katherine Quezada** discuss the close connection between information security and data protection law in the law enforcement sector. Information security is the set of processes aimed at protecting information from unauthorized access, modification, use or destruction. At the basis of these practices lies the so-called CIA-triad which envisions the preservation of the Confidentiality, Integrity and Availability of information. While European Union legislation has previously covered specific aspects of these security principles, it has been marked by a limited scope of application and has not introduced extensive obligations in the law enforcement sector. This might now be subject to change with the adoption of the DPLE Directive. While not explicitly conceived as an information security instrument, the Directive nevertheless harmonizes data management practices and institutes numerous data protection requirements for criminal justice authorities and police agencies in the European Union. The purpose of this chapter is to analyze to what extent the fundamental principles of information security are reflected in the provisions of the Directive and whether law enforcement agencies can rely on their compliance with data protection law to adhere to the fundamental principles of information security. Following an analysis of the three tenets of information security, the chapter reviews the current legal framework on cybersecurity and data protection in order to examine the relationship between both disciplines and assess whether the Directive mandates high standards of security which correspond to the triad. This assessment concludes with an overview of a number of concrete measures identified in EU research projects serving as a case study of the practical implementation of legal requirements as a means of realizing information security in a law enforcement context. The findings of this chapter convey that while information security and data protection are separate concepts with a diverging scope of application and general purpose, there exists a significant overlap between the two and compliance with the Directive is expected to result in a standard of security that satisfies and conforms with the fundamental tenets of information security.

Data protection law is also discussed in other contributions of the book, although from different angles. Chapter 6 discusses whether EU data protection law – and especially the GDPR – can constitute an international legal standard for a legal right to encryption by data subjects. Chapter 10 discusses data protection law as an illustration of a growing pattern in EU law to impose 'compliance by design' obligations in the ICT environment.

Chapter 6 ("Protecting human rights through a global encryption provision") by **Danaja Fabčič Povše** concentrates on encryption as a security measure for citizens to defend themselves against (perceived) intrusions by third parties, including public authorities. The elementary texts of human rights law, such as the Universal Declaration of Human Rights, the International Covenant on Civil and Political Rights, the European Convention on Human Rights, and the EU Charter of Fundamental Rights all provide for the right to privacy, including privacy of communications, with the EU Charter also explicitly providing for the right to personal data protection. None of those, however, mentions explicitly the need for security – let alone encryption – measures. More detailed rules on data protection can be found in regional instruments. Fabčič Povše's chapter examines the EU framework (GDPR, ePrivacy Directive and the proposed ePrivacy Regulation), Convention 108 of the Council of Europe, the ECOWAS's Model Data Protection Act and the APEC Privacy Framework. The EU legal framework specifically refers to encryption as a security or data masking measure, whereas the other instruments require data security measures in general. Recommendations on encryption by the OECD and ENISA both explicitly argue for use of encryption in order to facilitate online commerce and data security. The OECD 1997 guidelines provide, however, for potential backdoors or plaintext access by law enforcement, which puts the strength of encryption in jeopardy. Lastly, ensuring a global encryption obligation is discussed – a global treaty, possibly under the United Nations or World Trade Organisation, is unlikely. As an alternative, globalisation of the GDPR or of the Convention 108+ is proposed, although such globalisation does not come without drawbacks. Should the states decide to maintain the status quo, further ripple effects of seemingly domestic policy are to be expected.

Part III investigates the regulatory means that are or can be leveraged by the law-maker in its attempt to 'secure' products, organizations or entities in a technological and multi-actor' environment. In order to feed this delicate 'how' question, this part includes two types of pieces. Some contributions analyse various sector-specific case studies, such as security and online identity management or connected transport means. Others provide horizontal background on regulatory means leveraged by the EU law-maker. For instance, the 'by design' approach is increasingly gaining traction in EU legislation and recently culminated with the adoption of the Cybersecurity Act (Regulation (EU) 2019/881) laying down the ground for EU-wide cybersecurity certification.

The first sectorial case study is provided by **Jessica Schroers** in her chapter 7, "Identity management and security". She discusses security aspects of identification and authentication technologies. She describes the different requirements a user has to comply with and challenges the over-responsabilization of the users inherent to these requirements. The level of expertise required to address the risks is rather high, and no only the individual but also the community can be affected by the risks involved. She takes a look at the standard of care in tort law. The standard of care is generally interpreted in terms of the standard of reasonable care, the care an average person would take. Further research into this 'care an average person would take' with regard to the electronic identification means and the environment they are used in, is therefore deemed to be necessary.

The concern about over-responsibilizing certain (weak) actors in the value chain illustrates a more general challenge in the ICT and data-driven technological environment. While these technologies are inherently interconnected, who should be burdened with the obligation to secure? This question also lies at the core of the following chapter, with regard to the cybersecurity in the connected and automated driving environment. The right allocation of cybersecurity responsibilities and the (sometimes unexpected) case for *shared responsibility* are discussed in chapter 9 dealing with the liability consequently arising from NIS obligations. They also lie at the core of the enquiry about the legal status of cybersecurity obligations in international air law in chapter 13.

In chapter 8 "Towards an obligation to secure connected and automated vehicles "by design"?", **Charlotte Ducuing** provides another sectoral case-study. Road transport is undergoing significant changes by data-driven technologies. Two technological developments are especially visible, namely the development towards automated and autonomous driving on the one hand and the growing connected character of vehicles on the other. Both developments are increasingly converging for technical reasons but also for reasons of road safety, environment-friendly mobility and optimization of the use of infrastructure and vehicle capacity. They are referred to together here as 'connected and automated mobility' (CAM). CAM has a paradoxical relation to safety. Road safety constitutes one of the main political motives for moving to CAM. But increased connectivity and automation – or even autonomy – of vehicles will also result in increasing cybersecurity sensitivity. Both the European Union and the UNECE at an international level are active in revising type-approval legislation so as to include cybersecurity as part of vehicle safety requirements. The purpose of this book chapter is to evaluate whether and to what extent type-approval legislation, and the 'by design' approach at its heart, are fit for the purpose of ensuring cybersecurity of CAM vehicles. To do so, Ducuing analyses the two recently proposed recommendations of UNECE dealing with cybersecurity of CAM vehicles, as part of vehicle technical regulations, which interestingly reflect the changing nature of vehicles when growing in connectivity and autonomy.

Chapter 8 analyses the intrinsic limitations of the 'security by design' approach in the complex field of connected and automated vehicles. The discussion surrounding the 'by design' regulatory approach reverberates in several other chapters. Chapter 5 discusses the interactions between the data protection by design approach in the DPLE Directive and the discipline of information security. 'Security by design' is contemplated in chapter 7 as a potential factor in the assessment of a required standard of care in the field of identity management. Finally, chapter 10 is entirely dedicated to the 'by design' approach in both cybersecurity and data protection law, both being often intertwined.

After the sectoral case-studies in chapters 7 and 8, the remaining chapters of Part III provide horizontal analysis of cybersecurity legal frameworks, and especially aim to assess the regulatory 'toolbox' used by the EU law-maker. In chapter 9, "The cybersecurity requirements for operators of essential services under the NIS Directive – An analysis of potential liability issues from an EU, German and UK perspective", **Daniela Brešić** provides an overview of responsibilities and potential liability issues that may occur in the context of critical infrastructure protection for operators of essential services. She pays special attention to the NIS Directive as the first legislative initiative enhancing cybersecurity protection for the EU, and to the implementation of the Directive into national legislation in Germany and the United Kingdom. Her chapter concludes with a deliberation on potential drawbacks in terms of a shared responsibility between stakeholders, as well as on liability and critical infrastructure protection from a broader perspective.

The NIS Directive is also critically discussed in chapter 11 as one of the main components of EU cybersecurity legislation. In chapter 13, the NIS Directive is referred to as a measurement standard with regard to the qualification of a service as "essential", from an international law perspective.

In chapter 10 "The 'by Design' Turn in EU Cybersecurity Law: Emergence, challenges and ways forward", **Domenico Orlando** and **Pierre Dewitte** analyse the 'by Design' turn in the EU security and data protection legislative frameworks. The 'by design' approach in EU legislation is on the rise. Both data protection and cybersecurity law are involved in this trend, with the former ahead. After an introduction on definitions, the chapter describes the steps made by security by design, its focus in gaining attention and consideration in EU and soft law. Finally, the authors assess the challenges posed for consistent and effective development of the concept of 'by design' in general and of 'security by design' in particular.

Chapter 11 by **Alessandro Bruni** evaluates the regulatory initiatives from the EU institutions in the field of cybersecurity and pleads for "Promoting coherence in the EU cybersecurity strategy". Bruni explains how the commitment of the European Union to establish secure and trustworthy cyberspace resulted in two different but complementary European cybersecurity strategies. He explains why their coherence has been questioned and which factors have hampered the development of a coherent EU cybersecurity strategy. In his chapter, he intends to understand the impact, if any, of key elements and actors, namely, the EU cybersecurity agency ENISA and the role of public-private partnerships in the development of EU cybersecurity. By doing so, this chapter intends to assess if the progress that has been made that EU cybersecurity legislation can be labelled as coherent.

The final **part IV** discusses international aspects of ICT. On the one hand, their global, border-crossing, character requires appropriate international response to secure the EU. On the other hand, cybersecurity can represent an international collective good, especially in the case of safety-sensitive assets (e.g. aviation). In chapter 12, **Yuliya Miadzvetskaya** analyses the new regime concerning restrictive measures against cyber-attacks as a new tool of the EU Cyber diplomacy toolbox, in her contribution "Challenges of the cyber sanctions regime under the Common Foreign and Security Policy (CFSP)". She sheds some light on the main shortcomings for the efficient implementation of sanctions, notably relating to a spectrum of challenges, such as a problem of technical and political attribution of cyber-attacks, the lack of EU's common approach and will to name perpetrators and fundamental rights issues assessed on a case-by-case basis by the ECJ in sanctions related case-law.

Ivo Emanuilov discusses in chapter 13 cybersecurity obligations in public international law. "International (cyber)security of the global aviation critical infrastructure as a community interest" investigates whether cybersecurity obligations in the field of aviation can be considered as a 'community interest'. The international aviation system has become increasingly interconnected as a result of the proliferation of systems operated by both traditional stakeholders and new entrants. Civil aviation's critical infrastructure has therefore become exposed to an ever-growing number of physical, cyber and hybrid threats. While the Convention on International Civil Aviation and its Annexes have established a comprehensive and largely harmonised international legal framework of safety rules for civil aviation, the same cannot be said in so far as aviation (cyber) security is concerned. Cyber-attacks have unquestionably been considered an offence against the principles and arrangement for the safe and orderly development of the international civil aviation. While it has been argued that states have due diligence obligations under international law to prevent harmful international cyber operations, the nature and scope of these obligations in modern civil aviation is not always clear-cut. Furthermore, the extent and content of the obligations to ensure the (cyber)security of aviation critical infrastructure. This determination is further complicated by the emergence of a transnational (global) aviation critical infrastructure which exists across borders and which comprises a complex network of physical, virtualised and cyber components. This contribution aims to ascertain whether and in which cases States could be argued to bear primary obligations in international law to ensure the (cyber)security of such global aviation critical infrastructure. It also seeks to explore the source and nature of these obligations under public international law and asserts the view that the safety and certain safety-critical aspects of (cyber)security could plausibly be construed as being reflective of an interest of the international community as a whole. In light of virtualisation of physical infrastructure and the emergence of new categories of cyber(-physical) infrastructure, Emanuilov argues that this community interest could only be protected effectively by *erga omnes* obligations so as to ensure the continued "safe and orderly development" of international civil aviation.

CHAPTER 2
SAFETY, SECURITY AND ETHICS

Anton VEDDER*

1. INTRODUCTION

What are safety and security? Why should we value safety and security? These questions may sound redundant at first sight. Are safety and security not to be considered as elementary conditions for a minimally functioning human being? Exactly because of this apparent self-evidence, policy and law makers, as well as researchers of the legal dimensions or technical or economic aspects of safety and security might benefit from a more precise understanding of the concepts and the normative starting points behind them. This is especially so where specific measures or policies for ensuring or protecting safety and security must be balanced against other values or principles. In this chapter, the notions of security and safety will be clarified as normative concepts from an analytical ethical perspective. In the next section, current discussions on the definitions and conceptual distinctions with regards to the notion of security and the related notion of safety will be discussed. In section 3, the focus will be on security and safety as values. In section 4, the possibility of moral conflicts between safety and security on the one hand and individual rights and interests on the other, will be discussed.

2. DEFINITIONS AND DISTINCTIONS

Although the notions of safety and security have received an occasional modest dose of attention during the last decades from the side of philosophers in some subdomains of applied ethics, such as technology ethics and medical ethics,[1]

* Special thanks are due to Margaret Warthon, research intern at the KU Leuven Centre for IT and IP Law 2018–19, for her support with bibliographical research.

1 Of course, security and safety play important substantial normative roles in the development of technologies and in the regulatory field of standardization. The claim here merely concerns conceptual analysis.

they have been most intensively debated in philosophy of law[2] and in a branch of practical philosophy, perhaps best referred to as normative political theory. So-called "realist" or "neo-realist" political theorists – from Thucydides, over Machiavelli, Hobbes, Morgenthau to Waltz – start from the assumption that as individual human beings are fundamentally selfish and driven by a lust for power, only (voluntary) subjection to a sovereign state that is able to provide protection can offer security and safety for one individual from intrusions by others or for one state from others. In the controversies among realists themselves and in the debates between realists and their opponents, the notions of safety and security have therefore been articulated primarily on deep theoretical levels as global value-laden characteristics of individuals and of societies or states overall.[3] As a consequence, there exists an understandable tendency of philosophers when reflecting on the concepts of safety and security to treat these first and foremost as global concepts, indicating the overall security or safety of either individuals or societies or states. Walt defines the notion of security as such a global dimension when he claims that security is the "preservation of the state territorial integrity and the physical safety of its inhabitants," meaning that a state is secure when it is able to defend itself from hostile attacks and prevent other states from compelling it to adjust its behaviour in significant ways or to sacrifice important political values.[4] Focusing on the differences between security and safety, Rigterink contends that safety is the individual state of freedom from threats while security is the collective state of freedom from threats.[5]

Over the last decades, the theoretical debate on security and safety has incrementally expanded in scope and is slowly seeping into other fields than political philosophy. Boholm *et al.*, Ceccorulli and Lucarelli, Balzacq *et al.* have contributed to the debate with intricate linguistic and semantic analyses on the notions in general.[6] Especially in connection with technology, the interest in

---

2 See also section 3.1 in the chapter by Plixavra Vogiatzoglou and Stephano Fantin in this volume.

3 Lawrence Freedman, 'The concept of security' Encyclopedia of Government and Politics (2nd edn, 2003).

4 Stephen Martin Walt, 'Realism and Security' Oxford Research Encyclopedia of International Studies (2010) <https://oxfordre.com/internationalstudies/view/10.1093/acrefore/9780190846626.001.0001/acrefore-9780190846626-e-286> accessed 25 June 2019.

5 Anouk Rigterink, 'Does Security Imply Safety? On The (Lack of) Correlation Between Different Aspects of Security' (2015) (4) Stability: International Journal of Security & Development <http://doi.org/10.5334/sta.fw> accessed 24 June 2019.

6 Max Boholm, Niklas Möller, Sven Ove Hansson, 'The Concepts of Risk, Safety, and Security: Applications in Everyday Language' (2016) 36 Risk Analysis <https://doi 10.1111/risa.12464> accessed 24 June 2019; Michela Ceccorulli, Sonia Lucarelli, 'Security governance: making the concept fit for the analysis of a multipolar, global and regionalized world' 2014 41 Global Governance Programme-98; European, Transnational and Global Governance <http://hdl.handle.net/1814/31282> accessed 25 June 2019; Thierry Balzacq, Sarah Léonard, Jan Ruzicka "Securitization' revisited: theory and cases' (2016) 30 International Relations <https://doi.org/10.1177/0047117815596590> accessed 24 June 2019.

the conceptual aspects of the two notions and their differences in respect of one another has grown. A clear and consistent line with regards to the definitions and the differentiation of security, on the one hand, and safety, on the other, cannot be discerned in recent scholarly literature. It is, however, important to note from the outset that underlying many different explanations of the differences between the terms of security and safety is a tacit distinction. This distinction is one between:

- security as unimpaired integrity of an entity itself, e.g., of a technical device, communication, a society, or a state, et cetera, from external risks and dangers, and
- safety as the absence of harmfulness or possible adverseness of such an entity to persons, their health, or economic or environmental situation.

In line with this implicit definition and distinction are for example Maurice who defines security as the status of being protected from harm caused by intentional human actions or behaviours, and safety as the state of being protected from harm caused by accidental technical failure or human mistake,[7] and Heinz Peter Berg who contends that the safety of critical infrastructures such as nuclear infrastructures implies the protection of workers, the population and the environment against harm caused by accidents or radiological incidents.[8] Sametinger *et al.* also remain within this same line of thought with regards to the medical sector when they claim that safety "is about the protection of a device's environment, i.e., mainly the patient, from the device itself". According to them, a manufacturer will make sure that the device does not harm the patient, e.g., by not using toxic substances in implants or by careful development of an insulin pump's software. They also contend that security "is about the protection of the device from its environment, i.e., just the opposite to safety".[9]

Further distinctions come in broad varieties and seem to be inspired by particularities of the types of situations or technologies that form the main subject of consideration of the authors involved. In relation to safety, risk is

---

7 Pierre Maurice, 'Safety and safety promotion: definitions for operational developments' (2001) 8 Injury Control and Safety Promotion 238 <https://pdfs.semanticscholar.org/363d/81922697730c2ab49cca4f903d03ffe352b3.pdf> accessed 25 June 2019.

8 Heinz-Peter Berg, 'Safety and Security of Critical Infrastructures with regard to nuclear facilities' in I Žutautaitė, M Eid, K Simola, V Kopustinskas (eds) *Critical Infrastructures: Enhancing Preparedness & Resilience for the Security of Citizens and Services Supply Continuity. Proceedings of the 52nd ESReDA Seminar.* Lithuanian Energy Institute & Vytautas Magnus University (2017) <https://www.researchgate.net/profile/Mohamed_Eid19/publication/321027342_EUR_28803_EN_proceedings_52nd_esreda_seminar/links/5a097329aca272ed27a020f3/EUR-28803-EN-proceedings-52nd-esreda-seminar.pdf#page=64> accessed on 10 June 2019.

9 Johannes Sametinger, Jerzy Rozenblit, Roman Lysecky, Peter Ott, 'Security Challenges for Medical Devices' 2015 58 Communications of the ACM <https://www.se.jku.at/wp-content/uploads/2015/03/TR-SE-15.03.pdf> accessed 10 June 2019.

sometimes considered to be the eventual occurrence of unintentional events, while in security contexts risks are deemed to involve intentional malicious events. Amundrud and Flage define safety and security both as being without unacceptable risk and as antonyms of risk.[10]

Nicklas *et al.* argue that safety and security as key concepts in the protection of critical infrastructure have a common goal, i.e., the protection of individuals, society and the environment. The authors, however, further argue that security is often defined as a state of protection against deliberate threat, while safety should be considered as being unaffected by hazards: "Safety functions are designed to protect users from hazards, e.g. an accident. Security functions protect the system and its contents against attacks like an intentional misuse." In mixed cyber- and physical systems these functions often conflict, according to the authors, since "for reasons of safety, redundancies are designed to ensure safety in dangerous situations. Simultaneously these redundancies should not be implemented for reasons of security, because they result in additional attack vectors. Consequently, safety and security functions affect each other."[11] In the same vein, Nigam, Pretschner and Ruess stipulate that while safety is associated with "controlling catastrophic events caused by system malfunctions", security deals with "mitigating attacks by malicious agents to the system".[12] Serpanos and Wolf claim that the concepts of security and safety have traditionally been developed separately and in different domains. They think, however, that the evolution of integrated cyber-physical systems and the Internet of Things require both terms to be treated jointly, or rather in a "unified" manner.[13]

To sum up, the notions of security and safety traditionally play key roles in normative political theory, where they refer to individuals' or societies' overall dimensions of being unimpaired by the selfishness and power-lust of other individuals or other states. Concerning the distinction between safety and security, recent scholarly contributions have been far from unanimous. Underlying many explanations seems to be a tacit assumption, however, that safety is primarily concerned with the adverse effects which any entity might have on the integrity of human individuals or its environment in general, while

---

10 Øystein Amundrud, Terje Aven, Roger Flage 'How the definition of security risk can be made compatible with safety definitions' (2017) 3, Proceedings of the Institution of Mechanical Engineers, Part O: Journal of Risk and Reliability < https://doi.org/10.1177/1748006X17699145> accessed 24 June 2019.

11 Jan-Peter Nicklas, Michel Mamrot, Petra Winzer, Daniel Lichte, Stefan Marchlewitz, Kai-Dietrich) Wolf, 'Use case based approach for an integrated consideration of safety and security aspects for smart home applications' (2016) 11th System of Systems Engineering Conference (SoSE) Kongsberg <https://ieeexplore.ieee.org/stamp/stamp.jsp?tp=&arnumber=7542908> accessed 25 June 2019.

12 Vivek Nigam, Alexander Pretschner, Harald Ruess, 'Model-Based Safety and Security Engineering' (2019) ArXiv <https://arxiv.org/pdf/1810.04866.pdf> accessed 10 June 2019.

13 Dimitrios Serpanos, Marilyn Wolf, *Internet-of-Things (IoT) Systems – Architectures, Algorithms, Methodologies*, (Springer 2018).

security primarily is a dimension of integrity of the entity as such. With the introduction of the Internet of Things, where cyber- and physical environments are merging, e.g., in connected medical devices, in aviation, or in connected and automated vehicles, the notions of security and safety come to be used more and more interchangeably or exactly in order to refer to different aspects of one and the same dimension, as security flaws may more often than not be the flip-side of safety risks and vice versa.

3. SECURITY AND SAFETY AS VALUES IN ETHICS AND NORMATIVE POLITICAL THEORY

Notwithstanding their centuries-old elementary roles in philosophy of law and political theory, substantial analyses and positive ethical arguments in favour of the protection of the values of security and safety are rather scarce. Security and safety can not only – like all normative notions – be characterized as essentially contested concepts, meaning that the search will always have to be for the *for the time being* most adequate definition and not for the conclusively most adequate one[14]; they also are on a more practical, concrete level, relatively under-exposed concepts in ethics and normative political theory as topics in their own right. They often figure as the counterpart of values or normative starting points centred around the individual, such as autonomy, privacy, and data protection in debates on value conflicts between individualist and collectivist value notions, e.g. privacy versus public security. Whereas in these debates, however, a lot of attention is paid to the conflicting values and rights, security and safety as such receive relatively little attention as independent values. Nonetheless these discussions can give us indirectly some insights in the ways in which safety and security function as values (see section 4 of this chapter). Before focusing on that type of debates, however, it is important, first, to consider security and safety under their dimensions of public goods and common goods, and, second, to delve a little deeper into the typical valuable aspects of security and safety.

The notions of security and safety are often referred to as *public goods*, because the benefits of a safety or security protection measure to one person often cannot be completely individuated from those to another, while the burdens and benefits of safety and security measures affect different individuals and sub-groups of a population often in different manners. In economic theory, a public good is often defined as a type of good that members of a community would not possess if they were each motivated only by their own self-interest. The problem posed by a public good in economic theory is that the optimal course of action for each individual, from the vantage point of egoistic rationality, is not to

14 Walter Bryce Gallie, 'Essentially Contested Concepts' vol 56 (Proceedings of the Aristotelian Society, 1956) 167.

contribute to the provision of the good, even though everyone would be better off if they all would do so.[15] The notion of a *common good* refers to the interests that members have in common or to the facilities that serve common interests. Relevant facilities and interests together constitute the common good and generally serve as a more or less shared perspective for political deliberation, as Hussain puts it.[16] In both academic and non-academic discussions, people often refer to the common good as if it were a public good in the economic sense of those words. Although sophisticated distinctions can be made between the two notions,[17] the subject will not be dwelled on too extensively. What is important to keep in mind, is that the common good or a public good may be a benefit for society as a whole but not a net benefit to all individual members of society alike or in the same manner and that it may moreover conflict with individual rights and interests.

Safety and security, taken here for the time being as being protected from hazards and attacks, may be considered both public goods and substantial constituents of the common good. Both characterizations remind us (1) that safety and security measures may be important beneficial assets to society, while each individual member of that society might overall be better-off with a situation in which all of the other members of society contribute to it except for him- or herself, and (2) that individuals may have to contribute to the safety and security measures that are a benefit to society as a whole, whereas they themselves are not sharing in that benefit (to the same degree as others), or, even worse, have their interests or rights harmed or infringed by it. This raises not only complicated, deeply fundamental ethical questions concerning the moral conflicts involved that may ultimately hinge on the opposition between collectivist and individualist ethical outlooks, such as communitarian or utilitarian versus deontological approaches. It also gives rise to challenges concerning distributive justice: who exactly benefits from particular forms or instantiations of safety and security protection? Whose security and safety are we concerned with, and which sacrifices are acceptable to ask of individuals or societal groups in order to achieve them? These issues will be discussed in the next section.

Why are security and safety worth protecting or promoting? Which aspects of security and safety make these values so important? As was mentioned at the beginning of this chapter, raising this question sounds somehow superfluous. Although philosophers have the reputation of leaving nothing unquestioned, the exact reasons behind security and safety as values have not received much

---

15 Mancur Olson, *The Logic of Collective Action: Public Goods and the Theory of Groups*, (revised edition, Harvard University Press 1971).

16 Waheed Hussain, 'The Common Good' *The Stanford Encyclopedia of Philosophy* (Spring edn, 2018) <https://plato.stanford.edu/archives/spr2018/entries/common-good/> accessed 10 June 2019.

17 Ibid.

philosophical attention, except for general acclaim of their conditionality for many other values. Although for the ethical justification of security and safety protection measures and policies doubtlessly many intricate utilitarian arguments can be delivered, reflection on security and safety as values probably best starts with the works of a group of ethical theorists, often referred to as "need-consequentialists" such as Thomson, Wiggins and Braybrooke. Not only are their theories intuitively very appealing; as will become clear from references to recent work on security and safety in the course of this section, most of the views put forward in the recent and current debates on safety and security seem to come very close to the fundamental contentions of need-consequentialism. Need-consequentialists represent so-called objectivist value theories, which define or stipulate the good without taking the desires, preferences or personal conceptions of the good of individuals as their starting point. They claim that morality has an objective basis in reality in the form of basic, functional and social needs of human beings. This objectivism is often contrasted with the value subjectivism of for instance utilitarianism – also a branch of consequentialism, but one in which the central notion of utility is ultimately based on individual preferences. The claim for objectivity of need-consequentialism is sometimes criticized for denying or at least not taking into account the fact that needs do not speak for themselves but are always interpreted by human beings.[18] And indeed, one of the strong points of need consequentialism seems to be exactly the fact that they start from the quasi self-evidence of the normativity of needs. On the basis of this quasi self-evidence, need-consequentialists will – probably rightfully so – doubt the rational capacities of people who would claim that the moral desirability of feeding a hungry baby or sheltering it and protecting it from the cold or from fierce sunshine cannot be positively argued for. Since the objectivism-versus-subjectivism debate is not our primary concern here, we will leave that issue aside. It is worth noting, however, that the very few participants in the debate on possible conflicts between security, safety and individualist values such as autonomy and privacy, who try to provide the values of security and safety with some context, mostly tend to refer to utilitarianism as their natural habitat.[19] They thereby seem to overlook the aspect of (apparent) self-evidence of the value notions, which is much closer to the objectivism inherent to need-consequentialism, than to the subjectivism of utilitarianism.

The issue of self-evidence is a very relevant one for the purposes of this chapter. Need-consequentialists generally claim that human well-being minimally consists of the satisfaction of certain basic needs. A stereotypical conception of basic needs refers to biology and defines good in terms of sustainment of life and the possession and integrity of bodies, bodily parts, etc.

18 Brian Barry *Political Argument* (Routledge and Kegan Paul 1965) 47–49.

19 Mireille Hildebrandt, 'Balance or Trade-off? Online Security Technologies and Fundamental Rights' (2013) 26 Philosophy and Technology 357–379.

Normally, as was already suggested, proponents of this view are of the opinion that the duty to satisfy these needs does not call for further justification. Other things or states of affairs are considered goods insofar as they contribute to the satisfaction of basic needs. This kind of value theory automatically entails an urgency thesis: the more an asset or commodity contributes to satisfying basic needs, the more urgent it is for persons having the needs.[20] Because in modern welfare societies there is of course an abundance of all kinds of alternative means to provide, obtain or remain in possession of the things which according to this criterion are considered to be elementary goods, objectivist theorists of this kind often supply further criteria which see to the satisfaction of needs to be met in order to live by and large the kind of life which is actually lived by the average citizen of the society at stake. Basic needs then become a function of the general living standards of the community involved, yielding norms like 'subsistence level', 'decent standard of living' etc.[21] Sometimes, in addition to these, extra criteria are stated that must be satisfied in order to fulfil functions or tasks, defined within and through social constellations, such as those of parents, heads of families, workers, citizens etc., as well as criteria concerning the level of satisfaction of such basic, social and functional needs.[22]

Clearly, advocacy of protective measures regarding security and safety can build on objectivist need-consequentialist considerations of the latter kind. Security and safety policies and arrangements in our societies, e.g. military, police, medical and other services, see directly or indirectly to the satisfaction of basic needs, social needs or functional needs. Some protect life, health and shelter; some protect our institutions, our educational system, our economy, our democracy, in short: the better part of our way of life. Many of the relevant policies and arrangements aim to satisfy in part basic biological needs and in part social or functional needs, simultaneously. Military services may protect people from being killed; but they may also protect democratic institutions and a certain level of welfare. Cyber security measures protecting critical infrastructures for the provision of energy against attacks by hackers, may help to protect people from life threatening cold, but also enable them to live their lives comfortably according to the relevant standards in their societies.

This also explains why Nyman argues that the 'positive' or 'negative' postures given to the term security are confusing. While in the analytical and normative frame of security in its negative form, security is defined as the absence of threat and avoidance of something "bad", a positive version would be put in terms

---

20 Garrett Thomson, *Needs.* (Routledge and Kegan Paul, 1988) 77–89, 98–107, 121–122, 125–128; David Wiggins, *Needs, values, truth. Essays in the philosophy of value.* (Aristotelian Society series vol. 6, Blackwell, 1987) 48–49, 60–67, 117–121.

21 Stanley Isaac Benn, Richard Stanley Peters, *Social principles and the democratic state.* (Allen and Unwin 1975) 142–147.

22 David Braybrooke, *Meeting Needs* (Princeton University Press 1987) 48–49, 60–67, 117–121.

of conditions for human well-being.[23] Jeremy Waldron argues that national security in particular protects not the mere survival but a way of life that is shared by many in society. Waldron understands this way of life as a "common reservoir of values" which includes the protection of certain individual rights and liberties for "meaningful exercise".[24] When discussing conflicts between security and safety on the one hand and individual rights on the other, this view will be returned to.

The protection of ways of life is a relevant important ingredient for the justification of security and safety measures in many sectors, such as the security of energy supplies, hospital systems, and migration control, among many others. National security policies gradually focus more on networks and computer systems than on national territory. We depend on networks and computer infrastructures of critical infrastructures for the exercise of freedoms through which we form our ways of life and perform our "normal" daily activities.[25] This is why energy, transport and information systems are considered essential or critical services. If these systems are attacked, our standard ways of living are interfered with, possibly causing dramatic physical, psychological, or financial damage and considerable harm to the institutions substantiating democracy and the rule of law.[26]

4. SECURITY AND SAFETY IN CONFLICT

In the aftermath of the dramatic terrorist attacks at the beginning of this millennium, a debate flared up involving ethicists, political philosophers, legal scholars, and law and policy makers, on conflicts between public security and safety on the one hand and individual rights and liberties, such as the right to privacy and the right to data protection, on the other. Of course, the subject of the debate is a subspecies of the more generic issue of conflicts between the realization of public interests and the protection of the interests and rights of individuals and minorities. In most of these conflicts we are confronted with intangibles on both sides. Public interests to be realized may represent the most attractive perspectives, but still have to be realized, while the measures taken to realize the objective must yet prove their efficacy. Simultaneously, at the other

---

23 Jonna Nyman, 'What is the value of security? Contextualising the negative/positive debate' (2016) 42 Review of International Studies <https://doi.org/10.1017/S0260210516000140> accessed 24 June 2019.

24 Jeremy Waldron, 'Safety and Security' (2006) 85 Nebraska Law Review 454.

25 Mike Bourne, *Understanding Security*. (Macmillan International Higher Education 2013) 88.

26 Claudia Aradau, 'Security that matters: Critical infrastructure and objects of protection' (2010) 41 Security Dialogue <https://doi.org/10.1177/0967010610382687> accessed 24 June 2019; Myriam Dunn Cavelty and Kristian Søby Kristensen, *Securing the homeland: critical infrastructure, risk and (in)security* (Routledge, 2008) 1.

horn of the dilemma, the infringements of a right, e.g. the right to privacy, can be serious and significant, but nonetheless its impact can often be specified only with great difficulties.

As was suggested earlier on, security and safety on the one hand and liberties on the other are generally conceived of as very different types of values or even as incompatible concepts, due to the fact that they fit better with different moral outlooks: safety and security seem to be more related to outlooks that warm to collectivity, e.g., communitarianism, utilitarianism and need-consequentialism, whereas rights of the individual are closer to outlooks in which the individual is key, such as in deontological, Kantian theories. The problem of these moral outlooks is that they may be overlapping and reconcilable to a large degree, but not completely. In the end, they rest on irreconcilable normative views of the relationship between individuals and minorities on the one hand, and majorities and society as a whole, on the other. Many of us nowadays are – mostly unwittingly – ethical eclectics reasoning now with deontological premises, then with utilitarian ones, and then again with communitarian ones. Thanks to the overlap between them, this often does not lead us into irresoluble dilemmas. Problems occur exactly where we are confronted with bifurcations of individual-regarding considerations and collectivity-regarding ones. To the degree that the conflicting views are really substantially irreconcilable, not much more can be done than take a somewhat agnostic, pragmatic approach by respecting both horns of the dilemma and by asking: can the security or safety objective be achieved by means that impact the right or liberty involved less significantly than the one proposed? And: can the security or safety objective be achieved at all or at least to large degree by the measures proposed? By answering the less impacting alternatives and efficacy questions a decision can be reached that of course does not resolve the ethical dilemma, but nonetheless seems to be the best achievable reasonable way of coming to terms with the fundamental inconsistencies of the late modern or post-modern moral mind.

Concerning the conflict between security, safety and individual liberties, Hildebrandt claims that requests for giving up some of our liberty to achieve security have a rhetorical ring fitting "the political agenda" because of the utilitarian considerations that she believes to be behind the security objective.[27] Interestingly, Faden and Shebaya discuss the typically prospective nature of security measures and policies and, consequently, the uncertainties concerning their efficiency and efficacy. They consider this to be an important obstacle for policy and law makers who want to account for their (proposed) security policies and laws.[28] Be this, as it may be, Jeremy Waldron seems to offer a much

---

[27] Mireille Hildebrandt, 'Balance or Trade-off? Online Security Technologies and Fundamental Rights' (2013) 26 Philosophy and Technology 357–379.

[28] Ruth Faden and Sirine Shebaya, 'Public Health Ethics' *The Stanford Encyclopedia of Philosophy* (Winter edn, 2016) <https://plato.stanford.edu/archives/win2016/entries/public health-ethics/> accessed 10 June 2019.

more promising approach by not focusing on rhetorics and not restricting himself to the minimalist approach of applying less impacting alternatives and efficacy questions.[29] Waldron suggests that we go some steps further than just concluding that there are simply some basic irreconcilabilities at work in the *prima facie* conflicts. He argues that security and liberties should not be treated as completely incommensurable values. Fundamental liberties require security for their meaningful exercise; but also protecting our way of life does not make much sense if our liberties are treated as insignificant.[30] Moreover, touching on the issue of the distribution of benefits and burdens of security and safety protection policies and measures, Waldron claims that important values should not be maximized without paying any attention to their distribution. The balance between *prima facie* conflicting values should be "governed and constrained by egalitarian principles".[31] Extensive critical assessment of Waldron's claims would go far beyond the purposes of this chapter. His ideas about the practical connections between security, safety and individual liberties and rights – and we might want to add: the institutions typical of the democratic state and the state governed by the rule of law – *via* the notion of ways of life, however, seem to offer at least a promising way out of the dilemma as it does more justice to the intricate connections between security, safety and liberties and fundamental rights than the minimalist approach discussed in the previous paragraph. Whether this approach in the end can do completely without the auxiliary questions of less impacting alternatives and efficacy, however, remains to be seen.

5. CONCLUSION

By and large, many recent authors on safety and security seem to agree – albeit often tacitly – that safety is primarily concerned with the adverse effects which any entity might have on (the integrity of) human individuals, while security primarily is a dimension, i.e., the unimpairedness, of the integrity of the entity as such. Many authors, furthermore, distinguish, albeit in different manners, between safety as controlling catastrophic events caused by system malfunctions versus security as dealing with mitigating attacks by malicious agents. With the blending of the physical and virtual world through the Internet of Things, the notions of security and safety come to be used more and more interchangeably, as security flaws often turn out to be the flip-side of safety risks and vice versa.

Articulations and justifications of security and safety as value notions can build on objectivist need-consequentialist considerations. Security and safety policies and arrangements in our societies provide directly or indirectly for the

29 Jeremy Waldron, 'Safety and Security' (2006) 85 Nebraska Law Review 454.

30 Jeremy Waldron, 'Safety and Security' (2006) 85 Nebraska Law Review 454, 506.

31 Jeremy Waldron, 'Safety and Security' (2006) 85 Nebraska Law Review 454, 479.

satisfaction of basic, social, and functional needs. Some protect life, health and shelter; some protect our institutions, our educational systems, our economy, our democracy, some protect the facilities that make our lives comfortable, extra enjoyable. Many security and safety policies and arrangements happen to satisfy in part basic biological needs and in part social or functional needs, simultaneously.

The benefits and burdens of policies and other arrangements for the protection of security and safety are not automatically distributed equally, in the sense that the people who gain from them share the burdens equally, while people who do not gain, do not share the burdens. This raises questions of distributive justice in terms of fairness, equity etc. The issues of distributive justice can, but do not necessarily always, overlap with the delicate fundamental issues of moral conflict. The latter occur in situations in which the realization of a (proposed) policy or measure of security or safety protection collides with liberties or rights of individuals or specific groups. To the degree that the conflicting views derive from differences of moral outlook and therefore are really substantially irreconcilable, not much more can be done than to take a somewhat agnostic approach by respecting both horns of the dilemma and applying the questions of less impacting alternatives and efficacy in order to see whether it practically makes sense to tolerate infringements of rights and liberties for the sake of the interest at issue. It should be noted, however, that the latter approach is a pragmatic one. Its persuasiveness seems to hinge more on some idea of reasonableness than on substantial morality. If one would prefer to have a more substantial moral approach, one should try somehow to overcome the fundamental conflict or incommensurability between the moral outlooks involved. It is not clear whether such an undertaking can ever succeed. Waldron's approach in terms of the connection between rights and liberties and the protection of ways of life, however, seems to offer promising first steps in the exploration of a rationally satisfying moral justification.

At the end of this chapter, it may be good to make some comments on the role of ethics in the context of policy and law making especially with regards to the development of technologies involved in safety and security policies and arrangements. Elsewhere, an extensive argument was given for the role of ethics and law as important preconditions for the acceptance of technology regulation and for the adoption of the technologies themselves.[32] The reasoning behind this argument is relatively simple: by including ethical and legal considerations in the development of the technology or in accompanying regulatory schemes, the makers avoid adverse effects for users and in that way facilitate the uptake. For this reason, ethics, with the law in its wake, may also be viewed as an asset

32 Anton Vedder, 'Inclusive Regulation, Inclusive Design and Technology Adoption' in E Palmerini and E Stradella (eds), *Law and Technology: The Challenge of Regulating Technological Development* (Pisa University Press 2013) 205.

for the security and safety technology business.[33] Reducing it to an instrument for marketing strategy, however, will in the end not work. Recently, various authors have warned for the risk that in the context of (security) technology development, ethics may be reduced to an uncritical instrument of mere formality.[34] Indeed, such an approach is to be avoided if only because it may soon turn out to have counterproductive effects. The ideal situation is of course one in which engineers, policy and law makers, stakeholders and scholars from ethics and law make a sincere joint effort to work together on the realization of responsible safety and security arrangements.

ACKNOWLEDGEMENT

The research for this chapter was in part performed for the COMPACT (GA 740712) and SAURON (GA 740477) projects funded under the Horizon 2020 scheme of the European Union.

BIBLIOGRAPHY

Amundrud Ø, Aven T, Flage R, 'How the definition of security risk can be made compatible with safety definitions' (2017) 3, Proceedings of the Institution of Mechanical Engineers, Part O: Journal of Risk and Reliability <https://doi.org/10.1177/1748006X17699145> accessed 24 June 2019

Aradau C, 'Security that matters: Critical infrastructure and objects of protection' (2010) 41 Security Dialogue <https://doi.org/10.1177/0967010610382687> accessed 24 June 2019

Balzacq T, Léonard S, Ruzicka J, "Securitization' revisited: theory and cases' (2016) 30 International Relations <https: //doi 10.1177/0047117815596590> accessed 24 June 2019

Barry B, *Political Argument* (Routledge and Kegan Paul 1965) 47–49

Benn SI and Peters RS, *Social principles and the democratic state.* (Allen and Unwin 1975) 142–147

Berg H-P, 'Safety and Security of Critical Infrastructures with regard to nuclear facilities' in I Žutautaitė, M Eid, K Simola, V Kopustinskas (eds) *Critical Infrastructures: Enhancing Preparedness & Resilience for the Security of Citizens and Services Supply Continuity. Proceedings of the 52nd ESReDA Seminar.* Lithuanian Energy Institute & Vytautas Magnus University, 2017 <https://www.researchgate.net/profile/

[33] Myriam Dunn Cavelty, 'Breaking the cyber-security dilemma: aligning security needs and removing vulnerabilities' 2014 20 Science and Engineering Ethics 701 <https://doi: 10.1007/s11948-014-9551-y> accessed 25 June 2019.

[34] Matthias Leese, Kristoffer Lidén, Blagovesta Nikolova, 'Putting critique to work: Ethics in EU security research' (2019) 50 Security Dialogue 59 <https://doi.org/10.1177/0967010618809554> accessed 25 June 2019.

Mohamed_Eid19/publication/321027342_EUR_28803_EN_proceedings_52nd_esreda_seminar/links/5a097329aca272ed27a020f3/EUR-28803-EN-proceedings-52nd-esreda-seminar.pdf#page=64> accessed 10 June 2019

Boholm M, Möller N, Ove Hansson S, 'The Concepts of Risk, Safety, and Security: Applications in Everyday Language' (2016) 36 Risk Analysis <https: //doi 10.1111/risa.12464> accessed 24 June 2019

Bourne M, *Understanding Security* (Macmillan International Higher Education 2013) 88

Braybrooke D, *Meeting Needs* (Princeton University Press 1987) 48–49, 60–67, 117–121

Cavelty M and Søby Kristensen K, *Securing the homeland: critical infrastructure, risk and (in)security* (Routledge, 2008) 1

Cavelty M, 'Breaking the cyber-security dilemma: aligning security needs and removing vulnerabilities' 2014 20 Science and Engineering Ethics 701 <https://doi: 10.1007/s11948-014-9551-y> accessed 25 June 2019

Ceccorulli M and Lucarelli S, 'Security governance: making the concept fit for the analysis of a multipolar, global and regionalized world' 2014 41 Global Governance Programme-98; European, Transnational and Global Governance <http://hdl.handle.net/1814/31282> accessed 25 June 2019

Faden R and Shebaya S, 'Public Health Ethics' *The Stanford Encyclopedia of Philosophy* (Winter edn, 2016) <https://plato.stanford.edu/archives/win2016/entries/publichealth-ethics/> accessed 10 June 2019

Freedman L, 'The concept of security' *Encyclopedia of Government and Politics* (2nd edn, 2003)

Gallie WB, '*Essentially Contested Concepts*' vol 56 (Proceedings of the Aristotelian Society, 1956) 167

Hildebrandt M, 'Balance or Trade-off? Online Security Technologies and Fundamental Rights' (2013) 26 Philosophy and Technology 357–379

Hussain W, 'The Common Good' *The Stanford Encyclopedia of Philosophy* (Spring edn, 2018) <https://plato.stanford.edu/archives/spr2018/entries/common-good/> accessed 10 June 2019

Leese M, Lidén K, Nikolova B, 'Putting critique to work: Ethics in EU security research' (2019) 50 Security Dialogue 59 <https://doi.org/10.1177/0967010618809554> accessed 25 June 2019

Maurice P, 'Safety and safety promotion: definitions for operational developments' (2001) 8 Injury Control and Safety Promotion 238 <https://pdfs.semanticscholar.org/363d/81922697730c2ab49cca4f903d03ffe352b3.pdf> accessed June 25 2019

Nicklas J, Mamrot M, Winzer P, Lichte D, Marchlewitz S, Wolf K, 'Use case based approach for an integrated consideration of safety and security aspects for smart home applications' (2016) 11th System of Systems Engineering Conference (SoSE) Kongsberg <https://ieeexplore.ieee.org/stamp/stamp.jsp?tp=&arnumber=7542908> accessed 25 June 2019

Nigam V, Pretschner A, Ruess H, 'Model-Based Safety and Security Engineering' (2019) ArXiv <https://arxiv.org/pdf/1810.04866.pdf> accessed 10 June 2019

Nyman J, 'What is the value of security? Contextualising the negative/positive debate' (2016) 42 Review of International Studies <https://doi.org/10.1017/S0260210516000140> accessed 24 June 2019

Olson M, *The Logic of Collective Action: Public Goods and the Theory of Groups,* (revised edition, Harvard University Press 1971)

Rigterink AS, 'Does Security Imply Safety? On The (Lack of) Correlation Between Different Aspects of Security' (2015) 4 Stability: International Journal of Security & Development <http://doi.org/10.5334/sta.fw> accessed 24 June 2019

Sametinger J, Rozenblit J, Lysecky R, Ott P, 'Security Challenges for Medical Devices' 2015 58 Communications of the ACM <https://www.se.jku.at/wp-content/uploads/2015/03/TR-SE-15.03.pdf> accessed 10 June 2019

Serpanos D and Wolf M, *Internet-of-Things (IoT) Systems – Architectures, Algorithms, Methodologies,* (Springer 2018)

Thomson G, *Needs.* (Routledge and Kegan Paul 1988) 77–89, 98–107, 121–122, 125–128.

Vedder A, 'Inclusive Regulation, Inclusive Design and Technology Adoption' in E Palmerini and E Stradella (eds), *Law and Technology: The Challenge of Regulating Technological Development* (Pisa University Press 2013) 205

Waldron J, 'Safety and Security' (2006) 85 Nebraska Law Review 453 479 506

Walt SM, 'Realism and Security' *Oxford Research Encyclopedia of International Studies* (2010) <https://oxfordre.com/internationalstudies/view/10.1093/acrefore/9780190846626.001.0001/acrefore-9780190846626-e-286> accessed June 25 2019

Wiggins D, (1987) *Needs, values, truth. Essays in the philosophy of value.* (Aristotelian Society series vol. 6, Blackwell 1987) 48–49 60–67 117–121

CHAPTER 3

NATIONAL AND PUBLIC SECURITY WITHIN AND BEYOND THE POLICE DIRECTIVE

Plixavra VOGIATZOGLOU* and Stefano FANTIN*

1. INTRODUCTION

The Directive (EU) 2016/680, also referred to as the Data Protection Law Enforcement Directive, (hereinafter the DPLE Directive)[1] that accompanies the General Data Protection Regulation (hereinafter the GDPR)[2] is often left aside in most discussions around the EU Data Protection Reform of 2016 (also including the Passenger Name Records – hereinafter PNR – Directive[3]). On its own merit, the DPLE Directive was praised for broadening the scope of data protection in the criminal justice sector, from the previous cross-border regime (Council Framework Decision 2008/977/JHA, hereinafter the Framework Decision[4]) to a much wider territorial remit, extending its rules to purely internal data processing. During its drafting, however, the major European data protection supervisory bodies, i.e. the European Data Protection Supervisor (hereinafter EDPS), and the Article 29 Working Party (currently European Data Protection

* The authors contributed equally to this work. For correspondence please refer to plixavra.vogiatzoglou@kuleuven.be or stefano.fantin@kuleuven.be.

1 Directive (EU) 2016/680 of the European Parliament and of the Council of 27 April 2016 on the protection of natural persons with regard to the processing of personal data by competent authorities for the purposes of the prevention, investigation, detection or prosecution of criminal offences or the execution of criminal penalties, and on the free movement of such data, and repealing Council Framework Decision 2008/977/JHA [2016] OJ L119, 89.

2 Regulation (EU) 2016/679 of the European Parliament and of the Council of 27 April 2016 on the protection of natural persons with regard to the processing of personal data and on the free movement of such data, and repealing Directive 95/46/EC [2016] OJ L119, 1.

3 Directive (EU) 2016/681 of the European Parliament and of the Council of 27 April 2016 on the use of passenger name record (PNR) data for the prevention, detection, investigation and prosecution of terrorist offences and serious crime, [2016] OJ L119, 132.

4 Council Framework Decision 2008/977/JHA of 27 November 2008 on the protection of personal data processed in the framework of police and judicial cooperation in criminal matters, [2008] OJ L350, 60.

Board, hereinafter WP29), raised their concerns with regards to the scope of the directive, in particular the purpose of safeguarding public security. As the directive applies to the processing of personal data by competent authorities for the purposes of the prevention, investigation, detection or prosecution of criminal offences including the safeguarding against and the prevention of threats to public security, the EDPS[5] and WP29,[6] in their respective Opinions on the Proposal for the DPLE Directive, objected to the inclusion of this last phrase, pointing out the potential for legal uncertainty that such wording may lead to. More specifically, the directive does not further define the notion of public security, while explicitly juxtaposing the concept to national security, as the latter is excluded from the scope of application of the legislation.

At the time of writing, the European Commission has referred two Member States before the Court of Justice of the European Union for failing to transpose the DPLE Directive into national law.[7] Several months after the official deadline for the national transposition of the directive, the interpretative questions highlighted above have not been given any more thought by both regulators and scholarly literature.[8]

Against this backdrop, this chapter aims at triggering further reflections about the DPLE Directive in a number of communities, first and foremost Member States' legislators, data protection regulators and academics. Specifically, it will do so by seeking to clarify the scope of the directive and the meaning of public security within, by adopting a three-layered approach; first through its contraposition with the concept of national security, second through its operationalisation and third through the definition of competent authorities, as formulated in the text of the directive. With regard to the first of the above-mentioned objectives, this chapter will, by following a *reductio ad absurdum* approach, examine general theories and international law so as to identify the

5 European Data Protection Supervisor (EDPS), 'Opinion 6/2015 – A further step towards comprehensive EU data protection' (2015).

6 Article 29 Data Protection Working Party, 'Opinion 03/2015 on the draft directive on the protection of individuals with regard to the processing of personal data by competent authorities for the purposes of prevention, investigation, detection or prosecution of criminal offences or the execution of criminal penalties, and the free movement of such data' (2015).

7 European Commission – Press Release, 25 July 2019, IP/19/4261. Additionally, in 2018 nineteen Member States had been notified by the European Commission of an infringement procedure against them, due to their delay in implementing the Directive throughout their respective national processes, see European Commission, Seventeenth Progress Report towards an Effective and Genuine Security Union (2018).

8 Thomas Marquenie 'The Police and Criminal Justice Authorities Directive: Data protection standards and impact on the legal framework' (2017) 33 Computer Law & Security Review 324; Paul De Hert and Vagelis Papakonstantinou, 'The Police and Criminal Justice Data Protection Directive: Comment and Analysis' (2012) 7 New Journal of European Criminal Law 7(1); Teresa Quintel, 'European Union · Article 29 Data Protection Working Party Opinion on the Law Enforcement Directive' (2018) 4 European Data Protection Law Review 104.; Franziska Boehm, 'Data Processing and Law Enforcement Access to Information Systems at EU Level' (2012) 36 Datenschutz und Datensicherheit – DuD 339.

main elements that define national security in such domains. In order to achieve the second objective, public security within European Union primary and secondary law will be analysed. Lastly, as far as the third objective is concerned, the focus will shift to the concept of competent authorities within the meaning of the directive. For this notion to be clarified, examples from national laws transposing the directive will be considered.

2. THE SCOPE OF THE DATA PROTECTION LAW ENFORCEMENT DIRECTIVE

The DPLE Directive concerns the protection of natural persons with regard to the processing of personal data by competent authorities for the purposes of the prevention, investigation, detection or prosecution of criminal offences or the execution of criminal penalties. It has replaced the previous regime of the Framework Decision, as it entered into force on 5 May 2016 and was due to be transposed by the Member States by 6 May 2018.[9] While the GDPR regulates the processing of personal data in general context, the processing of personal data within the law enforcement and criminal justice sectors has been considered to require a separate legal instrument, due to the special nature of security-related data and activities.[10]

The scope of the DPLE Directive is significantly broadened in comparison to the previous regime, set out by the Framework Decision, which was limited to the processing of personal data transmitted or made available between the Member States and thus only to cross-border transfers of data. On the contrary, the DPLE Directive now also includes the purely domestic processing of personal data by competent authorities. What further differentiates the latter legal instrument is that it does no longer find its legal basis in the Area of Freedom, Security and Justice and the EU competence on police and judicial cooperation in criminal matters. In contrast, it is based on the Lisbon-introduced Article 16 TFEU, which provided for the legal basis to regulate comprehensively all rules on data protection at large.[11]

Delving deeper into the body of the directive and the defining contour of its scope, the two key concepts delineating the application of the DPLE Directive are, on the one hand, the purpose of the processing and on the other hand the notion of 'competent authorities'. More specifically, the DPLE Directive applies to the "*processing of personal data by competent authorities for the purposes of the prevention, investigation, detection or prosecution of criminal offences or the execution of criminal penalties, including the safeguarding against and*

---

9 Directive (EU) 2016/680 (n 1) Article 63, 64.

10 Paul De Hert and Vagelis Papakonstantinou (n 8) 1–2.

11 Marquenie (n 8).

the prevention of threats to public security" [emphasis added by authors].[12] Furthermore, a competent authority is defined as either "*any public authority competent for the prevention, investigation, detection or prosecution of criminal offences or the execution of criminal penalties, including the safeguarding against and the prevention of threats to public security*" or "*any other body or entity entrusted by Member State law to exercise public authority and public powers*" for the same abovementioned purposes.[13] It is also important to note that neither the DPLE Directive nor the GDPR apply to the processing of personal data in the course of an activity which falls outside the scope of Union Law (i.e. beyond the competences afforded to the EU by the Member States).[14] While the text of the initial proposal referred to national security explicitly within this provision,[15] the reference was eventually moved to the recitals of the DPLE Directive. In particular, recital 14 sheds light on what constitutes activities that fall outside the scope of Union Law, by referring to examples such as activities concerning national security and activities falling within the scope of Chapter 2 of Title V of the Treaty on European Union (TEU), that is the common foreign and security policy[16].

Despite there being three separate and cumulative conditions, they seem to be intertwined in the sense that they all depend, in one way or another, on the notion of security, whether public or national. Furthermore, the competence of the authorities that are subject to the DPLE Directive is defined through the purposes, '*including the safeguarding of public security*', and the entities' power to pursue those purposes, while activities concerning national security are excluded. It is thus safe to assume that the core concept on which the scope of the DPLE Directive depends is security and in particular public security. Therefore, in order to fully comprehend the scope of the directive and appraise its potential applicability in a context outside the strict realm of criminal justice, these three conditions (national security, purpose of public security and competent authority) must be further interpreted and clarified.

While the notion of public security is opposed to the notion of national security within the scope of the DPLE Directive, the latter does not provide for further definitions or analysis. It is not as clear, however, what these notions entail, as they depend on international and European law as well as on the national policy of each Member State and their different understandings.[17] Due

---

12 Directive (EU) 2016/680 (n 1) Article 1(1).

13 Directive (EU) 2016/680 (n 1) Article 3(7).

14 Directive (EU) 2016/680 (n 1) Article 2(3)(a); Regulation (EU) 2016/679 (n 2) Article 2(2)(a).

15 Proposal for a Directive of the European Parliament and of the Council on the protection of individuals with regard to the processing of personal data by competent authorities for the purposes of prevention, investigation, detection or prosecution of criminal offences or the execution of criminal penalties, and the free movement of such data, COM(2012) 10 final.

16 Directive (EU) 2016/680 (n 1) Rec. 14; Regulation (EU) 2016/679 (n 2) Rec. 16.

17 Directorate General for Internal Policies Policy Department C, Citizen's Rights and Constitutional Affairs, National Security and Secret Evidence in Legislation and before

to this lack of clarity, the major EU data protection authorities, i.e. the EDPS and the WP29, provided their opinion against the inclusion of the phrase 'including the safeguarding against and the prevention of threats to public security' in the determination of the scope of the Directive.

In particular, even though the observations by the EDPS in Opinion 6/2015 where made when the DPLE Directive was still in its drafting phase, many of the objections therein are still valid.[18] With respect to the scope of this chapter, three considerations were made explicit. Firstly, that the unclarity of the term 'public security' leads to the extension of the application of the Directive to those police activities which are not strictly related to a criminal offence that has happened or is taking place. This is the case, for instance, with the protection of public order, where extensive surveillance measures like video-monitoring are often applied in the context of rallies, demonstrations or sports events. Secondly, that the term 'competent authority' should be interpreted narrowly, thus keeping out of the scope of application of the DPLE Directive organizations such as telecommunications companies or airline carriers for which a stricter regime, the one of the GDPR, shall apply. Thirdly, with regard to the exclusion of the national security domain from the DPLE Directive, it was made clear that the exception shall not be misused to give a systematic legitimization to the processing of personal data falling outside the scopes of both the DPLE Directive and the GDPR. This implies that even though such a clause will be clarified by national legislators when implementing the DPLE Directive, a narrow interpretation would be recommended, as a safeguard against the risk of abuse or misuse.

Similarly, in its opinion 3/2015, WP29 points out a number of elements which follow the same reasoning of the EDPS in the Opinion mentioned above.[19] On the concept of 'public security' for instance, WP29 considers it as a complementary police activity, next to the core mandate of criminal investigation and prosecution. However, such an addition to the scope of the DPLE Directive might carry on quite a broad interpretation of this wording by Member States: in some countries for instance, the administration of public health or food safety is considered as falling within the scope of the term public security, departing from some other domestic legislations which, as we will be able to see, include health in the notion of national security. Both WP29 and EDPS thus claimed that the vagueness surrounding the concept of public security may therefore lead to the expansion of the scope of the directive beyond matters and authorities dealing purely with criminal justice.

---

the Courts: Exploring the Challenges, Study for the LIBE Committee 2014, 32–35, <www.europarl.europa.eu/RegData/etudes/STUD/2014/509991/IPOL_STU(2014)509991_EN.pdf> accessed 10 April 2019.

18 EDPS (n 5).

19 Article 29 Data Protection Working Party (n 6).

3. SECURITY IN INTERNATIONAL LAW

3.1. THEORETICAL BASES FROM PHILOSOPHY OF LAW

Philosophy of law and political theory do not often clearly distinguish between the concept of national security and the broad concept of security. Scholars have long debated on the boundaries between these two terms, many of them accepting that such an attempt has not brought meaningful results in the past,[20] some others criticizing the fact that a conceptual ambiguity was deliberately kept unclear for the benefit of policy-makers[21]. This exercise is made even more difficult by the fact that legal scholarship has so far developed the two concepts at times ambiguously or interchangeably.

One of the first striking elements when reviewing the above-mentioned scholarly literature is the relation between national security and sovereignty in the post-Augsburg[22] and post-Westphalian era. For example, Thomas Hobbes associates the two concepts extensively in its Leviathan. Before the age of governments, the world was populated by individuals in a state of nature, whereby each man enjoyed his personal sovereignty.[23] This led to individuals being at war with each other, in a perpetual state of instability and, most importantly, insecurity. Men therefore needed some sort of collective security, and it was from this impulse that governments originated. The *fil rouge* between the individual (main entity in the nature state) and the government (main entity in the next era) is the legitimation of the state towards the concept sovereignty, which shifts from being a singular and individual attribute to a collective one. However, while Hobbes conceptualized this theory in defence of the monarchy under which he was living, others departed from his ideas in order to establish the perception that democratic governments cannot transcend from individuals and the enjoyment of their rights. John Locke, for instance, developed the principle of reciprocity between governments and society: sovereignty did not mean saving humankind from a previous tragic era.[24] Rather, it consisted of

20 Klaus Knorr, 'National Security Studies: Scope and Structure of the Field' in Frank N. Trager and Philip S. Kronenberg (eds.), *National Security and American Society: Theory, Process and Policy* (Lawrence KS, 1973) 5.

21 Barry Buzan, 'Peace, Power, and Security: Contending Concepts in the Study of International Relations' (1984) 21 Journal of Peace Research 109, 111.

22 "*Significant modernisation of the national security concept occurred upon the adoption of the Doctrine on the inviolability of sovereignty dating back to the Augsburg Peace in 1555, which gave the right to a sovereign to decide on the religion in his country (cuius region, eius religion - whose country, his religion). This right was confirmed and revised by the Prague Peace of 1635 and the Peace of Westphalia of 1648*" Sasa Mijalkovic and Dusan Blagojevic, 'The Basis of National Security in International Law' [2014] Nauka, bezbednost, policija 49.

23 Thomas Hobbes, *Leviathan-Or the Matter, Form and Power of a Common-Wealth Ecclesiastical and Civil* (I Shapiro ed, first published 1651, Yale University Press 2010).

24 Alex Tuckness, 'Locke's Political Philosophy' in Edward N Zalta (ed), *The Stanford Encyclopedia of Philosophy* (Summer 2018, Metaphysics Research Lab, Stanford University

individuals entering into a mutual contract with reciprocal expectations, and the ultimate possibility to withdraw from it. The combination of these theories enables us to understand something fundamental. Sovereignty is seen as the expression of a state protecting the contract between itself and its citizens, not just a default attribution to each state-entity. For this reason, the government is accountable towards the citizens. Reflecting on this with modern eyes, this reasoning could have a translation in providing control to people with respect to the activities undertaken by the government on national security grounds. More specifically, national security and sovereignty are crucial elements of the identity of a government, although the exercise of these need some form of scrutiny against arbitrary and unaccountable powers.

The definition of national security (and its boundaries) has often taken different routes and interpretations, particularly in the last Century. For instance, definitions focused solely on the protection of a state from external threats[25] (Harold Brown), or included also non-military coercions[26] (Joseph Romm). Even in these conceptualizations, however, the link between national security and sovereignty keeps surviving. This correlation has become an established doctrine in international customary law, where sovereignty is one of the main legal principles to establish the integrity[27] and the authority of a state to exercise its power without interferences[28] (i.e., political independence and territorial integrity).

This assumption was further confirmed in the nineteen eighties by the approach to security by the Copenhagen School, the first group of international theorists to establish the *securitization*[29] doctrine, according to which modern security substantiates in the tendency of states to transform unrelated subjects into security items. In this doctrine, three levels of security are identifiable:

2018) <https://plato.stanford.edu/archives/sum2018/entries/locke-political/> accessed 20 May 2019.

25 Harold Brown, 'U.S. National Security: The Next 50 Years' (2000) Centre for Naval Analyses, https://www.cna.org/CNA_files/PDF/D0001565.A1.pdf

26 Joseph J. Romm, *Defining National Security: The Nonmilitary Aspects* (Council on Foreign Relations Press 1993).

27 Charter of the United Nations (signed 26 June 1945, published 24 October 1945), 1 UNTS XVI (UN Charter), Article 2(4).

28 Samantha Besson, 'Sovereignty' Oxford Public International Law (2011) Max Planck Encyclopedia of Public International Law [MPEPIL]<https://opil.ouplaw.com/ view/10.1093/law:epil/9780199231690/law-9780199231690-e1472> accessed 13 May 2019.

29 *"The concept of securitization provided a fresh take on the increasingly tiresome debate between those who claimed that threats are objective (i.e., what really constitutes a threat to international security) on the one hand, and those that maintained that security is subjective (what is perceived to be a threat) on the other. In an attempt to sidestep or bypass this debate, the Copenhagen school suggests that security should instead be seen as a speech act, where the central issue is not if threats are real or not, but the ways in which a certain issue (troop movements, migration, or environmental degradation) can be socially constructed as a threat"*, Rens van Munster, definition of 'Securitization – International Relations – Oxford Bibliographies' <https://www.oxfordbibliographies.com/view/document/obo-9780199743292/obo-9780199743292-0091.xml> accessed 13 May 2019.

individual, state and international. The second one is the closest to the expression of national security. In his book *People, States and Fear*, Buzan takes a stance which acknowledges the complexity of security threats according to the *referent object* (i.e., the threatened actor situation) which looks at it.[30] Such a methodological approach developed by the Copenhagen School, imposes to analyse what is the nature of a state, in order to delineate the contours of the threats under which a nation is subject to.

3.2. INTERNATIONAL LAW

The theoretical considerations discussed in section 3.1 have a concrete translation into legal constructs and codification.[31] Even though the law of international treaties has explored national security without attributing it a clear definition, a number of common approaches towards this subject can be found. For example, these can be inferred from the circumstances under which national security is invoked by states according to international treaties. National security is often included as a matter of exception, derogating from the adherence to an existing treaty obligation. Notwithstanding the fact that the room for manoeuvre of such an exception might vary from treaty to treaty, what is common is the explicitness of such an exception. As Ackerman argues, international customary law does not advocate an implicit national security exception into treaties.[32] Even if the nature of national security clauses in international customary laws provides for a margin of appreciation, very often such a clause is not interpreted as fully arbitrary. Eisenhut observes this when he exegetically differentiates between circumscribed security exceptions and *self-judging clauses*, often laid down by the wording '*as it considers necessary*'.[33] Regardless of the breadth of such a discretion, however, Eisenhut identifies in all such examples the presence of judicial review mechanisms (including in the self-judging clauses).[34]

---

30 Barry Buzan (Emeritus Professor at the London School of Economics and Political Science and Honorary Professor at the University of Copenhagen) is one of the most prominent scholars of the Copenhagen School alongside Professor Ole Waever.

31 Mijalkovic and Blagojevic (n 22).

32 Rather, the exceptions that are consolidated by the Vienna Convention and the customary evolution of international law are normally substantiated into four different cases: *rebus sic stantibus* (change of circumstances), reprisal (violation of the treaty by another party), self-defence or necessity. See also, Susan Rose-Ackerman and Benjamin Billa, 'Treaties and National Security' (2008) reprinted in Yale Law School Faculty Scholarship Series <https://digitalcommons.law.yale.edu/fss_papers/595/> accessed 27 June 2019.

33 Dominik Eisenhut, 'Sovereignty, National Security and International Treaty Law. The Standard of Review of International Courts and Tribunals with Regard to "Security Exceptions"' (2010) 48 Archiv des Völkerrechts 431.

34 For instance, the ICJ reviewed the extent of a such an exemption in its widely known 'Nicaragua case', whereby the Court remarked that the application of the self-judging clause must not be intended as totally arbitrary; Case Concerning Military and Paramilitary

Having said this, it is also useful to give an overview of the security exceptions amongst some of the main international law treaties. The General Agreement on Tariffs and Trade (GATT) for instance, includes a number of highly disputed national security exceptions (Article XXI – referring to '*essential security interests*').[35] The discretion that the self-judging clause leads to is not by-default absolute: according to a number of scholars, a WTO panel shall be entitled to evaluate the appropriateness of the invocation of this clause.[36]

Moving to another prominent treaty, the UN Charter includes among its primary objectives the promotion of international peace and security (inter alia, through the powers of the Security Council), where national security is seen as a concept misaligned from the collective protection of international security. Yet, the achievement of these global objectives also relate to the orderly maintenance of national interests, such as state's self-determination and sovereignty.[37] While Article 39 provides for a number of prerequisites for the Council's military powers to be actionable against a threat for international peace and security, Article 51 counterweights such a global vision of security, allowing for the exercise of the *inherent right of self-defence*, whereby an individual state may use the force to counter an armed attack prior to any Security Council action.[38]

The International Covenant on Civil and Political Rights (hereafter, the 'Covenant'), is one of the first and main instruments for the international protection of civil rights, including the right to privacy.[39] A general derogation for public emergencies is laid down in Article 4. It enables the unilateral departure from the rights enshrined in the Covenant while conditioning it to a number of safeguards.[40] Moreover, national security is mentioned as a way to exception

Activities In and Against Nicaragua (Nicaragua v. United States of America); Jurisdiction of the Court and Admissibility of the Application, International Court of Justice (ICJ), 26 November 1984.

35 To be exercised only when derogating from the disclosure of information on as nuclear materials, military goods or in case of emergency in the self-determination of a state in foreign affairs. See also Michael J Hahn, 'Vital Interests and the Law of GATT: An Analysis of GATT's Security Exception' (1991) 12 Michigan Journal of International Law 558.

36 Brandon J Murrill, 'The "National Security Exception" and the World Trade Organization' (2018) <https://fas.org/sgp/crs/row/LSB10223.pdf> accessed 27 June 2019 5.

37 Mijalkovic and Blagojevic (n 22).

38 UN Charter, Article 51: "*Nothing in the present Charter shall impair the inherent right of individual or collective self-defence if an armed attack occurs against a Member of the United Nations, until the Security Council has taken measures necessary to maintain international peace and security. Measures taken by Members in the exercise of this right of self-defence shall be immediately reported to the Security Council and shall not in any way affect the authority and responsibility of the Security Council under the present Charter to take at any time such action as it deems necessary in order to maintain or restore international peace and security*".

39 Comments and references: Claire Macken, 'Preventive Detention and the Right of Personal Liberty and Security under the International Covenant on Civil and Political Rights, 1966' (2005) 26 Adelaide Law Review 1.; United Nations, General Comment No. 16 Article 17 (The right to respect of privacy, family, home and correspondence, and protection of honour and reputation).

40 Rose-Ackerman and Billa (n 32).

to the exercise of a number of rights,[41] to be invoked only insofar as it is "taken to protect the existence of the nation or its territorial integrity or political independence against force or threat of force".[42] The invocation of these clauses is circumscribed and applied under specific conditions.[43] Two points of reflection are worth mentioning here. Firstly, that the wording of the Covenant in such exceptions clearly differentiates between national security as a distinct concept from *public order.*[44] Secondly, the interference with the right to privacy (Article 17) does not mention national security. Yet, the General Note on Article 17 provided by the Human Rights Committee, explains that interferences shall be provided by law and even in such case, must not be arbitrarily conducted, rather designed in accordance with the principles laid down by the Covenant.[45] Furthermore, the UN Special Rapporteur for the right to privacy has further clarified the meaning of Article 17 in the national security context: the latest Report in fact conceptualizes the need for an extension of the oversight powers of regulatory agencies involved in national security.[46] In its recommendations, the Rapporteur Joe Cannataci suggests the adoption of the principle "*If it's exchangeable, then it's oversightable, in relation to any personal information exchanged between intelligence services and law enforcement agencies within a country, and across borders*".[47] This underscores the increasing intersection between national security and law enforcement tasks in cross-border setting, on the one hand, and the call for extension of oversight powers over such practices, on the other.[48]

3.3. COUNCIL OF EUROPE

In the same vein, in the European Convention of Human Rights (hereinafter ECHR), national security is included as an exception to the full enjoyment of the

41 Freedom of movement (Article 12), right to judicial redress after an expulsion (Article 13), publicity of trials (Article 14), freedom of expression (Article 19), freedom of association (Article 22).

42 UN Sub-Commission on Prevention of Discrimination and Protection of Minorities, 'Siracusa Principles on the Limitation and Derogation of Provisions in the International Covenant on Civil and Political Rights Annex, UN Doc E/ CN.4/1984/4 (1984)' (2019) as reported in CCBE Recommendations on the protection of fundamental rights in the context of national security 6.

43 Specifically, the interference with the right must be foreseen by a law and it must pass the necessity test.

44 International Covenant on Civil and Political Rights, Articles 12, 14, 19 and 22.

45 United Nations, General Comment No. 16 Article 17 (The right to respect of privacy, family, home and correspondence, and protection of honour and reputation), Articles 3 and 4.

46 Human Rights Council, 25/117 Panel on the right to privacy in the digital age (2014) A/ HRC/25/117.

47 Human Rights Council, *Report of the Special Rapporteur on the right to privacy* (2019) A/ HRC/40/63.

48 United Nations Human Rights, 'States Must Bridge Privacy Gap in Intelligence Sharing, Says UN Human Rights Expert' (1 March 2019) <https://www.ohchr.org/EN/NewsEvents/Pages/DisplayNews.aspx?NewsID=24242&LangID=E> accessed 2 April 2019.

rights enshrined in the Convention. However, such a clause can only be exercised when explicitly mentioned, since a number of rights are defined as absolute, hence inalienable and non-derogable, such as the prohibition against torture or slavery (Articles 3 and 4.1) and against unlawful punishment (Article 7).[49] Beyond such absolute rights, the ECHR provides for a number of other civil and human principles which are instead either limited (i.e. circumscribed to a specific case, such as Article 5 – right to liberty) or qualified (i.e., which need to be balanced with other interests, such as Article 8 – respect for private life). When the interference with the latter category occurs, such a violation must meet the legality and necessity tests (foreseeable law and proportional measure to the end to be achieved), in order to be accepted. Within this strict interpretation of the interference, the ECHR mentions national security as an explicit cause for interfering with a qualified right on a number of occasions: Article 8 (private life), Article 10 and 11 (freedoms of expression, assembly and association).

A first consideration to be made, refers to the wording of the ECHR in Articles 8, 10 and 11. Next to national security, the ECHR explicitly lays down the term '*public safety*', as well as the '*prevention of disorders and crimes*'. In Article 10 and 11, the grounds are even more articulated, including as a standalone concept the notion of '*territorial integrity*' (an inherent element of the principle of sovereignty). Public safety and order and the protection of health and morals could be accumulated under the umbrella of public security.[50] However, delineating boundaries cannot be clearly drawn, while the States and Convention organs do not consider these clauses to be mutually exclusive. In this manner, a State would be able to invoke collectively national security and, for instance, public safety.[51]

Furthermore, when national security is invoked by a State, judicial scrutiny by the ECtHR over such an exercise is foreseen. In the context of the ECHR, this translates into a narrow interpretation of the exceptions laid out in Article 8, for example. It would go beyond the scope of this chapter to analyse in-depth the rather longstanding series of decisions of the European Court of Human Rights on this, even though it is important to mention the *Klass v Germany* case, where the ECtHR, in evaluating a German surveillance law against the legality test of the ECHR,[52] asserted that national security exceptions shall be assessed narrowly and shall exclude that "*Contracting States enjoy an unlimited discretion*".[53] The prohibition of unlimited discretion goes even further in certain domains, for

---

49 John Finnis, 'Absolute Rights: Some Problems Illustrated' (2016) 61 American Journal of Jurisprudence 195.

50 Sofie Stalla-Bourdillon, 'Privacy Versus Security … Are We Done Yet?' in Sophie Stalla-Bourdillon, Joshua Phillips and Mark D. Ryan (eds), *Privacy vs. Security* (Springer London, Springer Briefs in Cybersecurity 2014) 69.

51 Iain Cameron, *National Security and the European Convention on Human Rights* (Kluwer Law International 2000) 54.

52 Rose-Ackerman and Billa (n 32).

53 *Klass and others v. Germany* App. No. 5029/71 (ECtHR, 6 September 1978) paras 49–50.

instance with regard to the over-classification of documents, whereby "*[T]he individual must be able to challenge the executive's assertion that national security is at stake*", as elaborated by the Court in the *Janowiecz* case.[54] The ECtHR, therefore, does not by default provide for a wider margin of appreciation to States on acts of national security in contrast to acts of public security. Moreover, it should be noted that neither the ECHR defines national security in any way, nor the ECtHR discusses what sort of initiative constitutes a measure of national security. The Court relies rather on the Contracting States' claim that the measure in question aims to serve national security.[55] Nonetheless, espionage, terrorism,[56] subversion,[57] separatist organisations,[58] and inciting disaffection of military personnel[59] have been accepted by the Court as threats against national security.

The Convention 108 is a Council of Europe international instrument signed in 1981 for the protection of individuals against the automatic processing of personal data.[60] The Convention served as the basis for the modernization of data protection laws and policies for a very long time. After more than thirty years, in 2018 a significant modernization of the Convention was published in the form of the so-called Convention 108+. In comparing the two texts, a number of meaningful elements can be observed. To begin with, the term *national security* now replaces the old wording *state security*. However, the two concepts seem to overlap in terms of purposes, as Convention 108+ provides for the same exact exemptions as the 108 (fair and lawful processing, safeguard against special categories of data processing, information rights), alongside additional ones (data breach notifications, trans border data transfers notifications, enforcement powers of supervisory authorities).[61] While the same boundaries to as the ones in the ECHR apply (legality, necessity and proportionality), it is noteworthy to observe that, such exceptions are formulated less broadly than in the previous text, and protected by a number of more strict conditions, as confirmed by the wording of Article 11 of the Convention 108+ and the recommendations made by the UN Special Rapporteur for the Right to Privacy in his recent reports.[62]

---

54 *Janowiec and Others v. Russia* App. No. 55508/07 29520/09 (ECtHR, 21 October 2013) paras 213–214.

55 Iain Cameron (n 51), p. 36; Lyubomira Midelieva, 'The Elusive Cause and the Extensive Effect of the Principle of Supremacy of EU Law' (2017) 7 Southampton Student Law Review 21.

56 *Klass* (n 53) paras 48 to 50.

57 *Leander v. Sweden* App. No. 9248/81 (ECtHR, 26 March 1987) para 20.

58 *United Communist Party of Turkey and others v. Turkey* App. No. 19392/92 (ECtHR, 30 January 1998) paras 10, 48, 55.

59 *Arrowsmith v. the United Kingdom* App. No. 7075/75 (CoE, European Commission of Human Rights, 5 December 1978).

60 Council of Europe, 'Convention for the Protection of Individuals with regard to Automatic Processing of Personal Data' (European Treaty Number 108, 1981).

61 Convention for the protection of individuals with regard to the processing of personal data – Convention 108+, 128th session of the Committee of Ministers, Elsinore, 18 May 2018.

62 Human Rights Council, 'Report of the Special Rapporteur on the right to privacy' (2019) A/HRC/40/63 para 28.

4. SECURITY IN EUROPEAN UNION LAW

4.1. EU TREATIES

The Treaty of the European Union (TEU), in its Article 4(2), calls for the respect by the European Union for Member States' national identity and sovereignty. Member States are the first and foremost holders of their prerogatives towards their own national security.[63] However, it is believed that such derogations to EU Law do not fully exclude the principle of supremacy of EU Law[64]: "*Despite the inclusion of a national identity clause in Article 4(2) TEU (...) EU law still does not permit Member States to unilaterally decide to override EU obligations and give precedence to measures of national law, however framed*".[65] Yet, in the operationalization of EU primary and secondary law, this means that national security in Article 4(2), provides for a level of derogatory legislative and executive autonomy for Member States ("*In particular, national security remains the sole responsibility of each Member State*"), one which can be characterized by the exceptionality of the action under such realm.[66] Even though the following considerations are, at the time of writing, being challenged before the Court of Justice of the EU (ECJ) as will be explained subsequently,[67] it is useful to remark that part of the European legal tradition has so far agreed that Article 4(2) excludes the applicability of basic EU privacy principles, such as Article 8 of the EU Charter (right to protection of personal data) and Article 16 of the Treaty on the Functioning of the European Union (TFEU) (protection of personal data) "*to any national security matters governed by domestic law*"[68].

63 Consolidated version of the Treaty on the Functioning of the European Union [2016] OJ C 202, Article 73.

64 See also: Midelieva (n 55).

65 Monica Claes, 'The Primacy of EU Law in European and National Law' in Anthony Arnull and Damian Chalmers (eds), The Oxford Handbook of European Union Law (2015), 178-211 <www. oxfordhandbooks.com/view/10.1093/oxfordhb/9780199672646.001.0001/oxford hb9780199672646-e-8> accessed 5 April 2019; Christopher Kuner, Fred Cate, Orla Lynskey, Christopher Millard, Nora Ni Loideain and Dan Svantesson, 'An Unstoppable Force and an Immoveable Object? EU Data Protection Law and National Security' 3.Barbara Guastaferro, 'Beyond the Exceptionalism of Constitutional Conflicts: The Ordinary Functions of the Identity Clause' (2012) Yearbook of European Law 263–318 and Monica Claes, 'National Identity: Trump Card or Up for Negotiation?' in Alejandro Saiz Arnaiz and Carina Alcoberro Llivina, National Constitutional Identity and European Integration (Intersentia 2013) 109–140.

66 Consolidated version of the Treaty on the European Union [2016] OJ C 202, Article 4(2).

67 C-623/17 *Privacy International v Secretary of State for Foreign and Commonwealth Affairs and Others*, 31.10.2017; C-512/18 *French Data Network, La Quadrature du Net, Fédération des fournisseurs d'accès à Internet associatifs v Premier ministre, Garde des Sceaux, Ministre de la Justice*, 03.08.2018; C-520/18 *Ordre des barreaux francophones et germanophone, Académie Fiscale ASBL, UA, Liga voor Mensenrechten ASBL, Ligue des Droits de l'Homme ASBL, VZ, WY, XX v Conseil des ministers*, 02.08.2018.

68 Christopher Kuner and others (n 65).

The TFEU moreover considers security as an exception that derogates from EU competence. It does so in at least two occasions. On the one hand, Article 346 TFEU, allows for an exception to be made in order to prevent the supply of information by a Member State that is contrary to the '*essential interests of its security*', and Article 347 TFEU calls upon the Member State to fulfil its obligations in the area of protection of international security. On the other hand, '*public security*' may be invoked as an exception to the main rules and freedoms that the EU Internal Market brings forward.[69] It should be noted here that the freedom of movement of persons established in the TFEU has been codified in secondary law, that is in Directive 64/224/EEC, which has been repealed by the currently in force Directive 2004/38/EC.[70] These legal instruments include the same terminology and reference to 'public security' as the TFEU and have given rise to a plethora of rulings by the Court of Justice of the European Union (ECJ), to which mention will be made as follows.

In his analysis on the exceptions to the EU free movement law, Koutrakos (2016) strikes a noteworthy point in referring to the meaning of 'security' deriving from the TFEU as the closest principle to the concept of state sovereignty, encompassing both internal and external security.[71] On the contrary, another scholarly (Dimitrova and Brkan) approach assimilates 'public security' within the meaning of the Treaty to the security of the European public, its citizens and the EU territory. According to the latter, while national security may only revolve around the security of each individual Member State, public security may also be considered as a broader term encompassing the security within the whole EU.[72] These two different interpretations demonstrate the complexity surrounding the concepts of national security and public security, as well as the flexibility in which they may be understood depending on the context.

A final remark should be made in relation to the changes the Lisbon Treaties brought in regulating aspects of security. In particular, the role of the EU on matters of internal security and criminal law was strengthened through various institutional changes. Besides, offering an area of freedom, security and justice

---

69 Treaty on the Functioning of the European Union (n 63) Articles 36, 45, 52 and 65. These provisions allow for limitations to the free movement of goods, workers, services and capital respectively on grounds of public security.

70 Directive 2004/38/EC of the European Parliament and of the Council of 29 April 2004 on the right of citizens of the Union and their family members to move and reside freely within the territory of the Member States amending Regulation (EEC) No 1612/68 and repealing Directives 64/221/EEC, 68/360/EEC, 72/194/EEC, 73/148/EEC, 75/34/EEC, 75/35/EEC, 90/364/EEC, 90/365/EEC and 93/96/EEC (Text with EEA relevance) [2004] OJ L158, 77.

71 Panos Koutrakos, 'Public Security Exceptions and EU Freed Movement Law' in P. Koutrakos, N. Nic Shuibhne & P. Syrpis (eds), Exceptions from EU Free Movement Law: Derogation, Justification and Proportionality (Hart Publishing 2016) 190.

72 Anna Dimitrova and Maya Brkan, 'Balancing National Security and Data Protection: The Role of EU and US Policy-Makers and Courts before and after the NSA Affair' (2017) Journal of Common Market Studies 751.

to EU citizens lays amongst the highest priorities of the EU.[73] On the one hand, the 'Common Foreign and Security Policy' (hereinafter CFSP)[74] acquired a stronger structure and position, as will be explained below under 'EU Policy'. On the other hand, the EU has now been conferred upon the brand-new competence to define criminal offences *in areas of particularly serious crime with a cross-border dimension*, including terrorism.[75] It could then be concluded that, within this framework, the EU is moving towards a broader concept of security that encompasses all threats to its citizens, while national security remains confined to the limits of strictly state-related threats.

4.2. JURISPRUDENCE ON SECURITY AS DEROGATION

The examples from the TFEU help us understand how the European legislator might deliberately have relinquished the definition of national and public security, probably in favour of further contextualization by both jurisprudence and EU policy. More specifically, with regard to the judicial approach on security as a derogation, the ECJ has always tried to provide for a narrow interpretation of the exceptions at stake, although very few details explain us what national security really is with regard to European Union Law.[76] As the Council of Bars & Law Societies of Europe fairly points out,[77] the Court has never clearly defined national security except for providing it a collective scope in the *Promusicae v Telefonica* case, whereby it states that "*national security [...] constitutes activities of the State or of State authorities unrelated to the fields of activity of individuals*"[78].

Furthermore, in examining the security derogation within the meaning of the TFEU, the ECJ seems to endorse the doctrine under which any sort of security (either public or national) represents a dynamic and flexible concept that often tends to evolve or adapt to the circumstance or the legal scenario, thus imposing a case-by-case approach in its assessment.[79] For instance, in the *Commission v Spain*, a case before the ECJ about a person that was refused a visa on public security grounds, the Court explained that any measure taken on the grounds of public security should comply with the proportionality principle

73 Treaty on European Union (n 66) Article 3(2).
74 Treaty on European Union (n 66) Title V.
75 Treaty on the Functioning of the European Union (n 63) Article 83.
76 See Case C-72/83 *Campus Oil Limited and others v Minister for Industry and Energy and others* [1984] ECR 1984–02727, II A; Case C-112/91 *Hans Werner v Finanzamt Aachen-Innenstadt* [1993] ECR 1993 I-00429, I. See also: Eisenhut (n 33).
77 CCBE Recommendations on the protection of fundamental rights in the context of 'national security' – 2019, 8.
78 Case C-275/06 *Productores de Música de España (Promusicae) v Telefónica de España SAU* [2008] ECR I-00271 para 51.
79 Case C- 30–77 *Régina v Pierre Bouchereau* [1977] ECR 1977–01999, II A.

and not be based solely on an individual's conduct.[80] Therefore, Member States should corroborate the mere public security argument with additional information to assess the criminal predisposition of the individual.[81]

Later on, however, the Court found in *Tsakouridis* that public security could be affected by "*a threat to the functioning of the institutions and essential public services and the survival of the population, as well as the risk of a serious disturbance to foreign relations or to peaceful coexistence of nations, or a risk to military interests*".[82] These elements point to the interpretation that assimilates public security within the meaning of the TFEU to national security, as described above. Finally, the ECJ recently associated the concept of public security with the idea of fundamental interests of society, in another case on permissible derogations from the freedom of movement.[83] In particular, a threat to public security may include "*a particularly serious threat to one of the fundamental interests of society*". Interestingly, this approach has been implemented in the recitals of the DPLE Directive.[84] It has been argued, however, that the Court is adopting a very broad concept of public security, while this 'socialisation' of the concept strips public security from the very element that differentiates it from the notion of public policy.[85] These rulings are indicative of the room for manoeuvre the ECJ enjoys in interpreting (public) security as a derogation to fundamental freedoms of the EU Internal Single Market.

4.3. EU POLICY

A report from LIBE Committee of the European Parliament, aiming to analyse Member States' definition of national security, states that the term "*is nebulously defined across the Member States analysed, with no national definition meeting legal certainty and 'in accordance with the law' standards and a clear risk that the executive and secret services may act arbitrarily*".[86] Furthermore, the report argues that, whilst the term national security in the 50es was contextualized by any form of war threat from another state-actor, in the following decades the

---

80 Case C-503/03 *Commission of the European Communities v Kingdom of Spain* [2006] ECR I-01097, para 44.

81 Alan Dashwood and others, Wyatt and Dashwood's European Union Law (6th edition, Hart Publishing 2011) 482–485.

82 Case C-145/09 *Land Baden-Württemberg v Panagiotis Tsakouridis* [2010] ECR I-11979, para 44.

83 Case C-348/09 *P.I. v Oberbürgermeisterin der Stadt Remscheid* [2012] ECR General, paras 4, 8(2), 28, 30, 33, 34.

84 Directive (EU) 2016/680 (n 1) Rec 12.

85 Azoulai L and Coutts S, 'Restricting Union citizens' residence rights on grounds of public security. Where Union citizenship and the AFSJ meet: P.I.' (2013) Vol. 50 Common Market Law Review 553.

86 Study for the LIBE Committee (n 17); EDPS (n 5).

concept got *"broadened to include criminal activities, terrorism and migration"*. A change that, as observed by Bigo (1994), was also perceived in the evolution of European policing measures and strategies (which followed the evolution of historical events), changing from a mono-dimensional concept of security, typical for the Cold War, into a more sophisticated one, which takes into account modern challenges and hybrid threats, such as cross-border criminality and massive migrations.[87]

While national security remains a prerogative of Member States(*'domaine reserve'*, as Eisenhut puts it[88]), small steps ahead by the European Union have been made with the establishment of the CFSP, whereby for the EU arrogates itself the intergovernmental lead in the rollout of a pan-EU framework on security and defence.[89] In particular, the European Union has been assigned the task of ensuring a high level of security throughout a mandate that affirms the principles of shared and attributed competences, by ways of actions aimed at preventing crime, enabling police cooperation, supporting mutual judicial recognition and approximating criminal laws.[90] To date, such powers are limited to coordination only, and are highly susceptible to changes according to the evolution of the political scenario,[91] including on the definition and adoption of common policies on cyber defence[92].

What comes to light however is that the EU as a policy maker has not defined national security (probably, deliberately), derogating this exercise to the events and the circumstances of the moment. As we will see, such an approach is recurrent in many international and national[93] law instruments. However, this does not mean that the security exceptions in EU law do not give us any

---

87 Didier Bigo, 'The European internal security field: stakes and rivalries in a newly developing area of police intervention' in Malcolm Anderson and Monica Den Boer (eds), Policing Across National Boundaries (1994) 161.

88 Eisenhut (n 33).

89 Mary Dobbs 'Sovereignty, article 4(2) TEU and the respect of national identities: Swinging the balance of power in favour of the member states?' (2014) Yearbook of European Law 33(1) 298.

90 According to Articles 2–6 Treaty on the Functioning of the European Union, the EU enjoys three types of competences, exclusive, shared and supporting. However, the Common Foreign and Security Policy is considered to constitute a *sui generis* type of competence.

91 Stephen Weatherill, 'Distinctive Identity Claims, Article 4(2) TEU (and a Fleetingly Sad Nod to Brexit) Editorial Note' (2016) 12 Croatian Yearbook of European Law and Policy VII.

92 Steven Blockmans and others, *What Comes after the Last Chance Commission? Policy Priorities for 2019–2024* (Steven Blockmans ed, 2019); Krzysztof Feliks Sliwinski, 'Moving beyond the European Union's Weakness as a Cyber-Security Agent' (2014) 35 Contemporary Security Policy 468.

93 For instance, as Earl Howe (UK Government) states with regard to the situation in Britain: *"It has been the policy of successive Governments not to define National security in statute. National security is one of the statutory purposes of the security and intelligence agencies"*. Earl Howe, Parliamentary debate on the Investigatory Powers Bill (2017), as reported in CCBE Recommendations on the protection of fundamental rights in the context of 'national security' – 2019.

meaningful indication. To start with, national security in EU law might be intended as a concept which needs contextualization, more specifically legal operationalization. Secondly, even though national and public security shall be regarded as exceptions, scrutiny by the ECJ shall still be expected, particularly with regard to the proportionality of the call for exception by the Member State. Having outlined the state of the art of EU primary law, jurisprudence and CFSP, it is useful to draw now from other sources of law, to verify how we can consolidate some of the details listed above and further explore how data-specific branches of EU secondary law regard national and public security as legal concepts.

4.4. SECURITY AND PERSONAL DATA IN SECONDARY EU LAW

In order to be able to understand the scope of the DPLE Directive and to examine to what extent the aforementioned analysis on the interpretation of national and public security may be similarly applied on secondary law and by extension on the text of the directive, further research was conducted on the mention of these two concepts and their role and potential meaning, in the following legal instruments: GDPR,[94] DPLE Directive,[95] E-Privacy Directive,[96] Regulation (EU) 2018/1725,[97] Regulation on EUROPOL,[98] Framework Decision,[99] Data Retention Directive,[100] Anti-Money Laundering Directive,[101] PNR Directive[102] and

---

94 Regulation (EU) 2016/679 (n 2).

95 Directive (EU) 2016/680 (n 1).

96 Directive 2002/58/EC of the European Parliament and of the Council of 12 July 2002 concerning the processing of personal data and the protection of privacy in the electronic communications sector [2002] OJ L201, 37.

97 Regulation (EU) 2018/1725 of the European Parliament and of the Council of 23 October 2018 on the protection of natural persons with regard to the processing of personal data by the Union institutions, bodies, offices and agencies and on the free movement of such data, and repealing Regulation (EC) No 45/2001 and Decision No 1247/2002/EC (Text with EEA relevance) PE/31/2018/REV/1 [2018] OJ L 295, 39.

98 Regulation (EU) 2016/794 of the European Parliament and of the Council of 11 May 2016 on the European Union Agency for Law Enforcement Cooperation (Europol) and replacing and repealing Council Decisions 2009/371/JHA, 2009/934/JHA, 2009/935/JHA, 2009/936/JHA and 2009/968/JHA [2016] OJ L135, 53.

99 Council Framework Decision 2008/977/JHA (n 4).

100 Directive 2006/24/EC of the European Parliament and of the Council of 15 March 2006 on the retention of data generated or processed in connection with the provision of publicly available electronic communications services or of public communications networks and amending Directive 2002/58/EC [2006] OJ L 105, 54.

101 Directive (EU) 2018/843 of the European Parliament and of the Council of 30 May 2018 amending Directive (EU) 2015/849 on the prevention of the use of the financial system for the purposes of money laundering or terrorist financing, and amending Directives 2009/138/EC and 2013/36/EU (Text with EEA relevance), PE/72/2017/REV/1 [2018] OJ L 156, 43.

102 Directive (EU) 2016/681 (n 3).

Agreements,[103] and Privacy Shield[104]. These instruments have been selected as components of the overarching EU regime establishing rules on the processing of personal data altogether as well as within specific sectors or institutions, and within specific contexts. A deeper focus on the relevant provisions of the DPLE Directive will be provided in the following section of this chapter.

Overall, national security, often also referred to as State security,[105] and public security are mentioned on most occasions side by side without an accompanying definition or differentiation in treatment. More specifically, manifestations of security function as permissible derogations to the application either of the instrument in its totality or of specific provisions, referring namely to the rights of individuals. The GDPR and the DPLE Directive, as aforementioned, explicitly foresee an exemption from the application of the rules they establish, in the context of national security, as falling outside the scope of the EU competences.[106] It is worth mentioning that, formerly, activities of public security were also excluded from application as falling outside the scope of EU law.[107] It can also be observed that older texts refer to the ECHR and follow the verbal construction of Article 8(2) ECHR; a reference that faded away in most recent laws. Finally, both national and public security may be invoked to restrict data subject rights and namely the right of access in many of these instruments, including the GDPR, the DPLE Directive and the PNR Agreements.

The particularities presented in some of these legal instruments, nonetheless, should be given separate consideration. Some light on which elements may constitute national security is shed through its link to intelligence services and their activities,[108] as made by the legal texts of the Framework Decision, the Regulation on EUROPOL and the Privacy Shield.[109] Interestingly, there is

103 Agreement between the European Union and Australia on the processing and transfer of Passenger Name Record (PNR) data by air carriers to the Australian Customs and Border Protection Service [2012] OJ L 186 4 and Agreement between the United States of America and the European Union on the use and transfer of passenger name records to the United States Department of Homeland Security [2012] OJ L 215 5.

104 Commission Implementing Decision (EU) 2016/1250 of 12 July 2016 pursuant to Directive 95/46/EC of the European Parliament and of the Council on the adequacy of the protection provided by the EU-U.S. Privacy Shield (notified under document C(2016) 4176) (Text with EEA relevance), C/2016/4176 [2016] OJ L 207 1.

105 Directive 2006/24/EC (n 100) Rec 4, 9; Directive 2002/58/EC (n 96) Rec 11 and Article 15(1); Council Framework Decision 2008/977/JHA (n 4) Rec 5.

106 (n 14).

107 Directive 2002/58/EC (n 96) Article 1(3); Council Framework Decision 2008/977/JHA (n 4) Rec 5.

108 Traditionally law enforcement authorities are entrusted with internal security and safety and are regulated more transparently under a stronger judicial oversight. On the contrary, intelligence services are competent on matters of national security against external threats, while they also operate with a higher degree of secrecy and enjoy wider discretion with limited judicial control.

109 See for example Council Framework Decision 2008/977/JHA (n 4) Article 1(4) 'This Framework Decision is without prejudice to essential national security interests and specific intelligence activities in the field of national security'.

no mention of intelligence activities being exempted from application of the DPLE Directive, especially in light of the pending cases before the ECJ as will be discussed subsequently. Furthermore, the relevant EU legislative initiatives in the context of counter terrorism, i.e. the PNR Directive and the AML Directive, refrain from referencing to the terms of national and public security, rather they focus on the fight against (serious) crime including terrorism. For instance, the objectives of the PNR Directive is to "*ensure the security and the safety of the public* and ultimately to enhance the *internal security of the EU*".[110]

Bringing all these elements together, the ECJ is also called upon giving an answer to what national and public security comprise of in the field of data protection. In its now famous rulings on bulk transfers of electronic communications data from the service providers to law enforcement authorities, i.e. Digital Rights Ireland[111] and Tele 2 Sverige / Watson,[112] the ECJ acknowledges that the legitimate aim of public security includes the fight against serious crime, in particular organised crime and terrorism. Furthermore, the ECJ has provided through these rulings a set of criteria to which law enforcement authorities must abide in order to collect electronic communications data in bulk. The question that has been recently raised, however, by three Member States, is whether these criteria may be also applicable vis-à-vis intelligence services and hence in the context of national security.[113] Three references for preliminary request currently pending before the ECJ could potentially further blur the lines between national and public security. In this regard, Kuner (2018) argues that the Tele 2 Sverige / Watson ruling could already allow for a broad interpretation of public security, one that would encompass national security as well.[114]

In this vein, the recently adopted Regulation on the free flow of non-personal data, in contrast to the above listed instruments, is the only one providing for a formal definition of public security in its body of recitals.[115] Public security serves also in this case as a ground for derogation from the rules established by said Regulation, which states that "*the concept of public security, within the meaning of Article 52 TFEU and as interpreted by the Court of Justice, covers both the internal and external security of a Member State, as well as issues of public safety, in order, in particular, to facilitate the investigation, detection and prosecution of criminal offences*".[116] The texts continues by explaining that

110 Directive (EU) 2016/681 (n 3) Rec 5–6.

111 Case C-293/12 *Digital Rights Ireland Ltd v Minister for Communications, Marine and Natural Resources and Others and Kärntner Landesregierung and Others* [2014] para 51.

112 Case C-203/15 and C-698/15 *Tele2 Sverige AB v Postoch telestyrelsen and Secretary of State for the Home Department v Tom Watson and Others* [2016] ECR General para 111.

113 (n 67).

114 Christopher Kuner and others (n 65).

115 Regulation (EU) 2018/1807 of the European Parliament and of the Council of 14 November 2018 on a framework for the free flow of non-personal data in the European Union (Text with EEA relevance.) PE/53/2018/REV/1 [2018] OJ L 303, 59.

116 ibid Rec 19.

public security "*presupposes the existence of a genuine and sufficiently serious threat affecting one of the fundamental interests of society, such as a threat to the functioning of institutions and essential public services and the survival of the population, as well as the risk of a serious disturbance to foreign relations or the peaceful coexistence of nations, or a risk to military interests*".

This definition further complicates matters in a twofold manner. Firstly, by introducing the concept of safety as part of public security. Like the notion of security, safety is also what scholars call 'a contested concept'. Even though sometimes the two notions can be used interchangeably, law and security disciplines tend to differentiate between them. With regard to safety, Van den Berg and Prins (2017) consider it as the protection from inadvertent flaws and mistakes which can cause an accidental harm to individuals in a determined situation.[117] Secondly and most importantly, public security within these lines is essentially equated to national security. While in line with the interpretations provided above, this definition bears a fundamental controversy if applied in the context of the DPLE Directive.

4.5. EU MEMBER STATES

The EU Member States, in their turn, conceptualise national security through a number of different legal instruments within their legal regimes. Several derive this notion from constitutional law, some embed it into secondary legislation pertaining on defence and the military, while others formulate national security as an exception to law enforcement statutes. Recently, a study conducted by the Council of Bars & Laws Societies of Europe (CCBE), tried to look into the various Member States notions of national security.[118] What comes as a result of the comparison by CCBE of eleven Member States is indeed the different sources where national security is found as a concept. However, in spite of these

[117] While within the term security the 'acquired values' are harmed deliberately, safety describes instead a protection from a circumstance where the source of the danger is not necessarily human, with the subsequent exclusion of the intentional element in the conceptualization of the term. It is important to note that many challenges of our modern world are the result of a combined failure from both security and safety: Van den Berg and Prins (2017) well describe this with the example of the Fukushima events in 2011, where a tsunami caused by an earthquake provoked a chain reaction that led to a nuclear disaster. In this example, the clearly unintentional course of natural events mixed with human negligence and unpreparedness, putting at risk a significant number of human lives. 'A Multi-Actor Perspective on Security and Safety – Perspectives and Levels' (*Coursera*) <https://www.coursera.org/lecture/security-safety-globalized-world/a-multi-actor-perspective-on-security-and-safety-duiLA> accessed 13 May 2019.

[118] Council of Bars & Law Societies of Europe, 'CCBE Recommendations on the protection of fundamental rights in the context of 'national security' (2019) <https://www.ccbe.eu/fileadmin/speciality_distribution/public/documents/SURVEILLANCE/SVL_Guides_recommendations/EN_SVL_20190329_CCBE-Recommendations-on-the-protection-of-fundamental-rights-in-the-context-of-national-security.pdf> accessed 18 May 2019.

differences in the legal instruments, a number of similarities can be drawn from this exercise.

Interestingly enough, domestic conceptualizations of national security include an explicit reference to the notion of sovereignty, territorial integrity and the protection of democratic order[119] (for instance, this can be observed in the legal systems of Czech Republic,[120] France,[121] Greece,[122] Hungary,[123] Italy[124] and the United Kingdom[125]). This confirms the point made above on the strict interconnection between sovereignty and national security, which, as we have been able to determine, is not only present in political theories, but finds its explications in both international laws and national statutes, too.

Furthermore, in many national frameworks, the results from the CCBE Study underline how other policy domains are also included under the realm of national security, such as, for instance the protection of a nation's citizens and residents against serious threats to their life, health and human rights as well as the conduct and promotion of a nation's foreign relations and commitment to the peaceful coexistence of nations.[126] These domains, however, fall under the concept of public security in the EU secondary legislation as discussed in this section of this chapter.[127] In this respect, two conclusions can be drawn; firstly, even though the definition of national security is not clearly defined in Member States' frameworks, national laws are nevertheless much less vague than EU law when it comes to delineating what competences fall under national security. Secondly, it appears that the EU concept of public security overlaps to an extent with the Member States notions of national security.

5. COMPETENT AUTHORITIES UNDER THE DPLE DIRECTIVE

5.1. GENERAL GUIDANCE

Having established the uncertainty veiling the material scope of the DPLE Directive, we now turn our focus on the personal scope. As previously

119 ibid 10–11 13 14 18.
120 Constitutional Act, Article 1 (CZ).
121 Law L1111-1 Code of Defence (FR).
122 See Law 2292/1995 (GR).
123 National Security Services Act Para. 74 (HU).
124 See Law 124/2007, Articles 6 and 7 (IT).
125 House of Lords, on the Secretary of State for the Home Department v Rehman [2001] UKHL 47.
126 CCBE Recommendations on the protection of fundamental rights in the context of 'national security' (n 118) 18.
127 See the concept of public security within secondary law regulating fundamental freedoms (in particular through the analysis by Panos Koutrakos (n 71) and its definition within Regulation (EU) 2018/1807 (n 115). Similarly, public safety and health fall under the meaning of public security in the regime of the ECHR (see in particular Sofie Stalla-Bourdillon (n 50).

mentioned, the third condition for the applicability of the DPLE Directive is the concept of competent authorities, *i.e.* "*any public authority competent for the prevention [..] of criminal offences [...], including the safeguarding against and the prevention of threats to public security*' or '*any other body or entity entrusted by Member State law to exercise public authority and public powers*" for the same purposes.[128] While the former may be understood as falling strictly within the field of criminal justice latter, the latter may potentially allow for a broader applicability of the DPLE Directive, as this concern was voiced by the EDPS[129] and the WP29[130]. In this respect, the body of recitals of the Directive provides a high-level form of guidance through a small set of examples.

More specifically, according to recital 11, "*such competent authorities may include not only public authorities such as the judicial authorities, the police or other law-enforcement authorities but also any other body or entity entrusted by Member State law to exercise public authority and public powers for the purposes of this Directive. [...] For example, for the purposes of investigation detection or prosecution of criminal offences financial institutions retain certain personal data which are processed by them, and provide those personal data only to the competent national authorities in specific cases and in accordance with Member State law*". The recital continues by pointing out that, in case where an authority also processes personal data for purposes other than the ones falling under the DPLE Directive, said authority would then be considered as a processor, pursuant to the DPLE Directive, of the personal data that the authority is bound to process on behalf of competent authorities. The authority in question, therefore, must abide by the DPLE Directive obligations for processors as regards its processing activities for the purpose of safeguarding public security, and the GDPR for its processing activities for other purposes.

Furthermore, recital 12 attempts to explain the sort of activities may fall under the concept of prevention of criminal offences, including the safeguarding against and prevention of threats to public security. In particular, "*such activities can also include the exercise of authority by taking coercive measures such as police activities at demonstrations, major sporting events and riots. They also include maintaining law and order as a task conferred on the police or other law-enforcement authorities where necessary to safeguard against and prevent threats to public security and to fundamental interests of the society protected by law which may lead to a criminal offence*".[131]

---

128 (n 13).

129 EDPS (n 5).

130 Article 29 Working Party (n 6).

131 The recital further states that 'Member States may entrust competent authorities with other tasks which are not necessarily carried out for the purposes of the prevention, investigation, detection or prosecution of criminal offences, including the safeguarding against and the prevention of threats to public security, so that the processing of personal data for those other purposes, in so far as it is within the scope of Union law, falls within the scope of Regulation (EU) 2016/679'.

These recitals, nonetheless, do not draw a full and comprehensive picture. While some authorities, like law enforcement agencies or bank institutions when performing their tasks under anti-money laundering obligations,[132] will clearly fall under the scope of the Directive, others, like ones entrusted for instance with the management of Critical Infrastructures (hereinafter CI), could fall between the cracks. CI authorities are entrusted with the power to secure their facilities by national, European and international legal instruments.[133] In particular, according to the legal frameworks in question, CI authorities are under the obligation to prevent physical threats and attacks against their infrastructures or individuals on field, attacks which comprise of criminal offences in the realm of criminal laws, as well as a wide range of attacks attempted or committed against their information systems, which also constitute a criminal act and as such will have to be investigated and prosecuted.[134] Finally, as these instruments do not define these powers and authorities as public, it is up to the Member States to decide. Through the example of CI authorities, it is sought to demonstrate how further examination of the national regulation on such entities and on the DPLE Directive should be taken into account in order to clarify the ambiguity of whether such authorities may be considered as a *'public authority'* or *'other body with public authority and public powers'* within the meaning of the DPLE Directive.

Against this backdrop, we explore the national laws of six Member States, i.e. the United Kingdom, Republic of Ireland, Italy, Belgium, Germany and France implementing the DPLE Directive, and their understanding of the scope of the directive and the concept of a competent authority.

---

132 See for instance the obligations under EU and national law: European Commission, 'Anti-money laundering and counter terrorist financing' (19 July 2018) <https://ec.europa.eu/info/policies/justice-and-fundamental-rights/criminal-justice/anti-money-laundering-and-counter-terrorist-financing_en#eulegalframeworkonamlctf> accessed 19 May 2019.

133 See *inter alia* Council Directive 2008/114/EC of 8 December 2008 on the identification and designation of European critical infrastructures and the assessment of the need to improve their protection [2008] OJ L 345 75; Directive 2013/40/EU of the European Parliament and of the Council of 12 August 2013 on attacks against information systems and replacing Council Framework Decision 2005/222/JHA [2013] OJ L218; Directive (EU) 2016/1148 of the European Parliament and of the Council of 6 July 2016 concerning measures for a high common level of security of network and information systems across the Union [2016] OJ L194 30.

134 Directive 2013/40/EU of the European Parliament and of the Council of 12 August 2013 on attacks against information systems and replacing Council Framework Decision 2005/222/JHA [2013] OJ L218 8; Council of Europe, Convention on Cybercrime, 23.11.2001, European Treaty Series No 185.

5.2. NATIONAL IMPLEMENTATION

United Kingdom

The UK 2018 Data Protection Act (hereinafter, the Act),[135] which received the Royal Assent in May 2018, has been one of the first national laws in Europe to provide a full implementation of the whole EU privacy reform package, hence comprising both GDPR and DPLE Directive.[136] A third framework complements the first two, one which makes reference to the Council of Europe's Convention 108: it is the case of the data protection regime in the national security domain. Prominently, the United Kingdom therefore offers one of the most comprehensive legislations, including in the same act (but strictly separated in terms of provisions and obligations) ordinary regime (GDPR), law enforcement regime (DPLE Directive transposed into national law), and national security regime (Convention 108), mitigating the risk of legal uncertainty and fragmentation.

With regard to national security, the Act is structured as follows: within the GDPR implementation (Part2, Chapter 3), national security is considered as an exemption to the general GDPR application, alongside data processing for defence purposes. Furthermore, in Part 4, the Act lays down a proper set of provisions which do not use the wording 'national security' anymore, replaced by the narrower definition 'Intelligence Services Processing'.[137]

In addition, according to the implementation of the DPLE Directive within the Act, competent authorities are those with the statutory functions of public authority or law enforcement; From a mere public-sector perspective, the competent authorities falling under this definition are explicitly enlisted in Schedule 7 (Section 30) of the Act, which provides a long series of governmental bodies that meet the requirements of the DPLE Directive. It should be noted that such a list, might actually be amended at any time by the Secretary of State, who has got the power (by law) of adding or removing public bodies from it. Coming back to the general definition by the Act, according to the British Data Protection Authority the Information Commissioner's Office (hereinafter ICO), the wording *'competent authority'* translates into *"any public authority with powers to investigate and/or prosecute crimes and impose sentences; or any other organizations (such as a private company/contractor) empowered by law [..] to*

135 Data Protection Act 2018 (UK).

136 It is to be noted, for the sake of completeness, that the Data Protection Act does not only cover the implementation of these laws.

137 According to the common security governance of the United Kingdom and the commentary of the British Regulator, the Information Commissioner's Office, intelligence services (entrusted of protecting national security) are MI5, MI6 and GCHQ.

exercise those powers in a way that gives them control over the data i.e. as a data controller, as opposed to a data processor".[138]

As a consequence, competent authorities falling under the DPLE Directive for the British legislator are both public agencies and private ones, as long as the latter category has the status of a data controller (*ergo*: competent authorities cannot be private organizations acting in a data processing chain as data processors). Therefore, under such a provision, companies entrusted to undertake public functions in the criminal justice sector (for instance, organizations involved in the correctional system), will be considered competent authorities when meeting two conditions: being data controller and being empowered by a statutory law, which means that simple contractual arrangements might not be sufficient to fulfil this requirement. Conversely, if a private organization is asked to transfer data to a police agency for criminal investigation purposes, that same organization will still have to adhere to the GDPR: personal data will fall under the DPLE Directive regime only when they will be transferred to the law enforcement authority.[139]

Republic of Ireland

Similarly, the Republic of Ireland has included provisions on personal data processing for law enforcement purposes within a piece of legislation which comprises a number of general data protection principles deriving from the GDPR. The 2018 Irish Data Protection Act (hereinafter, the 'Irish Act'), dedicates its entire Part 5, constituted by six Chapters), to the implementation of the DPLE Directive in the national legal framework.[140] The legal regime outlined in Part 5 therefore applies when two conditions are met. Firstly, the data processing operation is carried out for law enforcement purposes, intended by Article 70 as prevention, investigation, detection, prosecution and execution of criminal offences, unless the processing of data is undertaken either for the purposes of safeguarding national security, defence or foreign state relations, or under the 2014 Criminal Justice Act on Forensic Evidence and DNA Database System or under the 2018 Automated Vehicle registration Searching Act. In this latter case, the 1988 Irish Data Protection Act will still apply and thus not be repealed by the 2018 Irish Act (Part 1, Article 8). The second condition to be met is indeed that the organization carrying out the data processing must fall under the definition of competent authority.

---

138 Information Commissioner's Office, Guide to Law Enforcement Provisions (Version 1.0.6, 2017) <https://www.dataprotection.ie/organisations/law-enforcement-directive> accessed 13 May 2019.

139 This is the case of financial institutions, for instance, processing personal data for anti-fraud or anti-money laundering finalities: in these circumstances, data will follow the ordinary GDPR regime of the Act until they are transferred to the police authority requesting it.

140 Data Protection Act 2018 (IE), 5.

In the Irish context, competent law enforcement authorities would naturally be the *An Garda Síochána*, although the definition extends to other organizations, as enshrined in the wording of the DPLE Directive. Differently from the British Act, the Irish one does not provide for an explicit list of competent authorities. Specifically, the Irish Act deliberately allows for a larger number of public organizations to fit in this definition. To prove the broadness of this wording, the Irish Data protection Commission (*An Coimisinéir Cosanta Sonraí*) makes the example of local authorities or public transport companies processing fines and sanctions, concluding that it is impossible to delineate exactly the contours of public competent authorities, and that therefore this will have to be done on a case-by-case basis.[141]

Furthermore, private organizations may fit, under the fulfilment of a number of requirements, within the definition of competent authorities, as dictated by the DPLE Directive definition of *'any other body or entity'*.[142] As a consequence, any private organization undertaking law enforcement activities must be entrusted by a legislation to do so, in order to be considered authority. Lastly, competent authorities must be data controllers. In the definition of data processors, in fact, the wording results to be broader, hence including any natural or legal person, public agency or other body.[143]

Italy[144]

The Decree 51/2018 (hereinafter Decree 51),[145] i.e. the Italian DPLE Directive implementing Act, defines its material scope of application as *"automated or semi-automated personal data processing of natural persons by competent authorities for the purposes of prevention, investigation, detection and prosecution of criminal offences and the execution of criminal sanctions"*.[146] The above data processing includes, *inter alia*, the processing for archiving purposes or the processing of the same data in a 'police database'. It should be noted that, according to some authors, the Italian legislator has exercised the flexibility clause of Article 45 of the DPLE Directive, deliberately leaving out from the supervision of the Italian Data protection Authority (*Garante per la Protezione dei Dati Personali*) the processing of personal data by the judiciary body when exercising its decisional activities, in order to respect the principle of judiciary

141 'Law Enforcement Directive | Data Protection Commission' (n 138).
142 Data Protection Act 2018, Article 69 (IE).
143 ibid.
144 All translations are the author's, unless otherwise indicated.
145 Rossi Copparoni & Partners, 'Approvato Il Decreto Di Attuazione Della Direttiva UE in Materia Di Trattamento Dei Dati Personali Da Parte Delle Autorità Competenti' (8 June 2018) <www.rpcstudiolegale.it/2018/06/08/approvato-il-decreto-di-attuazione-della-direttiva-ue-in-materia-di-trattamento-dei-dati-personali-da-parte-delle-autorita-competenti/> accessed 10 May 2019.
146 Legislative Decree 51/2018, Article 1 (IT).

independence.[147] In the same article, while the legislator specifies that the data processing operation undertaken for public security purposes falls within the scope of application of the Decree 51, national security is nevertheless explicated as an out-of-scope domain.[148]

With regard to public sector competent authorities, it is interesting to note that the Italian legislator made explicit that competent authorities are any public bodies undertaking law enforcement tasks, be it Italian, European or third-country ones.[149] In its opinion 86/2017,[150] issued during the drafting phase of the Decree 51, the Italian *Garante* explored this topic with regard to Italian public agencies, making an important series of operative distinctions within the term competent authority. For instance, the *Garante*'s opinion states that the Decree should not be applicable *a priori* to all public authorities' data processing with a link of any sort with police activities (for instance, in the case of data processing operations undertaken by Prefectures, Custom Agencies or local Police): in such cases in fact, the DPLE Directive will only apply insofar as the processing demonstrates a clear and strict link with the enforcement of a criminal provision.

The competent authorities which are not public bodies are further defined as "*any other entity or organization tasked by the national legal system with law enforcement activities*".[151] While the translation of this wording may not look particularly problematic, the Italian wording opens up for a broad interpretation of the term 'national legal system' (tr. *ordinamenti interni*), as it does not specify in narrow terms what sort of national law would suffice (would it be a Law, a Law Decree, a Legislative Decree?). Contextually, the wording seems to leave room for foreign organizations too, since "*as tasked by the national legal* system" could refer, interpreted broadly, to private organizations entrusted by foreign countries to undertake law enforcement tasks in those same countries. Lastly, and similarly to the British and Irish frameworks, the Decree 51 specifies what established organizations can undertake the functions of controllers and

---

147 See for instance, Monica A. Senor, 'Una Overview Sulla Data Protection in Ambito Di Polizia e Giustizia Penale – ICT Security Magazine' (17 September 2018) <https://www.ictsecuritymagazine.com/articoli/una-overview-sulla-data-protection-in-ambito-di-polizia-e-giustizia-penale/> accessed 10 May 2019.

148 According to the statutory Law No. 124 from 2007 [Sistema di Informazione per la Sicurezza della Repubblica e Nuova Disciplina del Segreto (tr., Intelligence System for the Republic's Security and New State Secret Framework)], these bodies result to be the DIS – Department for Information and Security (the general intelligence directorate), the Agency for Internal Information and Security – AISI (the internal security services) and the Agency for External Information and Security – AISE (the foreign intelligence agency).

149 Decree 51 (n 146), Article 2(g).

150 Italian DPA, Article 1, Capo 5.1, Registro dei provvedimenti n. 86 del 2 marzo 2017 'Parere Su Uno Schema Di d.P.R. Ai Sensi Dell'art 57 Del Codice, in Tema… – Garante Privacy' <https://www.garanteprivacy.it/web/guest/home/docweb/-/docweb-display/docweb/6197365> accessed 10 May 2019.

151 Decree 51 (n 146), Article 2(g).

processors: competent authorities are only controllers,[152] while processor tasks can be contracted to any legal or natural persons[153].

Belgium[154]

Alike the United Kingdom, Belgium also regulates in one law the processing of personal data by all entities, whether they fall within the scope of the GDPR (Title 1) or the DPLE Directive (Title 2), or outside the scope of both instruments (Title 3).[155] It should first be noted that national security is not mentioned explicitly as falling outside the scope. Furthermore, Belgium repeats in its national law verbatim the relative provision regarding the scope of the DPLE Directive (Article 27). Interestingly enough, it provides for a detailed definition of a competent authority within the meaning of the DPLE Directive through a seemingly exhaustive list of entities (Article 26.7). The additional particularity observed is that competent authorities also entail units within intelligence services. More specifically, the list of competent authorities includes *inter alia* the General Administration of Customs and Excise, the Passenger Information Unit, the Financial Information Processing Unit and the Investigation Service of the Standing Committee for the Control of Intelligence Services in the framework of it judicial missions.

According to the Belgian approach, then, an extensive part of rules and derogations specific to entities that to be regulated separately, follows the provisions implementing the GDPR and the DPLE Directive in the law.[156] The Belgian Data Protection Authority explain it its opinion that these entities fall outside the scope of the two legal instruments due to their link to national security.[157] This approach seems not to allow for a broadening of scope of the DPLE Directive rules to authorities other than the ones explicitly named in the Belgian law.

---

152 ibid, Article 2(h).

153 ibid, Article 2(i).

154 All translations are the author's, unless otherwise indicated.

155 Loi du 30 juillet 2018 relative à la protection des personnes physiques à l'égard des traitements de données à caractère personnel / Wet betreffende de bescherming van natuurlijke personen met betrekking tot de verwerking van persoonsgegevens, Moniteur Belge / Belgish Staatsblad, 05-09-2018.

156 Intelligence and security services other than the ones that fall within the definition of competent authorities, Armed Forces, in the context of classification and security clearings, safety certificates and safety advice, the coordination body for the threat analysis and the Passenger Information Unit.

157 Autorité de protection des données – APD / Gegevensbeschermingsautoriteit – GBA (Belgian DPA), Avis n° 33/2018 du 11 avril 2018 / Advies nr. 33/2018 van 11 april 2018.

France[158]

French law, in a rather complicated manner, excludes state security, defence and public security from the scope of application, unless otherwise prescribed by the chapter within the law transposing the DPLE Directive.[159] The chapter in question, nonetheless, refers to the DPLE Directive purpose of protection against threats to public security and the prevention of such threats (Article 70). Moreover, it provides for the same definition of competent authorities as the DPLE Directive, in a way that resembles a mere translation of the relevant provision.

The French data protection authority, Commission Nationale de l'Informatique et des Libertés (hereinafter CNIL) recently provided for an explanatory text as regards the transposition of the DPLE Directive.[160] Apart from law enforcement and judicial authorities, according to CNIL, the internal services of safety of CI authorities such as the Autonomous Operator of Parisian Transports (Régie Autonome des Transports Parisiens – RATP) and the French National Railway Company (Société nationale des chemins de fer français – SNCF), and the approved sports federations for the purpose of securing sports events consist of competent authorities. The examples provided by CNIL seem to confirm the hypothesis that competent authorities may encompass a wide range of authorities entrusted with security in the broad sense.

Germany

The German Federal Data Protection Act (hereinafter the Federal Act) defines controllers within the meaning of the DPLE Directive as public bodies competent for the prevention, investigation, detection or prosecution of criminal or administrative offences or the execution of criminal or administrative penalties, as far as they process data for the purpose of carrying out these tasks (Part 3).[161] It further clarifies that the prevention of criminal offences includes the protection against and prevention of threats to public security. The provisions transposing the DPLE Directive rules are also applicable vis-à-vis public bodies responsible for executing penalties, criminal measures, and educational or disciplinary measures as referred to in the Juvenile Court Act. Moreover, the

158 All translations are the author's, unless otherwise indicated.

159 LOI n° 2018-493 du 20 Juin 2018 relative à la protection des données personnelles, Journal Officiel de la République Française (JORF), 21-06-2018, Chapitre XIII (FR).

160 Commission Nationale de l'Informatique et des Libertés – CNIL (French DPA), 'Directive "Police-Justice": de quoi parle-t-on?' (20 February 2019) <https://www.cnil.fr/fr/directive-police-justice-de-quoi-parle-t> accessed 19 May 2019.

161 Gesetz zur Anpassung des Datenschutzrechts an die Verordnung (EU) 2016/679 und zur Umsetzung der Richtlinie (EU) 2016/680 (Datenschutz-Anpassungs- und -Umsetzungsgesetz EU – DSAnpUG-EU), Bundesdatenschutzgesetz vom 30. Juni 2017 (BGBl. I S. 2097), as translated by the Language Service of the Federal Ministry of the Interior.

Federal Act regulates processing activities that fall outside the scope of both GDPR and DPLE Directive (Part 4).[162]

What is interesting and exceptional about the Federal Act is that it includes entities entrusted with public security under the scope of the GDPR (Part 1). More specifically, the GDPR applies to a broad range of public and private bodies of the Federation and of the Länder. The processing of sensitive personal data by public bodies is permitted when it is "*urgently necessary for reasons of substantial public* interest"; "*necessary to prevent a substantial threat to public security*"; is "*urgently necessary to prevent substantial harm to the common good or to safeguard substantial concerns of the common good*"; or "*necessary for urgent reasons of defence or to fulfil supra- or intergovernmental obligations of a public body of the Federation in the field of crisis management or conflict prevention or for humanitarian measures*". The German law is innovative also in the sense of introducing this notion of 'urgent necessity'.

Finally, the processing activities of personal data in the context of video surveillance activities of publicly accessible spaces also fall under the GDPR. In particular, the Federal Act states that "*for video surveillance of large publicly accessible facilities, such as sport facilities, places of gathering and entertainment, shopping centres and car parks, or vehicles and large publicly accessible facilities of public rail, ship or bus transport*", the protection of the lives, health and freedom of persons present is regarded as a very important interest and hence as the legal basis for such processing activities (Chapter 2, section 4). According to German law, contrary to the national laws analysed above, a broad range of entities entrusted with public security, including for example CI authorities, have to abide by the GDPR and not the DPLE Directive.

6. CONCLUSIONS

Based on the three-layered examination of the scope of the DPLE Directive, a number of conclusions can be drawn. Starting with the first layer, the analysis of the sources under general theories of international law reveals the lack of effort by scholars and law-makers in defining national security. However, some recurring elements have been usefully pointed out in order to understand the contextualization of such a terminology. For example, the historical dependence of national security as an embodiment of the sovereignty principle is a trend

162 In particular, the law states that the transfer of personal data to a third country, to supranational or intergovernmental bodies or to international organizations in the context of activities outside the scope of GDPR and DPLE Directive shall be permitted in addition to the cases permitted under the GDPR, also when the processing is necessary to perform tasks for urgent reasons of defence or to fulfil *supra-* or intergovernmental obligations of a public body of the Federation in the field of crisis management or conflict prevention or for humanitarian measures.

that we encounter in political science, security studies, international treaties and even national laws. It is a building block of national security doctrine to refer to sovereignty and its exercise, seen as the explication of a social contract between the citizens and the executive, a relationship which calls for reciprocal acceptance, democratic accountability and control.

All sources in fact reveal, in different forms and fashions, that invocation of national security reasons is conditioned to the recurrence of exceptional conditions. As such, most of the treaties (even those including a *self-judging* clause), either circumscribe narrowly the national security exception (often considering it as a separate concept from the notions of '*public order*', '*public safety*', '*public security*' or '*crime prevention*'), or foresee a judicial scrutiny on the invocation of national security by states, often substantiated in a judicial evaluation of appropriateness, necessity, proportionality and legality.

In the second layer of the EU regime, while Union law refers to national security in order to delineate its competences and regulatory powers, it also refrains from providing a definition. The term seems to be understood as linked to the core, sovereignty and democratic nature of a state, in a similar way as analysed under general theories and international law. The concept of public security under EU law may also be invoked by Member States in order to repress the applicability of EU law. At the same time, it serves as one of EU's highest priorities; public security of EU citizens increasingly gives rise to EU policy and legislation, with counter-terrorism often as its centre-line. Public security, however, evolves through secondary legislation, as the latter is informed by the jurisprudence of the ECJ, into an autonomous concept. This concept appears expansive and inclusive of domains that under international or national law would have been considered to constitute national security.

Therefore, the paradox observed is that public security, when invoked as a derogation, may be as broad as to overlap with national security, even though it is still subject to judicial scrutiny and must be interpreted narrowly. The question then arises vis-à-vis the effects of this broadening of the term of public security, when it is established as the rule and no longer as an exception, for instance in the case of the DPLE Directive. It could be inferred that public security might continue to be as broad as consisting of both the internal and external security of a Member State, public safety, societal security, survival of the population and peaceful coexistence of states. One may then consider in the scope of public security all those bodies and entities tasked not only with the identification and criminalisation of a threat (strictly speaking, law enforcement authorities), but also organisations competent or tasked with the prevention and the minimisation of a broader range of security risks. As a consequence, it will then be up to Member States to name their exceptions under a more restricted notion of national security.

Finally, according to the analysis under the third layer, the distinction between data protection frameworks, i.e. GDPR, DPLE Directive or other, boils down to the level of strictness of rules. Contrary to the GDPR, the DPLE Directive is more flexible from a data controller's perspective, allowing for a more restricted exercise of data subject rights. Nonetheless, as observed in this chapter, several Member States (e.g. United Kingdom, Belgium and Germany) have opted for a granular regulatory approach affecting a wide range of authorities.

To conclude, on the grounds of national security, intelligence services seem to fall outside the scope of the GDPR and the DPLE Directive, while they may still be subject to some form of regulation. As regards the regulatory discretion states enjoy, international bodies, such as the UN, advocate more accountable and transparent intelligence oversight. Insofar as the concept of public security is concerned, it becomes expansive under EU law while it lacks clarity within the DPLE Directive. Brought together, these elements allow for various authorities entrusted by Member States with the public mandate to ensure internal and external security, inter alia critical infrastructures authorities as aforementioned, to be considered as competent authorities. In such case, they will have to comply with the DPLE Directive as opposed to the GDPR, in relation to their activities within this context. In practice, that may be a very fine line to draw.

ACKNOWLEDGEMENT

The research for this chapter has been performed and has been partially funded by the project *Infra*Stress (GA 833088) under the Horizon 2020 scheme of the European Commission and call SU-INFRA01-2018-2019-2020 and partially by the project SAURON (GA 740477) under the Horizon 2020 scheme of the European Commission and call CIP-01-2016-2017.

BIBLIOGRAPHY

Azoulai L and Coutts S, 'Restricting Union citizens' residence rights on grounds of public security. Where Union citizenship and the AFSJ meet: P.I.' (2013) Vol. 50 Common Market Law Review 553

Besson, S, 'Sovereignty' Oxford Public International Law (2011) Max Planck Encyclopedia of Public International Law [MPEPIL]<https://opil.ouplaw.com/ view/10.1093/ law:epil/9780199231690/law-9780199231690-e1472> accessed 13 May 2019

Bigo D, 'The European internal security field: stakes and rivalries in a newly developing area of police intervention' in Anderson M and Boer MD (eds), *Policing Across National Boundaries* (1994) 161

Blockmans S and others, *What Comes after the Last Chance Commission? Policy Priorities for 2019–2024* (Steven Blockmans ed, 2019)

Boehm F, 'Data Processing and Law Enforcement Access to Information Systems at EU Level' (2012) 36 Datenschutz und Datensicherheit – DuD 339

Brown H, 'U.S. National Security: The Next 50 Years' (2000) Centre for Naval Analyses, https://www.cna.org/CNA_files/PDF/D0001565.A1.pdf

Buzan B, 'Peace, Power, and Security: Contending Concepts in the Study of International Relations' (1984) 21 Journal of Peace Research 109

Cameron I, *National Security and the European Convention on Human Rights* (Kluwer Law International 2000) 54

Claes M, 'The Primacy of EU Law in European and National Law' in Arnull A and Chalmers D (eds), *The Oxford Handbook of European Union Law* <www.oxfordhandbooks.com/view/10.1093/oxfordhb/9780199672646.001.0001/oxfordhb-9780199672646-e-8> accessed 5 April 2019

Claes M, 'The Primacy of EU Law in European and National Law' in Anthony Arnull and Damian Chalmers (eds), *The Oxford Handbook of European Union Law* (2015), 178-211 <www. oxfordhandbooks.com/view/10.1093/oxfordhb/9780199672646.001.0001/oxfordhb9780199672646-e-8> accessed 5 April 2019

Council of Bars & Law Societies of Europe, 'CCBE Recommendations on the protection of fundamental rights in the context of 'national security' (2019) <https://www.ccbe.eu/fileadmin/speciality_distribution/public/documents/SURVEILLANCE/SVL_Guides_recommendations/EN_SVL_20190329_CCBE-Recommendations-on-the-protection-of-fundamental-rights-in-the-context-of-national-security.pdf> accessed 18 May 2019

Dashwood A and others, *Wyatt and Dashwood's European Union Law* (6th edition, Hart Publishing 2011) 482–485

De Hert P and Papakonstantinou V, 'The Police and Criminal Justice Data Protection Directive: Comment and Analysis' (2012) 7 New Journal of European Criminal Law 7

Dimitrova A and Brkan M, 'Balancing National Security and Data Protection: The Role of EU and US Policy-Makers and Courts before and after the NSA Affair' (2017) Journal of Common Market Studies 751

Dobbs M, 'Sovereignty, article 4(2) TEU and the respect of national identities: Swinging the balance of power in favour of the member states?' (2014) Yearbook of European Law 33(1) 298

Eisenhut D, 'Sovereignty, National Security and International Treaty Law. The Standard of Review of International Courts and Tribunals with Regard to "Security Exceptions"' (2010) 48 Archiv des Völkerrechts 431

Finnis J, 'Absolute Rights: Some Problems Illustrated' (2016) 61 American Journal of Jurisprudence 195

Gray C, 'A Crisis of Legitimacy for the UN Collective Security System?' (2007) 56 The International and Comparative Law Quarterly 157

Guastaferro B, 'Beyond the Exceptionalism of Constitutional Conflicts: The Ordinary Functions of the Identity Clause' (2012) Yearbook of European Law 263–318

Hahn MJ, 'Vital Interests and the Law of GATT: An Analysis of GATT's Security Exception' (1991) 12 Michigan Journal of International Law 558

Hobbes T, *Leviathan-Or the Matter, Form and Power of a Common-Wealth Ecclesiastical and Civil* (I Shapiro ed, first published 1651, Yale University Press 2010)

Information Commissioner's Office, *Guide to Law Enforcement Provisions* (Version 1.0.6, 2017) <https://www.dataprotection.ie/organisations/law-enforcement-directive> accessed 13 May 2019

Knorr K, 'National Security Studies: Scope and Structure of the Field' in Frank N. Trager and Philip S. Kronenberg (eds), *National Security and American Society: Theory, Process and Policy* (Lawrence KS, 1973) 5

Koutrakos P, 'Public Security Exceptions and EU Freed Movement Law' in P. Koutrakos, N. Nic Shuibhne & P. Syrpis (eds), *Exceptions from EU Free Movement Law: Derogation, Justification and Proportionality* (Hart Publishing 2016) 190

Kuner C and others, 'An Unstoppable Force and an Immoveable Object? EU Data Protection Law and National Security' 3

Macken C, 'Preventive Detention and the Right of Personal Liberty and Security under the International Covenant on Civil and Political Rights, 1966' (2005) 26 Adelaide Law Review 1

Marquenie T, 'The Police and Criminal Justice Authorities Directive: Data protection standards and impact on the legal framework' (2017) 33 Computer Law & Security Review 324

Midelieva L, 'The Elusive Cause and the Extensive Effect of the Principle of Supremacy of EU Law' (2017) 7 Southampton Student Law Review 21

Mijalkovic S and Blagojevic D, 'The Basis of National Security in International Law' [2014] Nauka, bezbednost, policija 49

Murrill BJ, 'The "National Security Exception" and the World Trade Organization' (2018) <https://fas.org/sgp/crs/row/LSB10223.pdf> accessed 27 June 2019 5

Quintel T, 'European Union · Article 29 Data Protection Working Party Opinion on the Law Enforcement Directive' (2018) 4 European Data Protection Law Review 104

Romm JJ, *Defining National Security: The Nonmilitary Aspects* (Council on Foreign Relations Press 1993)

Rose-Ackerman S and Billa B, 'Treaties and National Security' (2008) reprinted in Yale Law School Faculty Scholarship Series <https://digitalcommons.law.yale.edu/fss_papers/595/> accessed 27 June 2019

Rossi Copparoni & Partners, 'Approvato Il Decreto Di Attuazione Della Direttiva UE in Materia Di Trattamento Dei Dati Personali Da Parte Delle Autorità Competenti' (8 June 2018) <www.rpcstudiolegale.it/2018/06/08/approvato-il-decreto-di-attuazione-della-direttiva-ue-in-materia-di-trattamento-dei-dati-personali-da-parte-delle-autorita-competenti/> accessed 10 May 2019

Senor M A, 'Una Overview Sulla Data Protection in Ambito Di Polizia e Giustizia Penale – ICT Security Magazine' (17 September 2018) <https://www.ictsecuritymagazine.com/articoli/una-overview-sulla-data-protection-in-ambito-di-polizia-e-giustizia-penale/> accessed 10 May 2019

Sliwinski KF, 'Moving beyond the European Union's Weakness as a Cyber-Security Agent' (2014) 35 Contemporary Security Policy 468

Stalla-Bourdillon S, 'Privacy Versus Security … Are We Done Yet?' in Sophie Stalla-Bourdillon, Joshua Phillips, Mark D. Ryan (eds), *Privacy vs. Security* (Springer London, Springer Briefs in Cybersecurity 2014) 69

Van den Berg B and Prins R, 'A Multi-Actor Perspective on Security and Safety – Perspectives and Levels' (Coursera) <https://www.coursera.org/lecture/security-

safety-globalized-world/a-multi-actor-perspective-on-security-and-safety-duiLA> accessed 13 May 2019

UNHR, 'States Must Bridge Privacy Gap in Intelligence Sharing, Says UN Human Rights Expert' (1 March 2019) <https://www.ohchr.org/EN/NewsEvents/Pages/DisplayNews.aspx?NewsID=24242&LangID=E> accessed 2 April 2019

Weatherill S, 'Distinctive Identity Claims, Article 4(2) TEU (and a Fleetingly Sad Nod to Brexit) Editorial Note' (2016) 12 Croatian Yearbook of European Law and Policy VII

CHAPTER 4

CRIMINAL PROFILING AND NON-DISCRIMINATION: ON FIRM GROUNDS FOR THE DIGITAL ERA?

Laurens NAUDTS

1. INTRODUCTION

Within a democratic society, and governed by the rule of law, law enforcement and intelligence agencies serve the maintenance of public tranquillity, law and order. They seek to prevent, detect and combat crime, and provide assistance and service functions to the public.[1] Tasked with the protection against and prevention of threats to public and national security and to the fundamental interests of society, they are bound to protect and respect fundamental rights, and in particular those enshrined within the European Convention on Human Rights (hereinafter ECHR).[2] Nevertheless, for the performance of their functions, and in order to safeguard their independence, effectiveness and impartiality, they have been granted a wide degree of discretion.[3]

As guardians of public and national security, public authorities have found in big data analytics a new instrument to facilitate the performance of their core activities, i.e. the prevention, investigation, detection or prosecution of criminal offences or the execution of criminal penalties.[4] Data-driven technologies

---

1 See inter alia: Committee of Ministers of the Council of Europe, 'The European Code of Police Ethics' Recommendation (2001) 10, para 1; and The Council of Europe and the European Court of Human Rights, 'National Security and European Case-Law' (2013) <https://www.echr.coe.int/Documents/Research_report_national_security_ENG.pdf> accessed 03 July 2019.

2 Ibid.

3 See inter alia, Jim Murdoch and Ralph Roche, *The European Convention on Human Rights and Policing: A handbook for police officers and other law enforcement officials*, (Council of Europe Publishing, 2013) 154, 7; Commissioner for Human Rights, Opinion concerning independent and effective determination of complaints against the police (12 March 2009) para 15; Committee of Ministers of the Council of Europe (n 1) and the Council of Europe and the European Court of Human Rights (n 1).

4 See inter alia: Sarah Brayne, 'Big Data Surveillance: The Case of Policing' (2017) Vol. 82 American Sociological Review 977; Evelien De Pauw and others (eds), *Technology-Led*

in particular help public authorities in their battle against different forms of criminality.[5] One such application, is the collection, and subsequent analysis, of data for the purposes of building criminal profiles which can be deployed either in a predictive, real-time or post-fact manner. Criminal profiling has been described as the process whereby 'exhibited criminal behaviours are evaluated for the purpose of making some prediction concerning the characteristics of the probable offender, in order to provide information that can assist in criminal investigations'.[6] The increase in the availability of data, in combination with rapid technological developments in the fields of data analysis, have increased the potential for, and the scope at which, profiling strategies can be developed and deployed. Due to these advancements however, the associated risks criminal profiles may pose have increased as well. Whether they are scientifically sound or not, profiling tactics, or a variation thereof, are generally perceived as promising and beneficial for law enforcement endeavours, and therefor relied, and invested, upon.[7]

The validity and evaluation of profiling can be approached through many different angles, this paper aims to contribute to the current discourse by evaluating one specific risk of profiling: the potential discriminatory nature of profiling practices. In this regard, the chapter aims to clear one part of the confusion concerning the legality of criminal profiling, i.e. the role non-discrimination law, and more specifically non-discrimination grounds, can play in evaluating the valid and justified use of certain types of information where profiles are generated to serve decision-making for security purposes. It does so by looking at the legal building blocks that govern the inclusion of

Policing (Maklu 2011); Lina Dencik, Arne Hintz and Zoe Carey, 'Prediction, Pre-Emption and Limits to Dissent: Social Media and Big Data Uses for Policing Protests in the United Kingdom' (2018) Vol. 20 New Media & Society 1433; Greg Ridgeway, 'Policing in the Era of Big Data' (2018) 1 Annual Review of Criminology 401; Solon Barocas and Andrew D. Selbst, 'Big Data's Disparate Impact Essay' (2016) 104 California Law Review 671; Liza van Lonkhuyzen, 'Misdaad voorspellen, het kan echt' *NRC* (16 May 2017) <https://www.nrc.nl/nieuws/2017/05/16/misdaad-voorspellen-het-kan-echt-9100898-a1558837> accessed 8 March 2019; Lars Bové, 'Politie gaat criminaliteit via data voorspellen' *De Tijd* (30 August 2018) <https://www.tijd.be/politiek-economie/belgie/federaal/politie-gaat-criminaliteit-via-data-voorspellen/10044356.html> accessed 8 March 2019; CNIL, 'Comment Permettre à l'Homme de Garder La Main ? Rapport Sur Les Enjeux Éthiques Des Algorithmes et de l'intelligence Artificielle' (2017) <https://www.cnil.fr/en/node/24008> accessed 8 March 2019.

5 Committee of Ministers of the Council of Europe, 'The European Code of Police Ethics (n 1) para 42.

6 Richard N Kocsis, *Criminal Profiling: Principles and Practice* (Humana Press 2006) 9.

7 See for instance: Kocsis (n 6); Albert Meijer and Martijn Wessels, 'Predictive Policing: Review of Benefits and Drawbacks' [2019] International Journal of Public Administration 1; Richard N Kocsis and George B Palermo, 'Disentangling Criminal Profiling: Accuracy, Homology, and the Myth of Trait-Based Profiling' (2015) Vol. 59 International Journal of Offender Therapy and Comparative Criminology 313; De Pauw and others (n 4); Laurence Alison and others, 'Pragmatic Solutions to Offender Profiling and Behavioural Investigative Advice' (2010) Vol. 15 Legal and Criminological Psychology 115.

certain information in criminal profiles. After having briefly touched upon the nature of criminal and algorithmic profiling, in the first section, the chapter will analyse data protection legislation, which focuses on the data underlying the profiles – data that will moreover function as the constituents of the profile. Despite governing primarily the fundamental rights to privacy and data protection, current EU data protection laws remains sensitive towards the potential discriminatory nature of personal data processing. In the second section, it will be ascertained to what extent non-discrimination law considers the use of certain types of information as problematic where this information is used to differentiate amongst individuals or groups of individuals. Here, an evaluation will be made of the case law of the European Court of Human Rights (hereinafter ECtHR) and their discourse on the 'discrimination grounds'. As profiles consist of an amalgamation of information, the Court's case-law on the human right to non-discrimination may prove particularly interesting. Indeed, the grounds, such as ethnicity, gender or age, that underlie or serve as the basis for differentiation are often a crucial element in the Court's reasoning. In doing so, the second section aims to identify the criteria the ECtHR uses to delimit problematic from unproblematic forms of differentiation. Through the analysis of the ECtHR's case law, it will be ascertained whether, and to what extent, the ECHR non-discrimination clause is closed or open-ended, i.e. whether every form of differentiation can engage the ECHR's non-discrimination clause. The chapter will further analyse the justification that must be provided by nations for differential treatment to be considered legitimate.[8] The conclusion of this analysis will be juxtaposed to the new risks big data analytics pose to the human rights of equality and non-discrimination.

2. CRIMINAL AND ALGORITHMIC PROFILING

Like criminal profiles, algorithms too rely on differentiation. Both processes build upon finding patterns and connections in order to distinguish between groups and individuals in an effort to guide decisions that are relevant for the specific task at hand. Within a security setting, profiles serve towards the prediction, prevention and investigation of crimes or the apprehension of criminals. Whereas algorithms can be deployed for a variety of purposes, they can also be used to complement a criminal profile. Filtering, and learning

8 This chapter focuses upon the nature of differentiation grounds. It therefore only analyses one particular element of the legal framework governing profiling practices. Other rules will need to be considered in order to determine whether or not profiling practices are indeed lawful, such as the impact of big data analytics on the fundamental rights to privacy and data protection. Though data protection instruments will be discussed, they will only be assessed in so far as they are relevant for the equality and non-discrimination related evaluation of data-driven analytics and profiling.

from, large amounts of data, big data analytics can add better information to, or help in making more concrete and accurate, the criminal profile. Although the data-driven approach might reflect traditional, analogue methods of criminal profiling, they can nevertheless source larger pools of data, e.g. criminal databases, social media data and video material, in order to find more correlations relevant for crime solving. Due to the increased availability of data, profiles can become more complex, with a high granularity in the parameters deemed relevant for law enforcement purposes.

Through their application, profiles inherently instil different treatment upon specific segments of the population, or persons therein. Profiles might for example determine which neighbourhoods should be more closely monitored by police forces,[9] which individuals or communities should be tracked in fear of radicalization,[10] or which psychological traits indicate deviant behaviour[11]. As a consequence, and whether online or offline, predictive, real-time or post-fact, the question must be raised to what extent a difference in treatment can be justified. From a non-discrimination law perspective, the principle of equality stipulates that like situations should be treated alike, and unalike situations unalike, and that differences in treatment must have an objective justification.[12] Hence, what are the conditions for profiles to serve as a justification for differential treatment? Moreover, law enforcement agencies are likely to be subject to a heightened scrutiny. As the Council of Europe recently noted: *"Member states should apply the highest level of scrutiny when using AI systems in the context of law enforcement, especially when engaging in methods such as predictive or preventive policing. Such systems need to be independently audited prior to deployment for any discriminatory effect that could indicate de facto profiling of specific groups. If any such effects are detected, the system cannot be used."*[13]

---

9 See for instance the PredPol predictive policing system in the United States: Issie Lapowsky, 'How the LAPD uses data to predict crime' (*Wired*, 22 May 2018) <https://www.wired.com/story/los-angeles-police-department-predictive-policing/> accessed 03 July 2019 -and the CAS system in the Netherlands: Marc Schuilenburg, 'De burger moet kunnen weten hoe de misdaadvoorspeller werkt' (*NRC* 18 June 2018) <https://www.nrc.nl/nieuws/2018/06/18/de-burger-moet-kunnen-weten-hoe-de-misdaadvoorspeller-werkt-a1606978> accessed 03 July 2019.

10 Swati Agarwal and Ashish Sureka, 'Applying Social Media Intelligence for Predicting and Identifying On-Line Radicalization and Civil Unrest Oriented Threats' (2015) ArXiv <http://arxiv.org/abs/1511.06858> accessed 9 May 2019.

11 Brent E Turvey, *Criminal Profiling: An Introduction to Behavioral Evidence Analysis* (4th edn, Oxford: Academic 2011).

12 The preamble to Protocol 12 to the ECHR clarifies the relationship between both equality and non-discrimination: "the non-discrimination and equality principles are closely intertwined. For example, the principle of equality requires that equal situations are treated equally and unequal situations differently. Failure to do so will amount to discrimination unless an objective and reasonable justification exists."

13 Council of Europe, Commissioner for Human Rights, 'Unboxing Artificial Intelligence: 10 steps to protect Human Rights' (May 2019) 11 <https://rm.coe.int/unboxing-artificial-intelligence-10-steps-to-protect-human-rights-reco/1680946e64> accessed 03 July 2019.

Traditionally, non-discrimination laws have been considered as instruments that serve the protection of specific groups, represented by specific traits, such as ethnicity or gender, within society. Unlike traditional forms of profiling, big data analytics could allow for the generation of new groups, where relevant traits or parameters are not simply a reflection of specific, tangible characteristics or salient traits. Rather the elements that go into a profile can become more fluent and intangible.[14] Nevertheless, the treatment towards these groups might still be unfair, and the 'diverse' nature of these profiles does not necessarily imply their legality. Considering the inherent 'profiling' nature of big data analytics, the relevance of criminal profiles for security related decision-making processes, and the increasing reliance on data and big data analytics therein, it remains important to question the legal limits of profiling in a security context. The main question raised in this paper is the following: to what extent does the law regulate the potential discriminatory nature of data-driven criminal profiling, and to what extent can the law account for the potential risks associated with new forms of differentiation perpetuated by those technologies?

3. THE LAW ENFORCEMENT DIRECTIVE: SPECIAL CATEGORIES OF DATA AS NON-DISCRIMINATION GROUNDS

As profiling practices heavily rely on the processing of large amounts of (personal) data, the main point of departure for regulating analytics is the EU data protection framework. Within the public security context, the European Directive 2016/680 (hereinafter DPLE Directive) governs the processing of personal data by authorities competent for the prevention, investigation, detection or prosecution of criminal offences or the execution of criminal penalties, including the safeguarding against and the prevention of threats to public security.[15] The DPLE Directive's direct nature and scope of application

14 Laurens Naudts, 'How Machine Learning Generates Unfair Inequalities and How Data Protection Instruments May Help in Mitigating Them', in Ronald Leenes and others (eds) *Data Protection and Privacy: The Internet of Bodies* (Hart Publishing 2019) ch 3; Anton Vedder and Laurens Naudts, 'Accountability for the Use of Algorithms in a Big Data Environment' (2017) 31 International Review of Law, Computers & Technology 206.

15 Directive (EU) 2016/680 of the European Parliament and the Council of 27 April 2016 on the protection of natural persons with regard to the processing of personal data by competent authorities for the purposes of the prevention, investigation, detection or prosecution of criminal offences or the execution of criminal penalties, and on the free movement of such data, and repealing Council Framework Decision 2008/977/JHA (Data Protection Law Enforcement Directive). Hereinafter, the DPLE Directive. A competent authority has been defined as: "any public authority competent for the prevention, investigation, detection or prosecution of criminal offences or the execution of criminal penalties, including the safeguarding against and the prevention of threats to public security; or "any other body or

increase its potential value for evaluating the legality of profiling techniques. One caveat should nonetheless be drawn. The Directive might only be applicable to law enforcement agencies, and not intelligence agencies, due to the DPLE Directive's focus on public, rather than national security. The Directive does not apply to the processing of personal data in the course of activities concerning national security, activities or agencies or units dealing with national security and the processing of personal data by Member States when carrying out activities which fall within the scope of Chapter 2 of Title V of the Treaty on European Union, i.e. the common foreign and security policy.[16] Intelligence services are traditionally entrusted with the preservation of national security, which falls outside the scope of the DPLE Directive.[17]

The DPLE Directive lays down the framework with which law enforcement authorities should abide where personal data are processed during the performance of their activities.[18] The Directive thus covers the deployment of analytics techniques for the purposes of criminal profiling, where these procedures would rely on personal data. Primarily focusing upon the underlying data processes, the DPLE Directive does not remain insensitive towards the potential discriminatory nature of profiling practices however.[19]

The DPLE Directive foresees its own definition of what profiling entails. Under the Directive, profiling is described as a form of automated processing of personal data where the personal data is used to evaluate, analyse or predict certain personal aspects relating to a natural person.[20] Though the DPLE

entity entrusted by Member State law to exercise public authority and public powers for the purposes of the prevention, investigation, detection or prosecution of criminal offences or the execution of criminal penalties, including the safeguarding against and the prevention of threats to public security". DPLE Directive, Article 3 (7).

16 DPLE Directive Article 2 para 3(a), read in combination with DPLE Directive, recital 14.

17 See also: Davor Derencinovic and Anna-Maria Getos, 'Cooperation of law enforcement and intelligence agencies in prevention and suppression of terrorism' (2007) Vol. 78 Revue internationale de droit penal 79.

18 As recital 11 DPLE Directive notes: other authorities, such as financial institutions might retain certain personal data for the purposes of crime prevention and investigation and provide those data to the competent national authorities. These entities should be bound by a contract or other legal act and by the provisions applicable to processors pursuant to this Directive.

19 Recital 38 of the DPLE states for instance that "profiling that results in discrimination against natural persons on the basis of personal data which are by their nature particularly sensitive in relation to fundamental rights and freedoms should be prohibited under the conditions laid down in Articles 21 (non-discrimination) and 52 (scope of guaranteed rights) of the Charter."

20 DPLE Directive, Article 3 (4). The definition further specifies: "in particular to analyze or predict aspects concerning that natural person's performance at work, economic situation, health, personal preferences, interests, reliability, behavior, location or movements." A similar definition was also adopted by the Council of Europe, where profiling is described as: "automatic data processing technique that consists of applying a "profile" to an individual, particularly in order to take decisions concerning her or him or for analysing or predicting her or his personal preferences, behaviours and attitudes." See: Committee of Ministers of

Directive merely mimics the wording of the General Data Protection Regulation, making no reference to criminal profiling as such, the deployment of big data analytics to uncover aspects relevant for the prevention, prediction and investigation of crime, would easily enter the ambit of the Directive's definition on profiling. It should be noted that the DPLE Directive does not forbid profiling, rather the processing activities involved should comply with general data protection principles.[21]

What is subject to a heightened level of scrutiny, however, are automated individual decision-making processes, which could include profiling, and the processing of special categories of data. Automated individual decision-making is defined by the Directive as a decision-making mechanism that is based solely on automated processes and that moreover produces an adverse legal effect concerning the data subject or significantly affects him or her.[22] As noted by the Article 29 Working Party (currently European Data Protection Board, hereinafter WP29): *"Although profiling and automated decision-making can be combined activities of the same process, they can also be carried out separately. There may be cases of automated decisions made with (or without) profiling and profiling which may take place without making automated decisions. Profiling has to involve some form of automated processing – although human involvement does not necessarily take the activity out of the definition."*[23] As a matter of principle, no individual should be made subject to a decision that did not have any human

the Council of Europe, 'The protection of individuals with regard to automatic processing of personal data in the context of profiling' Recommendation CM/Rec (2013) 10.

21 More specifically, personal data should be: (a) processed lawfully and fairly; (b) collected for specified, explicit and legitimate purposes and not processed in a manner that is incompatible with those purposes; (c) adequate, relevant and not excessive in relation to the purposes for which they are processed; (d) accurate and, where necessary, kept up to date; every reasonable step must be taken to ensure that personal data that are inaccurate, having regard to the purposes for which they are processed, are erased or rectified without delay; (e) kept in a form which permits identification of data subjects for no longer than is necessary for the purposes for which they are processed; (f) processed in a manner that ensures appropriate security of the personal data, including protection against unauthorised or unlawful processing and against accidental loss, destruction or damage, using appropriate technical or organisational measures.

22 DPLE Directive, Article 11 (1). According to the WP29, a legal effect entails that someone's legal rights have been affected, but might also include something that affects a person's legal status or their rights under a contract. With regard to law enforcement, the WP29 further clarified that the term 'significantly' aims to exclude 'trivial effects' from the principled prohibition. In other words, the effect the data subject experiences should be "substantial enough to deserve attention and influence the individual". See: Article 29 Data Protection Working Party, Opinion on some key issues of the Law Enforcement Directive (EU 2016/680), (2017) 8 and Article 29 Data Protection Working Party, 'Guidelines on Automated Individual Decision-Making and Profiling for the Purposes of Regulation 2016/679' (2018) 21.

23 Article 29 Data Protection Working Party, 'Opinion on Some Key Issues of the Law Enforcement Directive (EU 2016/680)' (n 22) 11–12.

involvement.[24] Derogations to this general prohibition can however be foreseen by Union or Member State law under the condition that any derogation provides appropriate safeguards for the rights and freedoms of the data subject, and at least the right to obtain human intervention on the part of the controller. Even if one might not yet foresee criminal profiling to become a fully automated process, this does not mean that law enforcement agencies can simply engage into profiling.

Regardless of whether the deployment of profiling techniques constitutes a 'solely' automated process in the sense of the data protection framework, a higher level of protection is also afforded to 'special categories of data'. Profiles will often constitute specific intelligence and characteristics that could reveal sensitive information about individuals.[25] Where these types of information fall under a, following the wording of the DPLE Directive, 'special category' of data, their processing will be more strictly governed. In particular, the Directive considers that the processing of data that reveal information concerning an individual's racial or ethnic origin, political opinions, religious or philosophical beliefs, or trade union membership, should warrant more care.[26] The same goes for genetic data, biometric data for the purpose of uniquely identifying a natural person and data concerning health or a natural person's sex life or sexual orientation.[27] It has furthermore been argued that the special categories of data not only refers to data that directly reveal the sensitive information, but also infers such information. In other words, proxies for the abovementioned types of data, arguably enjoy an equally high degree of protection.[28]

The special categories of data are similar to the grounds typically associated with non-discrimination legislation. Contrary to the latter however, and as shall be seen in the following section, the DPLE Directive employs a closed and limited list of categories subject to higher protection. The Directive shows great reservation regarding the processing of special categories of data: their

---

24 According to the WP29, human involvement cannot simply be fabricated. For example, the routine application of automatically generated profiles to individuals without there being an actual influence of the human decision-maker on the automated results, would still constitute a solely automated process. In other words: "To qualify as human involvement, the controller must ensure that any oversight of the decision is meaningful, rather than just a token gesture. It should be carried out by someone who has the authority and competence to change the decision." Article 29 Data Protection Working Party, 'Guidelines on Automated Individual Decision-Making and Profiling for the Purposes of Regulation 2016/679' (n 22) 20–21.

25 Such data nonetheless often represent parameters of vital importance to law enforcement agencies, and as a consequence, could feed into the creation of a criminal profile.

26 DPLE Directive, Article 10 (1).

27 Ibid.

28 Article 29 Data Protection Working Party, 'Advice Paper on Special Categories of Data ("sensitive Data")' (2011); Sandra Wachter, 'Affinity Profiling and Discrimination by Association in Online Behavioural Advertising' (Social Science Research Network 2019) SSRN Scholarly Paper ID 3388639 11 <https://papers.ssrn.com/abstract=3388639> accessed 6 June 2019.

processing shall only be allowed where strictly necessary and where the processing is subject to appropriate safeguards for the rights and freedoms of the data subject.[29] Furthermore, the use of these data can only occur where this has been authorised by Union or Member State Law. Additionally, the use of the data should either be necessary to protect the vital interests of the data subject or of another natural person; or when the data involved have been manifestly made public by the data subject. Where solely automated processes are involved, the DPLE Directive stipulates that such processes should not rely on special categories of data, unless again suitable measures and safeguards have been put in place in order protect the fundamental rights and interests of individuals concerned. Where profiling would however result in the discrimination against natural persons on the basis of special categories of personal data, this shall be prohibited.[30]

It is also important to point towards the convergence of European non-discrimination law and the fundamental rights to privacy and data protection. In particular, the European Court of Justice's Huber case has been considered a landmark decision for indicating the relevance of equality and non-discrimination where personal data are processed.[31] The Huber case concerned an Austrian national who requested the deletion of his data from the German AZR (Ausländerzentralregister). The AZR was a central register storing data of foreign nationals who took residence in Germany. Such a database did not exist

---

29 According to WP29, strict necessity should be understood as "a call to pay particular attention to the necessity principle in the context of processing special categories of data, as well as to foresee precise and particularly solid justifications for the processing of such data." In this regard, the WP notes that a careful balance must be found between the right to privacy and data protection, and the public interest. The WP therefore recommends competent authorities to perform a data protection impact assessment. In particular, "it should be assessed and demonstrated whether the purpose of the processing cannot be achieved by processing which affects the rights and freedoms of the data subject less and if the processing of special categories of data does not represent a risk of discrimination for the data subject." Furthermore, the WP29 specified that legal safeguards can be provided through additional material or procedural requirements. The former can consist of additional limitations to the purpose of the processing, such as reserving the collection and processing of personal data to specific categories of crime, or where the collection occurs for preventive measures, the presence of a certain sense of urgency, such as an 'imminent danger with probably severe consequences for the vital interests of many people.' Procedural safeguards could be the need for prior authorization from a court or independent body, or the prohibition to transmit those data. Article 29 Working Party, 'Opinion on some key issues of the Law Enforcement Directive' (EU 2016/680), (n 22), p.8. DPLE Directive, recital 37 further lists the following safeguards: "the possibility to collect those data only in connection with other data on the natural person concerned, the possibility to secure the data collected adequately, stricter rules on the access of staff of the competent authority to the data and the prohibition of transmission of those data."

30 DPLE Directive, Article 11 (3).

31 Case C-524/06 *Heinz Huber v Germany* [2008]; Hans Lammerant and Paul de Hert 'Predictive Profiling and Its Legal Limits: Effectiveness Gone Forever' (2016) Vol. 32 Exploring the boundaries of big data 159–160.

in respect of German nationals.[32] Moreover, one of the purposes for processing the personal data was the fighting of crime. Focusing on the storage and access of personal data, the case illustrates the respect for non-discrimination considerations where criminal profiling is concerned.[33] According to the ECJ, the fight against crime "necessarily involves the prosecution of crimes and offences committed, irrespective of the nationality of their perpetrators." For the Court, it followed that, as regards the objective of fighting crime, the situation of German nationals should not have been different from that of other Union citizens. Rather, the difference in treatment, which arose "by virtue of the systematic processing of personal data relating only to Union citizens who are not nationals of the Member State concerned for the purposes of fighting crime", constituted a prohibited form of discrimination on the basis of nationality.[34]

In summary, the building of a profile for criminal purposes is not forbidden per se under the DPLE Directive, but shall be subject to more stringent safeguards under specific circumstances. First, in the case no parameters are used that represent, or could be considered, a special category of personal data, only solely automated decisions are prohibited, unless Member State laws implementing the Directive have foreseen a derogation thereto. Second, where special categories of data are involved, and regardless of the level of automation that has been integrated, the law imposes a higher level of protection for data subjects. The processing of such data is however not subject to a general prohibition. Finally, the processing of special categories of data, when combined with a solely automated profiling or decision-making practice, shall always be prohibited if this would result in discrimination on the basis of special categories of personal data.[35] The

32 *Huber* (n 31).

33 See also: Raphaël Gellert and others, 'A Comparative Analysis of Anti-Discrimination and Data Protection Legislations' in Bart Custers and others (eds), *Discrimination and Privacy in the Information Society: Data Mining and Profiling in Large Databases* (Springer Berlin Heidelberg 2013) <https://doi.org/10.1007/978-3-642-30487-3_4>. Hans Lammerant, Paul de Hert, 'Predictive Profiling and Its Legal Limits: Effectiveness Gone Forever' (2016) Exploring the boundaries of big data 159.

34 *Huber* (n 31), paras 78-81.

35 The Council of Europe's recommendation on the protection of individuals with regard to automatic processing of personal data in the context of profiling contains similar provisions to the DPLE Directive. The recommendation states that the "The collection and processing of sensitive data in the context of profiling is prohibited except if these data are necessary for the lawful and specific purposes of processing and as long as domestic law provides appropriate safeguards. When consent is required it shall be explicit where the processing concerns sensitive data." Sensitive data are however defined in a more limited fashion, referring to personal data that reveal racial origin, political opinions or religious or other beliefs, as well as personal data on health, sex life or criminal convictions, as well as other data defined as sensitive by domestic law. Interestingly however, the Council of Europe has added criminal convictions as a sensitive category of data upon which, in principle, profiling should not be based. Regarding the latter however, it should be noted that the recommendations do not target law enforcement, but rather data processing in general. In their recommendations on personal data processing for police use, the Council of Europe does refer back to its guidelines on profiling though.

latter processing can never benefit from a derogation rule. Still, in the assumption that a profiling practice does not fall under one of the abovementioned categories, following the Huber case, proper consideration should also be given to equality and non-discrimination principles during the criminal profiling process.[36]

4. EQUALITY AND NON-DISCRIMINATION IN THE EUROPEAN CONVENTION OF HUMAN RIGHTS

The EU Law Enforcement Data Protection framework takes into account the potential impact personal data processing has on other fundamental rights, such as the right to equality and non-discrimination. From its wording, the highest form of protection against discrimination provided through the data protection framework remains limited to the list of criteria that constitute the special categories of personal data. Therefore, only in small set of circumstances would a reading of the DPLE Directive actually result in the conclusion that a specific form of criminal profiling is prohibited.

Yet, the limited scope of DPLE Directive vis-à-vis equality does not necessarily entail that all profiling techniques are legal. Indeed, beyond the protection afforded by the data protection framework, one should also consider the human rights to equality and non-discrimination itself. As profiles can be used to support decision-making processes that impose differential treatment, they enter the domain of equality law. This section will explore how the interpretation of equality and non-discrimination in human rights case-law, and the case-law of the ECtHR in particular, could potentially affect the deployment, and the evaluation, of profiling techniques, including new risks associated with those techniques, and the formation of new differentiation grounds in particular. The ECHR, and its interpretation by the ECtHR, do moreover not suffer the abovementioned limitation regarding what agencies can be caught; as the ECHR covers measures taken by national states for the purpose of national and public security, and public authorities therein, it covers both law enforcement and intelligence agencies.[37]

The ECHR has enshrined the right to equality and non-discrimination as a fundamental human right in Article 14.[38] As law enforcement and intelligence agencies perform a public function, their actions can be scrutinized for human

[36] Under section 4.4, i.e. "Big Data Profiling: New Grounds?", the chapter will consider new forms of differentiation that are not necessarily captured by the limited representation of special categories of data.

[37] Though legal interpretation might differ depending on which authority is considered, they should not affect the basic principles laid out in this chapter, and the conclusions drawn.

[38] The term equality is never mentioned explicitly in the non-discrimination clauses of the Convention. Yet, non-discrimination and equality principles are closely intertwined: As mentioned at (n12), whereas the principle of equality requires that equal situations are treated

rights violations and discriminatory treatment during the performance of their functions. For instance, in the Lingurar case, the ECtHR found that a police raid was a discriminatory and forbidden case of ethnic profiling as the applicants were targeted, not due to their actual behaviour, but rather because the police *expected* the applicants to be criminals because they were Roma.[39] Indeed, the ECtHR's case law on ethnic profiling illustrates that actions by police forces, and certain forms of profiling, clearly fall within the ambit of the Convention.[40] Moreover, from the Convention's wording, one can consider that there is, in principle, no limitation with regard to which forms of discrimination can be considered illegal or undesirable. Indeed, the language of the Convention remains open ended. More concretely, Article 14 of the European Convention on Human Rights states that:

> *"The enjoyment of the rights and freedoms set forth in this Convention shall be secured without discrimination on any ground such as sex, race, colour, language, religion, political or other opinion, national or social origin, association with a national minority, property, birth or other status."*[41]

Mimicking the wording of Article 14, Article 1 of Protocol 12 to the ECHR stipulates that:

> *"the enjoyment of any right set forth by law shall be secured without discrimination on any ground such as sex, race, colour, language, religion, political or other opinion, national or social origin, association with a national minority, property, birth or other status."*[42]

---

equally and unequal situations differently, failure to do so will amount to discrimination unless an objective and reasonable justification exists. *Preamble to Protocol 12 ECHR*, 15.

39 *Lingurar v Romania* App no 48474/14 (ECtHR, 16 April 2019).

40 See also *Timishev v Russia* App no 55762/00 and 55974/00 (ECtHR, 13 March 2006).

41 Article 14 serves primarily as the protective article towards the distribution of the other human rights protected by the ECHR. Christopher McCrudden and Sacha Prechal, 'The Concepts of Equality and Non-Discrimination Inn Europe: A Practical Approach' (2009) European Network of Legal Experts in the Field of Gender Equality 21, in reference to: Sandra Fredman, 'Equality Issues' in Basil S. Markesinis, The Impact of the Human Rights Bill on English Law: The Clifford Chance Lectures Vol 3 (OUP, 1998) 111–132. Likewise, Article 21 of the European Charter of Fundamental Rights proclaims that any discrimination based on any ground such as sex, race, colour, ethnic or social origin, genetic features, language, religion or belief, political or any other opinion, membership of a national minority, property, birth, disability, age or sexual orientation shall be prohibited.

42 Whereas Protocol 12 installed equality and non-discrimination as a stand-alone right, Article 14 can only be invoked in conjunction with another substantive right. A violation of Article 14 can be found however, even if there was no violation of the other substantive right. See for example: *Sommerset v Germany* App no 31871/96 (ECtHR Grand Chamber 8 July 2013). Given the data-driven context, it could therefore easily be envisaged that Article 14 can be invoked in cases of criminal profiling, which will often also be related to amongst others Article 6, the right to fair trial and Article 8, the right to privacy. Rory O'Connell, 'Cinderella

The terminology used in both clauses, and in particular the reference to *'any ground'* and *'other status'* indicates that, at least to a certain degree, any type of differentiation amongst individuals, where such differentiation is not justified, can result in a human rights violation. In its explanatory memorandum to Protocol 12, the Council of Europe noted that, even though certain grounds, such as sexual orientation, age or mental or physical disability could perhaps have been included in drafting the protocol, their inclusion was expressly decided against. Arguing that this was *"not because of a lack of awareness that such grounds have become particularly important in today's societies as compared with the time of drafting of Article 14 of the Convention, but because such an inclusion was considered unnecessary from a legal point of view since the list of non-discrimination grounds is not exhaustive, and because inclusion of any particular additional ground might give rise to unwarranted a contrario interpretations as regards discrimination based on grounds not so included. It is recalled that the European Court of Human Rights has already applied Article 14 in relation to discrimination grounds not explicitly mentioned in that provision."*[43]

The question remains, however, to what extent the open-ended nature of Article 14 indicates openness? Could every differentiation mechanism used by law enforcement or intelligence agencies in the context of their activities ultimately be considered problematic? Or has the ECtHR prioritised certain grounds over others? And if the list is truly open, what are the conditions developed by the ECtHR to consider whether the use of a ground is problematic?

4.1. DISCRIMINATION GROUNDS AND THE EUROPEAN COURT OF HUMAN RIGHT'S CASE LAW

In cases where the profiling practices conducted by public bodies that represent the state, such as law enforcement and intelligence agencies, are proven to be discriminatory, non-discrimination law could be invoked in an effort to cease the discriminatory practices by these authorities.[44] Two notions within Article 14's non-discrimination clause are particularly important when considering new forms of profiling generated that are not linked to salient traits: *'any ground'* and *'other status'*.

According to Fredman, the notion 'discrimination grounds' has a certain 'elasticity', which has enabled the ECtHR to expand the ambit of non-

Comes to the Ball: Article 14 and the Right to Non-Discrimination in the ECHR' (2009) 29 *Legal Studies* 211.

43 Council of Europe, 'Explanatory Report to the Protocol No. 12 to the Convention for the Protection of Human Rights and Fundamental Freedoms (Rome, 4 XI. 2000)' <https://rm.coe.int/16800cce48> accessed 03 July 2019.

44 Wim Schreurs and others, 'Cogitas, Ergo Sum. The Role of Data Protection Law and Non-Discrimination Law in Group Profiling in the Private Sector', in Mireille Hildebrandt and Serge Gutwirth (eds) *Profiling the European citizen* (Springer 2008) Ch 13, 258–259.

discrimination law to also cover grounds which, looking at the list of grounds provided, in present day would seem 'conspicuously absent', such as disability, sexual orientation and age.[45] The notion 'other status' appears equally open-ended. Seemingly similar notions, they nonetheless appear to represent a difference in approach by the Court. As will be outlined in the following section, in cases where the Court has placed an emphasis on the notion of grounds, it favours an open-ended approach towards discrimination. Whilst focusing on status – which in itself can be considered a ground – seems to have resulted in a more restrictive approach towards equality and non-discrimination, whereby the condemnation of differential treatment has usually been linked to the requirement that a 'personal characteristic' should underlie a decision-making practice.[46]

4.2. GROUND OR STATUS: A DIVERGENT APPROACH BY THE ECTHR[47]

Over the years, the Court took different approaches towards Article 14, which resulted in a varying degree of conflicting and often confusing interpretations.[48] In *Engel,* where military rank underlied differential treatment, the ECtHR argued that the list set out in Article 14 is illustrative and not exhaustive, "as is shown by the words 'any grounds such as'". The word "status" was moreover wide enough so that it may include other grounds.[49] According to Gerards, through this wording of the Court, the application of the non-discrimination clause seemed quite straightforward. Following this formulation, each and every case of unequal treatment could be brought before the Court in order to assess the reasonableness thereof, regardless of the particular ground of discrimination underlying the state measure.[50] In principle, such an open-ended phrasing would allow new differentiation grounds used by law enforcement agencies to be scrutinized and brought before the ECtHR.

Shifting away from its focus on grounds, a divergent set of case law followed in the early 2010's, wherein the meaning of 'other status' became the focal point

45 Sandra Fredman, 'Emerging from the Shadows: Substantive Equality and Article 14 of the European Convention on Human Rights' (2016) Vol. 16 *Human Rights Law Review* 273, 277.

46 Janneke Gerards, 'The Discrimination Grounds of Article 14 of the European Convention on Human Rights' (2013) Vol. 13 *Human Rights Law Review* 99, 104–105.

47 The navigation of the ECtHR's case-law in the following section is indebted to the work of Janneke Gerards (n 46). Her work on the relevant case-law regarding the non-discrimination grounds has been an inspiration and main source of guidance for this section.

48 See also: Gerards (n 46); Oddný Mjöll Arnardóttir, 'The Differences That Make a Difference: Recent Developments on the Discrimination Grounds and the Margin of Appreciation under Article 14 of the European Convention on Human Rights' (2014) Vol. 14 *Human Rights Law Review* 647.

49 A similar approach was followed in Rasmussen v Denmark. *Engel and Others v Netherlands* (1976) Series A 22, para 72; *Rasmussen v Denmark* (1984) Series A 87, para 34.

50 Gerards (n 46) 104. See also: *Engel* (n 49) para 72; *Rasmussen* (n 49) para 34.

of the Court's reasoning. In *Kjeldsen, Busk Madsen and Pedersen v. Denmark*, the Court noted that what truly matters is whether discriminatory treatment has as its basis or reason *a* personal characteristic, i.e. "status", by which persons or groups are distinguishable from each other.[51] In *Carson*, the ECtHR maintained the more restrictive, further interpretation of the Convention stating that not every difference in treatment will amount to a violation of Article 14. Rather, "only differences in treatment based on a personal characteristic (or "status") by which persons or groups of persons are distinguishable from each other are capable of amounting to discrimination within the meaning of Article 14."[52] The Court recognized for instance that the specific grounds specified under Article 14, such as sex, race and religion, or in the case of Carson residence, constitute an aspect of personal 'status'. A similar wording was used in Clift where the Court argued that "Article 14 does not prohibit all differences in treatment but only those differences based on an identifiable, objective or personal characteristic, or "status", by which persons or groups of persons are distinguishable from one another".[53]

The difficulty in interpreting the Convention then lies in being able to determine what other grounds could be categorised as being a 'status' in the sense of Article 14. In this regard, the Court has noted on numerous occasions that the list set out in Article 14 ECHR is only illustrative, and therefore not exhaustive.[54] The Court further specified that the notion 'other status' should be given a wide meaning, and further specified that "their interpretation has not been limited to characteristics which are 'personal' in the sense that they are innate or inherent."[55] In *Clift*, the Court observed that whilst "a number of the specific examples [mentioned in Article 14 ECHR] relate to characteristics which can be said to be 'personal' in the sense that they are innate characteristics or inherently linked to the identity or the personality of the individual, such as sex, race and religion, not all of the grounds listed can be thus characterised."[56] The Court did observe that it is not surprising that the 'other status' notion has been interpreted to include characteristics that can be said to be personal in the sense that they are innate or inherent, yet in finding violations the Court has accepted that 'status' exists where the distinction upon which was relied did not involve

51 *Kjeldsen, Busk Madsen and Pedersen v Denmark* Series A 23 (1976) para 56.

52 *Carson and Others v. The United Kingdom* App no 42184/05, (ECtHR, 16 March 2010) para 70.

53 *Clift v The United Kingdom* App no 7205/07 (ECtHR, 13 July 2010) para 55.

54 *Carson* (n 52), para 70; *Clift* (n 53), para 55; *Engel* (n 49), para 72. The Court moreover refers to the French version of the Convention, (and a fortiori the French equivalent toute autre situation (see Carson, para 70.).

55 *Molla Sali v Greece* App no 20452/14 (ECtHR, 19 December 2018), para 133; see also *Carson* (n 52), para 70; *Clift* (n 53), para 56). In Carson, the Court seemed to have introduced the 'wide meaning' of "other status": "The Court further notes that the words "other status" (and a fortiori the French equivalent toute autre situation) have been given a wide meaning so as to include, in certain circumstances, a distinction drawn on the basis of a place of residence."

56 *Clift* (n 53) para 56.

a characteristic in that specific sense.[57] As an illustration, the Court referred to numerous previous cases. For instance, in *Shelley*, the Court considered that 'being a convicted prisoner' could fall within the notion of other status, which by reference it did not consider an innate or inherent characteristic.[58] Article 14 may even cover instances in which individuals are treated less favourably on the basis of another person's status or protected characteristics.[59] More importantly however, in *Clift*, the Court did seem to stress the need for a personal characteristic to underlie differential treatment in order to trigger Article 14, albeit one that should not be innate or inherent.[60] As such, the Court has concluded that Article 14 might also capture "ejusdem generis" constructions.[61]

In the same year as *Carson* and *Clift* however, the ECtHR again took a different approach in *Springett* and *Peterka*, where the innate or inherent nature of personal characteristics was deemed critical.[62] In *Peterka*, the Court seemed more flexible, but nonetheless noted that "the other status" notion should only apply to grounds that are sufficiently analogous or similar to the grounds expressly mentioned in Article 14. The sudden change of reasoning was not limited to the aforementioned cases. In *Cadek and Others v. The Czech Republic*, the ECtHR did not find a violation of Article 14. The *Cadek* case concerned a difference in treatment that was based on whether someone was an original restitution claimant or had bought a restitution claim. According to the Court, that difference was not a relevant ground under Article 14 as it was not based on "any personal choice in so far as this choice should be respected as elements of someone's personality, such as religion, political opinion, sexual orientation and gender identity, or on grounds of personal features in respect of which no choice at all can be made, such as sex, race, disability and age."[63]

---

57 *Clift* (n 53) para 56.para 57–59.

58 *Clift* (n 53) para 58. *Shelley v the United Kingdom* App no 23800/06 (ECtHR, 4 January 2008).

59 See *Guberina v. Croatia* App no 23682/13 (ECtHR, 22 March 2016), para 78, *Škorjanec v Croatia* App no 25536/14 (ECtHR 28 March 2017), para 55; and also *Weller v Hungary* App no 44399/05 (ECtHR 31 March 2009) para 37.

60 "The Court therefore considers it clear that while it has consistently referred to the need for a distinction based on a "personal" characteristic in order to engage Article 14, as the above review of its case-law demonstrates, the protection conferred by that Article is not limited to different treatment based on characteristics which are personal in the sense that they are innate or inherent.", *Clift* (n 53), para 59.

61 ibid.

62 Janneke Gerards (n 46) p. 112. See also: *Springett, Easto-Brigden and Sheffield v The United Kingdom* App no 34726/04, 14287/05, 34702/05 (ECtHR, 27 April 2010). In the former case, the Court noted that that the factor of having, or not having, acquired a right to a welfare benefit could not be considered to be an aspect of personal status within the meaning of Article 14 as, unlike the grounds listed therein, it is not an innate characteristic that applies from birth.

63 *Cadek and Others v The Czech Republic* App nos 31933/08, 60084/08, 6185/09, 46696/09, 52792/09, 53518/09, 10185/10, 42151/10, 3167/11 and 20939/11 (ECtHR, 22 November 2012) para 94.

4.3. RECENT ILLUSTRATIONS: SETTLING ON THE PAST?

In most recent judgments on equality and non-discrimination, the Court seems to have settled on the Clift and Carson approach.[64] In *Molla Sali* for instance, which concerned discriminatory treatment on grounds of religious beliefs, the Court again states that "only differences in treatment based on an identifiable characteristic, or 'status', are capable of amounting to discrimination within the meaning of Article 14."[65] Unlike those two cases however, where mention was made of "differences based on an identifiable, objective or personal characteristic, or 'status', by which persons or groups of persons are distinguishable from one another", *Molla Sali* omits reference to the notion "personal characteristic". That omission can also be found in the Fabian case.[66] The Court does however, when reiterating the wider meaning of 'other status', consider that the interpretation thereof has not been limited to characteristics that are personal in the sense that they are innate or inherent.[67]

At the same time, a different approach was taken by the Court in the *Big Brother Watch* case, which concerns mass-surveillance – and where the danger exists that collected data are also used to generate data-driven profiles. Though only briefly touched upon, the Court also considered a potential infringement of Article 14.[68] The applicants argued that persons outside the UK were disproportionately likely to have their private communications intercepted than persons inside the UK, and that moreover additional safeguards against the interception regime were only afforded to persons known to be in the British isles. As geographic location was the differentiator, the Court referred back to its Magee case, where it had already established that geographic location was not to be considered a "personal characteristic".[69] The ECtHR thus found in Big Brother Watch that the applicants' claims regarding Article 14 was inadmissible. Perhaps because it could refer back to older case-law in this specific instance, the Court nonetheless again introduced the relevance of the notion 'personal' vis-à-vis differential treatment. It should be noted however that, at the time of writing, the *Big Brother Watch* case has been referred to the Grand Chamber, which might come to a different conclusion.

---

64 Oddný Mjöll Arnardóttir, 'Vulnerability under Article 14 of the European Convention on Human Rights' (2017) Vol. 4 *Oslo Law Review* 150. See also: *Fabian v Hungary*, App no 78117/13 (ECtHR, 5 September 2017); *Molla Sali* (n 55), and *Lupeni Greek Catholic Parish and Others v Romania* App no 76943/11 (ECtHR Grand Chamber, 29 November 2016) para 163.

65 See amongst others: ECtHR, *Molla Sali* (n 55); para 133. Guberina v Croatia (Application no. 23682/13; 22 March 2016), para 68; *Eweida and others v The United Kingdom* App no 48420/10, 59842/10, 51671/10 and 36516/10 (ECtHR, 15 January 2013) para 86.

66 *Fabian* (n 64).

67 *Molla Sali v Greece* (n 55) para 133.

68 *Big Brother Watch and Others v The United Kingdom* App nos 58170/13, 62322/14 and 24960/15 (ECtHR 13 September 2018) para 516–518.

69 *Magee v the United Kingdom* App no. 28135/95 (ECtHR, 20 June 2000) para 50.

Over the past decades, the approach of the Court towards Article 14 does not seem to have always been consistent, and theoretical confusion may still arise. It appears from recent cases that the Court has settled for the approach it introduced in the Carson and Clift cases, through its focus on the "other status" notion. The relevance of "any other ground" does not seem forgotten however, as *Engel* has been referred to in other recent cases.[70] Still, some elements remain unclear. The wording of the Court is particularly vague regarding to what extent a relationship is required between differential treatment and the presence of a personal characteristic in order to engage Article 14.[71] Should a personal characteristic underlie differential treatment, or should it not? And does the Court, when they argue that different treatment should not be based on characteristics that are personal in the sense that they are innate or inherent, open the possibility for 'impersonal' characteristics to engage Article 14, or does it simply wishes to avoid a too strict interpretation of the notion 'personal'? As will be outlined in the next section, the potential for new forms of differentiation to be brought before the Court depends on how this question will be answered.

4.4. BIG DATA PROFILING: NEW GROUNDS?

The ECtHR's case law illustrates that the Court does indeed seem willing to consider decisions based on grounds that are not explicitly mentioned in Article 14 as discriminatory. In their analysis of the ECtHR case-law, the European Union Agency for Fundamental Rights (hereinafter FRA) and the Council of Europe note that over the years, *amongst others* the following 'grounds', not captured by the non-exhaustive list provided, have been granted protection: disability, age, sexual orientation, fatherhood,[72] marital status,[73]

---

70 See for instance, *Biao v Denmark* App no 38590/10 (ECtHR Grand Chamber 24 May 2015) para 89; and *Lupeni Greek Catholic Parish and Others v Romania* App no 76943/11 (ECtHR 29 November 2016) para 163.

71 According to Arnardóttir, the 'personal characteristic' notion, as it was introduced in Kjeldsen, Busk Madsen and Peterson (n 51), should not be interpreted as excluding non-personal discrimination grounds from the range of the Court. She hereby refers to the grounds listed in Article 14, and the inclusion of property and political opinion. In particular she notes that both property and political opinion "do not connote personal characteristics, have no links with immutable or inherent traits and in the case of property raise no issues of core personal choices." Arnardóttir (n 48) 665–667. In her analysis of the 2010 case-law, Gerards also noted that: "As matters presently stand, the Court either does not pay attention to the ground of discrimination, or it does not provide substantive reasons for holding that the case does (or does not) concern a ground protected by Article 14, or it applies the criterion of 'personal status' in unexpected and unfortunate ways. There are still many cases which do not evidently relate to a personal characteristic, yet are still assessed on their merits." (n 46), 112.

72 *Weller v Hungary* App no 44399/05 (ECtHR 31 March 2009).

73 Petrov v Bulgaria App no 15197/02 (ECtHR 22 May 2008).

membership of an organisation,[74] military rank,[75] parenthood of a child born out of wedlock,[76] place of residence,[77] health or any medical condition,[78] former KGB officer status,[79] retirees employed in certain categories of the public sector[80] and detainees pending trial.[81]

From the aforementioned examples, it is nonetheless clear that the Court has not yet been confronted by differentiation grounds that are not defined by, or comprised of, a single specific characteristic, but rather by an amalgam of characteristics. The Court has mainly dealt with discriminatory treatment where one specific element or trait underlies the decision-making processes. Data-driven profiling techniques will often consist of a multitude of characteristics, which do not necessarily have to be linked to salient or personal traits, but which, due to the ubiquitous nature of data in the digital world, can nevertheless have a large impact. Data driven analytics might indicate for instance that persons who visit a specific social media website, post political images and have a degree in engineering, might be more likely to commit violent crimes. They might even find a correlation between the colour car someone might have and the likelihood to commit traffic infringements. Some traits that constitute a data-driven profile will certainly represent or reflect a personal characteristic, such as education, political or philosophical beliefs. The group as a whole however, might be described general enough for the group level not to be considered 'personal'. A profile might underlie differential treatment, yet it is unlikely that the profile, or the combined use of the parameters therein, would be considered as an innate or inherent personal trait for those subject to the differential treatment. An approach where the presence of such a characteristic is a constitutive element for the Court to condemn differential treatment seems ill-equipped to deal with new profiling practices.

As seen in the previous section, the Court currently allocates a wider meaning to the 'other status' notion. It nonetheless seems to connect the 'other status' requirement with the presence of a personal link, albeit one that should not necessarily be innate or inherent. A personal characteristic or information related to a person could be present within a profile. Such information does not necessarily have to be decisive for a decision-making process, it can be one element that shapes a decision. Moreover, and as mentioned before, the data-

74 See inter alia: *Danilenkov and Others v Russia* App no 67336/01 (ECtHR, 30 July 2009) and *Grande Oriente d'Italia di Palazzo Giustiniani v Italy* App no 26740/02 (ECtHR 31 May 2007).

75 *Engel* (n 49).

76 *Sommerfeld v Germany* App no 31871/96 (ECtHR Grand Chamber, 8 July 2003); *Sahin v Germany* App no 30943/96 (ECtHR Grand Chamber, 8 July 2003).

77 *Carson* (n 52); *Pichkur v Ukraine* App no *10441/06* (ECtHR 7 November 2013).

78 *Novruk and Others v Russia* App no 31039/11 and others (ECtHR 15 March 2015).

79 *Sidabras and Others v Lithuania* App no 50421/08 and 56213/08 (ECtHR 23 June 2015).

80 *Fabian* (n 64).

81 *Varnas v Lithuania* App no 42615/06 (ECtHR, 9 July 2013) See also: European Union Agency for Fundamental Rights and the Council of Europe (eds), *Handbook on European Non-Discrimination Law* (2018 edition, Publications Office of the European Union 2018) 224–225.

driven profile as a whole might not be 'personal' at all. A profile might provide a general description of a person (or a group of persons) or be applied to them, the profile, and the criterion therein, that underlie differential treatment could be generalized enough for them not be considered personal. Exemplary in this regard are the on-going discussions between privacy and data protection scholars regarding the unclear scope of the notion 'personal data'. Often perceived as a highly individual notion, it has been argued that the way 'personal data' has been conceived, cannot be easily applied to groups of individuals or collectives formed through data-driven analytics techniques.[82] Considering this definitional confusion, it seems rather unlikely that an 'intangible' group profile, even though it might result in unfair differential treatment, would constitute a 'personal characteristic' as understood by the Court.

The inclusion of new, intangible grounds would more likely require a return to the open-ended grounds-based approach, i.e. towards a conception of equality and non-discrimination that is more instrumental and procedural in nature, as seen in Engel and Rasmussen. The non-discrimination clause could be conceived as a means to bring any form of differential treatment before the Court, allowing a case-by-case assessment to be made regarding the justified nature of differential treatment.[83] A procedural and instrumental approach can serve much better the uncertain futures associated with big data analytics, and the potential undesired effects that might follow from them on a societal scale.[84] A focus on 'personal' characteristics is likely more conducive to result in an approach where higher protection is afforded to suspect grounds, traditional forms of discrimination, or proxies thereof. It should be clearly understood however that new forms of differentiation perpetuated by big data analytics do not always correspond to protected characteristics, nor serve as a proxy thereto. Even where the group profile started out as a proxy of a protected characteristic, it could become detached from the latter.

---

82 See inter alia: Alessandro Mantelero, 'From Group Privacy to Collective Privacy: Towards a New Dimension of Privacy and Data Protection in the Big Data Era' in Linnet Taylor, Luciano Floridi and Bart van der Sloot (eds), *Group Privacy: New Challenges of Data Technologies* (Springer International Publishing 2017) <https://doi.org/10.1007/978-3-319-46608-8_8> accessed 26 June 2019; Alessandro Mantelero, 'Personal Data for Decisional Purposes in the Age of Analytics: From an Individual to a Collective Dimension of Data Protection' (2016) Vol. 32 *Computer Law & Security Review* 238; Brent Mittelstadt, 'From Individual to Group Privacy in Big Data Analytics' (2017) 30 Philosophy & Technology 475; Naudts (n 14); Anton Vedder, 'KDD: The Challenge to Individualism' (1999) 1 *Ethics and Information Technology* 275.

83 Gerards refers to such a rationale as the 'equal treatment' interpretation of Article 14, which she opposes against the 'non-discrimination' rationale. The former can more easily deal with "complex forms of unequal treatment, such as discrimination based on multiple or cumulative grounds or intersectional discrimination." The latter would interpret Article 14 as a prohibition of unequal treatment on the basis of grounds that are "a priori considered problematic or 'suspect'". Such an approach tends to focus on differential treatment related to personal characteristics, either in the sense that they are innate or immutable, or because they are closely related to the core of individual autonomy (n 46) 113–119.

84 See also (n 83), whereby data-driven profiles could be understood as complex forms of unequal treatment.

For example, big data analytics might show a correlation between geographic location, income and deviant behaviour. The combination of those parameters could serve as a proxy for ethnicity, e.g. when they would refer to a lower-income area where mainly minorities are living. A data-driven policy to heighten the control of that area however not only impacts those people that share the protected characteristic that is ethnicity. Due to the generalised nature of the profile, it will impact a larger group, i.e. all people living within that location, and as such the profile becomes, at least partially, detached from the parameter 'ethnicity'.[85] The differentiation ground that is the group profile as a whole might thus result in unfair treatment. The differentiation ground might moreover not represent 'ethnicity' in the first place, but might simply be a combination of parameters that, although seemingly 'relevant' for a security decision, nonetheless results in the unfair treatment of a group within society.[86] In other words, in an analytics era there is value in being able to engage non-discrimination law on the basis of those new differentiation grounds. The conclusion in favour for new differentiation grounds to trigger the ECHR's non-discrimination clause also holds value when considering the data protection framework. As was seen under section 3, where data-driven profiling is concerned, the DPLE finds as mainly problematic those forms of differentiation that are linked to the limited number of special categories of data, and, depending on the interpretation that is given to them, proxies of those categories. Though the specificity of a closed list increases certainty regarding what forms of profiling should be subject to higher scrutiny, The DPLE framework might not be phrased in a way that can adequately mitigate the risks associated with new forms of differentiation. An open-ended interpretation of Article14 ECHR could thus also help in closing the gap left open by data protection instruments.

Of course, an open approach towards non-discrimination would eventually result in more substantive interpretations of what equality and non-discrimination should entail. Yet, it would not exclude new differentiation grounds a priori. When confronted with new differentiation grounds the Court will need to consider whether or not they can enjoy protection, and that decision will affect subsequent case-law. Differential treatment should, in the words of the Court, be assessed taking into consideration all the circumstances of the case, as well as the aim of the Convention which is to guarantee "not rights that are theoretical or illusory, but rights that are practical and effective."[87] Arguing in favour of an open-ended approach, Arnardottir moreover rightfully notes that an "openness and indifference towards a 'precise definition of protected discrimination grounds" will nonetheless be complemented by a substantive

---

85 See also Naudts (n 14).

86 Put differently, a group profile does not need to be a proxy of a protected or personal characteristic in order for the impact on the group by application of the profile to be unfair.

87 *Clift* (n 53) para 60; See also: *Cudak v Lithuania* App no15869/02 (ECtHR Grand Chamber 23 March 2010), para. 36.

assessment of the case, for instance through the review of objective and reasonable justification.[88] In other words, whereas the open-ended approach could allow new grounds to be brought before the Court, Member States could still provide a reasonable and objective justification for why they instilled differential treatment.

It should furthermore not be ruled out that perceptions and values change over time, also with regard to intensive data-driven profiling activities. If the Court will one day have to shed light on how new technologies affect equality and non-discrimination, those altered perceptions might be taken into account, and as such shape how human rights are interpreted. An open grounds based approach could allow for the consideration of new forms of discrimination, the unfair nature of which might currently not yet be apparent. As the Court has already stated: "the Convention is a living instrument to be interpreted in the light of present-day conditions".[89]

4.5. DIFFERENTIAL TREATMENT: REASONABLE AND OBJECTIVE JUSTIFICATION

The ECHR could potentially be interpreted in a manner so as to include new differentiation grounds generated through machine learning. The latter could cover the group profile as a whole, or the individual traits that constitute it. This would not automatically entail that treating others differently on the basis thereof is discriminatory or problematic. In order for an issue to arise there must first of all be a difference in the treatment of persons in analogous or relevantly similar situations.[90] The ECtHR moreover considers that a difference in treatment is discriminatory only if it has no objective or reasonable justification. Discrimination exists if the decision or policy does not pursue a legitimate aim or if there is not a reasonable relationship of proportionality between the means employed and the aim sought to be realised.[91] Furthermore, the contracting states enjoy a margin of appreciation in assessing whether and to what extent differences in otherwise similar situations justify a different treatment.[92]

The 'reasonable and objective' justification test that the Court applies in the context of Article 14 contains several elements. In their analysis of the ECtHR case law, Prechal and McCrudden discern several steps in the Court's assessment.

88 Arnardóttir (n 48) 666. Moreover, according to Arnardóttir an open approach seemed to have always been present.
89 *Inze v. Austria* App no 8695/79 (ECtHR, 28 October 1987) para 41.
90 *Molla Sali* (n 55) para 133.
91 "The Court also reiterates that in the enjoyment of the rights and freedoms guaranteed by the Convention, Article 14 affords protection against different treatment, without an objective and reasonable justification, of persons in similar situations. *Molla Sali* (n 55), para 135. See also *amongst others*, *Clift* (n 53) para 73.
92 *Molla Sali* (n 55) para 136.

First, the Court evaluates whether the State has provided a justification for the difference in treatment. Second, it will be considered whether the differential treatment pursues a legitimate aim or aims. If a legitimate aim is present, a further analysis will be made in that the objective pursued should be sufficiently important to justify a limitation to the fundamental right; the measures envisaged to pursue the objective, including the difference in treatment, should be designed to meet the objective rationally connected to it; and finally, that the measures taken are proportionate to the objective pursued, i.e. they do not go further than what is necessary to accomplish the objective.[93]

Depending on the differentiation ground, the test is not always applied with the same degree of strictness. According to Fredman, the wide meaning given to the 'other status' notion has resulted in a filtering mechanism with a varying degree of scrutiny.[94] From its case law, it is apparent that the Court considers that differentiation based on certain grounds should be subject to higher scrutiny (implying that it will be harder to justify the discriminatory treatment in those cases).[95] For example, where the difference in treatment is based on race or ethnic origin, "the notion of objective and reasonable justification must be interpreted as strictly as possible."[96] Here the court would require particularly convincing and weighty reasons. In the field of policing and criminal profiling, ethnic profiling has been considered a practice for which such reasons should exist. It is reasonable to argue that, where other grounds are considered, it is more likely that in the future, the Court will uphold a higher level test for those grounds already explicitly mentioned within Article 14's open list, or to grounds that are related thereto. This should not necessarily be surprising: their explicit inclusion indicates that they concern those grounds for which society has deemed that, at least within critical contexts, they should not be considered relevant for decision-making, or that decisions where they serve as criteria should be subject to a higher level of scrutiny.

To what extent then, might new grounds of differentiation be considered as discriminatory if they would be scrutinized? It should be recalled that States enjoy a margin of appreciation in assessing "whether and to what extent differences in otherwise similar situations justify a different treatment."[97] According to the ECtHR, the scope of this margin will vary according to the circumstances, the subject matter and its background.[98] Moreover, the Court

---

93 McCrudden and Prechal (n 41) 22.

94 Fredman (n 45) 278.

95 Murdoch and Roche (n 3) 19.

96 See for instance, *Lingurar* (n 39) para 68 and D.H. and *Others v the Czech Republic* ECHR GC 2007-IV, para 196.

97 In a recent article, Gerards argues however that the Court has turned the margin of appreciation doctrine into a rather empty rhetorical device. Janneke Gerards, 'Margin of Appreciation and Incrementalism in the Case Law of the European Court of Human Rights' (2018) Vol. 18 *Human Rights Law Review* 495.

98 See inter alia: *Petrovic v Austria* App no 156/1996/775/976 (ECtHR, 27 March 1998) para 38.

considers that the margin of appreciation is narrower where the right(s) at stake are crucial to the 'individual's effective enjoyment of intimate or key rights'.[99] In certain spheres, such as social or economic policies, the margin tends to be wider.[100] In general, States also tend to have a wider measure of discretion in their evaluation of threats to national security and their approach to combat them, yet their margin of appreciation in this area is no longer absolute.[101] For instance, a wide margin of appreciation seems to be given also to the valuation of proof in criminal proceedings.[102]

Yet, where a wide margin of appreciation exists, the test applied might be one of mere rationality, i.e. it will be ascertained whether the difference in treatment was rational or not. According to McCrudden and Prechal, in cases where equality is considered as a form of rationality, courts tend to afford a favourable position to public bodies as they could suffice by simply indicating that a decision was seemingly rational.[103] The State's margin of appreciation, in combination with the reasonable relationship that should exist between the measure and the aims pursued, can make it easy to establish a rational claim towards differential treatment.[104] In cases where Member States enjoy a wide margin of appreciation, the Court's test can be rather arbitrary, wherein key factors such as the necessity, suitability and proportionality are only addressed superficially.[105] In a digital environment, this approach from the Court is more beneficial for public decision-makers in their ability to deploy big data technologies.

If decisions should simply appear rational, big data analytics, if not properly scrutinized, will likely remain uncontested. As noted by Barocas and Selbst: "By definition, data mining is always a form of statistical (and therefore seemingly rational) discrimination. Indeed, the very point [...] is to provide a rational basis upon which to distinguish between individuals and to reliably confer to the individual the qualities possessed by those who seem statistically similar."[106] In this sense, the relationship between big data analytics and equality and non-discrimination is rather paradoxical. Big data analytics can be used to argue both sides of the coin: it allows to see the similarities between individuals, as well as their differences. In other words, a rational ground to either treat

---

99 *Connors v The United Kingdom* App no 66746/01 (ECtHR, 27 May 2004) para 82; Chapman v. the United Kingdom [GC], no. 27138/95, ECHR 2001-I, para 92 and *Buckley v United Kingdom* ECHR 1996-IV para 76.

100 ibid.

101 Council of Europe, 'National Security and Euopean Case-Law' (2013) <https://www.echr.coe.int/Documents/Research_report_national_security_ENG.pdf> accessed 03 July 2019.

102 Janneke Gerards, 'Intensity of Judicial Review in Equal Treatment Cases' (2004) Vol. 51 Netherlands International Law Review 135, 177 at footnote 164.

103 McCrudden and Prechal (n 41) 22.

104 Nicholas Bamforth, Maleiha Malik and Colm O'Cinneide, *Discrimination Law: Theory and Context* (Sweet & Maxwell 2008) 73.

105 Gerards (n 102) 154.

106 Barocas and Selbst (n 4) 677.

similar situations differently, or different situations alike, can always be found where technologies are used that have as their exact goal to look for these commonalities or dissimilarities.

Notwithstanding the potentially wide margin of appreciation afforded by the Court to differentiate amongst individuals, profiling practices should not be applied without proper safeguards. The Court has argued that in determining the margin of appreciation, one should also take into account the procedural safeguards available to the individual.[107] For instance, in reference to Article 8 ECHR, the right to privacy, and the vulnerable position of gypsies as a minority, the Court has noted that it "must examine whether the decision-making process leading to measures of interference was fair and such as to afford due respect to the interests safeguarded to the individual."[108] Where profiling practices are concerned, the latter can be an important, additional component to take into account: as profiling will likely comprise both a prima facie infringement to the right to privacy and the right to non-discrimination, procedural safeguards, which in this case have partially been implemented by the EU data protection framework, should be upheld. For instance, in reference to automated decision-making, the DPLE Directive considers that safeguards could include the provision of specific information to data subjects, the right to obtain human intervention, in particular in the form of allowing the data subject to express his or her point of view, and to obtain an explanation of the decision reached after an automated decision, or to challenge that decision.[109]

An additional element taken into consideration by the Court is the existence or non-existence of common grounds, which can be reflected by the laws, that exist between Member States.[110] In this regard, it should be noted that, to a certain degree, such communalities will exist between a high number of Member States, due to the presence of national data protection laws implementing the DPLE, whereby profiling practices on the basis of personal data processing have been made subject to a higher level of scrutiny. For instance, non-binding, interpretative bodies, such as the WP29, have been known to interpret the directive and personal data protection legislation in

107 In Connors, the ECtHR noted that: "The procedural safeguards available to the individual will be especially material in determining whether the respondent State has, when fixing the regulatory framework, remained within its margin of appreciation." *Connors* (n 99) para 83. Moreover, the Court added that the existence of other procedural safeguards is also a crucial consideration in determining the proportionality of an interference (at para 92).

108 See inter alia: *Connors v The United Kingdom* App no 66746/01 (ECtHR, 27 May 2004) para 83; Chapman v. the United Kingdom App no 27138/95 (ECtHR Grand Chamber, 18 January 2011), para 92, and Though in Connors, the Court was also asked to consider the alleged violation of Article 14 of the Convention, the Court, having found a violation of Article 8, the right to privacy, found it unnecessary to consider this complaint further.

109 DPLE Directive, recital 37.

110 See also *Petrovic* (n 98) para 38.

equality and non-discrimination sensitive ways.[111] Moreover, given that the public discussion regarding the potential discriminatory and unfair effects of AI and big data analytics is highly present in modern debate, it is not unlikely that the application of profiling technologies, especially in light of problems experienced within American examples, could be faced by a certain sense of apprehension within Member States, and the public at large.[112] Moreover, both the Council of Europe and European Union Institutions have taken position vis-à-vis the deployment of AI, and in doing so have expressly addressed the potential discriminatory effects of AI.[113]

4.6. ETHNIC PROFILING: AN EXAMPLE?

The ECtHR's case-law does not provide adequate information regarding the validity and legality of differential treatment vis-à-vis newly formed groups. Drawing from established case-law on ethnic profiling, guidelines could perhaps be formulated regarding the accompanying factors that could be taken into account in order to justify the deployment of profiling techniques. In its case law on ethnic profiling, the Court has granted Member States a small margin of appreciation. The Court considers that where the difference in treatment is based on race, colour or ethnic origin, the notion of objective and reasonable justification must be interpreted as strictly as possible.[114] From a precautionary perspective, it might therefore be interesting to assess to what extent some of the guiding factors that have been developed in an effort to mitigate the risks of ethnic profiling could also accompany big data profiling practices.

---

111 See inter alia: Article 29 Data Protection Working Party, 'Opinion on Some Key Issues of the Law Enforcement Directive (EU 2016/680)' (n 22) 29; Article 29 Data Protection Working Party, 'Guidelines on Automated Individual Decision-Making and Profiling for the Purposes of Regulation 2016/679' (n 22); Article 29 Data Protection Working Party, 'Guidelines on Data Protection Impact Assessment (DPIA) and Determining Whether Processing Is "Likely to Result in a High Risk" for the Purposes of Regulation 2016/679' (2017). Also, the European Court of Justice has been known to consider the discriminatory aspects where the fundamental rights of data protection and privacy were at stake, such as in C-524/06 Heinz Huber v. Germany and C-293/12 and C-594/12, Digital Rights Ireland Ltd. v. Ireland.

112 See for instance Danielle Ensign and others, 'Runaway Feedback Loops in Predictive Policing' (2017) ArXiv <http://arxiv.org/abs/1706.09847> accessed 20 May 2019.

113 See inter alia: Frederik Zuiderveen-Borgesius, 'Discrimination, Artificial Intelligence, and Algorithmic Decision-Making' (Council of Europe, 2017) <https://rm.coe.int/discrimination-artificial-intelligence-and-algorithmic-decision-making/1680925d73> accessed 03 July 2019>; High-Level Expert Group on Artificial Intelligence, 'Ethics Guidelines for Trustworthy AI' (2019) <https://ec.europa.eu/digital-single-market/en/news/ethics-guidelines-trustworthy-ai> accessed 26 June 2019; Council of Europe, Commissioner for Human Rights, 'Unboxing Artificial Intelligence: 10 steps to protect Human Rights' (May 2019) 11 <https://rm.coe.int/unboxing-artificial-intelligence-10-steps-to-protect-human-rights-reco/1680946e64> accessed 03 July 2019.

114 See inter alia: *Lingurar* (n 39) para 67; *D.H. and Others* (n 96) para 196.

Ethnic profiling is the act to treat an individual less favourable than others who are in a similar situation, where the decision to treat that individual differently has been based only or mainly on that individual's race, ethnicity or religion.[115] The act of an authority to base a policy or decision-making process, solely, or mainly, on an individual's race, ethnicity or religion is generally forbidden under international and national human rights frameworks.[116] Still, parties can avoid that their practices, even though differentiating on the basis of ethnicity, are considered discriminatory and illegal.[117] This can be achieved by basing decisions on "factors additional to a person's race, ethnicity or religion, even when race, ethnicity or religion are relevant to the particular operation or policy."[118] The inclusion of additional characteristics could ensure that officers are not applying a procedure that automatically connects race, ethnicity or religion to criminal behaviour. The FRA adds that: "By basing 'reasonable grounds' for identifying a suspect on behavioural factors that single out a particular individual, the risk of engaging in discriminatory ethnic profiling is reduced." The FRA moreover considers that good intelligence on patterns of behaviour or events can increase objectivity of profiling: "actions based on specific and timely intelligence, such as information about a specific person and/ context, are more likely to be objective".[119]

115 European Union Agency for Fundamental Rights, 'Towards More Effective Policing – Understanding and Preventing Discriminatory Ethnic Profiling: A Guide' (2010) 15 < https://fra.europa.eu/sites/default/files/fra_uploads/1133-Guide-ethnic-profiling_EN.pdf> accessed 26 June 2019.

116 See for instance also the United Nations' International Convention on the Elimination of All Forms of Racial Discrimination. Under this convention, 'racial discrimination' has been defined as: "any distinction, exclusion, restriction or preference based on race, colour, descent, or national or ethnic origin which has the purpose or effect of nullifying or impairing the recognition, enjoyment or exercise, on an equal footing, of human rights and fundamental freedoms in the political, economic, social, cultural or any other field of public life." Article 2 urges States Parties to "condemn racial discrimination and undertake to pursue by all appropriate means and without delay a policy of eliminating racial discrimination in all its forms and promoting understanding among all races."

117 The FRA argues that: "In addition to intelligence and objective elements, information about protected characteristics such as actual or perceived race, ethnic origin, nationality, gender or religion may be used legitimately as an added component in profiling assessments in certain circumstances. For use of this information to be lawful, it must be regulated by law, respect the essence of the rights and freedoms affected, be proportionate (i.e. complying with a balance of interests) and necessary (i.e. there should not be any less restrictive means available). There must be a justifiable reason, other than the protected grounds, for the officers to treat an individual differently from other members of the public." European Union Agency for Fundamental Rights", 'Preventing Unlawful Profiling Today and in the Future: A Guide' (2018) 70 < https://fra.europa.eu/en/publication/2018/prevent-unlawful-profiling> accessed 26 June 2019.

118 European Union Agency for Fundamental Rights (n 115) 22-23.

119 European Union Agency for Fundamental Rights (n 117) 11. The FRA notes that removing race and ethnicity from a general criminal profile, and that profiles based upon behavioral factors, could help improve the 'hit rate' of policing and enhance the effectiveness of law enforcement (n 115) 35-36.

One difficulty with regard to big data analytics, and especially within the online environment, is that behavioural factors, which might, for instance, be necessary to establish whether or not an individual has radicalized, cannot be perceived directly in the data. Rather, analysis techniques are developed that seek to discern those characteristics that indicate radicalization. Because behaviour is usually something we perceive, rather than something that can be captured through data, one must be weary regarding the validity of the use of data-driven techniques in order to determine decision-making on 'behavioural' analytics. In this regard, it could be valuable to test certain types of data in practice in order to verify whether what the analytics and data say, can actually be verified on the ground. Perhaps only then, should those data subsequently be used as a means to determine suspicion. The behaviour an individual displays online might be entirely different from his or her actions, e.g. in the case of internet trolls.

Likewise, the belief that the more data there is, the more valuable analytics becomes, runs counter to European fundamental rights, under which blanket and indiscriminate retention of data has been scrutinized, and where mass-surveillance regimes risk violating fundamental rights by leading to discriminatory effects.[120] Following the above, it might also be important to consider the purpose for which, and the time when, profiling practices have been applied. If profiling is deployed for predictive purposes, behavioural factors are often inferred and data-driven, rather than perceived. In other words, the legality of profiling, where based on data, seems more likely to stand the test of time when they are used in a post-fact, rather than a real-time, preventive or predictive manner. Indeed, substantial post-fact evidence could provide information of perceived behaviour, which can subsequently be used in the profiling exercise.

5. FUTURE RESEARCH

The analysis presented in this chapter illuminates the relationship between profiling and non-discrimination law by focusing on the ECtHR's case law regarding the development of the grounds-based approach. The broader discussion on the desirability of data-driven investigatory techniques may benefit, however, from a further investigation of other approaches and problems that could not be dealt with in this chapter.

This chapter did, for instance, not touch upon other matters relevant within non-discrimination law, such as direct and indirect discrimination, the role of a comparator, and the evidence required to prove discrimination. These elements nonetheless help shape the answers regarding the justifiability of differential

120 See for instance *S. and Marper v UK* App no 30562/04 and 30566/04 (ECtHR Grand Chamber, 4 December 2008); and Franziska Boehm and Mark Cole, Data Retention after the Judgement of the Court of Justice of the European Union 26.

treatment. The distinction between direct and indirect discrimination is important in those instances where seemingly innocuous groups might serve as a proxy for a special category of data, or for one the protected grounds specified in the charters' open-ended list. Similarly, the principle of equality has been said to have various meanings, which could lead to different interpretations of international non-discrimination clauses, and their functioning.[121]

Second, legal scholars have debated the stereotyping or stigmatizing impact as potential negative effect of profiling.[122] This paper focused on the grounds-based approach, and the capability of new grounds to be found discriminatory by the Court, but did not specifically zoom in on the issue of stereotyping. The Court's case law has recently been analysed through the concepts of stereotyping and vulnerability, which could open new ways to discuss forms of differentiation under the ECtHR's case law.[123] For instance, the Court has recognized the stereotyping effects of ethnic profiling, in that it can, on the basis of ethnicity, extend the (criminal) behaviour of a few members of a community, to the whole community.[124]

Third, the chapter focused on the case-law of the ECtHR only. The case-law of the CJEU can nonetheless be relevant, both with regard to the deployment of data-driven practices for security purposes in general, as well as their potential discriminatory effects. For instance, in its opinion on the agreement on the transfer and processing of passenger name records, the ECJ noted that the compatibility of such an agreement with fundamental rights depends *amongst others* on the presence of safeguards in order to ensure that the models and criteria for automated processing of PNR are specific, reliable and non-discriminatory.[125] Likewise, the CJEU has the possibility to further guide the use of data-driven processes through its interpretation of the DPLE Directive.

---

121 In their analysis of EU non-discrimination law, McCrudden and Prechal discern four meanings of equality within EU fundamental rights frameworks: a) equality as rationality, b) equality as preserving fair distribution of specific prized goods, c) equality as the prohibition to distinguish between individuals on the basis of a group characteristic that should be considered irrational or unacceptable to base decision-making on, and d) equality as the positive duty to promote equality of opportunity and de facto equality. McCrudden and Prechal (n 43). See also: Gerards (n 46) (n 102) and Olivier De Schutter, 'Three Models of Equality and European Anti-Discrimination Law' (2006) 57 *Northern Ireland Legal Quarterly* 1.

122 Schreurs and others (n 44); Tal Z Zarsky, 'Understanding Discrimination in the Scored Society' (2014) 89 Wash. L. Rev. 1375; Danielle Keats Citron and Frank Pasquale, 'The Scored Society: Due Process for Automated Predictions' (2014) Vol. 89 *Washington Law Review* 33.

123 See inter alia Aleksandra Timmer, 'Toward an Anti-Stereotyping Approach for the European Court of Human Rights' (2011) 11 Human Rights Law Review 707; L Peroni and A Timmer, 'Vulnerable Groups: The Promise of an Emerging Concept in European Human Rights Convention Law' (2013) 11 *International Journal of Constitutional Law* 1056; Alexandra Timmer, *Strentghening the Equality Analysis of the European Court of Human Rights: The Potential of the Concepts of Stereotyping and Vulnerability.* (2014); Arnardóttir (n 64).

124 As the Court observed in *Lingurar*: "the applicants' own behaviour was extrapolated from a stereotypical perception that the authorities had of the Roma community as a whole that the authorities had of the Roma community as a whole." (n 39) para 75–76.

125 Opinion 1/15 of the Court (Grand Chamber) on the agreement envisaged between the European Union and Canada on the transfer of Passenger Name Record Data (27 July 2017).

Fourth, the deployment of analytics in itself has been argued to be discriminatory if no proper consideration is given to the socio-historical context in which automated processes are deployed. Where historical data shows biases reflecting past prejudice or injustice, algorithms are likely to reinforce societal disadvantages. Likewise, as coded constructs, implicit biases and values might creep in by design, which if prejudiced, in turn, might generate inequalities.

Finally, the profiling of individuals affects multiple fundamental rights, including privacy, data protection, fair trial, presumption of innocence and freedom to expression. Fundamental rights are to be balanced against other values that are hold dearly, such as national security and public safety. Though one might consider the potential negative effects of profiling, new techniques adopted for public and national security are here to stay. Hence, discussions regarding their value for security versus the fundamental rights they might infringe, should be continued, without disregarding their relative importance. In recent years, several claims related to mass-surveillance have been brought before the Court.[126] As such practices often constitute a particular threat to a variety of fundamental rights, including equality and non-discrimination, this line of cases will be important to follow.[127]

6. CONCLUSION

Law enforcement and intelligence agencies rely on ICT and data-driven technologies for the maintenance and protection of security in modern-day society. The deployment of those technologies can nonetheless affect other fundamental values, such as privacy, data protection and equality. A balance should therefore be maintained between the protection of the latter and the technological environment needed to ensure efficient and accurate decision-making for security purposes. The regulation of criminal profiling practices is complex and multi-layered. This chapter analysed how, from a legal perspective, new forms of differentiation generated by data-driving analytics tools, might constitute problematic from a non-discrimination perspective.

The DPLE provides clear and concrete guidelines regarding the use of specific types of information in building profiles, indicating quite well when, and under what conditions, profiling practices could be allowed. Moreover, the Directive

"The pre-established models and criteria should be specific and reliable, making its possible, [...] to arrive at results targeting individuals who might be under a 'reasonable suspicion' of participation in terrorist offences or serious transnational crime and should be non-discriminatory." *PNR Agreement*, para 172. In its opinion, the ECJ also stressed that the need for safeguards is greater where personal data is subject to automated processing, and even more so where those data are sensitive. *PNR Agreement*, para 141.

126 European Court of Human Rights, 'Mass-Surveillance Fact Sheet' (2019) <https://www.echr.coe.int/Documents/FS_Mass_surveillance_ENG.pdf> last accessed 26 June 2019.

127 The aforementioned *Big Brother Watch* case touched upon equality and non-discrimination, yet did so in a very concise manner (n 68).

includes equality-sensitive considerations, noting the potential discriminatory nature data-driven techniques might have. It does so in particular where special categories of data are involved. The latter present a limited list of data that are considered particularly problematic. Specific in nature, the DPLE ruleset might be inadequately equipped to tackle new forms of differentiation generated through data-driven analytics. Moreover, the DPLE Directive only applies to matters of public security, and might, as a consequence, only apply to law enforcement authorities, leaving matters of national security, and intelligence agencies, outside of its scope.

Considering the requirement that profiling practices should not be discriminatory, public bodies should still consider the fundamental right to equality and non-discrimination as it has been enshrined in the European Convention of Human Rights, and as it has been interpreted by the European Court of Human Rights. The Court's case law is at times both complex and confusing. Through the open-ended phrasing of Article 14, the Convention's non-discrimination clause can, in principle, allow the Court to condemn new forms of discrimination. The Court's reasoning might however be ill-equipped to tackle the risks new technologies pose. First, where the Court departs from an open, grounds-based approach to an approach where differential treatment can only be considered problematic if it is based on status – and whereby status is moreover understood as a personal characteristic – new grounds of differentiation might be general enough as to not fit the 'personal' criterion. This seems particularly true when that criterion is moreover linked to the condition that it should also entail a characteristic that is innate or inherent. Second, even if new forms of differentiation could enter the ambit of Article 14, the Court might still fail to apply a test that is truly capable of evaluating decision-making practices driven by big data analytics. Therefore, in order to tackle new differentiation grounds adequately, a return to the procedural and instrumental conception of equality might be necessary. This should furthermore be combined with a thorough insight into the data and tools used by public authorities. Perhaps then, a proper evaluation regarding the relevancy of profiles for decision-making can be made, where the 'rationale' for implementing data-driven techniques can be questioned, rather than taking their 'rationality' at face value. Still, as emphasized by the Court, the Convention remains a living instrument, where rights should not remain illusory.

A heightened level of awareness across society regarding the dangers that profiling techniques pose to the fundamental principles of equality and non-discrimination, could become a common ground amongst Member States and in turn increase the level of protection afforded to citizens in the case of criminal profiling. Of course, the desired nature of these techniques as a means to preserve public and national security does not solely depend upon equality and non-discrimination; a balancing exercise would still need to be made. The scope of this chapter was limited to considering the potential role of non-discrimination law. The discussion overall, however, will remain complex and likely open-ended itself.

BIBLIOGRAPHY

Agarwal S and Sureka A, 'Applying Social Media Intelligence for Predicting and Identifying On-Line Radicalization and Civil Unrest Oriented Threats' (2015) ArXiv <http://arxiv.org/abs/1511.06858> accessed 9 May 2019

Alison L and others, 'Pragmatic Solutions to Offender Profiling and Behavioural Investigative Advice' (2010) Vol. 15 Legal and Criminological Psychology 115

Arnardóttir OM, 'The Differences That Make a Difference: Recent Developments on the Discrimination Grounds and the Margin of Appreciation under Article 14 of the European Convention on Human Rights' (2014) Vol. 14 Human Rights Law Review 647

Arnardóttir OM, 'Vulnerability under Article 14 of the European Convention on Human Rights' (2017) Vol. 4 Oslo Law Review 150

Bamforth N, Malik M, O'Cinneide C, *Discrimination Law: Theory and Context* (Sweet & Maxwell 2008) 73

Barocas S and Selbst AD, 'Big Data's Disparate Impact Essay' (2016) 104 California Law Review 671

Bové L, 'Politie gaat criminaliteit via data voorspellen' *De Tijd* (30 August 2018) <https://www.tijd.be/politiek-economie/belgie/federaal/politie-gaat-criminaliteit-via-data-voorspellen/10044356.html> accessed 8 March 2019

Brayne S, 'Big Data Surveillance: The Case of Policing' (2017) Vol. 82 American Sociological Review 977

Citron DK and Pasquale F, 'The Scored Society: Due Process for Automated Predictions' (2014) Vol. 89 Washington Law Review 33

CNIL, 'Comment Permettre à l'Homme de Garder La Main ? Rapport Sur Les Enjeux Éthiques Des Algorithmes et de l'intelligence Artificielle' (2017) <https://www.cnil.fr/en/node/24008> accessed 8 March 2019

Council of Europe, Commissioner for Human Rights, 'Unboxing Artificial Intelligence: 10 steps to protect Human Rights' (May 2019) 11 <https://rm.coe.int/unboxing-artificial-intelligence-10-steps-to-protect-human-rights-reco/1680946e64> accessed 03 July 2019

Council of Europe, 'Explanatory Report to the Protocol No. 12 to the Convention for the Protection of Human Rights and Fundamental Freedoms (Rome, 4 XI. 2000)' <https://rm.coe.int/16800cce48> accessed 03 July 2019

Council of Europe, 'National Security and Euopean Case-Law' (2013) <https://www.echr.coe.int/Documents/Research_report_national_security_ENG.pdf> accessed 03 July 2019

De Pauw E and others (eds), Technology-Led Policing (Maklu 2011)

Dencik L, Hintz A, Carey Z, 'Prediction, Pre-Emption and Limits to Dissent: Social Media and Big Data Uses for Policing Protests in the United Kingdom' (2018) Vol. 20 New Media & Society 1433

Derencinovic D and Getos AM, 'Cooperation of law enforcement and intelligence agencies in prevention and suppression of terrorism' (2007) Vol. 78 Revue internationale de droit penal 79

Ensign D and others, 'Runaway Feedback Loops in Predictive Policing' (2017) ArXiv <http://arxiv.org/abs/1706.09847> accessed 20 May 2019

European Court of Human Rights, 'Mass-Surveillance Fact Sheet' (2019) <https://www.echr.coe.int/Documents/FS_Mass_surveillance_ENG.pdf> accessed 26 June 2019

European Union Agency for Fundamental Rights, 'Preventing Unlawful Profiling Today and in the Future: A Guide' (2018) 138 < https://fra.europa.eu/en/publication/2018/prevent-unlawful-profiling> accessed 26 June 2019

European Union Agency for Fundamental Rights, 'Towards More Effective Policing – Understanding and Preventing Discriminatory Ethnic Profiling: A Guide' (2010) <https://fra.europa.eu/sites/default/files/fra_uploads/1133-Guide-ethnic-profiling_EN.pdf> accessed 26 June 2019

European Union Agency for Fundamental Rights and the Council of Europe (eds), Handbook on European Non-Discrimination Law (2018 edition, Publications Office of the European Union 2018) 224–225

Fredman S, 'Emerging from the Shadows: Substantive Equality and Article 14 of the European Convention on Human Rights' (2016) Vol. 16 Human Rights Law Review 273, 277

Gellert R and others, 'A Comparative Analysis of Anti-Discrimination and Data Protection Legislations' in Bart Custers and others (eds), Discrimination and Privacy in the Information Society: Data Mining and Profiling in Large Databases (Springer Berlin Heidelberg 2013) <https://doi.org/10.1007/978-3-642-30487-3_4>

Gerards J, "Intensity of Judicial Review in Equal Treatment Cases" (2004) 51 Netherlands International Law Review 135

Gerards J, 'The Discrimination Grounds of Article 14 of the European Convention on Human Rights' (2013) Vol. 13 Human Rights Law Review 99

Gerards J, 'Margin of Appreciation and Incrementalism in the Case Law of the European Court of Human Rights' (2018) Vol. 18 Human Rights Law Review 495

High-Level Expert Group on Artificial Intelligence, 'Ethics Guidelines for Trustworthy AI' (2019) <https://ec.europa.eu/digital-single-market/en/news/ethics-guidelines-trustworthy-ai> accessed 26 June 2019

Kocsis RN, Criminal Profiling: Principles and Practice (Humana Press 2006) 9

Kocsis RN and Palermo GB, 'Disentangling Criminal Profiling: Accuracy, Homology, and the Myth of Trait-Based Profiling' (2015) Vol. 59 International Journal of Offender Therapy and Comparative Criminology 313

Lammerant H and Hert PD, 'Predictive Profiling and Its Legal Limits: Effectiveness Gone Forever' (2016) Vol. 32 Exploring the boundaries of big data 145

Lapowsky I, 'How the LAPD uses data to predict crime' (22 May 2018) <https://www.wired.com/story/los-angeles-police-department-predictive-policing/> accessed 03 July 2019

Mantelero A, 'Personal Data for Decisional Purposes in the Age of Analytics: From an Individual to a Collective Dimension of Data Protection' (2016) Vol. 32 Computer Law & Security Review 238

Mantelero A, 'From Group Privacy to Collective Privacy: Towards a New Dimension of Privacy and Data Protection in the Big Data Era' in Linnet Taylor, Luciano Floridi and Bart van der Sloot (eds), Group Privacy: New Challenges of Data Technologies (Springer International Publishing 2017) <https://doi.org/10.1007/978-3-319-46608-8_8> accessed 26 June 2019

McCrudden C, Prechal S, 'The Concepts of Equality and Non-Discrimination in Europe: A Practical Approach' (2009) European Network of Legal Experts in the Field of Gender Equality 21

Meijer A and Wessels M, 'Predictive Policing: Review of Benefits and Drawbacks' [2019] International Journal of Public Administration 1

Van Lonkhuyzen L, 'Misdaad voorspellen, het kan echt' *NRC* (16 May 2017) <https://www.nrc.nl/nieuws/2017/05/16/misdaad-voorspellen-het-kan-echt-9100898-a1558837> accessed 8 March 2019

Mittelstadt B, 'From Individual to Group Privacy in Big Data Analytics' (2017) 30 Philosophy & Technology 475

Murdoch J and Roche R, *The European Convention on Human Rights and Policing: A handbook for police officers and other law enforcement officials*. 154

Naudts L, 'How Machine Learning Generates Unfair Inequalities and How Data Protection Instruments May Help in Mitigating Them', in Ronald Leenes and others (eds) in, Data Protection and Privacy: The Internet of Bodies (Hart Publishing 2019) ch 3

O'Connell R, 'Cinderella Comes to the Ball: Art 14 and the Right to Non-Discrimination in the ECHR' (2009) 29 Legal Studies 211

Peroni L and Timmer A, 'Vulnerable Groups: The Promise of an Emerging Concept in European Human Rights Convention Law' (2013) 11 International Journal of Constitutional Law 1056

Ridgeway G, 'Policing in the Era of Big Data' (2018) 1 Annual Review of Criminology 401

Schreurs W and others, 'Cogitas, Ergo Sum. The Role of Data Protection Law and Non-Discrimination Law in Group Profiling in the Private Sector', in Mireille Hildebrandt and Serge Gutwirth (eds) Profiling the European citizen (Springer 2008) Ch 13

Schuilenburg M, 'De burger moet kunnen weten hoe de misdaadvoorspeller werkt' *NRC* (18 June 2018) <https://www.nrc.nl/nieuws/2018/06/18/de-burger-moet-kunnen-weten-hoe-de-misdaadvoorspeller-werkt-a1606978> accessed 03 July 2019

Schutter OD, 'Three Models of Equality and European Anti-Discrimination Law' (2006) Vol.57 Northern Ireland Legal Quarterly 1

Timmer A, 'Toward an Anti-Stereotyping Approach for the European Court of Human Rights' (2011) 11 Human Rights Law Review 707

Timmer A, Strentghening the Equality Analysis of the European Court of Human Rights: The Potential of the Concepts of Stereotyping and Vulnerability (2014)

Turvey B, *Criminal Profiling: An Introduction to Behavioral Evidence Analysis* (4th edn, Oxford: Academic 2011)

Vedder A, 'KDD: The Challenge to Individualism' (1999) 1 Ethics and Information Technology 275

Vedder A and Naudts L, 'Accountability for the Use of Algorithms in a Big Data Environment' (2017) 31 International Review of Law, Computers & Technology 206

Wachter S, 'Affinity Profiling and Discrimination by Association in Online Behavioural Advertising' (SSRN Scholarly Paper ID 3388639, Social Science Research Network 2019) <https://papers.ssrn.com/abstract=3388639> accessed 6 June 2019

Zarsky TZ, 'Understanding Discrimination in the Scored Society' (2014) 89 Wash. L. Rev. 1375

Zuiderveen-Borgesius F, 'Discrimination, Artificial Intelligence, and Algorithmic Decision-Making' (Council of Europe, 2018) 51 <https://rm.coe.int/discrimination-artificial-intelligence-and-algorithmic-decision-making/1680925d73 > accessed 03 July 2019

CHAPTER 5

OPERATIONALIZATION OF INFORMATION SECURITY THROUGH COMPLIANCE WITH DIRECTIVE 2016/680 IN LAW ENFORCEMENT TECHNOLOGY AND PRACTICE

Thomas MARQUENIE and Katherine QUEZADA

1. INTRODUCTION

Information and communication technologies are cornerstones of modern society. Automated computer processes and the continuous collection, analysis and creation of data are staples of each current industry, service and sector. As data analytics are now vital in both the public and private sphere, securing confidential and valuable information remains a key goal of computer science. To this end, the concept of information security revolves around the identification and implementation of concrete safeguards based on the three fundamental tenets of Confidentiality, Integrity and Availability. While these principles are generally accepted in the field of computer science,[1] they do not constitute universal or legally binding conditions. The current EU legal framework on cybersecurity[2] does not impose general or specific obligations on developers of information technologies for private or public actors. Still, as the undue disclosure or processing of confidential information can have serious consequences, the EU legislator recently finalized its data protection reforms to further safeguard personal data. In addition to the General Data Protection Regulation (GDPR), the reforms also consist of a Law Enforcement Directive

1 Bel G. Raggad, *Information Security Management: Concepts and Practice* (1st edn, CRC Press 2010).

2 An extensive overview of the legislative framework is provided in section 3.1. The so-called NIS Directive is the foremost current instrument; Directive (EU) 2016/1148 of the European Parliament and of the Council of 6 July 2016 concerning measures for a high common level of security of network and information systems across the Union [2016] OJ L194.

(DPLE) for the purpose of regulating the collection, processing and storage of personal information in the context of policing.

As innovative technologies are rapidly adopted by law enforcement agencies to detect, investigate and prevent crime, the negative impact of security breaches can significantly affect the safety and integrity of citizens and police practices.[3] It is in light of these developments that this chapter seeks to assess whether compliance with the recent European legislation on data protection may support the realization of fundamental principles of information security in a law enforcement context. To this end, it provides an outline of the principles of information security followed by an overview of the current legal framework on cybersecurity and data protection in the EU. The differences and similarities between information security and data protection are examined in order to determine to what extent law enforcement technology and practice could rely on the applicable data protection legislation to ensure sufficiently high standards of information security. Finally, to illustrate how the concrete implementation of security requirements in data protection might actually support the accomplishment of high standards of information security in practice, the chapter concludes with a brief assessment of security protocols applied in two law enforcement systems developed in the framework of European research projects. It has therefore been conceived as a contribution to the field of theoretical and comparative approaches in the study of data protection and security standards, particularly in the context of law enforcement.

2. PRINCIPLES OF INFORMATION SECURITY

In general terms, the study and realization of information security concerns the identification and implementation of measures and techniques for the protection of information from unauthorized access, use, modification, destruction, disclosure or disruption.[4] These measures are relevant and can be applied to all types of information, regardless of whether they contain personally identifiable details or are presented in a printed, electronic or other format. Information security measures aim to address a variety of different threats to the preservation of information.[5] These possible threats typically include human vulnerabilities and flaws in programming, non-human events such as power outages, and illegitimate actors which might be external, such as hackers seeking to steal or

3 International Association of Chiefs of Police (IACP), *Managing Cybersecurity Risk: A Law Enforcement Guide* (2017) <www.iacpcybercenter.org/wp-content/uploads/2015/04/Managing_Cybersecurity_Risk_2017.pdf> accessed 16 July 2019.

4 Michael E. Whitman and Herbert J. Mattord, *Principles of Information Security* (4th edn, Course Technology Press 2011).

5 Justin Peltier, 'Threats to Information Security' in Peltier TR (ed.), Information Security Fundamentals (2nd edn, CRC Press 2014).

sabotage data, or internal, such as employees who might be susceptible to social engineering or could mismanage information.[6]

For information to be considered secure, it is widely accepted[7] that it must satisfy three fundamental principles known as the CIA-triad.[8] While there exists no singular point of origin for this acronym, the general notions underlying it can be found dating back to the early years of modern computer science.[9] Only when adequate technical or organizational measures ensure the Confidentiality, Integrity and Availability of the information can it be regarded as secure.[10] In the European legal framework, these principles are recognized in the NIS Directive which defines the "security of network and information systems" as meaning the ability of such systems to resist actions which compromise the "availability, authenticity, integrity or confidentiality" of the data and service.[11] In the field of computer science, these general tenets consist of specific security goals upon which concrete controls and policies are based.[12] To adequately assess how specific policies might support the CIA principles, the following section provides

6 Per Oscarson, 'Information Security Fundamentals: Graphical Conceptualisations for Understanding' in Irvine C and Armstrong H (eds), Security Education and Critical Infrastructures (IFIP – The International Federation for Information Processing, Springer 2003); Jason Andress, *The Basics of Information Security: Understanding the Fundamentals of InfoSec in Theory and* Practice (Elsevier 2011); Darren Death, *Information Security Handbook: Develop a threat model and incident response strategy to build a strong information security network* (Packt Publishing 2017).

7 To illustrate the broad acceptance of the CIA-triad as the fundamentals of the information security discipline, reference can be made to the International Organization for Standardization (ISO) *Standard ISO/IEC 27000:2018 – Information Security Management Systems – Overview and Vocabulary* (available at <https://www.iso.org/standard/73906.html>, 2018) accessed 16 July 2019, which defines Information Security as the "preservation of *Confidentiality, Integrity* and *Availability* of information", as well as to the European Union Agency for Network and Information Security (ENISA) which considers the triad to be the primary model for managing information security. For more, see: European Union Agency for Network and Information Security (ENISA), 'Guidelines for SMEs on the Security of Personal Data Processing' (2016) <https://www.enisa.europa.eu/publications/guidelines-for-smes-on-the-security-of-personal-data-processing/at_download/fullReport> accessed 01 July 2019.

8 Sattarova Feruza and Tao-hoon Kim, 'IT Security Review: Privacy, Protection, Access Control, Assurance and System Security' (2007) 2 International Journal of Multimedia and Ubiquitous Engineering 17.

9 For example, the following paper by Bell and La Padula established an access control model for computer security that considered aspects of the confidentiality, integrity and accessibility of information in 1976: Elliott Bell and Leonard J. La Padula, *Secure Computer System: Unified Exposition and Multics Interpretation* (The MITRE Corporation 1976).

10 National Research Council, *Computers at Risk: Safe Computing in the Information Age* (The National Academic Press 1991).

11 Directive (EU) 2016/1148 of the European Parliament and of the Council of 6 July 2016 concerning measures for a high common level of security of network and information systems across the Union [2016] OJ L194 Article 4 (2).

12 Dieter Gollman, *Computer Security* (3rd edn, Wiley 2013).

an overview of the triad as well as concrete ways in which it is frequently implemented in practice.[13]

2.1. CONFIDENTIALITY

Under the principle of confidentiality, information must only be shared with and made available to authorized individuals.[14] Access is reserved for those with legitimate privileges while the information remains inaccessible and hidden from those who do not have the appropriate access rights. Information can be kept confidential for a number of reasons justifying its private nature. The information might concern personal data of individuals, intellectual property or business strategies, or governmental matters regarding public and national security.[15] In all of these instances, the undue disclosure of sensitive information can have significant negative consequences for society, businesses and individuals alike. Measures taken to safeguard the confidentiality of information can be aimed at both external and internal actors and threats.[16] The former are those who are foreign to the organization, such as competing businesses or criminals, who might seek access to confidential information by means of interception, infiltration or hacking. The latter are individuals who are part of the organization but might overstep their allotted access rights or unduly disclose information to others.

As such, security measures implementing this principle aim to prevent unauthorized individuals from accessing confidential information. In practice, these methods often include the adoption of access controls and identity verification protocols.[17] Individuals accessing computer systems or the facilities in which the information is kept might have to present ID cards, register themselves at an information desk, or provide a password and profile details before being able to retrieve any data. Subsequently, an automated control system might restrict which information they can access or alter based on the access rights granted to their particular profile. These measures are known as "layered"

---

13 For the sake of the clarity, the scope of this chapter is limited to the three CIA principles as they lay the groundwork for information security and the prevention of data breaches and misuse. Other aspects of cybersecurity, such as the governance of and response to security incidents, will not be considered in depth as part of this chapter.

14 Mariana Gerber, Rossouw von Solms and Paul Overbeek, 'Formalizing information security requirements' (2001) 9 Information Management & Computer Security 1.

15 David Kim and Michael G. Solomon, *Fundamentals of Information Systems Security* (3rd edn, Jones & Bartlett 2018).

16 European Union Agency for Network and Information Security (ENISA), 'Guidelines for SMEs on the Security of Personal Data Processing' (2016) <https://www.enisa.europa.eu/publications/guidelines-for-smes-on-the-security-of-personal-data-processing/at_download/fullReport> accessed 01 July 2019.

17 Kimberly Logan, 'Access Controls' in Thomas R. Peltier (ed.), *Information Security Fundamentals* (2nd edn, CRC Press 2014).

security solutions[18] and allow for different levels of access based on the sensitivity and confidentiality of a particular piece of information. Encryption protocols, as further discussed under the section on integrity, can secure and hide data which individuals are not authorized to view by obscuring the contents of files. In addition, internal policies or training might be provided to raise awareness among employees of the consequences of unintended or illegitimate disclosures of information.[19] Educating system operators on password security and proper methods of handling, storing and extracting private data can support and improve the confidentiality thereof. Finally, the performance of periodic security risk assessments as well as the consistent monitoring of system interactions and events allow for the identification of possible threats, weaknesses or instances of system misuse.[20]

2.2. INTEGRITY

The principle of informational integrity is to be understood as meaning that data must be kept reliable, accurate, consistent and complete.[21] This is to ensure that the information itself remains trustworthy and usable for its intended purposes. As a consequence, the integrity of information is considered damaged or lacking when its quality is affected through alteration, deletion or deterioration. This can occur when, for example, an unauthorized individual sabotages and makes changes to the data, or a non-human event causes corruption or deletion of system files. Data which is lacking in integrity is often no longer valid for its intended purpose and can cause the loss of significant value. This might be the case when the lost or compromised data contains personal information or is the result of extensive data mining, organizing or processing and cannot easily be replaced or verified.

In practice, this principle is frequently implemented by a number of complementary security measures.[22] A primary set of methods typically overlaps with those used to safeguard confidentiality. Techniques such as access controls, identity verification and secure storage constitute a first line of defence against outside interference and aim to prevent the information from being unduly

18 Clive Blackwell, 'A multi-layered security architecture for modelling complex systems' (2008) CSIIRW 35.

19 International Association of Chiefs of Police (IACP), *Managing Cybersecurity Risk: A Law Enforcement Guide* (2017) <www.iacpcybercenter.org/wp-content/uploads/2015/04/Managing_Cybersecurity_Risk_2017.pdf> accessed 01 July 2019.

20 Chunlin Liu and others 'The Security Risk Assessment Methodology' (2012) 43 Procedia Engineering.

21 J. Efrim Boritz, 'IS practitioners' views on core concepts of information integrity' (2005) 6 International Journal of Accounting Information Systems 260.

22 Fayez Hussain Alqahtani, 'Developing an Information Security Policy: A Case Study Approach' (2017) 124 Procedia Computer Science 691.

retrieved, accessed or altered. This is in contrast with the secondary set of methods which are not intended to prevent mismanagement of or unauthorized access to the data, but rather to maintain the system and ensure that the information does not lose its validity or accuracy in the event of a data breach or system failure.[23] Such security measures might include version controls and system back-ups that allow for the tracking of changes in system files over time and for deleted, overwritten or corrupted data to be restored. This might be supplemented by a logging module that provides system administrators with the tools to determine how and at what time a certain piece of information was accessed, deleted or modified by a certain actor.

Other safeguards might include techniques to validate the authenticity[24] and accuracy of information as well of the actor providing it through the adoption of file verification measures such as hashing algorithms which can establish whether files have been altered, viewed or tampered with.[25] This relates closely to the field of cryptography, which is another established method of preserving the integrity of information.[26] Encryption is the process of transforming data into illegible bits that can only be deciphered by the corresponding decryption key.[27] Encryption can be symmetric, when the same key is employed to alter and decrypt the bits of data, or asymmetric, where a publicly available key must match a corresponding private one to reveal the information. Thus, encryption is a key tool for the preservation of information confidentiality and integrity by making data unable to be read and altered by unauthorized parties.[28]

2.3. AVAILABILITY

Following the principle of availability, the information must be made available and accessible whenever necessary. This requires that the computer hardware, system processes and security protocols by means of which the data is accessed,

---

23 David T. Bourgeois and Dave Bourgeois, 'Information Systems Security' in David T. Bourgeois and Dave Bourgeois, *Information Systems for Business and Beyond* (Saylor Academy 2014).

24 From an information security perspective, authenticity is defined as "the property that an entity is what it claims to be", meaning that it hasn't been altered from its original state. For more, see: International Organization for Standardization (ISO), *Standard ISO/IEC 27000:2018 – Information Security Management Systems – Overview and Vocabulary* (available at <https://www.iso.org/standard/73906.html>, 2018), section 3.6.

25 Bart Preneel, 'Cryptographic Hash Functions: Theory and Practice' in Guang Cong and Kishan Chand Gupta (eds.), *Progress in Cryptology – IndoCrypt 2010* (Springer Berlin 2010).

26 Gustavus J. Simmons, *Contemporary Cryptology: The Science of Information Integrity* (IEEE Press 1994).

27 Harold Tipton and Micki Krause, *Information Security Management Handbook* (vol 2, 6th edn, CRC Press 2009).

28 Lina Gong and others, 'The application of data encryption technology in computer network communication security' (2017) AIP Conference Proceedings 1834.

altered and stored must be working reliably and as intended. It is therefore considered a security flaw when the data is not actively available to authorized persons. This might occur as a result of system failure due to hardware problems, software flaws or disruption by human actors. In technical terms, system availability is calculated in function of uptime, or the total amount of time that the system is accessible, and downtime, or the timespan during which the system is inaccessible.[29]

As the unavailability of key system processes can impact the reliability of the information and severely hamper time-critical tasks, practical safeguards and security measures underlying the principle of availability aim to ensure the ongoing accessibility of data.[30] These methods often consist of back-up systems and servers to which operators can switch if the main processes would fail. In addition to providing functionalities to retrieve lost data in case of corruption or undue deletion, these back-up measures serve as an immediate replacement while the necessary repairs are made to primary components.[31] Additional technical measures include emergency power supplies in the event of energy blackouts and counter-DDoS (Distributed Denial of Service) protocols such as ingress filtering and the blocking of suspicious POST-requests.[32] At the organizational level, availability might be supported by the continuous support of IT personnel as well as policies requiring ongoing maintenance, continued access to archived software versions during system updates or limiting simultaneous log-ins during emergency situations to avoid system overload.[33]

3. INFORMATION SECURITY IN DATA PROTECTION FOR LAW ENFORCEMENT

For information to be considered secure, it must satisfy the tenets of Confidentiality, Integrity and Availability. Despite the importance of these principles in the field of information security, there exists no binding legal instrument that requires their implementation for the general processing of

---

29 David Kim and Michael G. Solomon, *Fundamentals of Information Systems Security* (3rd edn, Jones & Bartlett 2018).

30 Yulia Cherdantseva and Jeremy Hilton, 'A reference model of information assurance and security' (2013) IEEE Proceedings of the International Conference on Availability, Reliability and Security (ARES).

31 European Union Agency for Network and Information Security (ENISA), 'Guidelines for SMEs on the Security of Personal Data Processing' (2016) <https://www.enisa.europa.eu/publications/guidelines-for-smes-on-the-security-of-personal-data-processing/at_download/fullReport> accessed 01 July 2019.

32 Suhail Qadir and S. M. K. Quadri, 'Information Availability: An Insight into the Most Important Attribute of Information Security' (2016) Journal of Information Security 7.

33 National Research Council, Computers at Risk: Safe Computing in the Information Age (The National Academic Press 1991).

information in the EU. This holds equally true in the context of law enforcement where police agencies collect, store and analyse highly personal and sensitive information in increasingly extensive and data-driven ways.[34]

Nevertheless, despite being marked by clear differences in their scope and objective, the discipline of information security shares several notable similarities with the current European framework on data protection. As incentivizing the security and protection of personal data remains a key goal of the recent EU legislative reforms,[35] this chapter will draw parallels between the Data Protection Directive 2016/680 for Law Enforcement (DPLE)[36] and the discipline of information security to determine whether competent authorities may rely on their compliance with the current data protection regime as means to implement and adhere to the basic tenets of information security. Thereto, the following section shall examine the relationship between the concepts of data protection and information security, and analyse the DPLE to assess to what extent the abovementioned principles are reflected in its provisions.

3.1. THE EU LEGAL FRAMEWORK ON CYBERSECURITY AND DATA PROTECTION

In order to fully understand the scope of the legal framework, a brief exposition must first be given regarding the concepts of cybersecurity and information security. While the terms are often used interchangeably due to a significant degree of overlap, there nevertheless exist several points of distinction.[37] Both disciplines aim to preserve confidentiality, integrity and availability[38] but are marked by a differing scope of application. Whereas information security seeks to protect information in any form, cybersecurity aims to safeguard vulnerabilities in the so-called "cyberspace" in particular.[39] As a result,

---

34 Jerry Ratcliffe, *Intelligence-Led Policing* (2nd edition, Routledge 2016).

35 European Commission, 'Questions and Answers – Data protection reform package' (*European Commission Press Release*, 24 May 2017) <http://europa.eu/rapid/press-release_MEMO-17-1441_en.htm> accessed 3 July 2019.

36 Directive (EU) 2016/680 of the European Parliament and of the Council on the protection of natural persons with regard to the processing of personal data by competent authorities for the purposes of the prevention, investigation, detection or prosecution of criminal offences or the execution of criminal penalties, and on the free movement of such data, and repealing Council Framework Decision 2008/977/JHA [2016] OJ L 119/89 (DPLE).

37 International Telecommunication Union (ITU), *The ITU National Cybersecurity Strategy Guide* (September 2011) <www.itu.int/ITU-D/cyb/cybersecurity/docs/ITUNationalCybersecurityStrategyGuide.pdf> accessed 03 July 2019.

38 International Organization for Standardization (ISO), *Standard ISO/IEC ISO/IEC 27032:2012 – Information Technology – Security techniques – Guidelines for cybersecurity* (2012).

39 This particular scope of application is confirmed by NIST which further specifies that cyberspace is "a global domain within the information environment consisting of the interdependent network of information systems infrastructures including the Internet, telecommunications networks, computer systems, and embedded processors and controllers."

cybersecurity is a concept which is both broader, by going beyond the mere protection of resources of information but also including vulnerable persons, networks and general interests in its scope, as well as narrower, as it only considers vulnerabilities which are at risk in a cyberspace context.[40] However, for the purpose of the following section, both concepts can be considered to be analogous. As the primary focus of the chapter lies on recent data protection legislation which was explicitly adopted to provide a framework for new technologies and data-driven police practices,[41] it is clear that many of these innovative tools fall squarely within the confines of cyberspace and are covered by the discipline of cybersecurity which, in turn, applies to all information in this sphere and reflects the same conditions present in information security. Due to the significant overlap between both concepts and their shared reliance on the CIA-triad, the term cybersecurity and the legislation underlying it can therefore be considered as identical to the concept of information security in this section.

Following that clarification, one can consider the current EU framework on cybersecurity as building upon the fundamentals of information security. This framework is multifaceted[42] and consists of a number of different instruments.[43] In addition to a number of high-level yet non-binding strategies and agendas,[44] the 2016 NIS Directive marks the first EU-wide legislation on cybersecurity[45] and aims to improve European security standards by requiring the establishment of incident response teams, further cooperation between Member States, and heightened security measures for providers of critical infrastructure and certain "digital" services.[46] In 2019, this Directive was supplemented by

See: National Institute of Standards and Technology (NIST), 'Security and Privacy Controls for Federal Information Systems and Organizations' (2013) NIST Special Publication 800-53.

40 Rossouw von Solms and Johan van Niekerk, 'From information security to cyber security' (2013) Computers & Security 38.

41 DPLE, recital 3.

42 William RM Long, Geraldine Scali and Francesca Blythe, 'European Union Overview' in Alan Charles Paul (ed.), *The Privacy, Data Protection and Cybersecurity Law Review* (5th edn, Law Business Research London 2018).

43 European Court of Auditors, 'Challenges to effective EU Cybersecurity Policy' (EU Briefing Papers 2019).

44 Joint communication to the European Parliament, the Council, the European Economic and Social Committee and the Committee of Regions, *Cybersecurity Strategy of the European Union: An Open, Safe and Secure Cyberspace* [2013] JOIN(2013)1; Communication from the Commission to the European Parliament, the Council, the European Economic and Social Committee and the Committee of the Regions, *A Digital Single Market Strategy for Europe* [2015] COM(2015)192; Communication from the Commission to the European Parliament, the Council, the European Economic and Social Committee and the Committee of the Regions, *The European Agenda on Security* [2015] COM(2015)185.

45 European Commission, 'Questions and Answers: Directive on Security of Network and Information systems, the first EU-wide legislation on cybersecurity' (*European Commission Press Release*, 4 May 2018) <http://europa.eu/rapid/press-release_MEMO-18-3651_en.htm>.

46 Directive (EU) 2016/1148 of the European Parliament and of the Council of 6 July 2016 concerning measures for a high common level of security of network and information systems across the Union [2016] OJ L194.

the Cybersecurity Act which introduces a currently optional certification scheme to guarantee that complying products, services and processes deliver a high standard of security.[47] As such, no current overarching cybersecurity instrument mandates compliance with the security principles for the processing of information.[48]

However, as further argued below, it is the contention of this chapter that the recently finalized EU data protection reforms partially mend this gap in the legal framework. Our data-dependent lifestyle and information-rich environment have increased the risks of intrusion into our private lives and the threats to the security of our personal data. In response to these challenges brought by technological advancements, the EU legislator has adopted innovative instruments to strengthen the protection of the rights to privacy and data protection.[49]

In 2016, the European Union took the next step in its data protection reforms to harmonize data protection standards among Member States. This legislative overhaul resulted in the adoption of two new legal instruments. These are the General Data Protection Regulation (GDPR)[50] replacing the Data Protection Directive 95/46/EC, which was the general framework regulating the processing of personal data within the European Union, and the Data Protection for Law Enforcement Directive (DPLE)[51] repealing the Council Framework Decision 2008/977/JHA which applied to the police processing of personal data in a cross-border context.

As such, the more comprehensive data protection regime of the GDPR covers a wide array of activities including those for private, commercial and general purposes, and is supplemented by the DPLE applying in the context of law enforcement and criminal justice.[52] The Directive pertains to the so-called competent authorities, as defined in Article 3 (7) of the DPLE as any public authority or body entrusted with the law enforcement duties of the state. This typically includes police agencies, prosecutor's offices and criminal courts but can be extended to cover any body or institution granted the authority to do so.[53]

---

47 Regulation (EU) of the European Parliament and of the Council on ENISA (The European Agency for Cybersecurity) and on information and communications technology cybersecurity certification and repealing Regulation (EU) No 526/2013 (Cybersecurity Act) [2019] 2017/0225 (COD).

48 Maria G. Porcedda, 'Patching the patchwork: appraising the EU regulatory framework on cyber security breaches' (2018) 34 Computer Law & Security Review 5.

49 European Agency for Fundamental Rights (FRA), *Handbook on European data protection law* (Publications Office of the European Union 2018).

50 Regulation (EU) 2016/679 of the European Parliament and of the Council on the protection of natural persons with regard to the processing of personal data and on the free movement of such data, and repealing Directive 95/46/EC [2016] OJ L 119/1.

51 (n 36).

52 Thomas Marquenie, 'The Police and Criminal Justice Authorities Directive: Data Protection Standards and Impact on the Legal Framework' (2017) 33 Computer Law & Security Report 324.

53 DPLE, recital 11.

In addition, the DPLE applies to those actors only when they process personal data for the prevention, investigation, detection or prosecution of criminal offences and the execution of criminal penalties. As such, it is not only the status of the data controller, being the organization or body that collects, processes and stores the data, but also the concrete purpose for which they process personal data that determines the applicable legislation. When competent authorities process data for the fighting, preventing and prosecuting of crime, the DPLE shall apply.[54] In contrast, the processing of personal data by those actors shall be subject to the GDPR if it is done for other purposes such as, for example, administrative matters relating to human resources.[55]

Apart from the difference in their scope of application,[56] the DPLE also differs from the GDPR in that it is a legal instrument taking the form of a directive rather than a regulation. As a consequence, the GDPR has an immediate and direct application within the internal law of each Member State.[57] The DPLE, on the other hand, lays down general principles and requirements with the aim of achieving a minimum common standard and harmonizing the processing of personal data for law enforcement and criminal justice. In doing so, it grants national legislators a broad discretion when implementing its provisions in national law.[58] This significant manoeuvrability[59] enjoyed by Member States when transposing the Directive may result in some countries having higher standards than others when implementing the provisions of the DPLE Directive into their domestic legislation.[60] The following sections provide an overview

---

54 DPLE, recital 11 and Article 1 (1).

55 FRA (n 49).

56 Pursuant to Article 2 GDPR, the material scope of the Regulation covers the processing of personal data, except when conducted by competent authorities for the purposes of the prevention, investigation, detection or prosecution of criminal offences or the execution of criminal penalties, which, according to Recital 19 of the GDPR, shall be governed by the DPLE Directive. Along the same lines, Articles 1 and 9 DPLE Directive specify that the scope of application of that Directive covers the processing of personal data by competent authorities for the prevention, investigation, detection or prosecution of criminal offences or the execution of criminal activities, and processing activities for purposes other than those fall within the scope of the GDPR.

57 Article 288 Treaty of the Functioning of the European Union (TFEU) governs the different legal acts of the Union and specifies how binding each instrument shall be in accordance with the legal form that they take. This Article provides that, while regulations have a general application within the EU and are fully binding in all Member States, directives are binding as to the result to be achieved and, thus, require national implementation by each Member State to give force to that legal act.

58 Pursuant to Article 288 TFEU, when a directive is adopted at EU level, it then needs to be transposed by each EU Member State, meaning that EU countries have to incorporate the provisions into their legal systems to make them part of their legislation, thereby providing the directive with effect at the national level.

59 William RM Long (n 42).

60 This significant degree of deviation at the national level was observed with regards to the implementation of the previous Data Protection Directive (95/46 EC). See: Douwe Korff, 'European Commission Study on the implementation of Data Protection Directive:

of these legal standards and evaluates how they relate to the principles of information security.

3.2. DATA PROTECTION PRINCIPLES

A cornerstone of the DPLE are the general data protection principles.[61] These general standards apply to all processing of personal data and are therefore relevant to the comparison with the fundamentals of information security. Of immediate relevance are the principles of data minimization,[62] purpose limitation,[63] data accuracy[64] and security.[65] To minimize the impact of the data processing, the processing activities must be adequate, relevant and limited to what is necessary for its purpose.[66] This is closely related to the principle of purpose limitation which requires data to be collected and used only for specified, explicit and legitimate purposes without it being transferred or made available to other actors.[67] Both of these principles tie into the security concept of Confidentiality by requiring that only the most relevant parts of information are disclosed to and processed by authorized persons for legitimate purposes.

The principle of accuracy requires every reasonable step to be taken to keep data up to date and accurate. This relates closely to the concept of Integrity, as they both refer to the necessity of maintaining the reliability and trustworthiness of information. Following this, the principle of security requires the implementation of measures protecting personal data against misuse and damage. It constitutes a general requirement that supplements the other principles and states that personal data must be "processed in a manner that ensures appropriate security of the personal data, including protection against unauthorized or unlawful processing and against accidental loss, destruction or damage, using appropriate technical or organisational measures".[68] In doing so, this principle evidently corresponds to all three pillars of information security and calls upon law enforcement agencies to implement concrete measures such as encryption and pseudonymization to ensure that the data can only be

---

Comparative Summary of National Laws' (2002) <https://gegevensbeschermingsrecht.nl/onewebmedia/douwe.pdf> accessed 03 July 2019.

61 IT Governance Privacy Team, *EU General Data Protection Regulation (GDPR). An implementation and compliance guide* (2nd edn, IT Governance Publishing 2017).

62 DPLE, Article 4 (1)(c).

63 DPLE, Article 4 (1)(b).

64 DPLE, Article 4 (1)(d).

65 DPLE, Article 4 (1)(f).

66 Lee Andrew Bygrave, *Data Privacy Law: An International Perspective* (Oxford University Press 2014).

67 Opinion 03/2013 on purpose limitation [2013] WP 203.

68 DPLE, Article 4 (1)(f).

accessed, altered, disclosed or deleted by authorized individuals, and that the accuracy, relevancy and completeness of the data is maintained.[69]

This general security principle is complemented by Article 29 which lists a number of specific technical and organizational measures to be implemented as to achieve an appropriate standard of security. In doing so, the nature, scope and risk associated with the processing must be taken into account for the development of a tailored security policy.[70] This overview considers that, under the different types of 'access control', the measures must prevent unauthorized persons from accessing processing equipment ('equipment access control') and using automated processing systems through data communication protocols ('user control'), and restrict authorized users from overstepping the boundaries of their access rights ('data access control'). In addition, 'data media control' must prevent the unauthorized reading or modification of data storage devices while 'data storage control' restricts the unauthorized input, deletion or modification of stored personal data. The measures of 'communication control' and 'input control' are mandated to allow for the verification and establishment of bodies to which data has been transmitted or made available as well as to determine when and by whom certain data has been entered in to the system. This ties into the requirement of 'transport control' which aims to prevent unauthorized interference or monitoring of data during transfer. Finally, the DPLE obliges measures ensuring that systems can be restored in case of interruption ('recovery'), that systems perform as intended and that faults are reported ('reliability'), and that stored personal data cannot be corrupted as the result of system malfunctions ('integrity'). Due to its technology-neutral approach,[71] which aims to prevent new and currently unspecified technologies from falling outside of its scope by targeting the processing in general rather than by means of a specific technique or system,[72] the DPLE provides no extensive technical details on how these requirements should be implemented. Instead, and in line with the principle of corporate responsibilization,[73] it allows and requires system developers and data controllers to implement appropriate and adequate measures corresponding to these requirements which, taken

69 FRA (n 49).

70 In this context, the notion of risk is to be understood as a legal concept referring to the threats posed to the freedoms and rights of the individuals whose data is being processed. This clarification is made in Article 29(1) Directive (EU) 2016/680 (DPLE) and contrasts the notion of risk from an information security perspective. This distinction and its impact are further discussed in section 3.7 of this chapter.

71 Recital 18 Directive (EU) 2016/680 (DPLE) states that "in order to prevent creating a serious risk of circumvention, the protection of natural persons should be technologically neutral and should not depend on the techniques used".

72 Winston Maxwell and Marc Bourreau, 'Technology Neutrality in Internet, Telecoms and Data Protection Regulation' (2015) Computer and Telecommunications Law Review 1.

73 Ronen Shamir, 'The age of responsibilization: on market-embedded morality' (2008) 37 Economy and Society 1.

together, allow law enforcement agencies to rely on their compliance with data protection law to adhere to and implement the three fundamental aspects of information security.

3.3. DATA PROCESSING OBLIGATIONS

Following the establishment of the general data protection principles and specific security measures, the Directive also contains a number of additional obligations for data controllers relating to system design and data processing.

As a first specific obligation, the legislation mandates that a clear distinction must be made between different categories of data. This ties into the concepts of Confidentiality and Integrity as it serves as a tool to protect the truthfulness and accuracy of information, and allows for the restriction of access to certain kinds of data only to persons with a specific need or authorization to do so. While, in itself, the mere separation of data categories does not improve the security of the information, this categorization is often tied to multi-layered access control mechanisms supporting more extensive security features for increasingly sensitive data. A concrete example of such a measure is discussed in the section on operationalization. The first distinction refers to the nature of the personal data itself as additional safeguards are required for particularly sensitive information.[74] These special categories of data include information revealing racial or ethnic origin, political opinions, religious or philosophical beliefs and trade union membership, as well as data relating to genetics, biometrics, health and sexuality. This type of data is subject to a special legal regime and, due to its high-risk potential, requires enhanced protection.[75] The DPLE allows the processing of special categories of data only when authorized by law, if necessary to protect the vital interests of the data subject or of another natural person, or in the event that the data being processed had been manifestly made public by the data subject. The required appropriate safeguards for the processing of this kind information can therefore consist of security and access control measures that hide sensitive details from regular system operators and allow only individuals with a specific authorization to access, alter or process them.

The second distinction must reflect the different types of data subjects based on their involvement in a criminal activity or previous encounters with the justice system.[76] For instance, a clear separation should be maintained between suspects of crime, meaning persons thought to be possibly guilty of having committed a criminal offence, known offenders and convicts, being individuals

74 DPLE, Article 10.

75 Paul Voigt and Axel von dem Bussche, *The EU General Data Protection Regulation (GDPR). A Practical Guide* (Springer International Publishing AG 2017).

76 DPLE, Article 6.

who have been convicted or have been found guilty of a crime, and victims, or those who suffer as a consequence of criminal acts. Additional categories of data subjects can include witnesses, informants or persons otherwise connected to an investigation. The purpose of this requirement is to avoid the misinterpretation of data by connecting identifiable persons with criminal acts without specifying the extent of their involvement. This distinction can support the implementation of fine-grain security measures which might include additional features for the protection of the more vulnerable data subjects such as victims or witnesses. The third categorization required by the DPLE is the distinction of the data based on their quality.[77] As a result of this requirement, factual data should be distinguished from opinions or observations made by the individual carrying out the processing of data. In practical terms, this allows data controllers to easily assess the reliability of information and differentiate between speculation and fact by adopting technical measures corresponding to intelligence grading systems such as the British 5x5x5 Intelligence Report.[78] The implementation of this distinction therefore supports the integrity of the data by allowing data controllers to easily verify and establish the accuracy, reliability and trustworthiness of the information.

In addition to the different categories of data, controllers must also follow the principles of data protection by design and by default.[79] This refers to the requirement of identifying data protection problems that are likely to arise and incorporating the data protection principles and obligations directly into the system's design[80] prior to engaging in technical development[81] and encouraging the application of privacy and data protection principles in any action concerning data processing.[82] The most privacy-oriented setting or approach should be taken or enabled by default to limit processing to the data necessary for the identified purposes. As such, this requirement mandates the adoption of technical and organizational measures to integrate technologies aimed at protecting the data into the system itself.

To this end, Privacy-Enhancing Technologies (PETs) have been identified as technical mechanisms that would enable the achievement of privacy and data protection by design. Two of the privacy-enhancing measures that not only can

---

77 DPLE, Article 7.

78 College of Policing, 'Intelligence Report' (2015) <https://www.app.college.police.uk/app-content/intelligence-management/intelligence-report/> accessed 03 July 2019.

79 DPLE, Article 20.

80 Pagona Tsormpatzoudi, Bettina Berendt and Fanny Coudert, 'Privacy by Design: From Research and Policy to Practice – the Challenge of Multi-Disciplinarity', in Preneel B and Ikonomou D (eds), *Privacy Technologies and Policy* (Springer 2015) 199.

81 Travis Breaux, *Introduction to IT privacy: A handbook for technologists* (International Association of Privacy Professionals 2014).

82 Vanessa Ayala-Rivera and Liliana Pasquale, 'The Grace Period Has Ended: An Approach to Operationalize GDPR Requirements' [2018] IEEE 26th International Requirements Engineering Conference 136.

help comply with this requirement but are also linked to the confidentiality principle of the CIA-triad, are the pseudonymization and anonymization of data.[83] Following the definition of pseudonymization provided by the DPLE, pseudonymized data can no longer be attributed to an identified or identifiable natural person without using additional information that is kept separately. Thus, pseudonimization can help curtail privacy risks and safeguard the confidentiality of data by hindering the possibility of individuals being identified. However, it is important to bear in mind that such data is still considered to be personal within the meaning of data protection laws, and may still pose a risk to the confidentiality principle due to the remaining possibility of that data being linked to an individual. The process of anonymization, on the other hand, results in a data which no longer has any ties to personally identifiable information and might therefore further support the confidentiality principle as this information can definitively no longer be attributed to a particular individual.

Finally, the Directive requires data controllers to keep extensive records and logs of the processing activities and their technical details in order to verify compliance with data protection law and assess the integrity of the data.[84] While these requirements do not prevent unauthorized access or modification of data, they do support the investigation of such instances and can assist in the identification of illegitimate actors. As system logs typically register user ID information as well as time, date and actions performed, they serve the purpose of holding individuals accountable and determining the exact ways in which information was altered or disclosed. In doing so, they support the tenets of integrity and confidentiality.

3.4. DATA PROTECTION IMPACT ASSESSMENT

Given its risk-based approach to data protection, the Directive requires data controllers to conduct a Data Protection Impact Assessment (DPIA) when a type of processing, in particular when using technologies, is likely to result in a high risk[85] to the rights and freedoms of natural persons.[86] The DPIA embodies an essential element of data protection by design.[87] Pursuant to the

83 Information Commissioner's Office (ICO), *Guide to the General Data Protection Regulation (GDPR)* (2018) <https://ico.org.uk/media/for-organisations/guide-to-the-general-data-protection-regulation-gdpr-1-0.pdf> accessed 01 July 2019.

84 DPLE, Articles 24–25.

85 Article 29 Data Protection Working Party, 'Guidelines on Data Protection Impact Assessment (DPIA) and Determining Whether Processing Is "likely to Result in a High Risk" for the Purposes of Regulation 2016/679' (2017).

86 DPLE, Article 27.

87 Bettina Berendt, 'Better Data Protection by Design through multicriteria decision making: On false tradeoffs between privacy and utility' in Erich Schweighofer and others (eds.), *Privacy Technologies and Policy* (Springer 2017).

DPLE, the DPIA is composed of three key elements. First, a DPIA must provide a general description of the envisaged processing operations. Second, it must identify and assess the severity of the risks to the rights and freedoms of data subjects. Third, it must list the envisaged measures to mitigate the established threats and diminish the risks. As such, this requirement obliges data controllers to review whether their current security mechanisms are sufficient in light of changing technologies, new risks and the purposes of the processing activities, and to determine new measures where necessary.[88] While not in its own right a concrete technical measure, it nevertheless enables and supports, *inter alia,* the thorough implementation of all three fundamental key concepts of information security by requiring data controllers to identify possible threats to and risks of their processing activities, and to take the necessary technical and organizational steps to prevent security breaches and preserve the confidentiality, integrity and availability of information.

3.5. REPORTING OF DATA BREACHES AND SUPERVISORY OVERSIGHT

While most of the security requirements in the DPLE aim to prevent the unauthorized processing of personal data, the Directive also imposes ex-post obligations on data controllers in case of disruption of the confidentiality and integrity of the data. In the event of a personal data breach resulting in the undue processing, deletion, alteration or disclosure of personal information,[89] the data controller is required to notify the supervisory and independent data protection authority (DPA) without undue delay unless it is unlikely to cause a risk to the rights and freedoms of the individuals concerned.[90] This notification shall contain information regarding the nature of the breach, the data affected, the expected consequences, and the measures taken to address and mitigate the impact. In addition, the controller must provide the individuals whose data is compromised with similar information if the breach is likely to result in a high risk to their rights and freedoms.[91] However, the controller remains exempt of this duty if subsequent measures ensure the risks are no longer likely to materialize, a public communication would suffice due to direct notifications constituting a disproportionate effort, or appropriate security measures such as encryption were in place to protect the personal data and render it unintelligible.

88 Christopher Kuner and others, 'Risk management in data protection' (2015) 5 International Data Privacy Law 2.

89 Article 3(11) Directive (EU) 2016/680 (DPLE) defines such a breach as "a breach of security leading to the accidental or unlawful destruction, loss, alteration, unauthorised disclosure of, or access to, personal data transmitted, stored or otherwise processed."

90 DPLE, Article 30.

91 DPLE, Article 31.

As such, this obligation of transparency and timely responsiveness to data breaches supports the implementation of information security principles by obliging controllers to address vulnerabilities and take measures to mitigate the negative consequences of the disruption of information.

Furthermore, the Directive provides an avenue for independent oversight by requiring that Member States empower the abovementioned DPA to monitor compliance with data protection legislation. This oversight body must be entirely independent and have extensive competences to inquire, investigate and sanction violations of data protection law.[92] Data controllers must cooperate with the DPA and, in the event that the abovementioned DPIA would reveal a high risk to human rights and freedoms or that the type of processing, in particular when involving new technologies, poses inherent risks thereto, are required to consult with the authority.[93] While the establishment of these oversight bodies does not constitute a technical security measure, it nevertheless allows for a thorough and independent review of security standards from a data protection perspective. System vulnerabilities and insufficient measures to preserve the confidentiality, integrity and availability of data can be identified by the DPA which can subsequently mandate such flaws to be addressed.[94] As such, these provisions further support the indication that ensuring the CIA-triad is an integral part of the DPLE compliance.

3.6. REPRESENTATION OF IS REQUIREMENTS IN THE DPLE

To illustrate the coverage of information security principles in the DPLE, the following table provides an overview of the extent to which specific data protection requirements reflect the tenets of Confidentiality, Integrity and Availability. The left hand column lists the most relevant provisions from the DPLE and matches them to the CIA-triad in the top row. For the purpose of clarity, it must be mentioned that the table considers a number of highly similar requirements jointly. 'Access control' consists of 'equipment access control', 'user control', and 'data access control'. Upon review, it is evident that, when considered jointly, the fundamental tenets of information security are reflected in the data protection obligations laid down in the DPLE. Compliance with

[92] DPLE, Chapter VI.

[93] DPLE, Article 28.

[94] Article 47 DPLE grants the data protection authorities extensive investigative and corrective powers to identify and address non-compliance with the Directive. As this extents to the security requirements in Articles 4(f) and 29 DPLE, the DPA could order the adoption of additional or more extensive security measures if the initial safeguards were insufficient to adequately protect the data.

these legal requirements will therefore result in a high standard of information security for law enforcement agencies and their processing of data.

Table 1. Representation of IS requirements in the DPLE

	Confidentiality	Integrity	Availability
Data minimization	(X)	(X)	
Purpose limitation	(X)	(X)	
Data accuracy		(X)	
Security	(X)	(X)	(X)
– 'Access control'	(X)	(X)	
– 'Media control'	(X)	(X)	
– 'Storage control'	(X)	(X)	
– 'Comm. control'	(X)		
– 'Input control'		(X)	
– 'Transport control'	(X)	(X)	
– 'Recovery'		(X)	(X)
– 'Reliability'			(X)
– 'Integrity'		(X)	
Categories of data	(X)	(X)	
DPIA	(X)	(X)	(X)
Breaches & Oversight	(X)	(X)	(X)

3.7. THE SCOPE AND PURPOSE OF INFORMATION SECURITY AND DATA PROTECTION

In light of the above, it is clear that there exists a strong connection between the discipline of information security and the data protection framework. The former envisions the protection of information by implementing technical and organizational measures to preserve its confidentiality, integrity and availability. The latter seeks to safeguard personal data by empowering individuals and obliging data controllers to comply with a number of fundamental principles and respect the rights, freedoms and interests of the persons whose data they process. The relationship between the two is equally clear in the sector of law enforcement as the DPLE, either directly or indirectly, contains numerous provisions reflecting and requiring compliance with the core tenets of information security from a data protection perspective. While the EU data protection legislation was not primarily conceived as an instrument for information security, they are nevertheless complementary fields.[95] The Council of Europe's (CoE) Convention no. 108[96] was the first legally binding international instrument concerning the protection of personal data[97] and immediately introduced the implementation of 'data security' measures as an important aspect of data protection policy.[98] Adding to this, the Convention's explanatory report noted how 'problems of data security' partially motivated the adoption of data protection legislation and its requirements of appropriate security standards.[99] The same approach to security was followed in the original EU Data Protection Directive that obliged controllers to maintain a level of security appropriate to the risks and the nature of the data to be protected.[100] The close and lasting connection between information security and data protection is further illustrated by the scholarly debate on the drafting of the GDPR suggesting that security risks posed by technological advancements would require data protection law to be altered accordingly.[101]

As such, the likelihood of not complying with data protection norms increases when lacking security standards are in place.[102] Conversely, if a data controller does not abide by data protection rules, the processed information is more likely to be insecure in turn.[103] These developments and changing technologies with increasingly advanced and extensive data analytics are therefore resulting in a growing convergence of the fields of security and privacy or data protection.[104] However, despite these clear similarities and the significant degree of overlap, there are numerous differences regarding the scope and purposes of these two

95 Ian J. Lloyd, *Information Technology Law* (Eight edn, Oxford University Press 2017).

96 Council of Europe (CoE), 'Convention for the Protection of Individuals with regard to Automatic Processing of Personal Data' (European Treaty Series – No. 108, 1981) (Convention 108).

97 Convention for the Protection of Individuals with regard to Automatic Processing of Personal Data 1981, ETS 108.

98 Article 7 CoE Convention no. 108 states that "appropriate security measures shall be taken for the protection of personal data stored in automated data files against accidental or unauthorised destruction or accidental loss as well as against unauthorised access, alteration or dissemination."

99 Council of Europe (CoE), 'Explanatory Report to the Convention for the Protection of Individuals with regard to Automatic Processing of Personal Data' (European Treaty Series – No. 108, 1981).

100 Directive 95/46/EC of the European Parliament and of the Council of 24 October 1995 on the protection of individuals with regard to the processing of personal data and on the free movement of such data (1995) OJ L 281.

101 Rebecca Wong, 'The Data Protection Directive 95/46/EC: Idealisms and Realisms' (2012) 26 International Review of Law Computers & Technology 2.

102 Information Commissioner's Office (ICO), *Guide to the General Data Protection Regulation (GDPR)* (2018) <https://ico.org.uk/media/for-organisations/guide-to-the-general-data-protection-regulation-gdpr-1-0.pdf> accessed 05 July 2019.

103 Jesper Zerlang, 'GDPR: A Milestone in Convergence for Cyber-security and Compliance' (2017) 6 Network Security 8.

104 Andrew Burt, 'Privacy and Security are converging. Here's why that matters for people and for companies' (2019) Harvard Business Review 1.

fields. Failure to comply with one does not necessarily imply incompatibility with the other. It is possible that an organization which is in compliance with data protection legislation does not sufficiently protect all of its information, or that the same entity has implemented extensive security measures while not abiding by all data protection conditions. The following section assesses this distinction and clarifies how data protection and information security are clearly delineated and independent notions.

A major difference between compliance with data protection and the discipline of information security relates to the type of data they seek to safeguard. Data protection is only applicable to personal data, which is legally defined as information relating to an identified or identifiable natural person.[105] As a result, even though the concept of personal data is broad and has expanded by the interpretation of the legal framework made by the European courts,[106] information which lacks these personal attributes does not fall under the scope of data protection legislation.[107] While some expect that the concept of personal data will in the future encompass nearly all information in our increasingly connected and 'smart' society,[108] the notion is currently still clearly delineated and restricted to only particular kinds of data. In contrast, information security principles are tools which can be leveraged for all types of information, typically defined in this context as referring to the output of the processing of data.[109] In other words, while all personal data can be considered as information, not all information is covered by data protection rules.

Another way in which the concepts diverge relates to their general purpose. Despite the high levels of protection it provides,[110] data protection legislation is focused more on protecting of personal data and strengthening the autonomy and rights of individuals over the use of their personal data than it relates to the security of information in general.[111] Whereas data protection empowers data subjects by allowing them to exert a certain degree over their data and by imposing obligations on data controllers, the discipline of information security is mainly designed so as to protect the interests of the "owner" and controller of the data by ensuring that the information preserves the values as originally

---

105 DPLE, Article 3 (1).

106 As evidenced, for instance, by the consideration of IP addresses as constituting personal data in the judgement of the Court of Justice of the European Union in the case *Patrick Breyer v Bundesrepublik Deutschland* (C-582/14 ECLI:EU:C:2016:779) para 49.

107 Regulation (EU) 2018/1807 of the European Parliament and of the Council on a framework for the free flow of non-personal data in the European Union [2018] OJ L 303/59.

108 Nadezdha Purtova, 'The law of everything. Broad concept of personal data and future of EU data protection law' (2018) 10 Law, Innovation and Technology 1.

109 Mark Charlton, *A Handbook of Information Technology* (Global Media 2009).

110 Ariadna Ripoll Servent, 'Protecting or Processing? Recasting EU Data Protection Norms' in W.J. Schünemann and others (eds), *Privacy, Data Protection and Cybersecurity in Europe* (Springer 2017).

111 Darra Hofman, Luciana Duranti and Elissa How, 'Trust in the Balance: Data Protection Laws as Tools for Privacy and Security in the Cloud' (2017) 10 Algorithms 2.

input in the system, remains accessible and is protected from corruption and infiltration.[112] As such, in a law enforcement context, security mechanisms in the framework of data protection would mainly seek to prevent the undue disclosure of sensitive information that might endanger people or the transgressions of police authority in the form of illegitimate processing out of personal or unfair motivations. However, from the perspective of information security, similar mechanisms would instead firstly aim to protect the interests of the police agency itself against the exposure of classified law enforcement practices and intelligence which could alert criminals of certain strategies. This distinction becomes apparent in several provisions of the law itself. For example, when the DPLE requires the implementation of security measures to mitigate possible risks, it does so primarily in the context of preventing negative consequences to the rights and freedoms of natural persons.[113] This is in contrast with its interpretation in the field of information security where the concept instead refers more to the potential exploitation of vulnerabilities that might adversely impact the organization.[114]

Even more so than constituting a mere difference between both fields, it is not inconceivable that these disparate goals could result in a certain conflict of interest where data controllers may be tempted to prioritize protecting their security interests rather than those of the individuals whose data they process. Nevertheless, it seems unlikely that such a conflict would have serious consequences. As the notion of personal data is broad and data protection law imposes legally binding obligations and sanctions for non-compliance on data controllers, law enforcement agencies are required to implement extensive security measures for all of their processing activities of personal information. As the existence of such a framework could likely be expanded to cover non-personal information as well, it stands to reason that police forces could adopt the same consistent and high security standard for all of their informational resources. Considering then that the same breaches of its systems, processes and information could cause significant harm to both the interests of the data subjects and the controllers alike, there is little reason to assume that the convergence of information security and data protection standards would be detrimental to the objectives of either.

Yet still, notwithstanding the several differences between the concepts, it is clear that they also share notable similarities. When assessing the relationship between data protection and information security, it becomes apparent that they

---

112 Hong Chan and Sameera Mubarak, 'Significance of Information Security Awareness in the Higher Education Sector' (2012) 60 International Journal of Computer Applications 10.

113 DPLE, Article 27(1) and 29(1).

114 According to the ISO, risk is defined as "the potential that a given threat will exploit vulnerabilities of an asset or group of assets and thereby cause harm to the organization". See: International Organization for Standardization (ISO), *ISO/IEC 27005:2011 Information technology -- Security techniques -- Information security risk management* (2011).

share a common reason for their existence and are inextricably linked to protect data and curtail its misuse.[115] They are both aimed at maintaining the security of information, allowing legitimate actors to exercise control, and preventing unintended or unauthorized data misuse. It is the fact that their fundamental values both concern the exercising of control over information and safeguarding it against undue and unjust processing that warrants the analysis in this chapter.

4. OPERATIONALIZATION OF SECURITY IN LAW ENFORCEMENT

In light of the above, it is evident that the fundamental principles of information security are reflected in the data protection Directive for law enforcement. The tenets of Confidentiality, Integrity and Availability are incorporated in numerous provisions mandating their implementation in data processing activities by police actors. To explore the concrete ways in which compliance with this legislation can result in high security standards in practice, this section provides an overview of how these abstract and technology-neutral requirements of the data protection framework might be implemented in actual law enforcement systems, and explores how these approaches to legal compliance with data protection requirements can result in the practical realization of information security in context of law enforcement. As such, the following section analyses two EU-funded research projects as case studies to illustrate some methods that may be used by competent authorities and developers to turn data protection obligations into practical security measures.

FP7 VALCRI (Visual Analytics for Sense-making in Criminal Intelligence Analysis) and H2020 MAGNETO (Multimedia Analysis and Correlation Engine for Organised Crime Prevention and Investigation) are European research projects responding to the need of law enforcement authorities to analyse massive volumes of data for the purposes of crime prevention, investigation and prosecution in the ongoing big data age.[116] Since the collection of personal data is a necessary aspect[117] of criminal intelligence analysis, both research projects

---

115 European Data Protection Supervisor (EDPS), 'Opinion of the European Data Protection Supervisor on the Joint Communication of the Commission and of the High Representative of the European Union for Foreign Affairs and Security Policy on a 'Cyber Security Strategy of the European Union: an Open, Safe and Secure Cyberspace', and on the Commission proposal for a Directive concerning measures to ensure a high common level of network and information security across the Union' (2013); European Data Protection Supervisor (EDPS) 'Information Security' <https://edps.europa.eu/data-protection/our-work/subjects/information-security_en> accessed 03 July 2019.

116 Omer Tene and Jules Polonetsky, 'Privacy in the Age of Big Data, A Time for Big Decision' [2012] Stanford Law Review <https://www.stanfordlawreview.org/online/privacy-paradox-privacy-and-big-data/> accessed 10 April 2019.

117 Luca Bolognini and Camilla Bistolfi, 'Pseudonymization and impacts of Big (personal/anonymous) data processing in the transition from the Directive 95/46/EC to the new EU

have been conceived with the goal of providing competent authorities with the technologies to extract useful intelligence from large amounts of information while also providing concrete techniques to support data protection compliance. VALCRI sought to extract valuable information from intelligence presented in different formats and visualize the outcomes in a manner supporting the reasoning of criminal analysts.[118] MAGNETO, on the other hand, is envisioned as a platform that will empower competent authorities with abilities to analyse and combine multiple data sources, reveal undetected connections between pieces of information, and compute trends of security-related events.

In this section, both projects are summarily assessed as a case study on potential methods for the implementation of security requirements as established in the data protection framework. In doing so, this section transitions from abstract legal provisions to an examination of the practical inclusion of security standards in the design and development of actual law enforcement systems in which technical and organizational measures aimed to implement data protection requirements and achieve security goals.

Among the measures considered during the development of the two research projects are the implementation of a top-level log-in requirement to control access to the system in order to comply with the requirement of the equipment access control set out in Article 29 of the DPLE. Similarly, another method adopted during both research projects is the identity and access management by creating user levels to allow access to different data depending on the user's profile. This is aimed at preventing access of unauthorized users to confidential and sensitive data, which merit a higher level of protection, and thereby further safeguards the rights and freedoms of the individuals involved. This type of access control is supplemented by the implementation of means to limit data processing activities according to the role of the agent within the organization, their access authorization and the nature of the case at hand. This allows the system to identify an operator and determine his or her access rights based on the user profile. For example, high-level tactical analysts might only be able to retrieve anonymized and aggregated data to review crime trends while operational analysts working on specific cases might have increased access rights to information relevant to their assignment.

In addition, both research projects have incorporated a logging system[119] capable of tracking the actions performed by the person analysing the data and tying those actions to the specific individual that performs them. Logs are kept so that it is possible to determine the justification, data and time of all the transactions carried out in the system, as well to identify the individuals

General Data Protection Regulation' [2017] 33 Computer Law & Security Report 171.

118 Thomas Marquenie and Fanny Coudert, 'Roadmap for the Operationalization of Legal and Privacy Requirements in VALCRI Analysis' [2017] VALCRI White Papers Series.

119 DPLE, Article 25.

who accessed, retrieved or disclosed personal data, and, when the data have been disclosed or transferred, the recipients of this data. In both projects, the logging system is tied closely to an extensive back-up protocol which allowed for the retrieval and recovery of information in the event of undue alterations or technical problems.

For its part, the principle of data minimization is intended to be achieved by avoiding and minimizing the amount of personal data to be used during the lifecycle of both systems. This involves conducting periodical assessments of the need to process certain data for the specified purposes and, when determining that some personal data is no longer needed, proceed to delete or anonymize it. This might occur both manually and automatically by linking to the source police database and flagging files for review or deletion after the expiration of a set time period.

Both law enforcement systems have also considered the implementation of different categories of data subjects. Following the DPLE, competent authorities should distinguish individuals in relation to whom serious grounds lead to believe that they have perpetrated or are about to commit a criminal offence (suspects), individuals that have been declared guilty of a criminal offence (convicts), victims of a criminal offence or individuals in relation to whom some elements give reason to believe that they could have been victims of a criminal offence (victims), other persons involved in a criminal offence, for instance individuals that have been called to give their testimony in relation to criminal offences (witnesses). This functionality can then be used to allow technical safeguards to prevent information relating to, for example, witnesses and victims to be revealed by default. In practice, this might be implemented by tying these categories to access control levels. By manually marking or automatically classifying the involvement of persons in a certain case based on police records and statements, the system could support data minimization and the confidentiality of information by only providing operators with the specific details necessary for a particular task. The identities of victims, witnesses and informants can be concealed by default and only made available when additional authorization or justification is provided. These measures can improve the security, confidentiality and integrity of the information by further restricting access thereto and maintaining a fine-grain and multi-layered access policy.

Not only categories of data subjects have been envisaged for VALCRI and MAGNETO, but also different categories of data, in compliance with the data protection requirement of data quality. Pursuant to Article 6 of the DPLE, the system should allow for labelling data depending on their quality, meaning that the analyst or user of the system should be able to specify whether the data are factual or based on personal assessments. This is most easily achieved through the addition of a tagging system which allows users to either directly import existing intelligence grading protocols into the software, such as the 5x5x5 grid described above, or by manually noting or filing certain types of information under specific categories. Such measures can contribute to the integrity of the data by allowing operators to establish the trustworthiness and reliability of information by applying an accepted and objective standard.

Encryption, pseudonymization and anonymization are three privacy-enhancing measures[120] that have been contemplated for both law enforcement systems, particularly with the purpose of ensuring the protection of data by design and by default.[121] Pseudonymized data pose less risks of re-identification of the data subject since the process ensures that the identity of the individual is masked.[122] Anonymization supports data protection by suppressing, generalizing or adding noise to data values,[123] thereby making non-identifiable data by breaking the link between the personal data and the individual concerned. As such, both techniques support the implementation of the principle of confidentiality.[124] These functionalities can be especially relevant in the context of facial recognition. In VALCRI, the system proved capable of automatically blurring out faces of individuals in video footage. Tied to the access control mechanisms, this module allowed for the selective anonymization of non-vital persons. Witnesses and victims could be made unrecognizable by default if their identity was not of key importance for the particular analyst or investigator working with the footage.

5. CONCLUSION

The discipline of information security relies on the three fundamental tenets of confidentiality, integrity and availability known as the CIA-triad. While these principles are widely accepted in the field of computer science, the current European legislative framework on cybersecurity is fragmented and does not require compliance with the triad for the general processing of information. Regardless, legally binding security obligations are present in the EU legal framework as there exist numerous similarities and a significant degree of overlap between information security and the legal concept of data protection. As the European Union legislator recently adopted two data protection instruments which, in part, aim to address security concerns in new technologies, this chapter assessed to what extent the principles of Confidentiality, Integrity

120 Johannes Heurix and others, 'A taxonomy for privacy enhancing technologies' (2015) 53 Computers & Security.

121 DPLE, Article 20.

122 Information Commissioner's Office (ICO), *Anonymisation: managing data protection risk code of practice* (Wilmslow, November 2012) <https://ico.org.uk/media/1061/anonymisation-code.pdf> accessed 15 May 2019.

123 Opinion 05/2014 on Anonymisation Techniques [2014] WP216.

124 Miranda Mourby and others, 'Are 'pseudonymised' data always personal data? Implications of the GDPR for administrative data research in the UK' (2018) 34 Computer Law & Security Review 222.

and Availability are reflected in the new Data Protection Directive for Law Enforcement.

Upon comparing the Directive with the security triad, it is clear that the latter is fully reflected in the provisions of the law. First, several of the general data protection principles indirectly support adherence to the tenets of information security. The principles of data minimization, purpose limitation and data accuracy all contribute to effectively securing the data and protecting it from unauthorized interference, deletion, disclosure or access. Second, the Directive includes a specific principle ensuring the security of the personal data. This is complemented by Article 29 which obliges data controllers to implement an extensive list of security measures such as access controls, recovery mechanisms and methods preserving the integrity and reliability of the data. Third, the Directive contains a number of specific requirements relating to the processing and categorizing of certain types of data and the development of systems to achieve data protection by design and default. Supplemented by provisions requiring controllers to conduct an impact assessment, cooperate with supervisory authorities and take concrete steps following breaches of data, these aspects of the law further contribute to a comprehensive security policy. When considered jointly, these legal obligations and principles cover and relate to all aspects of the CIA-triad, and compliance therewith results in the safeguarding of information security in law enforcement technology and practice.

However, it must be noted that there nevertheless exist significant differences in purpose and scope of application between the concepts of data protection and information security. While the latter covers all types of information, data protection applies only to data relating to a personally identifiable individual. In addition, information security primarily aims to protect the interests of the controller of the information whereas data protection intends to empower the person to whom the data refers and safeguard his or her interests, freedoms and rights. This distinction signifies that while the Directive does reflect the same principles underlying information security, compliance therewith does not necessarily accomplish the same objective or apply to the same kind of information.

Additionally, by virtue of its nature as a directive, the DPLE might also not achieve a maximum and consistent level of harmonization as it only requires Member States to achieve a particular result without specifying the means to accomplish that goal. As such, differences in its implementation in national law might not achieve full and uniform adherence to the information security standards across the European Union.

Regardless, it is clear that the Directive reflects and mandates compliance with fundamental information security principles in a law enforcement context. As the CIA-triad is both indirectly and directly present in the law, it can be concluded that compliance with the DPLE supports the achievement of information security standards with regards to the processing of personal data by police agencies. To illustrate this conclusion, a brief analysis of the practical measures implemented in two EU research projects, FP7 VALCRI and H2020 MAGNETO, serves as an indication of how compliance with the provisions of the data protection legislation may result in the application of all three pillars of information security in law enforcement practice.

ACKNOWLEDGEMENT

This work has been performed under the H2020 786629 project MAGNETO, which has received funding from the European Union's Horizon 2020 Programme. This paper reflects only the authors' view, and the European Commission is not liable to any use that may be made of the information contained therein.

BIBLIOGRAPHY

Andress J, *The Basics of Information Security: Understanding the Fundamentals of InfoSec in Theory and Practice* (Elsevier 2011)

Ayala-Rivera V and Pasquale L, 'The Grace Period Has Ended: An Approach to Operationalize GDPR Requirements' [2018] IEEE 26th International Requirements Engineering Conference 136

Bell E and La Padula L, *Secure Computer System: Unified Exposition and Multics Interpretation* (The MITRE Corporation 1976)

Berendt B, 'Better Data Protection by Design through multicriteria decision making: On false tradeoffs between privacy and utility' in Erich Schweighofer and others (eds.), *Privacy Technologies and Policy* (Springer 2017)

Blackwell C, 'A multi-layered security architecture for modelling complex systems' (2008) CSIIRW 35

Bolognini L and Bistolfi C, 'Pseudonymization and impacts of Big (personal/anonymous) data processing in the transition from the Directive 95/46/EC to the new EU General Data Protection Regulation' [2017] 33 Computer Law & Security Report 171

Boritz JE, "IS practitioners' views on core concepts of information integrity' (2005) 6 International Journal of Accounting Information Systems 260

Bourgeois DT and Bourgeois D, 'Information Systems Security' in David T. Bourgeois and Dave Bourgeois, *Information Systems for Business and Beyond* (Saylor Academy 2014)

Breaux T, *Introduction to IT privacy: A handbook for technologists* (International Association of Privacy Professionals 2014)

Burt A, 'Privacy and Security are converging. Here's why that matters for people and for companies' (2019) Harvard Business Review 1

Bygrave LA, *Data Privacy Law: An International Perspective* (Oxford University Press 2014)

Chan H and Mubarak S, 'Significance of Information Security Awareness in the Higher Education Sector' (2012) 60 International Journal of Computer Applications 10

Charlton M, *A Handbook of Information Technology* (Global Media 2009)

Cherdantseva Y and Hilton J, 'A reference model of information assurance and security' (2013) IEEE Proceedings of the International Conference on Availability, Reliability and Security (ARES)

College of Policing, 'Intelligence Report' (2015) <https://www.app.college.police.uk/app-content/intelligence-management/intelligence-report/> accessed 01 July 2019

Coudert F, Dumortier J and Verbruggen F, 'Applying the Purpose Specification Principle in the Age of 'Big Data': The Example of Integrated Video Surveillance Platforms in France' [2012] ICRI Research Paper

Danezis G, Domingo-Ferrer J and Hansen M, 'Privacy and Data Protection by Design – from Policy to Engineering' (2014) European Union Agency for Network and Information Security <https://www.enisa.europa.eu/publications/privacy-and-data-protection-by-design> accessed 28 June 2019

Death D, *Information Security Handbook: Develop a threat model and incident response strategy to build a strong information security network* (Packt Publishing 2017)

European Agency for Fundamental Rights (FRA), *Handbook on European data protection law*, (Publications Office of the European Union 2018)

European Commission, 'Questions and Answers: Directive on Security of Network and Information systems, the first EU-wide legislation on cybersecurity' (*European Commission Press Release,* 4 May 2018) <http://europa.eu/rapid/press-release_MEMO-18-3651_en.htm> accessed 17 July 2019

European Commission, 'Questions and Answers – Data protection reform package' (European Commission Press Release, 24 May 2017) <http://europa.eu/rapid/press-release_MEMO-17-1441_en.htm> accessed 3 July 2019.

European Court of Auditors, 'Challenges to effective EU Cybersecurity Policy' (EU Briefing Papers 2019)

European Union Agency for Network and Information Security (ENISA), 'Guidelines for SMEs on the Security of Personal Data Processing' (2016) <https://www.enisa.europa.eu/publications/guidelines-for-smes-on-the-security-of-personal-data-processing/at_download/fullReport> accessed 01 July 2019

Feruza S and Kim T, 'IT Security Review: Privacy, Protection, Access Control, Assurance and System Security' (2007) 2 International Journal of Multimedia and Ubiquitous Engineering

Gerber M, von Solms R and Overbeek P, 'Formalizing information security requirements' (2001) 9 Information Management & Computer Security 1

Gollman D, *Computer Security* (3rd edn, Wiley 2013)

Gong L and others, 'The application of data encryption technology in computer network communication security' (2017) AIP Conference Proceedings *1834*

Heurix J and others, 'A taxonomy for privacy enhancing technologies' (2015) 53 Computers & Security

Hofman D, Duranti L and How E, 'Trust in the Balance: Data Protection Laws as Tools for Privacy and Security in the Cloud' (2017) 10 Algorithms 2

Hussain Alqahtani F, 'Developing an Information Security Policy: A Case Study Approach' (2017) 124 Procedia Computer Science 691

Information Commissioner's Office (ICO), *Anonymisation: managing data protection risk code of practice* (Wilmslow, November 2012) <https://ico.org.uk/media/1061/anonymisation-code.pdf> accessed 15 May 2019

Information Commissioner's Office (ICO), *Guide to the General Data Protection Regulation (GDPR)* (2018) <https://ico.org.uk/media/for-organisations/guide-to-the-general-data-protection-regulation-gdpr-1-0.pdf> accessed 01 July 2019

International Association of Chiefs of Police (IACP), *Managing Cybersecurity Risk: A Law Enforcement Guide* (2017)

International Organization for Standardization (ISO), *Standard ISO/IEC ISO/IEC 27032:2012 – Information Technology – Security techniques – Guidelines for cybersecurity* (2012)

International Organization for Standardization (ISO), *Standard ISO/IEC 27001:2013 – Information Security Management Systems – Requirements* (2013)

International Organization for Standardization (ISO), *ISO Standard ISO/IEC 27000:2018 – Information Security Management Systems – Overview and Vocabulary* (5 edn, 2018)

International Telecommunication Union (ITU), *The ITU National Cybersecurity Strategy Guide* (September 2011)

IT Governance Privacy Team, *EU General Data Protection Regulation (GDPR). An implementation and compliance guide* (2nd edn, IT Governance Publishing 2017)

Kim D and Solomon MG, *Fundamentals of Information Systems Security* (3rd edn, Jones & Bartlett 2018)

Korff D, 'European Commission Study on the implementation of Data Protection Directive: Comparative Summary of National Laws' (2002)

Kuner C and others, 'Risk management in data protection' (2015) 5 International Data Privacy Law 2

Liu C and others 'The Security Risk Assessment Methodology' (2012) 43 Procedia Engineering

Lloyd IJ, *Information Technology Law* (Eight edn, Oxford University Press 2017)

Logan K, 'Access Controls' in Peltier TR (ed.), *Information Security Fundamentals* (2nd edn, CRC Press 2014)

Long WRM, Scali G and Blythe F, 'European Union Overview' in Charles Paul A (ed.), *The Privacy, Data Protection and Cybersecurity Law Review* (5th edn, Law Business Research London 2018)

Marquenie T and Coudert F, 'Roadmap for the Operationalization of Legal and Privacy Requirements in VALCRI Analysis' [2017] VALCRI White Papers Series

Marquenie T, 'The Police and Criminal Justice Authorities Directive: Data Protection Standards and Impact on the Legal Framework' (2017) 33 Computer Law & Security Report 324

Maxwell W and Bourreau M, 'Technology Neutrality in Internet, Telecoms and Data Protection Regulation' (2015) Computer and Telecommunications Law Review 1

Mourby M and others, 'Are 'pseudonymised' data always personal data? Implications of the GDPR for administrative data research in the UK' (2018) 34 Computer Law & Security Review 222

National Institute of Standards and Technology (NIST), 'Security and Privacy Controls for Federal Information Systems and Organizations' (2013) NIST Special Publication 800-53

National Research Council, *Computers at Risk: Safe Computing in the Information Age* (The National Academic Press 1991)

Oscarson P, 'Information Security Fundamentals: Graphical Conceptualisations for Understanding' in Irvine C and Armstrong H (eds), *Security Education and Critical Infrastructures* (IFIP – The International Federation for Information Processing, Springer 2003)

Peltier J, 'Threats to Information Security' in Peltier TR (ed.), *Information Security Fundamentals* (2nd edn, CRC Press 2014)

Porcedda MG, 'Patching the patchwork: appraising the EU regulatory framework on cyber security breaches' (2018) 34 Computer Law & Security Review 5

Preneel B, 'Cryptographic Hash Functions: Theory and Practice' in Cong G and Gupta K (eds.), *Progress in Cryptology – IndoCrypt 2010* (Springer Berlin 2010)

Purtova N, 'The law of everything. Broad concept of personal data and future of EU data protection law' (2018) 10 Law, Innovation and Technology 1

Qadir S and Quadri SMK, 'Information Availability: An Insight into the Most Important Attribute of Information Security' (2016) Journal of Information Security 7

Raggad, B, *Information Security Management: Concepts and Practice* (1st edn, CRC Press 2010)

Ratcliffe J, *Intelligence-Led Policing* (2nd edition, Routledge 2016)

Servent AR, 'Protecting or Processing? Recasting EU Data Protection Norms' in Schünemann WJ and others (eds), *Privacy, Data Protection and Cybersecurity in Europe* (Springer 2017)

Shamir R, 'The age of responsibilization: on market-embedded morality' (2008) 37 Economy and Society 1

Simmons GJ, *Contemporary Cryptology: The Science of Information Integrity* (IEEE Press 1994)

Tene O and Polonetsky J, 'Privacy in the Age of Big Data, A Time for Big Decision' [2012] Stanford Law Review <https://www.stanfordlawreview.org/online/privacy-paradox-privacy-and-big-data/> accessed 10 April 2019

Tipton H and Krause M, *Information Security Management Handbook* (vol 2, 6th edn, CRC Press 2009)

Tsormpatzoudi P, Berendt B and Coudert F, 'Privacy by Design: From Research and Policy to Practice – the Challenge of Multi-Disciplinarity', in Preneel B and Ikonomou D (eds), *Privacy Technologies and Policy* (Springer 2016) 199

Voigt P and von dem Bussche A, *The EU General Data Protection Regulation (GDPR). A Practical Guide* (Springer International Publishing AG 2017)

Von Solms R and Van Niekerk J, 'From information security to cyber security' (2013) Computers & Security 38

Whitman ME and Mattord HJ, *Principles of Information Security* (4th edn, Course Technology Press 2011)

Wong R, 'The Data Protection Directive 95/46/EC: Idealisms and Realisms' (2012) 26 International Review of Law Computers & Technology 2

Zerlang J, 'GDPR: A Milestone in Convergence for Cyber-security and Compliance' (2017) 6 Network Security 8

CHAPTER 6

PROTECTING HUMAN RIGHTS THROUGH A GLOBAL ENCRYPTION PROVISION

Danaja Fabčič Povše

1. INTRODUCTION

In a global digital economy, data pass through servers, located in different countries with diverse rules on data protection security. Different standards and requirements lead to the problem of the global system only being as strong (or weak) as cyber-security requirements in the "least trusted country".[1]

Encryption is often put forward by the crypto experts as an effective security measure. At its core, encryption transforms text-information into a seemingly random string of words and letters that can only be deciphered by using another bit of information, called the decryption key. The rules on use of encryption vary and some countries have adopted regimes that may compromise information and conversations despite use of appropriate encryption techniques.[2] Encryption is also an important measure contributing to human rights, especially freedom of expression and the right to privacy. It keeps communications inaccessible and safe from prying eyes, enabling the sharing of opinion, accessing online information and organising with others to counter injustices.[3] In data protection, encryption is a privacy preserving technique, that also contributes to security of processing personal data.[4]

---

1 Peter Swire and Kenesa Ahmad, 'Encryption and Globalization' (2011) 23 Columbia Science and Technology Law Review.

2 An overview of different laws, applicable to encryption, incl. references, is available on two websites:
'Crypto Law Survey – Page 2' <www.cryptolaw.org/cls2.htm> accessed 4 March 2019.
'World Map of Encryption Laws and Policies | Global Partners Digital' <https://www.gp-digital.org/world-map-of-encryption/> accessed 2 July 2019.

3 Amnesty International, 'Encryption: A Matter of Human Rights' (2016) <https://www.amnesty.nl/content/uploads/2016/03/160322_encryption_-_a_matter_of_human_rights_-_def.pdf?x68337> accessed 16 July 2019.

4 Gerald Spindler and Philipp Schmechel, 'Personal Data and Encryption in the European General Data Protection Regulation' (2016) 7 Journal of Intellectual Property, Information

The data protection framework has seen two important changes in 2018 and 2019: the General Data Protection Regulation (GDPR) becoming applicable, and the modernisation of the Convention for the Protection of Individuals with regard to Automatic Processing of Personal Data (so-called Convention no. 108+), respectively. Both instruments are oriented toward European states. However, due to their extraterritorial effects, the two instruments can be considered as means of *globalising* the data protection framework to achieve a worldwide adequate level of protection of personal data.[5]

A connected world with international data flows could therefore benefit from globalised data protection rules. However, as discussed in this paper, progress has been slow, and not all instruments explicitly contain a reference to encryption. Nevertheless, if the international community decided to push for an obligation to use encryption under international law, some potentially applicable rules are already in place. Such an obligation would apply globally.[6]

This paper attempts to address the challenge of finding such an obligation by examining provisions, relevant to encryption, that could potentially lead to a worldwide encryption requirement, thus obviating the problem of the least trusted country.[7] More specifically, it poses the question: in the absence of a global encryption treaty, which existing legal documents in the international law on privacy and data protection apply to encryption, and how could a binding legal obligation on states to mandate the use of encryption be imposed?

To answer the question, which is descriptive and normative in its nature, the following steps will be taken. First, encryption is explained from the perspective of concepts of cybersecurity and data protection, and its contribution to protection of human rights is examined. Applicable legal sources from Europe, Western Africa, Asia-Pacific and East Asia regions are analysed in order to find relevant provisions on encryption. Finally, three ways on binding states to impose encryption obligations are suggested: adoption of a relevant new international treaty on data protection or data security, globalisation of existing (European) rules, or keeping the status quo. Traditional desk research model is the most suitable method of choice, including analysis of legal state of the art in

---

Technology and Electronic Commerce Law [i].
Bruce Schneier, 'Essays: Why We Encrypt' (*Schneier on Security*, June 2015) <https://www.schneier.com/essays/archives/2015/06/why_we_encrypt.html> accessed 17 July 2019.

5 Graham Greenleaf, 'A World Data Privacy Treaty? "Globalisation" and "Modernisation" of Council of Europe Convention 108', *Emerging Challenges in Privacy Law: Comparative Perspectives* (Cambridge University Press 2014); Graham Greenleaf, 'The Influence of European Data Privacy Standards Outside Europe: Implications for Globalization of Convention 108' (2012) 2 International Data Privacy Law 68.

6 For the purposes of this article, the term 'globalisation' is understood in wider than by Greenleaf, i.e. applicable on an international scale to all states bound by the relevant instrument, instead of solely meaning accession by non-European countries.

7 Swire and Ahmad (n 1).

existing academic literature, legislation and soft law guidance. Due to its scarcity, relevant case law will be examined to a smaller extent.

This chapter will focus on analysis of encryption in the international human rights legal framework. More specifically, (1) general human rights framework on the right to privacy, especially confidentiality of communications, and/or data protection, (2) legal instruments specific to data protection, and (3) soft law, i.e. experts' and policy-makers' non-binding opinions and recommendations, will be analysed.

2. ENCRYPTION, (CYBER)SECURITY AND HUMAN RIGHTS

Encryption is the process of obscuring information to make it unreadable without special knowledge. It renders the original information, called plaintext, into unintelligible cyphertext. Typically, this is done in order to ensure secrecy, confidentiality and authenticity.[8] Encryption is a crucial factor in ensuring reliable communication through ICTs, since it enables sending and receiving information without exposure to prying eyes of third parties, as well as enabling the receiver to verify that the information had really been sent by the intended sender.

Encryption enables security of information since algorithms, upon which encryption is based, make data unreadable to anyone without the appropriate decryption key. Therefore, the data are virtually inaccessible to third parties without the decryption key to see the plaintext.[9]

There are different types of encryption based on who has access to the decryption (different key management systems). Cryptographic research talks about *public (asymmetric) key cryptography* and *private (symmetric) key cryptography*. The difference between the two is that with private cryptography, one can use the same private key to encrypt and decrypt the message, whereas in public cryptography always a key pair (two keys) exist, whereby what one key encrypts only the other can decrypt the private key encrypts the message, and the public one decrypts it.[10] For example, this is how digital signatures work.

Traditionally, encryption is at the heart of the privacy or security trade-off.[11] On the one hand, cryptographic research is clear on the need for strong

---

8 Kostas Zotos and Andreas Litke, 'Cryptography and Encryption' [2005] arXiv <http://arxiv.org/abs/math/0510057> accessed 4 March 2019.

9 Hal Abelson and others, 'The Risks of Key Recovery, Key Escrow, and Trusted Third-Party Encryption' (1997) 2 World Wide Web J. 241.

10 Steve Lloyd and Carlisle Adams, 'Key Management' in Henk CA van Tilborg and Sushil Jajodia (eds), *Encyclopedia of Cryptography and Security* (Springer US 2011) <https://doi.org/10.1007/978-1-4419-5906-5_85> accessed 6 June 2019.

11 See for example, Section 3.D, pp.320–329 of Marc Rotenberg, Paul M Schwartz and Daniel J Solove, *Information Privacy Law* (2nd ed., Aspen 2006); or Herbert S Lin, 'Cryptography and

encryption to protect against access by unauthorised third parties. Strong encryption is defined as encryption that is difficult to break[12] or unbreakable,[13] i.e. a "strong algorithm with keys properly secured, and not compromised through back doors, front doors or exceptional access",[14] without the law imposing measures, which render the algorithm less secure, and therefore weaker.[15] If the encryption method does not meet these criteria, the encryption itself cannot be considered strong and it may not provide good security.

Walking the tightrope between privacy and security is a difficult exercise. Recently, the issue has resurfaced as the law enforcement agencies re-iterate their fear of "going dark"[16] – sometimes, suspects use encrypted (or otherwise masked) communications, whose contents are inaccessible to law enforcement. Accordingly, they fear that by going dark and being unable to listen in, crime may not be prevented and public security could not be maintained. To solve the problem, governments have proposed ideas, such as using backdoors (secret access to plaintext),[17] key escrow (access to keys),[18] [19] or simply mandating actors to adopt weaker algorithms or keys.[20]

However, as cryptographic research has shown,[21] the tightrope is not only a question of privacy versus security, it is also a problem of more security

---

Public Policy' (1998) 25 Journal of Government Information 135.

12 Joris Van Hoboken and Wolfgang Schulz, *Human Rights and Encryption* (UNESCO Publishing 2016).

13 'The Importance of Strong Encryption to Security – Schneier on Security' (*Schneier on Security* 25 February 2016) <https://www.schneier.com/blog/archives/2016/02/the_importance_.html> accessed 27 March 2019.

14 Susan Landau, *Listening in: Cybersecurity in an Insecure Age* (Yale University press 2017).

15 Stephen Mason, 'Digital Signatures', *Electronic Signatures in Law* (School of Advanced Study, University of London 2016).

16 Famously referenced in the speech by James Comey in 2015, the then-director of the FBI, following terrorist attacks in the US – see: James Comey, 'Going Dark: Are Technology, Privacy, and Public Safety on a Collision Course?' (*Federal Bureau of Investigation,* October 16 2014) <https://www.fbi.gov/news/speeches/going-dark-are-technology-privacy-and-public-safety-on-a-collision-course> accessed 4 July 2019.

17 Very recently proposed by the G7 summit in April 2019 – see the Outcome Document at: G7, 'Outcome Document. Combatting the use of the internet for terrorist and violent extremist content' (*elysee.fr*) <https://www.elysee.fr/admin/upload/default/0001/04/287b5bb9a30155452ff7762a9131301284ff6417.pdf> accessed 4 July 2019.

18 Abelson and others (n 9).

19 Glyn Moody, 'Nobody Saw This Coming: Now China Too Wants Company Encryption Keys And Backdoors In Hardware And Software' (*Techdirt.*, 29 January 2015) <https://www.techdirt.com/articles/20150129/06262129848/nobody-saw-this-coming-now-china-too-wants-company-encryption-keys-backdoors-hardware-software.shtml> accessed 4 July 2019.

20 For example, India mandates using keys no longer than 40 bits in certain instances. See: Software Freedom Law Center India, 'FAQ: Legal Position of Encryption in India' (*SFLC.in*) <https://sflc.in/faq-legal-position-encryption-india> accessed 4 July 2019.

21 Susan Landau and Whitfield Diffie, *Privacy on the Line: The Politics of Wiretapping and Encryption* (<https://mitpress.mit.edu/books/privacy-line>, MIT Press 2007); Harold Abelson and others, 'Keys Under Doormats' (2015) 58 Commun. ACM 24.

versus less security.[22] Namely, setting up a system that would enable lawful and exceptional access either to keys or to plaintext would be very costly and technologically very difficult. In fact, such a system would be almost impossible to implement, highly impractical and it would not prevent access by hackers or foreign, unfriendly governments. It would decrease the cybersecurity of *all* communications and transactions.[23] Moreover, backdoors may not be necessary, since arguments have been made by cybersecurity experts and lawyers[24] that law enforcement can take alternative steps to access encrypted text or information.

The advent of the digital society through the internet and associated technologies has been beneficial to businesses, individuals and society at large; however, it has also made state surveillance and mass surveillance much easier. As Amnesty International notes in its report on encryption, tracking and discovering crime used to be a laborious, cost-ineffective exercise that required agents to install wiretaps or intercept communications, has now become "easily achievable through the deployment of inexpensive electronic surveillance technologies that can conduct analyses at a speed and volume that far outpaces the capacity of traditional law enforcement or intelligence services".[25]

Intelligence services globally have made use of the information technologies in order to spy on own and foreign citizens alike. Companies, especially social media networks and technological giants like Google, have had to hand over their customers' data to state agencies without disclosing it properly.[26] After the

22 See the 2016 testimony in front of US Congress by Susan Landau, 'The Encryption Tightrope: Balancing Americans' Security and Privacy | Committee Repository | U.S. House of Representatives' (*U.S. House of Representatives*, 1 March 2016) <https://docs.house.gov/Committee/Calendar/ByEvent.aspx?EventID=104573> accessed 4 July 2019.

23 Abelson and others (n 21).

24 For techno-legal analyses, see:
Orin S Kerr and Bruce Schneier, 'Encryption Workarounds' (2018) 106 Georgetown Law Journal;
Matt Olsen, Bruce Schneier and Jonathan Zittrain, 'Don't Panic: Making Progress on the "Going Dark" Debate' (The Berkman Centre for Internet & Society 2016) <https://dash.harvard.edu/handle/1/28552576 > accessed 28 June 2019.
Justin Gus Hurwitz, 'Encryption.Congress Mod (Apple + CALEA).(Communications Assistance for Law Enforcement Act of 1994)' (2017) 30 Harvard Journal of Law & Technology.

25 Amnesty International (n 3).

26 Google provides an interesting overview of its own compliance with user data request warrants at: Google, 'Requests for User Information – Google Transparency Report' (*Google*) <https://transparencyreport.google.com/user-data/overview> accessed 4 July 2019; A comparative analysis of other 'big tech' companies was compiled by Wong at: Joon Ian Wong, 'Here's How Often Apple, Google, and Others Handed over Data When the US Government Asked for It' (*Quartz*, 19 February 2016) <https://qz.com/620423/heres-how-often-apple-google-and-others-handed-over-data-when-the-us-government-asked-for-it/> accessed 4 July 2019. However, this does not take into account secret and undisclosed warrants whose scale was leaked by Snowden – see footnote 27.

revelation of NSA's secret programmes, the pervasiveness of surveillance is has gained traction and awareness.[27]

Encryption contributes to genuine enjoyment of the right to expression online by providing the opportunity to communicate confidentially. Together with anonymity, encryption creates a 'zone of privacy to protect opinion and belief'. This is especially important in environments, which are politically, socially or religiously hostile to members of certain communities – for example, artists in countries with strong censorship, or people who wish to explore their gender identity in socially conservative places. Confidential communication is also important for human rights defenders, lawyers and journalists, who wish to protect their sources or clients from societal or governmental repercussions. Nevertheless, like many other technologies, encryption can also be abused – for examples, when it is used to mask comprehensible behaviour of criminals, terrorists or cowardly cyberbullies. However, whenever states impose limitations on encryption they inadvertently affect both beneficent and maleficent users of encryption. Therefore, encryption deserves special protection.[28]

Human rights law traditionally reins in governments' powers by mandating negative obligations – i.e. the state must not interfere with the exercise of the right. Nonetheless, sometimes it is necessary to implement certain measures in order to ensure effective exercise of human rights, leading to the notion of positive obligations. Positive obligations are implied the International Covenant on Political and Civil Rights, whose Article 17(2) grants the right to the protection of the law against interferences with one's privacy rights. The European Court of Human Rights views positive obligations as necessary for the exercise of human rights in general[29] and in order to ensure private communications are not disclosed publically.[30] Accordingly, in a cyber-insecure world, where encryption has been proposed as the best line of defence against cyber-attacks,[31] positive state obligations on ensuring secure encryption is used, could be considered justifiable. Such obligations can include, but are not limited to, ensuring security of online communications, spreading awareness of internet security, encouraging vulnerability disclosure practices and facilitating the use of encryption.[32]

In a global digital economy, data traverse the globe easily and with relatively low costs. Data may pass through servers, located in different countries with

27 See: Luke Harding, *The Snowden Files: The Inside Story of the World's Most Wanted Man* (Vintage Books 2014).

28 David Kaye, 'Report of the Special Rapporteur on the Promotion and Protection of the Right to Freedom of Opinion and Expression' (*United Nations Human Rights Council* 2015) <www.ohchr.org/EN/HRBodies/HRC/RegularSessions/Session29/Documents/A.HRC.29.32_AEV.doc> accessed 28 June 2019.

29 *Airey v Ireland*, App. no. 6289/73 (ECtHR, 9 October 1979), para. 25: "...hindrance in fact can contravene the Convention just like a legal impediment..."

30 *Craxi v. Italy*, App. no. 25337/94 (ECtHR, 17 July 2003), paras. 68–76.

31 Peter Swire and Kenesa Ahmad (n 1).

32 Amnesty International (n 3).

diverse rules on data or general IT security. As Swire and Ahmad[33] point out, different standards and requirements on strength of encryption, lead to the problem of the global system only being as strong as cyber-security requirements in the "least trusted country" mandate. For example, if a country imposes secret backdoors for law enforcement and intelligence purposes, it creates the risk that another, potentially hostile, country could access seemingly secure encrypted data as well by exploiting the decreased strength of encryption.[34] Security holes multiply when more and more governments impose limitations on strong encryption and when data pass through such territories, there is a risk that important communications end up in the hands of the least trusted country, potentially unencrypted for unauthorised eyes to see.

While the problem of least trusted country could have been contained if data never left national borders in any form, that was not possible any more by the late 90s. By 1997, there were already millions of internet users throughout the world, using tens of millions (or more) private and public keys, and there were numerous law enforcement agencies interested in accessing information located in various countries.[35] Since then, while the use of internet has expanded rapidly and the society has become very dependent on the use of networks, the arguments against -or for, from the point of view of law enforcement- imposing either key escrows, backdoors or otherwise decreasing the strength of encryption, have remained the same. Cryptographic experts point out that constructing infrastructure that would satisfy the needs of secure but accessible key escrow or exceptional access to plaintext is technically too costly and too complicated to set up according to the current technical state of the art.[36]

Moreover, the systems would have to be aligned: either all the countries adopted a mandatory key escrow system, or none. A divergence in systems would decrease the usability and security of key escrows significantly.[37]

Adoption of standards has been proposed as a means of bridging the divergence in systems – a collaboration to use cryptography for good of all mankind.[38] Standardisation has a positive effect on innovation, leading to better products and services.[39] Standards, however, are voluntary, and most of the effort has been led by a limited amount of actors, thus risking that potentially

---

33 Peter Swire and Kenesa Ahmad (n 1).

34 Peter Swire and Kenesa Ahmad (n 1).

35 Hal Abelson and others (n 9).

36 Harold Abelson and others (n 21).

37 "And this prohibition would have to be enforced on a global scale, for if this kind of initiative were to be adopted only by a limited number of countries, its usefulness would be greatly undermined. Full international consensus on the matter would have to be achieved, and this is clearly an extremely complex ambition, given the particular interests at stake."
Hassan Aljifri and Diego Sánchez Navarro, 'International Legal Aspects of Cryptography: Understanding Cryptography' (2003) 22 Computers & Security 196.

38 ibid.

39 Knut Blind, 'The Impact of Standardization and Standards on Innovation' (Manchester Institute of Innovation Research 2013) 13/15 <www.innovation-policy.org.uk/compendium/section/Default.aspx?topicid=30> accessed 18 July 2019.

more secure encryption techniques and tools are not taken into consideration out of commercial interests.

Another way to harmonise rules is globalisation-driven regulatory convergence. Governments lay down rules for businesses to follow, and since there is an interest to explore foreign markets, the legal frameworks may start resembling each other. However, in the absence of formal harmonisation, the great powers will lead the effort, and set the rules for everyone else.[40] Since the United States are without doubt a leader in the technological development, the result could be that other legal systems would follow it without allowing for more nuanced frameworks.

Finally, there are rules on an international level. As discussed above, international human rights law could in certain instances bind states to adopt certain measures in order to protect human rights rather than prevent them from doing so, as is traditionally understood. Certain areas of law, such as private international law and commercial law have profited from unification at international or regional level. Traditionally, rules are laid down in a treaty or a convention, open to other countries. However, drafting countries must be careful not to make the text too inflexible lest conventional rules become too difficult to realise in practice.[41]

The benefits of international rules are also stressed by the Council of Europe in its Explanatory Report to the Convention for the Protection of Individuals with regard to Automatic Processing of Personal Data (Convention 108).[42] It cites reasons of unresolved jurisdiction issues – though those may not be entirely resolved by international conventions[43] – and facilitated exercise of data subjects' rights.

Adopting uniform rules on encryption – a global obligation on states to mandate the use of encryption – at international level therefore has its benefits and drawbacks. As a uniform flexible standard, it would enhance innovation in order to find a more secure encryption algorithm and other techniques, which would ensure a comparable level of protection of human rights in different legal system. On the other hand, if global superpowers, such as US and EU[44] were the only ones leading the effort, they could skew the rules in their favour, which could prevent better encryption tools being considered, and the decreased level of protection of human rights.

---

40 Daniel W Drezner, 'Globalization, Harmonization, and Competition: The Different Pathways to Policy Convergence' (2005) 12 Journal of European Public Policy 841.

41 Martin Gebauer, 'Unification and Harmonization of Laws', *Max Planck Encyclopedia of Public International Law* (Oxford University Press 2009) <http://opil.ouplaw.com/view/10.1093/law:epil/9780199231690/law-9780199231690-e1123> accessed 4 June 2019.

42 The report is available at 'Convention 108 and Protocols' (*Council of Europe*) <https://www.coe.int/en/web/data-protection/convention108-and-protocol> accessed 4 July 2019.

43 Aljifri and Sánchez Navarro (n 37).

44 US has by far the most encryption products available on the market, with EU member states (as a whole) not far behind it. China is surprisingly lagging behind despite their efforts at creating a home-grown encryption market. See: Bruce Schneier, Kathleen Seidel and Saranya Vijayakumar, 'A Worldwide Survey of Encryption Products' (2016) Social Science Research Network SSRN Scholarly Paper <https://papers.ssrn.com/abstract=2731160> accessed 18 July 2019.

However, the questions remains – is there already a provision obliging states to mandate the use of encryption? This will be explored in the next section.

3. FRAGMENTED PROVISIONS IN INTERNATIONAL HUMAN RIGHTS LAW

On the international law level, cryptography can trigger questions in relation to human rights, law enforcement and jurisdiction, intelligence, trade and economy, as well as export controls.[45] Data gathering as a result of breaking or limiting encryption can be seen as encroachment upon another state's territory, and lead to jurisdiction issues, which are not completely resolved by the existing legal framework.[46]

As the UN special rapporteur David Kaye has noted, encryption and/or anonymity are capable of creating "a zone of privacy to protect opinion and belief", and that any restrictions on encryption must be provided for by the law, can be imposed only if legitimate grounds exist, and such a restriction must meet the tests of necessity and proportionality.[47]

3.1. GENERAL HUMAN RIGHTS FRAMEWORK

The right to privacy is enshrined in several international human rights legal documents.

The Universal Declaration of Human Rights (UDHR),[48] arguably the most important and well-known human rights instrument despite its non-binding character,[49] provides for the right to be free from interference with, inter alia, privacy and communications in its Article 12. Any restrictions placed upon the privacy of communications, incl. restrictions on encryption, must not be arbitrary (as set out in Article 12), nor can they be arbitrary and unlawful (as laid down in Article 17).

The International Covenant on Civil and Political Rights (ICCPR)[50] likewise provides for freedom from arbitrary or unlawful interference with privacy and communications in its Article 17.

---

45 Ashley Deeks, 'The International Legal Dynamics of Encryption' <https://www.hoover.org/sites/default/files/research/docs/deeks_webreadypdf.pdf> accessed 28 June 2019 28.

46 Grant Hodgson, Breaking Encryption and Gathering Data: International Law Applications, 20 J. Tech. L. & Pol'y 39 (2015).

47 Kaye (n 28).

48 Universal Declaration of Human Rights (adopted 10/12/1948 UNGA Res 217 A(III) (UDHR).

49 See esp. pp. 32–38 of Gordon Brown (ed.), *The Universal Declaration of Human Rights in the 21st Century* (Open Book Publishers 2016).

50 International Covenant on Civil and Political Rights (adopted 16/12/1966, entered into force 23 March 1976) 999 UNTS 171 (ICCPR).

On regional European level, the *European Convention on Human Rights*[51] in its Article 8 provides for the right to respect for private and family life, home and correspondence. The provision applies to private and family life, home and correspondence. The European Court of Human Rights has ruled that the notion of correspondence covers not only physical means, such as letters, but also email and internet,[52] as well as instant messaging.[53] Case law has also confirmed that this right extends to interception of communications[54] in a mass surveillance scenario.[55]

The Council of Europe's Convention no. 108[56] protects an individual's right to privacy, with regard to automatic processing of personal data relating to him ("data protection"). Unlike the other human rights international conventions, it specifically applies to protection of personal data, and contains provisions about data security, which will be discussed in the next section.

The European Union legal framework provides for both rights to privacy and data protection in Articles 7 and 8 of the *Charter of Fundamental Rights of the European Union,*[57] respectively.

However, while all of the above provisions provide for either the right to privacy, or the right to data protection, they do not explicitly require the states to mandate adoption of any type of cryptography measures. While most of the provisions require *confidentiality* of communications, encryption is far from the only confidentiality measure. For example, measures such as access controls, integrity checking, intrusion detection systems and non-disclosure agreements can also contribute toward confidentiality.[58]

Since many national security agencies' efforts involve listening in to private communications, and storing information about them (metadata), masking communications through use of encryption has been put forward as a viable solution.[59]

---

51 Council of Europe, 'Convention for the Protection of Human Rights and Fundamental Freedoms' European Treaty Number 005.

52 *Copland v. the United Kingdom*, app no. 62617/00 (ECtHR, 3 March 2007).

53 *Barbulescu v. Romania*, app. no 61496/08 (ECtHR, 12 January 2016).

54 *Halford v. the United Kingdom*, app. no. 20605/92 (ECtHR, 25 June 1997), *Copland v. the United Kingdom* (cited at fn. 52).

55 *Big Brother Watch v. the United Kingdom*, apps. no. 58170/13 62322/14 24960/15 (ECtHR, 13 September 2018).

56 Council of Europe, 'Convention for the Protection of Individuals with regard to Automatic Processing of Personal Data' European Treaty Number 108.

57 European Union, 'Charter of Fundamental Rights of the European Union' C326.

58 Matthew Scholl and others, 'An Introductory Resource Guide for Implementing the Health Insurance Portability and Accountability Act (HIPAA) Security Rule' (National institute of standards and technology 2008) <https://csrc.nist.gov/publications/detail/sp/800-66/rev-1/final> accessed 19 July 2019.

59 See, among others, Edward Snowden's 2014 speech reported at Lauren C Williams, 'Edward Snowden Says Encryption Is The Only Way To Counter Mass Surveillance' (*ThinkPogress*, 10 March 2014) <https://thinkprogress.org/edward-snowden-says-encryption-is-the-only-way-to-counter-mass-surveillance-ee450433dca8/> accessed 4 July 2019. See also Joris VJ

An implicit link between mass surveillance and encryption has been made by the European Court of Human Rights (ECtHR) in the Big Brother Watch case.[60] While ruling on the mass surveillance regime in the UK, the court indirectly acknowledged the importance of encryption as a measure against such surveillance, as it blocks intelligence services from accessing the content of a telecommunication, in para. 356 of the judgment. Moreover, as already discussed above in the introductory section, the UN Special Rapporteur's reports have explicitly linked encryption to the right to privacy and freedom of expression; however, unlike the judgment, which is binding for the country addressed, and may become a precedent in the court's case law, the reports are non-binding and recommendatory in their nature.

The Court of Justice of the EU (CJEU) has a wide-ranging jurisprudence on privacy and data protection.[61] The case law has set high standards to protect the rights and interests of individuals in mass surveillance scenarios in cases such as Digital Rights Ireland, Schrems, Tele2 Sverige and in its Opinion 1/15, having ruled on data retention rules and transfer of personal data to the United States. According to Directive 2006/24/EC (Data Retention Directive), telecom providers were required to keep metadata of their users from 6 months to 2 years, which was justified by the blanket provision of "investigating, detecting and prosecuting serious crime". Metadata retention in itself falls under the "private life" provision of Article 7 of the Charter of Fundamental Rights, as it makes people feel that their private lives are the subject of constant surveillance.[62] In principle, general-blanket-data retention is incompatible with European data protection rules, while targeted data retention may be permissible if Tele2 Sverige criteria are met.[63] The need for data retention is assessed upon the strict necessity and proportionality test. As the CJEU reiterates in its Opinion 1/15 on the EU-Canada Agreement on the transfer of Passenger Name Record data (PNR), general data retention and processing is not strictly necessary and does not meet the threshold of the test.[64] Further, in the Maximillian Schrems case on transfer of data to the US under its PRISM surveillance program, the CJEU

Van Hoboken, 'Privacy and Security in the Cloud: Some Realism about Technical Solutions to Transnational Surveillance in the Post-Snowden Era Symposium: Who's Governing Privacy: Regulation and Protection in a Digital Era' (2013) 66 Maine Law Review 487; as well as Seda Gürses, Arun Kundnani and Joris Van Hoboken, 'Crypto and Empire: The Contradictions of Counter-Surveillance Advocacy' (2016) 38 Media, Culture & Society 576.

60 *Big Brother Watch v. the United Kingdom* (n 55), paras. 353–356.

61 See, inter alia: C-293/12 *Digital Rights Ireland Ltd v Minister for Communications, Marine and Natural Resources and Others and Kärntner Landesregierung and Others* (8 April 2014); C-362/14 *Maximilian Schrems v Data Protection Commissioner* (6 October 2015); joined cases C-203/15 and C-698/15 *Tele2 Sverige AB v Post- och telestyrelsen and Secretary of State for the Home Department v Tom Watson and Others AB* (21 December 2016); and Opinion of the Court (Grand Chamber) 1/15 on PNR agreement with Canada (26 July 2017).

62 *Digital Rights Ireland Ltd.* (n 61).

63 *Tele2 Sverige*, (n 61), para. 77.

64 Opinion 1/15 on PNR agreement with Canada (n 61).

pointed out the need of data subjects – surveilled population – to have adequate control and access to court, and to have their data processed without the risk of unauthorised third party interference.[65]

3.2. SECURITY MEASURES AND STANDARDS IN DATA PROTECTION LAWS

Contrary to the human rights frameworks, data protection laws contain explicit provisions on security of (personal) data. This section will discuss the regional frameworks in Europe, Asia-Pacific and Western Africa, although it should be kept in mind that certain national legal systems, for example health data regulation in the United States under the Healthcare Insurance Portability and Accountability Act, also require the adoption of security measures.

3.2.1. European Union (EU)

The European Union is known for its strict data protection laws. Building upon the German, Swedish and French traditions of regulating data protection as early as the 1970's[66] the EU adopted the Data Protection Directive in 1995 (Directive 95/46/EC),[67] recently replaced by the General Data Protection Regulation (GDPR, Regulation (EU) 2016/679).[68] Moreover, Member States are under a duty to protect data transmitted over public communication networks under the so-called ePrivacy Directive[69] (Directive 2002/58/EC of the European Parliament and of the Council of 12 July 2002 concerning the processing of personal data and the protection of privacy in the electronic communications sector (Directive on privacy and electronic communications).

The Directive 95/46/EC was adopted in 1995. It applied to the processing of personal data wholly or partly by automatic means, and to the processing

65 *Maximilian Schrems* (n 61), paras. 86–87.

66 For a historical overview of data protection legislation in Europe, see Meg Leta Jones, 'The Right to a Human in the Loop: Political Constructions of Computer Automation and Personhood' (2017) 47 Social Studies of Science 216; or for a systemic comprehensive overview, see: Brendan Van Alsenoy, 'Regulating Data Protection : The Allocation of Responsibility and Risk among Actors Involved in Personal Data Processing' (Doctoral thesis, KU Leuven 2016) 163–206.

67 Directive 95/46/EC of the European Parliament and of the Council of 24 October 1995 on the protection of individuals with regard to the processing of personal data and on the free movement of such data (1995) OJ L 281, 31–50.

68 Regulation (EU) 2016/679 of the European Parliament and of the Council of 27 April 2016 on the protection of natural persons with regard to the processing of personal data and on the free movement of such data, and repealing Directive 95/46/EC (2016) OJ L 119, 1–88.

69 Directive 2002/58/EC of the European Parliament and of the Council of 12 July 2002 concerning the processing of personal data and the protection of privacy in the electronic communications sector (2002) OJ L201, 37–47.

otherwise than by automatic means of personal data which form part of a filing system or are intended to form part of a filing system. Recital 46 spelled out the need for security measures: when the protection of the rights and freedoms of data subjects required adoption of technical and organisational security measures, their adoption should be performed by taking into account the state of the art and the costs of their implementation in relation to the risks inherent in the processing and the nature of the data to be protected. Article 17 followed the recital, requiring controllers to adopt security measures having regard to the state of the art and the cost of their implementation. The level of security had to be appropriate to the risks represented by the processing and the nature of the data to be protected. However, encryption was not specifically mentioned in the text.

In 2018, the Directive was replaced by the GDPR, which entered into force on May 25 2018.

The GDPR similarly applies to processing of personal data wholly or partly by automated means and to the processing other than by automated means of personal data which form part of a filing system or are intended to form part of a filing system, according to its Article 2.

In the regime established in the GDPR, encryption plays a double role.

Firstly, according to Article 32 of the GDPR, encryption is a relevant measure in ensuring the security of personal data processing. The provision is risk-based, meaning that state of the art, the costs of implementation and the nature, scope, context and purposes of processing as well as the risk of varying likelihood and severity to human rights must be taken into account when assessing the need for encryption or during its implementation. The risk assessment takes into account human rights – could the data processing lead to discrimination, or will there be government intervention. If so, the risks are considered to be significant (in the words of recital 75), and a higher level of security measures, including stronger encryption, is required.,[70] [71]

Secondly, encryption may contribute toward depersonalising personal data in the sense that it renders them unintelligible to third parties without the possession of the decryption key. There are, however, varying opinions on how anonymous encrypted data truly are. In its opinion on anonymisation techniques,[72] the Article 29 Working Party suggests that as long as the keys or the original,

70 Paul Voigt and Axel von dem Bussche, 'Organisational Requirements' in Paul Voigt and Axel von dem Bussche (eds), *The EU General Data Protection Regulation (GDPR): A Practical Guide* (Springer International Publishing 2017).

71 In some instances, encryption can be used a data breach counter-measure. See, inter alia, Article 29 Working Party, 'Guidelines on Personal Data Breach Notification under Regulation 2016/679 (Wp250rev.01)' (European Commission 2018) <https://ec.europa.eu/newsroom/article29/item-detail.cfm?item_id=612052> accessed 28 June 2019; Ian Edwards, 'GDPR the Security Angle' (2018) 60 ITNOW 42.

72 Article 29 Working Party, 'Opinion 05/2014 on Anonymisation Techniques' (European Commission 2014) <https://ec.europa.eu/justice/article-29/documentation/opinion-recommendation/index_en.htm> accessed 7 June 2019.

unencrypted data, are available, it is still possible to identify the data subject. On the other hand, in its Breyer[73] judgment, the CJEU has introduced the criterion "lawful means reasonably likely", when assessing the notion of identifiability of a data subject. Accordingly, some authors have suggested that encrypted data could be considered anonymous for actors, which do not possess the key and are reasonably unlikely to obtain it by lawful means. This also means that when assessing the anonymous nature of encrypted data, the strength of the encryption algorithm, the key length, and the key management system must be taken into account; and the decryption key(s) must be kept separate from the data.[74]

The rules on privacy in electronic communications in the EU have been harmonised through the ePrivacy Directive, which is scheduled to be replaced by a newer ePrivacy Regulation[75] (COM/2017/010).

Articles 4 and 5 of the ePrivacy Directive require that providers of public communications networks adopt security and confidentiality measures. While the Directive talks about such measures generally, the proposed Regulation, in its Recital 37, specifically recommends service providers, such as telecoms or internet service providers, to use encryption techniques as part of their products. Article 5 of the current ePrivacy Directive prohibits listening, tapping, storage or other kinds of interception or surveillance of communications and the related traffic data. A similar provision is included in Article 5 of the proposed Regulation. However, both the Directive and the proposed Regulation explicitly exempt typical law enforcement actions out of their scope, such as prevention, investigation, detection or prosecution of criminal offences or the execution of criminal penalties. This means that the security and confidentiality measures of the ePrivacy framework will not apply to the extent that law enforcement and security agencies are involved in wiretapping or otherwise interfering with electronic communications, as specified in Article 1(3) of the Directive.[76]

Nevertheless, this does not mean free rein for the agencies – as already mentioned above, data retention resulting from communications network monitoring for purposes of crime prevention has been subject to close scrutiny by the CJEU.,[77] [78]

---

73 The test of lawful means reasonably likely to be used was defined in the Patrick Breyer case of the European Court of Justice, and answers several questions posed in (n 70).

74 Gerald Spindler and Philipp Schmechel (n 4).

75 Commission, 'Proposal for a Regulation of the European Parliament and of the Council concerning the respect for private life and the protection of personal data in electronic communications and repealing Directive 2002/58/EC (Regulation on Privacy and Electronic Communications)' COM/2017/010 final – 2017/03 (COD).

76 See Directive 2002/58/EC of the European Parliament and of the Council of 12 July 2002 concerning the processing of personal data and the protection of privacy in the electronic communications sector [2000] OJ L 201, Article 1(3).

77 See CJEU cases Digital Rights Ireland Ltd (C-293/12), Tele2 Sverige AB (C-203/15).

78 Frederik J Zuiderveen Borgesius and Wilfred Steenbruggen, 'The Right to Communications Confidentiality in Europe: Protecting Privacy, Freedom of Expression, and Trust' (2019) 20 Theoretical Inquiries in Law.

3.2.2. Convention no. 108 of the Council of Europe

The Council of Europe is an international organisation of 47 member states spanning across the geographical Europe.[79] The legislative efforts of the Council and the case law of the European Court of Human Rights have resulted in important contributions to European data protection and privacy law.

In 1981, the Council of Europe adopted the first international binding treaty on data protection, the Convention no. 108. It applies to protection of personal data, which are defined in Article 2(a) as 'any information relating to an identified or identifiable individual'. Chapter II, which lays out the basic principles of the Convention, contains a provision on data security, which requires that appropriate security measures are taken for the protection of personal data stored in automated data files against accidental or unauthorised destruction or accidental loss as well as against unauthorised access, alteration or dissemination. According to the Explanatory report to the Convention 108, there should be specific security measures for every file, taking into account its degree of vulnerability, the need to restrict access to the information within the organisation, requirements concerning long-term storage, and so forth. The security measures must be appropriate, i.e. adapted to the specific function of the file and the risks involved. They should be based on the current state of the art of data security methods and techniques in the field of data processing.

The Convention has been amended twice and modernised in 2018; since the last update, it has been referred to as Convention 108+.[80] Unlike the original 1981 version, the modernised convention extends its scope to non-automated data processing.

The security rule contained in the Convention 108+ is slightly extended compared to its previous iteration. The first paragraph requires controllers and processors to put in place appropriate security measures against risks such as accidental or unauthorised access to, destruction, loss, use, modification or disclosure of personal data. The second paragraph obliges the controller to notify the supervisory authority if the security of personal data has been breached and the breach could impact the rights and fundamental freedoms of data subjects.

As with its previous version, an explanatory report is provided for Convention 108+ as well. The security provision is interpreted in paragraphs 62–66, which state that the implementation of technical and organisational security measures must take into account the nature of the personal data, the volume of personal data processed, the degree of vulnerability of the technical architecture used for the processing, the need to restrict access to the data.

[79] 'Council of Europe' <https://www.coe.int/en/web/portal/home> accessed 4 July 2019.

[80] Full text of the original Convention, Additional Protocols and Convention 108+ available at: 'Convention 108 and Protocols' (n 42).

Moreover, they must be adopted according to the current state of the art, taking into account the implementation costs proportional to the potential risks.

3.2.3. Economic Community of West African States (ECOWAS)

The ECOWAS is an economic union of 15 states in the Western part of Africa with legislative powers; hence, the rules it adopts are binding for its member states.[81]

Its Model Data Protection Act,[82] adopted in 2010, obliges the member states to adopt their own data protection laws. The framework is similar to the pre-GDPR regime in the European Union regarding its basic definitions, principles and obligations; however, the enforcement mechanisms among different states lack coordination and harmonisation, nor does the act provide for judicial remedy nor civil liability.[83]

The Act specifically provides for security of personal data in two provisions. First, in Article 28, the principle of confidentiality and security requires the protection of personal data especially in transit – although whether that obliges data controllers to implement encryption at rest is debatable. Secondly, according to Article 43, data controllers must adopt measures to ensure that data are not deformed, damaged or accessible to unauthorised third parties.[84]

3.2.4. Asia-Pacific Economic Cooperation (APEC)

The APEC is an intergovernmental forum, set up by 21 states around the Pacific Rim in the 1980's with the aim of promoting free trade in the region.[85] Its Privacy Framework, first adopted in 2005[86] and renewed in 2015,[87] was adopted in order to promote electronic commerce in Asia and the Pacific, by inter alia facilitating trans-border flows of personal data. The Framework is based upon OECD's 2013 Guidelines on the Protection of Privacy and Trans-Border Flows of Personal Data and is not binding for member states. It contains a preamble, scope

---

81 'Economic Community of West African States (ECOWAS)' <https://www.ecowas.int/> accessed 18 July 2019.

82 Supplementary Act A/SA. 1/01/10 on Personal Data Protection within ECOWAS (adopted at the 37th session of the Authority of ECOWAS Heads of State and Government on 12/02/2010, Abuja, Nigeria).

83 Uchenna Jerome Orji, 'Regionalizing Data Protection Law: A Discourse on the Status and Implementation of the ECOWAS Data Protection Act' (2017) 7 International Data Privacy Law 179.

84 Economic Community of West African States (ECOWAS) (n 81).

85 'Asia-Pacific Economic Cooperation' <https://www.apec.org/> accessed 4 July 2019.

86 Full text of the 2005 Privacy Framework is available at 'APEC Privacy Framework' (*Asia-Pacific Economic Cooperation*) <http://publications.apec.org/Publications/2005/12/APEC-Privacy-Framework> accessed 4 July 2019.

87 Privacy Framework (adopted in 2015 by Ministers of Member States of Asia-Pacific Economic Cooperation). Full text likewise available at ibid.

provisions, nine information privacy principles and provisions on domestic and international implementation.

Information Privacy Principle no. VII of the 2015 Privacy Framework[88] requires controllers of personal data to adopt appropriate safeguards against risks, such as loss or unauthorized access to personal information, or unauthorized destruction, use, modification or disclosure of information or other misuses. Similarly to the GDPR, the security requirements are balanced against other criteria, such as sensitivity of the information and the context in which it is held, they must be proportionate to the likelihood and severity of the harm threatened, and periodically reviewed and reassessed.[89]

3.3. RECOMMENDATIONS OF EXPERT BODIES

This section will explore expert opinions on cryptography and encryption by international bodies and national expert agencies. While such opinions are non-binding (so-called soft law), they are nevertheless important as they can represent an important contribution to the scientific and practical state of the art in the field.

The OECD was set up in 1961 to promote international trade and progress. Today, it counts 36 member countries from mainly Western or Western-style economies, including the US, Canada, Japan and several EU member states.

In the 90's, during the first crypto war, talks resulted in the 1997 Recommendation concerning Guidelines for cryptography policy.[90] The Guidelines address policy-makers with the goal of decreasing obstacles in international trade and evolution of information and communication networks by reducing policy disparities. Encryption is linked to both privacy and data protection as well as security, similarly to the approach adopted by the European legislator. The Guidelines stipulate eight principles to be taken into account when designing cryptography policies at government level: (1) user trust into cryptography to facilitate electronic and online commerce, (2) user choice in using specific cryptographic techniques, (3) market-driven development rather than top-down requirements, (4) voluntary standardisation, (5) cryptography as a privacy and data protection preserving technique, (6) lawful access to

88 The provision in the 2015 Privacy Framework is identical to the 2005 one.

89 The APEC Framework has been criticised as unambitious and purposefully legislating lower standards than the European ones – see Graham Greenleaf, 'APEC's Privacy Framework Sets a New Low Standard for the Asia-Pacific' in Andrew T Kenyon and Megan Richardson (eds), *New Dimensions in Privacy Law* (Cambridge University Press 2006) <https://www.cambridge.org/core/product/identifier/CBO9780511494208A012/type/book_part> accessed 20 May 2019.

90 Stewart A Baker and Paul R Hurst, *The Limits of Trust: Cryptography, Governments, and Electronic Commerce* (Kluwer law international 1998).

encrypted communications, (7) the need for liability provisions, and (8) international cooperation to ensure compliant free flow of data across borders.[91]

While the Guidelines seem to promote strong encryption, the background of the talks must be taken into account. The impetus for discussion were cryptographic export controls in the US and its erstwhile administration's attempts to impose the use of specific cryptographic products, called the Clipper Chip, which enabled lawful access to communications by the FBI. This explains the notions of lawful access (Principle 6) and the use of cryptographic methods subject to applicable law (Principle 2).[92] In the end, the Clipper Chip initiative was dropped due to serious concerns following the outcry of civil rights advocates and the crypto community, while the principles remained in the text.[93]

United Nations adopted brief guidelines on computerised files in 1990. Principle no. 7 deals with security of files, requiring adoption of appropriate measures to protect the files against both natural dangers, such as accidental loss or destruction and human dangers, such as unauthorized access, fraudulent misuse of data or contamination by computer viruses.[94] A follow-up report was discussed in 1999, though the series seem to have been discontinued.

ENISA is the EU agency responsible for network and systems security to the benefit of individuals, society and member states with the aim of facilitating smooth functioning of the EU single digital market. According to the upcoming Cybersecurity Act,[95] ENISA will play an important role in the upcoming certification scheme of cyber security products – however, cryptographic products are conspicuous by their absence from the Regulation. In fact, encryption is mentioned only once throughout the Act, in recital 40, which prompts ENISA to raise awareness about it as a counter-measure against cyber-attacks.

ENISA has tackled encryption in its non-binding recommendatory work, both from the perspective of privacy by design and the security/law enforcement access aspects.

---

91 Recommendation Concerning Guidelines for Cryptography Policy (adopted on 27/03/1997 by the Council of the Organisation for Economic Cooperation and Development on the proposal of the Committee for Information, Computer and Communications Policy) (the OECD Guidelines). See Organisation for Economic Cooperation and Development, 'OECD Guidelines for Cryptography Policy – OECD' (*OECD.org*) <https://www.oecd.org/sti/ieconomy/guidelinesforcryptographypolicy.htm> accessed 4 July 2019.

92 Baker and Hurst (n 90).

93 See Landau and Diffie (n 21).

94 Louis Joinet, 'Revised Version of the Guidelines for the Regulation of Computerized Personal Data Files' (*United Nations Commission on Human Rights,* 1990) <http://digitallibrary.un.org/record/43365> accessed 17 July 2019.

95 Regulation (EU) 2019/881 of the European Parliament and of the Council of 17 April 2019 on ENISA (the European Union Agency for Cybersecurity) and on information and communications technology cybersecurity certification and repealing Regulation (EU) No 526/2013 (Cybersecurity Act) OJ L 151, 7.6.2019, p. 15–6.

The 2014 Report on Privacy by design[96] addresses policy-makers and engineers involved in different levels of privacy design processes. Encryption plays different roles; as a privacy-enhancing technique, privacy preserving technique, a tool to secure conversations, enable secure storage of data at rest, and as a computational tool. However, it does not address larger concerns about encryption, such as backdoors or access to plaintext.

ENISA's Opinion paper on encryption[97] focuses on cryptography as a confidentiality and authentication measure, both from design perspective, as well as in the context of lawful access for law enforcement and intelligence services context. Its position is strongly negative toward backdoors and key escrow due to their previous ineffectiveness, arguing that criminals will always find a way around the law, and that backdoors will decrease the level of cyber-security across the board, making criminals' work easier. More specifically, ENISA and Europol in their Joint Statement on Encryption[98] argue for 'encryption circumvention', echoing 'encryption workarounds' from Kerr and Schneier's work.[99]

On the other side of the Atlantic, the *National Institute of Standards (NIST)*, part of the US Department of Commerce has led many important initiatives in the field of cryptography, for example promoting the Data Encryption Standard from 1970 until its eventual obsolescence.[100] It published cryptography guidelines in 2016 and in 2019.

NIST's report on Cryptographic Standards and Guidelines Development Process[101] suggests to base crypto development processes on balance of interests of government, industry and academia. The standards developed must be strong and practical, and they must be capable of meeting the needs of (federal) government, as well as the user community in the broad sense. Standards adopted should be globally acceptable since encrypted products, developed in the US, are sold internationally. The document also stresses the need for consultation with government agencies, such as the National Security Agency

---

96 George Danezis, Josep Domingo-Ferrer and Marit Hansen, 'Privacy and Data Protection by Design – from Policy to Engineering' (ENISA 2014) <https://www.enisa.europa.eu/publications/privacy-and-data-protection-by-design> accessed 7 June 2019.

97 Ioanna Kampouraki, 'ENISA's Opinion Paper on Encryption' (2016) <https://www.enisa.europa.eu/publications/enisa-position-papers-and-opinions/enisas-opinion-paper-on-encryption> accessed 7 June 2019.

98 ENISA and Europol, 'ENISA- Europol Issue Joint Statement' (*ENISA*, 23 May 2016) <https://www.enisa.europa.eu/news/enisa-news/enisa-europol-issue-joint-statement> accessed 4 July 2019.

99 Kerr and Schneier (n 24).

100 Later on, DES turned out to be relatively easy to crack, and was replaced by the AES – advanced encryption standard.

101 Computer Security Division, Information Technology Laboratory, 'Crypto Standards Development Process | CSRC' (*CSRC* | *NIST*, 24 May 2016) <https://csrc.nist.gov/Projects/Crypto-Standards-Development-Process> accessed 16 July 2019.

(NSA) and the Department of Homeland Security. Cooperation with NSA is especially advised due to its high level of expertise.

The 2019 Guidelines for Using Cryptographic Standards in the Federal Government[102] exhort the government to use cryptography in order to protect important data it stores as part of its daily business. While the report does not address backdoors or access to plaintext, it does provide for key storage principles under section 5.4.3. Some keys might have to be stored for longer periods of time should there be a legal order to decrypt text. However, the report also addresses an older standard which would have enabled key escrow if it had been implemented. The use of such a standard as part of an algorithm, called Skipjack, is disallowed, according to section 3.2.1.4.[103]

3.4. OTHER UPCOMING INITIATIVES BY REGIONAL ORGANISATIONS

In the wake of the digital economy, several other regional international organisations are adopting, or considering adopting, relevant legislation on encryption, either in a data protection context or as part of cybersecurity measures.

MERCOSUR, i.e. the Common Southern Market, is a trading bloc in Latin America, established in 1991. Its member states include Argentina, Brazil, Paraguay and Uruguay, with associated countries such as Chile and Peru, thus unifying a major part of South American economies.[104] While MERCOSUR's focus areas are agriculture, social development and human rights, it has recently tackled development and cooperation in the digital economy. It has been noted[105] that MERCOSUR countries are interested in laying down rules on data protection, but a GDPR-type of legislation is considered to be too inflexible. Under current Argentinian leadership, expert groups are consulting on future direction of the organisation's digital agenda,[106] though no legislation

102 The Guidelines are not final – a draft version is available for public perusal, and the final version should be available in September 2019. Thelma A Allen, 'Guideline for Using Cryptographic Standards in the Federal Government – Cryptographic Mechanisms: NIST Releases Draft NIST SP 800–175B Rev. 1' (*NIST*, 3 July 2019) <https://www.nist.gov/news-events/news/2019/07/guideline-using-cryptographic-standards-federal-government-cryptographic> accessed 16 July 2019.

103 There have been some allegations that NIST endorses standards, which include a secret backdoor for NSA's exclusive use. Thomas C Hales, 'The NSA Back Door to NIST' (2014) 61 Notices of the American Mathematical Society.

104 'MERCOSUR Official Website' (*MERCOSUR*) <https://www.mercosur.int/en/> accessed 15 July 2019.

105 Kati Suominen, 'Fueling Digital Trade in Mercosur: A Regulatory Roadmap' (*Inter-American Development Bank* 2018) <https://publications.iadb.org/handle/11319/9339> accessed 15 July 2019.

106 'Avanza la agenda digital en el Mercosur' (*MERCOSUR*, 27 June 2019) <https://www.mercosur.int/avanza-la-agenda-digital-en-el-mercosur/> accessed 15 July 2019.

has been proposed yet. Moreover, MERCOSUR is collaborating with the Pacific Alliance, a trading bloc in the same area, on topics such as digital trade and cybersecurity.[107]

ASEAN, Association of Southeast Asian Nations, is an intergovernmental organisation which was set up in 1967.[108] Its 2016–2020 ICT Masterplan, adopted in 2015,[109] lists development of regional data protection principles, as part of establishing information security in the regional framework.[110] However, as per the Masterplan's Annex A, only sharing best practices is currently planned. The adoption of cyber-norms foreseen in the Masterplan would be a major step forward, though its effective use is in doubt due to costly barriers to market entry and lack of user trust into using digital services.[111]

To conclude, while privacy and data protection are strongly recognised human rights at international level, very few legal instruments specifically provide for encryption. Since the 80's, when computers became more ubiquitous, regional instruments on data protection have emerged, such as the APEC Privacy Framework, the Convention 108, and the European Union data protection legislation; however, none of these apply globally. In the next section, three potential pathways to ensure global encryption obligations will be explored.

4. ENABLING GLOBAL ENCRYPTION OBLIGATIONS IN THE ABSENCE OF SPECIFIC TREATY PROVISIONS

4.1. OPTION 1 – A GLOBAL TREATY WITH ENCRYPTION REQUIREMENTS

The first scenario is to have a relevant international organisation (United Nations, International Telecommunications Union) adopt treaty on encryption, which would be open to accession for all states. A provision mandating encryption could also be part of a broader treaty, e.g. on data protection, confidentiality of communications, or a more general instrument on law of ICT or cybersecurity should the UN decide to adopt a treaty on those matters. However, the UN is

---

107 Mikio Kuwayama, 'Pacific Alliance: A Latin American Version of "Open Regionalism" in Practice' [2019] IDEAS Working Paper Series from RePEc <http://search.proquest.com/docview/2188997245/> accessed 18 July 2019.

108 'ASEAN | One Vision One Identity One Community' (*ASEAN.org*) <https://asean.org/> accessed 16 July 2019.

109 Association of Southeast Asian Nations, 'ASEAN ICT Masterplan 2020 (AIM 2020) – ASEAN THAILAND 2019' (2015) <https://www.asean2019.go.th/en/infographic/asean-ict-masterplan-2020-aim-2020/> accessed 16 July 2019.

110 Ibid pt. 8.1.1.

111 Candice Tran Dai and Miguel Alberto Gomez, 'Challenges and Opportunities for Cyber Norms in ASEAN' (2018) 3 Journal of Cyber Policy 217.

unlikely to adopt a non-binding resolution on end-to-end encryption,[112] let alone adopt a comprehensive treaty (geo- and cyber-political interests would not allow for one).[113]

A potential forum for discussion could be the UNCTAD,[114] the UN Conference on Trade and Development, since its ICT policy work includes data protection, e-commerce and development of the digital economy.[115] Another possible forum is the UNCITRAL, the UN Commission on International Trade Law. The UNCITRAL has adopted the Model Law on Electronic Signatures,[116] which inter alia lays down the rules on signature authenticity, including certificates. It does not, however, contain specific rules on cryptographic techniques or protocols, which are left to national legislation.[117]

However, in order for the UN to adopt a treaty, there must be enough consensus in the General Assembly to pass the vote. Could countries, which use the international forums as a battleground for asserting geopolitical and geostrategic interests, ever agree on issues such as backdoors, access to plaintext, key disclosure and key strength? In the words of Greenleaf – "the likelihood of a new UN treaty being developed from scratch are miniscule"[118]; or, according to Bygrave, there is "realistically, scant chance".[119]

The World Trade Organisation is another potential candidate to adopt a treaty including encryption requirements. One if its policy areas is e-commerce in the context of trade development[120]; however, its progress in legislating has been slow since the 1998 adoption of its ecommerce work programme. Moreover, as Bygrave has noted, any WTO legislation would have a commercial bias,[121] and thus regulate protection of personal data from a trade/competition point of view rather than a human rights one.

---

112 Grant Hodgson, 'Breaking Encryption and Gathering Data: International Law Applications' (2015) 20 Journal of Technology Law & Policy 39.

113 'Data Privacy Law: An International Perspective by Lee Andrew Bygrave' (2014) 25 King's Law Journal 497.

114 'UNCTAD | Home' <https://unctad.org/en/Pages/Home.aspx> accessed 4 July 2019.

115 For example, the UNCTAD has addressed authentication measures, security measures and encryption in Chapter One of its report on e-commerce development: United Nations Conference on Trade and Development, 'Building Confidence – Electronic Commerce and Development' (*UNCTAD*) <https://unctad.org/en/pages/PublicationArchive.aspx?publicationid=1532> accessed 4 July 2019.

116 'UNCITRAL Model Law on Electronic Signatures (2001)' (*United Nations Commission on International Trade Law*) <www.uncitral.org/uncitral/uncitral_texts/electronic_commerce/2001Model_signatures.html> accessed 4 July 2019.

117 Apollònia Martínez-Nadal and Josep Lluís Ferrer-Gomila, 'Comments to the UNCITRAL Model Law on Electronic Signatures' in Agnes Hui Chan and Virgil Gligor (eds), *Information Security* (Springer Berlin Heidelberg 2002); United Nations (ed), *UNCITRAL Model Law on Electronic Signatures: With Guide to Enactment 2001* (United Nations 2002).

118 Greenleaf, 'A World Data Privacy Treaty?' (n 5).

119 Lee Andrew Bygrave, 'Data Privacy Law: An International Perspective' (2014) 25 King's Law Journal 497.

120 'WTO | Electronic Commerce Gateway' (*World Trade Organization*) <https://www.wto.org/english/tratop_e/ecom_e/ecom_e.htm> accessed 4 July 2019.

121 Bygrave (n 119).

4.2. OPTION 2A – GLOBALISATION BY MEANS OF ACCESSION

As explored above, several regional data protection instruments provide for security requirements, which may specifically include encryption. To globalise an existing treaty or framework, non-regional actors would accede to the treaty according to its rules, thus extend its scope onto a larger scene. According to the Vienna Convention on the law of Treaties,[122] accession is only possible if the treaty implicitly or explicitly provides for it, or if the states signatories agree on it.[123]

The ECOWAS Act does not provide for non-member accession, nor does the APEC Privacy Framework. Unlike them, Convention 108+ allows non-member accession in its Article 27(1), which states that the Committee of Minister of the Council of Europe may invite any non-member state or an international organisation to accede to the Convention. Member states must agree to this accession. So far, only Uruguay has acceded to the treaty, whereas nine non-member states acceded to the 1981 Convention.[124] As already discussed above, the treaty does not explicitly provide for encryption, but it is recommended that data controllers adopt it. Therefore, globalisation of the Convention 108+ could be a viable option to ensure global encryption requirements, although it goes without saying that the economic powers of acceding non-members should be taken into account as well when assessing the Convention's globalisation success.

4.3. OPTION 2B – GLOBALISATION BY GDPR'S 'ADEQUATE PROTECTION' STANDARD

Under Chapter V of the GDPR, there are special rules for transferring personal data outside the EU.[125] There are three possible legal grounds to justify cross-border transfer:

1. transfer based on an adequacy decision,
2. transfer based on appropriate safeguards and
3. transfer based on exemptions for specific situations.

An adequacy decision is a decision by the European Commission that a non-EU country guarantees an adequate level of protection of personal data according to

122 Vienna Convention on the Law of Treaties (adopted on 23/5/1969, entered into force on 27/1/1980), UNTS 1155 (Vienna Convention).

123 SeeArticle 15 of the Vienna Convention.

124 'Chart of Signatures and Ratifications of Treaty 223' (*Council of Europe*) <https://www.coe.int/en/web/conventions/full-list/-/conventions/treaty/223> accessed 4 July 2019.

125 The GDPR applies also in Norway, Iceland and Liechtenstein, therefore personal data can be transferred to those countries without reference to Chapter V.

the criteria set down in Article 45 of the GDPR, such as the rule of law, respect for human rights and fundamental freedoms, legislation dealing with security, law enforcement access to data, personal data regulation etc., as well as their enforcement in practice, and possible international contractual obligations with regards to personal data protection. One of the criteria is also meeting the requirement of security and confidentiality measures.

As long as these criteria are met, then the personal data flow freely between the EU and the state whose level of protection has been deemed adequate. Currently, these are Andorra, Argentina, Canada (applies only to Canadian commercial organisations), Faroe Islands, Guernsey, Israel, Isle of Man, Japan, Jersey, New Zealand, Switzerland, Uruguay and the United States of America.,[126] [127]

Unlike the GDPR, the current proposal for the ePrivacy Regulation, which covers other data involved in a communication context that are not personal data, does not include a similar clause, thus restricting its scope to EU proper instead of globalising its standards.

Nevertheless, there are some possible drawbacks to globalising European standards (Europeanising?) through the Convention 108+ and the GDPR. As Greenleaf points out, there is a pro-European bias in the current enforcement system of the Convention 108+. There is no adjudication forum for non-European countries who accede to the treaty: while European countries, members of the Council of Europe, can be directly challenged in the European Court of Human Rights, the Court's jurisdiction does not extend to non-members regardless of their accession to the Convention 108+, therefore depriving local data subjects of effective remedies against violations of the Convention.[128] Another drawback are data localisation rules, such as data export restrictions in the GDPR's Chapter V. Such rules can bring high costs to outside actors seeking to enter the system and who are not yet compliant with it and may bring welfare losses to national economies.[129]

Moreover, what if a new (cryptographic or other) technology were to emerge; one that is better at promoting human rights than the current encryption requirements imposed by European instruments? Of course, if the security provisions are interpreted broadly enough, then the rules should be flexible

126 European Commission, 'Adequacy Decisions' (*European Commission*) <https://ec.europa.eu/info/law/law-topic/data-protection/international-dimension-data-protection/adequacy-decisions_en> accessed 4 July 2019.

127 After the invalidation of the Safe Harbour agreement, the US negotiated the Privacy Shield framework, in which participating companies are certified to comply with the criteria laid down by the Federal Trade Commission.

128 Greenleaf, 'A World Data Privacy Treaty?' (n 5).

129 Data localization rules have recently been implemented by inter alia EU, Brazil, China and India. See: Matthias Bauer and others, 'The Costs of Data Localisation: Friendly Fire on Economic Recovery' (2014) European Centre for International Political Economy <http://hdl.handle.net/10419/174726> accessed 19 July 2019.

enough to accommodate such new technologies; nevertheless, this is a question that can be better answered in the future by case law (especially decisions by the CJEU), further expert work and industry effort.

4.4. OPTION 3 – MAINTAIN THE STATUS QUO

Last but not the least, it may be business as usual for the foreseeable future. In this scenario, the legal frameworks will apply regionally or nationally as currently provided with or without reference to encryption. However, when governments change policies – especially when the government's geo-political weight is significant – the ripple effects emanating from their actions could be sizeable. For example, requiring a foreign company to disclose decryption keys to the law enforcement could lead to loss of consumer trust in confidential communication, and potentially to competitive advantages for domestic companies. Such ripple effects could be mitigated by informal talks and coordination between governments, or by assessing policy impact ahead of its adoption.[130]

5. CONCLUSION

This paper explored instruments, applicable to encryption in an international human rights legal framework, and given the absence of an international encryption treaty, discussed a potential imposition of a binding legal obligation on states to mandate the use of encryption.

First, the connection between encryption, privacy/data protection and human rights was explained. Encryption functions as a measure to prevent unauthorised parties from seeing the data in their plaintext form. It enables safe communications and data transactions. It holds a very important role in a global economy, where data are transferred between different countries with different levels of data protection. Moreover, thanks to these functions, encryption facilitates the exercise of human rights, such as freedom of expression and the right to privacy.

Then, applicable legal instruments were analysed. The elementary texts of human rights law, such as the Universal Declaration of Human Rights, the International Covenant on Civil and Political Rights, the European Convention on Human Rights, and the EU Charter of Fundamental Rights all provide for the right to privacy, including privacy of communications, with the EU Charter also explicitly providing for the right to personal data protection. None of those,

---

130 Ryan Budish, Herbert Burkert and Urs Gasser, 'Encryption Policy and Its International Impacts: A Framework for Understanding Extraterritorial Ripple Effects' Stanford University 28.

however, mentions explicitly the need for security – let alone encryption – measures.

More detailed rules on data protection were found in regional instruments. This chapter examined the EU framework (GDPR, ePrivacy Directive and the proposed Regulation), Convention 108 of the Council of Europe, the ECOWAS's Model Data Protection Act and the APEC Privacy Framework, as well as some upcoming legislative initiatives by other regional organisations. The EU legal framework specifically refers to encryption as a security or data masking measure, whereas the other instruments require data security measures in general.

Recommendations on encryption by the expert bodies argue for use of encryption in order to facilitate online commerce and data security. The OECD 1997 guidelines provide, however, for potential backdoors or plaintext access by law enforcement, which puts the strength of encryption in jeopardy.

Lastly, a global encryption obligation is discussed – a global treaty, possibly under the United Nations or World Trade Organisation, is unlikely. As an alternative, globalisation of the GDPR or of the Convention 108+ is proposed, although such globalisation does not come without drawbacks, such as bias. Should the states decide to maintain the status quo, further ripple effects of national encryption policies are to be expected.

ACKNOWLEDGEMENT

The research for this paper was carried out as part of a Horizon 2020 research and innovation programme funded by the European Commission under grant agreement No 780108 (FENTEC – Functional ENcryption TEChnologies).

BIBLIOGRAPHY

–, 'APEC Privacy Framework' (*Asia-Pacific Economic Cooperation*) <http://publications.apec.org/Publications/2005/12/APEC-Privacy-Framework> accessed 4 July 2019

–, 'ASEAN | ONE VISION ONE IDENTITY ONE COMMUNITY' (*ASEAN.org*) <https://asean.org/> accessed 16 July 2019

–, 'Asia-Pacific Economic Cooperation' <https://www.apec.org/> accessed 4 July 2019

–, 'Chart of Signatures and Ratifications of Treaty 223' (*Council of Europe*) <https://www.coe.int/en/web/conventions/full-list/-/conventions/treaty/223> accessed 4 July 2019

–, 'Crypto Law Survey – Page 2' <www.cryptolaw.org/cls2.htm> accessed 4 March 2019

–, 'Economic Community of West African States (ECOWAS)' <https://www.ecowas.int/> accessed 4 July 2019

–, 'The Encryption Tightrope: Balancing Americans' Security and Privacy | Committee Repository | U.S. House of Representatives' (*U.S. House of Representatives*, 1 March 2016) <https://docs.house.gov/Committee/Calendar/ByEvent.aspx?EventID=104573> accessed 4 July 2019

–, 'World Map of Encryption Laws and Policies | Global Partners Digital' <https://www.gp-digital.org/world-map-of-encryption/> accessed 2 July 2019

–, 'UNCTAD | Home' <https://unctad.org/en/Pages/Home.aspx> accessed 4 July 2019

–, 'UNCITRAL Model Law on Electronic Signatures (2001)' (*United Nations Commission on International Trade Law*) <www.uncitral.org/uncitral/uncitral_texts/electronic_commerce/2001Model_signatures.html> accessed 4 July 2019

Abelson H and others, 'The Risks of Key Recovery, Key Escrow, and Trusted Third-Party Encryption' (1997) 2 World Wide Web J. 241

Abelson H and others, 'Keys Under Doormats' (2015) 58 Commun. ACM 24

Aljifri H and Sánchez Navarro D, 'International Legal Aspects of Cryptography: Understanding Cryptography' (2003) 22 Computers & Security 196

Allen TA, 'Guideline for Using Cryptographic Standards in the Federal Government – Cryptographic Mechanisms: NIST Releases Draft NIST SP 800–175B Rev. 1' (*NIST*, 3 July 2019) <https://www.nist.gov/news-events/news/2019/07/guideline-using-cryptographic-standards-federal-government-cryptographic> accessed 16 July 2019

Amnesty International, 'Encryption: A Matter of Human Rights' (2016) <https://www.amnesty.nl/content/uploads/2016/03/160322_encryption_-_a_matter_of_human_rights_-_def.pdf?x68337> accessed 16 July 2019

Association of Southeast Asian Nations, 'ASEAN ICT Masterplan 2020 (AIM 2020) – ASEAN THAILAND 2019' (2015) <https://www.asean2019.go.th/en/infographic/asean-ict-masterplan-2020-aim-2020/> accessed 16 July 2019

Baker SA and Hurst PR, *The Limits of Trust : Cryptography, Governments, and Electronic Commerce* (Kluwer law international 1998)

Bauer M and others, 'The Costs of Data Localisation: Friendly Fire on Economic Recovery' (European Centre for International Political Economy 2014) <http://hdl.handle.net/10419/174726> accessed 19 July 2019

Blind K, 'The Impact of Standardization and Standards on Innovation' (Manchester Institute of Innovation Research 2013) 13/15 <www.innovation-policy.org.uk/compendium/section/Default.aspx?topicid=30> accessed 18 July 2019

Brown (ed.) G, *The Universal Declaration of Human Rights in the 21st Century* (Open Book Publishers 2016)

Budish R, Burkert H and Gasser U, 'Encryption Policy and Its International Impacts: A Framework for Understanding Extraterritorial Ripple Effects' Stanford University 28

Bygrave LA, 'Data Privacy Law: An International Perspective' (2014) 25 King's Law Journal 497

Computer Security Division, Information Technology Laboratory, 'Crypto Standards Development Process | CSRC' (*CSRC | NIST*, 24 May 2016) <https://csrc.nist.gov/Projects/Crypto-Standards-Development-Process> accessed 16 July 2019

Danezis G, Domingo-Ferrer J and Hansen M, 'Privacy and Data Protection by Design – from Policy to Engineering' (ENISA 2014) <https://www.enisa.europa.eu/publications/privacy-and-data-protection-by-design> accessed 7 June 2019

Deeks A, 'The International Legal Dynamics of Encryption' Stanford University 28

Drezner DW, 'Globalization, Harmonization, and Competition: The Different Pathways to Policy Convergence' (2005) 12 Journal of European Public Policy 841

Edwards I, 'GDPR the Security Angle' (2018) 60 ITNOW 42

ENISA and Europol, 'ENISA – Europol Issue Joint Statement' (*ENISA*, 23 May 2016) <https://www.enisa.europa.eu/news/enisa-news/enisa-europol-issue-joint-statement> accessed 4 July 2019

European Commission, 'Adequacy Decisions' (*European Commission*) <https://ec.europa.eu/info/law/law-topic/data-protection/international-dimension-data-protection/adequacy-decisions_en> accessed 4 July 2019

G7, 'Outcome Document. Combatting the use of the internet for terrorist and violent extremist content.' (*elysee.fr*) <https://www.elysee.fr/admin/upload/default/0001/04/287b5bb9a30155452ff7762a9131301284ff6417.pdf> accessed 4 July 2019

Gebauer M, 'Unification and Harmonization of Laws', *Max Planck Encyclopedia of Public International Law* (Oxford University Press 2009) <http://opil.ouplaw.com/view/10.1093/law:epil/9780199231690/law-9780199231690-e1123> accessed 4 June 2019

Google, 'Requests for User Information – Google Transparency Report' (*Google*) <https://transparencyreport.google.com/user-data/overview> accessed 4 July 2019

Greenleaf G, 'APEC's Privacy Framework Sets a New Low Standard for the Asia-Pacific' in Andrew T Kenyon and Megan Richardson (eds), *New Dimensions in Privacy Law* (Cambridge University Press 2006) <https://www.cambridge.org/core/product/identifier/CBO9780511494208A012/type/book_part> accessed 20 May 2019

Greenleaf G, 'A World Data Privacy Treaty? "Globalisation" and "Modernisation" of Council of Europe Convention 108', Emerging Challenges in Privacy Law: Comparative Perspectives (Cambridge University Press 2014)

Greenleaf G, 'The Influence of European Data Privacy Standards Outside Europe: Implications for Globalization of Convention 108' (2012) 2 International Data Privacy Law 68

Gürses S, Kundnani A and Van Hoboken J, 'Crypto and Empire: The Contradictions of Counter-Surveillance Advocacy' (2016) 38 Media, Culture & Society 576

Hales TC, 'The NSA Back Door to NIST' (2014) 61 Notices of the American Mathematical Society

Harding L, *The Snowden Files: The Inside Story of the World's Most Wanted Man* (Vintage Books 2014)

Hodgson G, 'Breaking Encryption and Gathering Data: International Law Applications' (2015) 20 Journal of Technology Law & Policy 39

Hurwitz JG, 'Encryption.Congress Mod (Apple + CALEA).(Communications Assistance for Law Enforcement Act of 1994)' (2017) 30 Harvard Journal of Law & Technology

Joinet L, 'Revised Version of the Guidelines for the Regulation of Computerized Personal Data Files' (United Nations Commission on Human Rights 1990) <http://digitallibrary.un.org/record/43365> accessed 17 July 2019

Jones ML, 'The Right to a Human in the Loop: Political Constructions of Computer Automation and Personhood' (2017) 47 Social Studies of Science 216

Kampouraki I, 'ENISA's Opinion Paper on Encryption' (2016) <https://www.enisa.europa.eu/publications/enisa-position-papers-and-opinions/enisas-opinion-paper-on-encryption> accessed June 7 2019

Kaye D, 'Report of the Special Rapporteur on the Promotion and Protection of the Right to Freedom of Opinion and Expression' (United Nations Human Rights Council 2015) A/HRC/29/32 <www.ohchr.org/EN/HRBodies/HRC/RegularSessions/Session29/Documents/A.HRC.29.32_AEV.doc> accessed 28 June 2019

Kerr OS and Schneier B, 'Encryption Workarounds' (2018) 106 Georgetown Law Journal

Kuwayama M, 'Pacific Alliance: A Latin American Version of"Open Regionalism"in Practice' [2019] IDEAS Working Paper Series from RePEc <http://search.proquest.com/docview/2188997245/> accessed 18 July 2019

Landau S, *Listening in: Cybersecurity in an Insecure Age* (Yale University press 2017)

Landau S and Diffie W, *Privacy on the Line* <https://mitpress.mit.edu/books/privacy-line> accessed March 5 2019

Lin HS, 'Cryptography and Public Policy' (1998) 25 Journal of Government Information 135

Lloyd S and Adams C, 'Key Management' in Henk CA van Tilborg and Sushil Jajodia (eds), *Encyclopedia of Cryptography and Security* (Springer US 2011) <https://doi.org/10.1007/978-1-4419-5906-5_85> accessed 6 June 2019

Martínez-Nadal A and Ferrer-Gomila JL, 'Comments to the UNCITRAL Model Law on Electronic Signatures' in Agnes Hui Chan and Virgil Gligor (eds), *Information Security* (Springer Berlin Heidelberg 2002)

Mason S, 'Digital Signatures', *Electronic Signatures in Law* (School of Advanced Study, University of London 2016)

Mercosur, 'Avanza la agenda digital en el Mercosur' (*MERCOSUR*, 27 June 2019) <https://www.mercosur.int/avanza-la-agenda-digital-en-el-mercosur/> accessed 15 July 2019

Mercosur, 'MERCOSUR Official Website' (*MERCOSUR*) <https://www.mercosur.int/en/> accessed 15 July 2019

Moody G, 'Nobody Saw This Coming: Now China Too Wants Company Encryption Keys And Backdoors In Hardware And Software' (*Techdirt.*, 29 January 2015) <https://www.techdirt.com/articles/20150129/06262129848/nobody-saw-this-coming-now-china-too-wants-company-encryption-keys-backdoors-hardware-software.shtml> accessed 4 July 2019

Olsen M, Schneier B and Zittrain J, 'Don't Panic: Making Progress on the "Going Dark" Debate' (The Berkman Centre for Internet & Society 2016)

Organisation for Economic Cooperation and Development, 'OECD Guidelines for Cryptography Policy - OECD' (*OECD.org*) <https://www.oecd.org/sti/ieconomy/guidelinesforcryptographypolicy.htm> accessed 4 July 2019

Orji UJ, 'Regionalizing Data Protection Law: A Discourse on the Status and Implementation of the ECOWAS Data Protection Act' (2017) 7 International Data Privacy Law 179

Rotenberg M, Schwartz PM and Solove DJ, *Information Privacy Law* (2nd ed., Aspen 2006)

Schneier B, 'Essays: Why We Encrypt' (*Schneier on Security*, June 2015) <https://www.schneier.com/essays/archives/2015/06/why_we_encrypt.html> accessed 17 July 2019

Schneier B, 'The Importance of Strong Encryption to Security' (*Schneier on Security*) <https://www.schneier.com/blog/archives/2016/02/the_importance_.html> accessed 27 March 2019

Schneier B, Seidel K and Vijayakumar S, 'A Worldwide Survey of Encryption Products' (Social Science Research Network 2016) SSRN Scholarly Paper <https://papers.ssrn.com/abstract=2731160> accessed 18 July 2019

Scholl M and others, 'An Introductory Resource Guide for Implementing the Health Insurance Portability and Accountability Act (HIPAA) Security Rule' (National institute of standards and technology 2008) <https://csrc.nist.gov/publications/detail/sp/800-66/rev-1/final> accessed 19 July 2019

Software Freedom Law Center India, 'FAQ: Legal Position of Encryption in India' (*SFLC.in*) <https://sflc.in/faq-legal-position-encryption-india> accessed 4 July 2019

Spindler G and Schmechel P, 'Personal Data and Encryption in the European General Data Protection Regulation' (2016) 7 Journal of Intellectual Property, Information Technology and Electronic Commerce Law [i]

Suominen K, 'Fueling Digital Trade in Mercosur: A Regulatory Roadmap' (Inter-American Development Bank 2018) <https://publications.iadb.org/handle/11319/9339> accessed 15 July 2019

Swire P and Ahmad K, 'Encryption and Globalization' (2011) 23 Columbia Science and Technology Law Review

Tran Dai C and Gomez MA, 'Challenges and Opportunities for Cyber Norms in ASEAN' (2018) 3 Journal of Cyber Policy 217

United Nations (ed), *UNCITRAL Model Law on Electronic Signatures: With Guide to Enactment 2001* (United Nations 2002)

United Nations Conference on Trade and Development, 'Building Confidence – Electronic Commerce and Development' (*UNCTAD, 2000*) <https://unctad.org/en/pages/PublicationArchive.aspx?publicationid=1532> accessed 4 July 2019

Van Alsenoy B, 'Regulating Data Protection : The Allocation of Responsibility and Risk among Actors Involved in Personal Data Processing' (Doctoral thesis, KU Leuven 2016)

Van Hoboken J and Schulz W, 'Human Rights and Encryption – UNESCO Digital Library' (2016) <https://unesdoc.unesco.org/ark:/48223/pf0000246527> accessed 31 January 2019.

Van Hoboken JVJ, 'Privacy and Security in the Cloud: Some Realism about Technical Solutions to Transnational Surveillance in the Post-Snowden Era Symposium: Who's Governing Privacy: Regulation and Protection in a Digital Era' (2013) 66 Maine Law Review 487

Voigt P and von dem Bussche A, 'Organisational Requirements' in Paul Voigt and Axel von dem Bussche (eds), *The EU General Data Protection Regulation (GDPR): A Practical Guide* (Springer International Publishing 2017) <https://doi.org/10.1007/978-3-319-57959-7_3> accessed 16 May 2019

Williams LC, 'Edward Snowden Says Encryption Is The Only Way To Counter Mass Surveillance' (*ThinkProgress*, 10 March 2014) <https://thinkprogress.org/edward-

snowden-says-encryption-is-the-only-way-to-counter-mass-surveillance-ee450433dca8/> accessed 4 July 2019

Wong JI, 'Here's How Often Apple, Google, and Others Handed over Data When the US Government Asked for It' (*Quartz*, 19 February 2016) <https://qz.com/620423/heres-how-often-apple-google-and-others-handed-over-data-when-the-us-government-asked-for-it/> accessed 4 July 2019

WTO, 'WTO | Electronic Commerce Gateway' (*World Trade Organization*) <https://www.wto.org/english/tratop_e/ecom_e/ecom_e.htm> accessed 4 July 2019

Zotos K and Litke A, 'Cryptography and Encryption' [2005] arXiv <http://arxiv.org/abs/math/0510057> accessed 4 March 2019

Zuiderveen Borgesius F J and Steenbruggen W, 'The Right to Communications Confidentiality in Europe: Protecting Privacy, Freedom of Expression, and Trust' (2019) 20 Theoretical Inquiries in Law 291.

CHAPTER 7
IDENTITY MANAGEMENT AND SECURITY

Jessica SCHROERS

1. INTRODUCTION

"Identity management (or IdM for short), consists of the processes and all underlying technologies for the creation, management, and usage of digital identities."[1]

The relation of identity management to security is two-fold, since identity (and access) management systems are a security measure, which can in principle be for physical security (e.g. access to specific areas upon authentication) as well as for cybersecurity (e.g. access to data bases). This security measure is only useful if the identity management system itself is secure, which needs to be ensured by different parties. As the focus of this chapter is on the user security requirements for online identity management systems, especially national public electronic identity schemes, the relevant area of security addressed in this chapter is cyber security.

This chapter introduces the reader to identity management and shows the different legal requirements the users, such as citizens using governmental electronic identification means, might have to comply with. The main research problem to be discussed is whether identity management users can and should be able to comply with these requirements. The research is based upon an analysis of literature, legislation of Belgium, Germany and Estonia, and various statements of terms and conditions of different electronic identification schemes to identify different types of obligations for users. However, this is not intended to be a positivist analysis of all possible requirements that exist, but to show that various requirements exist and to question the applicability of certain

---

1 Gergely Alpár, Jaap-Henk Hoepman and Johanneke Siljee, 'The Identity Crisis. Security, Privacy and Usability Issues in Identity Management' [2011] ArXiv <http://arxiv.org/abs/1101.0427> accessed 11 January 2018;

requirements for users, based upon the analysis of risk regulation regimes and cultures by Renaud et al.

The chapter is structured as follows. First, an explanation of basic concepts of identity management is given. In the second part examples of different identity management systems are provided and obligations on users will be analysed in the third part. Finally, based on the analysis of risk regulation regimes and cultures by Renaud et al., the concept of reasonable care and the possibility of security by design are taken into account as potential influential factors.

2. WHAT IS IDENTITY MANAGEMENT?

A main function of identity management systems is to make it possible to *authenticate* entities online, since on the internet no general system to authenticate entities exists.[2] Authentication is related to identification but nonetheless different. In simple terms, identification serves to identify a person, answering the question 'who are you?'. Authentication is to confirm the claim, i.e. verify that a specific person is indeed that specific person. Often a further difference is made between authentication (verifying that you are who you claim you are) and authorisation (verifying that you are permitted to do what you are trying to do).[3]

2.1. ATTRIBUTES

In order to identify a person, attributes are used. An attribute is a "distinct, measurable, physical or abstract named property belonging to an entity."[4] A person can have many attributes, such as nationality, date of birth, name, address or unique identification number. Some of these might be identifiers by themselves (e.g. a unique identification number), or several attributes may be

2 Entities can be persons but also computers, cars, Internet of Things (IoT) devices, etc., but for the purposes of this chapter, we will focus solely on the authentication of persons.

3 This difference will not be elaborated in this chapter; instead, authentication will be considered as a general prerequisite for authorisation. In the literature, the difference is also not always clearly indicated. As a short explanation: For example, a driver's license is at the same time an authentication token (authenticating the driver's license holder) and an authorisation token (authorizing the license holder to drive). Even though the holder of an authorisation token does not necessarily need to be identified (e.g. a ticket giving access to a festival authorises the holder of it to access the festival, while the holder can stay anonymous), it does authenticate the holder as somebody who may access the festival (verifying that this person is a person which is allowed on the festival).

4 European Commission, 'Modinis Study on Identity Management in EGovernment – Common Terminological Framework for Interoperable Electronic Identity Management' (2005) <https://ec.europa.eu/newsroom/dae/document.cfm?doc_id=2794> accessed 27 June 2019.

used together to form an identifier (e.g. name and date of birth and address). An identifier uniquely identifies a person *within a certain context*. For example, the Belgian unique identification number can be used to identify a person within the group of Belgian registered inhabitants. However, even within a certain context is the authenticity of a stated attribute or identifier not guaranteed, as it is not ensured that for example a person stating that a certain number is their unique identification number is indeed the person to whom that unique identification number refers to. Therefore, credentials are needed.

2.2. CREDENTIALS

An attribute in itself is often not very useful for authentication, as it needs to be verified that it is correct and indeed belongs to a certain user. This is generally done by using credentials, which can be defined as a "*piece of information attesting to the integrity of certain stated facts*".[5] Real life, non-digital, examples of credentials are for example passports or membership cards, which attest to the integrity of a certain stated attribute (e.g. nationality, membership, unique identification number). Quite often digital credentials are contained in so-called tokens, which can have the form of hardware (e.g. smartcards) or software.[6] Sometimes the term 'assertion' is preferred instead of the term credentials, since the use of the term credential is often misunderstood as a term for digital certificates in the public key infrastructure (PKI) environment, while assertion can take various forms.[7] Credentials can generally be categorised into three different types of authentication factors: 1) 'something you know': e.g. password, security question; 2) 'something you have': e.g. ID card, bankcard, phone; 3) 'something you are': e.g. fingerprint, pattern of the iris. Often multifactor authentication is used for extra security. In the case of 2F authentication, two factors such as for example possession of a smart card and knowledge of a PIN, or possession of a smartphone/SIM card and fingerprint can be used in order to authenticate a person.

2.3. PKI

As will also be shown further below, for identity management often Public Key Infrastructure (PKI) is used in case a high level of evidence and legal

---

5 Ibid.

6 Ibid.

7 European Commission and others, *Report on Feasibility Study on an Electronic Identification, Authentication and Signature Policy (IAS)* (Publications Office 2013) 9 <http://dx.publications.europa.eu/10.2759/25928> accessed 20 April 2016. The IAS study uses the term 'Identity Attribute Assertions' in order to avoid confusion.

certainty is required.[8] Therefore, it is useful to give a short basic introduction to asymmetric encryption and certificates (see also chapter 6). In case of asymmetric encryption, a key pair is used, consisting of a public and a private key. These keys are related in such a way that information which has been encrypted with one key can only be decrypted with the other key of the key pair. The private key is kept secret, while the public key can be disclosed to the public.[9] This technology is also used for digital signatures, where the signatory encrypts a hash of the information with the private key, while a certificate shows who the signatory and the corresponding public key is.[10] In case the information can be decrypted with the public key of the certificate, it is assumed that the signatory has digitally signed it and is therefore authenticated, since he/she should be the only one who has access to the private key. Within a PKI system, certificates are a common type of credential. The identity provider in this case is the Certification Service Provider, which identified the user/signatory and provided the certificate.[11]

2.4. IDENTITY MANAGEMENT SYSTEMS

Identity management systems include different parties. In most cases, these are at least the user, the identity provider and the relying party.[12] The identity provider establishes the identity of the user and provides the possibility for the user to authenticate themselves for the relying party, who then relies upon the information for different purposes, e.g. to give roles and authorisation to this user.

The simplest version of identity management systems consists of isolated/siloed solutions, where every relying party employs its own identity system: the relying party identifies the user and establishes credentials that are specific for their service (usually username and password). The relying party therefore acts essentially as their own identity provider, keeping the information about the user in a 'data silo'.[13]

---

8 United Nations, 'Promoting Confidence in Electronic Commerce: Legal Issues on International Use of Electronic Authentication and Signature Methods' (United Nations 2009) 71.

9 Marten Voulon, 'Digitalisering En Het Nederlands Burgerlijk Wetboek' (2018) 3 Tijdschrift voor Privaatrecht 969, 983.

10 Ibid 989.

11 Czesław Kościelny, Mirosław Kurkowski and Marian Srebrny, 'Public Key Infrastructure' in Czesław Kościelny, Mirosław Kurkowski and Marian Srebrny, *Modern Cryptography Primer* (Springer Berlin Heidelberg 2013) 176.

12 Alpár, Hoepman and Siljee (n 1) 2.

13 Ijlal Loutfi and Audun Jøsang, '1,2, Pause: Lets Start by Meaningfully Navigating the Current Online Authentication Solutions Space' in Christian Damsgaard Jensen and others (eds), *Trust Management IX* (Vol. 454, Springer International Publishing 2015).

Quite often the relying party does not have the resources or abilities to establish their own identity system, especially if the risk level requires a more thorough identity verification (e.g. in case of online tax declarations, access to health data). Additionally users are generally not in favour of an ever increasing amount of credentials such as passwords, which can be the result if every relying party they interact with has their own identity system.[14] To avoid that every party has to establish their own identity system, trusted third parties are used, to act as identity providers and provide the credentials for the authentication at the services of relying parties.

Alpár et al. make a difference between network-based identity management and claim-based identity management.[15] In network-based identity management, the relying party directly contacts the identity provider in order to verify the token of the user. Examples of this are OpenID, Liberty Alliance and Shibboleth.[16] In claim-based identity management the relying party does not contact the identity provider, but defines which user information it needs, which the user can then obtain from different identity providers (statements expressed and signed by the identity provider) by authenticating himself to the identity provider and then forwarding the claim to the relying party.[17] Examples of this are Idemix and U-Prove.[18]

At least three different phases can be identified in identity management: the configuration phase, the operation phase and the termination phase.[19] The configuration phase includes the step of registration by the user at the identity provider. In the operation phase, the user uses the authentication credentials in order to be authenticated for the relying party.[20] The relying party then needs to verify the credentials.[21] The security issues of these two phases are different. In the first phase the risk for the user is mainly that somebody else registers their identity, e.g. with personal data or stolen credentials of the user. To prevent this form of identity theft, taking better care of personal data is often advised.[22] However, as Whitson and Haggerty explain, much of the personal data is coming from leaks of companies, and therefore the number of actions a user can take is

14 Thomas J Smedinghoff, 'Solving the Legal Challenges of Trustworthy Online Identity' (2012) 28 Computer Law & Security Review 532.
15 Alpár, Hoepman and Siljee (n 1) 2.
16 Alpár, Hoepman and Siljee (n 1).
17 Ibid.
18 Ibid The IRMA system can also be named as an example of claims-based IdM.
19 Audun Jøsang, 'Assurance Requirements for Mutual User and Service Provider Authentication' in Joaquin Garcia-Alfaro and others (eds), *Data Privacy Management, Autonomous Spontaneous Security, and Security Assurance*, (Vol 8872, Springer International Publishing 2015) 27.
20 Ibid.
21 Ibid.
22 Jennifer R Whitson and Kevin D Haggerty, 'Identity Theft and the Care of the Virtual Self' (2008) 37 Economy and Society 572, 577.

limited.[23] Here it is worth considering whether a higher responsibility for identity providers or relying parties to verify information before registering users could be effective against identity theft. It should not be overlooked that in the operation phase, the problem sits mainly with stolen or cloned authentication credentials, such as passwords, PINs, smartcards or smartphones. The last phase is the termination phase, in which authorisations can be revoked and credentials and accounts deactivated.[24] Thanks to the activities in the termination phase, a former student, for example, cannot use the student credentials to access the university library anymore after graduation. In case of PKI systems, a certificate can be revoked. Certificate Revocation Lists (CRL) or Online Certificate Status Protocol (OCSP) are then often used to make it possible for another party to assess the status of a certificate.

2.5. LEVELS OF ASSURANCE (LOA)

LoAs "characterise the degree of confidence in electronic identification means in establishing the identity of a person, thus providing assurance that the person claiming a particular identity is in fact the person to which that identity was assigned".[25] LoAs are used as an indication of the degree of confidence in the system. Different definitions and systems of assurance levels exist, resulting from projects such as the STORK project, and different standardisation activities.[26] The eIDAS Regulation[27] is an EU Regulation which aims to provide a regulatory environment to enable secure and seamless electronic interactions between businesses, citizens and public authorities. Its two main parts focus on electronic identity and trust services. The part on electronic identity provides for the possibility of cross-border use and mutual recognition of existing electronic identity systems for access to online public services, if the electronic identity

23 Ibid 589.

24 Jøsang (n 19) 2.

25 Regulation (EU) No 910/2014 of the European Parliament and of the Council of 23 July 2014 on electronic identification and trust services for electronic transactions in the internal market and repealing Directive 1999/93/EC 2014 [2014] OJ L 257/73, recital 16 (eIDAS Regulation).

26 E.g. STORK Quality Authentication Assurance (QAA) model (Described in B. Hulsebosch, G. Lenzini, and H. Eertink, 'STORK D2.3 Quality authenticator scheme' (2009) <https://joinup.ec.europa.eu/sites/default/files/document/2014-12/STORK%20Deliverable%20D2.3%20-%20Quality%20authenticator%20scheme.pdf> accessed 17 July 2019); International Organisation for Standardization, 'ISO/IEC 29115:2013 – Information Technology – Security techniques – Entity authentication assurance framework' (2013) <https://www.iso.org/standard/45138.html> accessed 17 July 2019; International Telecommunication Union, 'Recommendation X.1254 (2012) Erratum 1' (2013) <https://www.itu.int/Rec/T-REC-X.1254-201305-I!Err1/en> accessed 17 July 2019.

27 Regulation (EU) No 910/2014 of the European Parliament and of the Council of 23 July 2014 on electronic identification and trust services for electronic transactions in the internal market and repealing Directive 1999/93/EC [2014] OJ L 257/73.

schemes have been notified to the Commission and fulfil certain requirements. Mainly based upon the results of the STORK project and on the ISO standard 29115,[28] the eIDAS Regulation defines three levels of LoA in Article 8 eIDAS Regulation. When Member States notify to the Commission their electronic identity schemes, which can be used to access their online public services, they must indicate the LoA of the notified scheme. Three levels are defined: low, substantial and high. LoA 'low' indicates identification means which only provide a limited degree of confidence, and the specifications, standards, procedures and controls have the purpose to decrease the risk of misuse or alteration of the identity.[29] 'Substantial' refers to identification means which provide a substantial degree of confidence, and the specifications, standards and procedures intend to decrease the risk of misuse or alteration of the identity substantially.[30] The LoA 'high' finally refers to identification means which provide a higher degree of confidence than identification means with the LoA 'substantial', and the purpose of the technical specifications, standard, procedures and technical controls is to prevent misuse or alteration of the identity.[31] The Commission issued an Implementing Regulation on assurance levels.[32] The Implementing Regulation sets specifications and procedures in its Annex for determining the three different levels. This is done by considering not only the reliability and quality of the enrolment but also the electronic identification means management and the authentication itself.[33] Furthermore, the general management and organisation of participants which provide a service related to electronic identification in a cross-border context, is considered in assessing the assurance level.[34]

3. EXAMPLES OF DIFFERENT SYSTEMS

This section will provide an overview of different electronic identification systems, describing examples for siloed identity management and solutions using passwords as authentication factor, as well as stronger public and private electronic identity solutions, often using PKI. In the next section, examples

28 Ibid recital 16.
29 eIDAS Regulation, Article 8 (2) (a).
30 eIDAS Regulation, Article 8 (2) (b).
31 eIDAS Regulation, Article 8 (2) (c).
32 Commission Implementing Regulation (EU) 2015/1502 of 8 September 2015 on setting out minimum technical specifications and procedures for assurance levels for electronic identification means pursuant to Article 8 (3) of Regulation (EU) No 910/2014 of the European Parliament and of the Council on electronic identification and trust services for electronic transactions in the internal market [2015] OJ L 235/7 (Commission Implementing Regulation (EU) 2015/1502).
33 Commission Implementing Regulation (EU) 2015/1502, Article 1 (2).
34 Commission Implementing Regulation (EU) 2015/1502, Article 1 (2).

of obligations for users, derived from applicable legislation and terms and conditions of the electronic identification systems presented here, will be shown.

The login at Amazon can be used as an example of normal password-based authentication. When registering for the first time at Amazon, the user is requested to fill in their e-mail address, name and a self-chosen password. Afterwards Amazon verifies that the e-mail address indeed exists by sending a code to the provided e-mail address, which then needs to be filled in at the website to finalise the registration. Afterwards the user can use the e-mail address and the password in order to authenticate at Amazon, and can add further information to the account.

'Login with Facebook' is the possibility to use an existing Facebook username and password to log in at other websites. Facebook is an example of a 'soft eID provider' as defined by Zarsky and Andrade, who make a difference between 'soft eID providers', identity providers for whom providing identity related services is not the core business, and 'hard eID providers', which are identity providers who focus on providing secure eID services.[35] Jøsang explains that social websites became 'de facto' federated identity providers, "although this was never the intention when these websites first started."[36] In 2008 Facebook Connect was introduced with the aim to "allow users to "connect" their Facebook identity, friends and privacy to any site."[37] Any website could integrate Facebook Connect.[38] In 2013, Facebook Connect was rebranded into Facebook Login during the announcement of an updated version of the service.[39] Currently, Facebook Login is one of the most used social logins.[40] It provides the possibility to log in on a multitude of services across different platforms with the Facebook credentials (username-password).

National governments issue identity cards to authenticate their citizens, and likewise many States also started to issue electronic identities in order to enable their citizens to authenticate themselves online, e.g. to use e-government services. For national solutions, different concepts and technologies are used. Quite often

35 Tal Z Zarsky and Norberto Nuno Gomes de Andrade, 'Regulating Electronic Identity Intermediaries: The Soft EID Conundrum' (2013) 74 Ohio St. LJ 1335.

36 Audun Jøsang, 'Identity Management and Trusted Interaction in Internet and Mobile Computing' (2014) 8 IET Information Security 67, 73.

37 Dave Morin, 'Announcing Facebook Connect' (*Facebook for Developers*, 5 September 2008) <https://developers.facebook.com/blog/post/2008/05/09/announcing-facebook-connect/> accessed 17 June 2019.

38 'Facebook Expands Its Social Platform across the Web Through General Availability of Facebook Connect | Facebook Newsroom' (12 April 2008) <https://newsroom.fb.com/news/2008/12/facebook-expands-its-social-platform-across-the-web-through-general-availability-of-facebook-connect/> accessed 17 June 2019.

39 Facebook, 'Updates to Facebook Login | Facebook Newsroom' (22 August 2013) <https://newsroom.fb.com/news/2013/08/updates-to-facebook-login/> accessed 17 June 2019.

40 2nd quarter 2016: Facebook has a share of 53,1%, Google+ 44,8% and Twitter, LinkedIn and others around 1% or below – Statista Research Department, 'Preferred Global Social Login ID 2016 | Statistic' <https://www.statista.com/statistics/459601/preferred-social-login-id-global/> accessed 12 August 2019.

digital signatures/PKI play an important role. The solutions described below have been notified under the eIDAS Regulation, and are (with exception of the Belgian 'itsme', which is currently in the pre-notification stage) considered to be sufficiently secure for cross-border e-government authentication.[41]

In Belgium different types of governmental electronic identities exist, which all have a high LoA: on the one hand the official governmental electronic identities such as the 'elektronische identiteitskaart' (eID), Kids-ID and 'elektronische vreemdelingenkaart', and on the other hand private solutions which can also be used to access e-government services, such as 'itsme'. The Belgian eID card has different functions, including (digital) identification and the creation of (authentication) signatures. The card's chip contains five X.509v3 certificates.[42] Two of these certificates are tied to the cardholder. These two certificates are the authentication certificate which enables the cardholders to authenticate themselves online and the electronic signature certificate which can be used to produce qualified electronic signatures. Only the authentication and electronic signature certificate contain an additional field (SerialNumber), where the national unique identification number of the cardholder is included.[43] A Belgian non-governmental solution is 'itsme', provided by Belgian Mobile iD (a consortium of Belgian banks and mobile network operators).[44] The solution works with an app on a smartphone, and requires a sign up with the use of a Belgian eID and a Belgian SIM card.[45] 'Itsme' can also be used to access Belgian e-government services and has been prenotified under eIDAS.[46]

Estonia has six types of official solutions, which all have a high LoA: Three smart cards which are also physical identification documents: ID card, RP card[47] and diplomatic identity card, and three other solutions: Digi-ID, Mobiil-ID/Smart-ID,[48] and e-Residency Digi-ID (transnational electronic

41 eIDAS Regulation, Article 6 and 7; for an overview of notified eID schemes see: https://ec.europa.eu/cefdigital/wiki/display/EIDCOMMUNITY/Overview+of+pre-notified+and+notified+eID+schemes+under+eIDAS.

42 Danny De Cock and others, 'The Belgian EID Approach' in Walter Fumy and Manfred Paeschke (eds), *Handbook of eID Security. Concepts, Practical Experiences, Technologies* (Publicis Publishing 2011) 124.

43 Ibid 125.

44 Itsme, 'Questions & Answers' <https://www.itsme.be/en/faq> accessed 15 July 2019.

45 Ibid.

46 See M. Eichholtzer, 'Overview of pre-notified and notified eID schemes under eIDAS' (8 May 2019) <https://ec.europa.eu/cefdigital/wiki/display/EIDCOMMUNITY/Belgium+-+Itsme> accessed on 14 June 2019. Prenotification on 18.4.2019. Notification under eIDAS allows that identification means can also be used to authenticate to e-government services in other Member States, but requires the notifying Member State to assume a certain responsibility for the notified eID scheme.

47 Residence Permit card.

48 Mobile phone ID based on a special Mobile-ID SIM card and a mobile application for those who do not have a SIM card in their device, 'e-identity – mobile-id' <https://e-estonia.com/solutions/e-identity/mobile-id> accessed 15 July 2019.

identity).[49] All solutions are PKI-based with the private key on a secure module of the chip.[50] At least two X.509 certificates are included: one for authentication (for electronic identification, encryption and digital signing of e-mails) and a digital signature certificate for creating electronic signatures.[51] The certificates contain only the user's name (first name and last name) and Personal Identification Code (PIC), the authentication certificate additionally stores the user's unique e-mail address (the governmental e-mail address).[52] The electronic signature certificate is considered qualified, which means that the user can use the certificate to make qualified electronic signatures, which are considered to have the equivalent legal effect of a handwritten signature.[53] The authentication certificate has deliberately not that label for concerns of legal certainty, since, even though the technology is the same, the authentication certificate is not supposed to be used for signing and therefore in principle won't have the same legal effect.[54] Except for the mobile solution, all solutions use smart cards as tokens. In case of the Mobiil ID, a SIM card with Mobiil-ID readiness needs to be obtained under a contractual agreement from Estonian mobile operators.[55]

In Germany the nPA (neuer Personalausweis) is the governmental digital identity with a high LoA.[56] If the user has the nPA function on the identity card activated, it can be used to authenticate for online public services as well as private services. The user has to approve the transmission of data to the relying party.[57] Furthermore, the principle of data minimisation is central, therefore, the relying parties need to obtain a certificate to be able to request data, whereby they may only request data which has been approved as necessary for them.[58] For example if the information is required that a user is over 18, the relying party will not receive the birthdate but a binary yes/no answer based upon the birthdate.[59]

---

49 Republic of Estonia, 'Notification Form for Electronic Identity Scheme under Article 9 (5) of Regulation (EU) No. 910/2014' (2018) <https://ec.europa.eu/cefdigital/wiki/download/attachments/62885749/Estonian%20eID%20notification%20form%20for%20electronic%20identity%20scheme%20under%20article%209%20of%20eIDAS%20Regulation.pdf?version=1&modificationDate=1531759817709&api=v2> accessed 15 July 2019.

50 Ibid 3.

51 Ronald Leenes and others, 'D2.2 – Report on Legal Interoperability' (2009) STORK project Deliverable D2.2 66.

52 Ibid.

53 eIDAS Regulation, Article 25 (2).

54 Ronald Leenes and others (n 51) 68.

55 Republic of Estonia (n 49) 3.

56 Federal Office for Information Security, 'German EID Based on Extended Access Control v2 – Overview of the German EID System, Version1.0' (2017) 4.

57 Jens Bender and others, 'Privacy-Friendly Revocation Management without Unique Chip Identifiers for the German National ID Card' (2010) 2010 Computer Fraud & Security 14, 14.

58 Federal Office for Information Security (n 56) 7, 9.

59 Bender and others (n 57) 15.

4. SECURITY OBLIGATIONS FOR USERS

In order to be secure, all participants need to comply with certain requirements.[60] The security requirements are often to be found across different sources such as applicable legislation, standards, terms and conditions, etc. Provisions for users are often detailed in legislation and/or terms and conditions. The level of detail of the provisions varies considerably. Nevertheless, certain common requirements have been identified in an analysis of three different legislations (Belgium, Germany and Estonia) and three terms and conditions, which give examples of different sources of obligations from a small variety of electronic identification schemes, including public and private systems.[61]

4.1. EXCLUSIVE CONTROL

One of the main requirements imposed on users by identity providers (via terms and conditions) or the government (via legislation) is to keep the means of electronic identification under exclusive control. The exact requirements differ from one legal system to another and from one terms and conditions to another. For example, Belgian law simply requires to "take all necessary measures to keep the electronic identification means under his exclusive control",[62] while the German legislation requires specifically that the user must take reasonable measures so that no other person gains knowledge of the Personal Identification Number (PIN).[63] It is mentioned in particular that the PIN may not be noted down on the identity card or be otherwise stored with it.[64] If the user is aware that the PIN number has been disclosed to third parties, they should immediately change it or have the electronic proof of identity function blocked.[65]

---

60 See for example on data protection requirements an analysis of the requirements for controllers and processors, also in the IdM area Brendan Van Alsenoy, '*Data protection in the EU: roles, responsibilities and liability*' (Cambridge: Intersentia, 2019).

61 Belgian Law of 19 July 2017 on electronic identification (Belgisch Staatsblad, 'Wet inzake elektronische identificatie, B.S. 9 August 2017, p. 78183' (18 July 2017)), German Act on Identity Cards and Electronic Identification (Personalausweisgesetz vom 18. Juni 2009 (BGBl. I S. 1346), das zuletzt durch Artikel 3 des Gesetzes vom 21. Juni 2019 (BGBl. I S. 846) geändert worden ist), Estonian Identity Documents Act (Riigi Teataja, 'Identity Documents Act' (RT I 1999, 25, 365)); terms and conditions from Belgian itsme, Estonian SK, Amazon.com and Amazon.de.

62 Belgisch Staatsblad, 'Wet inzake elektronische identificatie, B.S. 9 August 2017, p. 78183' (18 July 2017) Article 11.

63 Bundesgesetzblatt, ‚Personalausweisgesetz vom 18. Juni 2009 (BGBl. I S. 1346), das zuletzt durch Artikel 3 des Gesetzes vom 21. Juni 2019 (BGBl. I S. 846) geändert worden ist , §27 (2) (PAuswG).

64 Ibid.

65 Ibid.

The terms and conditions of the Estonian SK simply provide that the user has to ensure that the private key is used under their control,[66] while the terms and conditions of the Belgian 'itsme' specifies[67]:

- the 'itsme' code must be kept secret: the code should never be written down, not even in coded form; it must be discreetly entered in the app and the user should always ensure that the 'itsme' code cannot be seen;
- a secure code must be chosen (e.g. not part of a date of birth, telephone number, postcode etc.), and immediately changed if the suspicion arises that somebody else knows the code. The terms and conditions further specify to use strong passwords and that a strong password is comprised of upper- and lowercase text as well as (a) number(s) and (a) symbol(s).

The terms and conditions specify that failure to adhere to the above mentioned requirements are considered gross negligent conduct. The failure to choose an appropriately secure 'itsme' code or failure to take the necessary precautionary measures to safeguard the 'itsme' code and/or the device on which the 'itsme' app is installed would for instance qualify as gross negligence. But also recording of the 'itsme' code in a readable form on the device or on an object or document that the user keeps or carries together with the device, or disclosure of the 'itsme' code to a third party is specified within the terms and conditions as gross negligent conduct.

Furthermore, the 'itsme' terms and conditions state that the device (smartphone) should never be left unsupervised, no third party (including spouse/partner, family members or friends) may be authorised to use the device. In case the fingerprint is registered for use of the 'itsme' app, it needs to be ensured that no other fingerprints are registered on the device.

The Amazon terms and conditions are much less detailed, and simply state, in the version from Amazon.com, that "*You are responsible for maintaining the confidentiality of your account and password and for restricting access to your account, and you agree to accept responsibility for all activities that occur under your account or password*".[68] The German version is a little more extensive, explaining additionally that the user should take all relevant measures to ensure that the password stays secret and is stored in a secure way.[69]

---

66 SK ID Solutions, 'Terms and Conditions for Use of Certificates for ID-1 Format Identity Documents of the Republic of Estonia' <https://www.id.ee/public/SK-TCU-ESTEID2018-EN-20190117.pdf> accessed 27 June 2019 para 5.2.7.

67 Itsme, 'Terms & Conditions of the itsme® app' (30 March 2018). <https://www.itsme.be/en/legal/app-terms-and-conditions> accessed 27 June 2019.

68 Amazon, 'Conditions of Use' (21 May 2018) <https://www.amazon.com/gp/help/customer/display.html/ref=ap_register_notification_condition_of_use?ie=UTF8&nodeId=508088> accessed 28 May 2019.

69 Amazon, 'Amazon.de Allgemeine Geschäftsbedingungen' (11 July 2018) <https://www.amazon.de/gp/help/customer/display.html/ref=ap_register_notification_condition_of_use?ie=UTF8&nodeId=505048> accessed 28 May 2019.

4.2. NOTIFICATION OBLIGATION

Another very important obligation that can be found in almost all analysed sources is the obligation to notify in case of loss: Belgian law provides that the user should prevent theft, loss or distribution of the electronic identification means (though it's not further specified how), and to have them immediately withdrawn in the event of theft, loss or dispersal.[70] The German §27 PAuswG[71] also obliges the user to inform the ID card authority immediately in case of a loss of the card, while the Estonian §14 of the Identity Documents Act specifies that the government authority should be informed within 24 hours if the documents becomes unusable, are lost or destroyed. The 24 hour limit is also found in the terms and conditions of the Belgian 'itsme', which require to inform the police of the loss or the theft of the Device within 24 hours of becoming aware of it, while requiring immediate notification in case of awareness of loss or theft of the device or the risk of fraudulent use (a failure to report is considered to be gross negligence). The Estonian terms and conditions also require to immediately notify the Police and Boarder Guard in case of loss, theft or inoperability. If there is a possibility of unauthorised use of the private key the certificate with the related public key must be immediately suspended by calling a number provided in the terms and conditions. Another possibility is to submit a signed application at the Police and Border Guard Customer Service Point, which is also the only way to revoke a certificate. The users are obliged to do this if they have the suspicion that the electronic identification means have gone out of their control. In case of Amazon, only the German version includes an obligation to inform Amazon in case there is reason to worry that a third party got knowledge of the password, or when it might be possible that the password is used in an unauthorised way.[72]

4.3. NO LONGER USING ELECTRONIC IDENTIFICATION MEANS IN CASE OF WITHDRAWAL/REVOCATION

This requirement applies after the termination phase. The obligation not to use the electronic means in case the electronic identification means have expired or revoked is only found in the analysed set in the Belgian legislation and the Estonian legislation and terms and conditions. Belgium requires that "in case the electronic means of identification expires or is withdrawn, the holder may

70 Belgisch Staatsblad, 'Wet inzake elektronische identificatie, B.S. 9 August 2017, p. 78183' (18 July 2017) 78183' (n 62).

71 Bundesgesetzblatt, ‚Personalausweisgesetz vom 18. Juni 2009 (BGBl. I S. 1346), das zuletzt durch Artikel 3 des Gesetzes vom 21. Juni 2019 (BGBl. I S. 846) geändert worden ist (PAuswG).

72 Amazon, 'Amazon.de Allgemeine Geschäftsbedingungen' (n 69) para 7 Ihr Konto.

no longer use the electronic means of identification knowingly after the expiry date or after the withdrawal"[73] and Estonia requires generally that the user return the document promptly in case it is revoked[74] while the Estonian terms and conditions focus again on the use of the private key, which may no longer be used after the user has been informed that their certificate has been revoked or that the issuing CA has been compromised.[75]

4.4. SECURE ENVIRONMENT

The Belgian and Estonian legislation and the Amazon terms and conditions do not include provisions on ensuring a secure environment for the use of the electronic identification means, while the other analysed documents did have various requirements for this. For example the German legislation provides that the user must ensure "by means of technical and organisational measures that the nPA is only used in an environment which, according to the respective state of the art, can be considered secure. They should in particular use such technical systems and components that are assessed by the Federal Office for Security in Information Technology as safe for this purpose."[76]

The Estonian terms and conditions focus on the private keys and specify that the user should use their private keys and certificates solely on a secure cryptographic device handed over to them at Customer Service Point of the Police and Border Guard[77] and use their private keys solely for creating Qualified Electronic Signatures. The Belgian 'itsme' terms and conditions are far more explicit, requiring that the user should take all reasonable measures to ensure that the 'itsme' app is used in accordance with the security rules on correct internet conduct and secured equipment and, to the extent applicable, secured (WIFI) networks. Specific recommendations in the 'itsme' terms and conditions are to:

- use antivirus software and a firewall;
- keep the operating systems and software up to date;
- never download pirated or cracked software;
- not use jailbroken or rooted Devices;

---

73 'Wet inzake elektronische identificatie, B.S. 9 august 2017, p. 78183' (n 62).

74 Riigi Teataja, 'Identity Documents Act' (RT I 1999, 25, 365) <https://www.riigiteataja.ee/en/eli/504112013003/consolide> accessed 27 June 2019) para 14.

75 SK ID Solutions, 'Terms and Conditions for Use of Certificates for ID-1 Format Identity Documents of the Republic of Estonia' <https://www.id.ee/public/SK-TCU-ESTEID2018-EN-20190117.pdf> accessed 27 June 2019 (n 66) para 5.2.6.

76 PAuswG, §27 (3).

77 SK ID Solutions, 'Terms and Conditions for Use of Certificates for ID-1 Format Identity Documents of the Republic of Estonia' <https://www.id.ee/public/SK-TCU-ESTEID2018-EN-20190117.pdf> accessed 27 June 2019 (n 66) para 5.2.4.

- not click on popup windows or hyperlinks that tell you that the device is infected with a virus;
- be careful with incoming email attachments;
- be aware of what kind of information you share on social media sites.

5. CAN AND SHOULD USERS BE RESPONSIBLE?

The previous analysis of the legislation and terms and conditions but also general literature shows that users are considered to be responsible for certain online security aspects. For example Whitson and Haggerty analysed the responses of different Canadian and North American institutions to identity theft, and found that "many of the recommended risk avoidance measures involve forms of responsibilization, a process of encouraging individuals to become more centrally involved in managing the risks they face".[78] The most dominant one is "a form of individualised responsibility to take steps to reduce a person's risk of victimisation."[79] They conclude that in the context of identity theft, "institutionally promoted methods for the *care for the virtual self* transcend what is reasonably practicable for most citizens and mask the role played by major institutions in fostering the preconditions for identity theft".[80]

Though not specifically talking about identity management, the process of responsibilization of the user for their online security has been heavily criticised by Renaud et al.[81] They analyse cyber security risk from the vantage point of different government risk cultures (individualist, hierarchist and egalitarian), based on Hood et al.[82] Pivotal to their view are the questions whether the community or the individual is affected, and whether expertise is required to manage the risk. In individualist risk cultures, the responsibility to manage risk is assigned to the individual citizen, who is normally also the only one who bears the consequences.[83] In an egalitarian culture, the risks can impact the community and in response, the government provides structures which the community can use. The differentiating factor from the hierarchist risk culture is that it requires no special knowledge to use these structures (e.g. public transportation).[84] Finally, in a hierarchist risk culture, which affects

78 Whitson and Haggerty (n 22) 576.
79 Ibid.
80 Ibid 572.
81 Karen Renaud and others, 'Is the Responsibilization of the Cyber Security Risk Reasonable and Judicious?' (2018) 78 Computers & Security 198.
82 Christopher Hood, Henry Rothstein and Robert Baldwin, The Government Of Risk (Oxford University Press 2001).
83 Renaud and others (n 81) 202.
84 Ibid 203.

the community and requires expert knowledge, whole-society solutions are developed, "informed by expert forecasting and management".[85]

In their analysis, Renaud et al. argue that currently cyber security risk for normal users is most often approached by an individualist risk regime, which means that full responsibility is placed upon users to manage cyber security risks.[86] Considering that expert knowledge is needed to gauge this risk and that it can have a community-impacting effect, they advocate a shift to a hierarchist risk regulation regime, which requires that whole-society solutions are developed.[87] They propose that the responsibility for cyber security should be "shared between the individual and the state, with the individual being required to take certain simple preventive measures and the state taking care of the rest."[88] The question is then which obligations can be considered simple preventive measures that can be taken care of by the user, and which ones should be better addressed by the government. Renaud et al. consider the responsibility of the user mainly in prevention and deterrence, whereby the user should be given a list of preventive measures to take, with easy instructions and help-centres to support them.[89] Governments, on the other hand, have broader responsibilities and "ought to act on three fronts: (1) standard setting to prevent and ease management, (2) information gathering by encouraging reposting of cybercrime and establishing skilled cybercrime units to provide advice and help citizens to manage such risks; and (3) behavioural modification by applying sanctions to those who do not follow preventative advice or adhere to standards."[90]

Can this also be applied to identity management? Renaud et al. consider two dimensions that indicate a hierarchist culture should be established: 1) specialised expertise is required to manage the risk; and 2) the community is impacted by the risk.[91] It is possible to argue that in case of identity management failures the community is at risk, because for example an identity theft does not only affect the 'identity owner' but also everybody else who relies upon the stolen identity (relying party) which would generally undermine trust in electronic identification. Also, specialised expertise is often required, since identity management systems are often complicated and the user is often not able to see or understand what exactly is happening. Therefore, a more hierarchist approach to risk in this area could be useful.

---

85 Ibid 202–203.

86 Ibid 202–204 Renaud et al focus in their analysis on normal computer users/average citizens as victims of cyber attacks. The result of the analysis might look different when considering for example the protection of critical infrastructure.

87 Ibid 202–205.

88 Ibid 207.

89 Ibid 208.

90 Ibid.

91 Ibid 204.

6. SOME ASPECTS TO TAKE INTO ACCOUNT

The aspect of expert knowledge as specified by Renaud et al deserves further attention. When looking at the obligations identified earlier on for users in different identity management systems, it becomes clear that some obligations are easier to comply with than others are, and therefore not all obligations require expert knowledge. Two obligations are to refrain from using the electronic identification means after they have been declared unusable and to notify in case they might not be secure. No expert knowledge is required for a user to not use the electronic identification means after they have been declared unusable (often it is simply automatically not possible anymore), and, under the assumption that an uncomplicated notification point is available, to notify in case the user becomes aware that the identification means are not secure anymore.

The other obligations are to keep the electronic identification means secure and to only use them in a secure environment. To keep the identification means secure has been found in all analysed legislation and terms and conditions with the exception of the Estonian Identity Documents Act, while the requirement to use a secure environment is only found in the terms and conditions of 'itsme' and the Estonian identity documents, and the German Act on Identity Cards and Electronic Identification. These requirements can be considered to require expert knowledge, taking into account that even big companies and national States, who have budget and expertise for IT security are not always able to keep their systems secure – although they might also face higher skilled adversaries. Assigning the obligation to do exactly this to the user could be considered keeping the user responsible for more than they can fulfil. In this case, in line with the analysis of Renaud et al, the hierarchist approach to risk could be relevant and require the government to intervene.

Nevertheless, also in this case some reservations can be made. One consideration is that it depends whether the obligation phrased in the legislation or terms and conditions is an obligation of means (obligation to make reasonable efforts to do something)[92] or an obligation of result. Obligations of result such as in the Belgian legislation to "take all necessary measures"[93] or the Estonian terms and conditions to "ensure that Subscriber's Private Key is used under its control"[94] are less likely to be possible to be fulfilled by the user as they require expert knowledge, than obligations of means such as the German obligation to take reasonable measures so that no other person gains knowledge of the PIN.[95] Also in the UNCITRAL Model Law on electronic signatures, for example, the

---

92 See on this also Brendan Van Alsenoy (n 60) 84 with regard to data protection obligations.

93 'Wet inzake elektronische identificatie, B.S. 9 august 2017, p. 78183' (n 62) Article 11.

94 'Terms and Conditions for Use of Certificates for ID-1 Format Identity Documents of the Republic of Estonia' (n 66) para 5.2.7.

95 PAuswG §27 (2).

obligations of the signatory are phrased as obligations of means (to exercise reasonable care, to use reasonable efforts).[96]

Some responsibility has to remain with the user, since even the most secure system could still be undermined by the user, e.g. if the user gives the authentication means to another party. The question is which level of responsibility is reasonable. A useful consideration for future research could be the relevant standard of care of a user in tort law. The standard of care which is required in tort law is often the standard of 'reasonable care'.[97] In civil law jurisdictions, the concept of reasonable care is often referred to as the *bonus pater familias* standard.[98] The *bonus pater familias* is a model of an average person, "not exceptionally gifted, careful or developed, neither underdeveloped nor someone who recklessly takes chances or who has no prudence".[99] For some countries the concept can be adapted to the personal circumstances or time and place ('reasonable surgeon', 'careful barkeeper') and for specialists generally a higher 'due care' is evaluated according to their above average capacities.

Another consideration with regard to a hierarchist approach with governmental involvement is that this approach could be seen as paternalistic, as the government may be tempted to exactly prescribe which equipment the user should use in what manner. Moreover, if it would become very burdensome to use the electronic identification means, the user might decide not to use them, barring themselves from using the advantages of, for instance, e-government services, or, to feel motivated to use less secure but more user-friendly solutions, if available.

In this regard, it is interesting to consider the problem of usability vs security, not only for identity management but also for security in general. The problem is that "when technology interferes with desired activities, users devise shortcuts, often undermining security in the process".[100] Users are often unwilling to invest much time or money in security improvements.[101] Especially since identity management is normally not the primary goal, but something to facilitate another task.[102] Users must, for instance, manage an increasing number of identifiers, leading to an effect often called 'password fatigue' where the user, as a consequence, often chooses the same passwords and usernames again and again for different services.[103]

---

96 United Nations (ed), *UNCITRAL Model Law on Electronic Signatures: With Guide to Enactment 2001* (United Nations 2002) Article 8.

97 United Nations (n 8) 83.

98 Ibid.

99 Pierre Widmer, *Unification of Tort Law: Fault* (Kluwer 2015); Pierre Widmer, *Unification of Tort Law: Fault* (Kluwer 2015).

100 R Dhamija and L Dusseault, 'The Seven Flaws of Identity Management: Usability and Security Challenges' (2008) 6 IEEE Security Privacy 24, 25.

101 Ibid; Robert LaRose, Nora J Rifon and Richard Enbody, 'Promoting Personal Responsibility for Internet Safety' (2008) 51 Communications of the ACM 71, 73.

102 R Dhamija and L Dusseault (n 100) 24.

103 R Dhamija and L Dusseault (n 100) 25.

LaRose explains that "users perform a mental calculus of the rewards and costs associated with both safe and unsafe behaviour. The advantages of safe behaviour are not always self-evident and there are negative outcomes (the cons) associated with safe behaviour. [...] The negatives must be countered so that fearful users don't invoke them as rationalisations for doing nothing."[104] Users are able and willing to use slightly more complex interfaces, if there is a perceived value for dealing with them.[105] This also means that users might often be willing to use more complicated systems in order to access something they perceive as more valuable or important (e.g. online banking, health information), while the security of access to systems deemed less important might be thwarted by unsafe behaviour.

Usability and security by design could be solutions. Dhamija states that identity management scheme designers should take into account the cognitive scalability of the users, looking not only at their own identity management system, but also at the whole system of different identity management systems the user has to interact with.[106] In this regard, the earlier mentioned Levels of Assurance can also be a factor that could be taken into account. Gutmann and Grigg explain that security comes with certain costs in terms of usability, but the problem is that it is often considered as merely a second thought.[107] They state that the primary goal of security efforts should be to make the existing security technology usable for normal people.[108] The easiest solution would be that the user is not required to be actively involved in security arrangements.[109] This could be an interesting angle for governmental intervention, requiring security by design (more information on security by design can be found in chapter 10) for usable identity management systems. Security by design could also play a role in the assessment of reasonable care, since if usable secure solutions exist which do not require expert knowledge, it is more reasonable to expect an average person to use them.

7. CONCLUSION

This chapter introduced the reader to identity management. It showed different requirements a user has to comply with. Based upon the analysis of risk regulation regimes and cultures by Renaud et al. and taking into account

---

104 Robert LaRose, Nora J Rifon and Richard Enbody, 'Promoting Personal Responsibility for Internet Safety' (2008) 51 Communications of the ACM 71, 73.

105 P Gutmann and I Grigg, 'Security Usability' (2005) 3 IEEE Security and Privacy Magazine 56, 57.

106 Dhamija and Dusseault (n 100) 25.

107 Gutmann and Grigg (n 105) 56.

108 Ibid.

109 Steven Furnell, 'The Usability of Security – Revisited' (2016) 2016 Computer Fraud & Security 5, 10.

the concept of reasonable care and the possibility of security by design, the contention that identity management users can and should be able to comply with these requirements was challenged. It has been concluded that also in identity management a more hierarchist approach could be useful in order not to over-responsibilize the user, since the level of expertise required to address the risks is rather high, and the community, not only the individual, can be affected by the risks involved. From the analysis of Renaud et al., it does not become clear which obligations exactly can be assigned to the user and which should be better addressed to other parties or the government. A look at the standard of care in tort law was taken. The standard of care is generally interpreted in terms of the standard of reasonable care, the care an average person would take. Further research into the care an average person should take with regard to the electronic identification means and the environment they use it in, is therefore necessary. The analysis, in particular of the discussion on usability and security and the upcoming 'security by design' principle, already showed that the way in which systems are developed might influence the standard of care as the care might be easier achieved and better guaranteed if it is easier to fulfil the requirements involved due to simple security systems.

BIBLIOGRAPHY

Alpár G, Hoepman J-H and Siljee J, 'The Identity Crisis. Security, Privacy and Usability Issues in Identity Management' [2011] arXiv <http://arxiv.org/abs/1101.0427> accessed 11 January 2018

Amazon, 'Amazon.Com Conditions of Use' (21 May 2018) <https://www.amazon.com/gp/help/customer/display.html/ref=ap_register_notification_condition_of_use?ie=UTF8&nodeId=508088> accessed 28 May 2019

Amazon, 'Amazon.de Allgemeine Geschäftsbedingungen' (11 July 2018) <https://www.amazon.de/gp/help/customer/display.html/ref=ap_register_notification_condition_of_use?ie=UTF8&nodeId=505048> accessed 28 May 2019

Bender J and others, 'Privacy-Friendly Revocation Management without Unique Chip Identifiers for the German National ID Card' (2010) 2010 Computer Fraud & Security 14

De Cock D and others, 'The Belgian EID Approach' in Walter Fumy and Manfred Paeschke (eds), *Handbook of eID Security. Concepts, Practical Experiences, Technologies* (Publicis Publishing 2011)

Dhamija R and Dusseault L, 'The Seven Flaws of Identity Management: Usability and Security Challenges' (2008) 6 IEEE Security Privacy 24

European Commission, 'Modinis Study on Identity Management in EGovernment – Common Terminological Framework for Interoperable Electronic Identity Management' (2005) <https://ec.europa.eu/newsroom/dae/document.cfm?doc_id=2794> accessed 27 June 2019

European Commission and others, *Feasibility Study on an Electronic Identification, Authentication and Signature Policy (IAS) Final Report* (Publications Office 2013) <http://dx.publications.europa.eu/10.2759/25928> accessed 20 April 2016

Facebook, 'Facebook Expands Its Social Platform across the Web Through General Availability of Facebook Connect | Facebook Newsroom' (12 April 2008) <https://newsroom.fb.com/news/2008/12/facebook-expands-its-social-platform-across-the-web-through-general-availability-of-facebook-connect/> accessed 17 June 2019

Facebook, 'Updates to Facebook Login | Facebook Newsroom' (22 August 2013) <https://newsroom.fb.com/news/2013/08/updates-to-facebook-login/> accessed 17 June 2019

Furnell S, 'The Usability of Security – Revisited' (2016) 2016 Computer Fraud & Security 5

German Federal Office for Information Security, 'German EID Based on Extended Access Control v2 – Overview of the German EID System, Version1.0' (2017) < https://ec.europa.eu/cefdigital/wiki/download/attachments/48762401/2017_02_20_German%20eID_01_Whitepaper_final.pdf?version=1&modificationDate=1499172188962&api=v2> accessed 18 July 2019

Gutmann P and Grigg I, 'Security Usability' (2005) 3 IEEE Security and Privacy Magazine 56

Itsme, 'Terms & Conditions of the itsme® app' (30 March 2018) < https://www.itsme.be/en/legal/app-terms-and-conditions> accessed 27 June 2019

Jøsang A, 'Assurance Requirements for Mutual User and Service Provider Authentication' in Joaquin Garcia-Alfaro and others (eds), *Data Privacy Management, Autonomous Spontaneous Security, and Security Assurance* (Vol 8872, Springer International Publishing 2015)

Jøsang A, 'Identity Management and Trusted Interaction in Internet and Mobile Computing' (2014) 8 IET Information Security 67

Kościelny C, Kurkowski M and Srebrny M, 'Public Key Infrastructure' in Czesław Kościelny, Mirosław Kurkowski and Marian Srebrny, *Modern Cryptography Primer* (Springer Berlin Heidelberg 2013) <http://link.springer.com/10.1007/978-3-642-41386-5_7> accessed 5 September 2018

LaRose R, Rifon NJ and Enbody R, 'Promoting Personal Responsibility for Internet Safety' (2008) 51 Communications of the ACM 71

Leenes R and others, 'D2.2 – Report on Legal Interoperability' (2009) STORK Project Deliverable D2.2

Loutfi I and Jøsang A, '1,2, Pause: Lets Start by Meaningfully Navigating the Current Online Authentication Solutions Space' in Christian Damsgaard Jensen and others (eds), *Trust Management IX* (Vol 454, Springer International Publishing 2015) <http://link.springer.com/10.1007/978-3-319-18491-3_12> accessed 13 September 2018

Morin D, 'Announcing Facebook Connect' (*Facebook for Developers*, 5 September 2008) <https://developers.facebook.com/blog/post/2008/05/09/announcing-facebook-connect/> accessed 17 June 2019

Renaud K and others, 'Is the Responsibilization of the Cyber Security Risk Reasonable and Judicious?' (2018) 78 Computers & Security 198

Republic of Estonia, 'Notification Form for Electronic Identity Scheme under Article 9 (5) of Regulation (EU) No. 910/2014' (2018)

Smedinghoff TJ, 'Solving the Legal Challenges of Trustworthy Online Identity' (2012) 28 Computer Law & Security Review 532

SK ID Solutions, 'Terms and Conditions for Use of Certificates for ID-1 Format Identity Documents of the Republic of Estonia' <https://www.id.ee/public/SK-TCU-ESTEID2018-EN-20190117.pdf> accessed 27 June 2019

Smedinghoff TJ, 'Solving the Legal Challenges of Trustworthy Online Identity' (2012) 28 Computer Law & Security Review 532

Statista Research Department, 'Preferred Global Social Login ID 2016 | Statistic' <https://www.statista.com/statistics/459601/preferred-social-login-id-global/> accessed 24 September 2018

United Nations, 'Promoting Confidence in Electronic Commerce: Legal Issues on International Use of Electronic Authentication and Signature Methods' (United Nations 2009) <http://www.uncitral.org/pdf/english/texts/electcom/08-55698_Ebook.pdf> accessed 18 July 2019

United Nations (ed), *UNCITRAL Model Law on Electronic Signatures: With Guide to Enactment 2001* (United Nations 2002)

Van Alsenoy B, *'Data protection in the EU: roles, responsibilities and liability'* (Cambridge: Intersentia, 2019)

Voulon M, 'Digitalisering En Het Nederlands Burgerlijk Wetboek' (2018) 3 Tijdschrift voor Privaatrecht 969

Whitson JR and Haggerty KD, 'Identity Theft and the Care of the Virtual Self' (2008) 37 Economy and Society 572

Widmer P, *Unification of Tort Law: Fault* (Kluwer 2015)

Zarsky TZ and Andrade NNG de, 'Regulating Electronic Identity Intermediaries: The Soft EID Conundrum' (2013) 74 Ohio St. LJ 1335

CHAPTER 8

TOWARDS AN OBLIGATION TO SECURE CONNECTED AND AUTOMATED VEHICLES "BY DESIGN"?

Charlotte Ducuing

1. INTRODUCTION

Driving automation is expected to result in a drop of road fatalities "since human error is estimated to play a role in 94 per cent of accidents".[1] Increased connectivity of vehicles and of the road transport environment is also strongly grounded in the expectation that it will enhance road safety. It is additionally regarded as a prerequisite for automated or autonomous vehicles to drive safely.[2] On the other hand, increased connectivity of vehicles results in cybersecurity sensitivity and increasing risks.[3] The developments of driving autonomy can therein be viewed as an additional layer of sensitivity: "the more a car is capable of doing itself, the larger the potential for damage is if the control of the car is taken over by malicious minds".[4] Generally, digitization is expected to "change the nature of risk" and especially of road "safety-related

---

1 Commission, 'On the road to automated mobility: An EU strategy for mobility of the future' (Communication 'On the road to automated mobility') COM(2018) 283 final, 1.

2 Dorothy J Glancy, 'Sharing the Road: Smart Transportation Infrastructure Symposium: Smart Law for Smart Cities: Regulation, Technology, and the Future of Cities' (2013) 41 Fordham Urban Law Journal 1617, 1664; Olivia Tambou, 'Le Point de Vue Européen sur la Libre Circulation des Voitures Connectées' (2019) in La Libre Circulation des Automobilistes en Europe, 193–212. This is especially so with regard to cooperative intelligent transport systems (C-ITS), see section 2.1 below.

3 This is recognized by the European Commission, 'A European strategy on Cooperative Intelligent Transport Systems, a milestone towards cooperative, connected and automated mobility' (Communication) COM(2016) 766 final, 7: "As the transport system becomes more and more digitized, it may also become more vulnerable to hacking and cyber-attacks".

4 Maurice Schellekens, 'Car Hacking: Navigating the Regulatory Landscape' (2016) 32 Computer Law & Security Review 307, 309. For a similar view, see Stig Ole Johnsen and others, *Risk Based Regulation and Certification of Autonomous Transport Systems* (2018) 1794–1795.

risks".[5] In other words, the emergence of CAM implies, to some extent, a shift of safety risks to cybersecurity sensitivity.

This book chapter focusses on 'CAM vehicles', namely on road vehicles in the context of "connected and automated mobility", after the Communication from the European Commission 'On the road to automated mobility'.[6] Although the Communication does not lay down a definition of CAM (vehicles), the following features are covered. First, the vehicle grows in connectivity, and especially *vis-à-vis* its environment. Second, the vehicle is increasingly automated and even autonomous ("driverless vehicle"). These features are further clarified in the first section.

For the purpose of this book chapter, cybersecurity is defined broadly, following the definition of the International Telecommunication Union (ITU) as "the collection of tools, policies, security concepts, security safeguards, guidelines, risk management approaches, actions, training, best practices, assurance and technologies that can be used to protect the cyber environment and organization and user's assets. Organization and user's assets include connected computing devices, personnel, infrastructure, applications, services, telecommunications systems, and the totality of transmitted and/or stored information in the cyber environment. Cybersecurity strives to ensure the attainment and maintenance of the security properties of the organization and user's assets against relevant security risks in the cyber environment. The general security objectives comprise the following: availability, integrity, which may include authenticity and non-repudiation, and confidentiality".[7]

The European Union ("EU") is very active in the field of CAM, and especially with regard to cybersecurity viewed as a prerequisite to CAM deployment. In its Communication 'Europe on the Move', the European Commission was generally confident that "much of the necessary legal framework is already in place in the EU"[8] especially hinting at the recent overhaul of vehicle type-approval framework. Before being placed on the market, road vehicles have to be (type-) approved by competent authorities, the responsibility to get this certification lying with the manufacturer. Both the type-approval certification procedure and the substantive vehicle technical regulations covered by this certification (e.g. safety requirements) are harmonized at EU level. The Commission hereby praises the recent introduction in EU type-approval legislation of "market surveillance

5 Vitor Sousa and I. Meireles, Risk management prospects with the digitization of road infrastructures (2018) Network Industries Quarterly Vol 20 number 4.

6 Communication 'On the road to automated mobility' 1.

7 International Telecommunication Union (ITU), Series X: Data networks, Open System Communications and Security – Telecommunication security – Overview of cybersecurity, International Telecommunication Union (2008) Point 3.2.5 "cybersecurity". Confidentiality, integrity and availability objectives are generally referred to as the "CIA triad" in the field of information security.

8 Commission, 'Europe on the Move – Sustainable Mobility for Europe: safe, connected and clean' (2018) COM(2018) 293 final, 6.

rules [which would] ensure that a genuine EU internal market is in place for vehicle, including for driverless vehicles".[9] While reckoning that there is yet "no sector specific approach on the protection of the vehicles against cyberattacks",[10] the Commission proposed to include cybersecurity requirements as part of the on-going revision of type-approval safety regulation.[11] The report of the Committee of the European Parliament on the Internal Market and on Consumer Protection ("IMCO Committee") on the proposal[12] further wishes to ensure that security is "ensured from cradle to grave and addressed *by design* for security of a connected vehicle, making it technically very difficult and economically unattractive to tamper with it, be it physically or remotely over-the-air" (emphasis added).[13] At international level, the United Nations Economic Commission for Europe ('UNECE'), in charge of developing harmonized vehicle technical regulation, is simultaneously striving to set up new vehicle technical regulations dealing with cybersecurity risks of CAM vehicles, and recently issued two proposals for recommendations, respectively on cybersecurity and software update management.

The purpose of this book chapter is to legally evaluate whether, as asserted by the European Commission and the IMCO Committee respectively, type-approval legislation, including already market surveillance and in the future cybersecurity and software update requirements, can ensure cybersecurity of CAM vehicles. Type-approval legislation is based on vehicle technical regulation, with the "by design" approach at its heart. Is this regulatory instrument appropriate and sufficient for that purpose? EU type-approval legislation is based on vehicle technical regulations developed by the UNECE. Against this background, the book chapter analyses the two proposals for recommendations recently issued by the UNECE on respectively cybersecurity and software update management of vehicles. The proposals are interesting for two reasons. Firstly, they reflect the *de facto* changing nature of CAM vehicles as opposed to traditional ones. Secondly, they constitute a concrete illustration of how

---

9 Ibid 6.

10 European Commission (n 6) 12.

11 Commission, 'Proposal for a Regulation of the European Parliament and of the Council on type-approval requirements for motor vehicles and their trailers, and systems, components and separate technical units intended for such vehicles, as regards their general safety and the protection of vehicle occupants and vulnerable road users, amending Regulation (EU) 2018/858, and repealing Regulations (EC) 78/2009, 79/2009 and 661/2009' 2018/0145 (COD).

12 Report on the proposal for a regulation of the European Parliament and of the Council on type-approval requirements for motor vehicles and their trailers, and systems, components and separate technical units intended for such vehicles, as regards their general safety and the protection of vehicle occupants and vulnerable road users, amending Regulation (EU) 2018/... and repealing Regulations (EC) No 78/2009, (EC) No 79/2009 and (EC) No 661/2009 (COM(2018)0286 – C8-0194/2018 – 2018/0145(COD)) Committee on the Internal Market and Consumer Protection Rapporteur: Róża Gräfin von Thun und Hohenstein.

13 Justification laid down by the report, ibid. 12, for the introduction of a new Rec 18b.

vehicle technical regulations and type-approval legislation could be designed to accommodate cybersecurity.

The second section (2) introduces the technological developments at stake with CAM vehicles. Then, the third section (3) outlines the EU and international (UNECE) legislative framework on vehicle type-approval. In this context, the fourth section (4) analyses the two recent proposed recommendations issued by the UNECE regarding cybersecurity of CAM vehicles. Against this background, the fifth section (5) evaluates whether and to what extent type-approval legislation as a regulatory instrument is fit for the purpose of ensuring cybersecurity of CAM vehicles. The sixth section (6) points to further implications that the analysis conducted in the book chapter may have beyond the field of cybersecurity regulation and finally, the seventh and last section (7) concludes the analysis.

2. TECHNOLOGICAL DEVELOPMENTS IN CAM

CAM vehicles were characterized as including both features of external connectivity on the one hand and automation – and even autonomy – on the other hand. These technical features will be now presented in turn.

2.1. INCREASED CONNECTIVITY OF VEHICLES

Many cars are already "connected devices"[14] to some extent. According to ENISA, existing connectivity in road vehicles includes: (a) "telematics", such as "in the context of fleet management or geo-fencing", but also for eco-driving, insurance ("pay-as-you-drive" models) or driving assistance and remote diagnosis; (b) "connected infotainment" in the sense of added value services "such as the access to an application store", which can include access to driving information; and (c) "intra-vehicular communication, where the infotainment connections can be shared with user devices".[15] In that sense, the connectivity of vehicles already covers both driving capabilities – even safety-critical features – and user's experience features (driving comfort or info/entertainment).[16] Intra-

---

14 Commission, 'A European strategy on Cooperative Intelligent Transport Systems, a milestone towards cooperative, connected and automated mobility' COM(2016) 766 final, 1.

15 ENISA, 'Cyber Security and Resilience of smart cars – Good practices and recommendations' December 2016, 13 <https://www.enisa.europa.eu/publications/cyber-security-and-resilience-of-smart-cars> accessed 05 July 2019.

16 Ibid. Similar finding is made in the US where communications in and from/to connected cars were recently described as covering, in the current state: "powertrain (e.g., engine, transmission, drive-shaft) and chassis control (including steering, brakes, airbag, windshield wipers), as well as infotainment systems (e.g., navigation, telephone, entertainment) and

vehicle communications shall be distinguished from external communications, where the latter obviously poses more severe cybersecurity risks than the former. Connectivity is mostly provided by devices embedded in the vehicles (the computerized "Electronic Control Units" or ECUs) or by (the driver's) cell phone.[17] External communications of the vehicles consist mostly, until now, in *bilateral* communications from and to the vehicle and pre-defined entities,[18] such as the manufacturer but also other actors in the automotive value chain (e.g. aftermarket suppliers for the purpose of remote diagnosis, remote maintenance) or insurance companies. While most of communications are provided on a commercial basis, the EU imposed on new vehicles the deployment of the eCall based on the 112 service for safety purposes, as from March 2018.[19] The eCall consists of a post-crash call which is automatically triggered by the vehicle – it can also be triggered manually – to the harmonized 112 emergency number with the location data of the vehicle, in case of serious road accident.

The vehicles are also expected to experience new forms of external communications,[20] referred to as "V2V", V2I" and "V2X" or alternatively as "C-ITS", based on which vehicles send and receive messages to non-predetermined entities. V2V refers to "Vehicle to Vehicle" communications, "V2I" to "Vehicle to Infrastructure" communications – such as "traffic signals, roadside and horizontal infrastructure"[21] – and "V2X" to "Vehicle to Everything", including communications to and from other road users (e.g. pedestrians).[22] The emphasis is hereby placed *on the entities with which vehicles communicate*. The expression "C-ITS" rather places the emphasis *on the means by which* communications are performed, namely "cooperatively". The 'Article 29 Working Party' defined C-ITS as "a peer-to-peer solution for the exchange of data between vehicles and other road infrastructure facilities [...] without the intervention of a network operator. [...] [P]eers can directly inform each other about their own status (elaborating data gathered by sensors with which

telematics (e.g., crash reporting and emergency warning)", in Roland L Trope and Thomas J Smedinghoff, 'Why Smart Car Safety Depends on Cybersecurity' (2018) 14 Scitech Lawyer 8.

17 ENISA (n 15).

18 Commission Delegated Regulation (EU) .../... of 13.3.2019 supplementing Directive 2010/40/EU of the European Parliament and of the Council with regard to the deployment and operational use of cooperative intelligent transport systems, C(2019) 1789 final, Rec 2 (Proposed C-ITS Regulation).

19 Regulation (EU) 2015/758 of the European Parliament and of the Council of 29 April 2015 concerning type-approval requirements for the deployment of the eCall in-vehicle system based on the 112 service and amending Directive 2007/46/EC (2015) OJ L 123, 77.

20 V2X / C-ITS communications are not broadly deployed in the EU but are already being tested in the territory of various Member States, see Proposed C-ITS Regulation, 3–4.

21 European Parliament resolution of 13 March 2018 on a European strategy on Cooperative Intelligent Transport Systems (2017/2067(INI)), 4.

22 While the "V2..." phrase focusses on vehicles, the Proposed C-ITS Regulation (see 9) also mentions communications between infrastructure assets (Infrastructure to Infrastructure communications, or "I2I"), see 1.

they are equipped), receiving in return similar information, and thus allowing the creation of an overview (for each peer) of the status of the environment surrounding the vehicle or infrastructural facility".[23] For instance, the messages can include "hazardous location notifications" such as "emergency vehicle approaching" sent by a vehicle to neighbouring vehicles,[24] or "traffic information and smart routing".[25] Such communications are expected to benefit road safety but also "traffic efficiency"[26] and "comfort of driving".[27]

2.2. DRIVING AUTOMATION, TOWARDS VEHICLE AUTONOMY

While they obviously overlap to such a point that they are sometimes confused,[28] driving *automation* shall be distinguished from vehicle *autonomy*.[29] An *automated* vehicle "can replace the driver for some or all of the driving tasks".[30] While an automated vehicle could thus be *pre-determined*, qualification as *autonomous* implies a certain level of *operational decision-making*. Concretely, an autonomous system "rel[ies] […] solely on its on-board equipment to collect information, *take decisions and inform tasks*" (emphasis added) without direct intervention of a human driver.[31] An autonomous vehicle "develop[s] and maintain[s] its internal structure and functioning through mechanisms like self-organization, evolution adaptation and learning".[32] For operational decision-

23 Opinion 03/2017 Processing personal data in the context of Cooperative Intelligent Transport Systems (C-ITS) [2017] WP 252, 3.

24 Day 1 C-ITS service, as listed in the Communication of the Commission […], a European strategy on Cooperative Intelligent Transport Systems, a milestone towards cooperative, connected and automated mobility, 6.

25 Day 1.5 C-ITS service, ibid.

26 Explanatory Memorandum of the Proposed C-ITS Regulation, 2.

27 Communication of the Commission, A European strategy on Cooperative Intelligent Transport Systems, 3.

28 See the "Proposal for the Future Certification of Automated / Autonomous Driving Systems, submitted by the experts from International Organization of Motor Vehicle Manufacturers, United Nations Economic and Social Council (UNECE), ECE/TRANS/WP.29/GRVA/2019/13. "Autonomy" is sometimes substituted by "fully automated" (as opposed to mere "automated"), see in Federal Public Service Mobility and Transport, Autonomous vehicles – Code of Practice for testing in Belgium, 2016 (Code of Practice for testing in Belgium). The document is available here: <https://mobilit.belgium.be/sites/default/files/resources/files/code_of_practice_en_2016_09.pdf> accessed 8th July 2019).

29 Johnsen and others (n 4) 1791–1792.

30 DG GROW, GEAR 2030 – High Level Group on the Competitiveness and Sustainable Growth of the Automotive Industry in the European Union, final Report (2017), 41.

31 Roberta Frisoni and others, 'Research for TRAN Committee – Self-Piloted Cars: The Future of Road Transport?' (European Union, 2016) 19 http://www.europarl.europa.eu/RegData/etudes/STUD/2016/573434/IPOL_STU(2016)573434_EN.pdf.

32 ENISA, 'Towards a framework for policy development in cybersecurity Security and privacy considerations in autonomous Agents' (14 March 2019) <https://www.enisa.europa.eu/

making to be delegated to the – thereby – *autonomous* vehicle "in the face of uncertainty",[33] artificial intelligence ('AI') is required.[34] There is yet no common agreement on definitions[35] but expressions such as "driverless cars", "self-piloted cars"[36] or "self-driving cars"[37] are broadly used. By emphasizing the absence of a driver, they appear to refer to vehicles being both automated *and* autonomous.

Automated driving assistance is already broadly used as of today, however fully automated *and autonomous* vehicles are not (yet) available on the market. They are being tested and contemplated for deployment in the medium term.[38] Until then, we are experiencing intermediary to high levels of automation and autonomy of vehicles, where a human driver is, however, ultimately responsible for taking over the control at a certain point.[39]

Against this background, *autonomous* driving appears to be based on the *connected* character of the vehicle. The "task of monitoring the driving environment" indeed "shifts completely from the human driver" to what Knieps

publications/considerations-in-autonomous-agents/at_download/fullReport> accessed 08 July 2019, 8.

33 Hazel Si Min Lim and Araz Taeihagh, 'Autonomous Vehicles for Smart and Sustainable Cities: An In-Depth Exploration of Privacy and Cybersecurity Implications' (2018) 11 Energies 1062, 4. See also Araz Taeihagh and Hazel Si Min Lim, 'Governing Autonomous Vehicles: Emerging Responses for Safety, Liability, Privacy, Cybersecurity, and Industry Risks' (2019) 39 Transport Reviews 103, 105.

34 The legal scholarship therein discusses how to adapt the applicable legal framework according to the behaviors of autonomous systems, and especially in the field of autonomous vehicles with regard to traffic law, see Henry Prakken, 'On the Problem of Making Autonomous Vehicles Conform to Traffic Law' (2017) 25 Artificial Intelligence and Law 341, 1–3.

35 Frisoni and others (n 30).

36 Ibid.

37 *Inter alia*, Nynke E Vellinga, 'From the Testing to the Deployment of Self-Driving Cars: Legal Challenges to Policymakers on the Road Ahead' (2017) 33 Computer Law & Security Review 847. It should be noticed that "autonomous driving" does not necessarily imply full automation: this is the situation of "partial delegation" of driving decision-making to the autonomous vehicle. On this, see Jérémy and Alain Bensoussan, Les voitures intelligentes (2015), in Larcier (ed) *Droit des Robots*, 81–89. The authors distinguish autonomous vehicles (in French "voiture autonome") from self-driving vehicles (in French "voiture indépendante"), while the later would be entirely delegated driving decision-making and no further human intervention would be needed.

38 For a different opinion, see Günter Knieps, 'Internet of Things, Big Data and the Economics of Networked Vehicles' (2019) 43 Telecommunications Policy 171, 173. While the author broadly uses the expressions "automated" or "driverless vehicles", he opposes the use of the expression "autonomous vehicle", based on the consideration that "even fully automated (driverless) cars will typically be obliged to *follow rules* based on the requirements of networked vehicles implemented by networked automated vehicle operators" (emphasis added). Similar position is held in Jack Stilgoe, 'Machine Learning, Social Learning and the Governance of Self-Driving Cars' (2018) 48 Social Studies of Science 25, 25.

39 Levels 3 and 4 of driving automation, pursuant to the International Society of Automotive Engineers (SAE international) SAE Standard J3016, which is broadly referred to with regard to the levels of automation, see for instance in DG GROW, GEAR 2030 – High Level Group on the Competitiveness and Sustainable Growth of the Automotive Industry in the European Union, final Report (2017), 41, or in Frisoni and others (n 30).

calls "the networked vehicle sensor systems".[40] More generally, "the environment in which the software agent operates" should be considered as making part of the "AI system".[41] Additionally, the expected (economic) benefits[42] of autonomous vehicles to "increase[e] road capacity, improve[e] traffic flow, and reduc[e] congestion" require a "manage[ment] and distribut[ion of] data on the go", based on V2X communications.[43] ENISA hereby refers to "connected self-driving car systems", where connected and autonomous features of vehicles will be brought together. ENISA especially notes that "connected self-driving car systems may upload their data to the cloud and share their data that will be then used to train the systems of other vehicles".[44] Truck platooning is often cited as a case in point, but cooperative connectivity is more generally expected to "add collective intelligence and action to automation, thus improving the overall efficiency of transport flows"[45] in the longer term.[46] This alignment of both (cooperative) connectivity and automation is reflected in the expression "Connected, cooperative and automated mobility" (CCAM).

3. OVERVIEW OF VEHICLE TECHNICAL REGULATIONS AND TYPE-APPROVAL LEGISLATION

3.1. EU TYPE-APPROVAL PROCESS LEGISLATION IN A NUTSHELL

EU legislation provides for "harmonized rules and principles for the type-approval of motor vehicles".[47] Both content and process of (type-)approval are

---

40 Knieps (n 38) 172. See also Jean-Paul Skeete, 'Level 5 Autonomy: The New Face of Disruption in Road Transport' (2018) 134 Technological Forecasting and Social Change 22, Introduction; Madeline Roe, 'Who's Driving That Car?: An Analysis of Regulatory and Potential Liability Frameworks for Driverless Cars' (2019) 60 Boston College Law Review 317, 324.

41 ENISA (n 32).

42 For a study of the "risks and unintended consequences" of autonomous vehicles, see Taeihagh and Lim (n 32) 106; Dimitris Milakis, Bart van Arem and Bert van Wee, 'Policy and Society Related Implications of Automated Driving: A Review of Literature and Directions for Future Research' (2017) 21 Journal of Intelligent Transportation Systems 324.

43 Lim and Taeihagh (n 32) 5.

44 ENISA (n 32).

45 DG GROW, GEAR 2030 – High Level Group on the Competitiveness and Sustainable Growth of the Automotive Industry in the European Union, final Report (2017), 45. See also among others Knieps (n 38) 171.

46 Commission, 'A European strategy on Cooperative Intelligent Transport Systems, a milestone towards cooperative, connected and automated mobility' COM (2016) 766 3.

47 Regulation (EU) 2018/858 on the approval and market surveillance of motor vehicles and their trailers, and of systems, components and separate technical units intended for such vehicles, amending Regulations (EC) No 715/2007 and (EC) 595/2009 and repealing Directive 2007/46/EC [2018] OJ L 151/1 (Type-Approval Regulation), Rec 7.

harmonized at EU level, while the implementation and enforcement activities remain to a great extent national competence. Type-approval is "the procedure whereby an approval authority certifies that a type of vehicle, system, component or separate technical unit satisfies the relevant administrative provisions and technical requirements".[48] Neither the vehicles nor their systems, components and separate technical units shall indeed be allowed to be placed on the market without prior acquisition of (type-)approval by the manufacturer.[49] The manufacturer, as product aggregator, is indeed responsible for conformity of the production with the substantive technical requirements attached to the type-approval. Successful type-approval results in the granting of a certification,[50] which includes an "information package" describing the functionalities of the *type* of vehicle or component.[51] The vehicle manufacturer is responsible for ensuring that *individual* vehicles are produced "in conformity with the type-approval requirements" for which the type-approval certificate was granted, which he certifies by "issuing a certificate of conformity for every vehicle".[52] Individual vehicles having a valid certificate of conformity are permitted to be made available on the EU market.[53]

EU type-approval legislation has recently been undergoing important modifications. The regulation of the *process* of vehicle type-approval was overhauled in 2018, with the adoption of the new Type-Approval Regulation, applicable as from the 1st of September 2020.[54] Following the so-called "Dieselgate",[55] the Type-Approval Regulation especially introduces stringent market surveillance rules to strengthen the enforcement competences of national authorities vis-à-vis manufacturers, including *after the placing on the market of vehicles.*[56]

---

48 Type-Approval Regulation, Article 3 (1).

49 Type-Approval Regulation, Article 13 (1).

50 Type-Approval Regulation, Article 28.

51 For more details, see Type-Approval Regulation, Article 28 (1), 24 and 26 (4).

52 Type-Approval Regulation, Rec 40.

53 Type-Approval Regulation, see in particular Article 36, 36 and 48.

54 Type-Approval Regulation, Article 91. See also Article 89 organizing a transition period.

55 In this regard, the Type-Approval Regulation justifies the introduction of market surveillance regime by the "technical progress [which] has increased the risk of technical services [competent national authorities] not possessing the necessary competence to test new technologies or devices that emerge with their scope of designation", Rec 13.

56 Further explanation of the concept and rationale of market surveillance in EU product legislation can be found in section 7 ('market surveillance') of the 'Blue Guide' from the Commission on the implementation of EU products rules, (2016/C 272/01) (Blue Guide), 97. See Type-Approval Regulation, Article 1 (2), 8, 9 and 13 (6). In addition to greater surveillance competences granted to national competence authorities, the Type-Approval Regulation also stipulates that the Commission shall organize (or have organized) "compliance verifications" by means of tests and inspections, see Article 9. Finally, the Commission shall assess the procedures put in place by national competent authorities, see Article 10.

3.2. THE PROPOSAL FOR A GENERAL SAFETY REGULATION: CYBERSECURITY AS PART OF SAFETY REQUIREMENTS

Additionally, with the proposal to adopt a new General Safety Regulation in 2018,[57] the European Commission aims to recast the various EU legal regimes pertaining to the safety requirements of vehicles, as part of substantive regulation of type-approval. At the time of writing, the last version of the proposed Regulation consists of the one that the European Parliament adopted in April 2019,[58] which is therefore the one considered here unless indicated otherwise (the "Proposed General Safety Regulation"). The proposed General Safety Regulation includes new provisions addressing the specific risks brought about by the growing connected and automated features of vehicles. The remainder of this book chapter focusses, however, exclusively on (cyber-) security requirements. Based on the observation that "the connectivity and automation of vehicles increases the possibility for unauthorized, remote access to in-vehicle data and illegal modification of software over-the-air",[59] the proposed Regulation introduces "security" requirements as part of vehicle safety regulation,[60] with regard to "cyber security" on the one hand and "security measures" of "software update processes" on the other hand.[61] With growing connectivity and automation of vehicles, security and safety appear to get intertwined as part of "cybersecurity".

At this point, both terms need to be further distinguished. "Safety" generally refers to "the degree to which accidental harm is prevented, reduced and properly reacted to",[62] while "security" can be defined as "the degree to which malicious harm is prevented, reduced and properly reacted to".[63] CAM is hereby a case in point, in that "a security vulnerability has the potential to become a

57 Proposal for a Regulation of the European Parliament and of the Council on type-approval requirements for motor vehicles and their trailers, and systems, components and separate technical units intended for such vehicles, as regards their general safety and the protection of vehicle occupants and vulnerable road users, amending Regulation (EU) 2018/858, and repealing Regulations (EC) 78/2009, 79/2009 and 661/2009, 2018/0145 (COD).

58 European Parliament legislative resolution of 16 April 2019 on the proposal for a regulation of the European Parliament and of the Council on type-approval requirements for motor vehicles and their trailers, and systems, components and separate technical units intended for such vehicles, as regards their general safety and the protection of vehicle occupants and vulnerable road users, amending Regulation (EU) 2018/... and repealing Regulations (EC) No 78/2009, (EC) No 79/2009 and (EC) No 661/2009 (COM(2018)0286 – C8-0194/2018 – 2018/0145(COD)) (Proposed General Safety Regulation).

59 Proposed General Safety Regulation, Rec 18a.

60 It should be further noted that the word "security" itself was not inserted in the proposal from the Commission.

61 Proposed General Safety Regulation, Rec 18a and 18b.

62 Firesmith (2003), as quoted in Johnsen and others (n 4) 1791.

63 Ibid.

safety issue".[64] Inclusion of security considerations in safety requirements is not entirely new. Safety regulations already lay down requirements for the design of vehicles and of their components to prevent "unauthorized use".[65] Security as part of safety requirements is however growing significantly with CAM vehicles.

3.3. THE UNECE MANDATE TO DEVELOP VEHICLE TECHNICAL REGULATIONS

While extending the scope of vehicles safety requirements to cybersecurity, the proposed General Safety Regulation does, however, not expressly lay down *substantive* norms in that respect. The development of vehicle technical regulations is indeed delegated to the UNECE, by virtue of the so-called "1958 Agreement".[66] The vehicle technical regulations developed by the UNECE, once adopted as "UN Regulation",[67] become legally binding within the EU, as part of type-approval legislation, upon the procedure foreseen in the Type-Approval Regulation.[68] UNECE is actively involved in adapting international legislation to CAM.

The remainder of the book chapter only focusses on cybersecurity, about which two recommendations were made by the new Working Party on "Automated / autonomous and connected vehicles" (GRVA)[69] of the forum of the permanent working group 29 in the institutional framework of the United Nations.[70] In 2018, the GRVA issued a "Proposal for a Recommendation on Cyber Security"[71] and a "Draft recommendation on Software Updates of the Task Force on Cyber Security

64 Maurice Schellekens, 'Self-Driving Cars and the Chilling Effect of Liability Law' (2015) 31 Computer Law & Security Review 506, Section 4.2.5.

65 Regulation (EC) No 661/2009 concerning type-approval requirements for the general safety of motor vehicles, their trailers and systems, components and separate technical units intended therefore [2009], OJ L 200/1, Article 5 (2) (j).

66 Agreement Concerning the Adoption of Harmonized Technical United Nations Regulations for Wheeled Vehicles, Equipment and Parts which can be Fitted and/or be Used on Wheeled Vehicles and the Conditions for Reciprocal Recognition of Approvals Granted on the Basis of these United Nations Regulations, ECE/TRANS/WP.29/2016/2 (1958 Agreement).

67 1958 Agreement, Article 1 (2) and 12.

68 Type-Approval Regulation, Rec 48 and 49 and Article 57. Essentially, the UN Regulations and the amendments thereto must have been voted in favour of by the EU, or the EU applies them "in accordance with Decision 97/836/EC". As a result, the UN Regulations "listed in Part II of Annex II [of the Type-Approval Regulation] are recognized as being equivalent to the corresponding regulatory acts to the extent they share the same scope and subject-matter" (Article 58 (1)) and as a result "the approval authorities of the Member States shall accept type-approvals granted in accordance with [them] (Article 58 (2)).

69 See the website of GRVA for further details: www.unece.org/trans/main/wp29/meeting_docs_grva.html (last visited 8th of July 2019).

70 See the website of the permanent working group 29 here: www.unece.org/trans/main/wp29/meeting_docs_wp29.html (last visited 8th July 2019).

71 Proposal for a Recommendation on Cyber Security submitted by the experts of the Task Force on Cyber Security and Over-the-air issues, 19.11.2018, ECE/TRANS/WP.29/GRVA/2019/2 (Proposal for a Cyber Security Recommendation).

and Over-the-air issues" (the "Draft Software Update Recommendation").[72] Both proposed recommendations include respectively a draft vehicle technical regulation.[73] A third recommendation is still expected to be issued on data protection, which would also partly address cybersecurity aspects.[74] Although aimed to tackle cybersecurity issues of connected *and automated / autonomous vehicles,* these recommendations barely mention automated / autonomous features *as such*. For the sake of completion, the "Proposal for the Future Certification of Automated / autonomous Driving Systems" (the "Proposal for ADS")[75] should hereby be mentioned. Although still at a preliminary stage, it outlines options for certification of autonomous features of vehicles. The focus is placed on "safety", which is considered as including "security" and especially "cyber security" and "software updates".[76] At the time of writing, none of these texts has led to the adoption of acts having legal binding value in the EU legal order.

4. LEGAL ANALYSIS OF THE PROPOSED RECOMMENDATIONS OF UNECE ON CYBERSECURITY

The study of both the proposed Cyber Security and the Software update recommendations indicates common patterns, in the sense that UNECE essentially suggests to *extend the scope* of vehicle technical regulations in order to secure CAM vehicles. Such extensions are visible in three main directions.

4.1. AN EXTENSIVE INTERPRETATION OF 'THE CAM VEHICLE' *IN SPACE*

The shift to CAM was described as profoundly changing "the very essence of cars, which have been stand-alone products since they were invented. [They

72 Draft Recommendation on Software Updated of the Task Force on Cyber Security and Over-the-air issues, 19.11.2018, ECE/TRANS/WP.29/GRVA/2019/3 (Draft Recommendation on Software). They follow the general "Guidelines on cybersecurity and data protection", adopted in 2017, see the Consolidated Resolution on the Construction of Vehicles (R.E.3), Revision 6, 11.08.2017, (ECE/TRANS/WP.29/78/Rev.6). The 'Guidelines on cybersecurity and data protection – Guidelines on measures ensuring cybersecurity and data protection of connected vehicles and vehicles with Automated Driving Technologies' are adopted as Annex 6 (p. 114–117).

73 They are respectively referred to as the "Proposed Cyber Security Regulation" and the "Draft Software Update Regulation".

74 Proposal for a Cyber Security Recommendation, Pt 1.2 and Fig 1.

75 Proposal for the Future Certification of Automated / Autonomous Driving Systems, submitted by the experts from International Organization of Motor Vehicle Manufacturers, 19.11.2018, ECE/TRANS/WP.29/GRVA/2019/13 (Proposal for ADS).

76 Proposal for ADS, the table "Comparison of published Safety Principles" in Chapter IX "Mapping of safety Principles and the Pillars".

are] now developing into ecosystems because they communicate with other cars, the traffic management centre and the infrastructure, and are integrated into a network of mobility services".[77] The question is then: are these external communications an integral part of the vehicle? More generally, what about the digital layer required for CAM vehicles to operate? While CAM is still emerging, various architecture models are being discussed with regard to the computing and storage of vehicle data, ranging from in-vehicle or manufacturer-specific solutions to shared cloud environments.[78] Are these servers and data part of the (CAM) vehicle – or should they be?

Both the Cyber Security and the Software Update recommendations reflect this growing uncertainty surrounding the *delineation of the CAM vehicle with respect to its environment ('in space')*. They appear to bring clarity by an *extensive interpretation of what is to be considered as 'the vehicle'*. In other words, they both include part of the digital layer as part of the scope *rationae materiae* of vehicle technical regulation. *For the purpose of cybersecurity requirements*, the Proposal for a Cyber Security Recommendation includes "dedicated environments of the vehicle type (*if provided*) for the storage and execution of aftermarket software, services, applications or data" (emphasis added),[79] as part of what manufacturers shall secure. The Proposal for a Cyber Security Recommendation provides a list of threats and vulnerabilities "which shall be considered in the design of a new or modified product or service".[80] As part of threats to vehicles arising from their "external connectivity and connections", the Recommendation covers "hosted third party software, e.g. entertainment applications [...]".[81] It also considers threats regarding "back-end services",[82] and threats to vehicles "regarding their communication channels" which especially includes "messages received by the vehicle (for example X2V or diagnostic messages), or transmitted within it [...]".[83] As for the Draft Software Update Recommendation, "software" is broadly defined as embracing both "instructions" and "digital data" being part of an Electronic Control System.[84] While the former seems to reflect the notion

77 Ruppert Stadler, Walter Brenner and Andreas Hermann, 'Evolutions and Revolutions in Mobility', *Autonomous Driving: How the Driverless Revolution will Change the World* (Emerald Publishing Limited 2018) 19.

78 Mike McCarthy and others, 'Access to In-Vehicle Data and Resources' (2017) Publications Office of the European Union 57–58.

79 Proposal for a Cyber Security Recommendation, Pt 7.3.5.

80 Proposal for a Cyber Security Recommendation, Pt 4.3.

81 Proposal for a Cyber Security Recommendation, Pt 4.3.5 (b).

82 Proposal for a Cyber Security Recommendation, Pt 4.3.1.

83 Proposal for a Cyber Security Recommendation, Pt 4.3.2 (h).

84 Draft Software Update Recommendation, Pt 2.9. The "Electronic Control System" is defined as "a combination of units, designed to co-operate in the production of the stated vehicle control function by electronic data processing. Such systems, often controlled by software, are built from discrete functional components such as sensors, electronic control units and actuators and connected by transmission links. They may include mechanical, electronic-pneumatic or electro-hydraulic elements", Draft Software Update Recommendation, Pt 2.4.

of "computer program" within the meaning of EU law,[85] the latter may, as it is, go as far as to cover data *merely used by* computer programs.[86] Such data may additionally stem from external and heterogeneous sources, as "digital data" would be covered by the definition of "software" *based solely on their role* in the "production of the stated vehicle control function".[87]

4.2. EXTENDING THE SCOPE OF VEHICLE TECHNICAL REGULATIONS TO THE WHOLE LIFECYCLE OF VEHICLES

Vehicle technical regulations are applicable in the phase of *manufacturing* of vehicles (and of the components), in the lifecycle of the vehicles. Compliance is verified by the granting of the (type-)approval, upon which the vehicle (type) can be placed on the market, namely for the first time supplied[88] "for [the then phase of] distribution [and] use on the market [...]".[89] Both the Cyber Security and the Software Update recommendations extend the scope of vehicle technical regulations *beyond the traditional manufacturing phase*.

On the one hand, the Proposal for a Cyber Security Recommendation lays down the requirement to protect "critical elements of the vehicle type [against] identified risks identified in the vehicle manufacturer's risk assessment".[90] This requirement shall be applicable, beyond the "development [and] production phase",[91] *to the "post-production phase"* (emphasis added). In other words, cybersecurity requirements shall remain applicable throughout "the whole lifecycle of the vehicle", from the vehicle's "initial development through the period of marketing and active use until it is decommissioned".[92] This extension is justified by "the changing cyber threats [...]".[93] On the other hand, the Draft

85 Software is defined for the purpose of the Computer Program Directive as including "programs in any form" (Directive 2009/24/EC on the legal protection of computer programs (Codified version) [2009], OJ L 111/16, Rec 7). It was clarified by the CJEU as including "the source code and the object code of a computer program", the criterion being whether it makes it then possible to "lead[...] to the reproduction or the subsequent creation of such a program", Case C-406/10 *SAS Institute Inc.* v *World Programming Ltd.*, 2 May 2012, ECLI:EU:C:2012:259, para. 38.

86 On the distinction between software and information (that software may also contain), see Geraint Howells, Christian Twigg-Flesner and Chris Willett, 'Product Liability and Digital Products' in Tatiana – Eleni Synodinou and others (eds), *EU Internet Law* (Springer, Cham 2017).

87 Draft Software Update Recommendation, Pt 2.4 (definition of "Electronic Control Systems", the latter being referred to in the definition of "Software", Pt 2.4).

88 Type-Approval Regulation, Article 3 (50).

89 Type-Approval Regulation, Article 3 (51).

90 Proposed Cyber Security Regulation, Pt 7.3.4.

91 Proposed Cyber Security Regulation, Pt 7.2.2.1.

92 Proposed Cyber Security Regulation, Pt 2.9.

93 Proposed Cyber Security Regulation, Pt 6.4.2.

Software Update Recommendation places obligations on manufacturers to ensure "software updates", defined as "a package used to *upgrade* software to a new version" (emphasis added). A further note clarifies that "the terms 'update' and 'upgrade' are used synonymously to refer to installing new versions of software. The update may "*contain a fix for a specific problem* or *introduce new product functionality*" (emphasis added).[94] The "specific problem" could especially consist of (new) cybersecurity threats, described as dynamic so that fixes as countermeasures should also be dynamic. While the Recommendation does not explicitly anticipate automated and autonomous features of vehicles, "new product functionality" could especially result from software update or upgrade as part of the learning process of AI.

For comparison, EU (product) legislation would be generally interpreted in that both the "fix" and the "new product functionality" would result in a *new product*. As clarified by the European Commission in its "Blue Guide" of 2016 on the implementation of EU product rules, product maintenance does in principle not result in a new product, even when the performance of the product is (positively) affected due to technical progress. On the contrary, a product "which has been subject to *important changes* or overhaul aiming to modify its original performance, purpose and type after it has been put into service [...] must be considered as a new product" (emphasis added).[95] The magnitude of the change brought to the product matters, with regard to its design and purpose. The European Commission also highlights that "if the *nature of the hazard has changed* or the *level of risk has increased*, then the modified product has to be considered as a new product" (emphasis added).[96] The determining criterion is therefore the *intended* use and maintenance "*at the design stage* of the product" (emphasis added). The timeline in the lifecycle of the product hereby plays a crucial role. The manufacturer is responsible for manufacturing and placing the product on the market, in compliance with "the legal requirements that were in place *at the time of its placing on the market*" (emphasis added).[97] Once placed on the market and consumed – or in the parlance of the Blue Guide "once it reaches the end-user" – it is no longer considered as a new product and EU harmonization legislation no longer applies.[98] EU product legislation incumbent on the manufacturer *does consequently not include* an obligation to monitor and update the product according to circumstances developing *after the placing on the market*. This is confirmed by the grounds for exonerations of the manufacturer's

94 Draft Software Update Regulation, Pt 7.1.4.

95 Blue Guide (n 56), section 2.1 'product coverage'.

96 Ibid.

97 Ibid.

98 Ibid. A specific mention is included with reference to software updates or repairs which "could be assimilated to maintenance operations provided that they do not modify a product already placed on the market in such a way that compliance with the applicable requirements may be affected".

liability for damages arising out of defective products, within the meaning of the Product Liability Directive.[99] The manufacturer[100] may especially invoke two grounds for exemption, namely where the defect did probably not exist when the product was placed on the market, or alternatively where "the state of scientific and technical knowledge at the time of [placing on the market] was not such as to enable the existence of the defect to be discovered" on the other.[101] As a result, software updates / upgrades aimed at "fixing" a problem which came into existence after the placing of the vehicle on the market, or at introducing "new functionalities" are considered as *not making part of the manufacturing* phase (and therefore manufacturing specific legislation) in EU law.

To sum up, both Recommendations propose to extend the scope of vehicle technical regulations to the whole lifecycle of the vehicle, by including requirements arising *after its placing on the market*. Such extension is considered as necessary to tackle the "changing cyber threats" and more generally reflects the changing nature of the CAM vehicle. In this regard, the autonomous features of the vehicles relying on the "learning loop" of AI seem also to require regular software updates and upgrades within the meaning of the Recommendations, although they are not *explicitly* covered.

4.3. EXTENSION OF THE SCOPE OF TECHNICAL REGULATION TO THE MANUFACTURER'S ORGANIZATION

The third and last extension of the scope of vehicle technical requirements appears to result logically from the two former ones. While vehicle technical regulation regards the condition of the vehicle and of its components as certified by the vehicle (type-)approval, both the draft Cyber Security and Software Update Recommendations propose to also include regulation and certification of the manufacturer.

---

99 Council Directive 85/374/EEC on the approximation of the laws, regulations and administrative provisions of the Member States concerning liability for defective products [1985] OJ L 210/29 (Product Liability Directive).

100 Within the meaning of the Product Liability Directive, the "producer" is essentially the "manufacturer", see the definition of the producer as "the manufacturer of a finished product, the producer of any raw material or the manufacturer of a component part and any person who, by putting his name, trade mark or other distinguishing feature on the product presents himself as its producer" (Article 3 (1)).

101 Product Liability Directive, Article 7 (b) and (e). This issue is further discussed in Hervé Jacquemin and Jean-Benoît Hubin, 'Aspects contractuels et de responsabilité civile en matière d'intelligence artificielle' [2017] Intelligence artificielle et droit 73. Although the authors mostly discuss the impact of the 'learning loop' of artificial intelligence on the application of the Product Liability Directive regime, they also address the issue of software updates. This issue is also discussed in Jan De Bruyne and Jarich Werbrouck, 'Merging Self-Driving Cars with the Law' (2018) 34 Computer Law & Security Review 1150.

They both include the creation of a new *certification regime* applying to, respectively, *the internal cybersecurity and software update management systems of the manufacturer*, aside the (type-) approval certification applying to vehicle (types). The scope of this regime essentially covers the above-mentioned extensions of the vehicle technical regulations, such as post-production security and software update requirements. The Cyber Security Recommendation proposes the creation and certification of a new "Cyber Security Management System" (CSMS) of the manufacturer. According to the Cyber Security Recommendation, the CSMS consists of "a systemic risk-based approach defining organizational processes, responsibilities and governance to mitigate cyber threats and protect vehicles from cyber-attacks".[102] The scope of the CSMS extends not only to the protection of vehicles, but also to the "organization",[103] namely the manufacturer, but also "[...] dependencies that may exist with contracted suppliers and service providers [...]".[104] The CSMS covers "processes used within the manufacturer's organization to manage cybersecurity",[105] which includes in particular "assessment, categorization and treatment of the risks identified", "monitoring for, detection and response to cyber-attacks on vehicle types", "identification of new and evolving cyber threats and vulnerabilities".[106] The certification of the manufacturer's CSMS would be a prerequisite for him to apply for vehicle type-approval.[107]

The Software Update Recommendation similarly proposes to create and certify the manufacturer's "Software Update Management System" (SUMS), namely the "systemic approach defining organizational processes and procedures to comply with the requirements for delivery of software updates [...]".[108] As part of his SUMS, the manufacturer shall "identify target vehicles for a software update",[109] which appears to amount to an obligation to monitor and update the product *after the placing of the vehicle (and software) on the market*. The manufacturer shall essentially assess and make a first line decision as for whether the software update would result in a 'new product', and shall appropriately apply for new type-approval.[110] The manufacturer shall also ensure the safe and secure implementation of the software update, with a view to the "interdependencies of the updated system with other systems",[111] which can

102 Proposed Cyber Security Regulation, Pt 2.3.

103 Proposed Cyber Security Regulation, Pt 2.18. The "Organization" is defined as including "a person or group of people that has its own functions with responsibilities, authorities and relationships to achieve its objectives" (pt. 2.12).

104 Proposed Cyber Security Regulation, Pt 7.2.2.4.

105 Proposed Cyber Security Regulation, Pt 7.2.2.2 (a).

106 Proposed Cyber Security Regulation, Pt 7.2.

107 Proposed Cyber Security Regulation, Pt 7.3.1.

108 Draft Software Update Recommendation, Pt 2.13.

109 Draft Software Update Regulation, Pt 7.1.1.6.

110 Draft Software Update Regulation, Pt 8.

111 Draft Software Update Regulation, Pt 7.1.1.5.

be qualified as a compatibility obligation. Acquisition of the certification of his SUMS is a prerequisite for the manufacturer to apply for vehicle type-approval vehicles.[112]

Based on this study, what can be concluded as for the fitness of vehicle type-approval legislation to deal with cybersecurity risks of CAM vehicles? Is the expectation right that the recent introduction of market surveillance rules and the up-coming introduction of cybersecurity requirements "by design" as part of safety regulation of vehicles will provide an appropriate legal framework?

5. IS TYPE-APPROVAL LEGISLATION FIT FOR THE PURPOSE OF SECURING CAM VEHICLES?

Assessing the technical fitness of the measures proposed in the Cyber Security and Software Update recommendations is obviously not a legal endeavour. The present contribution rather aims to assess the fitness of type-approval legislation *as a regulatory means* to deal with the cybersecurity challenges of CAM vehicles. Although they have not (yet) led to legally binding acts, the proposed recommendations developed by UNECE are hereby valuable in two respects. They reflect the *changing nature of vehicles* when growing in connectivity and autonomy and they constitute an illustration of how type-approval legislation could tackle these challenges. Already in 2016 – namely *before* the proposed recommendations were published – Schellekens expressed reservations as for the appropriateness of type-approval regulations to deal with cybersecurity of CAM vehicles. He considered that "rules about type-approval of vehicles tend to be very specific and also *specifying means*" (emphasis added).[113] Rules that "specify means" can be qualified as "rule-based regulation", as opposed to "principle-based regulation". The former "prescribes or prohibits specific behaviours" while the latter "emphasizes general and abstract guiding principles for desired regulatory outcomes".[114] In other words, Schellekens considers that the inherent rule-based character of type-approval regulation would not enable them to "deal with the [...] dynamic threat environment", which is "critical with security".[115] Based on the study of the proposed recommendations of UNECE, are his criticisms confirmed? The first sub-section (1) will discuss how, essentially, the proposed recommendations attempt to overcome the limitations observed by Schellekens. The attempt (and maybe success) to deal with the

112 Draft Software Update Regulation, Pt 3.1.

113 Schellekens (n 4) Section 4.2.3.

114 Mark Fenwick, Wulf A Kaal and Erik PM Vermeulen, 'Regulation Tomorrow: Strategies for Regulating New Technologies' in Toshiyuki Kono, Mary Hiscock and Arie Reich (eds), *Transnational Commercial and Consumer Law: Current Trends in International Business Law* (Springer Singapore 2018) Section 5.2.

115 Schellekens (n 4) Section 4.2.3.

dynamic cybersecurity threat environment within the framework of vehicle technical regulations paradoxically comes at the price of 'overfilling' vehicle type-approval legislation. The second sub-section (2) outlines another limitation of type-approval legislation which seems unsurpassable: the integration of the CAM vehicle in its spatial environment.

5.1. WHERE TECHNICAL REGULATION CALLS FOR FURTHER REGULATION OF THE MANUFACTURER

Precisely because of the "dynamic [cybersecurity] threat environment", both the above-mentioned recommendations propose to shift from a rule-based approach toward a principle-based approach. Essentially, they introduce general principles of security risk management, to be set up by the manufacturers (CSMS and SUMS).

These risk management systems share similarities with cybersecurity obligations found in other legislative frameworks, such as the NIS Directive[116] or the European Electronic Communications Code.[117] These frameworks have in common a *broad room of manoeuver* granted to the regulated entities, who are in particular responsible for identifying and evaluating the risks, identifying and taking appropriate incident mitigation measures, auditing, detecting and responding to attacks (or "incidents").[118] This broad room of manoeuver is considered necessary in all these cases *to adapt security management to the dynamic nature of cybersecurity threats*.[119] Although still at an early phase, the Proposal for the Future Certification of Automated / Autonomous Driving Systems appears to follow the same pattern. Therein, the traditional "function-by-function"[120] and "design restrictive"[121] certification of vehicle-types is viewed as insufficient to deal with the autonomous features of vehicles, because of their "system complexity"[122] and of the fast-evolving technological developments.[123] In addition to existing certification, the Proposal pleads in favour of "flexible" and "pragmatic" strategies, based on the concept of "functional safety" of

116 Directive (EU) 2016/1148 concerning measures for a high common level of security of network and information systems across the Union [2016] OJ L 194/1 (NIS Directive).

117 Directive (EU) 2018/1972 establishing the European Electronic Communications Code (Recast) [2018] OJ L 321/36 (European Electronic Communications Code).

118 European Electronic Communications Code, Title V; NIS Directive, Article 14 and 16; Proposal for a Cyber Security Recommendation, Chap 7.2.

119 NIS Directive, Rec 44: "[...] a culture of risk management, involving risk assessment and the implementation of security measures appropriate to the risks faced [...]"; see recital (94) of the European Electronic Communications Code: "[...] those measures shall ensure a level of security of networks and services appropriate to the risks posed [...]".

120 Proposal for ADS, Chap II.

121 Ibid.

122 Proposal for ADS, Chap VI A.

123 Proposal for ADS, Pt II.9.

the whole system.[124] This "new approach" to certification would result in manufacturers "giv[ing] evidence that their system has been designed and tested in a way that complies with established safety principles [or in other words] "make its safety case".[125] Given its yet early stage, the work of the UNECE on the certification of autonomous features of vehicles should however be further monitored in the future.

Following the categorization of risk regulation elaborated by Hood et al.[126] and used by Renaud et al.[127] to explain cybersecurity regulation, these cybersecurity risk management regimes can be qualified as mainly "individualist". Individualist risk regulatory approach is based on the rationale that the law "supports markets and underpins informed choice but responsibility is essentially the individual citizen's".[128] Such "responsibilization" is characterized by two elements: (a) "Individuals [are required] to take reasonable precautions thereby minimizing their risk of becoming victims" and (b) "if they fail to take all the right precautions and fall victims, a certain degree of responsibility for the consequences rests with them".[129] A major distinction however lies here between entities regulated by the European Electronic Communications Code and the NIS Directive on the one hand, and vehicle type-approval regulation on the other. The former entities provide services, namely "the making available of electronic communications network"[130] and respectively "electronic communication services"[131] with regard to the European Electronic Communications Code, "digital services"[132] and "essential services"[133] with regard to the NIS Directive. As opposed to that, the proposed recommendations of the UNECE are expected to apply to *product (vehicle) manufacturers.*

---

124 Proposal for ADS, Chap VIII, A "Concept of certification – the three pillars".

125 Bryant Walker Smith, 'Regulation and the Risk of Inaction' in Markus Maurer and others (eds), *Autonomous Driving: Technical, Legal and Social Aspects* (Springer Berlin Heidelberg 2016). The author considers that shifting the burden of proof onto the manufacturer would enable the regulator to acquire technical knowledge.

126 Christopher Hood, Henry Rothstein and Robert Baldwin, *The Government of Risk: Understanding Risk Regulation Regimes* (Oxford University Press 2001).

127 Karen Renaud and others, 'Is the Responsibilization of the Cyber Security Risk Reasonable and Judicious?' (2018) 78 Computer & Security 198.

128 The characterization developed by Hood et al. (2001) includes three other types: the "fatalist" approach consists in that "little is done to avert the risk but a response is formulated by government, as and when the event occurs [such as when] natural disasters [occur]". The "egalitarian approach" is characterized in that "the government supports communities in managing the risks and encourages local participation. Government will step in once an event occurs [such as in the case of] pollution reduction by providing public transport alternatives". Ibid Section 3.3. For the "hierarchist approach", see below.

129 Ibid Quoting Yan (2015).

130 European Electronic Communications Code, Article 2 (1) and (16).

131 European Electronic Communications Code, Article 2 (4).

132 NIS Directive, Article 4 (5).

133 NIS Directive, Article 4 (4), 5 (2) and Annex II.

Essentially, and to sum up, the UNECE recommendations propose to shift from a rule-based to a principle-based regulation to deal with dynamic cybersecurity threats of vehicles. To do so, they propose to partly depart from the product (vehicle)-centred "by design" approach towards an approach centred on the *entity*, namely the 'manufacturer'. The extensions of the scope *rationae materiae* of vehicle technical regulations appear to constitute the regulatory means designed to deal with the *de facto* blurring contours of the CAM vehicle with regard to its integration in its environment (in space) and its lifecycle (in time).

In view of the above-mentioned opinion of Schellekens, this results in a paradox. The proposed recommendations would accommodate cybersecurity, but only at the price of partly shifting the regulatory focus on the manufacturer. By doing so, type-approval legislation however appears to reach its limit. As the proposed recommendations also acknowledge, enforcement of the certification of the manufacturer for its CSMS and SUMS would require "further legal framework".[134] In this regard, the expectation that the new market surveillance regime inserted in EU type-approval law would suffice appears to be misplaced. New market surveillance legal provisions accommodate for additional *enforcement means*, which take place after the placing of the vehicle on the market (in addition to the 'mere' type-approval procedure). While the breach of vehicle technical regulation may be discovered – thanks to market surveillance – *after the placing of the vehicle on the market*, this does not affect the fact that the technical regulations are applicable with regard to the *manufacturing phase*. Mandating dynamic risk management on the manufacturer throughout the whole lifecycle of the vehicle is conceptually different. In this case, obligations indeed *arise after the placing on the market*. To put it another way, dynamic risk management implies *continuous obligations*. The concrete regulatory means proposed by the recommendations to embed these obligations – namely to certify the manufacturer for its CSMS and SUMS –, require further legislation at EU level to simply make it happen (e.g. to regulate the certifying process, the enforcement of the certification, etc.).

It also remains to be analysed whether legally binding acts which would follow these proposals would be compliant with the '1958 Agreement', by virtue of which UNECE is delegated the competence to develop technical vehicle regulation as UN Regulation (see above). While not imposing on Contracting Parties type-approval as mandatory or exclusive regulatory procedure, the 1958 Agreement is deeply based on type-approval.[135] More generally, the 1958 Agreement has been oriented towards the objective of laying down "technical requirements" applying to *vehicles(-types)*, which is reflected in the scope of the

---

134 Proposal for a Cyber Security Recommendation, Pt 7.6.1.

135 See for example 1958 Agreement, Article 2. The rooting in type-approval procedure runs throughout the whole Agreement.

UN Regulation to be developed by UNECE.[136] Whether technical requirements can be developed as UN Regulation with the purpose of regulating and even *certifying* the *manufacturer*, even if viewed as ancillary to the regulation of *vehicles(-types)*, calls for further legal analysis.

5.2. A LIMIT OF TYPE-APPROVAL LEGISLATION: THE INTEGRATION OF THE CAM VEHICLE IN ITS SPATIAL ENVIRONMENT

In addition to the above, it remains questionable whether the proposed recommendations of UNECE can account for the blurring contours of vehicles *in space*, in other words the growing integration of the vehicle in its environment. The technical imbrication of the CAM vehicle in its environment, discussed above, thereby means an imbrication of stakeholders. The CAM ecosystem is indeed expected to involve many stakeholders, having both cooperative and competitive relations.[137] The interactions between them may be constitutive of cybersecurity risks. Not only shall every piece of the puzzle be secured, but also "a global and coordinated effort" is needed to secure the puzzle as a whole.[138] Coordination of actors is a key component of cybersecurity, although often lacking.[139] Communication between actors and coordination have been considered as a cornerstone for various security activities, such as "resol[ution of incidents] and mitigat[ion of] threats", "the collection of information about vulnerabilities and the provision of support in the form of patches".[140] Even the very first step of security, namely setting security objectives, was found to require a "systemic and holistic" perspective.[141]

As discussed above, the proposed recommendations of UNECE aim to cover (and 'secure') part of the digital environment of the vehicles likely to constitute threats, such as "back-end services" and "external messages received by the vehicle (for example X2V [...])" (see above).[142] However, type-approval regulation is inherently focused on vehicles(-types) and on the manufacturer. The underlying premise is that the manufacturer is the entity best placed to "retain the overall control for the product and ensure that he receives all the information

136 See the scope of UN Regulation, 1958 Agreement, Article 1 (2).
137 Schellekens (n 4) Section 4.2.
138 Jonathan Petit, 'Automated Vehicles Cybersecurity: Summary AVS'17 and Stakeholder Analysis' in Gereon Meyer and Sven Beiker (eds), *Road Vehicle Automation 5* (Springer, Cham 2019) 176.
139 Tarun Chaudhary and others, 'Patchwork of Confusion: The Cybersecurity Coordination Problem' (2018) 4 Journal of Cybersecurity.
140 Schellekens (n 4) Section 4.2.
141 Anupam Chattopadhyay and Kwok-Yan Lam, 'Autonomous Vehicle: Security by Design' [2018] ArXiv <http://arxiv.org/abs/1810.00545> accessed 6 May 2019.
142 Proposal for a Cyber Security Recommendation, Pt 4.3.1 and 4.3.2 (h).

that is necessary to fulfil his responsibilities according to the relevant [product regulation]".[143] Is the manufacturer, *as a matter of fact*, able to retain control over, for instance, external C-ITS communications sent to the vehicle by third parties? Similarly, the proposed General Safety Regulation from the European Commission (see above) envisages "*multi-brand* vehicle platooning" (emphasis added), and proposes to "harmonize format for the exchange of data" as a specific requirement "relating to automated vehicles".[144] While the "who will do what" remains unclear at this stage, the learning process of autonomous vehicles is also expected to require sharing of behavioural data "to train the systems of other vehicles" potentially cross-(or multi-)brand[145] ("collective learning").[146] One can doubt that vehicle manufacturers would be indeed able and well-placed to retain control and secure information stemming from such third parties (who may be their competitors).

The proposal for a C-ITS Delegated Regulation notified by the European Commission to the European Parliament and to the Council in March 2019[147] (the 'proposed C-ITS Regulation') constitutes an interesting development in this regard. Based on the Directive on Intelligent Transport Systems ("ITS Directive"),[148] the proposed C-ITS Regulation aims to prevent "fragmentation of the internal market in the field of C-ITS" and to "ensure their coordinated and coherent deployment". With this text, the European Commission wants to "ensure compatibility, interoperability and continuity of C-ITS services in the deployment and operational use of Union-wide C-ITS services based on trusted and secure communications".[149] The proposed C-ITS Regulation does not *make it mandatory to equip vehicles* (and/or road infrastructure) with C-ITS stations,[150] namely the components "required to collect, store, process, receive and transmit secured and trusted messages in order to enable the provision of a C-ITS service".[151] However, C-ITS stations and C-ITS services can be deployed and made available on the market *only provided compliance* with requirements of the proposed Regulation.[152] Based on the systemic and peer-to-peer character of

---

143 Blue Guide, (n 56) Section 3.1.

144 Proposed General Safety Regulation from the Commission, Article 11.

145 ENISA (n 32) 13.

146 Khuram Shahzad, 'Cloud Robotics and Autonomous Vehicles' (2016) Autonomous Vehicle section 3.4.

147 Proposed C-ITS Regulation

148 Directive 2010/40/EU of the European Parliament and of the Council of 7 July 2010 on the framework for the deployment of Intelligent Transport Systems in the field of road transport and for interfaces with other modes of transport Text with EEA relevance, OJ L 207, 6.8.2010 (ITS Directive), 1–13.

149 Proposed C-ITS Regulation, Rec 3.

150 Proposed C-ITS Regulation, see the explanatory memorandum of the Commission: "compliance with the Delegated Regulation would be mandatory only where C-ITS service or stations were deployed", 3.

151 Proposed C-ITS Regulation, Article 2 (3).

152 Proposed C-ITS Regulation, Article 3 and 6.

C-ITS communications and with a view to interoperability, the proposed C-ITS Regulation lays down technical harmonization of C-ITS stations and services. In order to ensure that C-ITS communications are trustworthy, it provides for a whole security management system, with the creation of the so-called "European C-ITS trust model" based on public key infrastructure (PKI) delivering certificates.[153] A range of new central entities are proposed to be established[154] so as to safely coordinate and govern the new "C-ITS network" comprised of "all operational C-ITS stations in the EU".[155]

In this respect, the proposed C-ITS Regulation creates a new and crucial legal role of "C-ITS station operator", defined as the person "responsible for the putting in service and the operation of C-ITS stations [...]".[156] The C-ITS station operator bears substantial security obligations. It shall set up and "operate an information security management system (ISMS)".[157] Without prejudice to the responsibility of the C-ITS station manufacturer,[158] it shall "ensure that all [its] C-ITS stations are put in service and operated in accordance with [the proposed Regulation]".[159] It shall especially enrol the C-ITS stations in the "EU C-ITS security credential management system",[160] namely the "[...] framework for the provision of trusted and secure communications using a public key infrastructure (PKI)",[161] to which all C-ITS stations are enrolled.

In the context of our study, the proposed C-ITS Regulation is interesting in two main respects. Firstly, it creates the new legal role as "C-ITS station operator", which disrupts the traditional central figure of the vehicle manufacturer as product aggregator. The name "operator" reflects the continuous supervisory role that it should undertake for security purposes, throughout the exchange of C-ITS communications. This can be opposed to the role as "C-ITS station manufacturer", who 'only' bears obligations pertaining the design and manufacturing of the C-ITS station, targeted at the manufacturing phase until the "placing [of] C-ITS stations on the market".[162]

---

153 Annex III of the Proposed C-ITS Regulation defines "requirements for the management of public key certificates for C-ITS applications by issuing entities and their usage by end-entities in Europe." For further details, see the Introduction of Annex III.

154 With regard to the security management, Proposed C-ITS Regulation establishes the "C-ITS certificate policy authority" (Article 24), the "trust list manager" (Article 25) and the "C-ITS point of contact" (Article 26). The proposed regulation also establishes a centralized body to deal with both governance and supervision activities (e.g. the supervision of "the management of security incidents") (Article 29).

155 Proposed C-ITS Regulation, Article 2 (29).

156 Proposed C-ITS Regulation, Article 2 (16).

157 Proposed C-ITS Regulation, Article 27 and Annex IV.

158 Proposed C-ITS Regulation, Article 7.

159 Proposed C-ITS Regulation, Article 22 (1).

160 Proposed C-ITS Regulation, Article 22 (2) and 23 (3).

161 Proposed C-ITS Regulation, Article 2 (27) and 23.

162 Proposed C-ITS Regulation, Article 7 (1).

Secondly, by enacting harmonized standards on the one hand, and by creating central entities for the purpose of coordinating and securing the whole C-ITS network, the (cyber-)security risk management contemplated in the proposed C-ITS Regulation is mainly illustrative of the "hierarchist" approach, in the categorization of risk management Regulation used by Renaud et al.[163] (see above). This approach is characterized by two elements: (a) based on the observation that managing the risks requires "special skills", it involves "expert forecasting and management"; and (b) based on the observation that "failure to adequately deal with the risk [would] affect the community at large", security measures consist of "whole-society solutions", at various steps of risk management. For instance, the public authority may "enact legislation to ensure that preventative measures are taken", or "provide agents to [perform] remediation (including information gathering).[164] With regard to cybersecurity, such an approach appears to be better equipped to deal with the risks brought about by the very features of the C-ITS communications technology, namely its highly "integrated nature" and the peer-to-peer nature of interactions between the C-ITS stations.[165]

The proposed C-ITS Regulation has been introduced here for illustrative as well as comparative purposes. Further research appears to be yet needed to evaluate whether the EU legislative framework, beyond type-approval legislation, is fit for the purpose of ensuring the cybersecurity of the CAM ecosystem at large.

6. IMPLICATIONS OF THE ANALYSIS BEYOND TYPE-APPROVAL LEGISLATION

The analysis conducted in this book chapter has implications beyond the scope of type-approval legislation and hereby calls for further research. The first sub-section (1) reflects upon the changing – although yet unnamed – role of the manufacturer of CAM vehicles. The second sub-section (2) indicates how the above analysis also feeds the scholarly debate on the liability regime for the future CAM ecosystem.

163 Renaud and others (n 127).

164 Ibid Section 3.4.

165 The role of public authorities in C-ITS coordination and implementation has also been discussed in the US, under the auspices of NHTSA, see Daniel Crane, Kyle Logue and Bryce Pilz, 'A Survey of Legal Issues Arising from the Deployment of Autonomous and Connected Vehicles' (2017) 23 Michigan Technology Law Review 191.

6.1. THE EXTENSION OF THE ROLE AS MANUFACTURER... OR AN EMERGING ROLE AS FLEET OPERATOR?

Our analysis has shown that the activities considered above as required to "secure" CAM vehicles, namely cybersecurity risk management and software update management, partly overstretch the traditional legal function of (vehicle) manufacturing. Securing CAM vehicles thus partly implies to perform activities qualifying rather as services. Our hypothesis is that such activities, considered in the proposed recommendations as falling within the ambit of the (thus extended) "manufacturing function" seem to qualify as (part of) "fleet operation".[166]

A fleet operator can generally be defined as the entity "in charge of the maintenance and operation of fleet vehicles".[167] Aside cybersecurity and software update management as studied above, the role as operator has been observed to be technically required "with level 4 – 5 autonomous vehicles, [where] a fleet operator will require remote control of the vehicle in order to resolve deadlocks", this function being "critical to secure such capabilities".[168] Although the testing may not entirely foreshadow future real-life deployments, signs of a similar role as operator *can already be observed* in the testing of autonomous vehicles. The so-called "Code of Practice for testing of autonomous vehicles" issued by the Federal Belgian administration therein defines the "test operator" as "the person who oversees testing of an automated vehicle. The test operator [...] must at all times be able to override the automated operation of the vehicle, especially when there is no test driver in the vehicle".[169] The role as operator is interestingly attached to "safety" responsibilities.[170] Beyond technical safety and security operational reasons, fleet management or operation is also expected to be needed for CAM to deliver the policy expectations, which is already visible with vehicle platooning, where coordination is required to optimize vehicle, road infrastructure capacity and/or energy consumption.[171] As the CAM ecosystem is

166 For a similar opinion, see Bryant Smith, 'Automated Driving and Product Liability' (2017) 2017 Michigan State Law Review 1, 16. The author notes that, for safety reasons "vehicles with automated driving systems are likely to be operated either in fleets or with the ongoing involvement of their developers." He especially mentions the quick maintaining process allowed by over-the-air software updates.

167 Petit (n 138).

168 Ibid. See also Johnsen and others (n 4) 1796.

169 Code of Practice for testing in Belgium (n 28), para 2.9.

170 Ibid, para 1.1. According to this Code of Practice, the test operator (or also possibly the test driver) is assisted by a "test assistant", who would for instance "monitor the information relayed via screens or other information systems designed to provide feedback and [...] observe the reactions of other road users", see Para 2.10. The function as test assistant may be considered as making part of test operations.

171 Ion Nicolae Stancel and Maria Claudia Surugiu, 'Fleet Management System for Truck Platoons – Generating an Optimum Route in Terms of Fuel Consumption' (2017) 181 Procedia Engineering 861.

still in the making, the contours of fleet operation or fleet management remain unclear, especially vis-à-vis vehicle manufacturers on the one hand and the also changing nature of traffic management on the other hand. Further research is therefore needed to clarify the disruption brought by CAM to the role as vehicle manufacturer. Consequently, research is also required to clarify what should be regulated as part of vehicle technical regulation, as opposed to the potential regulation of an emerging role as fleet operator.

6.2. CONSEQUENCES FOR LIABILITY

Firstly, considering that the draft recommendations of UNECE essentially proposed to extend the reach of vehicle technical regulations beyond traditional product legislation, the consistency of such policy proposal with EU existing product legislation inevitably calls for further analysis.[172]

Secondly, the above study more generally invites to readjust scholarly discussion on the liability regime for the future CAM environment. The vehicle manufacturer has mostly been designated in the literature as the most appropriate entity to bear the burden of first-line liability for damage caused 'by' (or rather 'in relation to') CAM vehicles and suffered by third parties.[173] More or less strict liability regimes have been envisaged,[174] for that purpose. The reasoning is often based on the observation that operation of the vehicle would gradually shift from the human driver to the CAM (and especially "autonomous") vehicle, in the context of breaches of traffic law.[175] Three nuances can be derived from our study. First, the focus on the operation of the vehicle shifting from the human driver to "the autonomous vehicle" may overlook the changing nature of the *vehicle* itself in the CAM context. The above analysis suggests that the delineation of the contours of the CAM vehicle is blurring, as the vehicle becomes increasingly connected to its environment.[176] Second,

---

172 This item is also briefly touched upon in Schellekens (n 4) Section 4.2.5.1.

173 See Lisa Collingwood, 'Privacy Implications and Liability Issues of Autonomous Vehicles' (2017) 26 Information & Communications Technology Law 32, 40–44. The author presents the theoretical framework in which liability issues are being mostly tackled, namely the gradual shift of traffic decisions from the human driver to the "vehicle". She also outlines the scholarly debate on the identification of entity(ies) to hold liable in case of accidents and mentions the strong scholarly focus on the manufacturer. Further, she interestingly indicates her view that "no one of these stances, taken in isolation, is necessarily the most correct because there are several interconnected elements of the autonomous vehicle conundrum". Finally, she mentions cybersecurity obligations as potential grounds for liability, especially as part of criminal law.

174 See for instance, Melinda Florina Lohmann, 'Liability Issues Concerning Self-Driving Vehicles' (2016) 7 European Journal of Risk Regulation 335.

175 See for example, Schellekens (n 64).

176 In this regard, the report from the European Parliament evaluating CAM risks which may not be covered by EU law identify as "new risks" "software failure", "network failure" and

but related to the first, the focus on "the manufacturer" may overlook the (upcoming) emergence of other relevant roles and entities.[177] For illustration, the proposed C-ITS Regulation, if adopted, would create new legal roles, such as this as "C-ITS station operator". Additionally and as discussed in the previous sub-section, the manufacturing function may be getting *overstretched*, should the UNECE proposed recommendations or similar regulation be implemented to secure CAM vehicles. The manufacturing function appears to be undergoing major transformations with CAM developments, which would first need to be carefully analysed. The potential emergence of a function as fleet operator should especially be considered. Third and final, the (sometimes implicit) focus on *traffic law* as relevant legal standard may overlook the changing nature of risks and of the causation of road accidents in the CAM context. In fault-based liability regimes, liability implications are analysed in the legal field *in second logical instance*. Liability as the legal responsibility to compensate a damaged third party in case of *breach of (a) certain legal standard(s)*, can be logically established only based on the prior identification of the legal standard(s). Although the future CAM ecosystem remains yet unknown, a shift of safety-related risks to cybersecurity sensitivity has already been found to exist (see above). Traffic law as legal standard for liability in case of damages caused to third parties *is therefore likely to be complemented* by *inter alia* (cyber-)security legal frameworks, which calls for further legal analysis. In other words, we are looking at the CAM future with the lenses of the present situation, while claiming that the CAM future will look incredibly different from the present situation.[178] This conclusion meets the opinion of Gasser that, "to a great extent, the [above-described] argumentation follows the assumption that the cause of accidents today is regularly due to improper control decisions on the part of the driver. However, the (in future potentially automated) vehicle control may represent *only one of multiple possible accident causes*" (emphasis added).[179]

"hacking / cybercrime". Tatjana Evas and others, A Common EU Approach to Liability Rules and Insurance for Connected and Autonomous Vehicles: European Added Value Assessment Accompanying the European Parliament's Legislative Own-Initiative Report (Rapporteur: Mady Delvaux) : Study (European Parliament, 2018).

177 The calls for the attribution of legal personhood to autonomous robots (and especially autonomous vehicles) may also be found to fall short of taking both elements sufficiently into account, see for instance E Palmerini and others, 'RoboLaw: Towards a European Framework for Robotics Regulation' (2016) 86 Robotics and Autonomous Systems 78.

178 This is otherwise called the "Jetsons fallacy", namely "predictions made by extrapolating individual items of interest into the future while holding everything else in the world – other technologies, law, norms, values and markets – constant". See Bryant Walker Smith, 'How Governments Can Promote Automated Driving' (2017) 47 New Mexico Law Review 99, 102. Apart from cybersecurity legal frameworks, other legislations may be found relevant, or may be implemented in the future. They may for instance relate to the "Mobility as a Service" ecosystem, which is expected from CAM, and may have a huge impact on allocation of liability.

179 Tom Michael Gasser, 'Fundamental and Special Legal Questions for Autonomous Vehicles' in Markus Maurer and others (eds), *Autonomous Driving: Technical, Legal and Social Aspects*

7. CONCLUSION

Based on the analysis of the two recent proposed recommendations of the UNECE for vehicle technical regulations on cybersecurity, this book chapter has evaluated to what extent vehicle type-approval legislation is fit for the purpose of ensuring cybersecurity of CAM vehicles. It was found to be insufficient given the changing nature of CAM vehicles and therefore of risks. Firstly, our analysis confirmed the opinion of Schellekens that type-approval legislation cannot accommodate the dynamic character of cybersecurity threats. The draft recommendations of UNECE do propose means to tackle these challenges as part of vehicle technical regulations, by essentially shifting in part the regulatory focus from the vehicle to the manufacturer. The manufacturer would have to acquire certification for its risk management internal systems, which would however result in exceeding the scope of type-approval legislation. This is quite simply evidenced by the need to elaborate further legislation to arrange and enforce this new certification regime. Secondly, the analysis also finds that type-approval legislation seems to be insufficient to deal with the risks arising from the growing integration of CAM vehicles in their environment, which also means a growing imbrication of various stakeholders. This limitation is already somehow accounted for by the European Commission, at least with regard to C-ITS communications, with the proposed C-ITS Regulation to secure these peer-to-peer communications.

Against this background, it remains to be further explored how the EU legislative framework can ensure the overall cybersecurity of CAM vehicles. As this study shows, looking at the future road vehicles, otherwise applauded for revolutionizing mobility, only with the glasses of present times may not be the right way to go. The uncertainty about the future CAM ecosystem is likely to constitute a "chicken-and-egg" obstacle. Yet, signs of the upcoming future can already be observed and should therefore be carefully scrutinised. The paper identified the role that fleet operation may increasingly play, aside vehicle manufacturing, to ensure cybersecurity of CAM vehicles, which definitely calls for future interdisciplinary research.

BIBLIOGRAPHY

Chattopadhyay A and Lam K-Y, 'Autonomous Vehicle: Security by Design' [2018] ArXiv <http://arxiv.org/abs/1810.00545> accessed 6 May 2019

(Springer Berlin Heidelberg 2016) Section 25.5.1.2. Against this background, the author expressly questions the mainstream view that vehicle manufacturers would be liable for accidents caused by autonomous vehicles, while he concludes with an open question.

Chaudhary T and others, 'Patchwork of Confusion: The Cybersecurity Coordination Problem' (2018) 4 Journal of Cybersecurity

Collingwood L, 'Privacy Implications and Liability Issues of Autonomous Vehicles' (2017) 26 Information & Communications Technology Law 32

Crane D, Logue K and Pilz B, 'A Survey of Legal Issues Arising from the Deployment of Autonomous and Connected Vehicles' (2017) 23 Michigan Technology Law Review 191

De Bruyne J and Werbrouck J, 'Merging Self-Driving Cars with the Law' (2018) 34 Computer Law & Security Review 1150

Evas T and others, A Common EU Approach to Liability Rules and Insurance for Connected and Autonomous Vehicles: European Added Value Assessment Accompanying the European Parliament's Legislative Own-Initiative Report (Rapporteur: Mady Delvaux) : Study (European Parliament, 2018)

Fenwick M, Kaal WA and Vermeulen EPM, 'Regulation Tomorrow: Strategies for Regulating New Technologies' in Toshiyuki Kono, Mary Hiscock and Arie Reich (eds), *Transnational Commercial and Consumer Law: Current Trends in International Business Law* (Springer Singapore 2018)

Frisoni R and others, 'Research for TRAN Committee – Self-Piloted Cars: The Future of Road Transport?' (European Union, 2016) http://www.europarl.europa.eu/RegData/etudes/STUD/2016/573434/IPOL_STU(2016)573434_EN.pdf

Gasser TM, 'Fundamental and Special Legal Questions for Autonomous Vehicles' in Markus Maurer and others (eds), *Autonomous Driving: Technical, Legal and Social Aspects* (Springer Berlin Heidelberg 2016)

Glancy DJ, 'Sharing the Road: Smart Transportation Infrastructure Symposium: Smart Law for Smart Cities: Regulation, Technology, and the Future of Cities' (2013) 41 Fordham Urban Law Journal 1617

Hood C, Rothstein H and Baldwin R, *The Government of Risk: Understanding Risk Regulation Regimes* (Oxford University Press 2001)

Howells G, Twigg-Flesner C and Willett C, 'Product Liability and Digital Products', *EU Internet Law* (Springer, Cham 2017)

Jacquemin H and Hubin J-B, 'Aspects contractuels et de responsabilité civile en matière d'intelligence artificielle' [2017] Intelligence artificielle et droit 73

Johnsen SO and others, *Risk Based Regulation and Certification of Autonomous Transport Systems* (2018)

Knieps G, 'Internet of Things, Big Data and the Economics of Networked Vehicles' (2019) 43 Telecommunications Policy 171

Lim HSM and Taeihagh A, 'Autonomous Vehicles for Smart and Sustainable Cities: An In-Depth Exploration of Privacy and Cybersecurity Implications' (2018) 11 Energies 1062

Lohmann MF, 'Liability Issues Concerning Self-Driving Vehicles' (2016) 7 European Journal of Risk Regulation 335

McCarthy M and others, 'Access to In-Vehicle Data and Resources' (2017) Publications Office of the European Union

Milakis D, Arem B van and Wee B van, 'Policy and Society Related Implications of Automated Driving: A Review of Literature and Directions for Future Research' (2017) 21 Journal of Intelligent Transportation Systems 324

Palmerini E and others, 'RoboLaw: Towards a European Framework for Robotics Regulation' (2016) 86 Robotics and Autonomous Systems 78

Petit J, 'Automated Vehicles Cybersecurity: Summary AVS'17 and Stakeholder Analysis', *Road Vehicle Automation 5* (Springer, Cham 2019)

Prakken H, 'On the Problem of Making Autonomous Vehicles Conform to Traffic Law' (2017) 25 Artificial Intelligence and Law 341

Renaud K and others, 'Is the Responsibilization of the Cyber Security Risk Reasonable and Judicious?' ScienceDirect (2018) 78 Computer & Security 198

Roe M, 'Who's Driving That Car?: An Analysis of Regulatory and Potential Liability Frameworks for Driverless Cars' (2019) 60 Boston College Law Review 317

Schellekens M, 'Car Hacking: Navigating the Regulatory Landscape' (2016) 32 Computer Law & Security Review 307

Schellekens M, 'Self-Driving Cars and the Chilling Effect of Liability Law' (2015) 31 Computer Law & Security Review 506

Shahzad K, 'Cloud Robotics and Autonomous Vehicles' (2016) Autonomous Vehicle section 3.4

Skeete J-P, 'Level 5 Autonomy: The New Face of Disruption in Road Transport' (2018) 134 Technological Forecasting and Social Change 22

Smith B, 'Automated Driving and Product Liability' (2017) 2017 Michigan State Law Review 1

Smith BW, 'Regulation and the Risk of Inaction' in Markus Maurer and others (eds), *Autonomous Driving: Technical, Legal and Social Aspects* (Springer Berlin Heidelberg 2016)

Stadler R, Brenner W and Hermann A, 'Evolutions and Revolutions in Mobility', *Autonomous Driving: How the Driverless Revolution will Change the World* (Emerald Publishing Limited 2018)

Stancel IN and Surugiu MC, 'Fleet Management System for Truck Platoons – Generating an Optimum Route in Terms of Fuel Consumption' (2017) 181 Procedia Engineering 861

Stilgoe J, 'Machine Learning, Social Learning and the Governance of Self-Driving Cars' (2018) 48 Social Studies of Science 25

Taeihagh A and Lim HSM, 'Governing Autonomous Vehicles: Emerging Responses for Safety, Liability, Privacy, Cybersecurity, and Industry Risks' (2019) 39 Transport Reviews 103

Trope RL and Smedinghoff TJ, 'Why Smart Car Safety Depends on Cybersecurity' (2018) 14 Scitech Lawyer 8

Vellinga NE, 'From the Testing to the Deployment of Self-Driving Cars: Legal Challenges to Policymakers on the Road Ahead' (2017) 33 Computer Law & Security Review 847

Walker Smith B, 'How Governments Can Promote Automated Driving' (2017) 47 New Mexico Law Review 99

CHAPTER 9

THE CYBERSECURITY REQUIREMENTS FOR OPERATORS OF ESSENTIAL SERVICES UNDER THE NIS DIRECTIVE – AN ANALYSIS OF POTENTIAL LIABILITY ISSUES FROM AN EU, GERMAN AND UK PERSPECTIVE

Daniela Brešić

1. INTRODUCTION

The number of cyberattacks is increasing and with it the fear of attacks on highly vulnerable infrastructures, such as energy or healthcare infrastructures. This is crucial, as for instance, the intrusion on an energy supplier's computer systems may affect the supply and distribution of energy which may have impact on thousands of people's lives.[1] Such infrastructures are being considered as critical infrastructures (CIs) due to their importance for the maintenance of crucial "societal functions, health, safety, security, economic or social well-being of people"[2]. These infrastructures play a vital role for society and are essential for a successfully operating internal market. In that respect, disruptions may become very dangerous for the interests of the general public due to the interconnected concept of CIs. For instance, energy networks may be highly interdependent and the unavailability of energy supply provided by CI can constitute a major vulnerability to energy suppliers (i.e. electricity, oil and gas) that can be caused through cyber-attacks. Malicious attacks are not limited by borders and malfunctioning CI may have effects on other infrastructures, also in a cross-sector manner resulting from interdependencies between different CIs.

---

1 Commission, 'Recommendation of 3.4.2019 on cybersecurity in the energy sector {SWD(2019) 1240 final}' C (2019) 2400 final 1.

2 Council Directive 2008/114/EC of 8 December 2008 concerning the identification and designation of European critical infrastructures and the assessment of the need to improve their protection [2008] OJ L345/75, Article 2(a) (European Critical Infrastructure Directive).

Therefore, a common trans-boundary approach within Europe must be ensured. However, disruptions of CI may also be caused through other technological disasters than cyberattacks, or through natural disasters.[3] As far as the first type is concerned, a disaster may also be caused through human failure, for instance, if counter-measures have not been implemented sufficiently. Natural disasters on the other hand, are often considered as force majeure and consequently it may be difficult to identify a tortfeasor in this context. The scope for the application of liability regulation therefore becomes rather relevant in the context of technological disasters, rooted in human error which may be traced back to an individual's behaviour.[4]

Responsibility may become a crucial issue in the context of cybersecurity and CI, as the ownership of CIs, such as power suppliers, is primarily in the hand of private entities. The Directive on Security of Network and Information Systems[5] (NIS Directive) is the first European legislation that introduces minimum cybersecurity criterions in order to ensure a high level of security of network and information systems while focusing on operators of essential services and digital service providers. Precaution and the incorporation of specific cybersecurity measures are of importance in order to be prepared for the prevention of cyberattacks and non-cyberattacks against their network and information systems. Cybersecurity measures may be of technical (e.g. state of the art technology) or physical (e.g. access control or camera) nature. Nevertheless, taking into account that realistically not every disaster can be efficiently impeded, the question about liability in the context CI cybersecurity has to be raised. The NIS Directive does not cover regulatory issues on liability as this remains part of the national civil law but may provide indications on this issue. Given the nature of a Directive, the NIS Directive applies on a European Union level and is (generally) not directly applicable in the Member State. The Directive has to be transposed into national law by each EU country, which demands to achieve the objectives foreseen by the Directive but also allows discretion in favour of the national legislator as regard to the choice of the measures to be taken in order to achieve the result. In this respect, national legislations are likely to differ from one another but malfunctioning CIs may have a cross-border impact when affecting a CI in another country. It may be necessary to define obligations for OES in a clear and precise manner in order to maintain cybersecurity on an EU level. Moreover, a vague or unclear definition of obligations may impact on the allocation of responsibility, and hence on the allocation or distribution of liability as well. In this regard, the following chapter

3 Michael Faure, 'Private Liability and Critical Infrastructure' (2015) 6 European Journal of Risk Regulation 229, 242.

4 Ibid.

5 Council Directive (EU) 2016/1148 of 6 July 2016 concerning measures for a high common level of security of network and information systems across the Union [2016] OJ L194/1 (NIS Directive).

aims at providing an analysis on how and to what extent the NIS Directive provides first reference points from an EU level on responsibility issues as regards to liability as well as their potential impact on the distribution of liability by using a *sui generis* approach. Moreover, the transposition of the cybersecurity requirements of OES under the NIS Directive into German and UK national law shall be analysed, i.e. how the national legislation interprets and specifies the obligations set out for OES, and what problems this may bring to liability will be examined. The application of a two-stage comparative research in form of an external comparison of national legislation is predestined to uncover similarities and differences of harmonization measures.[6] Therefore, in order to analyse the cybersecurity requirements for OES from an EU as well as national level, the chapter will be structured as follows: Firstly, the chapter will introduce the EU regulatory framework on CI and explain the connection between the CI and OES, i.e. the scope of CI protection (CIP). The focus in this chapter will be put on OES instead of digital service providers, as the NIS Directive emphasizes the implementation of stricter security requirements for OES than for digital service providers.[7] The chapter then continues with the specification of the definitions of CI and OES under German and UK law. In a second step, it will be followed by the description of the responsibilities obliging OES under the NIS Directive, and the implementation of these responsibilities into the German und UK cybersecurity legislation. In that respect, the provisions will be compared more extensively by uncovering similarities and differences between the EU and national legislation (vertical comparison) and between the German and UK cybersecurity legislation (horizontal comparison). Moreover, the results of the comparison will be evaluated by analysing the potential impact on the distribution of liability in the context of OES, while also considering potential drawbacks from a broader perspective, namely the problem of identifying fault and public authority liability.

2. THE SCOPE OF CI PROTECTION ON AN EU AND NATIONAL LEVEL

2.1. THE EU REGULATORY FRAMEWORK OF CI PROTECTION COMPARED TO THE SCOPE OF THE NIS DIRECTIVE

The European Commission established the so-called "European Programme for Critical Infrastructure Protection" (EPCIP), setting out principles and

---

6 Lina Kestemont, *Handbook on Legal Methodology. From Objective to Method* (Intersentia Ltd 2018), 12–13, 47–48.

7 NIS Directive (n 5) Rec 57.

instruments while establishing an "all-hazards approach"[8] for the protection of national critical infrastructure (CI) and European critical infrastructure (ECI) in the European Union.[9] Article 2 (a) of Directive 2008/114/EC[10] defines CI as "an asset, system or part thereof located in Member States which is essential for the maintenance of vital societal functions, health, safety, security, economic or social well-being of people, and [where] the disruption or destruction of which would have a significant impact in a Member State as a result of the failure to maintain those functions", whereas ECI "means critical infrastructure located in Member States the disruption or destruction of which would have a significant impact on at least two Member States"[11]. The EPCIP particularly aims at addressing human-made, technological attacks and natural disasters while giving priority to terroristic threats.[12] The Critical Infrastructure Warning Network (CIWIN) forms part of the EPCIP Framework and supports CIP by enhancing CIP-related information sharing between Member States on an EU level, for instance as on shared threats, potential measures, or good practices.[13] However, the Council adopted conclusions stressing the primary responsibility of Member States and operators to establish sufficient European critical infrastructure protection (ECI), and implemented the Council Directive 2008/114/EC of 8 December 2008 on the identification and designation of European critical infrastructures,[14] which however only applies to the energy and transport sector.[15] The Directive on Security of Network and Information Systems (NIS Directive)[16] as the first piece of legislation on cybersecurity entered into force in August 2016, and forms part of the defence against cyberattacks, which is often associated with critical information infrastructure protection (CIIP). The definition of CIIP has its origin in the Council Directive 2008/114/EC and reflects the need to enhance the protection of "ICT systems that are [c]ritical [i]nfrastructure for themselves or that are essential for the operation of [c]ritical [i]nfrastructures"[17]. The Directive increases the level of cybersecurity by establishing "a global approach at Union level covering common [...] exchange of information, cooperation and common security requirements for

8 European Critical Infrastructure Directive (n 2) Rec 3.

9 Commission, 'European Programme for the Critical Infrastructure Protection' (Communication) COM (2006) 786 final.

10 European Critical Infrastructure Directive (n 2).

11 European Critical Infrastructure Directive (n 2) Article 2(b).

12 European Critical Infrastructure Directive (n 2) Rec 3.

13 European Commission, 'Critical Infrastructure Warning Information Network (CIWIN)' (*Migration and Home Affairs – European Commission*, 6 December 2016) <https://ec.europa.eu/home-affairs/what-we-do/networks/critical_infrastructure_warning_information_network_en> accessed 4 June 2019.

14 European Critical Infrastructure Directive (n 2) Rec 4, 6.

15 European Critical Infrastructure Directive (n 2) annex I.

16 NIS Directive (n 5).

17 ENISA, 'Critical Infrastructure and Services' <https://www.enisa.europa.eu/topics/critical-information-infrastructures-and-services/cii> accessed 20 May 2019.

essential services and digital service providers"[18]. The NIS Directive hereby intends to prevent or mitigate breaches of security of network and information systems and services by laying down provision on CI incidents. With regard to breaches, the Directive seems to differ between breaches related to security in recital 33, as well as to personal data in recital 63 and Article 15(4).[19] Security of network and information systems is defined as "the ability of network and information systems to resist, at a given level of confidence, any action that compromises the availability, authenticity, integrity or confidentiality of stored or transmitted or processed data or the related services offered by, or accessible via, those network and information systems",[20] and "comprises the security of stored, transmitted and processed data",[21] meaning personal or non-personal data.[22] Furthermore, the NIS Directive introduces reporting obligations for entities referred to as "operators of essential services"[23] (OES).[24] As OES may be identified who fulfils the following requirements: "an entity provides a service which is essential for the maintenance of critical societal and/or economic activities"(1), "the provision of that service depends on network and information systems"(2), and "an incident would have significant disruptive effects on the provision of that service"(3).[25] By referring to "OES", the NIS Directive uses a different terminology that is similar to the term "CI" in the EU Framework, as CIs may provide essential services. The sectors providing essential services are laid down in annex II NIS Directive, which are namely the energy, transportation, banking, financial market, health, water and digital infrastructure sector. As per Article 4(4), as OES shall be considered any private or public entity. Micro and small enterprises however do not fall under the scope of the NIS Directive.[26] Given that the NIS Directive introduces a minimum harmonisation of cybersecurity standards for OES, it is eventually up to the Member States to specify the transposition of the requirements, including the specification on which entities may be defined as OES.[27]

18 NIS Directive (n 5) Rec 5.

19 Maria Grazia Porcedda, 'Patching the patchwork: appraising the EU regulatory framework on cyber security breaches' (2018) 34 Computer Law & Security Review 1077, 1081.

20 NIS Directive (n 5) Article 4(2).

21 NIS Directive (n 5) Rec 46.

22 Porcedda (n 19) 1082.

23 NIS Directive (n 5) Article 4(4).

24 NIS Directive (n 5) Rec 4.

25 NIS Directive (n 5) Article 5(2).

26 Microenterprises as defined by the Commission Recommendation (EC) 2003/361 concerning the definition of micro, small and medium-sized enterprises [2003] OJ L124/36.

27 NIS Directive (n 5) Articles 5(1), 5(3), and Rec 19.

2.2. THE SCOPE OF CI PROTECTION FROM THE GERMAN PERSPECTIVE

As directives generally do not entail direct effect, they are to be transposed by the Member States. Germany transposed the NIS-Directive into national law through the IT-Security Act[28] and had a good starting position for its implementation due to well established pre-existing security standards. Nevertheless, in Germany, the implementation of the novel requirements for CIs resulted in significant amendments on the Act on the Federal Office for information Security (BSI Act)[29]. In addition, further laws regulating specific provisions for certain CIs (e.g. the Energy Industry Act[30] which is relevant for energy suppliers) are applicable as leges speciales. Germany has had a pioneering role in regards to the implementation of cybersecurity and its approach focuses on the implementation of standards and reporting obligations, similar to the approach newly established in the NIS Directive.[31] Germany followed a cooperative approach for more than ten years before the transposition of the NIS Directive, and also intends to continue with this approach after the implementation of the NIS Directive. The cooperative approach has been guided by the "principle of joint action" to which public and private actors contribute. The state, society, business and industry work on a partnership basis ("BSI UP KRITIS") and aim at developing common safeguards, such as in form of concepts, voluntary undertakings or legal rules governed by the state.[32] In 2016, a national cyber security strategy has been developed, which emphasises again the importance of the public-private cooperation for the fight against cyber threats, minimum security standards, and the need to introduce trusting information sharing.[33]

---

28 IT-Security Act of 17 July 2015 (Federal law Gazette I p. 1324) *(Gesetz zur Erhöhung der Sicherheit informationstechnischer Systeme (IT-Sicherheitsgesetz) vom 17. Juli 2015 (Bundesgesetzblatt I S. 1324)).*

29 Act on the Federal Office for Information Security (BSI Act – BSIG) of 14 August 2009 (Federal Law Gazette I p. 2821) last amended by Article 1 of the Act of 23 June 2017 (Federal Law Gazette I p. 1885) *(Gesetz über das Bundesamt für Sicherheit in der Informationstechnik (BSI-Gesetz – BSIG) BSI-Gesetz vom 14. August 2009 (BGBl. I S. 2821), das zuletzt durch Artikel 1 des Gesetzes vom 23. Juni 2017 (BGBl. I S. 1885) geändert worden ist)* (BSI Act).

30 Energy Industry Act of 7 July 2005 (Federal law Gazette I p. 1970, 3621) last amended by Article 3 of the Act of 17 December 2018 (Federal law Gazette I p. 2549) *(Gesetz über die Elektrizitäts- und Gasversorgung (Energiewirtschaftsgesetz – EnWG) vom 7. Juli 2005 (BGBl. I S. 1970, 3621), das zuletzt durch Artikel 1 des Gesetzes vom13. Mai 2019 (BGBl. I S. 706) geändert worden ist).*

31 Gerarld Spindler, 'IT-Sicherheitsgesetz Und Zivilrechtliche Haftung – Auswirkungen Des IT-Sicherheitsgesetzes Im Zusammenspiel Mit Der Endgültigen EU-NIS-Richtlinie Auf Die Zivilrechtliche Haftung' (2016) 5 Computer und Recht 297, 304.

32 Federal Ministry of the Interior, 'Building and Community, National Strategy for Critical Infrastructure Protection (CIP Strategy)' 3 <https://www.kritis.bund.de/SharedDocs/Downloads/BBK/EN/CIP-Strategy.pdf?__blob=publicationFile> accessed 17 June 2019.

33 Federal Ministry of the Interior, 'Cyber-Sicherheitsstrategie für Deutschland' (2016) <www.bmi.bund.de/cybersicherheitsstrategie/> accessed 3 July 2019.

When defining the essential services, the German BSI Act[34] uses the term critical infrastructure instead and refers to the BSI-KritisV[35] of the Federal Office for Information Security,[36] which defines who can be considered as CI. However, similarly as on EU level, the term CI used in the German IT-Security Act matches with the term OES in the NIS Directive,[37] and will therefore be used interchangeably in the following analysis. The provisions cover several sectors, namely energy, water, nutrition, information technology and telecommunication, health, transportation and traffic, and the finance and insurance industry,[38] while the German legislation covers more sectors, in particular the nutrition and the insurance industry. Even though Article 4(4) NIS Directive intends to address public and private entities, the BSI Act's scope of application does not cover the federal administration level.[39] Moreover, in order to be considered as CI, the infrastructure has to be of high importance to the functioning of the community in a sense that would result in supply shortage or danger to public safety.[40] As an example, for the energy sector, the BSI-KritisV requires that the infrastructure provides more than 500.000 people with life important services. The calculated threshold presumes that the interruption of this service would result in a supply crisis if more than 500.000 people would not be provided with the essential service. The legislator had industry-specific threshold, which enables operators to identify whether they can be considered critical or not. Accordingly, the law needs to determine the criteria in a sufficiently concrete manner in order to comply with the principle of legal certainty, which is required for the law to be enforceable.[41]

2.3. THE SCOPE OF CI PROTECTION FROM THE UK PERSPECTIVE

The UK's initial approach aims for resilience against attacks from an "all risk perspective", which shall enable to adequately respond against all types of threats and hazards. Similarly as in Germany, it is accompanied by the general approach of partnership with industry and academia in order to secure adequate

---

34 BSI Act (n 29).

35 Verordnung zur Bestimmung Kritischer Infrastrukturen nach dem BSI-Gesetz (BSI-Kritisverordnung - BSI-KritisV) vom 22. April 2016 (BGBl. I S. 958), die durch Artikel 1 der Verordnung vom 21. Juni 2017 (BGBl. I S. 1903) geändert worden ist (Germany) (BSI-KritisV).

36 Courtesy Translation for 'Bundesamt für Sicherheit und Information (BSI)'.

37 Dennis-Kenji Kipker, 'The EU NIS Directive Compared to the IT Security Act – Germany Is Well Positioned for the New European Cybersecurity Space' [2016] ZD-Aktuell 05363.

38 BSI-KritisV (n 35) sec 2–8.

39 Gerrit Hornung, 'Neue Pflichten Für Betreiber Kritischer Infrastrukturen: Das IT-Sicherheitsgesetz Des Bundes' [2015] Neue Juristische Wochenschrift 3334, 3335–3336.

40 BSI Act (n 29) sec 2(10).

41 Hornung (n 39) 3335.

cybersecurity.[42] However, the UK government may support CI operators to protect against cyberattacks but does not take the responsibility to manage the risk, as the responsibility sits with the CI operator.[43] In order to contribute to secure CI which are resilient to cyber threats, the UK's strategy foresees the government, amongst others, to share threat information with industry to increase the knowledge about what CI must protect themselves against, to provide guidance and to conduct exercises with CI on how to manage cyber risks, to provide training facilities, consultancy services and security standards.[44] In the UK, the NIS Directive has been transposed into the Network and Information Systems Regulation,[45] which came into force on 10 May 2018 and defines an essential service as "a service which is essential for the maintenance of critical societal or economic activities"[46]. Hereby, the UK Regulation uses the same terminology as the EU NIS Directive when referring to "essential services". However, while Germany covers more sectors than deliberated by the NIS Directive, the UK NIS Regulation covers only partially the same sectors as the NIS Directive, which are namely the energy, transport, health sector, drinking water supply and distribution, and digital infrastructure, without including the banking and financial market infrastructures into the scope of the UK NIS Regulation.[47] An OES as per section 8(1) NIS Regulation means an entity which "relies on network and information systems" and fulfils "the threshold requirement described for that kind of essential service". Schedule 2 NIS Regulation provides a comprehensive overview with criteria for the assessment of the threshold requirements. In comparison to the above-mentioned example on energy supply, the threshold requirement for the service of electricity supply foresees 250.000 final customers in Great Britain, or if the electricity undertakings would have a total capacity greater than or equal to 2 gigawatts in terms of input to a transmission system.[48] However, even if an OES does not meet the threshold requirements,[49] a competent authority may designate an entity as OES if conditions of section 8(3) NIS Regulation are fulfilled, requiring amongst others that an incident is likely to have significant disruptive effects[50] on the provision of the essential service.[51] In that respect, the UK NIS Regulation provides further discretion to competent authorities for defining essential services when comparing the German legislation. The supervisory

42 HM Government, 'National Cyber Security Strategy 2016–2021' (2016) 15 <https://assets.publishing.service.gov.uk/government/uploads/system/uploads/attachment_data/file/567242/national_cyber_security_strategy_2016.pdf> accessed 03 July 2019.

43 Ibid 40.

44 Ibid 41.

45 The Network and Information Systems Regulations 2018 [No. 506] (NIS Regulation).

46 NIS Regulation (n 45) sec 1(2).

47 NIS Regulation (n 45) schedule 2.

48 NIS Regulation (n 45) schedule 2, sec 1(2)(a).

49 NIS Regulation (n 45) sec 8(1)(b).

50 See also NIS Directive (n 5) Articles 5(2)(a), 6.

51 NIS Regulation (n 45) sec 8(3)(c), 4.

responsibility for competent authorities is distributed among different entities designated for the subsector in relation to the essential service provided.[52]

3. THE SECURITY REQUIREMENTS AND INCIDENT NOTIFICATION FOR OPERATORS OF ESSENTIAL SERVICES FROM AN EU AND NATIONAL PERSPECTIVE

3.1. THE SECURITY REQUIREMENTS AND INCIDENT NOTIFICATION SET OUT BY THE NIS DIRECTIVE, ARTICLE 14 AND 15

By legislating the NIS Directive, the European Commission has mainly focused on the implementation of standards and reporting obligations, and hereby lays down the security requirements and incident notification in Article 14(1) NIS Directive.

Firstly, the provision requires that Member States shall ensure that OES take appropriate and proportionate technical and organisational measures to manage the risks[53] that may affect the security of network and information systems. The NIS Directive enforces OES in form of private or public entities to comply with the requirements set out under the Directive hereby follows a cooperative approach between private entities and competent authorities. These obligations may be considered as preventive measures aiming at limiting or impeding potential damaging events.[54]

Secondly, the NIS Directive foresees risk management and incident reporting obligations for OES, which constitutes a major milestones when implementing cybersecurity obligations. In particular, the NIS Directive requires reporting obligations for OES in cases where incidents occur. An "incident" is being defined as "any event having an actual adverse effect on the security of network and information systems"[55]. In this regard, OES shall notify the competent authority or the Computer Security Incident Response Team (CSIRT)[56] of incidents having a significant impact on the continuity of the essential service. It is common that liability issues arise where reporting obligations have not been sufficiently met. The NIS Directive however does not follow this approach and states explicitly that "[n]otifications shall not make the notifying party

52 NIS Regulation (n 45) sec 1(3)(d), 3(1).

53 The term "risk" is being defined in Article 4(9) NIS Directive, meaning "any reasonably identifiable circumstance or event having a potential adverse effect on the security of network and information systems".

54 Hornung (n 39) 3334.

55 NIS Directive (n 5) Article 4(7).

56 NIS Directive (n 5) Rec 32.

subject to increased liability"[57]. It is debateable whether this also applies if the OES provides incorrect information, as the provision may imply that the information from the notification will not be used to hold the notifying entity liable. Nevertheless, Article 14(3) NIS Directive is the only paragraph that explicitly uses the term "liability" when looking at provisions concerning OES' obligations. Conversely, it could be argued that this may be considered as an indicator that the behavioural obligations set out under the NIS Directive may provide guidance for the assessment of liability concerns on a national level.

Another milestone set under the NIS Directive, is the transposition of an increased cooperation on EU level. In order to enforce the actual transposition of the Directive, Article 15 NIS Directive requires Member States to ensure the transposition of these measures as foreseen under Article 14 NIS Directive in cases where OES are not complying with the Directive's requirements.[58] Member States therefore shall designate a national competent authority monitoring the application of this directive on a national level[59] as per Article 8 NIS Directive, and they shall designate a single point of contact, which functions as a connection point for cross-border cooperation between EU countries.[60] In particular, national competent authorities may be empowered to demand the necessary information and the evidence of the effective implementation, such as security audit results, in order to enable the assessment whether OES comply with the obligations stated under Article 14 NIS Directive.[61] The competent authority may also issue binding instructions to remedy identified deficiencies.

3.2. THE SECURITY REQUIREMENTS SET OUT BY THE GERMAN BSI ACT, SECTION 8, 8A AND 8B BSI ACT

The BSI Act, just as the NIS Directive, does not contain specific provisions with regard to civil liability. However, the responsibilities set out in the legislation may become important under the general rules of contractual and tortuous claims, as the regulation of behavioural obligations may provide an indication for the assessment of liability issues.

The general obligations for CI operators are provided in Article 8a and 8b BSI Act. The act requires the implementation of appropriate organizational and technical precautionary measures in order to avoid disruptions of the availability, integrity, authenticity and confidentiality of their information technology systems, components or processes, if the effort is not disproportionate to

57 NIS Directive (n 5) Article 14(3).
58 See, for instance, NIS Directive (n 5) Article 15(3).
59 NIS Directive (n 5) Article 8(1) and (2).
60 NIS Directive (n 5) Article 8(3) and (4).
61 See NIS Directive (n 5) Article 15(1) and (2).

the consequences of a failure or an impairment.[62] The provision contains a "should"-stipulation, requiring precautionary measures to be ideally in accordance with the state of the art. In the context of section 8a and 8b BSI Act, it has been debated whether the derogation from the state of the art would lead to an increased liability. The estimates to be found in the literature negate an increased liability and consider negligent act if, for instance, a security software has not been regularly updated.[63] On the other hand, even though the legislation is formulated as a "should"-stipulation, the draft bill points out that this provision does not confer discretion.[64] The deviation from the state of the art shall remain an exemption, for instance, if update to the state of the art would jeopardize the functionality of complex interconnected CI systems.[65] Moreover, as previously indicated, reporting obligations do establish an important goal in the transposition of the NIS Directive. The German legislator went one step further than foreseen under the NIS Directive, which only requires the reporting for incidents that have actually happened. Under German law, the reporting obligations to the national competent authority, the Federal Office for Information Security,[66] goes further as the national BSI Act does not only require the reporting of incidents that have resulted but that may result in failure or material impairment of the functionality of the critical infrastructure.[67] Section 8b(4) BSI Act requires OES to immediately report these incidents and specifies what kind of information the notification shall include, which are: "information on the interference, possible cross-border effects and the technical framework, in particular the assumed or actual cause, the information technology concerned, the type of facility or equipment concerned as well as the provided critical service, and the effects of the incident on this service." The specification of the operator however has only to be provided if the incident resulted in an actual failure or impairment.

Moreover, the BSI Act requires CI to prove compliance at least every two years, and to provide evidence for having done so.[68] The German BSI Act hereby foresees farther-reaching obligations than the NIS Directive by defining an interval for a

62 BIS Act (n 29) sec 8a(1).

63 Klaus Beucher and Julia Utzerath, 'Cybersicherheit – Nationale Und Internationale Reguliserungsinitiativen – Folgen Für Die IT-Compliance Und Die Haftungsmaßstäbe' [2013] MultiaMedia und Recht 362, 367.

64 Referentenentwurf des Bundesministeriums des Inneren, Entwurf eines Gesetzes zur Erhöhung der Sicherheit informationstechnischer Systeme (IT-Sicherheitsgesetz) vom 20.09.2017 (Germany) 35.

65 Cleary Gottlieb, 'Das Neue IT-Sicherheitsgesetz – Erweiterte Sicherungs- Und Berichtspflichten Für Betreiber Kritischer Infrastrukturen (Alert Memorandum)' (7 July 2015) 3 <https://www.clearygottlieb.com/-/media/organize-archive/cgsh/files/publication-pdfs/das-neue-it-sicherheitsgesetz-erweiterte-pflichten-fur-betreiber-kritischer-infrastrukturen.pdf> accessed 03 July 2019.

66 Courtesy translation for 'Bundesamt für Sicherheit in der Informationstechnik'.

67 BSI Act (n 29) sec 8b(4).

68 BSI Act (n 29) sec 8a(3).

continues proof of compliance with the security requirements. Evidence may be provided by means of security audits, reviews or certifications. In case of security deficiencies, the Federal Office may request their remedy.[69] The Federal Office may review compliance with the requirements at the operator of CIs and may make use of an independent third party.[70] In that respect, considering that the operator of a CI has been informed about potential or actual insufficiencies, he may act in bad faith if he does not initiate an immediate verification of the organizational and technical measures.[71] Moreover, operators and their industry associations can suggest the implementation of industry-specific security standards. Upon formal request, the Federal Office determines whether the suggested standards are suitable for complying with the requirements.[72]

3.3. THE SECURITY REQUIREMENTS SET OUT BY THE UK NIS REGULATION, SECTION 10 AND 11

The NIS Directive has been transposed into the NIS Regulation in the United Kingdom in May 2018, focusing on the governance of key obligations in form of appropriate and proportionate technical and organisational measures for operators of essential services in the field of energy, healthcare, transportation, utilities and digital infrastructure. In terms of obligations relevant to OES, the NIS Regulation contains two provisions regulating security duties of OES as per section 10 NIS Regulation, and the duty to notify incidents as per section 11 NIS Regulation. The security duties of OES require an operator to take appropriate and proportionate technical and organisational measures, having regard to the state of the art, which must ensure a level of security appropriate to the risk posed in order to manage risks posed to the security of the network and information system.[73] Moreover, operators must have appropriate and proportionate technical and organisational measures in place to prevent and minimise the impact of incidents to the systems used for the provision of an essential service.[74] In any case, operators must have regard to guidance issued by the relevant competent authority when carrying out their security duties.[75] When comparing to German law, sections 10(1) and (2) of the UK NIS Regulation describe the need for the implementation of precautionary measures from two perspectives, once to manage risks posed to the security of the network and information system, and secondly, to prevent and minimise the impact of incidents affecting their security system. The UK NIS Regulation is hereby rather broader defining the duty of OES

69 BSI Act (n 29) sec 8a(3).
70 BSI Act (n 29) sec 8a (4).
71 Spindler (n 31) 308.
72 BSI Act (n 29) sec 8a (2).
73 NIS Regulation (n 45) sec 10(1), 10(3).
74 NIS Regulation (n 45) sec 10(2).
75 NIS Regulation (n 45) sec 10(4).

as the German BSI Act in contrast aim is "to avoid disruptions of the availability, integrity, authenticity and confidentiality of their information technology systems, components or processes that are decisive for the functionality of the critical infrastructure operated by them."[76] In this regard, the more concrete a duty is being defined, the clearer are the instructions to the OES. This may also enable the identification of their violation and the allocation of responsibility, hence the identification of a potential tortfeasor in the context of liability cases. Besides, relevant competent authorities have the right to conduct an inspection as per section 16(1) NIS Regulation in order to assess whether the OES has fulfilled the duties required by section 10 and 11 NIS Regulation. In this regard, critics have argued that the requirements set out in the NIS Regulation rather focus on security issues than on resilience or the prevention of supply disruption.[77]

Section 11 NIS Regulation, moreover, governs notification duties about any incident which has a significant impact on the continuity of the essential service, also described as "a network and information ('NIS') incident".[78] An "incident" as per section 1(2) NIS Regulation "means any event having an actual adverse effect on the security of network and information systems". Here, the UK legislator follows the path of the NIS Directive and foresees notification duties for incidents insofar as they actually occurred and as they have a significant impact on the continuity of the service. Section 11(2) NIS Regulation defines the factors to determine the significance of the impact of an incident, namely the duration of the incident, the number of users and geographical area affected by the incident. Section 11(3)(a) NIS Regulation determines what kind of information the notification to the competent authority must contain. The provision requires particularly to mention (i) the operator's name and the essential services it provides, (ii) the time the NIS incident occurred, (iii) the duration of the NIS incident, (iv) information concerning the nature and impact of the NIS incident, (v) information concerning any, or any likely, cross-border impact of the NIS incident, and (vi) any other information that may be helpful to the competent authority. The information however must only be provided if it can be reasonably expected to be within the knowledge of the OES.[79] Moreover, the information must be provided in a form determined by the competent authority and without undue delay; in any event no later than 72 hours after the operator got aware of the incident occurred.[80] Compared to the German BSI Act, which requires to notify *immediately*, the UK legislation provides a specific timeframe of maximum 72 hours and hereby provides further clarification and minimizes a potential misinterpretation in terms of a notification timeframe. However, the

76 BSI Act (n 29) sec 8a(1).

77 Department for Digital, Culture Media & Sport, 'Security of Network and Information Systems – Analysis of Responses to Public Consultation' (January 2018) 11, 13–14 <https://assets.publishing.service.gov.uk/government/uploads/system/uploads/attachment_data/file/677066/NIS_Consultation_Response_-_Analysis_of_Responses.pdf> accessed 16 May 2019.

78 NIS Regulation (n 45) sec 11(1).

79 NIS Regulation (n 45) sec 11(3)(a), (4).

80 NIS Regulation (n 45) sec 11(3)(b).

notification obligations under UK law contains a subjective component, i.e. the awareness of the operator that a NIS incident has occurred, which might be difficult to determine when allocating responsibility in the light of liability.

4. DELIBERATIONS ON LIABILITY ISSUES FROM AN EU AND NATIONAL PERSPECTIVE

4.1. THE UNCERTAIN MEANING OF THE NIS DIRECTIVE, ARTICLE 14 NIS DIRECTIVE

The aim of the NIS Directive is to respond to the challenges of the security of network and information systems in the European Union by embracing Member States to achieve an equal high level of protection in their territory particularly through the implementation of cybersecurity measures.[81] From the EU NIS Directive's perspective, however, it is debateable whether the implementation of such measures provide implications on the allocation of liability within the Directive. This could be assumed as the NIS Directive seems to consider potential liability issues with regard to the implementation of cybersecurity requirements, i.e. technical measures. In particular, the deliberations made in recital 50 pay attention to the existence of product liability rules which may concern hardware manufactures and software developers with regard to their products provided to OES in order to enhance the security of network information systems. Recital 50 obviously does not allocate liability to the OES, but it does take potential liability issues into account; here with regard to the developers of the hardware and software products used by OES. Even though it appears that the NIS Directive tends to highlight circumstances which shall not lead to a potential liability of OES, recital 44 NIS Directive seems to subtly point into this direction by allocating the responsibility to the OES. In particular, the recital states that the "[r]esponsibilities in ensuring the security of network and information systems lie, to a great extent, with operators of essential services". It mentions further that a "culture of risk management, involving risk assessment and the implementation of security measures appropriate to the risks faced, should be promoted and developed through appropriate regulatory requirements and voluntary industry practices." Regardless of a potential public authority liability, it could be argued that complying with standards or guidelines issued or confirmed by public authorities may provide an indication for the necessary diligence in favour of the OES.[82] Whereas recommendations provided by the European Commission as on cybersecurity in the energy sector[83] are not binding for the Member States, and

[81] NIS Directive (n 5) Rec 4, 74.
[82] Beucher and Utzerath (n 63) 367.
[83] Commission (n 1).

therefore may not have legal consequences, however, at the time of writing the EU Cybersecurity Act,[84] a framework which foresees the establishment of European cybersecurity certification schemes, has been released. These certification schemes aim at harmonising cybersecurity practices within the EU[85] and may become mandatory for OES[86].[87] This certificate shall attest that a product, service or process,[88] forming part of a network or information system, complies with the cybersecurity requirements laid down in the European cybersecurity certification scheme.[89] ENISA together with Member States and other relevant stakeholders as from the industry shall establish advice, guidelines and best practice for the security requirements related to OES.[90] This may raises the question whether complying with EU certification schemes or guidelines, may provide an indication of acting with due diligence. It seems, however, that recital 77 Cybersecurity Act pleads against this assumption. In particular, recital 77 Cybersecurity Act states that a certification cannot guarantee that the certified service or process as such are "cyber secure" but "that they comply with certain cybersecurity requirements laid down elsewhere, for example in technical standards". With a view to liability, however, it remains necessary to elaborate the responsibility for the tortious act on a case-by-case basis, as each liability case has to be assessed separately considering the particular violation of technical or organisational requirements which causes the damage under the specific circumstances.[91] Besides, infringements of European cybersecurity certification schemes may lead to further penalties for OES.[92]

When looking at the OES' obligation to the notification of incidents as per Article 14(3) NIS Directive, the Directive explicitly negates a potential increased liability for notifications made by the notifying party. In this regard, it could be assumed that a false or negligent incorrect reporting may not have a negative impact on the OES, even though the provision indicates that notifications should include relevant information that enables to determine any cross-border impact of the incident. Trust and information sharing are crucial for the realisation of cybersecurity in CIs.[93] Nevertheless, The NIS Directive considers in recital 8 that a Member State is not obliged "to supply information the disclosure of which it

---

84 Council Regulation (EU) 2019/881 of 17 April 2019 on ENISA (the European Union Agency for Cybersecurity) and on information and communications technology cybersecurity certification and repealing Regulation (EU) No 526/2013 [2019] OJ L151/15 (Cybersecurity Act).

85 Cybersecurity Act (n 84) Rec 95.

86 The definition of OES in the EU Cybersecurity Act corresponds with the NIS Directive (Article 2(4) Cybersecurity Act, which refers to Article 4(4) NIS Directive).

87 Cybersecurity Act (n 84) Article 56(3).

88 The EU Cybersecurity Act uses the term ICT product, ICT service and ICT process, which are defined in Article 2(12–14).

89 Cybersecurity Act (n 84) Article 56(1), Article 2(9).

90 Cybersecurity Act (n 84) Article 8, Article 9(c); NIS Directive (n 5) Article 19(2).

91 Spindler (n 31) 308.

92 Cybersecurity Act (n 84) Article 65.

93 Commission (n 1) 2.

considers to be contrary to the essential interests of its security". Similarly, an OES may also simply be restricted in the amount of information the entity can share with public authorities due to legal or other obligations. For instance, private entities may only disclose their knowledge to the extent as the information is not sensitive or may not be considered as a business secret.[94] Moreover, with regard to incidents involving personal data, the OES will have to ensure that he complies with the data protection regulation, i.e. the General Data Protection Regulation[95] and Member State law, before transferring and disclosing personal data to another entity. This may cause further restrictions with regard to information sharing, as OES may fear penalties when infringing the General Data Protection Regulation.[96] Therefore, it is likely that the OES primarily remains the entity with comprehensive and detailed knowledge about the internal operations, and hence, remains mainly responsible for errors caused through discrepancies by the infrastructure in question.

4.2. THE NATIONAL IMPLEMENTATION OF ARTICLE 14 NIS DIRECTIVE FROM AN UK AND GERMAN PERSPECTIVE

Yet, however, it appears that the NIS Directive is too vague when defining OES and cybersecurity requirements, which leads to varying cybersecurity standards between different sectors. Given the variety of definitions of CI between the EU and Member States, it appears that a potential conflict may arise due to the differing levels of sophistication of various CI protection strategies.[97] Developing the consideration on a diverging applicable scope and differing technical and organisation measures between different Member States further with a view to the allocation of liability, Member States may introduce diverging liability provisions and issues. The discrepancies, which are occurring through diverging national definitions and cybersecurity requirements are characterised by the transposition of a minimum harmonisation as per Article 114 TFEU,[98] which allows Member States to regulate within the discretion permitted by the NIS Directive. However, it seems that both the UK and the German legislator follow a rather broader concept of OES but in different ways. Germany, in comparison to the NIS Directive and the UK, includes additional sectors, in particular nutrition, telecommunication, and the finance and insurance industry, whereas

---

94 Christer Pursiainen, 'The Challenges for European Critical Infrastructure Protection' (2009) 31 Journal of European Integration 721, 734.

95 Council Regulation (EU) 2016/679 of 27 April 2016 on the protection of natural persons with regard to the processing of personal data and on the free movement of such data, and repealing Directive 95/46/EC [2016] OJ L119/1 (General Data Protection Regulation).

96 General Data Protection Regulation (n 95) Articles 82–84.

97 Pursiainen (n 94) 725.

98 Consolidated version of the Treaty on the Functioning of the European Union [2012] OJ C326.

the competent UK authorities reserve the right to determine organisations as critical if an incident may have an significant effect on society.[99] Implementing broader approaches may enhance the protection of more organisations and the cooperation amongst different sectors within a country, which vice versa may reduce potential liability risks by implementing security counter-measures and creating awareness through information sharing.

When looking at the implementation of technical and organisational measures, the relevant measures are not determined within the German BSI Act and the UK NIS Regulation itself. In Germany, as per section 8a(2) BSI Act, OES themselves can define precautionary measures in each sector in form of security standards, which need to be approved by the competent authority. On the one hand, such an approach allows for flexibility to constantly adopt adequate measures according to the state of the art. On the other hand, public authorities are being provided with the right to supervise the transposition of the measures concerned.[100] Similarly, the UK imposes technical methods, frameworks and standards for operators to comply with.[101] With that in mind, one could argue that the responsibility of public authorities to investigate potential violations and to supervise the realisation of technical and physical measures may lead towards a "shared responsibility". However, it may be to far-reaching to consider this degree of involvement as "shared responsibility", considering that the responsibility to maintain the overall security of the infrastructure may regularly be assigned to the OES as the entity responsible for the implementation of technical and organisational measures specifically tailored to the particular stakeholder. Also, shared responsibility may require that all stakeholders have obtained full details about the transposition of security measures.

Moreover, it may be highlighted the broader approach of the BSI Act including the reporting of incidents which may have occurred. The German legislator went one step further than the EU NIS Directive or the UK NIS Regulation, which only require the reporting of incidents that have actually resulted in failure or material impairment of the functionality of the CI. A remarkable difference compared to the German BSI Act is that the NIS Regulation requires the OES to provide "any other information that may be helpful to the competent authority"[102]. The wording of this particular section may cause uncertainty when looking to assess what kind of information could be relevant to the authority, and may enhance the penalties in terms of negligent

---

99 See NIS Directive (n 5) annex II; BSI-KritisV (n 35) sec 2-8; NIS Regulation (n 45) schedule 2 and sec 8(3).

100 Patricia Wiater, 'On the Notion of "Partnership" in Critical Infrastructure Protection' (2015) 6 European Journal of Risk Regulation 255, 257–259.

101 Parliamentary Office of Science and Technology (Houses of Parliament), 'Cyber Security of UK Infrastructure (POSTNOTE)' 3 <https://researchbriefings.parliament.uk/ResearchBriefing/Summary/POST-PN-0554> accessed 03 July 2019.

102 NIS Regulation (n 45) sec 11(3)(b).

behaviour. In the analysis of responses to UK's public consultation, it has been criticised that the incident reporting for operators of essential services may cause an undue burden due, especially for smaller companies, to an over-reporting of incidents or duplication of reporting at a time that should be committed to mitigate an incident.[103] This may cause tension between the reporting and mitigation of incidents with a view to liability as well. Nevertheless, gaining information on different aspects may allow public authorities to gain more experience on how to deal with potential threats and could be shared with other national and international stakeholder. Information sharing becomes important, as the obstacles aggravating CI protection are that CI risks are highly complex and cannot be easily determined due to the interplay of several factors, accumulating risks, and, as yet, only limited experience of the entities concerned. The diverging needs of each sector and the differing interests of public and private stakeholders impede the possibility to tackle the challenges associated with a view to sector-specific stakeholders.[104] In this respect, an obstacle for cross-sector information exchange may occur as the supervisory responsibility for competent authorities in the UK is distributed among different entities designated for the subsector in relation to the essential service provided.[105] As an example of good practices, establishing organised information sharing schemes may enable an efficient information exchange among the relevant stakeholders.[106] Also, the distribution of the supervisory authority among different entities may lead to the application of diverse standards between different sectors, as some might be determined more detailed than others, and thereby may disadvantage certain sectors. However, the EU Cybersecurity Act goes into the right direction as it foresees that ENISA may support information sharing between OES within and among sectors by establishing best practices and guidance.[107] Nevertheless, in that respect, a further obstacle will occur once the UK leaves the European Union. The NIS Directive will continue to apply after withdrawal of the UK from the EU as it has been transposed into national law. However, on 7 March 2019, a new draft[108] has been brought up, which aims to amend the currently applicable UK NIS Regulation. The draft foresees, amongst

103 Department for Digital, Culture, Media & Sport (n 77) 13–14.

104 Marjolein BA van Asselt, Ellen Vos and Isabelle Wildhaber, 'Some Reflections on EU Governance of Critical Infrastructure Risks' (2015) 6 European Journal of Risk Regulation 185, 186.

105 NIS Regulation (n 45) sec 1(3)(d), 3(1).

106 ENISA, 'Stocktaking, Analysis and Recommendations on the Protection of CIIs' (ENISA, January 2016) 16-17 <https://www.enisa.europa.eu/publications/stocktaking-analysis-and-recommendations-on-the-protection-of-ciis> accessed 03 July 2019. The reference also refers to Germany as an example for the implementation of information sharing schemes enabled through UP KRITIS and the Alliance for Cyber Security.

107 Cybersecurity Act (n 84) Articles 4(4), 5(2), 6(2), and Rec 29.

108 The Network and Information Systems (Amendment etc.) (EU Exit) Regulations 2019 (UK) <https://www.gov.uk/eu-withdrawal-act-2018-statutory-instruments/the-network-andinformation-systems-amendment-etc-eu-exit-regulations-2019> accessed 16 May 2019.

others, to remove the obligations on national authorities "to liaise, co-operate and share information with the European Commission and authorities in other Member States"[109]. Accordingly, cybersecurity and reporting obligations with other Member States may become voluntarily for the UK after its withdrawal from the EU.[110] The problem of UK's withdrawal from the EU shows the need for more specific cross-border arrangements among non-EU Member States in order to improve international CIP, however, cross-border information sharing may not be further discussed in detail.

4.3. THE PROBLEM OF FAULT / THE BURDEN OF PROOF

A problem may occur in terms of the burden of proof. The obligation to proof the cause and causality of a damage lies regularly on the side of the damaged party. Getting access, however, to the relevant information containing evidence on the cause and causality of the damage can become a hurdle due to a lack of information that is either confidential or only internally accessible to persons involved in CI operations.[111] Also audit results may not provide an indication for incorrectly implemented measures, as scholars argue that audits rather represent a snapshot of the moment in which the auditing has taken place and thereby does not reflect the moment in which the damage occurred. With that in mind, scholars are of the opinion that audits neither relieve from any liability in favour of the operator, nor do audits have impact on the burden of proof.[112]

Defining responsibilities in the various sectors is a key pre-condition for allocating liability, but may become a problem where the physical and cyber world collide. Paying attention to the responsibility of the OES to ensure the security of network and information systems, recital 57 NIS Directive highlights the need to take an approach in the light of the direct link of OES with physical infrastructure. Physical measures may concern aspects "such as culture, people, business continuity, risk and disaster management"[113]. Accordingly, it is advisable that organisations should assign tasks, determine roles, and prepare a specific cyber

---

109 Department for Digital, Culture, Media & Sport, 'Explanatory Memorandum to the Network and Information Systems (Amendments Etc.) (EU Exit) Regulations 2019' (March 2019) 1 <https://assets.publishing.service.gov.uk/media/5c7fb16940f0b6332d0ecf66/Network_EM.pdf> accessed 20 May 2019.

110 The Network and Information Systems (Amendment etc.) (EU Exit) Regulations 2019 (n 108) 1-2.

111 Spindler (n 31) 311–312.

112 Ibid 312.

113 Roberto Setola, Eric Luiijf and Marianthi Theocharidou, 'Critical Infrastructure, Protection and Resilience' in Roberto Setola and others (eds), *Managing the Complexity of Critical Infrastructures*, vol 90 (Springer Open 2016) 15.

incident response plan in order to identify, investigate and respond to risks.[114] However, given that CI are often complex operating systems, the issue on liability is getting more complicated as regards to localise the actual problem that caused the damage. Considering that many people are involved in the operations of CIs, difficulties may lie in the structure of the organisation itself. This would be the case, for instance, if potential creators may have known about the issues arisen in the information technology system, but may not have had the authority to resolve the issue.[115] Besides, it appears that most of the attacks are caused by insiders,[116] whether they may be initiated with malicious intention or by well-meaning employees.[117] Many root causes therefore seem difficult to be identified.[118] This holds true for the damaged party who does not have an insight on CI operations and likely be hindered in getting comprehensive information on internal procedures.

4.4. STATE LIABILITY IN THE CONTEXT OF CI

The elaboration of the legal status quo may create the impression that legal boundaries are becoming blurry in a vertical and horizontal sense; vertically due to the cross-border cooperation among countries and the delegation to international organizations, and horizontally due to the cooperation between private and public stakeholders.[119] However, when it comes to private liability, the scope of application remains limited to the particular Member State in accordance with public international law and its territoriality principle.[120] Unaffected hereby may remain state liability claims in the case of malfunctioning CIs that have an impact in other Member States. These have the potential to lead to liability issues due to a lack of an international agreement.[121] More importantly, however, becomes public authority liability if a failure of the government may lead to damages due to insufficient preventive measures undertaken by the public authority.[122] This may be relevant as, for instance in

114 Michał Choraś, Rafał Kozik, Adam Flizikowski, Witold Hołubowicz and Rafał Renk, 'Cyber Threats Impacting Critical Infrastructures' in Roberto Setola and others (eds), *Managing the Complexity of Critical Infrastructures*, vol. 90 (Springer Open 2016) 147.

115 Dennis F Thompson, 'Responsibility for Failures of Government: The Problem of Many Hands' (2014) 44 The American Review of Public Administration 259, 261.

116 Jaeseung Hong, Jongwung Kim and Jeonghun Cho, 'The Trend of the Security Research for the Insider Cyber Threat' in Dominik Ślęzak and others (eds), *Security Technology*, vol 58 (Springer Berlin Heidelberg 2009) 100-107.

117 David S Wall, 'Enemies within: Redefining the Insider Threat in Organizational Security Policy' (2013) 26 Security Journal 107–108.

118 Porcedda (n 19) 1078.

119 Anne van Aaken and Isabelle Wildhaber, 'State Liability and Critical Infrastructure: A Comparative and Functional Analysis' (2015) 6 European Journal of Risk Regulation 244.

120 Spindler (n 31) 298.

121 Van Aaken and Wildhaber (n 119) 246.

122 Faure (n 3) 230.

Germany, the Federal Office forming the central notification body, has, amongst others, the obligation to inform the OES immediately of relevant information to prevent threats to the security of information and network systems.[123] Such an approach might benefit OES which then would not carry the responsibility for correctly functioning CI alone, and hence might not be the only party that could be held liable. However, public authority liability has often been neglected, or at least considered to be limited, with the argument that public authorities need to be treated different than private stakeholders as they are entrusted with multiple tasks which require discretion.[124]

5. CONCLUSION

Private liability pursues mainly two functions: to prevent potential damages by introducing legal duties and obligations, and to compensate for a loss occurred through damages caused.[125] This chapter introduced an overview of responsibilities and analysed potential liability issues that may occur in the context of CI protection when looking at OES. The overview of responsibilities and obligations set out under the NIS Directive and its transposition into national law in Germany and the UK has shown the difficulties of allocating responsibilities due to an undefined common standard of cybersecurity requirements and the involvement of many actors in the private-public partnership. Issues arise as German and UK legislation consider different actors as OES, which are supposed to comply with the foreseen cybersecurity requirements. This leads to different standards for different operators when comparing the group of addressees internationally. However, when aiming at achieving EU-wide resilience and a common standard for OES on an EU level, it may be necessary to define the recipients of cybersecurity requirements EU-wide uniformly. Particularly, a lack of regulation which defines specifically what steps and measures CI need to adapt leads to a lack of a common "standard of care"[126]. Yet, only when a common ground for the implementation of a standard of cybersecurity care will be found, negligence liability, attesting that an action or omission has resulted in failure when deviating from a standard of care, may be applicable.[127] A uniform legislation on an EU level, which defines concrete

123 See BIS Act (n 29) sec 8b(2)(Nr. 4)(a).

124 Gerrit De Geest, 'Who Should Be Immune from Tort Liability?' (2012) 41 The Journal of Legal Studies 291, 317.

125 Faure (n 3) 230.

126 Scott J Shackelford, Andrew A Proia, Brenton Martell, Amanda N Craig, 'Toward a Global Cybersecurity Standard of Care?: Exploring the Implications of the 2014 NIST Cybersecurity Framework on Shaping Reasonable National and International Cybersecurity Practices' (2015) 50 Texas International Law Journal 305.

127 Ibid 314.

cybersecurity measures, may enable to actually ensure a common high level of cybersecurity among different sectors on an EU level. A clear allocation of responsibilities may lead to better CIP, also by using a liability regime as a mechanism to prevent damage indirectly, and may introduce a common EU-wide standardization of cybersecurity requirements. According to Article 14(3) NIS Directive, notification shall not make the notifying party subject to increased liability. In this regard, however, it may be debateable whether this approach should be maintained as information sharing is essential to obtain knowledge on how to defend cyberattacks as well as to determine any cross-border impact, and hence on how to achieve the NIS Directive's objective, namely security, integrity and resilience of network and information systems.[128] However, a reason speaking against this is that OES often are not able to share all the information due to business secrets or legal obligations. The German BSIG and the UK NIS Regulation foresee penalties in case of non-compliance with the cybersecurity legislation.[129] In particular with regard to notifications, the BSIG foresees fines for reports concerning significant incidents that have been submitted improperly, incompletely or not due in time.[130] Also, the NIS Regulation foresees a penalty for OES when failing to notify a NIS incident or to comply with the notification requirements.[131] As with regard to the cybersecurity obligations, at this point, the NIS Directive seems to provide rather an indication for the allocation of responsibility and liability, which needs to be specified by the national legislator and may lead to different level of standards among different sectors between the Member States. The EU Cybersecurity Act recognizes "the need for definitions of common norms of behaviour (...) [and] the adoption of codes of conduct",[132] but however does not introduce a uniform code of behaviour within the regulation itself. It remains to be seen if and how common norms will be established. Besides, in order to avoid liability cases, OES may need to consider that the organisational component forms part of CI protection in order to maintain the operability of the essential service under potential disruptions as much as the technical aspect. The competent national authority may collaborate with and supervise CI operators in order to successfully counter security risks and incidents. In conclusion, however, it seems that public and private stakeholders do not share their responsibility equally in order to affirm collective liability when looking at the implementation of security measures and the mitigation of security incidents.

---

128 NIS Directive (n 5) Rec 13.

129 See BSI Act (n 29) sec 14 and NIS Regulation (n 45) sec 17, 18.

130 BSI Act (n 29) sec 14(1)(4).

131 NIS Regulation (n 45) sec 17(1)(b and c), sec 18.

132 Cybersecurity Act (n 84) Rec 54.

BIBLIOGRAPHY

Beucher K and Utzerath J, 'Cybersicherheit – Nationale Und Internationale Reguliserungsinitiativen – Folgen Für Die IT-Compliance Und Die Haftungsmaβstäbe' [2013] MultiaMedia und Recht 362

Choraś M, Kozik R, Flizikowski A, Hołubowicz W and Renk R, 'Cyber Threats Impacting Critical Infrastructures' in Roberto Setola and others (eds), *Managing the Complexity of Critical Infrastructures,* vol. 90 (Springer Open 2016)

De Geest G, 'Who Should Be Immune from Tort Liability?' (2012) 41 The Journal of Legal Studies 291

Department for Digital, Culture, Media & Sport, 'Explanatory Memorandum to the Network and Information Systems (Amendments Etc.) (EU Exit) Regulations 2019' (March 2019) <https://assets.publishing.service.gov.uk/media/5c7fb16940f0b6332d0ecf66/Network_EM.pdf> accessed 20 May 2019

Department for Digital, Culture, Media & Sport, 'Security of Network and Information Systems – Analysis of Responses to Public Consultation' (January 2018) <https://assets.publishing.service.gov.uk/government/uploads/system/uploads/attachment_data/file/677066/NIS_Consultation_Response_-_Analysis_of_Responses.pdf> accessed 16 May 2019

ENISA, 'Critical Infrastructure and Services' <https://www.enisa.europa.eu/topics/critical-information-infrastructures-and-services/cii> accessed 20 May 2019

ENISA, 'Stocktaking, Analysis and Recommendations on the Protection of CIIs' (*ENISA*, January 2016) <https://www.enisa.europa.eu/publications/stocktaking-analysis-and-recommendations-on-the-protection-of-ciis> accessed 03 July 2019

European Commission, 'Critical Infrastructure Warning Information Network (CIWIN)' (*Migration and Home Affairs – European Commission*, 6 December 2016) <https://ec.europa.eu/home-affairs/what-we-do/networks/critical_infrastructure_warning_information_network_en> accessed 4 June 2019

Faure M, 'Private Liability and Critical Infrastructure' (2015) 6 European Journal of Risk Regulation 229

Federal Ministry of the Interior, 'Building and Community, National Strategy for Critical Infrastructure Protection (CIP Strategy)' <https://www.kritis.bund.de/SharedDocs/Downloads/BBK/EN/CIP-Strategy.pdf?__blob=publicationFile> accessed 17 June 2019

Federal Ministry of the Interior, 'Cyber-Sicherheitsstrategie für Deutschland' (2016) <www.bmi.bund.de/cybersicherheitsstrategie/> accessed 3 July 2019

Gottlieb C, 'Das Neue IT-Sicherheitsgesetz – Erweiterte Sicherungs- Und Berichtspflichten Für Betreiber Kritischer Infrastrukturen (Alert Memorandum)' (7 July 2015) <https://www.clearygottlieb.com/-/media/organize-archive/cgsh/files/publication-pdfs/das-neue-it-sicherheitsgesetz-erweiterte-pflichten-fur-betreiber-kritischer-infrastrukturen.pdf> accessed 03 July 2019

HM Government, 'National Cyber Security Strategy 2016–2021' (2016) <https://assets.publishing.service.gov.uk/government/uploads/system/uploads/attachment_data/file/567242/national_cyber_security_strategy_2016.pdf> accessed 03 July 2019

Hong J, Kim J and Cho J, 'The Trend of the Security Research for the Insider Cyber Threat' in Dominik Ślęzak and others (eds), *Security Technology*, vol 58 (Springer Berlin Heidelberg 2009)

Hornung G, 'Neue Pflichten für Betreiber kritischer Infrastrukturen: Das IT-Sicherheitsgesetz des Bundes' [2015] Neue Juristische Wochenschrift 3334

Kestemont L, *Handbook on Legal Methodology. From Objective to Method* (Cambridge: Intersentia Ltd 2018)

Kipker D-K, 'The EU NIS Directive Compared to the IT Security Act – Germany Is Well Positioned for the New European Cybersecurity Space' [2016] ZD-Aktuell 05363

Parliamentary Office of Science and Technology (Houses of Parliament), 'Cyber Security of UK Infrastructure (POSTNOTE)' <https://researchbriefings.parliament.uk/ResearchBriefing/Summary/POST-PN-0554> accessed 03 July 2019

Porcedda MG, 'Patching the patchwork: appraising the EU regulatory framework on cyber security breaches' (2018) 34 Computer Law & Security Review 5 1077

Pursiainen C, 'The Challenges for European Critical Infrastructure Protection' (2009) 31 Journal of European Integration 721

Setola R, Luiijf E and Theocharidou M, 'Critical Infrastructure, Protection and Resilience', in Roberto Setola and others (eds), *Managing the Complexity of Critical Infrastructures*, vol. 90 (Springer Open 2016)

Shackelford SJ, Proia AA, Martell B, Craig AN, 'Toward a Global Cybersecurity Standard of Care?: Exploring the Implications of the 2014 NIST Cybersecurity Framework on Shaping Reasonable National and International Cybersecurity Practices' (2015) 50 Texas International Law Journal 305

Spindler G, 'IT-Sicherheitsgesetz Und Zivilrechtliche Haftung – Auswirkungen Des IT-Sicherheitsgesetzes Im Zusammenspiel Mit Der Endgültigen EU-NIS-Richtlinie Auf Die Zivilrechtliche Haftung' (2016) 5 Computer und Recht 297

Thompson DF, 'Responsibility for Failures of Government: The Problem of Many Hands' (2014) 44 The American Review of Public Administration 259

Van Aaken A and Wildhaber I, 'State Liability and Critical Infrastructure: A Comparative and Functional Analysis' (2015) 6 European Journal of Risk Regulation 244

Van Asselt MBA, Vos E and Wildhaber I, 'Some Reflections on EU Governance of Critical Infrastructure Risks' (2015) 6 European Journal of Risk Regulation 185

Wall DS, 'Enemies within: Redefining the Insider Threat in Organizational Security Policy' (2013) 26 Security Journal 107

Wiater P, 'On the Notion of "Partnership" in Critical Infrastructure Protection' (2015) 6 European Journal of Risk Regulation 255

CHAPTER 10

THE 'BY DESIGN' TURN IN EU CYBERSECURITY LAW: EMERGENCE, CHALLENGES AND WAYS FORWARD

Domenico ORLANDO and Pierre DEWITTE

1. INTRODUCTION

The aim of this chapter is to analyse 'Security by Design' (SbD) as an emerging concept in EU Law, especially in the fields of information security and data protection. This is especially relevant in light of the growing amount of data breaches and ever-increasing pervasiveness of Internet of Things (IoT) devices. This is even more so if we take into account the worrying trend, especially from important market players, to tolerate risks of data breaches and therefore keep IT security investments relatively low.[1] The first part of this chapter will substantiate the notion of SbD by deciphering the exact meaning of the concepts of 'design' and 'security', with a strong focus on the IT sector. The second part will then explore the emergence of SbD as a principle in the EU legislative framework. In that context, a comparison will be made with the 'Data Protection by Design' (DPbD) paradigm, which has been one of the cornerstones of the data protection reform. The last part will then highlight some of the challenges inherent to the 'by design' approach.

2. DECODING 'SECURITY BY DESIGN': A TALE OF 'SECURITY' AND 'DESIGN'

Before delving into the substance and challenges of the SbD paradigm, it is crucial to clarify the exact scope of the notions that lie at the heart of that

1 Erik Sherman, 'Massive Data Leaks Keep Happening Because Big Companies Can Afford to Lose Your Data' [2018] Motherboard<https://www.vice.com/en_us/article/bje8na/massive-data-leaks-keep-happening-because-big-companies-can-afford-to-lose-your-data>accessed 21 May 2019.

approach, namely: 'security' and 'design'. In the ICT context, 'security' has been defined by the European Union Agency for Network and Information Security (ENISA) as the protection against the threat of theft, deletion or alteration of data stored or transmitted within a system.[2] Such a definition echoes the so-called 'CIA triad' – namely confidentiality, integrity and availability – which has been recognised as the basis of information security over the last decade.[3] While the notion of security traditionally encompasses the protection of both physical (*e.g.* a data centre) and non-physical (*e.g.* the data processed on the said servers) assets,[4] the present contribution will – for the sake of conciseness – be limited to the analysis of the second component.

'Design', on the other hand, refers to "the process by which an agent creates a specification of a software artefact intended to accomplish goals, using a set of primitive components and subject to constraints".[5] Alternatively, the notion of 'software design' has been referred to as "all the activities involved in conceptualising, framing, implementing, commissioning, and ultimately modifying complex systems".[6] In other words, the activity following requirements specification and before programming (*cf.* fig. 1). More specifically, the design stage focusses on the high-level outline of software solutions to overcome a given set of issues. As it clearly appears from the definition, the design phase merely represents a fraction of the whole software development lifecycle, preceded and followed by different phases from which it is ontologically and practically distinct.[7]

---

2 ENISA, 'Definition of Cybersecurity – Gaps and overlaps in standardization' (2016).

3 David Guretz, Jason Andress and Mark Leary, *Building a Practical Information Security Program* (Elsevier Science & Technology Books 2016) <http://ebookcentral.proquest.com/lib/kuleuvenul/detail.action?docID=4711748> accessed 17 May 2019.

4 Umesh Hodeghatta Rao and Umesha Nayak, 'Introduction to Security' in Umesh Hodeghatta Rao and Umesha Nayak (eds), *The InfoSec Handbook: An Introduction to Information Security* (Apress 2014) 3–4 <https://doi.org/10.1007/978-1-4302-6383-8_1> accessed 17 May 2019.

5 Paul Ralph and Yair Wand, 'A Proposal for a Formal Definition of the Design Concept' in Kalle Lyytinen and others (eds), *Design Requirements Engineering: A Ten-Year Perspective* (Springer Berlin Heidelberg 2009), 109.

6 Peter Freeman and David Hart, 'A Science of Design for Software Intensive Systems' (2004) 47 Commun. ACM 19, 20; See also: Arthur M Langer, *Guide to Software Development: Designing and Managing the Life Cycle* (2nd edn, Springer-Verlag 2016) <https://www.springer.com/gp/book/9781447167976> accessed 17 May 2019.

7 Alan M Davis, *201 Principles of Software Development* (McGraw-Hill, Inc 1995) 101; See, for more information: Suresh Seema and others, 'A Review on Various Software Development Life Cycle (SDLC) Models' (2014) 3 International Journal of Research in Computer and Communication Technology 2320.

Figure 1. Traditional software development lifecycle[8]

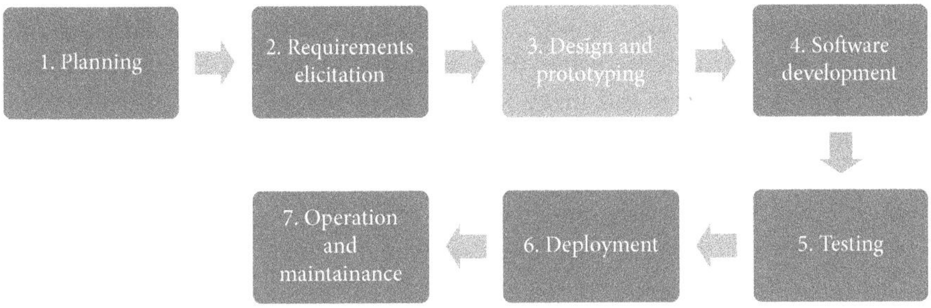

In the same vein, it is important to acknowledge a recent trend in software engineering, namely agile software development. While traditional software engineering methodologies – often referred to as waterfall models – require the completion of each step of the software development lifecycle before starting with the next one, agile software development methods put more emphasis on user centricity, continuous testing, greater simplicity and shorter development cycles.[9] As a result, the design phase is more likely to evolve over time to address issues that arise after the initial development cycle has been completed. This is all the more relevant when it comes to integrating policy recommendations or legal requirements into the design of a given information system.

3. THE 'BY DESIGN' TURN IN THE EUROPEAN LEGISLATIVE FRAMEWORK

3.1. INTEGRATING LEGAL REQUIREMENTS IN THE SOFTWARE DEVELOPMENT LIFECYCLE

The 'by design' approach has garnered the attention of legal scholars and policymakers over the last decade. As such, its influence is perceptible in various legislative instruments, especially in the context of information security and data protection. This, in turn, reflects the willingness to consider compliance with a complex set of rules as a continuous exercise rather than a one-shot,

8 Dave Swersky, 'The SDLC: 7 Phases, Popular Models, Benefits & More [2019]' (*Raygun Blog*) <https://raygun. com/blog/software-development-life-cycle/> accessed 17 May 2019.

9 Bruce Powel Douglass, *Agile Systems Engineering* (Elsevier 2016) <https://linkinghub.elsevier. com/retrieve/ pii/C20140021028> accessed 7 May 2019; Seda Gurses and Joris van Hoboken, 'Privacy after the Agile Turn' [2017] SocArXiv <https://osf.io/preprints/socarxiv/9gy73/> accessed 22 March 2018. See the definition of AI System Lifecycle in Recommendation of the Council on Artificial Intelligence (adopted on 22 May 2019), OECD/LEGAL/0449, I.

static assessment performed at a given point in time. In the same vein, it echoes the growing complexity inherent to multi-layered information systems whose functioning evolve rapidly over time. Addressing regulatory issues at the design stage also allows software developers and security experts to orient the development process and make the necessary changes before it is too late. As emphasised by Danezis et al., architectural matters "are the carriers of the earliest and hence most fundamental hardest-to-change design decisions; in addition, they reduce design and system complexity because they make it possible to abstract away unnecessary details and to focus on critical issues".[10] In that sense, the 'by design' paradigm aims at solving regulatory issues at the beginning, rather than adding a clunky layer of inefficient countermeasures after the development process has been finalised.

While the 'by design' paradigm requires taking appropriate measures to ensure compliance with legal obligations at the design stage (*i.e.*, as hinted above, before any tangible progress has been made vis-à-vis the development of the product itself), it often goes hand in hand with a 'risk-based' approach. This is especially the case for DPbD. Under Article 25(1) of the General Data Protection Regulation (GDPR),[11] controllers are indeed required to tailor their compliance exercise according to the risks posed by their processing activities to data subject's rights and freedoms (see *infra*).

The growing interest for the 'by design' approach can be seen as an alignment of what Lessig has called the West Coast and the East Coast Code.[12] The East Coast Code (a reference to Washington DC, USA) is the Law as it has been intended so far, namely all the statutes that prescribe how to behave following the logic of 'command and control' (*i.e.* the establishment of standards and targets as well as sanctions in case of non-compliance). This system is as old as the institutional government. The West Coast Code, on the other hand, is the code that the computer engineers 'enact', the instructions embedded in the software and the hardware that make the cyberspace work. In that theoretical conceptualisation, SbD and DPbD would represent the contact points between both Codes, allowing law to overcome technological barriers and to be more efficient.

---

10 George Danezis and others, 'Privacy and Data Protection by Design – from Policy to Engineering' (European Union Agency for Network and Information Security (ENISA) 2014) <http://bookshop.europa.eu/uri?target= EUB:NOTICE:TP0514111:EN:HTML> accessed 16 November 2017.

11 Regulation 2016/679 of the European Parliament and of the Council of 27 April 2016 on the protection of natural persons with regard to the processing of personal data and on the free movement of such data, and repealing Directive 95/46/EC [2016] O.J.E.U., L119/1 (General Data Protection Regulation).

12 Lawrence Lessig, Code and other laws of cyberspace (New York, Basic Books 1999), 72–74.

3.2. DATA PROTECTION (AND SECURITY) BY DESIGN IN THE GDPR

While the GDPR has certainly brought Data Protection by Design under the spotlight, the concept itself is far from a novelty. More than 20 years before the GDPR, Recital 46 of the Directive 95/46[13] – its predecessor – already highlighted the importance of technical and organisational measures to protect the rights and freedoms of individuals with regard to the processing itself and to the 'design' of the processing of personal data. The actual term, however, was first coined by former Information and Privacy Commissioner of Ontario Ann Cavoukian, who also outlined its seven foundational principles.[14] That approach has since garnered the attention of policymakers and has been acknowledged in many subsequent guidance instruments such as the Resolution on Privacy by Design,[15] the European Data Protection Supervisor (EPDS)'s Opinion on Promoting Trust in the Information Society by Fostering Data Protection and Privacy,[16] the Article 29 Working Party (WP29)'s Opinion 1/2012 on the data protection reform[17] as well as countless initiatives in the field of standardisation.[18] In the wake of the entry into force of the Regulation, the EDPS has also endorsed that approach in its Preliminary Opinion 5/2018 on Privacy by Design.[19]

Therefore, it's only recently that the concept of DPbD has made its way into an official, legally binding instrument of the European Union (EU). Since the entry into force of the GDPR, controllers are indeed obliged to adopt a proactive

13 Directive 95/46/EC of the European Parliament and of the Council of 24 October 1995 on the protection of individuals with regard to the processing of personal data and the free movement of such data [1995] O.J.E.U., L281/31 (Data Protection Directive).

14 Ann Cavoukian, 'Privacy by Design The 7 Foundational Principles' 5.

15 Resolution on Privacy by Design, adopted by the 32nd International Conference of Data Protection and Privacy Commissioner, Jerusalem 27–29 October 2010.

16 European Data Protection Supervisor, 'Opinion of the European Data Protection Supervisor on Promoting Trust in the Information Society by Fostering Data Protection and Privacy' adopted on 16 October 2010.

17 Article 29 Working Party, 'Opinion 01/2012 on the data protection reform proposals', adopted on 23 March 2012 (WP191).

18 See, *a.o.* the following standardisation efforts: International Organization for Standardization, 'ISO/IEC 29100:2011 Information technology – Security techniques – Privacy framework' <https://www.iso.org/standard/45123.html> accessed 14 July 2019; International Organization for Standardization, 'ISO/IEC 29134:2017 Information technology – Security techniques – Guidelines for privacy impact assessment' <https://www.iso.org/standard/62289.html> accessed 14 July 2019; International Organization for Standardization, 'ISO/IEC 27552 Security techniques – Extension to ISO/IEC 27001 and ISO/IEC 27002 for privacy information management – Requirements and guidelines' <https://www.iso.org/standard/71670.html> accessed 14 July 2019; International Organization for Standardization, 'ISO/IEC PRF TR 27550 – Information technology – Security techniques – Privacy engineering for system life cycle processes' <https://www.iso.org/standard/72024.html> accessed 14 July 2019.

19 European Data Protection Supervisor, 'Preliminary Opinion 5/2018 on privacy by design', 31 May 2018.

approach vis-à-vis their duties under data protection law. Article 24(1) GDPR compels them to "implement appropriate technical and organisational measures to ensure and demonstrate compliance with the Regulation", while Article 25(1) GDPR requires them to do so "both at the time of the determination of the means for processing and at the time of the processing itself". The GDPR also provides a list of criteria in light of which the said measures are to be evaluated, namely: (i) the state of the art, (ii) the cost of implementation, (iii) the nature, scope, context and purposes of the processing and (iv) the risks of varying likelihood and severity for rights and freedoms of natural persons posed by the processing.

In other words, controllers must (i) tailor the extent of their compliance efforts to the actual risks posed by their processing operations and (ii) embed privacy-conscious features in their systems at the design stage and throughout the entire personal data processing life cycle. Doing so is far from trivial. Compliance with the above-mentioned provisions will usually require controllers to (i) perform a comprehensive analysis of all the risks posed by their processing operations for data subjects' rights and freedoms, (ii) implement appropriate technical and organisational mitigation strategies into their systems to ensure compliance with all the requirements stemming from the Regulation – including but not limited to security –, (iii) demonstrate a certain degree of accountability for the assessment performed and the measures implemented and (iv) ensure the consistency and relevance of the trade-offs made during the design phase throughout the entire personal data processing lifecycle. Therefore, DPbD is not limited to legal countermeasures nor can it be reduced to the ex-post implementation of purely technical Privacy Enhancing Technologies (PETs) into existing systems.[20]

Despite not being expressly mentioned in the Regulation, the wording of Article 25(1) and Recital 78 GDPR, read together with Article 32(1) GDPR, nonetheless suggests that DPbD also encompasses the obligation for controllers to implement appropriate technical and organisational measures to ensure the security of their processing operations by design. As hinted above, Article 25(1) GDPR indeed obliges controllers to proactively embed suitable measures which are designed to "implement data protection principles" and "to integrate the necessary safeguards in the processing in order to meet the requirements of this Regulation and protect the rights of data subjects". Not only is security one of the general principles governing the processing of personal data (Article 5(1)f GDPR), but Article 32 GDPR also introduces a general obligation to guarantee an appropriate level of security. Jointly reading the above-mentioned provisions, one could therefore reasonably assume that security is also part of the requirements that controllers should comply with at the design phase, and

[20] George Danezis and others, 'Privacy and Data Protection by Design – from Policy to Engineering' (European Union Agency for Network and Information Security (ENISA) (2014) <http://bookshop.europa.eu/uri?target=EUB:NOTICE:TP0514111:EN:HTML> accessed 16 November 2017.

throughout the entire data processing life cycle. This is further supported by the flagrant parallel between the respective structure of Articles 25(1) and 32(1) GDPR, as well as the mention of 'security features' in Recital 78. In other words, the integration of DPbD in the GDPR is likely to result in a general obligation to proactively implement all the requirements stemming from the Regulation – including but not limited to security.

3.3. SECURITY BY DESIGN IN REGULATION 45/2001

Article 22(2)*j* of the Data Protection Regulation for EU Institutions and Bodies,[21] which is entitled 'Security of data processing', suggests the emergence of a SbD principle since it states that, "where personal data are processed by automated means, measures shall be taken as appropriate in view of the risks in particular with the aim of (...) designing the organisational structure within an institution or body in such a way that it will meet the special requirements of data protection". In this already dated piece of legislation, the lawmaker demonstrated a future-proof vision by tackling the organizational dimension of security and requiring specific attention when designing the organisational structure of the body. The said organisational measures represent, together with the technical ones, the two aspects that are also prescribed in the context of DPbD and SbD under Article 25 and 32 of the GDPR (see *supra*).

3.4. SECURITY BY DESIGN IN THE NEW CYBERSECURITY ACT REGULATION

SbD has made its express debut in the new Cybersecurity Act Regulation.[22] The Cybersecurity Act, published in the Official Journal on the 7 June 2019, is divided in two parts. The first is dedicated to the permanent mandate assigned to ENISA as well as to the agency's structure and organisation. The second establishes a European cybersecurity certification scheme in which SbD will play a significant role. In fact, Article 51 of the Cybersecurity Act, which describes the minimum security objectives of the certification scheme, provides more precision about SbD. Under the letter *i*, it is indeed stated that ICT products, services and processes must be 'secure by default and by design' in order to be certified. It is also worth noting that the existence of such a certification mechanism echoes Article 32(3) GDPR which considers 'appropriate certification mechanisms' as a

---

21 Regulation on the protection of individuals with regard to the processing of personal data by the Community institutions and bodies and on the free movement of such data [2001] O.J.E.U. 2 008/01.

22 Regulation on ENISA and on information and communications technology cybersecurity certification [2019] OJ 2 151/15 (Cybersecurity Act).

valid way to demonstrate compliance with the security obligation contained in the GDPR. Finally, the 'by design' approach is here coupled with a 'by default' requirement – exactly as under the GDPR for DPbD.

In Recital 2, the current 'lack of SbD' is unsurprisingly associated with the IoT sector. Recital 12 nonetheless emphasises the necessity to encourage "organizations, manufacturers and providers" to implement "measures at the earliest stages of design and development to protect the security of those products, services and processes to the highest possible degree, in such a way that the occurrence of cyber-attacks is presumed and their impact is anticipated and minimised". While merely included in a Recital, this could nonetheless be considered as a meaningful definition of the SbD paradigm.

3.5. SECURITY BY DESIGN IN THE IOT SECTOR

Two recent reports emphasize the importance of SbD in the context of IoT, namely: (i) the 'Secure by Design' report published in March 2018 by the Department for Digital, Culture Media & Sports of the UK Government[23] and (ii) the 'IoT Security Standards Gap' published in January 2019 by the ENISA.[24] According to the former document, security by design is "a design-stage focus on ensuring that security is in-built within consumer IoTs products and connected services".[25] This definition is quite tautological but, at the same time, highlights the consumer-oriented approach that is pursued.

The UK Government is aware of the actual risks posed exclusively on consumers when speaking of the security of IoT, and tries to distribute this burden more equally throughout the production and supply chains. The adopted strategy suggests the development of guidelines in the form of codes of practice and economic incentives. SbD will be introduced in those codes like a 'security mindset' encouraging companies to "design products and services with security in mind, from product development through to the entire product lifecycle".[26] Moreover, a voluntary labelling is envisaged in order to build trust among consumers and the industry in terms of security.[27] This soft law approach made of codes of conduct and labelling systems could, however, prove inefficient on

---

23 Department for Digital, Culture, Media & Sport at UK Government, 'Secure by Design: Improving the cybersecurity of consumer Internet of things Report' (2018) <https://assets.publishing.service.gov.uk/government/uploads/system/uploads/attachment_data/file/775559/Secure_by_Design_Report_.pdf> accessed 15 July 2019.

24 ENISA, IoT Security Standards gap Analysis: Mapping of existing standards against requirements on security and privacy in the area of IoT (Version 1.0, 2018), <https://www.enisa.europa.eu/publications/iot-security-standards-gap-analysis>, accessed 7 August 2019.

25 Secure by Design, UK Gov. (n 24) 33.

26 Ibid, 16.

27 Ibid, 25–26.

the long run since there is no legal obligation and the whole system at the end relies upon consumers' choice.

The EU's intentions regarding SbD in the IoT sector are also worth noting. In fact, the certification scheme is considered as a way to operationalise SbD. The Cybersecurity Act introduces the mentioned cybersecurity scheme, while ENISA will support its implementation. In its last IoT Security Standards Gap published last December, ENISA lists existing standards that could already be used to build up a secure by design IoT.[28]

4. CHALLENGES OF THE 'BY-DESIGN' APPROACH

4.1. A CALL FOR INTERDISCIPLINARITY

By essence, the 'by design' paradigm requires a close collaboration between many disciplines, including but not limited to computer science, law, economics, psychology, sociology, management and ethics. This is especially true when it comes to DPbD. Article 25(1) GDPR indeed instructs controllers to implement appropriate *technical* and *organisational* measures. As it appears from the wording of that provision, the countermeasures that must be implemented are not limited to purely technical mitigation strategies. Rather, it encompasses solutions ranging from physical access control to the drafting of policy documents to the development of a refined approach towards traditional software development methodologies. As a result, compliance with Article 25(1) is not – and shouldn't be left to – legal experts acting on their own. The need for such an interdisciplinary stance has long been emphasised by academics[29] and policymakers.[30]

This can be illustrated in practice by the conceptual and methodological gap between security-focussed risks assessment methods – such as threat

---

28 IoT Security Standards, ENISA (n 25) 12.

29 Zhendong Ma and others, 'Towards a Multidisciplinary Framework to Include Privacy in the Design of Video Surveillance Systems' in Preneel B and Ikonomou D (eds), Privacy Technologies and Policy (Springer 2014); Pagona Tsormpatzoudi, Bettina Berendt and Fanny Coudert, 'Privacy by Design: From Research and Policy to Practice – the Challenge of Multi-Disciplinarity', in Preneel B and Ikonomou D (eds), Privacy Technologies and Policy (Springer 2015); Troncoso C and others, 'PRIPARE Deliverable 5.3 – Recommendations and Research Agenda' (2015) <http://pripareproject.eu/wp-content/uploads/2013/11/PRIPARE_Deliverable_D5.3_v1.0.pdf> accessed 04 July 2019.

30 Danezis and others (n 10); EDPS, 'Preliminary Opinion of the European Data Protection Supervisor Privacy and Competitiveness in the Age of Big Data: The Interplay between Data Protection, Competition Law and Consumer Protection in the Digital Economy' <https://edps.europa.eu/sites/edp/files/publication/14-03-26_competitition_law_big_data_en.pdf> accessed 9 March 2018.

modelling –[31] and legal impact assessment procedures – such as Data Protection Impact Assessments (DPIA). Although individual tool support and guidelines exist to perform both exercises, they are usually performed by different stakeholders in complete isolation.[32] Despite security being an integral part of the requirements stemming from the GDPR, it is usually dealt with by computer scientists acting with little – if no – oversight by legal experts. And vice-versa. Similarly, software engineers – who are tasked with the elicitation and implementation of technical countermeasures – and lawyers – in charge of interpreting and substantiating data protection rules – do not operate on the basis of a common conceptual framework. Therefore, core notions such as, for instance, 'privacy', 'data protection', 'lawfulness' or 'security' are interpreted differently by both communities. This, in turn, leads to architectural discrepancies, incoherent trade-offs and sub-optimal mitigation strategies being rolled out in the system. A similar reasoning can be held for any other discipline involved in the software development lifecycle.

4.2. SPECIFIC CHALLENGES OF SECURITY BY DESIGN

The GDPR and Cybersecurity Act have tried to introduce the principle of SbD in the EU legislative framework, recognizing its importance and potential utility. Nevertheless, the introduction of SbD as a self-standing value is not comparable to the DPbD paradigm which, as highlighted above, has already been widely discussed by legal and software engineering scholars. In fact SbD is not directly mentioned in the GDPR, while the Cybersecurity Act merely lists it as one of the ten objectives pursued by the certification schemes regulated under Title III (Articles 46–65). The certification schemes could lack effectiveness because of their voluntary nature, even if both Member States and the EU could introduce exceptions to render them compulsory (Article 56.2). Further assessments made by the Commission could also lead to mandatory certification schemes for products, services and processes within the end of 2023 and later on, every two years (Article 56.3).

The voluntary certification scheme system puts the burden of understanding complex issues related to cybersecurity on consumers, who will decide and

---

31 Michael Howard and Steve Lipner, The Security Development Lifecycle (Microsoft Press, Redmond 2016); Adam Shostack, Threat Modeling: Designing for Security (Wiley Publishing 2014); Mina Deng, Kim Wuyts, Riccardo Scandariato, Bart Preneel, and Wouter Joosen, 'A privacy threat analysis framework: supporting the elicitation and fulfillment of privacy requirements' (2011) 16 Requirements Engineering 1, 3–32; Kim Wuyts, Privacy Threats in Software Architectures (Ph.D. Dissertation KU Leuven, 2015); Adam Shostack, Threat Modeling: Designing for Security (Wiley Publishing 2014).

32 Laurens Sion and others, 'An Architectural View for Data Protection by Design' (2019) IEEE; Pierre Dewitte and others, 'A Comparison of System Description Models for Data Protection by Design' (2019) IEEE.

purchase accordingly. This is particularly problematic, especially in an environment like the Internet where the damages propagate easily from the private to the public field. In fact, one of the intrinsic characteristics of the Internet is that it is interconnected, which implies that a single violation might put the whole system at risk. Besides, ENISA, despite a deep restructuring, is not able to directly enforce SbD in the same way as supervisory authorities can enforce the implementation of DPbD through, for instance, the imposition of fines. A good opportunity has been missed because the Cybersecurity Act does not provide ENISA with effective means to enforce the matter for which it is competent. This misalignment between the creation of a European certification scheme and its enforcement at a national level could therefore generate a fragmented approach towards Security by Design.[33]

4.3. THE INTERACTION BETWEEN SBD AND DPBD

Now that DPbD and SbD principles are established in the legal system, it will be interesting to see how the two principles will relate to each other and how potential conflict between those two principles will be solved, whereas the law itself is reticent on the point. Data protection and security share many similarities through properties such as confidentiality, integrity and data quality. If those were ensured 'by design', it would fulfil both data protection and security requirements. Yet, they also present noteworthy differences. Availability, for instance, is considered as the data property of being accessible and usable upon demand by an authorized entity.[34] A controller might, for instance, be required to delete some personal data in order to accommodate data subject's rights under the GDPR. This, in turn, will directly impact the availability of the said information and, therefore, might undermine security. Whether data protection or security should prevail is yet to be determined. This will place developers in front of an analogue conundrum when in charge of designing software with or without backdoors. The presence of backdoors would guarantee more availability of data, while the absence would ensure more confidentiality. Another term of contradiction between data protection and security directly follows from their respective scope of application. While data protection only deals with personal data, security is much broader.

---

33 The European Cockpit Association (ECA), the body that represents European pilots, has expressed its concerns about the risks of 'certification shopping'. Negreiro M, 'Eu legislation in process – on ENISA and a new Cybersecurity Act' (3rd edition, 2019) <www.europarl.europa.eu/RegData/etudes/BRIE/2017/614643/EPRS_BRI(2017)614643_EN.pdf> accessed 28 June 2019.

34 Efrim J Boritz, 'IS Practitioners' Views on Core Concepts of Information Integrity ' [2005] 6(4) International journal of Accounting Information Systems 277–278.

5. CONCLUSIONS

The SbD principle, in line with the broader 'by design' trend pushed by the EU lawmaker, has garnered the attention of legal scholars and now plays a growing role in the realisation of the Digital Single Market. The conceptualisation of that approach has, quite logically, put more emphasis on the design phase. Such a proactive mindset could wield benefits for the industry and users by substituting the traditional norm-control-sanction model with one based on security embedded in the product development lifecycle. Nevertheless, SbD raises significant issues such as the need to foster interdisciplinary efforts and problems related to the choice of including it in the implementation of certification schemes rather than giving it a self-standing value. The lawmaker should also provide a more certain legal position for the possible conflicts that could arise in the future between Security and Data protection in the designing process. SbD will only produce the desired effects once all the above-mentioned challenges have been addressed.

ACKNOWLEDGEMENTS

Domenico Orlando is currently involved in SNIPPET, a project about designing and testing peer-to-peer energy markets in a secure and privacy-friendly environment. SNIPPET is funded by the Flemish Fonds Wetenschappelijk Onderzoek (FWO).

Pierre Dewitte's contribution to the present Chapter is based on the research carried out in the context of PRiSE, a KU Leuven-funded interdisciplinary project which explores Data Protection by Design in close collaboration with imec-DistriNet.

BIBLIOGRAPHY

Boritz E, 'IS Practitioners' Views on Core Concepts of Information Integrity ' [2005] 6(4) International Journal of Accounting Information Systems 260–279.

Cavoukian A, 'Privacy by Design and the Emerging Personal Data Ecosystem' (*Information and privacy Commissioner of Ontario*, October 2012) <https://www.ipc.on.ca/wp-content/uploads/Resources/pbd-pde.pdf> accessed 17 May 2019.

Cavoukian A, 'Privacy by Design. The 7 Foundational Principles' <https://iapp.org/resources/article/privacy-by-design-the-7-foundational-principles/> accessed 01 July 2019, 5.

Danezis G and others, 'Privacy and Data Protection by Design – from Policy to Engineering' (European Union Agency for Network and Information Security (ENISA) 2014) <http://bookshop.europa.eu/uri?target=EUB:NOTICE:TP0514111:EN:HTML> accessed 16 November 2017

Davis AM, *201 Principles of Software Development* (McGraw-Hill, Inc 1995)

Department for Digital, Culture, Media & Sport at UK Government, 'Secure by Design: Improving the cybersecurity of consumer Internet of things Report' (2018) <https://assets.publishing.service.gov.uk/government/uploads/system/uploads/attachment_data/file/775559/Secure_by_Design_Report_.pdf > accessed 15 July 2019.

Dewitte P and others, 'A Comparison of System Description Models for Data Protection by Design' (2019) IEEE

Directive 95/46/EC of the European Parliament and of the Council of 24 October 1995 on the protection of individuals with regard to the processing of personal data and the free movement of such data [1995] *O.J.E.U.*, L281/31.

Douglass BP, *Agile Systems Engineering* (Elsevier 2016) <https://linkinghub.elsevier.com/retrieve/pii/C20140021028> accessed 7 May 2019.

EDPS, 'Preliminary Opinion of the European Data Protection Supervisor Privacy and Competitiveness in the Age of Big Data: The Interplay between Data Protection, Competition Law and Consumer Protection in the Digital Economy' <https://edps.europa.eu/sites/edp/files/publication/14-03-26_competitition_law_big_data_en.pdf> accessed 9 March 2018.

ENISA, 'Definition of Cybersecurity - Gaps and overlaps in standardization' (2016) <https://www.enisa.europa.eu/publications/definition-of-cybersecurity> accessed 28 June 2019.

ENISA, IoT Security Standards gap Analysis. Mapping of existing standards against requirements on security and privacy in the area of IoT (V 1.0, 2018), <https://www.enisa.europa.eu/publications/iot-security-standards-gap-analysis>, accessed 7 August 2019.

Freeman P and Hart D, 'A Science of Design for Software Intensive Systems' (2004) 47 Commun. ACM 19.

Guretz D, Andress J and Leary M, *Building a Practical Information Security Program* (Elsevier Science & Technology Books 2016)

Gurses S and Hoboken J van, 'Privacy after the Agile Turn' [2017] SocArXiv <https://osf.io/preprints/socarxiv/9gy73/> accessed 22 March 2018.

Hodeghatta Rao U and Nayak U, 'Introduction to Security' in Umesh Hodeghatta Rao and Umesha Nayak (eds), The InfoSec Handbook: An Introduction to Information Security (Apress 2014) 3–4

International Organization for Standardization, 'ISO/IEC 27552 Security techniques - Extension to ISO/IEC 27001 and ISO/IEC 27002 for privacy information management - Requirements and guidelines' <https://www.iso.org/standard/71670.html> accessed 14 July 2019

International Organization for Standardization, 'ISO/IEC 29100:2011 Information technology - Security techniques - Privacy framework' <https://www.iso.org/standard/45123.html> accessed 14 July 2019;

International Organization for Standardization, 'ISO/IEC 29134:2017 Information technology - Security techniques - Guidelines for privacy impact assessment' <https://www.iso.org/standard/62289.html> accessed 14 July 2019;

International Organization for Standardization, 'ISO/IEC PRF TR 27550 - Information technology - Security techniques - Privacy engineering for system life cycle processes' <https://www.iso.org/standard/72024.html>.accessed 14 July 2019

Langer AM, *Guide to Software Development: Designing and Managing the Life Cycle* (2nd edn, Springer-Verlag 2016)

Lessig L, *Code and other laws of cyberspace* (New York, Basic Books 1999) 72–74

Ma Z and others, 'Towards a Multidisciplinary Framework to Include Privacy in the Design of Video Surveillance Systems' in Preneel B and Ikonomou D (eds), Privacy Technologies and Policy (Springer 2014)

Negreiro M, 'Eu legislation in process – on ENISA and a new Cybersecurity Act' (3rd edition, 2019) <www.europarl.europa.eu/RegData/etudes/BRIE/2017/614643/EPRS_BRI(2017)614643_EN.pdf> accessed 28 June 2019

Ralph P and Wand Y, 'A Proposal for a Formal Definition of the Design Concept' in Kalle Lyytinen and others (eds), *Design Requirements Engineering: A Ten-Year Perspective* (Springer Berlin Heidelberg 2009).

Rao UH and Nayak U, 'Introduction to Security' in Umesh Hodeghatta Rao and Umesha Nayak (eds), *The InfoSec Handbook: An Introduction to Information Security* (Apress 2014) <https://doi.org/10.1007/978-1-4302-6383-8_1> accessed 17 May 2019.

Regulation 2001/45 on the protection of individuals with regard to the processing of personal data by the Community institutions and bodies and on the free movement of such data [2001] *O.J.E.U.*, L008/01.

Regulation 2016/679 of the European Parliament and of the Council of 27 April 2016 on the protection of natural persons with regard to the processing of personal data and on the free movement of such data, and repealing Directive 95/46/EC (General Data Protection Regulation) [2016] *O.J.E.U.*, L119/1.

Regulation 2019/881 of the European Parliament and of the Council on ENISA (the European Union Agency for Cybersecurity) and on information and communications technology cybersecurity certification and repealing Regulation (EU) no. 526/2013 (Cybersecurity Act) [2019] OJ 2 151/15.

Seema S and others, 'A Review on Various Software Development Life Cycle (SDLC) Models' (2014) 3 International Journal of Research in Computer and Communication Technology 2320.

Sherman E, 'Massive Data Leaks Keep Happening Because Big Companies Can Afford to Lose Your Data' [2018] 1 <https://www.vice.com/en_us/article/bje8na/massive-data-leaks-keep-happening-because-big-companies-can-afford-to-lose-your-data>accessed 21 May 2019

Sion L and others, 'An Architectural View for Data Protection by Design' (2019) IEEE

Swersky D, 'The SDLC: 7 Phases, Popular Models, Benefits & More [2019]' (Raygun Blog, 2019) <https://raygun.com/blog/software-development-life-cycle/> accessed 17 May 2019

Troncoso C and others, 'PRIPARE Deliverable 5.3 – Recommendations and Research Agenda' (2015) <http://pripareproject.eu/wp-content/uploads/2013/11/PRIPARE_Deliverable_D5.3_v1.0.pdf> accessed 04 July 2019.

Tsormpatzoudi P, Berendt B and Coudert F, 'Privacy by Design: From Research and Policy to Practice – the Challenge of Multi-Disciplinarity', in Preneel B and Ikonomou D (eds), *Privacy Technologies and Policy* (Springer 2015)

CHAPTER 11

PROMOTING COHERENCE IN THE EU CYBERSECURITY STRATEGY

Alessandro Bruni

1. INTRODUCTION

According to Accenture, in 2019, each private company experienced, on average, 145 (cyber)security breaches, an increase of 11% in respect to 2017. The average cost of cybercrime for an organisation increased from 1.4 million to 13.0 million dollars.[1] The economic impact of such attacks and their cross-border nature require collective action. Aware of the necessity to develop joint actions to address the technical and operational cybersecurity challenges, EU policymakers have started developing legislative initiatives with the intent of establishing a secure and trustworthy environment within the EU area.[2] Nevertheless, the initial cybersecurity legislative initiatives developed at the EU level have not declared by the EU itself to be entirely coherent so far.

Considering this, this chapter is divided into two complementary sections to describe and assess the coherence of an EU cybersecurity framework. To do so, in the first part of this chapter, a comprehensive overview of the different interpretations that have been developed on the concept of coherence will be provided. Indeed, when it comes to defining what should be considered coherent action at the EU level, there is no clear, unique interpretation of such terminology.[3] According to the context, policy or legally, the concept of coherence has been differently interpreted. Nevertheless, the latest legislative initiatives have demonstrated a positive change in this trend. Additionally, the key elements and actors that characterise the legislative development of EU cybersecurity initiatives are briefly described, namely, the EU cybersecurity

---

1 Accenture Security, 'The Cost of Cybercrime' (2019) <https://www.accenture.com/_acnmedia/PDF-96/Accenture-2019-Cost-of-Cybercrime-Study-Final.pdf#zoom=50> accessed 22/05/2019.

2 European Commission, 'Joint Communication to the European Parliament, the Council, the European Economic and Social Committee and the Committee of the Regions, Cybersecurity Strategy of the European Union: An Open, Safe and Secure Cyberspace' Join/2013/1/Final 14.

3 Helena Carrapico and André Barrinha, 'The EU as a Coherent (Cyber)Security Actor?: The EU as a Coherent (Cyber)Security Actor?' (2017) 55 *Journal of Common Market Studies* 1254.

agency ENISA and the role of public-private partnerships in the development of EU cybersecurity.

Subsequently, once having provided an overview of such crucial elements, the second part of the research aims to interpret the evolution of EU cybersecurity legislative initiatives. The chapter concludes by offering several normative reflections on the EU cybersecurity strategy that has been developed so far.

2. THE CONCEPT OF COHERENCE

Article 349, Treaty on the Functioning of the European Union (TFEU)[4] states that the Council should adopt measures coherent with the Union legal order. Also considering these provisions and the way the European Union has been structured according to its Treaties, Gauttier has defined coherence as "*the principle of action and organisation*", interpreting it from a policy-organisational perspective.[5] In the EU, this concept can be found in primary law (Article 249 TFEU and 13 Treaty of the European Union-TEU), but regardless of the multiple references, it remains challenging to substantiate. According to the interpretative angle, use of the concept of coherence assumes a different connotation. Furthermore, the concept of coherence is frequently used interchangeably with that of coordination.[6] Besides, different authors over the years have expressed diverging opinions regarding the value of such an idea within the EU acquis.[7]

Following Gauttier's perspective, Cremona and Nuttall utilize the concept of coherence to describe the rules governing the legislative initiative power of the EU regarding the Member States. According to these scholars, the concept of coherence describes, from a policy-organisational perspective, the intricate horizontal and vertical power relations that characterise the EU and determine the competences of the different actors. As a result of this intricate allocation of skills, two ties can be recognised. The former refers to the rules governing the legislative powers between the EU and Member States (Inter-Level relationship).[8]

---

4 European Union, 'Consolidated version of the Treaty on the Functioning of the European Union' [2012] OJ C 326, 26.10.

5 Pascal Gauttier, 'Horizontal Coherence and the External Competences of the European Union' (2004) 10 *European Law Journal* 23, 19.

6 Helena Carrapico and André Barrinha, 'The EU as a Coherent (Cyber)Security Actor?: The EU as a Coherent (Cyber)Security Actor?' (2017) 55.6 *Journal of Common Market Studies* 1257.

7 According to Cremona coherence provides a context and rationale for the operation of fundamental legal principles governing the relations between Member States and the EU institutions and between the institutions themselves, including the principle of primacy, the duty of cooperation and the principle by which the Community acquis is protected from being affected by the exercise of CFSP powers. Marise Cremona, 'Coherence through Law: What Difference Will the Treaty of Lisbon Make?' Hamburg review of social sciences, Vol. 3, (2008).

8 Florian Trauner, 'The Internal-External Security Nexus: More Coherence Under Lisbon?' [2011] SSRN Electronic Journal <www.ssrn.com/abstract=1885322> accessed 21 May 2019.

The latter are those that occur between EU bodies (Inter-Institutional Level). Moving forward from such an interpretation, Missiroli proposes a three-level analysis of the concept of coherence.[9] The first one governs and avoids a potential conflict of competence; also termed the *"rules of hierarchy"*.[10] The predominance of EU law over national law is an exemplification of this level. The second rule of coherence establishes the rules for areas where the EU and its bodies share competence with the Member States: the *"rules of delimitation"*, which corresponds to the EU principles of subsidiarity and proportionality.[11] The third level of coherence governs the cooperation between the EU and the Member States (principle of cooperation and complementary) and establishes, according to the area and the scope pursued, how the different actors should cooperate towards achieving a specific purpose.[12] Concurring with this analysis, the European Court of Justice has repeatedly recognised the rules of hierarchy, delimitation and cooperation when dealing with conflicts of competences among the EU and its bodies on one side, and between the EU and the Member States on the other.[13] Even if these interpretations seem to have a correspondence in the EU primary law as also recognised by the European Court of Justice, they have not been substantiated in any secondary law. The developments that have occurred and taken place within the European Union regarding the revision of the treaties, from the Single European Act to the Lisbon Treaty, do not seem to have affected such multi-layered conceptualisation.[14]

2.1. COHERENCE VS CONSISTENCY

The notion of coherence has been interchangeably used with that of consistency, and even if the two terms have similarities, there are substantial differences between these two concepts. As pointed out by Missiroli, consistency, from a legal perspective describes and characterizes a series of acts that are compatible and not in contradiction, while coherence marks those legislative initiatives that, synergistically combined, bring an added value to a specific framework. While the former notion does not leave space to interpretation, something can be consistent or not when it comes to coherence, since we can have a different perspective of it.

9 Simon J. Nuttall, *European Foreign Policy* (2000), New York (N.Y.): Oxford UP 25.

10 Marise Cremona, 'Coherence through Law: What difference will the Treaty of Lisbon make?', Hamburg review of social sciences, Vol. 3, (2008) <https://www.researchgate.net/publication/237541410_Coherence_through_Law_What_difference_will_the_Treaty_of_Lisbon_make> accessed 02 July 2019.

11 Ibid.

12 Simon J. Nutall, *European Foreign Policy* (Oxford UP 2000) 25.

13 Cremona (n 9).

14 Antonio Missiroli, 'European Security Policy: The Challenge of Coherence' European Foreign Affairs Review 6.2 (2001) 177–96.

Regarding these two notions, two implications should be considered in the EU legal and policy context. The first one concerns the use of these two notions in the EU primary legislation, while the second, from a more political angle, is related to the effectiveness and efficiency of measures that are characterized by their coherence and consistency.

From the Single European Act until the Treaty of the European Union, the two concepts have been used interchangeably in the different official translations. As amended by the Lisbon Treaty, the Treaty of the European Union in Article 13(1) refers, in the English version, to consistency, stating that the Union shall have an institutional framework which shall aim to promote its values, advance its objectives, serve its interests and those of its citizens and the Member States, and ensure the consistency, effectiveness and continuity of its policies and actions.[15] On the other hand, such a notion becomes coherence in the French, Italian and German versions. There is no doubt that this different approach has been a source of misconceptions, leaving the door open to legal uncertainty when assessing the coherence of a certain policy.

From a policy perspective, the notions of consistency and coherence are traditionally used when assessing the efficiency and effectiveness of a particular policy. The EU's architecture, especially when it comes to the development of legislative initiatives where unanimity or majority among Member States is necessary, entails that coherence is frequently sacrificed to achieve agreement, resulting in approving measures that are neither effective or efficient.

Considering this, it should, therefore, be questioned whether a distinction between the notion of coherence and consistency is necessary. Indeed, while from a policy perspective the evaluation of an EU policy that is not appropriate requires differentiation between these two concepts, from a legal angle such separation might be useful to understanding the development and the interaction between the horizontal and vertical relations that characterize the EU and the policies developed within it.

2.2. COHERENCE PRINCIPLE IN THE EU CYBERSECURITY LEGISLATIVE FRAMEWORK

Within the EU cybersecurity legislative framework, the interpretation of coherence as an organisational principle that governs the legislative initiative powers between Member States and EU bodies carried out by authors such as Missiroli, has been challenged by Carrapico and Barrinha. According to the two scholars to have coherent coordination it is necessary that involved actors have

[15] Consolidated versions of the Treaty on European Union and the Treaty on the Functioning of the European Union Consolidated version Declarations annexed to the Final Act of the Intergovernmental Conference which adopted the Treaty of Lisbon signed on 13 December 2007 (2016) OJ C 202, Article 13 TEU.

a shared understanding of the field they intend to regulate.[16] According to their thesis, without a universal acknowledgement of the risks and threats posed to the Member States, any EU cybersecurity legislation risks to to be lacking in coherence.

When it comes to defining the level of risk of a specific asset or service, the different perspectives that the Member States might have on the same assets might determine a different approach to secure the same asset or service. Considering this, in the next sections, the thesis developed by Carrapico and Barrinha will be used to describe and analyse the EU cybersecurity legislative initiatives.

3. THE EU CYBERSECURITY CONTEXT

The Cybersecurity Act entered into force on 27 June 2019 and is the latest building block in the field of cybersecurity at EU level. The legislative binding and not-binding legislative initiatives that have been developed by the EU have paved the way to this latest Regulation, trying to assess all challenges that characterise the cybersecurity environment. In parallel with the development of these initiatives, the concept of coherence has been developed since it has always been considered as a prodromal element for achieving a secure EU digital ecosystem.

3.1. THE EU AND CYBERSECURITY

The first difficulty when assessing the coherence of EU cybersecurity legislation comes from the absence of a definition of cybersecurity.[17]

While at the national level, many Member States have developed their definitions of cybersecurity, at the EU level, there is no binding definition. The only comprehensive description of cybersecurity is the one included in the EU Cybersecurity Strategy of 2013 (2013 EUCSS), where cybersecurity is defined as "*the safeguard, and the actions that can be used to protect the cyber domain, both in the civilian and military fields, from those threats that are associated with or that, may harm its interdependent networks and information infrastructure. Cyber-security strives to preserve the availability and integrity of the networks and infrastructure and the confidentiality of the information contained therein*".[18]

16 Helena Carrapico and André Barrinha, 'The EU as a Coherent (Cyber)Security Actor?: The EU as a Coherent (Cyber)Security Actor?' (2017) 55 Journal of Common Market Studies 1257.

17 Tatiana Tropina and Cormac Callanan, *Self- and Co-Regulation in Cybercrime, Cybersecurity and National Security* (Springer International Publishing 2015).

18 European Commission, 'Joint Communication to the European Parliament, the Council, the European Economic and Social Committee and the Committee of the Regions, Cybersecurity Strategy of the European Union: An Open, Safe and Secure Cyberspace'.

For this book chapter, it is also useful to analyse the definition that is provided for cybercrime in the same communication. The European Union Cybersecurity Strategy 2013 defines cybercrime as *"a broad range of different criminal activities where computers and information systems are involved either as a primary tool or as a primary target. Cybercrime comprises traditional offences (for example, fraud, forgery and identity theft), content related offences (for example, online distribution of child pornography or incitement to racial hatred) and offences unique to computers and information systems (for examples, attacks against information systems, denial services and malware)"*.[19]

According to the given definitions, these two notions have a lot in common but at the same time in regards to the area, the cybercrime area is broader than that of cybersecurity. Also, the characteristics of the cybercrime result to be described more precisely while the cybersecurity ones remain vague.[20]

3.2. THE INITIAL EU CYBERSECURITY LEGISLATIVE INITIATIVES

Cybersecurity and in particular, the security of Network and Information Systems have become a key priority for EU legislators, aware of the essential role of this sector in a society that is increasingly reliant on technology. The first initiatives taken by the EC, through multiple communications, stressed the necessity of having harmonised substantial and procedural measures at EU level address criminal activities.

In 2001, the European Commission (EC), through the Communication *on Network and Information Security*,[21] began developing its cybersecurity regulatory approach. In this Communication, the EC declares that *"policy measures can reinforce the market process and at the same time improve the functioning of the legal framework"*.[22] Against this background, the Communication provides a list of actions for enhancing cooperation among all stakeholders, namely, Member States, private entities and EU bodies, and stresses the importance of internationally agreed standards.[23]

---

19 Ibid.

20 George Christou, 'Introduction' in *Cybersecurity in the European Union book* (1st 978-1-137-40051-2, Palgrave Mcmillan UK 2016) 7.

21 European Commission, 'Communication from the Commission to the Council, the European Parliament, the European Economic and Social Committee and the Committee of the Regions – Network and Information Security: Proposal for A European Policy Approach' /* COM/2001/0298 Final.

22 Ibid 19.

23 *"In the Communiqué adopted in Washington on 9/10 December 1997 on Principles and 10 Points Action Plan to combat high-tech crime, G8 Ministers of Justice and of the Interior declared that: 'it is the industrial sector that is designing, deploying and maintaining these global networks and is primarily responsible for the development of technical standards. Thus, it is incumbent on the industrial sector to play its part in developing and distributing secure*

The need for improved cooperation and coordination among stakeholders has been stressed not only by the Commission, but also by the Council in some of its decisions.[24] The first cybersecurity legislative initiative developed by the Council is the Council Decision 92/242/EEC.[25] The Council Decision 92/242/EEC has settled the baseline for the development of the EU legislative initiatives in this field at Council Level. In response to the Directive, 92/242/EEC and Council Recommendation 1995/144/EC on common information technology security criteria had led to the creation of the Senior Officers Information System Security (SOG-IS), an organisation that is still active nowadays. The SOG-IS participants work together to *"coordinate the standardisation of Common Criteria protection profiles and certification policies between European Certification Bodies to have a common position in the fast-growing international CCRA group"*.[26] The SOG-IS, which is not recognised by all Member States, has been used by the Commission as a baseline for the certification system foreseen in the Cybersecurity Act. Approximately ten years later, the Council Framework Decision 2005/222/JHA[27] had highlighted the limits of EU action in this field, calling for an effective response to cyber threats. To do so, the Council, in line with the *eEurope Action Plan*,[28] which recognized the importance of information infrastructure protection, demanded a comprehensive approach to network and information security. Framework Decision 2005/222, which has as a primary aim the harmonisation of criminal offences related to cyber-attacks, stresses the importance of increasing *'the understand and awareness of the problems related to information security'*.[29]

---

systems designed to help detect computer abuse, preserve electronic evidence and assist in ascertaining the location and identity of criminals.' European Commission, 'Communication from the Commission to the Council, the European Parliament, the European Economic and Social Committee and the Committee of the Regions – Network and Information Security: Proposal for A European Policy Approach' /* COM/2001/0298 Final.

24 *(1) The objective of this Framework Decision is to improve cooperation between judicial and other competent authorities, including the police and other specialised law enforcement services of the Member States, through approximating rules on criminal law in the Member States in the area of attacks against information systems.* Council Framework decision 2005/222/JHA.

25 Council Decision 92/242/EEC of 31 March 1992 in the field of security of information systems (1992) OJ L 123 19–25.

26 Senior Officials Group Information Systems Security, https://www.sogis.eu, accessed 18/06/2019.

27 Council Framework Decision 2005/222/JHA of 24 February 2005 on attacks against information systems (2005) OJ L 69 67–71.

28 *The eEurope 2002 Action Plan is an integral part of the Lisbon strategy for making the European Union the world's most dynamic knowledge-based economy by 2010. The measures were grouped according to three key objectives to be met by the end of 2002: (i) a cheaper, faster and secure Internet, (ii) investing in people and skills,(iii) stimulate the use of the Internet.* Commission Communication of 13 March 2001 on eEurope 2002: Impact and Priorities A communication to the Spring European Council in Stockholm, 23–24 March 2001 COM(2001) 140 final.

29 Council Framework Decision 2005/222/JHA of 24 February 2005 on attacks against information systems

In line with such an approach, the EC *Strategy for a Secure Information Society,*[30] which was linked to the launch of initiative *i2010 A European Information Society for Growth and Employment*[31] calls on Member States to establish a "*dynamic, global strategy in Europe, based on a culture of security and founded on dialogue, partnership and empowerment*". The EC Strategy for a Secure Information Society moves on from the necessity of ensuring security through a coordinated fight to cybercrime and recognises the necessity to implement specific security measures for network and information systems. Such a need has to be fulfilled through the development of a particular regulatory framework. With its Strategy for a Secure Information Society, the EC intends to develop through information sharing practices, a cybersecurity culture at the private and public level.[32]

The necessity to harmonise cybercrimes and consequently have a coherent approach in securing information systems is the rationale behind the adoption of *Directive on Attacks Against Information Systems.*[33] What is still missing, adopting the Carrapico and Barrinha's thesis, is a shared understanding among all Member States of the risks and threats related to networks and information systems that might harm information systems, with a consequential impact on our internal market.[34]

In the 2012 EC Communication on Security Industrial Policy, the EC substantiating the thesis of the two scholars stated that cybercrime '*forms an integral part of efforts to develop an overarching EU strategy to strength cybersecurity*'.[35] Therefore, the Commission listed some of the problems that have hampered the development of an effective and coherent EU strategy in this field.[36] According to the EC, the main criticalities that affect the EU regarding cybercrime are: "*jurisdictional boundaries, insufficient intelligence-sharing capabilities, technical difficulties in tracing the origin of cybercrime perpetrators,*

(2005) OJ L 69 67–71.

30 Communication from the Commission to the Council, the European Parliament, the European Economic and Social committee and the Committee of the Regions – A strategy for a Secure Information Society – "Dialogue, partnership and empowerment" {SEC(2006) 656}, COM/2006/0251 final.

31 Communication from the Commission to the Council, the European Parliament, the European Economic and Social Committee and the Committee of the Regions, '*i2010- A European Information Society for growth and employment*', COM(2005) 229 final.

32 Carrapico and Barrinha (n 4).

33 Directive 2013/40/EU of the European Parliament and of the Council of 12 August 2013 on attacks against information systems and replacing Council Framework Decision 2005/222/JHA (2013) OJ L218 8–14.

34 George Christou, 'Introduction' in Cybersecurity in the European Union: Resilience and Adaptability in Governance Policy (1st edition, Palgrave Mcmillan UK 2016) 98.

35 European Commission, 'Communication from the Commission to the European Parliament, the Council and the European Economic and Social Committee, Security Industrial Policy Action Plan for an innovative and competitive Security Industry' (2012) COM/2012/0417 final.

36 Ibid.

scarcity of trained staff, and inconsistent cooperation with other stakeholders responsible for cybersecurity."[37]

Even if much progress has been made, it seems that some of these critical issues are still relevant today and represent some of the reasons why the EU has not established a comprehensive and coherent approach to cybersecurity yet. In light of the concept of coherence, it should be noted that the legislative initiatives analysed so far, while stressing the importance of coordinated actions, do not provide a substantive definition of core components of cybersecurity, such as the risks and threats.

The implementation of measures and concepts embedded in the Budapest Cybercrime Convention[38] through the already mentioned Framework Decision 2005/222 and the 2013 Cybercrime Directive (replacing the Framework Decision)[39] have enabled the harmonisation of what constitutes cybercrime- among the Member States. Unfortunately, the Budapest Convention and implementing EU legislative initiatives focus on criminal law and do not deal as such with the security angle.[40]

4. EU CYBERSECURITY ACTORS

The development of legislative initiatives in the field of cybersecurity and the attempt to create a coherent framework has been influenced by the activities of ENISA, the EU Agency that has been created to deal with the challenges related to the Network and Information Systems. Also, due to the characteristics of this field, the role of private parties in the development of the latest initiatives has been essential.

4.1. ENISA

The attempt to establish a cybersecurity culture within the EU has been supported by the activities carried out by ENISA, the EU Agency on Network and Information Security. ENISA, established in 2004 with the Regulation

---

37 Ibid.

38 Council of Europe, 'Convention on Cybercrime' (23 November 2011) <www.europarl.europa.eu/meetdocs/2014_2019/documents/libe/dv/7_conv_budapest_/7_conv_budapest_en.pdf> accessed 11 June 2001.

39 In Particular, Art. 1 states that "This Directive establishes minimum rules concerning the definition of criminal offences and sanctions in the area of attacks against information systems. It also aims to facilitate the prevention of such offences and to improve cooperation between judicial and other competent authorities. Directive 2013/40/EU of the European Parliament and of the Council of 12 August 2013 on attacks against information systems and replacing Council Framework Decision 2005/222/JHA (2013) OJ L218 8–14.

40 Tropina and Callanan (n 17).

(EC) No 460/2004[41] and operative since 2005, has provided, through its coordination and information exchange activities, a legal and technical common baseline for a common understanding of cybersecurity within the EU. With its action, the EU Agency has provided the necessary support to the Member States and private actors in developing an EU cybersecurity strategy.

Moreover, ENISA, through its activities, mainly related to develop and promote a culture of network and information security within the European Union, have contributed to strengthening the cooperation and coordination of all relevant stakeholders. The central role of the EU Agency has also been stressed by Rec 44 Directive 2009/140/EC[42] that states ENISA *"contribute[s] to the enhanced level of security of electronic communication by, among other things, providing expertise and advice, and promoting the exchange of best practices."*[43]

The creation of ENISA, like this of many other regulatory agencies, must be contextualised. According to Carrapico and Farrand,[44] the flourishing of agencies at the EU and national level has to be read from an economic and efficiency angle. The state institutional apparatus has been seen to rely on electoral results increasingly and therefore not reliable from an economic perspective to implement long-term actions. Consequently, the allocation of responsibility by the law-maker to entities independent from both market players and even to some extent, the lawmaker has been hailed as a solution that could support the fast-evolving market's needs. The activities carried out not only by ENISA illustrates this trend and have resulted in offering multiple technical, procedural, and regulatory solutions to EU Institutions, Member states and private entities.[45]

In its Cyber Europe 2012 Report[46] ENISA defines coherence as one of the critical pillars that policymakers have to consider when developing an EU cybersecurity strategy. The Report highlights the discrepancies due to the different evaluation of risks and threats in the management of cybercrime by the various Member States. The different approach is also reflected in the way each

---

41 Regulation (EC) No 460/2004 of the European Parliament and of the Council of 10 March 2004 establishing the European Network and Information Security Agency (2004) OJ L 77 1–11.

42 Directive 2009/140/EC of the European Parliament and of the Council of 25 November 2009 amending Directives 2002/21/EC on a common regulatory framework for electronic communications networks and services, 2002/19/EC on access to, and interconnection of, electronic communications networks and associated facilities, and 2002/20/EC on the authorisation of electronic communications networks and services (2009) OJ L337 37–69.

43 Ibid.

44 Helena Carrapico and Benjamin Farrand, '"Dialogue, Partnership and Empowerment for Network and Information Security": The Changing Role of the Private Sector from Objects of Regulation to Regulation Shapers' (2017) 67 Crime, Law and Social Change 245.

45 Ibid.

46 ENISA, 'Cyber Europe 2012' (*Key Findings and Recommendations*, December 2012) <https://www.enisa.europa.eu/publications/cyber-europe-2012-key-findings-report/at_download/fullReport> accessed 21 May 2019.

Member State has organised its public-partnership.[47] Considering this, in its 2012 Report, ENISA called for the implementation of cyber exercises to improve the actions and activities taken by national governments in cybersecurity at the technical and operational level. The ENISA-organised cyber exercise for the Member States that can be used to analyse and assess Member States technical skills to cyber-attacks. Doing so, the activities organised by ENISA support the development of standard procedures that are necessary to be implemented by each Member State. As a result, the activity carried out by ENISA with these exercises has supported the development of a shared understanding of threats characteristics, developing procedures, allocating roles and responsibilities, improving resilience and reducing asymmetries among the Member States.[48] Before the publication of the European Union Cybersecurity Strategy 2013 (EUCSS) the activities of ENISA, had been expanded, including, together when the organisation of cyber drills, seminars and training sessions, but also the publication of guidelines for Member states and stakeholders. As highlighted by Christou the activities that have characterised the ENISA mandate have had a role in building a cybersecurity culture among the different Member states, enhancing the strategic and operational dimensions at the EU.[49]

4.2. PUBLIC-PRIVATE PARTNERSHIP

Increasingly sophisticated cyber-attacks requires close collaboration between private and public actors, and information sharing mechanisms result fundamental to develop standard practices and tools that can effectively provide cybersecurity solutions. The involvement of private parties has always characterised the cybercrime, and cybersecurity legislative frameworks have contributed to the development of a common understanding of the technical aspects that distinguish this sector. Private involvement in the regulatory initiatives has generated an interesting debate on the role institutional government has currently.[50] Security has always been one of the most important prerogatives of a state. The technical complexity generated by the information technology sector has required to open the regulatory debate to private actors working in this sector due to the fact of technical knowledge of the

47 Oldrich Bures and Helena Carrapico, 'Private Security Beyond Private Military and Security Companies: Exploring Diversity Within Private–Public Collaborations and Its Consequences for Security Governance' (2016) Springer Science+Business Media Dordrecht <https://link.springer.com/content/pdf/10.1007%2Fs10611-016-9651-5.pdf> accessed 04 July 2019, 6.

48 George Christou, 'Introduction' in *Cybersecurity in the European Union: Resilience and Adaptability in Governance Policy* (Palgrave Macmillan UK 2016) 121.

49 Ibid.

50 Raphael Bossong and Ben Wagner, 'A Typology of Cybersecurity and Public-Private Partnerships in the Context of the EU' (2017) 67 Crime, Law and Social Change 265 226.

field. At the same time, finding a balance between private and public entities has always proven to be a challenge for the EU.

On the one hand, the public authorities have ever tried to enhance security, requesting private companies to share information. On the other hand, when it comes to information sharing activities, the private groups, led by the economic interests, have always been reluctant to share voluntarily information related to the activities they carry out since they believe this could harm their businesses.[51]

Defining the Private Public Partnership is a challenging exercise and is out of the scope of this chapter.[52] This cooperation between public and private entities varies according to the actors and the services that characterise their activity.[53] As a result, in the network and information systems, the different group of actors involved in this sector will determine according to the characteristics of their activities, a relationship more or less stringent between private and public actors. In the network and information systems context, the actors carrying out activities at the physical infrastructure layer have a marginal relationship with the public sector authorities. Contrary, the private entities providing services and products to consumers have a stringent relationship with public authorities at the EU and national level.[54]

Analysing the EU cybersecurity legislative initiatives some authors interpret the public-private partnership as part of the state's strategy (at the national level, EU at European Union one) to transfer risk from the state to the private sector, with a significant beneficial effect for state economic resources. From an economic-oriented perspective, the private-public partnership is the result of the privatisation of critical information infrastructure from the public sector to the private one.[55] An example of such organisation between public and private in the EU legislation is given by Article 49 Cybersecurity Act where it is stated that an EU cybersecurity certification for ICT products, services and processes will be developed consulting all relevant stakeholders.[56]

---

51 Philip Everts and Pierangelo Isernia, *Public Opinion, Transatlantic Relations and the Use of Force* (Palgrave McMillan UK 2015) 236.

52 Oldrich Bures, 'Contributions of Private Business to the Provision of Security in the EU: Beyond Public-Private Partnership' in Oldricht Bures and Helena Carrapico (eds), *Security privatization: how non-security-related private businesses shape security governance* (Springer Berlin Heidelberg 2017).

53 According to Bovis: ' *the principal benefit from involving the private sector in the delivery of public services through a public-private partnership format has been attributed to the fact that the public sector does not have to commit its own capital resources …and that substantial transfer of risks to the private sector offers value for money.*' Oldrich Bures, 'Contributions of Private Business to the Provision of Security in the EU: Beyond Public-Private Partnership' in Oldrich Bures and Helena Carrapico H (eds), *Security privatization: how non-security-related private businesses shape security governance* (Springer Berlin Heidelberg 2017).

54 Tropina and Callanan (n 17).

55 Oldrich Bures and Helena Carrapico (n 48).

56 Regulation (EU) 2019/881 of the European Parliament and of the Council of 17 April 2019 on ENISA (the European Union Agency for Cybersecurity) and on information and

There is no doubt that the information exchange between private entities and public bodies has contributed to enhancing a shared understanding of cyber risks and threats and the necessary measures to enhance security against potential cyber-attacks. The know-how developed at the technical and management level of private entities has resulted in a major resource to increase the security of private and national assets within the EU. Such approach is recognised in Rec 33 ENISA Regulation[57] where is stressed "*the necessity of developing an efficient network and information security policies that should be based on well-developed risk assessment methods, both in the public and private sector. [...] Promoting and developing best practices for risk assessment and for interoperable risk management solutions in public- and private-sector organisations will increase the security level of networks and information systems in the Union.*" As a result, the involvement of the private sector has had, fundamental for developing a coherent approach, in the way Carrapico has interpreted such concept when analysing EU legislation.[58] As a result, the EU has recognised such contribution in many cybersecurity legislative initiatives. Recital 18, 33, 47 and Article 2(5) ENISA Regulation.

5. THE EU CYBERSECURITY STRATEGIES

5.1. THE EUROPEAN UNION CYBERSECURITY STRATEGY 2013

The Digital Agenda for Europe[59] represents one of the pillars of the Europe 2020 Program that programmatically sets the objectives for the growth of the EU. One of the priorities of the Digital Agenda is the strengthening of trust and security of consumers in the ICT. The European Union Cybersecurity Strategy 2013 (EUCSS 2013) published by the EC on 7 February 2013 includes a set of binding and non-binding legal measures aimed to establish an open, safe, and secure cyberspace.[60] To achieve this purpose the EC delineates its actions

communications technology cybersecurity certification and repealing Regulation (EU) No 526/2013 (Cybersecurity Act) (2019) OJ L151, 15–69.

57 Regulation (EU) No 526/2013 of the European Parliament and of the Council of 21 May 2013 concerning the European Union Agency for Network and Information Security (ENISA) and repealing Regulation (EC) No 460/2004 Text with EEA relevance (2013) OJ L165, 41–58.

58 Bossong and Wagner (n 50).

59 Communication from the Commission to the European Parliament, the Council, the European Economic and Social Committee of the Regions, A Digital Agenda for Europe /* COM/2010/0245 f/2 */.

60 European Commission, 'Joint Communication to the European Parliament, the Council, the European Economic and Social Committee and the Committee of the Regions, Cybersecurity Strategy of the European Union: An Open, Safe and Secure Cyberspace' COM /*Join/2013/01 final */.

through three main guidelines: (i) Protect the EU and its internal market against cybercrime; (ii) Protect Critical Information Infrastructure, Network and Information Security (NIS), Critical infrastructures (CIP) and Critical Information Infrastructure (CIIP); (iii) Develop an EU Cyber defence Strategy.[61]

The NIS Directive and the Cybersecurity Strategy Joint Communication, are the two legislative initiatives that compose the EUCSS 2013 package and focus on the protection of those assets considered essential for each Member State. In doing so, the EUCSS has stressed the importance of cooperation, not only at governance level EU Member states, EU institutions and agencies, but also between the public and private sector.

In line with such purposes, with the ENISA Regulation the EU Agencies mandate was overhauled, and its tasks, listed in Article 2[62] enhanced, to support a coherent and coordinate development of cybersecurity legislative initiatives at the EU and national levels.[63]

Concerning the role of private actors the 2013 EUCSS, in the NIS Directive (i.e. Recital 35,[64] Article 7(1)), ENISA Regulation and Cybersecurity Strategy Joint Communication, recognises the role of private entities and their active involvement in the development of the cybersecurity framework, providing the necessary competencies and capabilities. The private contribution would prove useful also to building a more effective and efficient national strategy.[65]

The NIS Directive

The Directive 2016/1148 on the security of network and information systems is the first EU binding horizontal legislative initiative in the cybersecurity area (NIS)[66] and represents the cornerstone of the EUCSS 2013.[67] The NIS Directive has been developed following two complementary objectives, both listed in Article 1(1).[68] The first one, prodromal to the second, is related to the protection

---

61 George Christou, 'Introduction' in *Cybersecurity in the European Union: Resilience and Adaptability in Governance Policy* (Palgrave Macmillan UK 2016).

62 Regulation (EU) No 526/2013 of the European Parliament and of the Council of 21 May 2013 concerning the European Union Agency for Network and Information Security (ENISA) and repealing Regulation (EC) No 460/2004 (2013) OJ L 165, Article 2.

63 Carrapico and Farrand (n 44).

64 Rec. 33 *inter alia* states that "cooperation between the public and private sectors is essential"

65 Ibid.

66 Directive (EU) 2016/1148 of the European Parliament and of the Council of 6 July 2016 concerning measures for a high common level of security of network and information systems across the Union (2016) OJ L194 1–30.

67 The Directive came into force on 6 July 2016 and required Member States to put in place adequate measures foreseen in the text by 9 May 2018. So far Belgium has still to implement the measures embedded in the NIS while other states have done it later than requested.

68 Art. 1(1) NIS Directive: "*This Directive lays down measures with a view to achieving a high common level of security of network and information systems within the Union so as to improve the functioning of the internal market*".

of critical infrastructure against terrorist attacks. The other, more economic-oriented, is linked to the promotion and enhancement of the EU internal market.[69]

The legal basis for the NIS Directive is Article 116 TFEU, where the EU has exclusive competence to legislate.[70] According to the explanatory memorandum of the NIS proposal,[71] the mandate to regulate the security of network and related systems is considered necessary to support the development of the internal single market.[72] This decision has been criticised by numerous authors and also by Member States since the NIS deals with security, an area where the EU and the Member States share legislative competences.[73]

Recital 5 NIS Directive, confirming the different level of preparedness among the Member States, stresses how the lack of harmonised approaches within the EU has created asymmetries in the level of protection for business and users. Therefore, NIS regime applies respectively to the Member States, operators of essential services and Digital Services Providers (DSP) since, due to their role, they have a significant impact in a state. For this paper, the analysis of this legislation will mainly focus on the provisions related to DSP, for the implications these provisions have in the public-private partnership context.[74]

DSP *"any legal persons providing a digital service"*.[75] In particular, the NIS Directive identifies in Annex III as types of Digital Service Providers: Online marketplaces, Online search engines and Cloud computing services. Nowadays

---

69 In the Communication for a Secure information Society the EC already stated that *'the availability, reliability and security of networks and information systems are increasingly central to our economies and to the fabric society.'*, Strategy for a secure information society (2006 communication).

70 Art. 116 TFEU: "*Where the Commission finds that a difference between the provisions laid down by law, regulation or administrative action in Member States is distorting the conditions of competition in the internal*
market and that the resultant distortion needs to be eliminated, it shall consult the Member States concerned.
If such consultation does not result in an agreement eliminating the distortion in question, the European, Parliament and the Council, acting in accordance with the ordinary legislative procedure, shall issue the necessary directives. Any other appropriate measures provided for in the Treaties may be adopted." Consolidated version of the Treaty on the Functioning of the European Union (n 15) 47–390.

71 Proposal for a Directive of the European Parliament and of the Council concerning measures to ensure a high common level of network and information security across the Union, /* COM/2013/048 final - 2013/0027 (COD).

72 Andreas Mitrakas, 'The Emerging EU Framework on Cybersecurity Certification' (2018) 42 Datenschutz und Datensicherheit - DuD 411.

73 Carrapico and Farrand (n 44).

74 Christou (n 61).

75 Directive 2009/140/EC of the European Parliament and of the Council of 25 November 2009 amending Directives 2002/21/EC on a common regulatory framework for electronic communications networks and services, 2002/19/EC on access to, and interconnection of, electronic communications networks and associated facilities, and 2002/20/EC on the authorisation of electronic communications networks and services (2009) OJ L 337, Article 4(5).

DSP represents *"an important resource for their users, including operators of essential service"*.[76] Therefore, *"A disruption of such a digital service could prevent the provision of other services which rely on it and could thus have an impact on key economic and societal activities in the Union"*.[77] Consequently, DSP has to ensure the integrity and security of their services that have to be achieved complying with the security and incident information requirements.[78] Precisely, Member States will have to ensure that DSP *"identify and take appropriate and proportionate technical and organisational measures to manage the risks posed to the security of network and information systems which they use in the context of offering services."*[79]

In line with the Directive 2009/140/EC,[80] the NIS Directive foresees mandatory information requirements in regards to cyber incidents that have to be reported to national authorities. Differently from Directive 2009/140/EC, the entities that are subjected to such obligations are not providers of electronic communications networks and services but all Digital Service Providers listed in Annex III NIS Directive. At the same time, considering that most of the electronic communications network and service providers usually offer services included in Annex III NIS Directive, these actors are included in the NIS provisions for the aspects related to such services (i.e. cloud). Article 16(3) NIS Directive establishes standard steps regarding the incidents handling and incident notification mechanisms requiring the Member States to ensure such obligations.[81] The requirements listed in Article 16 are characterised for a high level of harmonisation obliging the Member States do not impose any further security or notification requirements on digital service providers.[82] To enforce such obligation, the NIS Directive has foreseen penalties for DSP in case of non-compliance with such obligation in Article 21.[83]

The EC justifies the necessity to have mandatory information requirements stating that 'the current situation in the EU, reflecting the purely voluntary approach followed so far, does not provide sufficient protection against NIS

---

[76] Ibid Rec. 48.

[77] Ibid.

[78] Ibid Article 16.

[79] Ibid Article 16 (1).

[80] Ibid.

[81] On this regard ENISA has published 'Technical Guidelines on Incident Reporting 2013 to give 'guidance to NRSs about the implementation of these two types of incident reporting mentioned in Art. 13: the annual summary reporting of significant incidents to ENISA and EC and ad hoc notification of incidents to other NRAs in case of cross-border incidents'. See also Christou (n 61).

[82] (n 74) Article 16(10).

[83] Art. 21 NIS, Penalties: 'Member States shall lay down the rules on penalties applicable to infringements of national provisions adopted pursuant to this Directive and shall take all measures necessary to ensure that they are implemented. The penalties provided for shall be effective, proportionate and dissuasive'.

incidents and risks across the EU'.[84] According to some scholars, to make it mandatory for DSP to report competent national authorities incidents, foreseeing sanctions in case of non-compliance with such obligations will have an impact on the current information sharing systems. Such an obligation will oblige DSP to focus part of their activity to the compliance aspects related to the development of an efficient and effective report mechanism with their competent national authorities. As a result, the effort put in the compliance activities might diminish the DSP contribution in the information sharing with other relevant stakeholders, consequently decreasing cybersecurity culture coming from such activity.[85]

In conclusion, the NIS directive develops two complementary obligations for the Member States on the one hand and public and private entities on the other hand. The formers obligations require Member States to develop capabilities (legal, technical, financial) and establish monitoring activities to ensure compliance of DSP and Operators of Essential Services (OES) with the requirements foreseen in the NIS Directive. The latter imposes DSP and OSES and relevant public administration specific technical and organisational measures to manage the risks posed to the security of network and information systems.[86] As a result, the EU expects an enhancement of competencies, skills, and abilities for the creation of securer cyberspace.

The NIS is the result of almost ten years of legislative initiatives in the field of cybersecurity. It embeds most of the claim included in the multiple EC Communication, ENISA reports and EU Council Framework Decision 2005/222/JHA. Analysing the EU cybersecurity strategy from a coherence perspective, it

---

84 Opinion of the European Economic and Social Committee on the 'Proposal for a directive of the European Parliament and of the Council concerning measures to ensure a high common level of network and information security across the Union' COM(2013) 48 final – 2013/0027. See also Bossong and Wagner (n 50).

85 Art. 16 NIS: '*1. Member States shall ensure that digital service providers identify and take appropriate and proportionate technical and organisational measures to manage the risks posed to the security of network and information systems which they use in the context of offering services referred to in Annex III within the Union. Having regard to the state of the art, those measures shall ensure a level of security of network and information systems appropriate to the risk posed, and shall take into account the following elements: (a) the security of systems and facilities; (b) incident handling; (c) business continuity management; (d) monitoring, auditing and testing; (e) compliance with international standards. 2. Member States shall ensure that digital service providers take measures to prevent and minimise the impact of incidents affecting the security of their network and information systems on the services referred to in Annex III that are offered within the Union, with a view to ensuring the continuity of those services.*
3. Member States shall ensure that digital service providers notify the competent authority or the CSIRT without undue delay of any incident having a substantial impact on the provision of a service as referred to in Annex III that they offer within the Union. Notifications shall include information to enable the competent authority or the CSIRT to determine the significance of any cross-border impact. Notification shall not make the notifying party subject to increased liability.'

86 (n 74) Article 16.

seems that the NIS Directive focuses more on harmonising procedural aspects to manage risks rather than providing substantial clarification regarding such cyber risks. While coordination and incident notification procedures are well established in details; some key substantial elements aspects that characterise the evaluation of risks are left to Member States implementation procedures. Concretely, NIS Directive does not clarify in concrete when a cyber-incident has a substantial impact on the provision of a service, but only which are the elements that should be considered for such evaluation.

Analysing the NIS Directive, two considerations need to be done in regards to the public-private partnership. First, the NIS Directive, confirming what was already stated in the 2013 EUCSS,[87] foresees an active role for private companies in the development of strategies for the enhancement of cooperation and information sharing in Article 11 NIS. On the other hand, the incident notification mechanism foreseen in Article 16 NIS Directive might have an impact on the information sharing between private a public partnership due to the mandatory incident notification obligations.

From a coherence point of view, the NIS Directive, due to its binding nature reinforces and strengthens the inter-institutional coordination and enhances cooperation among all relevant stakeholders. Nonetheless, due to its top-down approach lacks in providing a substantive legal basis to all relevant stakeholders. While Article 4(9) defines what should be considered as a risk, the NIS Directive specifically left it to the Member States to evaluate the level of risk represented by a particular product, services or event. Regardless the definition of risk, or the elements that should be considered in the evaluation of an incident, under the NIS Directive regime, Member States can still put in place different national procedures to secure their network systems. As a result of the EUCS, even if establishing a coordinate action within the EU when it comes to putting in place common procedure to secure Member States Networks and Information systems, does not provide a coherent and substantial understanding of cybersecurity substantial elements.

As a proof of this criticality, the EC, in the Communication "Making the most of NIS"[88] included in the Cybersecurity Package, provides additional clarifications for all those entities falling in the NIS Directive scope to support the NIS implementation process.[89] Also, the EC, with the implementing of

87 European Commission, 'Joint Communication to the European Parliament, the Council, the European Economic and Social Committee and the Committee of the Regions, Cybersecurity Strategy of the European Union: An Open, Safe and Secure Cyberspace' COM /*Join/2013/01 final */.

88 Communication from the Commission to the European Parliament and the Council, Making the most of NIS – towards the effective implementation of Directive (EU) 2016/1148 concerning measures for a high common level of security of network and information systems across the Union COM/2017/0476 final.

89 Ibid.

Regulation to NIS in 2018[90] (ECIR), specifies key aspects that had not been substantiated in the NIS Directive. As an example, Article 4 ECIR, referring to the NIS provisions on incident having substantial impact, describes which are the elements that should be taken into account in the evaluation of an incident.[91] Doing so, the recent initiatives published by the EC substantiate and harmonise at EU level crucial aspects related to cyber risks and incident handling procedures.

5.2. THE EUROPEAN UNION 2017 CYBERSECURITY STRATEGY

Taking into account the evolution of the cybersecurity technical and operational solutions and the increasing role that ICT actors are having in the EU economy, the European Commission revisited its cybersecurity strategy in 2017 with the publication of the *Cybersecurity Package*.[92] The set of legislative initiatives published within the Cybersecurity Package, which include both binding and non-binding legislative measures have a twofold purpose. On the one hand,

---

90 Commission Implementing Regulation (EU) 2018/151 of 30 January 2018 laying down rules for application of Directive (EU) 2016/1148 of the European Parliament and of the Council as regards further specification of the elements to be taken into account by digital service providers for managing the risks posed to the security of network and information systems and of the parameters for determining whether an incident has a substantial impact, C/2018/0471 (2018) OJ L26, 48–51.

91 Art. 4 ECIR: *"1. An incident shall be considered as having a substantial impact where at least one of the following situations has taken place: (a) the service provided by a digital service provider was unavailable for more than 5 000 000 user-hours whereby the term user-hour refers to the number of affected users in the Union for a duration of 60 minutes; (b) the incident has resulted in a loss of integrity, authenticity or confidentiality of stored or transmitted or processed data or the related services offered by, or accessible via a network and information system of the digital service provider affecting more than 100 000 users in the Union;*
(c) the incident has created a risk to public safety, public security or of loss of life; (d) the incident has caused material damage to at least one user in the Union where the damage caused to that user exceeds EUR 1 000 000. 2. Drawing on the best practice collected by the Cooperation Group in the exercise of its tasks under Article 11(3) of Directive (EU) 2016/1148 and on the discussions under point (m) of Article 11(3) thereof, the Commission may review the thresholds laid down in paragraph 1".

92 The 2017 Cybersecurity package includes: a) EC Communication 'Resilience, Deterrence and Defence: Building strong cybersecurity for the EU', b) Proposal for a Regulation on ENISA, the "EU Cybersecurity Agency", and on Information and Communication Technology cybersecurity certification ("Cybersecurity Act"), c) Commission Recommendation on Coordinated Response to Large Scale Cybersecurity Incidents and Crises, d) Communication "Making the most of NIS – towards effective implementation of Directive (EU) 2016/1148 concerning measures for a high common level of security of network and information systems across the Union, e)Commission staff working document assessment of the EU 2013 cybersecurity strategy, e) Proposal for a Directive on combating fraud and counterfeiting of non-cash means of payment, f) Report assessing the extent to which the Member States have taken the necessary measures in order to comply with Directive 2013/40/EU on attacks against information systems.

support Member States and Digital Service providers listed in Annex III of the NIS Directive in implementing NIS provisions. On the other hand, harmonise through the enhancement of ENISA capabilities the cybersecurity certification process for ICT products, services and processes. In particular, the Cybersecurity Act, the only binding legislative initiative of the Cybersecurity Package, shows a shift in the new EC's strategy from the NIS' approach, mainly focus on inter-institutional coordination and information exchange procedures, to one oriented towards building a shared understanding of the cybersecurity risks within the EU. The new EU's strategy takes into account not only operational and technical security aspects linked to the cybersecurity context but also explores the economic issues and opportunities that may come from this area for establishing a secure Digital Single Market.[93]

The Cybersecurity Act

The most important legislative initiative included in the 2017 Cybersecurity Package is the so-called Cybersecurity Act Regulation, published during the State of the Union on 13 September 2017.[94]

The Cybersecurity Act can be divided into two complementary sections: the first focuses on the implementation of ENISA capabilities and tasks while the second establishes the creation of an EU cybersecurity certification scheme for ICT products, services, and processes as established by Article 46(2) Cybersecurity Act Regulation.[95] Overall, the new Regulation aims to enhance the role of the EU in the global scenario, improving cross-border coordination, implementing common understanding of cyber threats for the EU Member States and promoting EU standards. According to the EC Communication 'Resilience, Deterrence and Defence: Building strong cybersecurity for the EU',[96] the adoption of EU standards in the cybersecurity context will enhance

---

93 European Commission, Joint Communication to the European Parliament and the Council, Resilience, Deterrence and Defence: Building strong cybersecurity for the EU Join/2017/0450 final.

94 Regulation (EU) 2019/881 of the European Parliament and of the Council of 17 April 2019 on ENISA (the European Union Agency for Cybersecurity) and on information and communications technology cybersecurity certification and repealing Regulation (EU) No 526/2013 (Cybersecurity Act) (2019) OJ L151 15–69.

95 Art. 46(2) Cybersecurity Act: "*The European cybersecurity certification framework shall provide for a mechanism to establish European cybersecurity certification schemes and to attest that the ICT products, ICT services and ICT processes that have been evaluated in accordance with such schemes comply with specified security requirements for the purpose of protecting the availability, authenticity, integrity or confidentiality of stored or transmitted or processed data or the functions or services offered by, or accessible via, those products, services and processes throughout their life cycle.*"

96 European Commission, Joint Communication to the European Parliament and the Council, Resilience, Deterrence and Defence: Building strong cybersecurity for the EU Join/2017/0450 final.

trust in EU products, services, and processes and will consequently promote EU companies outside the EU borders.[1]

The EU cybersecurity certifications for ICT products, services and processes will be developed under the EC initiative by ENISA together with relevant stakeholders coming from academia, public and private sector.[2] As foreseen by Article 56 Cybersecurity Act, the recourse to the developed certificates by industries and companies will initially be voluntary.[3] Each cybersecurity certification scheme will foresee different assurance levels that are considered the basis for users' confidence. The different assurance levels will depend *"on the risk associated with the intended use of the ICT product, ICT service or ICT process, in terms of the probability and impact of an incident."*[4] The type of assurance level chosen by the applying company will determine the accuracy and the kind of evaluation necessary for granting the certification, but also the marketing value of the certificate. In particular, each cybersecurity certification scheme will foresee different assurance levels that are considered the basis for users' confidence. The different assurance levels will depend *'on the risk associated with the intended use of the ICT product, ICT service or ICT process, in terms of the probability and impact of an incident.'*[5] The type of assurance level chosen by the applying company will determine the accuracy and the kind of evaluation necessary for granting the certification, but also the marketing value of the certificate.

The approach taken by the EU with the Cybersecurity Act is linked to the cross-border nature of the cybercrime phenomenon. The EU considers it necessary to adopt globally recognised standards that can contribute to harmonise and consequently enhance cybersecurity across the EU.[6]

From a Public-Private Partnership perspective, such an approach is the result of the evolution at EU level of this relationship between the Public and Private sector. Nowadays, international standards such as those developed by the

---

1 Art. 46 (1) Cybersecurity Act "*The European cybersecurity certification framework shall be established in order to improve the conditions for the functioning of the internal market by increasing the level of cybersecurity within the Union and enabling a harmonised approach at Union level to European cybersecurity certification schemes, with a view to creating a digital single market for ICT products, ICT services and ICT processes*".

2 Art. 49(3) Cybersecurity Act: "*When preparing a candidate scheme, ENISA shall consult all relevant stakeholders by means of a formal, open, transparent and inclusive consultation process.*"

3 Art. 56(2) Cybersecurity Act: "*The cybersecurity certification shall be voluntary, unless otherwise specified by Union law or Member State law*"

4 Regulation (EU) 2019/881 of the European Parliament and of the Council of 17 April 2019 on ENISA (the European Union Agency for Cybersecurity) and on information and communications technology cybersecurity certification and repealing Regulation (EU) No 526/2013 (Cybersecurity Act) (2019) OJ L 151, Article 52(1).

5 Ibid.

6 European Commission, 'Joint Communication to the European Parliament, the Council, the European Economic and Social Committee and the Committee of the Regions, Cybersecurity Strategy of the European Union: An Open, Safe and Secure Cyberspace' Join/2013/1/Final 5.

International Organisation for Standardisation (ISO) for ICT services, products and products are *de facto* shaping the activities of private actors that operate in such context. Their development is the result of a close dialogue between industries entities and the adoption by private parties is voluntary.[7]

When it comes to the EU standards, according to Mitrakas the EU certification scheme foreseen in the Cybersecurity Act and will not create new standards, but it will be based on the ones already established and recognised at an international level.[8] In line with such interpretation, the Cybersecurity Act stresses the importance for manufacturers and providers of ICT products, service and process to adopt such international recognised standards to raise security standards.[9] In addition, Cybersecurity Act stresses in multiple provisions (i.e. Recital 54, Article 52(4), 54(1)(b) and 62(4)) the correlation between the existing national and international recognised standards and the EU certification one, highlighting how the former should be used as a baseline for the development of the latter.

The decision to support the adoption of the standard by industries had been already stressed in previous EC communication on EU Cybersecurity Strategy 2013 and NIS Directive. Rec 66 NIS dealing with the standardisation of security requirements and recognising the market value in adopting such standards stress the importance of choosing at national level specific standards "*to ensure a high level of security of network and information systems at Union level.*"[10] Moreover, Article 19 encourage the use of standards (European and International one) to have a convergent implementation of the procedures for OES and DSP. In particular, such standardised procedures should concern technical and organisational measures necessary to manage the risks posed to the security of network and information systems and those concerning the prevention and minimisation of the impact of incidents.[11] The Cybersecurity Act, reinforcing the approach already established in the NIS Directive on international recognised standards foresees the creation of EU standards. The Cybersecurity Act, which has as a legal basis Article 114 TFEU that deals with the approximation of laws of the Member States to achieve the proper functioning of the internal market, aims to strengthen trust in the Digital Single Market. Also, the foreseen mutual recognition by Member States of EU cybersecurity certifications intends to increase the opportunities for EU

---

7 Carrapico and Farrand (n 44).

8 Mitrakas (n 72).

9 Regulation (EU) 2019/881 of the European Parliament and of the Council of 17 April 2019 on ENISA (the European Union Agency for Cybersecurity) and on information and communications technology cybersecurity certification and repealing Regulation (EU) No 526/2013 (Cybersecurity Act) (2019) OJ L 151, Rec. 50.

10 Ibid Rec. 66.

11 Ibid Article 19.

organisation, organisations, manufacturers and providers of ICT products, services and processes within and outside the EU.[12]

The Cybersecurity Act, moving forward from the NIS approach reinforce the presence and role of private stakeholders, foreseeing for them an active role in the development of the ICT certifications. In the context of the public-private partnership, the market-driven approach taken by the EU has a twofold explanation.

First, the decision to involve private parties in the development of EU cybersecurity certifications can be interpreted as a necessary step for enhancing EU cybersecurity culture. Consequently the know-how resulting from such partnership could be used to develop measures that aim ensure the security of the cyberspace and consequently strength trust in the Digital Single Market.[13]

Second, the EU approach in the Cybersecurity Act is related to governance. Embedding private standards under in EU certification schemes could be seen as an EU strategy to enhance the hands-on governance approach over private entities. Such certification procedure will *de facto* determine an EU institutional control over an area, the certification and standards one, that has been so far regulated by private entities.[14]

6. CONCLUSION

This chapter has provided a brief description of the evolution of the EU's regulatory approach towards cybersecurity in light of the coherence principle. The creation of a cybersecurity framework has been considered necessary for integrated and well-functioning cooperation in the long term among all the different stakeholders and forms an essential step for enhancing cybersecurity standards within the EU. At the national level, the transnational nature of the security regulatory framework put in place by the EU will influence and shape Member States' national policy, creating a coordinated ecosystem.

Analysing the current situation from the coherence perspective, and utilising the interpretation provided by Carrapico and Barrinha, it can be observed that asymmetries between the Member States exist. In particular, the lack of a coherent approach within the EU is reflected in the allocation of resources and capacities (legal, financial, and political) by the Member States. At the same time, the legislative development of an EU cybersecurity strategy has reduced the asymmetries between the Member States when it comes to cybersecurity legislative initiatives. As a result of the activity carried out over the last twenty years, a coherent approach, from a procedural and substantial angle, has almost

12 Mitrakas (n 72).
13 Carrapico and Farrand (n 44).
14 Ibid.

been achieved. In doing so, the EU is creating a trustworthy environment – a necessary step for enhancing the EU Digital Single Market and the private actors that operate within it.

BIBLIOGRAPHY

Accenture Security, 'The Cost of Cybercrime' (2019) <https://www.accenture.com/_acnmedia/PDF-96/Accenture-2019-Cost-of-Cybercrime-Study-Final.pdf#zoom=50> accessed 22/05/2019

Bossong R and Wagner B, 'A Typology of Cybersecurity and Public-Private Partnerships in the Context of the EU' (2017) 67 Crime, Law and Social Change 265

Bures O and Carrapico H (eds), 'Contributions of Private Business to the Provision of Security in the EU: Beyond Public-Private Partnership' in Bures O and Carrapico H (eds), Security privatization: how non-security-related private businesses shape security governance (Springer Berlin Heidelberg 2017)

Carrapico H and Barrinha A, 'The EU as a Coherent (Cyber)Security Actor?: The EU as a Coherent (Cyber)Security Actor?' (2017) 55 Journal of Common Market Studies 1254

Carrapico H and Farrand B, '"Dialogue, Partnership and Empowerment for Network and Information Security": The Changing Role of the Private Sector from Objects of Regulation to Regulation Shapers' (2017) 67 Crime, Law and Social Change 245

Christou G, 'Introduction' in *Cybersecurity in the European Union: Resilience and Adaptability in Governance Policy* (Palgrave Macmillan UK 2016)

Cremona M, 'Coherence through Law: What difference will the Treaty of Lisbon make?', Hamburg review of social sciences (2008) Vol. 3 <https://www.researchgate.net/publication/237541410_Coherence_through_Law_What_difference_will_the_Treaty_of_Lisbon_make> accessed 02 July 2019

ENISA, 'Cyber Europe 2012' (*Key Findings and Recommendations,* December 2012) <https://www.enisa.europa.eu/publications/cyber-europe-2012-key-findings-report/at_download/fullReport> accessed 21 May 2019

Everts P and Isernia P, *Public Opinion, Transatlantic Relations and the Use of Force* (Palgrave McMillan UK 2015) 236

Gauttier P, 'Horizontal Coherence and the External Competences of the European Union' (2004) 10 European Law Journal 23

Missiroli A, 'European Security Policy: The Challenge of Coherence' (2001) European Foreign Affairs Review 6.2

Mitrakas A, 'The Emerging EU Framework on Cybersecurity Certification' (2018) 42 Datenschutz und Datensicherheit – DuD 411

Nutall S, *European Foreign Policy* (2000), New York (N.Y.): Oxford UP 25

Trauner F, 'The Internal-External Security Nexus: More Coherence Under Lisbon?' [2011] SSRN Electronic Journal <www.ssrn.com/abstract=1885322> accessed 21 May 2019

Tropina T and Callanan C, *Self- and Co-Regulation in Cybercrime, Cybersecurity and National Security* (Springer International Publishing 2015)

CHAPTER 12

CHALLENGES OF THE CYBER SANCTIONS REGIME UNDER THE COMMON FOREIGN AND SECURITY POLICY (CFSP)

Yuliya MIADZVETSKAYA[1]

1. INTRODUCTION

"This has a whiff of August 1945. Somebody just used a new weapon and this weapon will not be put back in the box."[2]

That is how the former Central Intelligence Agency (CIA) and National Security Agency (NSA) director Michael Hayden referred to the computer virus StuxNet that silently accelerated a few hundred Iranian nuclear centrifuges leading to their self-destruction.[3] Then the quintessential cyberwar scenario became reality in Ukraine in 2015 with the electricity blackout following the unprecedented hack of Ukraine's power grid.[4] On top of that, WannaCry and NotPetya displayed across the globe the extent of the damage for people and infrastructure that malicious cyber-attacks can inflict.[5]

---

1 Yuliya Miadzvetskaya is a researcher at CiTiP. Prior to joining CiTiP, she worked as an academic assistant at the College of Europe in Bruges and was a trainee in the Legal Service of the European Parliament in Brussels and at the United Nations offices in Minsk. Many thanks to all the reviewers. All errors and omissions are my own.

2 Paul D. Shinkman, 'Former CIA Director: Cyber Attack Game-Changers Comparable to Hiroshima' *U.S. News* (20 February 2013) <https://www.usnews.com/news/articles/2013/02/20/former-cia-director-cyber-attack-game-changers-comparable-to-hiroshima>_ accessed 1 April 2019.

3 Andy Greenberg, 'How An Entire Nation Became Russia's Test Lab for Cyberwar' (*Wired*, 20 June 2017) <https://www.wired.com/story/russian-hackers-attack-ukraine/> accessed 7 April 2019.

4 Ibid.

5 Andy Greenberg, 'The Untold Story of NotPetya, the Most Devastating Cyberattack in History' (*Wired*, 22 August 2018) <https://www.wired.com/story/notpetya-cyberattack-ukraine-russia-code-crashed-the-world/> accessed 7 April 2019.

Faced with widespread cyber-attacks and a deadlock in the global negotiations about international law and state responsible behaviour in cyberspace,[6] the EU decided to develop its own framework to combat malicious cyber activities and build stronger cybersecurity.[7] While the Union has foreseen some measures[8] aimed at increased prevention and early warning mechanisms with regard to cyber-attacks, until recently it was lacking an appropriate framework for a joint EU diplomatic response to malicious cyber operations. And contrary to some Member States, which publicly attributed cyber-attacks, the EU has not taken any act of attribution or follow up with regard to potential perpetrators.[9] Thus, the further development of a common and comprehensive approach on cyber diplomacy was necessary in order to contribute to the "*mitigation of cybersecurity threats, conflict prevention and greater stability in international relations through the use of diplomatic and legal instruments*".[10]

In 2016, the Dutch presidency submitted a Non-paper on "*Developing a joint EU diplomatic response against coercive cyber operations*".[11] This non-paper argues that while resilience and security of networks are essential for preventing certain cyber operations, broader response and a comprehensive use of a multitude of policy instruments may be required. The EU's reaction must be proportionate to the scope, scale and duration of an aggressive behaviour in cyberspace. The use of cyber diplomacy tools is meant to influence rational cost-benefit analysis of state and non-state actors carrying out cyber-attacks for politico-military purposes.[12]

In June 2017, the Council continued its work on the issue and presented its draft conclusions on a Framework for a Joint EU Diplomatic Response to Malicious Cyber Activities.[13] Those conclusions refer to a range of diplomatic measures to be undertaken by the EU and Member States, including preventive

6 See François Delerue 'International Cooperation on the International Law Applicable to Cyber Operations' (2019) Vol.24 European Foreign Affairs Review, 297: "*The participating experts in the 2016–2017 UNGGE failed to reach a consensus in June 2017, and thus they did not produce a report.*"

7 Council Conclusions on Cyber Diplomacy 6122/15 of 11 February 2015.

8 For instance, the 2013 EU Cyber Security Strategy, the 2014 EU Cyber Defence Policy Framework, the 2016 Global Strategy for the European Union's Foreign and Security Policy, the 2016 Network and Information Security (NIS) Directive, the activities of the European Network and Information Security Agency (ENISA), the European Cyber Crime Centre (EC3) at Europol and CERT-EU.

9 Paul Ivan, 'Responding to cyberattacks: Prospects for the EU Cyber Diplomacy Toolbox' (2019) European Policy Center 5 <www.epc.eu/pub_details.php?cat_id=17&pub_id=9081> accessed 6 June 2019.

10 Council Conclusions on Cyber Diplomacy 6122/15 of 11 February 2015 (n 7) 4.

11 'Non-paper: Developing a joint EU diplomatic response against coercive cyber operations 5797/6/16 of 19' (May 2016) <http://statewatch.org/news/2016/jul/eu-council-diplomatic-response-cyber-ops-5797-6-16.pdf> accessed 6 May 2019.

12 Ibid.

13 Draft Council Conclusions on a Framework for a Joint EU Diplomatic Response to Malicious Cyber Activities ("Cyber Diplomacy Toolbox") 9916/17 of 7 June 2017.

measures, cooperative measures, stability measures and restrictive measures within the Common Foreign and Security Policy (CFSP). EU's competences in the field of the CFSP *"cover all areas of foreign policy and all questions relating to the Union's security, including the progressive framing of a common defence policy that might lead to a common defence"*.[14]

Restrictive measures were considered as a suitable foreign policy instrument for mitigating cyber threats and influencing the change of the behaviour of aggressors in the long term.[15] The need to take forward the EU's capacity to deter cyber-attacks through restrictive measures was further emphasized in the conclusions of the European Council last October.[16] However, the European capitals were rather divided on how the above-mentioned restrictive measures should work and some Member States were even reluctant to mandate this issue at the EU level.[17] For instance, Italy was allegedly strongly opposed to a new cyber sanctions framework and even called for the de-escalation of current tensions with some crucial economic partners.[18]

This May parliamentary elections deemed as *'Europe most hackable ones'* due to their dispersed nature and relatively long duration, made it even more urgent to finalize all the cybersecurity proposals. It comes as no surprise that a new cyber sanctions regime was approved on the 17th of May just a couple of days before the EU citizens headed to polls to decide on the future composition of the European Parliament. A newly established framework allows for restrictive measures to be applied in order to deter and respond to cyber-attacks in conformity with the CFSP objectives set out in Article 21 of the Treaty on European Union (TEU). Accordingly, the Union's action on the international scene, inter alia, aims at *"preserving peace, preventing conflicts and strengthening international security, in accordance with the purposes and principles of the United Nations Charter, with the principles of the Helsinki Final Act and with the aims of the Charter of Paris"*.[19] The EU upholds that cyber-enabled activities should be guided by the same principles, and respect for international law, notably the United Nations Charter, is crucial for maintaining peace and stability.

---

14 Consolidated version of the Treaty on European Union (TEU) [2016] OJ C202/1, Article 24(1).

15 "Cyber Diplomacy Toolbox" 9916/17 of 7 June 2017 (n 13) 5.

16 Conclusions of the European Council meeting EUCO 13/18 of 18 October 2018, <https://www.consilium.europa.eu/media/36775/18-euco-final-conclusions-en.pdf> accessed 6 June 2019.

17 Laurens Cerulus, 'Europe hopes to fend off election hackers with 'cyber sanctions' *Politico* (11 February 2019) <https://www.politico.eu/article/europe-cyber-sanctions-hoped-to-fend-off-election-hackers/> accessed 4 May 2019.

18 Francesco Guarascio, 'Italy resisting EU push to impose sanctions over cyberattacks' *Reuters* (12 October 2018) <https://www.reuters.com/article/us-italy-russia-sanctions/italy-resisting-eu-push-to-impose-sanctions-over-cyberattacks-idUSKCN1MM2CP> accessed 6 March 2019.

19 Consolidated version of the Treaty on European Union (TEU) [2016] OJ C202/1, Article 21 TEU.

The aim of this contribution is to analyse to what extent the current legal framework and rationale for sanctions are suitable for responding to increased cyber security challenges of the 21st century. The introduction of a new regime concerning restrictive measures to deter and respond to cyber-attacks marks a new stage in the development of the EU Cyber Diplomacy Toolbox and will be explained in the second part of this chapter. In the third part of this chapter, some light will be shed on the main difficulties for the efficient implementation of the cyber sanctions framework. First of all, its operationalisation might encounter a problem of technical and political attribution of cyber-attacks. In addition, existing divergences between Member States in foreign policy matters along with the challenge of providing solid and convincing evidence constitute a hindrance to a common action. Last but not least, targeted sanctions must ensure the respect for fundamental rights as established in the *Kadi* saga[20] in order to withstand the review in front of the Court of Justice of the European Union (CJEU). The overview of the European cyber sanctions framework will not be complete without comparing it against the American cyber sanctions regime, which will be done in the fourth part of this chapter.

2. CURRENT EU SANCTIONS FRAMEWORK

Sanctions constitute a pivotal instrument of the CFSP aimed at maintaining and restoring international peace and security, fighting terrorism and the proliferation of weapons of mass destruction and upholding respect for human rights, democracy and the rule of law.[21] With 42 sanctions programs in place, the EU has become the "*second-most active user of restrictive measures*", bypassed only by the US.[22] Commonly, sanctions were viewed as a method of exercising pressure and bringing about a political change in line with the objectives set out in each of the Council decisions on sanctions.[23]

The new regime concerning restrictive measures in response to cyber-attacks was introduced following the traditional two steps approach: first, the CFSP decision[24] adopted by the Council on the basis of Article 29 TEU laying down the overall sanctions framework. Secondly, the CFSP decision is accompanied by

---

20 Joined Cases C-402/05 P and C-415/05 P *Kadi I* [2008] ECLI:EU:C:2008:461; Joined Cases C 584/10 P, C 593/10 P and C 595/10 P *Kadi II* [2013] ECLI:EU:C:2013:518.

21 Council 10198/1/04 Basic Principles on the Use of Restrictive Measures (Sanctions) of 7 June 2004.

22 Martin Russell, 'EU sanctions: A key foreign and security policy instrument', (European Parliamentary Research, 2018). <www.europarl.europa.eu/thinktank/en/document.html?reference=EPRS_BRI%282018%29621870> accessed 25 June 2019.

23 Council Decision (CFSP) 2019/797 of 17 May 2019 concerning restrictive measures against cyber-attacks threatening the Union or its Member States [2019] OJ L129I, 13–19.

24 Ibid.

the associated regulation[25] adopted on the basis of Article 215 TFEU. While the Commission was traditionally involved in some specific sanctions regimes and provided a constantly updated consolidated public list of persons and entities subject to restrictive measures, the entry into force of the Lisbon Treaty extended the Council's prerogatives to manage sanctions lists upon a proposal from a Member State or from the High Representative of the Union for Foreign Affairs and Security Policy.[26]

The conventional approach towards sanctions was based on the assumption "*that hardships inflicted on the civilian population of a targeted state will lead to grassroots political pressure on that state's leaders to change their behavior*".[27] But traditional sanctions were largely criticized for its political ineffectiveness and tactlessness.[28] Thus, we could witness a shift from broad economic sanctions, affecting the entire population of the country, to a more targeted approach resulting in an increased use of restrictive measures or so-called '*smart sanctions*' directed at individuals or entities connected to problematic political regimes.[29] Such a sanctions toolkit includes wide-ranging measures from travel bans to asset freezes.

The established cyber sanctions regime mirrors the recently approved EU framework on restrictive measures addressing the use and proliferation of chemical weapons[30] and follows up on the smart sanctions approach. While the guidelines of the Council of October 2017 refer to the possibility of the adoption of sanctions against the State when it carries out the malicious cyber activity or when it is deemed responsible for the actions of a non-state actor,[31] the Council Decision adopted in May 2019 emphasizes the targeted nature of restrictive measures, excluding any attribution of responsibility for cyber-attacks to a third State.[32] Moreover, any measure under the proposed cyber diplomacy framework should take into account the broader context and objectives of the EU external relations, should be proportionate to malicious activities and should be based on a shared situational awareness agreed among the Member States.[33]

The new regime concerning restrictive measures in response to attacks in the cyber domain applies to performed and attempted cyber-attacks

---

25 Council Regulation (EU) 2019/796 of 17 May 2019 concerning restrictive measures against cyber-attacks threatening the Union or its Member States [2019] OJ L129I, 1–12.

26 Charlotte Beaucill, 'On opening up the horizon: the ECJ's new take on country sanctions' (2018) Vol. 55 Common Market Law Review 399.

27 Arne Tostensen, Beate Bull, 'Are Smart Sanctions Feasible?' (2002) Vol. 54 World Politics 375.

28 Ibid 377.

29 Piet Eeckhout, *EU External Relations Law* (2nd edition, Oxford University Press, 2011) 502.

30 Council Decision (CFSP) 2018/1544 of 15 October 2018 concerning restrictive measures against the proliferation and use of chemical weapons OJ L259/25.

31 Draft implementing guidelines for the Framework on a Joint EU Diplomatic Response to Malicious Cyber Activities, 13007/17, Brussels, 9 October 2017.

32 Council Decision (CFSP) 2019/797 of 17 May 2019 concerning restrictive measures against cyber-attacks threatening the Union or its Member States (n 23).

33 "Cyber Diplomacy Toolbox" 9916/17 of 7 June 2017 (n 13).

with a significant effect, constituting an external threat to the Union or its Member States, including cyber-attacks against third States or international organisations.[34] The notion of '*external threat*' encompasses attacks which originate or are carried out from outside the Union; or by, with the support, at the direction or under the control of any natural or legal person, entity or body established or operating outside the Union; or use infrastructure outside the Union.[35] Such cyber-attacks may involve access to information systems, information system interference, data interference or interception.[36] The notion of threat also applies when critical infrastructure or services necessary for the essential social activities are affected, for instance in the sectors of energy or transport. The disturbance of critical State functions, of the storage or processing of classified information or government emergency response teams qualifies as threat as well.[37]

3. CHALLENGES OF THE CYBER SANCTIONS REGIME

While the development of the cyber sanctions regime lays down the foundation for a joint EU action, there are still risks that its practical implementation will be limited due to a number of challenges. Even though the technical side of the problem of attribution of cyber-attacks (3.1) attracted more attention than its legal, political and contextual framework, the latter should not be ignored. Once the attribution is completed, there is a need for taking action, and the lack of a joint EU approach constitutes a barrier for internal cohesiveness and external effectiveness (3.2) with regard to cyber sanctions.

Moreover, sanctions must be based on a strong compelling evidence and withstand fundamental rights test (3.3) established in the seminal *Kadi* cases[38] where the CJEU made a powerful statement that international security considerations shall be balanced against fundamental rights of involved individuals. In recent years, we witnessed how the CJEU struck down several sanctions on the basis of failure to state reasons and provide sufficient evidence (3.4) which is deeply interconnected with the right to effective judicial remedy. The sensitive nature of the evidence supporting the cyber sanctions regime, including classified or partially classified information detained by the secret

34 Council Regulation of 17 May 2019 concerning restrictive measures against cyber-attacks (n 25).
35 Ibid.
36 Ibid.
37 Ibid.
38 Joined Cases C-402/05 P and C-415/05 P *Kadi I* [2008] ECLI:EU:C:2008:461; Joined Cases C 584/10 P, C 593/10 P and C 595/10 P *Kadi II* [2013] ECLI:EU:C:2013:518 (n 20).

services, might entail a number of difficulties of compliance with the high threshold of fundamental right test set out in the *Kadi* cases.[39]

3.1. CHALLENGE OF ATTRIBUTING CYBER-ATTACKS[40]

"Electrons don't wear uniforms."[41]

"Attribution is the art of answering a question as old as crime and punishment: who did it?"[42] It can be described as a core act of tracking and identifying perpetrators of a cyber-attack. The most crucial political decisions at the highest levels cannot be taken, if attribution, at first place, was not correctly performed.[43] The attribution problem has raised its profile high in the aftermath of the US presidential campaign. The story of Russian hackers and trolls meddling into presidential elections in the US has lived long on after the announcement of the results. The Kremlin spokesperson Dmitry Peskov dismissed all the CIA conclusions and qualified all the allegations of Russia's interfering in the US and any other elections as "*absolute nonsense*".[44] According to Kremlin's position, you either produce a solid evidence or stop talking about it,[45] and therein lies the problem.

The structural design and anonymity of the internet, while being its intrinsic features, constitute barriers to forensic-based technical attribution.[46] Different

39 Ibid.

40 This section will not delve into a detailed overview of issues of technical and legal attribution of cyber-attacks, but will just provide some preliminary ideas. In addition, the author considers that State Responsibility is not relevant in the context of restrictive measures since the wording of the Council CFSP Decision reads as follows: "Targeted restrictive measures should be differentiated from the attribution of responsibility for cyber-attacks to a third State. The application of targeted restrictive measures does not amount to such attribution, which is a sovereign political decision taken on a case-by-case basis. Every Member State is free to make its own determination with respect to the attribution of cyber-attacks to a third State."

41 Herbert Lin, 'Attribution of Malicious Cyber Incidents From Soup to Nuts' (*Hoover Institution*, 19 September 2016) <https://www.hoover.org/sites/default/files/research/docs/lin_webready.pdf> accessed 5 March 2019.

42 Thomas Rid, Ben Buchanan, 'Attributing Cyber Attacks' (2015) Vol. 3 Journal of Strategic Studies 1–2, 4–37 <https://ridt.co/d/rid-buchanan-attributing-cyber-attacks.pdf> accessed 6 March 2019.

43 Ibid 30.

44 David Filipov, 'Kremlin calls talk of Russian interference in U.S. elections 'absolute nonsense'' *The Washington Post* (13 December 2016)<https://www.washingtonpost.com/world/kremlin-calls-talk-ofrussian-interference-in-us-elections-absolute-nonsense/2016/12/13/cbb30130-c0a6-11e6-b527-949c5893595e_story.html?noredirect=on&utm_term=.8363df012882> accessed 10 March 2019.

45 Laura Smith-Spark, 'Russia Challenges US to Prove Campaign Hacking Claims or Shut Up' (2016) CNN <http://edition.cnn.com/2016/12/16/europe/russia-us-hacking-claims-peskov/index.html> accessed 17 March 2019.

46 W. Earl Boebert, 'A Survey of Challenges in Attribution', in Committee on Deterring Cyberattacks (2011) Proceedings of a Workshop on Deterring Cyberattacks, 43 <https://www.nap.edu/read/12997/chapter/5#42> accessed 16 April 2019.

deception techniques via 'spoofing' and 'false flags' are commonly displayed in cyberspace for covering the tracks of potential aggressors.[47] To remedy the current situation of impunity, "suggestions floated by the European Commission to reform IP addresses in order to facilitate tracking down terrorists groups by limiting the anonymity of web traffic".[48] Nevertheless, no concrete measures followed and it is not clear to what extent it is possible to limit the anonymity of web traffic at all.

For a successful attribution there has to be compelling proof, certainty and confidentiality because one can point a finger, but not with the needed precision. The credibility at source is crucial for being able to retaliate and avoid reputational damage. As such a few lines of malicious code and IP addresses can be manipulated by any number of state or non-state actors. But establishing a link between a geographical area and persons behind the attack or finding complicity between hackers and states is a difficult exercise, which has to be performed based on all-source intelligence, different technical traceback techniques and taking into consideration possible interests of aggressors.[49]

Though attribution has been mainly viewed as a technical problem, it involves a number of legal issues related to procedural aspects and the accumulation of evidence. At times, the attribution of an attack can be easier made in relation to its context, such as the North Korean fingerprint in the Sony incident, hindering the theatrical release of "The Interview" featuring the assassination of Kim Jong Un.[50] In addition, geopolitical interests, ability to interpret provided evidence and other logical considerations play a crucial role in establishing a link between an attack and perpetrators. In this regard, the scale of StuxNet virus, targeted state (Iran), targeted data (Iranian nuclear program), exploited vulnerabilities, the immense resources, that went into it, helped to deduce that there was a state behind it, allegedly the United States and Israel.[51]

Even if the attribution issue is solved from a technical point of view, it still amounts to a complex political challenge to publicly attribute an attack by a block of 28 member states. The attribution still remains the prerogative of individual states which deploy different methods and techniques[52] and have a

---

47 Antonio Missroli, 'The Dark Side of the Web: Cyber as a Threat' (2019) Vol.24 European Foreign Affairs Review.

48 Ibid 145.

49 "Cyber Diplomacy Toolbox" 9916/17 of 7 June 2017 (n 13) 13.

50 Andrea Peterson, 'The Sony pictures hack, explained' *The Washington Post* (18 December 2014) <https://www.washingtonpost.com/news/the-switch/wp/2014/12/18/the-sony-pictures-hack-explained/?utm_term=.73f1ff4615d3> accessed 15 April 2019.

51 Ellen Nakashima and Joby Warrick, 'Stuxnet was the Work of U.S. and Israeli Experts, Officials Say' *The Washington Post* (02 June 2012) <https://www.washingtonpost.com/world/national-security/stuxnet-was-work-of-us-and-israeli-experts-officials-say/2012/06/01/gJQAlnEy6U_story.html?utm_term=.541ba9a6bcfb> accessed 15 March 2019.

52 "Cyber Diplomacy Toolbox" 9916/17 of 7 June 2017 (n 13) 13.

tendency to overclassify information relating to cyber-attacks.[53] Moreover, the value of forensic methods and intelligence sources used may be compromised by their disclosure, while not presenting the required evidence leaves some room for plausible deniability.[54] In addition, the collective action on the basis of a shared situational awareness is limited in the cyber domain since there is no equivalent multilateral agencies such as the Organisation for the Prohibition of Chemical Weapons (OPCW).[55]

The newly adopted cyber sanctions framework differentiates between the issue of targeted restrictive measures and the attribution of responsibility for cyber-attacks to a third State. According to the wording of the Council Decision,[56] the application of targeted restrictive measures does not amount to such attribution, which remains a sovereign political decision taken on a case-by-case basis by every Member State. Such a delimitation between perpetrators of an attack targeted by sanctions and a state potentially relating to them comes from the necessity to overcome a possible deadlock in the EU's decision-making in the area of the CFSP, which will be discussed in more details in the next section. However, it will be difficult to avoid the public attribution, since in most of the cases entities behind cyber-attacks representing high threat to the EU's security are likely to have connections with third states authorities.

3.2. CHALLENGE OF A COMMON APPROACH

Divided in diversity?

One of the main challenges of the CFSP consists in the decision-making process in this area relying on the complex system of governance requiring unanimity. This high threshold cannot be easily attained due to some internal divisions in the EU. The '*otherness*' of the CFSP as a separate pillar to other areas of the European integration takes its roots in the Maastricht Treaty and is still maintained as a horizontal pillar in the Lisbon Treaty due to the presence of several intergovernmental elements.[57] The coherence of the EU's external policies can be compromised by divergences in economic and political interests between countries. While some Member States may be in favour of cyber sanctions, others may opt for a more accommodating line. Moreover, it

53 Antonio Missroli, 'The Dark Side of the Web: Cyber as a Threat' (2019) Vol.24 European Foreign Affairs Review (n 47) 142.

54 Ibid.

55 Ibid.

56 Council Decision (CFSP) 2019/797 of 17 May 2019 concerning restrictive measures against cyber-attacks threatening the Union or its Member States (n 23).

57 Paul James Cardwell, 'The legalisation of European Union foreign policy and the use of sanctions' (2015) Vol 17 Cambridge Yearbook of European Legal Studies 287–310.

already happened in the past that the EU's unitary and affirmative approach was undermined by some leaders with different opinions. For instance, during the EU-Russia summit while the European institutions condemned the Russian military activities in Chechnya, Berlusconi wanted to act as Putin's advocate.[58]

The implementation of cyber sanctions may encounter similar difficulties. Having technical and institutional means for attributing cyber-enabled attacks will not necessarily lead to a common reaction.[59] The prioritisation of good diplomatic relations over a common stance of the EU will lead to a shift of the issue to a bilateral basis. The effectiveness of such bilateral initiatives is rather doubtful.[60] For instance, the UK publicly attributed cyber campaigns against global Managed Service Providers (MSPs) to a group APT 10 associated with the Chinese Ministry of State Security.[61] Despite the dialogue with the Chinese authorities undertaken by the British side, malicious cyber-attacks enabled by Chinese actors continued.[62]

Moreover, the EU Member States diverge in their risk assessment strategies due to different levels of digitisation and cyber capabilities. In addition, they might rely on different evidence produced by intelligence agencies. Since wrongly attributing a cyber-attack entails reputational and diplomatic consequences, some states display a very high level of cautiousness with regard to strong common measures. For instance, Italy was a firm opposer to a new cyber sanctions framework.[63] Belgium, Finland and Sweden advocated for a '*gradual response*' with sanctions as a last resort.[64] Whereas, the United Kingdom, France, Estonia, the Netherlands, Romania, Slovakia, Latvia, Lithuania and Poland supported the introduction of sanctions.[65] This vast spectrum of views undermines the EU's solidarity on the issue.

On top of that, the issue of collective attribution of cyber-attacks by the EU was passed under silence on multiple occasions. While the UK and Denmark attributed the NotPetya cyberattack to the GRU (Russian Military Intelligence) and some Member States issued statements of support, the April 2018 Council

---

58 Anna-Sophie Maass, *EU-Russia Relations, 1999–2015: From courtship to confrontation* (1st edn, Routledge, 2016) 46.

59 Paul Ivan, 'Responding to cyberattacks: Prospects for the EU Cyber Diplomacy Toolbox' (2019) European Policy Center 7 <www.epc.eu/pub_details.php?cat_id=17&pub_id=9081> accessed 6 June 2019 (n 9).

60 Ibid 7.

61 Foreign & Commonwealth Office, National Cyber Security Centre, and The Rt Hon Jeremy Hunt MP, 'Press Release: UK and allies reveal global scale of Chinese cyber campaign' (2018) <https://www.gov.uk/government/news/uk-and-allies-reveal-global-scale-of-chinese-cyber-campaign> accessed 18 March 2019.

62 Paul Ivan, 'Responding to cyberattacks: Prospects for the EU Cyber Diplomacy Toolbox' (2019) European Policy Center (n 9) <www.epc.eu/pub_details.php?cat_id=17&pub_id=9081> accessed 6 June 2019.

63 Francesco Guarascio, 'Italy resisting EU push to impose sanctions over cyberattacks' (n 18).

64 Ibid.

65 Ibid.

conclusions were limited to a formal "*condemnation of the malicious use of information and communications technologies (ICTs)*".[66] In addition, the attacks on the offices of the Organisation for the Prohibition of Chemical Weapons (OPCW) in The Hague constituted another test of the EU's common action.[67] The United Kingdom and the Netherlands pointed out at Russia's involvement in the attack and pushed for swift action, Italy and France, however, were reluctant in publicly acknowledging Russia's responsibility.[68] The same discrepancies became obvious at the institutional level. Presidents Tusk and Juncker and High Representative Mogherini in their Joint statement[69] attributed the attack to some Russian actors, whereas the European Council failed to come up with such a statement and again only condemned in general terms the hostile cyber-attack carried out against the OPCW.[70]

Even though the Decision of the Council highlights that targeted sanctions should not be viewed as the attribution of responsibility to a state, this delimitation between individual perpetrators and states remains rather artificial. The practice shows that a vast majority of cyber-attacks with high impact consequences, such as StuxNet, WannaCry and NotPetya, were orchestrated at the request and with the support of governments and not just by some random hacktivists. Therefore, the challenge of a common EU stance will remain on the agenda. Attributing cyber-attacks can put diplomatic relations at stake, but failing to take measures may be perceived as green light for similar malicious actions in total impunity.

3.3. CHALLENGE OF THE FUNDAMENTAL RIGHTS TEST

Despite the general exclusion of the CJEU jurisdiction from the area of the CFSP, according to the wording of the second subparagraph of Article 24 (1) TEU and the first paragraph of Article 275 TFEU, targeted sanctions are not immune to judicial review. As noted by van Elsuwege, the CJEU was given significant powers in the area of the CFSP by the Lisbon Treaty abolishing the pillar structure and providing for the integration of the CFSP in the EU legal order.[71] Thus, the CJEU

---

66 Ibid.

67 Joint statement by Presidents Tusk and Juncker and High Representative Mogherini on Russian cyber-attacks of 4 October 2018 <https://www.consilium.europa.eu/en/press/press-releases/2018/10/04/joint-statement-by-presidents-tusk-and-juncker-and-high-representative-mogherini/> accessed 19 March 2019.

68 Laurens Cerulus, 'Russia dodges bullet of EU sanctions on cyber – for now' (2018) Politico <https://www.politico.eu/article/russia-dodges-eu-sanction-on-cyber-for-now/> accessed 23 February 2019.

69 Joint statement by Presidents Tusk and Juncker and High Representative Mogherini on Russian cyber-attacks (n 67).

70 European Council meeting Conclusions of 18 October 2018.

71 Peter van Elsuwege, 'Judicial Review of the EU's Common Foreign and Security Policy: Lessons from the Rosneft case' (2017) Verfassungsblog <https://verfassungsblog.de/judicial-

was empowered by the Lisbon Treaty to assess the legality of sanctions and their respect for fundamental rights of natural or legal persons.[72] Article 275(2) TFEU constitutes an "*exception to an exception*" or a so-called "*claw back*" provision, as observed by Advocate General Wathelet in his opinion on the *Rosneft* case.[73]

While the adoption of cyber sanctions would follow a fully legitimate objective of restoring international peace and security in cyberspace, it should be by itself subject to guarantees and safeguards ensuring the respect for fundamental rights, "*enshrined in Article 6(1) TEU as a foundation of the Union*".[74] As held by the Court in the *Kadi I* judgment,[75] "*the Courts of the European Union must ensure the full review of the lawfulness of all Union acts in the light of the fundamental rights forming an integral part of the European Union legal order*", irrespective of whether they stem from UN regime or have been decided by the EU autonomously. While in the *Kadi* cases the Court focused its analysis mainly on the fundamental rights of defence and of the right to effective judicial review, the impact of the Court's conclusions on further restrictive measures is much broader and should be read as establishing the general requirement of ensuring the compatibility of sanctions with EU fundamental rights. The intensity of the standard of review was further explained in the *Kadi II* judgement,[76] setting out that at least one of the reasons invoked by the Council as a listing criteria must be sufficiently substantiated by evidence.[77]

The obligation to state reasons, "*corollary of the principle of respect for the rights of the defence*",[78] constitutes an essential principle under the EU law, as provided for in the second paragraph of Article 296 TFEU and Article 41(2)(c) of the Charter of Fundamental Rights of the European Union. According to the

---

review-of-the-eus-common-foreign-and-security-policy-lessons-from-the-rosneft-case/> accessed 12 March 2019.

72 Consolidated version of the Treaty on the Functioning of the European Union (TFEU) [2016] OJ C202/1, Article 275 (2) reads as follows: 'However, the Court shall have jurisdiction to monitor compliance with Article 40 of the Treaty on European Union and to rule on proceedings, brought in accordance with the conditions laid down in the fourth paragraph of Article 263 of this Treaty, reviewing the legality of decisions providing for restrictive measures against natural or legal persons adopted by the Council on the basis of Chapter 2 of Title V of the Treaty on European Union.'

73 Case C-72/15 PJSC *Rosneft Oil Company v Her Majesty's Treasury and Others* [2016] ECLI:EU:C:2016:381, Opinion of AG Wathelet, paras 51–72.

74 Joined Cases C-402/05 P and C-415/05 P *Kadi I* [2008] ECLI:EU:C:2008:461, para 303.

75 Ibid, para 326.

76 Joined Cases C 584/10 P, C 593/10 P and C 595/10 P *Kadi II* [2013] ECLI:EU:C:2013:518, para 119.

77 Armin Cuyvers, '"Give me one good reason": The unified standard of review for sanctions after Kadi II' (2014) 51 Common Market Law Review 1759–1788, 1768.

78 Joined Cases T-533/15 and T-264/16 of 14 March 2018, *Il-Su Kim and Korea National Insurance Corporation v Council* of 14 March 2018 ECLI:EU:T:2018:138, para 69; Case C-417/11 P *Council v Bamba* of 15 November 2012, EU:C:2012:718, para 49; Case C-176/13 P *Council v Bank Mellat* of 18 February 2016, EU:C:2016:96, para 74; Case C-459/15 P *Iranian Offshore Engineering & Construction v Council* of 8 September 2016 EU:C:2016:646, para 23.

established case law, this obligation implies providing the person concerned in a clear and unequivocal fashion the reasoning behind the measure.[79] Since persons concerned by sanctions regulation do not usually dispose of the right to be heard before their adoption, the obligation to state reasons constitutes the sole safeguard enabling them to ascertain the reasons for an act and challenge it in front of the Courts where deemed that it is not well founded.[80] It should be duly noted that sanctions can achieve their objective only if they have a '*surprise effect*' and a person concerned cannot mitigate their impact by some preliminary measures, such as closing of bank accounts or moving assets. Therefore, the information on the listing and their reasons can be exceptionally provided at the same time as the act is published in the Official Journal, "*for failure to state the reasons cannot be remedied by the fact that the person concerned learns the reasons for the act during the proceedings before the Courts of the European Union*".[81]

If reasons for imposing sanctions were sufficiently substantiated by the Council, the Court will perform an assessment of proportionality and appropriateness of a measure with regard to its objective and its impact on fundamental rights and freedoms. Some restrictions can be placed on fundamental rights, provided they respect three conditions of Article 52(1) of the Charter. First of all, they should be set out by law, in other words, there should be a legal basis. Secondly they must be genuinely necessary to achieve an objective of general interest recognised by the EU. Last but not least, they must comply with the principle of proportionality. The same logic of balancing of foreign policy objectives against fundamental rights will apply to sanctions in response to cyber-attacks.

According to the Council Decision,[82] the EU authorities may impose travel bans and asset freezes against individuals responsible for cyber-attacks. The freeze of assets could, inter alia, lead to the violation of the right to property and the freedom to conduct a business. For instance, this line of argumentation was followed by the lawyers of *Rosneft* and *Rotenberg* in their respective sanctions related cases.[83]

---

79 Judgment of the Court (Full Court) of 22 June 2004, *Portuguese Republic v Commission of the European Communities*, Case C-42/01 *Portugal v Commission* ECLI:EU:C:2004:379, para 66.

80 Case C-417/11 P *Council of the European Union v Nadiany Bamba* of 15 November 2012, ECLI:EU:C:2012:718, para 51.

81 Cases T-307/12 and T-408/13 *Adib Mayaleh v Council of the European Union* of 5 November 2014 ECLI:EU:T:2014:926, para 85; Case C-417/11 P *Council of the European Union v Nadiany Bamba* of 15 November 2012, ECLI:EU:C:2012:718, para 49.

82 Council Decision (CFSP) 2019/797 of 17 May 2019 concerning restrictive measures against cyber-attacks threatening the Union or its Member States (n 23).

83 Case T-720/14 *Rotenberg v Council* of 30 November 2016 ECLI:EU:T:2016:689, para 166, Judgment of the Court (Grand Chamber) of 28 March 2017; Case C-72/15 PJSC *Rosneft Oil Company v Her Majesty's Treasury and Others* [2016] ECLI:EU:C:2016:381, Judgment of the General Court, para 197.

The incorrect attribution of cyber-attacks may cause some reputational damage for targeted individuals and violate their right to the protection of personal data in case if a wrong assessment was performed and erroneous information was published. The data protection related pleas were invoked in the case of sanctions imposed on Korea National Insurance Corporation, which argued the violation of Articles 14 and 16 of Regulation (EC) No 45/2001[84] on the protection of individuals with regard to the processing of personal data by the European institutions.[85]

As mentioned earlier, the infringement of the rights of the defence and of the right to effective judicial review are the first ones to be affected, if the Council fails to comply with its obligation to state reasons supporting listing criteria or substantiate them with sufficient evidence. In this regard, Declaration 25 attached to the Treaty on Articles 75 and 215 TFEU recalls that the respect for fundamental rights and freedoms implies "*the observance of the due process rights of the individuals concerned*".[86] A thorough judicial review can be ensured only if restrictive measures are based on "*clear and distinct criteria tailored to the specifics of each restrictive measure*".[87] It is the task of the EU authorities to present "*sufficiently solid factual basis*" supporting the justification for sanctions and not the task of the listed person to prove that the measure is not well founded.[88] The challenge of providing evidence is further examined in the next section.

3.4. CHALLENGE OF PROVIDING EVIDENCE

The justifications supporting listing criteria should have plausible factual bases to withstand a potential challenge of targeted sanctions in front of the CJEU. However, the sensitive nature of the information upon which the sanctions listings are based can be compromised by its disclosure. And this constitutes the main difficulty for complying with the requirement to state the reasons and sufficiently substantiate them by evidence. Sanctions lists are updated by the Council, which has access to partially classified information through the security services of the Member States.[89] The latter may not want to disclose their confidential sources for some legitimate considerations, such as avoiding

---

84 Regulation (EC) No 45/2001 of the European Parliament and of the Council of 18 December 2000 on the protection of individuals with regard to the processing of personal data by the Community institutions and bodies and on the free movement of such data, OJ 2001 L 8, 1.

85 Joined Cases T-533/15 and T-264/16 *Il-Su Kim and Others v Council of the European Union and European Commission* of 14 March 2018 ECLI:EU:T:2018:138, para 164.

86 Declaration 25 attached to the Treaty on Articles 75 and 215 TFEU.

87 Ibid.

88 Joined Cases C 584/10 P, C 593/10 P and C 595/10 P *Kadi II* [2013] ECLI:EU:C:2013:518, para 121.

89 Charlotte Beaucill, 'On opening up the horizon: the ECJ's new take on country sanctions' (2018) Vol. 55 Common Market Law Review (n 26) 398.

that hackers learn from their mistakes in hiding their fingerprints. Since "*the entitlement to disclosure of evidence as part of the rights of the defence is not an absolute right*",[90] some compelling reasons touching upon the security of the EU or of its Member States may be invoked in order to prevent the disclosure of the sensitive information.

The Council in the past adopted restrictive measures only on the basis of the explanatory memorandum submitted by a Member State, where the latter was not able to disclose material coming from confidential sources.[91] This approach, according to the Council, was consistent with the principle of mutual trust prevailing between Member States and the principle of sincere cooperation, as set out in Article 4(3) TEU.[92] Nevertheless, the CJEU did not agree with the Council and struck down the sanctions in question because individuals concerned were not in a position to defend themselves against the allegations and the judicial authorities were not in a position to decide whether the acts at issue were well founded.[93] Thus, no evidence should mean no sanction. The Court, however, recognises the need to strike a right balance between legitimate interests of preserving confidentiality of evidence, on the one hand, and the respect for the right to be heard and the provision of effective judicial protection, on the other hand.[94] And this task is far from being easy.

Last but not least, due to divergences in cyber capabilities between Member States, they may rely on different evidence in their attribution activities. To overcome this gap and strengthen a common culture of attribution, the European External Action Service (EEAS) suggests to empower the EU Intelligence Analysis Centre (INTCEN) with the attribution of cyber-attacks using its own intelligence materials.[95] INTCEN is a network of security services of Member States under the auspices of the EEAS. They do not produce new evidence, but process the materials gathered at national levels. Allegedly, Member States are reluctant to grant new attribution powers to INTCEN.[96] On top of that, recent Germany's allegations against sharing intelligence with the Austrian government because of the misuse of the data by the far-right party in the governing coalition shed some light on the boundaries of the principles

---

90 *Jasper v. United Kingdom* App no 27052/95 (ECtHR 2000), para 52.

91 Case C-280/12 P *Council of the European Union v Fulmen and Fereydoun Mahmoudian* of 28 November 2013 ECLI:EU:C:2013:775, para 44.

92 Ibid.

93 Ibid para 80.

94 Joined Cases C 584/10 P, C 593/10 P and C 595/10 P *Kadi II* [2013] ECLI:EU:C:2013:518, para 128.

95 Matthias Monroy 'Security Architectures and Police Collaboration in the EU' (2019) <https://digit.site36.net/2019/03/22/eu-intelligence-centre-facing-new-challenges/ > accessed 14 June 2019.

96 EEAS, Implementation of the Framework for a Joint EU Diplomatic Response to Malicious Cyber Activities – Attribution of malicious cyber activities (discussion of a revised text) 6852/1/19 [2019] <www.statewatch.org/news/2019/mar/eu-council-cyber-6852-REV-1–19.pdf > accessed 14 July 2019.

of mutual trust and sincere cooperation in practice.[97] Nevertherless, in order to guarantee the efficiency of a new cyber sanctions framework, the EU needs to take further steps contributing to a better exchange of confidential information between Member States and increasing their situational awareness.

4. OVERVIEW OF THE US CYBER SANCTIONS

The present chapter will provide some insight into the US cyber-related sanctions program and see how it compares to the European framework on sanctions in response to malicious cyber activities. While the EU is just in the beginning of putting in place its cyber-attacks deterrence strategies, the US, benefitting from a less fragmented decision-making and better cyber capabilities,[98] was already more effective in applying sanctions or criminal charges against government-sponsored hackers. For instance, a North Korean programmer was accused by the US Department of Justice of the involvement in several cyber-attacks, including the WannaCry attack.[99] In October 2018, the US charged seven Russian GRU officers for compromising computer networks used by various sporting and anti-doping organisations, a US nuclear power company, the Netherlands-based OPCW and the Switzerland-based Spiez laboratory.[100] The latter ones were involved in the investigation of the poisoning of the former Russian spy Skripal in Salisbury.

The US cyber-related sanctions program came into force with the Executive Order issued by the American president in April 2015, which provided for the imposition of sanctions against persons responsible for malicious cyber-enabled activities.[101] In December 2016, Barack Obama issued another Order authorizing sanctions related to interfering with or undermining election processes or

97 Jon Stone, 'Austrian government cannot be trusted with intelligence due to far-right links, German security service warns' (2019) Independent <https://www.independent.co.uk/news/world/europe/austria-germany-intelligence-security-services-russia-bfv-a8921966.html> accessed 22 May 2019.

98 North Korean Regime-Backed Programmer Charged With Conspiracy to Conduct Multiple Cyber Attacks and Intrusions, Department of Justice, Office of Public Affairs (6 September 2018) <https://www.justice.gov/opa/pr/north-korean-regime-backed-programmer-charged-conspiracy-conduct-multiple-cyber-attacks-and> accessed 15 July 2019.

99 Executive Order 13757 of December 28 2016, Taking Additional Steps to Address the National Emergency With Respect to Significant Malicious Cyber-Enabled Activities (2016) Federal Register Vol. 82 No. 1.

100 Department of Justice, Office of Public Affairs, October 4, 2018, U.S. Charges Russian GRU Officers with International Hacking and Related Influence and Disinformation Operations <https://www.justice.gov/opa/pr/us-charges-russian-gru-officers-international-hacking-and-related-influence-and> accessed 13 April 2019.

101 Office of Foreign Assets Control, 'Cyber-related sanctions program' (*US Treasury*, July 2017) <https://www.treasury.gov/resource-center/sanctions/Programs/Documents/cyber.pdf> accessed 20 May 2019.

institutions.[102] Similarly to the European cyber sanctions framework, three main elements can be observed in the American approach, such as the presence of an external element indicating that an attack comes from the outside, likelihood of a threat to national security and the conduct of all those events in the cyber domain.

In addition, the American cyber sanctions framework also provides for the blocking of the property of certain persons engaged in significant malicious cyber-enabled activities originating from, or directed by persons located, in whole or in substantial part, outside the United States.[103] The cyber sanctions may be applied when there is a reasonable likelihood that an attack "*will result in or contribute to a significant threat to the national security, foreign policy, or economic health or financial stability of the United States*".[104] This may include "*harming, or otherwise significantly compromising the provision of services in a critical infrastructure sector, disrupting the availability of a computer or network of computers, causing a significant misappropriation of funds or economic resources, trade secrets, personal identifiers*", or of information with the purpose or effect of interfering with or undermining election processes or institutions.[105]

The Office of Foreign Assets Control (OFAC) administers the American economic sanctions programs in a similar way to the Council in the EU. The American sanctions also include a range of measures from comprehensive ones, blocking the entire government or inflicting trade restrictions, to limited sanctions program targeting only specific individuals and entities. The names of affected individuals, which are designated or identified as blocked by the OFAC, are indicated in the OFAC's Specially Designated Nationals And Blocked Persons (SDN) List. However, the prohibition of transactions can be very broad and extend beyond the scope of SDN List by covering the property of an entity that is 50 percent or more directly or indirectly owned by one or more blocked persons or the property entities owned or controlled by the Government.

Both in the US and in the EU the listed persons can request for lifting of restrictive measures by sending a written petition with all the supporting documents to the OFAC or the Council respectively. The judicial review of sanctions is also available. However, in the US the standard of review to be delisted is rather high to meet.[106] For this very reason, Kadi was less successful in challenging his listing in the US Courts than in the EU.[107]

---

[102] Executive Order 13757 Taking Additional Steps to Address the National Emergency With Respect to Significant Malicious Cyber-Enabled Activities (2016) Federal Register Vol. 82 No. 1 (n 99).

[103] Ibid.

[104] Ibid.

[105] Ibid.

[106] Section 706(2)(A) of the Administrative Procedure Act (APA) instructs courts reviewing regulation to invalidate any agency action found to be "*arbitrary, capricious, an abuse of discretion, or otherwise not in accordance with law.*"

[107] *Kadi v Geithner*, F. Supp. 2d, 2012 WL 898778, at 19 (D.D.C. 19 March 2012).

5. CONCLUSION

In the present chapter we analysed the newly introduced regime relating to restrictive measures to deter and respond to malicious activities in cyberspace. The development of the EU's cyber diplomacy is a positive trend providing for further incentives for cooperation and, thus, contributing to greater stability and peace worldwide. Even though the effectiveness of those restrictive measures will be tested at a later stage, this chapter sheds some light on the main difficulties for the efficient implementation of the cyber sanctions framework.

First of all, the structural design and anonymity of the internet constitute barriers to forensic-based technical attribution. In case if attribution, at first place, was difficult and its source is not deemed as fully reliable, the effectiveness of a common action will be compromised. Thus, the credibility at source is crucial for being able to retaliate and avoid reputational damage. Therefore, establishing a link between a geographical area and persons behind the attack or finding complicity between hackers and states is a difficult exercise, which has to be performed based on all-source intelligence, different technical traceback techniques and taking into consideration possible interests of aggressors.[108]

Secondly, the adoption of restrictive measures by the EU requires unanimity at the Council. Since the issue of collective attribution of cyber-attacks by the EU was passed under silence on multiple occasions, it is questionable whether the current divergences in economic and political interests between countries could be overcome in the future. While some Member States may be in favour of cyber sanctions, others may opt for a more accommodating line. Consequently, having technical and institutional means for attributing cyber-attacks will not necessarily lead to a common action.

Thirdly, the seminal *Kadi* cases[109] set a high standard of fundamental rights protection to be ensured in the process of implementation of sanctions at the EU level, irrespective of whether they stem from the UN regime or have been decided by the EU autonomously. While in the *Kadi cases* the Court focused its analysis mainly on the fundamental right to be heard and effective judicial review, the impact of Court's conclusions on further restrictive measures is much broader and should be read as establishing the general requirement of ensuring the respect for fundamental rights. Thus, the Council will have to perform a difficult task of balancing of foreign policy objectives against fundamental rights in order to withstand a potential challenge of targeted sanctions in front of the CJEU.

And finally, since the decision on the adoption of cyber sanctions will most probably rely on the information provided by the security services of Member

108 "Cyber Diplomacy Toolbox" 9916/17 of 7 June 2017 (n 13) 13.

109 Joined Cases C-402/05 P and C-415/05 P *Kadi I* [2008] ECLI:EU:C:2008:461; Joined Cases C 584/10 P, C 593/10 P and C 595/10 P *Kadi II* [2013] ECLI:EU:C:2013:518.

States, they may want to keep it confidential in order to prevent hackers from learning from their mistakes in hiding their fingerprints. Since "*the entitlement to disclosure of evidence as part of the rights of the defence is not an absolute right*",[110] some compelling reasons touching upon the security of the EU or of its Member States may be invoked in order to prevent the disclosure of the sensitive information. But this may be counter to the obligation to state reasons and substantiate them by evidence, which constitutes an essential principle under the EU law[111] and is intrinsically linked with the right to the defence and the right to effective judicial protection. Thus, the courts will be confronted with a challenging task of striking a right balance between legitimate interests of preserving confidentiality of evidence, on the one hand, and the respect for the right to be heard and the provision of effective judicial protection, on the other hand.[112]

The introduction of the cyber sanctions framework marks a new stage in the development of a joint EU response to malicious cyber-enabled activities. Nevertheless, some underlined challenges may still constitute an obstacle to its complete operationalisation. And since in the 21st century "bits and bytes can be as threatening as bullets and bombs",[113] the EU will need to take appropriate measures in order to improve its technical and political attribution capabilities and enhance sincere cooperation and mutual trust between member states in cyber domain.

BIBLIOGRAPHY

Beaucill C, 'On opening up the horizon: the ECJ's new take on country sanctions' (2018) Vol. 55 Common Market Law Review 387–416

Cardwell PJ, 'The legalisation of European Union foreign policy and the use of sanctions' (2015) Vol. 17 Cambridge Yearbook of European Legal Studies 287–310

Cerulus L, 'Europe hopes to fend off election hackers with 'cyber sanctions' *Politico* (11 February 2019) <https://www.politico.eu/article/europe-cyber-sanctions-hoped-to-fend-off-election-hackers/> accessed 4 May 2019.

Delerue F, 'International Cooperation on the International Law Applicable to Cyber Operations' (2019) Vol. 24 European Foreign Affairs Review

Dutch Presidency, 'Non-paper: Developing a joint EU diplomatic response against coercive cyber operations 5797/6/16 of 19' (May 2016) <http://statewatch.org/news/2016/jul/eu-council-diplomatic-response-cyber-ops-5797-6-16.pdf>_ accessed 6 May 2019.

110 *Jasper v. United Kingdom* App no 27052/95 (ECtHR 2000), para 52.

111 Case C-42/01 *Portugal v Commission* of 22 June 2004 ECLI:EU:C:2004:379, para 66.

112 Joined Cases C 584/10 P, C 593/10 P and C 595/10 P *Kadi II* [2013] ECLI:EU:C:2013:518, para 128.

113 Pauline C. Reich and Eduardo Gelbstein, *Law, Policy, and Technology: Cyberterrorism, Information Warfare, and Internet Immobilization* [2012] 173.

Eeckhout P, *EU External Relations Law* (2nd edition, Oxford University Press, 2011) 502
Elsuwege PV, 'Judicial Review of the EU's Common Foreign and Security Policy: Lessons from the Rosneft case' (2017) Verfassungsblog <https://verfassungsblog.de/judicial-review-of-the-eus-common-foreign-and-security-policy-lessons-from-the-rosneft-case/> accessed 12 March 2019.
Filipov D, 'Kremlin calls talk of Russian interference in U.S. elections 'absolute nonsense'' *The Washington Post* (13 December 2016) https://www.washingtonpost.com/world/kremlin-calls-talk-ofrussian-interference-in-us-elections-absolute-nonsense/2016/12/13/cbb30130-c0a6–11e6-b527–949c5893595e_story.html?noredirect=on&utm_term=.8363df012882 accessed 10 March 2019.
Foreign & Commonwealth Office, National Cyber Security Centre, and The Rt Hon Jeremy Hunt MP, 'Press Release: UK and allies reveal global scale of Chinese cyber campaign' (2018) <https://www.gov.uk/government/news/uk-and-allies-reveal-global-scale-of-chinese-cyber-campaign> accessed 18 March 2019.
Greenberg A, 'How An Entire Nation Became Russia's Test Lab for Cyberwar' (Wired, June 2017) <https://www.wired.com/story/russian-hackers-attack-ukraine/> accessed 7 April 2019.
Greenberg A, 'The Untold Story of NotPetya, the Most Devastating Cyberattack in History' (Wired, 22 August 2018) <https://www.wired.com/story/notpetya-cyberattack-ukraine-russia-code-crashed-the-world/> accessed 7 April 2019.
Guarascio F, 'Italy resisting EU push to impose sanctions over cyberattacks' Reuters (12 October 2018) <https://www.reuters.com/article/us-italy-russia-sanctions/italy-resisting-eu-push-to-impose-sanctions-over-cyberattacks-idUSKCN1MM2CP> accessed 6 March 2019.
Ivan P, 'Responding to cyberattacks: Prospects for the EU Cyber Diplomacy Toolbox' (2019) European Policy Center <www.epc.eu/pub_details.php?cat_id=17&pub_id=9081> accessed 6 June 2019
Lin H, 'Attribution of Malicious Cyber Incidents From Soup to Nuts' (*Hoover Institution*, 19 September 2016) <https://www.hoover.org/sites/default/files/research/docs/lin_webready.pdf> accessed 5 March 2019.
Maass AS, *EU-Russia Relations, 1999–2015: From courtship to confrontation* (1st edn, Routledge, 2016) 46
Missiroli A, 'The Dark Side of the Web: Cyber as a Threat' (2019) Vol.24 European Foreign Affairs Review
Nakashima E and Warrick J, 'Stuxnet was the Work of U.S. and Israeli Experts, Officials Say' *The Washington Post* (02 June 2012) <https://www.washingtonpost.com/world/national-security/stuxnet-was-work-of-us-and-israeli-experts-officials-say/2012/06/01/gJQAlnEy6U_story.html?utm_term=.541ba9a6bcfb> accessed 15 March 2019.
Office of Foreign Assets Control, 'Cyber-related sanctions program' (*US Treasury*, July 2017) <https://www.treasury.gov/resource-center/sanctions/Programs/Documents/cyber.pdf> accessed 20 May 2019.
Peterson A, 'The Sony pictures hack, explained' *The Washington Post* (18 December 2014) <https://www.washingtonpost.com/news/the-switch/wp/2014/12/18/the-sony-pictures-hack-explained/?utm_term=.73f1ff4615d3> accessed 15 April 2019.

Rid T, Buchanan B, 'Attributing Cyber Attacks' (2015) Vol. 3 Journal of Strategic Studies 1–2, 4–37 <https://ridt.co/d/rid-buchanan-attributing-cyber-attacks.pdf> accessed 6 March 2019.

Russel M, 'EU sanctions: A key foreign and security policy instrument', (European Parliamentary Research, 2018) <www.europarl.europa.eu/thinktank/en/document.html?reference=EPRS_BRI%282018%29621870> accessed 25 June 2019

Shinkman PD, 'Former CIA Director: Cyber Attack Game-Changers Comparable to Hiroshima' U.S. News (20 February 2013) <https://www.usnews.com/news/articles/2013/02/20/former-cia-director-cyber-attack-game-changers-comparable-to-hiroshima> accessed 1 April 2019.

Stone J, 'Austrian government cannot be trusted with intelligence due to far-right links, German security service warns' (2019) Independent <https://www.independent.co.uk/news/world/europe/austria-germany-intelligence-security-services-russia-bfv-a8921966.html> accessed 22 May 2019

Tostensen A, Bull B, 'Are Smart Sanctions Feasible?' (2002) Vol. 54 World Politics 375.

CHAPTER 13

INTERNATIONAL (CYBER)SECURITY OF THE GLOBAL AVIATION CRITICAL INFRASTRUCTURE AS A COMMUNITY INTEREST

Ivo Emanuilov

1. (CYBER)SECURITY IN AN INTERCONNECTED INTERNATIONAL COMMUNITY

As early as 1758, Emer de Vattel, one of the most prominent international lawyers, crafted an eloquent definition of what the right to security entails. In his treatise on the law of nations, he argued that "[e]very nation, as well as every man, has (...) a right to prevent other nations from obstructing her preservation, her perfection, and happiness, – that is, to preserve herself from all injuries".[1] Almost three centuries later this definition still holds true in a world shaped by globalisation, growing uncertainty and emergence of new risks rocking the foundations of the international community.

While the main tenets of what constitutes 'security' have remained largely the same since Vattel's treatise, the complexity of global governance, scientific and technological developments have engendered new dimensions in the notion of security. A recent example is the growing importance of (cyber)security. The International Telecommunication Union ('ITU') defines cybersecurity as the "collection of tools, policies, security concepts, security safeguards, guidelines, risk management approaches, actions, training, best practices, assurance and technologies that can be used to protect the cyber environment and organization and user's assets".[2] Cybersecurity aims to "ensure the attainment

---

1 Emer de Vattel, *The Law of Nations, Or, Principles of the Law of Nature, Applied to the Conduct and Affairs of Nations and Sovereigns, with Three Early Essays on the Origin and Nature of Natural Law and on Luxury* (book 2, ch IV, Liberty Fund 2008) 288 para 49.

2 International Telecommunication Union (ITU), Series X: Data networks, Open System Communications and Security – Telecommunication security – Overview of cybersecurity, International Telecommunication Union (2008) Point 3.2.5 "cybersecurity".

and maintenance of the security properties of the organization and user's assets against relevant security risks in the cyber environment".[3]

As the offspring of information and communication technologies ('ICTs'), cybersecurity has been recognised as a tangible issue by the international community.[4] This has occurred against the background of globally interconnected users, devices and systems of systems, particularly in the realm of critical infrastructures, such as systems used for generation, distribution and transmission of energy, banking and financial services, public health and food, and transport.[5] Their interconnectedness through the cyber environment has led to the emergence of cyber-physical systems. These systems could be described as "hybrid systems of interacting digital, analogue, physical, and human components in systems engineered for function through integrated physics and logic."[6] These cyber-physical systems are no longer based on isolated but rather on open and interconnected technical architectures. This creates new attack vectors for unlawful interference, a problem which is particularly manifest in safety-critical domains, such as international civil aviation.

The global aviation system has become increasingly interconnected as a result of the proliferation of systems under the control of both traditional stakeholders, e.g. air navigation service providers, and new entrants, such as commercial data providers or providers of traffic management solutions for unmanned aircraft. Nowadays, its functioning depends upon a complex system of distributed cross-border critical infrastructure which has become equally exposed to an ever-growing number of physical, cyber and hybrid threats.[7] Furthermore, the inherently international nature of aviation and its global supply chain have led to the coming of shared physical infrastructure across the borders of more than one State.[8] Against this background, both the International Civil Aviation Organisation ('ICAO') and some regional international organisations, such as Eurocontrol and the European Union ('EU'), have launched multiple initiatives aimed at tackling the evolving threats at a global level. ICAO, for example, has

---

3 Ibid.

4 See, for example, the United Nations General Assembly (UNGA)'s UNGA Res 55/63 adopted 22 January 2001 UN Doc A/RES/55/63, UNGA Res 56/121 adopted 23 January 2002 UN Doc A/RES/56/121, UNGA Res 57/239 adopted 31 January 2003 UN Doc A/RES/57/239, UNGA Res 58/199 adopted 30 January 2004 UN Doc A/RES/58/199, UNGA Res 64/211 adopted 21 December 2009 UN Doc A/RES/64/211 2.

5 UNGA Res 58/199 adopted 30 January 2004 UN Doc A/RES/58/199 (n 4) 1.

6 See an extensive overview of the various definitions of cyber-physical systems and their relationship with the Internet of Things in Christopher Greer and others, 'Cyber-Physical Systems and Internet of Things' (National Institute of Standards and Technology 2019) NIST SP 1900-202 28–29 <https://nvlpubs.nist.gov/nistpubs/SpecialPublications/NIST.SP.1900-202.pdf> accessed 6 June 2019.

7 'The Protection of Critical Infrastructures against Terrorist Attacks: Compendium of Good Practices' (United Nations 2018) 117 <https://www.un.org/sc/ctc/wp-content/uploads/2019/01/Compendium_of_Good_Practices_Compressed.pdf> accessed 7 May 2019.

8 Ibid.

already made strong calls for the implementation of global, regional and national strategies and has advocated a collaborative approach to cybersecurity in civil aviation.[9]

While the Convention on International Civil Aviation[10] and its Annexes have established a comprehensive and largely harmonised international legal framework of safety rules for civil aviation, the same cannot be said regarding aviation cybersecurity. A welcome move was the adoption and recent entry into force of the Beijing Convention on the Suppression of Unlawful Acts Relating to International Civil Aviation[11] and the Protocol Supplementary to the Convention for the Suppression of Unlawful Seizure of Aircraft.[12] These instruments reflect progressive development in that they establish an obligation upon Contracting States to criminalise cyber attacks against air navigation facilities, incl. signals, data, information etc. Being primarily an instrument of international criminal air law, however, their impact is limited to mandating positive obligations for criminalisation of certain conduct and addressing *ex post* factum institution of criminal proceedings and jurisdictional issues.

The scope, nature and content of the international obligations for the protection of the aviation critical infrastructure from (cyber)security threats, however, are still unclear and have not been sufficiently addressed in scholarship. The aim of this chapter is therefore to identify whether such obligations exist under customary or treaty international law and, if so, to determine their nature. The main research problem resides in identifying the existence and place in the international legal system of international obligations to ensure the (cyber) security of the global aviation critical infrastructure, describing their content, defining their nature and delineating the scope of their recipients.

The chapter is structured as follows. **Section 2** provides an international outlook on the status of critical infrastructure in international law, with a focus on aviation infrastructure which defines the subject of analysis. **Section 3** then analyses the international (cyber)security obligations to protect critical infrastructure from the perspective of human rights law and due diligence obligations under general international law. **Section 4** focuses on the specific obligations of States under international air law from the angle of

9 Regional AVSEC Ministerial Conference, 'Dubai Declaration on Cyber Security in Civil Aviation: Reasons and Prospect' (GASeP: The Roadmap to Foster Aviation Security in Africa and the Middle East, Sharm El Sheikh Egypt, 22 August 2017) <https://www.icao.int/Meetings/AVSEC-RMC-Egypt/Documents/PPTs/session3-6.pdf> accessed 18 April 2019.

10 Convention on International Civil Aviation 1944 (adopted 07 December 1944, entered into force 04 April 1947) 15 UNTS 295 (Convention on International Civil Aviation).

11 Convention on the Suppression of Unlawful Acts Relating to International Civil Aviation (adopted 10 September 2010, entered into force 01 July 2018) ICAO Doc 9960 (Beijing Convention).

12 Protocol Supplementary to the Convention for the Suppression of Unlawful Seizure of Aircraft (adopted 10 September 2010, entered into force 01 January 2018) ICAO Doc 9959 (Beijing Protocol).

the intertwining of safety and (cyber)security. It suggests a conceptualisation of safety-critical aspects of (cyber)security as an interest of the international community as a whole. **Section 5** examines whether *de lege lata* this community interest is protected by *erga omnes* obligations embedded in a peremptory norm of international law and how this conceptualisation could facilitate the protection of the global aviation critical infrastructure.

2. CRITICAL (AVIATION) INFRASTRUCTURE: AN INTERNATIONAL OUTLOOK

Prior to embarking on a discussion of the existence of international obligations to ensure the (cyber)security of critical aviation infrastructure, it is necessary to define the notion of (global) critical aviation infrastructure and how a particular infrastructure becomes 'critical'.

2.1. DEFINING CRITICAL INFRASTRUCTURE

There is no binding legal definition of 'critical infrastructure' in international law. Without defining it, in the preamble to Resolution 2341 (2017) the UN Security Council ('UNSC') recognised that it is the responsibility of each State to determine "what constitutes its critical infrastructure, and how to effectively protect it".[13] Although in the context of counter-terrorism, the UNSC also noted the "increasing cross-border critical infrastructure interdependencies between countries, such as those used for, inter alia, (...) air, land and maritime transport (...)".[14] It further highlighted that increasing interdependency among critical infrastructure sectors exposes the infrastructure to new threats and vulnerabilities which in turn engender new security concerns.[15] The UNSC recognised cybersecurity as one of many efforts aimed at protecting critical infrastructure. It also acknowledged in Resolution 2396 (2017) that ICT could be used for malicious purposes to carry out terrorist acts[16] which could "significantly disrupt the functioning of government and private sectors alike and cause knock-on effects beyond the infrastructure sector".[17]

Thus, while there is no definition of critical infrastructure in international law *per se*, the following core elements of a definition could be discerned: (1) the designation of certain domains or sectors as 'critical infrastructure' is the

13 UNSC Res 2341 adopted 13 February 2017 UN Doc S/RES/2341, 2.
14 Ibid.
15 Ibid.
16 UNSC Res 2396 adopted 21 December 2017 UN Doc S/RES/2396, 4.
17 UNSC Res 2341 adopted 13 February 2017 (n 13), 2.

responsibility of States[18]; (2) broadly, critical infrastructure concerns assets and systems providing core functions linked to the operation of a State, such as energy generation, transmission and distribution, transport, banking and financial services, water supply, food distribution and public health; and (3) attacks on critical infrastructure could have disruptive or even debilitating effects vis-à-vis both the public and the private sectors in a State.

It flows from the principle of sovereignty that the responsibility for the designation of critical infrastructure lies with the State. However, international law does not provide criteria for determination of the 'criticality' of one infrastructure compared to another. Thus, it is within a State's discretion to determine the yardstick of criticality, being mindful of the fact that different States may have different priorities.[19] While recently States have been more inclined to designate an ever-growing number of 'important' infrastructures as 'critical', this creates additional risks of diluting the task of protection by distributing resources in different directions. Ultimately, the problem of designation boils down to a distinction between infrastructures which, while performing important functions, are not critical in the sense that they do not impinge upon the core functions related to a State's day-to-day operation.

2.2. CRITERIA FOR THE DESIGNATION OF CRITICAL INFRASTRUCTURE

That international law does not provide a definition of 'critical infrastructure' does not mean criteria for its designation cannot be discerned from it. Some commentators have suggested approaches to the determination of 'criticality' of an infrastructure which could be described, respectively, as function-based and effects-based.[20] They are essentially two sides of the same coin as they ultimately lead to the same outcome.

---

18 Thus, for example, in the EU see Council Directive 2008/114/EC of 8 December 2008 on the identification and designation of European critical infrastructures and the assessment of the need to improve their protection [2008] OJ L345/75, Article2(a) (ECI Directive), which defines 'critical infrastructure' as "asset, system or part thereof located in Member States which is essential for the maintenance of vital societal functions, health, safety, security, economic or social well-being of people, and the disruption or destruction of which would have a significant impact in a Member State as a result of the failure to maintain those functions". See also African Union Convention on Cyber Security and Personal Data Protection (adopted 27 June 2014) (2014) EXCL/846 (XXV) (Malabo Convention), Article 24 which reads that "each State Party shall adopt such legislative and/or regulatory measures as they deem necessary to identify the sectors regarded as sensitive for their national security and well-being of the economy, as well as the information and communication technology systems designed to function in these sectors as elements of critical information infrastructure".

19 'The Protection of Critical Infrastructures against Terrorist Attacks: Compendium of Good Practices' (n 7) 38, 42.

20 Ibid 39.

The function-based approach is basically a positive human rights-oriented approach of determining criticality by reference to the essential societal functions performed and values protected by a particular infrastructure.[21] Thus, an infrastructure would be designated as 'critical' if it plays a crucial role in the protection or the realisation of a particular human right. For example, the definition of 'critical infrastructure' in EU law refers particularly to the right to life, security, economic and social well-being etc.[22] Therefore, the assessment should probably account for the full spectrum of human rights. It is not the scope of the assessed rights that matters here as much as the extent to which any particular right could be encroached upon. Thus, if an infrastructure plays a paramount role in the realisation of the right to life, such as essential healthcare or water supply infrastructure, it would likely fall within the ambit of 'criticality'.

The effects-based approach focuses on the negative consequences the disruption, damaging or destruction of a particular infrastructure could have on the realisation of human rights.[23] For example, it is precisely the devastating effects of inflicting damage upon or destructing such infrastructure that underpin the rationale of the provisions of arts 54–56 of Protocol Additional to the Geneva Conventions of 12 August 1949, and relating to the protection of victims of international armed conflicts ('Additional Protocol I')[24] which prohibit attacks on objects indispensable to the survival of the civilian population (Article 54), the natural environment (Article 55) and works and installations containing dangerous forces (Article 56). The effects-based approach is grounded in the criterion of how intensive a violation of a particular human right the disruption, damaging or destruction or an infrastructure would constitute. Arguably, if the disruption, damage or destruction of the infrastructure would infringe the very 'essence', or core,[25] of a right, it is reasonable to consider the respective infrastructure 'critical'.

These approaches could be instrumental also in the prioritisation phase in which particular sectors or sub-sectors are identified as critical.[26] A human rights-based impact assessment would equip decision-makers with the tool necessary to evenly distribute resources and efforts in the protection of the

21 Such functions could be the provision of healthcare services, protection of the environment or essential water or energy supply resources etc.

22 ECI Directive, Article 2(a) (n 18).

23 'The Protection of Critical Infrastructures against Terrorist Attacks: Compendium of Good Practices' (n 7) 39.

24 Protocol Additional to the Geneva Conventions of 12 August 1949, and relating to the protection of victims of international armed conflicts (adopted 8 June 1977, entered into force 7 December 1978) 1125 UNTS 3 (Additional Protocol I), arts. 54–56.

25 See on the concept of 'essence of fundamental rights', particularly in an EU context, Maja Brkan, 'The Concept of Essence of Fundamental Rights in the EU Legal Order: Peeling the Onion to Its Core' (2018) 14 European Constitutional Law Review 332, 333.

26 'The Protection of Critical Infrastructures against Terrorist Attacks: Compendium of Good Practices' (n 7) 41.

respective sectors. Furthermore, prioritisation need not necessarily take place (only) at the level of specific assets or systems; it could equally concern critical processes as in the example of the Netherlands.[27] The Netherlands transitioned from identification of critical sectors to determination of critical processes since not all processes within a sector were critical. This shift has allegedly enabled the State to allocate resources more efficiently and therefore address better concerns related to the interconnectedness of critical infrastructures and the risk of cascade effects in case of failure of one of them.[28] Analysing the impact on human rights at both the level of systems and processes would allow for a better assessment of the involved risks and would ultimately contribute to a more evidence-based rather than 'intuitive' allocation of resources.

2.3. CRITICAL INFORMATION INFRASTRUCTURE

Critical infrastructure protection is fundamentally challenged also by digitalisation and global connectivity.[29] The control and delivery of certain industrial and public goods has long been supported by supervisory control and data acquisition ('SCADA') systems. They are increasingly being connected with other systems and devices which has made them more vulnerable to cyber attacks. The assemblages of legacy physical systems, new cyber-physical infrastructure and electronic communications networks has led to the emergence of a distinct over-the-top layer of cyber infrastructure. An example of this layer is the virtualisation of physical infrastructure in air traffic control whereby the physical controller working position is decoupled from the remote provision of air traffic management ('ATM') data and other technical services.[30]

This cyber infrastructure, also termed 'critical information infrastructure',[31] consists of "those interconnected information systems and networks, the disruption or destruction of which would have serious impact on the health, safety, security, or economic well-being of citizens, or on the effective

---

27 Ibid 43–44.

28 National Coordinator for Security and Counterterrorism, 'Resilient Critical Infrastructure' <https://english.nctv.nl/binaries/Factsheet%20Critical%20Infrastructure%20ENG%202018_tcm32-240750.pdf>.

29 'The Protection of Critical Infrastructures against Terrorist Attacks: Compendium of Good Practices' (n 7) 47.

30 See more on the virtual centre model in Skyguide, *The Virtual Centre Model* (2013) 1–2 <https://www.skyguide.ch/wp-content/uploads/fileadmin/user_upload/publications/corporate/concept_paper_VCM_2013-04.pdf> accessed 6 June 2019. See also on the decoupling of service provision from the local infrastructure in SESAR Joint Undertaking, 'A Proposal for the Future Architecture of the European Airspace' (Publications Office of the European Union 2019) 3 <https://www.sesarju.eu/sites/default/files/documents/reports/Future%20Airspace%20Architecture%20Proposal.pdf> accessed 12 May 2019.

31 See, for example, UNGA Res 58/199 adopted 30 January 2004 UN Doc A/RES/58/199 (n 4).

functioning of government or the economy".[32] The list of protected assets could also be complemented by data, machine learning models etc. The 'cyber link' between physical and cyber infrastructure could spawn a swirling vortex, pulling in virtually all kinds of (hitherto) non-critical infrastructure.[33] In other words, the interconnectedness and the ensuing interdependence between providers cutting across different critical infrastructure sectors and sub-sectors form complex linkages. This gives rise to new physical, cyber and hybrid risks originating from multiple sources. These risks could have particularly grave manifestations in safety-critical, time- and space-constrained environments, such as that of international civil aviation.

2.4. (GLOBAL) CRITICAL INFRASTRUCTURE IN AVIATION

Although there is no definition of 'critical aviation infrastructure' in international air law, the ICAO Aviation Security Manual,[34] in clarifying the provisions of Annex 17[35] to the Convention on International Civil Aviation, refers to the concept 'vulnerable point'. A vulnerable point is defined as "any facility on or connected with an airport which, if damaged or destroyed, would seriously impair the functioning of the airport". Vulnerable points include air traffic control towers, communication facilities, radio navigation aids, power transformers, primary and secondary power supplies and fuel installations, both on and off the airport.

While these vulnerable points refer to infrastructure largely confined to the territory of individual States, examples of cross-border critical aviation infrastructure include Eurocontrol,[36] an international organisation

---

32 Organisation for Economic Co-operation and Development (OECD), 'Recommendation of the Council on the Protection of Critical Information Infrastructures' (17–18 June 2008) C(2008)35, 4.

33 'The Protection of Critical Infrastructures against Terrorist Attacks: Compendium of Good Practices' (n 7) 48.

34 International Civil Aviation Organization (ICAO), 'Aviation Security Manual' (2017) ICAO Doc 8973.

35 ICAO, 'Annex 17 to the Convention on International Civil Aviation – Security', 10th edition (2017) 17.

36 See for more details on the scope of the Network Manager's functions Commission Regulation (EU) No 677/2011 of 7 July 2011 laying down detailed rules for the implementation of air traffic management (ATM) network functions and amending Regulation (EU) No 691/2010 [2011] OJ L185/1, to be superseded by Commission Implementing Regulation (EU) 2019/123 of 24 January 2019 laying down detailed rules for the implementation of air traffic management (ATM) network functions and repealing Commission Regulation (EU) No 677/2011 [2019] OJ L28/1. See also Commission Implementing Decision (EU) 2019/709 of 6 May 2019 on the appointment of the network manager for air traffic management (ATM) network functions of the single European sky (notified under document C(2019) 3228) [2019]

designated as ATM Network Manager.[37] In its new approach to European critical infrastructures, the European Commission ('EC') takes note of the interdependencies between critical infrastructures and various State and non-State actors. It also highlights the domino effects that the disruption of a part of this cross-border infrastructure in one State could have on others.[38]

The advent of a complex of systems, assets and services extending across borders and spaces, which could be termed collectively 'global aviation critical infrastructure', is corroborated by the intertwining of various technical artefacts. As aircraft become "complex data networks",[39] new dependencies emerge between flight management systems, airborne and ground-based air traffic management systems, satellite infrastructure etc.[40] Furthermore, the rollout of the System-Wide Information Management ('SWIM')[41] system as the "global ATM intranet",[42] is expected to redefine the ATM system by serving as a single point of access for aviation data. The distributed nature of ATM, rooted in State sovereignty, will be transformed into a cross-border public-private multi-actor system based on a "many-to-many model of information distribution where the producer is decoupled from the user of the information".[43] In other words, the 'cyber link' between physical aviation critical infrastructure and cyber infrastructure has gradually transformed global aviation into a 'system of systems' environment which extends above and beyond the jurisdiction of any individual State.

Thus, broadly speaking, there are two dimensions to aviation critical infrastructure: physical and cyber. Unlike the physical layer, the cyber layer is much more difficult to delineate as it may include physical and information infrastructure with ground, airborne, cyber and space segments which may fall under different jurisdictional regimes. The cross-border intertwining of

---

OJ L120/27 on the reappointment of Eurocontrol as Network Manager for the period 2020–2029.

37 The Network Manager function includes coordination of air traffic flow management and air traffic control, but it is also related function of network crisis management within the European Aviation Crisis Coordination Cell.

38 Commission, 'Commission Staff Working Document on a New Approach to the European Programme for Critical Infrastructure Protection Making European Critical Infrastructures More Secure' SWD (2013) 318 Final 2, 6–8.

39 Pete Cooper, 'Aviation Cybersecurity: Finding Lift, Minimizing Drag' (Atlantic Council Brent Scowcroft Center on International Security 2017) 90.

40 New dependencies will arise, for example, between the Global Positioning System ('GPS'), Aircraft Communications Addressing and Reporting System ('ACARS'), Automatic Dependent Surveillance – Broadcast ('ADS-B') technologies, controller-pilot data link communications, airborne collision avoidance systems ('ACAS'), remote tower services ('RTS') and many others.

41 For more details on the technical aspects of SWIM, see ICAO, 'Manual on System Wide Information Management (SWIM) Concept' (2015) ICAO Doc 10039.

42 Cooper (n 39) 125.

43 Anna Masutti, 'Single European Sky – a Possible Regulatory Framework for System Wide Information Management (SWIM)' (2011) 36 Air and Space Law 275, 278.

infrastructural elements brings about new cyber threats,[44] such as cyber jacking, State-sponsored disruption of airport operations, cyber attacks by State and non-State actors against communication, navigation and surveillance facilities and aircraft.[45] Such attacks could have disastrous consequences for the safety and security of international civil aviation which requires cyber resilience building through cooperation and shared responsibility.[46]

Public international air law is grounded in the principle of complete and exclusive sovereignty of States over the airspace above their territory.[47] While there are multiple exceptions whereby States have relinquished partially their sovereignty in pursuit of their common interest of maintaining adequate safety and security levels of international civil aviation,[48] the classicism of the Convention on International Civil Aviation[49] has generally prevailed. The prevailing view therefore is that ensuring civil aviation's (cyber)security, while revealing a collective dimension, is considered first and foremost the responsibility of individual States.[50] In light of this responsibility, which will be analysed in the following sections, the question remains unsettled as to who exactly should ensure the (cyber)security of this emerging global critical aviation infrastructure and whether there exist any general obligations under international law to do so.

3. (CYBER)SECURITY OBLIGATIONS UNDER GENERAL INTERNATIONAL LAW

States have certain general duties under international law regarding the security of infrastructure operating on their territory. These duties derive from international human rights law and the due diligence obligations of States to act as good neighbours in the international community. Their analysis is important as some of these obligations originate in customary international law and exist

44 See, Elinor Mills, 'Report: Hackers Broke into FAA Air Traffic Control Systems' (*CNET*) <https://www.cnet.com/news/report-hackers-broke-into-faa-air-traffic-control-systems/> accessed 8 May 2019.

45 Cooper (n 39) 104.

46 ICAO, 'Assembly Resolution A39-19: Addressing Cybersecurity in Civil Aviation' (06 October 2016) A39-19 ICAO Doc 10075; Cooper (n 39) 97.

47 Convention on International Civil Aviation, Article 1.

48 Paul Stephen Dempsey, 'Introduction: Multilateral Conventions and Customary International Law' in Paul Stephen Dempsey and Ram S Jakhu (eds), *Routledge Handbook of Public Aviation Law* (Routledge 2016) 6.

49 SG Sreejith, 'Legality of the Gulf Ban on Qatari Flights: *State Sovereignty at Crossroads*' (2018) 43 Air and Space Law 191, 199.

50 ICAO, 'Assembly Resolution A39-18: Consolidated statement on continuing ICAO policies related to aviation security' (06 October 2016) A39-18 ICAO Doc 10075 Appendix C, para 3*bis*, Appendix E, para 5. See also Regional AVSEC Ministerial Conference (n 9).

in parallel to a State's obligations under international treaty law, such as the Convention on International Civil Aviation.

This section analyses the internal and external dimensions of (cyber) security in international law from a State perspective. It first reflects upon the internal dimension through the place, content and role of the right to security in the universal system of human rights. The analysis then turns to examine the external dimension of security in inter-State relations from a due diligence standpoint.

3.1. RIGHT TO SECURITY AS AN INTERNATIONAL HUMAN RIGHT

States have a general obligation under international law to ensure the right to liberty and security of persons as an international human right[51] built upon the foundations laid down by Article 3 of the Universal Declaration of Human Rights of 1948.

In its General Comment No 35 to Article 9 of the International Covenant on Civil and Political Rights ('ICCPR'), the UN Human Rights Committee highlighted that "[l]iberty and security of person are precious for their own sake, and also because the deprivation of liberty and security of person have historically been principal means for impairing the enjoyment of other rights".[52] The commentary specifies that "security of person concerns freedom from injury to the body and the mind, or bodily and mental integrity", highlighting a State's negative obligation.[53] However, this right also implies a positive international obligation for States to "protect individuals from foreseeable threats to life or bodily integrity proceeding from any governmental or private actors".[54] While it does not address the full spectrum of risks to the physical or mental integrity of a person, it is clear the ambit of the right to security is broad and could potentially implicate other rights such as the right to life (Article 6), the prohibition of torture, cruel, inhuman or degrading treatment or punishment (Article 7), the liberty of movement (Article 12) etc. The paramountcy of the right to security is emphasised by the fact that, while it does not belong to the list of non-derogable rights under Article 4, there are still limits to the discretion of States.[55]

51 International Covenant on Civil and Political Rights (adopted 16 December 1966, entered into force 23 March 1976) 999 UNTS 171, Article 9 (ICCPR).

52 UN Human Rights Committee (UNHRC), 'General comment No. 35 Article 9 (Liberty and security of person)' (16 December 2014) CCPR/C/GC/35 para 2.

53 UNHRC, 'General comment No. 35 Article 9 (Liberty and security of person)' (16 December 2014) CCPR/C/GC/35 para 3.

54 UNHRC, 'General comment No. 35 Article 9 (Liberty and security of person)' (16 December 2014) CCPR/C/GC/35 para 9.

55 UNHRC, 'General comment No. 35 Article 9 (Liberty and security of person)' (16 December 2014) CCPR/C/GC/35 para 65, 66. Any derogation must be in line with the State's obligations

A closer analysis of the content of the right to security under international human rights law invites a discussion on its relationship with safety. Security is a manifold concept which takes on different shapes in different contexts.[56] Human rights law alone seems to invoke four different concepts of security.[57] It seems generally accepted that security concerns external risks while safety deals with internal risks. This, of course, depends on the perspective from which either security or safety is assessed. In fact, as argued in scholarship, looking at both concepts through the lens of the 'internal-external' dichotomy allows to gain a better understanding of the phenomenon in question.[58]

This dichotomy is inherent in the right to security. Thus, the negative obligation not to inflict harm on a person's bodily or mental integrity depicts the internal, safety perspective whereby a State is obliged to abstain from engaging in activities whence risks of inflicting such harm may emerge. This obligation has also been termed 'negative individual security against the state'.[59] Conversely, the positive obligation of a State to protect individuals from foreseeable threats from governmental forces or private activities portrays the external perspective. Under this obligation, a State must take measures to proactively manage external threats aimed at compromising a person's bodily or mental integrity. An example of this external perspective could be the actions taken by a State to protect individuals against detention or abduction by insurgents operating on its territory or to proactively scan its critical information infrastructure for security vulnerabilities. This has also been conceptualised as the 'positive security of individuals'.[60]

The relationship between safety and security reveals distinct characteristics in aviation which will be analysed in the following sections. Suffice it to say for the time being that this relationship is intrinsic to the essence of the human right to security which entails both positive and negative international obligations on States.

Since the right to security encompasses both safety and security considerations, the question arises whether the right is limited to physical safety and security or cybersecurity may also be justified as fitting. It is submitted here that the right to security encompasses both physical and cyber security provided certain conditions are met. Since States have a positive obligation to protect individuals from foreseeable threats to life or bodily integrity, this

---

under international law. Thus, for example, as pointed out by the UNHRC, derogations from the prohibitions against taking of hostages, abductions or unacknowledged detention are not allowed.

56 Kimmo Nuotio, 'Security and Criminal Law: A Difficult Relationship' [2013] Law and Security in Europe: Reconsidering the Security Constitution 197, 199.

57 Piet Hein van Kempen, 'Four Concepts of Security – A Human Rights Perspective' (2013) 13 Human Rights Law Review 1, 2.

58 Nuotio (n 56) 199–201.

59 Van Kempen (n 57) 9.

60 This is the positive State obligation to offer security to individuals. See ibid 16.

obligation encompasses proactive measures. These measures should be aimed at safeguarding, inter alia, critical infrastructure, both physical and cyber, whose disruption, damaging or destruction could inflict such harm. This would likely involve measures of cybersecurity, at least as far as safety- or mission-critical functions of the infrastructure are concerned. An example is a non-kinetic cyber attack capable of inflicting physical damage on individuals, e.g. by producing kinetic effects through destruction or damaging physical artefacts. Failure of States to protect the infrastructure from such threats could amount to a breach of their security obligations. Equally, States have a negative obligation not to interfere with an individual's personal security. This entails, for example, an obligation not to employ unlawful surveillance techniques or install backdoors on individuals' personal devices which may be used by malevolent States or non-State actors to cause damage to their mental or bodily integrity, e.g. by tracking their physical whereabouts and/or engaging in cyber torture practices.[61]

3.2. (CYBER)SECURITY DUE DILIGENCE OBLIGATIONS

States have a duty to protect not only their citizens, but also aliens on their territory. In his treatise E. de Vattel argued that "[t]he sovereign ought not to grant an entrance into his state for the purpose of drawing foreigners into a snare: as soon as he admits them, he engages to protect them as his own subjects, and to afford them perfect security, *as far as depends on him*" (emphasis added).[62] It is within this context that the obligation of due diligence emerged in international law.

Due diligence is a relatively old concept. While present in the writings of Grotius, it matured only in the 19th century with the emergence of nation-States. It gradually became "both a duty and a constraint upon State behaviour" on the international plane.[63] These early manifestations are linked first and foremost to the protection of aliens on a State's territory. In the *Alabama Claims Arbitration* case the arbitrators argued that "'due diligence' (…) ought to be exercised by *neutral* governments in exact *proportion* to the *risks* to which either of the belligerents may be exposed, from a failure to fulfil the obligations of neutrality on their part" (emphasis added).[64] The tribunal elaborated a dynamic concept of due diligence whence neutral States must exercise diligence in proportion to the risk to which belligerents may be exposed, should the State fail in performing its neutrality obligations.

61 Samantha Newbery and Ali Dehghantanha, 'Torture-Free Cyberspace – a Human Right' (2017) 2017 Computer Fraud & Security 14.

62 Vattel (n 1) 313 Book II, Ch VIII, §104 'Protection due to foreigners'.

63 Duncan French and Tim Stephens, 'ILA Study Group on Due Diligence in International Law: Final Report' (2014) 2.

64 *Alabama Claims Arbitration* (1872) 29 RIAA 125 129.

This stance was reiterated, albeit in a different context, several decades later in the *S.S. Lotus* case before the Permanent Court of International Justice ('PCIJ') where, in dissent, Judge Moore noted that "[i]t is well settled that a State is bound to use *due diligence* to *prevent* the commission within its dominions of *criminal acts against another nation or its people*" (emphasis added).[65] However, it was not until the ruling of the International Court of Justice ('ICJ') in the *Corfu Channel* case[66] that the concept took centre stage in international law and, most prominently, in the preventive principle in environmental law.[67]

Despite ensuing fragmentation, dissimilar approaches and even fundamental discussions about the very nature of due diligence as a primary or secondary rule, it is almost universally accepted that its content should be assessed against the yardstick of international law, discarding any references to municipal law standards.[68] It is beyond the ambition of this chapter to capture all the nuances in these discussions. The following paragraphs thus represent only a brief account of due diligence obligations in international law for the purpose of identifying what general (cyber)security obligations States may have in their inter-State relations.

Prior to embarking on a discussion of due diligence in the jurisprudence of international courts and tribunals, a word of caution must be mentioned. Due diligence is a concept that transpires many specialised branches of international law. This has spurred debates among international lawyers as to whether due diligence has an immutable content at all.[69] Setting these debates aside, certain material obligations could be discerned from customary international law[70] to support the argument that States have discrete general (cyber)security due diligence obligations towards other States regarding the use of critical infrastructure located on their territory.

Three main factors have been suggested as playing a role in the determination of the content of due diligence: degree of effectiveness of State control over a

---

65 *Case of the S.S. "Lotus" (France v Turkey)* PCIJ Series A no 10 4, Dissenting Opinion of Judge Moore 88–89.

66 *Corfu Channel Case (UK v Albania)* (Merits) [1949] ICJ Rep 4.

67 James Crawford, *Brownlie's Principles of Public International Law* (Oxford University Press 2012) 356–357.

68 Duncan French and Tim Stephens (n 63) 4.

69 Akiko Takano, 'Due Diligence Obligations and Transboundary Environmental Harm: Cybersecurity Applications' (2018) 7 Laws 36, 2. This was also recognised by the International Tribunal on Law of the Sea ('ITLOS') in its advisory opinion in the *Responsibilities and obligations of States with respect to activities in the Area* case where it argued that due diligence is a "variable concept" that "may change over time as measures considered sufficiently diligent at a certain moment may become not diligent enough in light, for instance, of new scientific or technological knowledge. It may also change in relation to the risks involved in the activity". See *Responsibilities and obligations of States with respect to activities in the* Area (Advisory Opinion, 1 February 2011) ITLOS Reports 2011, 117.

70 Russell Buchan, 'Cyberspace, Non-State Actors and the Obligation to Prevent Transboundary Harm' (2016) 21 Journal of Conflict and Security Law 429.

territory; degree of predictability of a harm; and paramountcy of the interest at stake.[71] Accordingly, three main due diligence obligations could be distinguished from customary international law: duty to warn, the principle of 'no harm' and the principle of non-intervention.[72]

The duty to warn, also known as the general obligation of good neighbourliness, was first elaborated in the *Corfu Channel* case where the ICJ held that "every State's obligation not to allow knowingly its territory to be used for acts contrary to the rights of other States" is a "well-recognized principle".[73] In the case, British warships set off a mine while passing through an international strait in Albania's territorial waters. While the ICJ was unable to establish whether it was Albania that planted the mines, it construed the State should have had knowledge of the mines and therefore had a duty to warn passing ships. This articulation of the ICJ could equally support the existence of a customary obligation for States to prevent the use of (cyber) infrastructure located on their territory in a way harmful to the rights of other States. The obligation encompasses two distinct duties: (1) to build capacity by instigating laws and institutions capable of preventing the use of the territory in such a way and (2) provided there is actual or constructive knowledge of a threat, to utilise this capacity to quash it or, lacking capacity, to at least notify and warn likely victim States.[74] Reading this rationale in a cyber(security) context, States can be argued to have a duty to disclose the existence of vulnerabilities in their (critical) information infrastructure to other States whose rights may be negatively affected. This is particularly so in cases where harm may originate from a non-commercial infrastructure, e.g. an air traffic management system under the effective control of a State, which could serve as a presumption of knowledge.[75]

While the application of due diligence to cyber-physical infrastructure under the control of a State seems to defy questions of jurisdiction in cyberspace,[76] this is certainly not the case as far as shared global cyber infrastructure is concerned. Thus, it is uncertain whether States have a duty to warn of vulnerabilities regarding virtualised infrastructures, such as the SWIM intranet whereby a global network of connected assets and data suppliers will extend far beyond the territory of any particular State.[77] On the one hand, if a State's duty to warn

---

71 Kristen E Boon, 'Are Control Tests Fit for the Future? The Slippage Problem in Attribution Doctrines' (2014) 15 Melbourne Journal of International Law; Melbourne 1, 38.

72 Scott J Shackelford, Scott Russell and Andreas Kuehn, 'Unpacking the International Law on Cybersecurity Due Diligence: Lessons from the Public and Private Sectors' (2016) 17 Chicago Journal of International Law; Chicago 1, 9.

73 *Corfu Channel Case (UK v Albania)* (Merits) [1949] ICJ Rep 4 (n 66) 22.

74 Buchan (n 70) 445, 451.

75 Shackelford, Russell and Kuehn (n 72) 11.

76 Luke Chircop, 'A Due Diligence Standard of Attribution in Cyberspace' (2018) 67 International & Comparative Law Quarterly 643, 392.

77 Francis Schubert, 'The Technical Defragmentation of Air Navigation Services – The Legal Challenges of Virtualisation' [2013] From Lowlands to High Skies: A Multilevel Jurisdictional

of known or foreseeable harms[78] is to be extended to infrastructure beyond the realms of its territory, this may come in conflict with the principle of non-intervention. On the other hand, in a global virtualised environment, it is infeasible to claim a duty on the State to actively monitor solely 'its' part of this shared infrastructure as this part can hardly be discerned, notwithstanding the prevailing opinion that State sovereignty applies equally in cyberspace. It is also unclear to what extent a State has a duty to intervene, for example, to counter an ongoing cyber attack in a segment of this infrastructure spanning across the cyberspace of several countries. Figuratively speaking, the question is essentially whether a State is expected to be not just a good neighbour, but also a vigilant member of the international community.

The 'no harm' principle, also known as the preventive principle, was articulated in the *Trail Smelter* case[79] and has since played a prominent role in international (environmental) law. The tribunal in this case argued that it is a principle of international law that "no State has the right to use or permit the use of its territory in such a manner as to cause injury (...) in or to the territory of another or the properties or persons therein, when the case is of serious consequence and the injury is established by clear and convincing evidence".[80] Thus, the essence of the preventive principle crystallised in an obligation for States to ensure that activities taking place within their jurisdiction are not detrimental to the rights of other States.

While this principle has been interpreted broadly in international law, an important caveat has to be added. The *Trail Smelter* case concerned environmental damage caused by fumes. Whether this principle could be considered a general principle of international law is still debatable. Provided there is a general obligation on States to prohibit the use of their territory in a manner injurious to other States,[81] in a cyber(security) context this obligation could be interpreted as requiring States to prohibit cyber activities which may result in "serious consequences" ensuing from harmful 'cyber emissions'. Arguably, such serious consequences may involve, for example, cyber attacks emanating from a State's territory, e.g. by a non-State actor, against air navigation facilities of another State resulting in disruption of air traffic or even an accident. Whether it also concerns similar attacks against global virtualised infrastructures, i.e. not directed against any particular State, resulting, for example, in widespread air traffic disruptions or accidents, is not as clear-cut. This problem will be reflected upon in more details in the following sections in

Approach Towards Air law 43, 49.

78 Shackelford, Russell and Kuehn (n 72) 9.

79 *Trail Smelter Case (US v Canada)* [1938] UN Rep Int'L Arb Awards 1905 1949.

80 *Trail Smelter Case (US v Canada)* [1938] UN Rep Int'L Arb Awards 1905 (n 79) 1965.

81 Commentators have noted the principle does not enjoy widespread State practice. See Shackelford, Russell and Kuehn (n 72) 11.

light of the international obligations of States in the domain of aviation safety and (cyber)security.

The non-intervention principle derives its authority from customary international law, as reflected in the UN Charter.[82] Its content was eloquently articulated by the ICJ in the *Military and Paramilitary Activities in and against Nicaragua* case.[83] The Court argued that the "principle forbids all States or groups of States to intervene directly or indirectly in internal or external affairs of other States".[84] It defined prohibited intervention as "one bearing on matters in which each State is permitted, by the principle of State sovereignty to decide freely".[85] The Court identified as one such matter the choice of a political, economic, social and cultural system, and the formulation of foreign policy. In the Court's view, intervention is wrongful when coercion is used in respect of choices within the *domain reservé* of States.

Unlike the preventive principle, which is concerned with the transboundary effects of harmful activity, the principle of non-intervention is deeply rooted in and derives from the principle of State sovereignty. Thus, while a violation of the principle of no harm is focused on the extraterritorial effects of a harmful activity, intervention interferes with the core elements of the principle of sovereignty.[86] This distinction has a particular merit in a cyber(security) context since the international community seems to have united around the view that State sovereignty applies equally in physical and cyberspace.[87] Therefore, in their international relations States can be argued to have an obligation of cyber non-intervention as an extension of sovereignty in cyberspace,[88] encompassing its physical, logical and social dimensions.[89]

---

82 Charter of the United Nations (adopted 24 October 1945, entered into force 24 October 1945) 1 UNTS XVI (UN Charter) Article 2(7) and Article 2(4).

83 *Military and Paramilitary Activities in and against Nicaragua (Nicaragua v United States of America)* (Merits) [1986] ICJ Rep 14 108 para 205.

84 *Military and Paramilitary Activities in and against Nicaragua (Nicaragua v United States of America)* (Merits) [1986] ICJ Rep 14 108 (n 83) para 205.

85 *Military and Paramilitary Activities in and against Nicaragua (Nicaragua v United States of America)* (Merits) [1986] ICJ Rep 14 108 (n 83) para 205.

86 Shackelford, Russell and Kuehn (n 72) 13.

87 Zhixiong Huang and Kubo Mačák, 'Towards the International Rule of Law in Cyberspace: Contrasting Chinese and Western Approaches' (2017) 16 Chinese Journal of International Law 271, 279.

88 See on the concept of sovereignty in cyberspace manifested as power rather than territory Nicholas Tsagourias, 'The Legal Status of Cyberspace', *Research Handbook on International Law and Cyberspace* (Edward Elgar Publishing 2015) 18 <www.elgaronline.com/view/9781782547389.xml> accessed 3 March 2019.

89 On the different dimensions of cyberspace, see a recent account in Michael N Schmitt (ed), *Tallinn Manual 2.0 on the International Law Applicable to Cyber Operations: Prepared by the International Groups of Experts at the Invitation of the NATO Cooperative Cyber Defence Centre of Excellence* (2nd edn, Cambridge University Press 2017) 12 <http://ebooks.cambridge.org/ref/id/CBO9781316822524> accessed 24 February 2019.

The content of this obligation of cyber non-intervention is all but clear. It seems there is some level of acceptance that cyber attacks failing to meet the threshold of use of force under Article 2(4) of the UN Charter could nonetheless constitute a breach of the principle of non-intervention.[90] It has been argued also that sophisticated malware, such as Stuxnet and possibly NotPetya, would certainly qualify as intervention.[91] Equally, the use of 'cyber force' against civil aviation or critical information infrastructure should easily qualify (at least) as intervention. However, it seems that there is a growing consensus around the stance that cyberspace's global and open technical architecture dictates that the principle of non-intervention is viewed not as a negative obligation of the intervening State, but rather as a positive obligation of the victim State to preclude intervention by implementing technical measures.[92] This implies that if a State wants to prevent coercive intervention into its cyberspace, it is incumbent upon that State to take proactive measures to prevent such intervention. If supported by State practice, this posture could signify further erosion of the principle of non-intervention or, at best, its fragmentation into low- and high-intensity thresholds of intervention in cyberspace, suggesting the emergence of different approaches. Furthermore, it seems to encourage a cyberspace policy of censorship and surveillance which equally goes against the free and open nature of cyberspace.

This brief overview of due diligence obligations in the context of (cyber) security calls for two remarks. First, in these cases due diligence obligations were construed in narrow, geographically defined contexts. This has raised reasonable concerns regarding the applicability of these cases to the essentially non-territorial cyberspace[93] in light of the tensions between the principle of sovereignty and effects-based jurisdiction. Inspired by the 'global commons' aspects of cyberspace, commentators have thus advocated a shift towards common responsibilities modelled after environmental obligations in pursuit of a community interest of keeping (other States') cyberspace free from harm.[94] Another word of caution concerns the invocation by States of national security exceptions[95] available in customary international law, allowing them to suspend the performance of their international obligations.[96] Recently, this has become a

90 Ibid 330, Rule 68, para 6.

91 Shackelford, Russell and Kuehn (n 72) 13.

92 A good example being the Great Firewall of China or the recently announced intention of Russia to physically disconnect itself from cyberspace.

93 Shackelford, Russell and Kuehn (n 72) 22.

94 Ibid 22–23. This argument will be revisited in section 5 in the context of aviation safety and security obligations.

95 These being *clausula rebus sic stantibus* (fundamental change of circumstance), law of reprisal, self-defence and necessity. See more in Susan Rose-Ackerman and Benjamin Billa, 'Treaties and National Security' (2008) reprinted in Yale Law School Faculty Scholarship Series <https://digitalcommons.law.yale.edu/fss_papers/595/> accessed 27 June 2019 as quoted by Shackelford, Russell and Kuehn (n 72) 23.

96 Shackelford, Russell and Kuehn (n 72) 23.

contentious issue in the dispute between Ukraine and Russia before the World Trade Organization's Dispute Settlement Body. In the case, Russia invoked the national security exception of Article XXI of the General Agreement on Trade and Tariffs ('GATT') to justify transit restrictions.[97] The panel defined narrowly 'emergency' in international relations as implying "a situation of armed conflict, or of latent armed conflict, or of heightened tension or crisis, or of general instability engulfing or surrounding a state", while excluding from its scope mere "political or economic differences".[98] In certain circumstance, cybersecurity itself could be a legitimate ground to invoke a national security exception to impose limitations to human rights[99] or stay the performance of (due diligence) obligations. In essence, this could easily undermine the practical usefulness of due diligence obligation in the context of (cyber)security.[100]

It follows from these discussions that while States have certain customary due diligence obligations which have a bearing on (cyber)security, these have emerged in geographically-constrained settings where the harm is relatively easy to measure. Also, the tensions between effects-based jurisdiction and sovereignty questions the relevance of these obligations in cyberspace in the first place. Finally, the availability of a continuum of customary national security exceptions could render these obligations inoperable should States decide to resort to them. This uncertainty indicates that the due diligence obligations derived from general international law are lacking in their own right to serve as a sufficient guarantee for the (cyber)security of the global aviation critical infrastructure. It is therefore necessary to turn to an analysis of the nature of the obligations of States in international air law and the interest(s) they protect.

4. SAFETY AND (CYBER)SECURITY OBLIGATIONS IN INTERNATIONAL AIR LAW

Apart from the general due diligence international obligations of States, which apply with a varying degree to cyber and cyber-physical infrastructure, the obligation for criminalisation of certain offences in accordance with the principle *aut dedere, aut iudicare*,[101] and human rights obligations, there are

---

97 WTO, *Russia – Measures Concerning Traffic in Transit (Ukraine v Russian Federation) – Report of the Panel* (5 April 2019) WT/DS512/R, 1.

98 WTO, *Russia – Measures Concerning Traffic in Transit (Ukraine v Russian Federation) – Report of the Panel* (5 April 2019) WT/DS512/R, 1 paras 7.75, 7.76.

99 Van Kempen (n 57) 13.

100 Shackelford, Russell and Kuehn (n 72) 24.

101 Which has been recognised by commentators as a sign of emerging *opinio iuris* for an international obligation of criminalisation and prosecution of certain criminal offences in the cyber realm. See more in ibid 7. The principle was formally acknowledged for the first time in an international criminal air law treaty in Convention for the Suppression of unlawful seizure of aircraft (adopted 16 December 1970, entered into force 14 October 1971)

hardly any other rules in general international law concerning cybersecurity. However, as far as international civil aviation is concerned, certain specific obligations could be distinguished.

This section explores the symbiotic relationship between safety and security in civil aviation and analyses the content and nature of the international obligations of States regarding aviation safety and (cyber)security.

4.1. AVIATION (CYBER)SECURITY OBLIGATIONS

There is no legal definition of security in international air law. It has been argued that security is not an independent concept but it is always linked to a system of individual and collective values.[102] Doctrinal definitions tend to focus on the protection against *external* dangers to civil aviation, such as hijacking, acts of sabotage, attacks with explosives or other criminal acts.[103] Unlike security's external outlook, aviation safety seems to be more concerned with the *internal* dangers. Safety has been used to refer to "the state of freedom from unacceptable risk of injury to persons or damage to aircraft and property".[104] Annex 19 to the Convention on International Civil Aviation defines it as "the state in which risks associated with aviation activities, related to, or in direct support of the operation of aircraft are reduced and controlled to an acceptable level".[105] Safety is therefore concerned with the elimination or reduction of risks of injury to persons or damage to property which may result from aviation activities which are related or directly support the operation of the aircraft. The articulated distinction between safety and security in a human rights context seems to have some relevance in this setting too. However, as will be shown in the following paragraphs, there is a specific relationship between safety and security in aviation which has a bearing on the obligations of States regarding the protection of critical aviation infrastructure.

Security was mentioned for the first time in the context of civil aviation in the wake of a series of hijackings, terrorist acts and other unlawful interferences in the 1950–60s. The first edition of Annex 17 'Security' to the Convention on International Civil Aviation, containing standards and recommended practices on aviation security, left the definition of the concept to the discretion of

---

860 UNTS 105 (Hague Convention) Article 7. Its nature as a reflection of general customary international law is still highly questionable though.

102 Anna Masutti and Filippo Tomasello, 'The Challenge of Security' in Elgar Edward (ed), *International regulation of non-military drones* (2018) 161.

103 Stephan Hobe, Nicolai von Ruckteschell and David Heffernan, *Cologne Compendium on Air Law in Europe* (Hardcover, Carl Heymanns Verlag 2013) 779.

104 ICAO, 'ICAO Working Paper AN-WP/7699 "Determination of a Definition of Aviation Safety"' (11 December 2001) AN-WP/7699 para 2.2.

105 ICAO, 'Annex 19 to the Convention on International Civil Aviation – Safety Management', 2nd edition (2016) 19.

the Contracting States. It was not until 1986 that 'security' was defined as "a combination of measures of human and material resources intended to safeguard civil aviation against acts of unlawful interference".[106] In the current edition of Annex 17 security is defined as "safeguarding civil aviation against acts of unlawful interferences".[107] The objectives of Annex 17 refer to strengthening of the responsibility of States to protect civil aviation from unlawful interference, establish efficient security organisation and implement measures to protect passengers, crews, personnel and the general public. Annex 17 further demands that States "have as its primary objective the safety of passengers ... the general public in all matters related to safeguarding against acts of unlawful interference with civil aviation".[108]

As an international organisation, ICAO does not possess any sovereign powers and the standards adopted by the ICAO Council under Article 54 (l) and Article 37 of the Convention on International Civil Aviation are not enforceable as such, absent national implementation.[109] Furthermore, States may depart from such standards by relying on the mechanism of 'filing of differences' enshrined in Article 38 which requires notification to the ICAO Council. Therefore, the aviation security standards and alleged responsibilities designated as Annex 17 to the Convention on International Civil Aviation do not *ipso facto* translate into international obligations.[110]

Understandably, in the early stages of 'securitisation' of civil aviation, the focus was on criminalisation and prosecution of certain offences against aircraft and infrastructure. In a series of treaties adopted under the auspices of ICAO, States came to an agreement to establish criminal jurisdiction over offences committed on board aircraft and unlawful seizure,[111] hijacking,[112] sabotage, incl. attacks against the safety of international civil aviation or air navigation facilities,[113] and new and emerging threats such as cyber attacks on air navigation facilities.[114] International aviation security law, however, extends far beyond the mere establishment of criminal jurisdiction over certain offences.

106 Masutti and Tomasello (n 102) 159.

107 Convention on International Civil Aviation, Annex 17 (n 35) 17.

108 Convention on International Civil Aviation, Annex 17 (n 35) 17.

109 Hobe, von Ruckteschell and Heffernan (n 103) 780.

110 Jane Hong, 'Liability of Aviation Security Service Providers and Responsibility of States' (2010) 35 Air and Space Law 9, 30.

111 Convention on offences and certain other acts committed on board aircraft (adopted 14 September 1963, entered into force 4 December 1969) 704 UNTS 219 (Tokyo Convention).

112 Hague Convention (n 101).

113 Convention for the suppression of unlawful acts against the safety of civil aviation (adopted 23 September 1971, entered into force 26 January 1973) 974 UNTS 177 (Montreal Convention).

114 Beijing Convention superseding the Montreal Convention; Beijing Protocol supplementing the Hague Convention; Protocol to Amend the Convention on Offences and Certain Other Acts Committed on Board Aircraft (adopted 4 April 2014) ICAO Doc 10034 (Airport Protocol).

Aviation security law is a corollary of the objective of the Convention on International Civil Aviation to "insure the safe and orderly growth of international civil aviation".[115] It was born out of a compromise between sovereign States to establish criminal jurisdiction over offences which were not conceived by the convention's drafters at the time.[116] Furthermore, States have assumed a general negative obligation not to use civil aviation for any purpose inconsistent with the aims of the convention.[117] States may be argued to have also a duty to implement certain preventive measures in order to attain the objective of safe and orderly development.

While the provisions of Annex 17 are not binding *per se*, States remain, as argued above, under a general duty to protect the life and safety of individuals on their territory. This implies a reading of the principle of sovereignty not only as a manifestation of power, but also as a responsibility embedding a "minimum content of international citizenship".[118] Consequently, this obligation would entail the implementation of (cyber)security measures by States to protect critical aviation infrastructure so as to least meet their good neighbourliness and human rights obligations. While there is an inextricable link between aviation safety and security, not all aspects of aviation security would fall within the ambit of safety, as discussed in the following paragraphs.

In the wake of the 9/11 terrorist attacks, ICAO adopted a Global Aviation Security Plan of Action aimed at improving aviation security in line with the duties in the implementation of UNSC Resolution 2309 (2016).[119] A core element of the plan was the establishment of regular, mandatory, systematic and harmonised security audits in all Contracting States. Thus, in 2002 the ICAO Universal Security Audit Programme ('USAP') came into being. The programme is implemented at two levels as it concerns directed airport security arrangements (airport level) and civil aviation security programmes (governmental level).[120] The carrying out of mandatory security audits is usually reconciled with the absence of any specific conferral of such powers to ICAO in the Convention on International Civil Aviation through the doctrine of inherent powers.[121]

---

115 Convention on International Civil Aviation, Article 44 (a).

116 Hobe, von Ruckteschell and Heffernan (n 103) 860.

117 Convention on International Civil Aviation, Article 4.

118 A finding that is also confirmed by the positive obligations of States to provide security. See International Commission on Intervention and State Sovereignty, 'The Responsibility to Protect' (International Commission on Intervention and State Sovereignty 2001) 8, 13 <http://responsibilitytoprotect.org/ICISS%20Report.pdf> accessed 26 May 2019 as noted also by Hong (n 110) 31.

119 ICAO, 'Global Aviation Security Plan' (2017) ICAO Doc 10118 2–1; UNSC Res 2309 (22 September 2016) UN Doc S/RES/2309.

120 ICAO, 'Assembly Resolution A33–1: Declaration on misuse of civil aircraft as weapons of destruction and other terrorist acts involving civil aviation' (06 October 2016) A33–1 ICAO Doc 10075 para 7.

121 Ruwantissa Abeyratne, 'Aviation Security Audits' in Ruwantissa Abeyratne (ed), *Aviation Security Law* (Springer Berlin Heidelberg 2010) 273–274.

Aviation security law has also faced the challenges of digitalisation of legacy infrastructures. Its initial focus on physical security, that is kinetic attacks on aircraft and infrastructure or acts otherwise constituting unlawful interference with the physical operation of aviation, has now shifted to the intertwining and virtualisation of cyber and physical infrastructure and the related cybersecurity risks. While Annex 17 does not define 'aviation cybersecurity', it prescribes that "[c]ontracting State[s] shall ensure that operators or entities as defined in the national civil aviation security programme or other relevant national documentation identify their critical information and communications technology systems and data used for civil aviation purposes and, in accordance with a risk assessment, develop and implement, as appropriate, measures to protect them from unlawful interference".[122] Furthermore, in Assembly Resolution A39–18: Consolidated statement on continuing ICAO policies related to aviation security, ICAO highlighted the need of protecting civil aviation against cyber attacks and cyber threats.[123]

Based on ITU's definition of cybersecurity, the ICAO Secretariat elaborated the following definition of 'cyber security' in the aviation domain: "the collection of tools, policies, security concepts, security safeguards, guidelines, risk management approaches, actions, training, best practices, assurance and technologies that can be used to *protect* the *cyber environment* as well as organizations' and *user's assets*. It encompasses, among others, the protection of electronic systems from malicious electronic attack and the means by which to deal with the consequences of such attacks" (emphasis added).[124] This definition refers to 'cyber environment' and 'user's assets' without defining them. However, it seems to recognise the distinct nature of cyberspace and cyber-physical infrastructure as worthy of specific protective measures.

Such an interpretation is also supported by the ICAO Assembly's Resolution Addressing Cybersecurity in Civil Aviation which highlighted that the "threat posed by cyber incidents on civil aviation is rapidly and continuously evolving" which requires identification of threats and risks from possible cyber incidents as well as clarification of the legal consequences for activities compromising aviation safety by exploiting cyber vulnerabilities.[125] The resolution explicitly emphasised the link between (cyber)security and safety in observing that "not all cybersecurity issues affecting the safety of civil aviation are unlawful and/or intentional, and should therefore be addressed through the application of safety management systems".[126] This is a fundamental distinction which seems to suggest

122 Convention on International Civil Aviation, Annex 17 (n 35), 17.

123 ICAO, 'Assembly Resolution A39–18: Consolidated statement on continuing ICAO policies related to aviation security' (n 50) Appendix C, para 7.

124 ICAO, 'Report on Civil Aviation and Cybersecurity' (21 April 2015) C-WP/14266 2.

125 ICAO, 'Assembly Resolution A39–19: Addressing Cybersecurity in Civil Aviation' (n 46) 3, 4.

126 ICAO, 'Assembly Resolution A39–19: Addressing Cybersecurity in Civil Aviation' (n 46) 3.

that aviation (cyber)security is a twofold concept.[127] On the one hand, it concerns acts or omissions of unlawful and/or intentional character, most of which are dealt with by the international treaties and respective national laws epitomising criminal air law. On the other hand, it also encompasses unintentional acts (and perhaps omissions) which have a bearing on safety and should therefore be dealt with as part of safety management. This latter category shall be referred to as 'safety-critical aspects of (cyber)security'.

4.2. RELATIONSHIP BETWEEN THE OBLIGATIONS FOR AVIATION SAFETY AND (CYBER)SECURITY: PROTECTING COMMUNITY INTERESTS?

Being ICAO's primary objective, safety is recognised as "the responsibility of Contracting States both collectively and individually".[128] Unlike security oversight obligations, safety oversight obligations have a much more prominent place in the Convention on International Civil Aviation.[129] In light of the principle of complete and exclusive sovereignty which States enjoy over the airspace above their territory,[130] the obligation to ensure the safety of life and the well-being of individuals is a manifestation of this principle. It is important to clarify that while Annex 2 and Annex 6 to the Convention on International Civil Aviation prescribe that it is the pilot-in-command who bears the ultimate responsibility for compliance with the rules of the air and the conformity with safety regulations, this responsibility does not translate into a legal obligation. While the aircraft operator has to ensure compliance, the safety and security obligations ultimately lie with the State.

The determination of adequate safety levels in a State's territory thus seems to be a matter within a State's reserved domain, subject to its prescriptive and enforcement jurisdiction.[131] However, this posture has been challenged by commentators who argued that global aviation's shared risks require that safety oversight be a shared responsibility too.[132] Such a conclusion could find support in

127 O. Mironenko also argues aviation security is a two-dimensional concept. However, she conceptualises it from the perspective of, on the one hand, its protective and, on the other, its contributory role to the right to life, seemingly elevating the right to life into a peremptory norm of international law. See more in, Olga Mironenko Enerstvedt, 'Introduction' in Olga Mironenko Enerstvedt (ed), *Aviation Security, Privacy, Data Protection and Other Human Rights: Technologies and Legal Principles* (Springer International Publishing 2017) 5.

128 ICAO, 'Assembly Resolution A37-5: The Universal Safety Oversight Audit Programme (USOAP) continuous monitoring approach' (06 October 2016) A37-5 ICAO Doc 10075.

129 See, for example, Convention on International Civil Aviation, Article 33.

130 Convention on International Civil Aviation, Article 1.

131 Jiefang Huang, 'Aviation Safety, ICAO and Obligations Erga Omnes' (2009) 8 Chinese Journal of International Law 63, 64.

132 Ibid.

the practice accumulated since the adoption of the Convention on International Civil Aviation and the gradual relinquishment of sovereignty to the benefit of the "common interest of ensuring safety and security of commercial aviation".[133]

Perhaps one of the most obvious examples of the tensions between this common interest and the principles of sovereignty concerns ICAO's Universal Safety Oversight Audit Programme ('USOAP'). The programme was launched by ICAO to tackle the growing problem of safety standards fragmentation and their diverging implementation among the Contracting States.[134] Similarly to USAP, which was modelled after USOAP, the programme involves safety oversights at governmental level. These unprecedented auditing powers of an international organisation raised concerns regarding their compatibility with the principle of sovereignty.[135] ICAO defied these allegations by arguing that any such audit is based on the execution of a Memorandum of Understanding with the consent of the audited State.[136]

The functions of safety oversight have been defined as aimed at "ensur[ing] effective implementation of the safety-related Standards and Recommended Practices ['SARPs'] and associated procedures contained in the Annexes to the Convention on International Civil Aviation and related ICAO documents".[137] Commentators have identified eight critical elements of a safety oversight system, including: primary aviation legislation, specific operating regulations, civil aviation authority's structure and safety oversight functions, technical guidance, qualified technical personnel, licencing and certification obligations, continued surveillance obligations and resolution of safety issues.[138] Safety oversight, therefore, has a broad scope which demands concerted efforts within the international community and coordination. It also involves a level of dependency between States in order to achieve a level playing field among them. Striving for global governance and the ensuing tensions with the principle of State sovereignty are telling of the emergence of a concept of aviation safety as a shared (legal) responsibility incumbent upon the international community.

International safety obligations have been discerned in three main groups of duties: duty to provide safety oversight, duty to refrain from use of weapons against civil aircraft in flight, and duty to prosecute criminal acts against the

---

133 Dempsey (n 48) 6.

134 Mikołaj Andrzej Ratajczyk, 'Regional Aviation Safety Organisations: Enhancing Air Transport Safety through Regional Cooperation' (Dissertatie, Leiden University 2014) 24 <https://openaccess.leidenuniv.nl/handle/1887/29759> accessed 3 April 2019.

135 Dempsey (n 48) 7.

136 Huang (n 131) 71.

137 Jiefang Huang, *Aviation Safety through the Rule of Law: ICAO's Mechanisms and Practices (Aviation Law and Policy Series)* (Kluwer Law International, BV 2009) 23–24.

138 Ibid 42–43. See also, Jimena Blumenkron, 'International Safety Requirements' in Paul Stephen Dempsey and Ram S Jakhu (eds), *Routledge Handbook of Public Aviation Law* (Routledge 2016) 34–63.

safety of civil aviation.[139] It is submitted here that certain (cyber)security-related duties, which may impact the level of safety, also fall within the ambit of these obligations. For example, cyber attacks against air navigation facilities would fall within the duty to prosecute criminal acts against the safety of civil aviation, but they could also implicate the duty to provide safety oversight to the extent they result from failures of States to mitigate safety-critical cyber threats. Therefore, the prevention and mitigation of such 'cyber' occurrences would be seen as protecting aviation safety as much as protecting aviation (cyber)security.[140]

This view seems to be supported by the growing importance of addressing safety hazards and security threats in an integrated manner. This is evident also from ICAO's approach to look at the overall risk of an activity as such rather than focusing on whether a particular risk compromises its safety or security.[141] For example, the interest of protecting aviation against disrupting or denial of service attacks against the flight controls or collision avoidance system of an aircraft or an air traffic management system can be said to belong as much to the (cyber)security as to the safety domain. In contrast, cyber attacks against, for example, information displays at an airport or even the infotainment system within an aircraft, while obnoxious, would likely fail to meet the threshold of being a safety risk since they would not endanger the bodily integrity of a person or damage property.

This distinction between safety- and non-safety critical aspects of (cyber) security has a bearing on the legal nature and content of certain (cyber) security obligations. If the responsibility for addressing safety-critical aspects of cyber(security) falls within the remit of safety, certain (cyber)security obligations could end up being (also) safety obligations pursued in a collective interest of the international community as a whole.

It has been argued in scholarship that safety obligations are not merely individual obligations assumed on a reciprocal basis, but that they represent the pursuit of a collective interest concerning the international community as a whole.[142] Judge Simma's classical definition of what constitutes 'community interests' in international law reads into such interests "a consensus according to which respect for certain fundamental values is not to be left to the free disposition of States individually or inter se but is recognized and sanctioned by international law as a matter of concern to all states".[143] Noteworthy

139 Huang (n 137) 231.

140 That safety includes security as an external element thereof is also supported in scholarship. See ibid 7.

141 Andreas Meyer and Catalin Radu, 'Integrated Risk Management: A Holistic Approach to Managing Aviation Risk' (*Uniting Aviation*, 4 February 2019) <https://www.unitingaviation.com/strategic-objective/safety/integrated-risk-management/> accessed 25 May 2019; ICAO 'Safety Management Manual' (2018) ICAO Doc 9859.

142 Huang (n 131) 71.

143 Bruno Simma, 'From Bilateralism to Community Interest in International Law (Volume 250)' [1994] Collected Courses of the Hague Academy of International Law 233 <https://

examples of such community interests include international peace and security, environmental protection, human rights protection, solidarity between developed and developing States etc.[144]

It is submitted here that, as a matter of principle, aviation safety could sit comfortably in Simma's definition of 'community interests'. It reflects a consensus that the safe and orderly development of international civil aviation is a fundamental value that is recognised by international law as a 'matter of concern to all States'. This is supported also by a closer reading of the Convention on International Civil Aviation which shows the implausibility of construing reciprocal obligations into the safety oversight obligations. It is one of the main objectives of the convention to ensure the safe and orderly development of aviation as a global activity by definition. If safety obligations are interpreted as reciprocal obligations, this would imply that a State would be willing to ensure the safety of its own aviation system and critical infrastructure only to the extent these actions have been reciprocated by other States. However, as rightly observed in scholarship, there is hardly any case in which a State would diminish its own levels of safety in response to non-compliance by other States.[145] This finding is furthermore backed by the virtually universal membership of the Convention on International Civil Aviation[146] and the practice of the ICAO Assembly which could serve as evidence of the existence of state practice promoting safety as a collective responsibility. So, if safety truly represents a community interest, the same would probably hold true at least of the safety-critical aspects of (cyber) security too.

As aviation safety is increasingly dependent upon distributed but interconnected and shared cyber-physical infrastructure, on the one hand, and virtualised infrastructure operating entirely in cyberspace, on the other, it could be argued that the protection of this global infrastructure also constitutes part of this community interest. In other words, the uninterrupted operation of this infrastructure is crucial for States to discharge their international safety oversight obligations. The potential for transboundary effects 'pierces' the veil of sovereignty and calls for international cooperation justifying the elaboration of norms of international law.

---

referenceworks.brillonline.com/entries/the-hague-academy-collected-courses/from-bilateralism-to-community-interest-in-internationallaw-volume-250-ej.9789041104199.217_384> accessed 22 May 2019.

144 See Isabel Feichtner, 'Community Interest', *Max Planck Encyclopedia of Public International Law* (Oxford University Press 2007) <https://opil.ouplaw.com/abstract/10.1093/law:epil/9780199231690/law-9780199231690-e1677> accessed 22 May 2019 quoting Simma (n 144) 235.

145 Huang (n 131) 73.

146 On 15th April 2019 Dominica became ICAO's 193rd Member States following its accession to the convention. For comparison, the UN General Assembly is also made up of 193 Member States, following the admission of South Sudan on 14 July 2011.

The consequences of construing aviation safety as an interest of the international community has an important bearing on the nature and content of the obligations in question. In light of this discussion, it has been suggested in scholarship that safety obligations have an *erga omnes* character and perhaps even a rudimentary *ius cogens* nature. The next and final section develops the argument that while safety oversight obligations may have been endowed with an *erga omnes* character, this is certainly not the case as far as their peremptory nature is concerned. It also submits that the community interest construction could explain and justify why States have obligations to protect the emerging global cyber-physical and virtualised infrastructure as an emanation of protecting this community interest.

5. TOWARDS *ERGA OMNES* AVIATION (CYBER) SECURITY OBLIGATIONS

5.1. *ERGA OMNES* OBLIGATIONS

The fundamental importance of community interests is reflected in their endowed with various doctrinal expressions,[147] such as attribution of a special hierarchical place in the international legal system by recognising, inter alia, (1) a status of *ius cogens*[148] or constitutional order[149] of certain norms or (2) *erga omnes* status when parallel conduct is required to protect certain community interests.[150]

Early indications of the recognition of community interests in the practice of international courts and tribunals could be traced back to the case of *S.S. Wimbledon* before the PCIJ on the right to passage. In the case, the Court hinted that the obligation to allow free access to the Kiel Canal in time of war as in time of peace may be one owed "to the vessels of all nations".[151] Furthermore, in its advisory opinion in the case of *Reservations to the Convention on the Prevention and Punishment of the Crime of Genocide*, the ICJ held that "[i]n such a convention the contracting States do not have any interests of their own; they merely have, one and all, a common interest, namely, the accomplishment of those high purposes which are the raison d'être of the convention".[152]

However, it was not until its landmark decision in the *Barcelona Traction* case that the ICJ, for the first time, pronounced an essential distinction between obligations towards the international community as a whole, and reciprocal

147 Feichtner (n 144) para 39.
148 Ibid para 41.
149 Ibid para 42.
150 Ibid paras 43–46.
151 *Case of The SS 'Wimbledon' (UK and ors v Germany)* [1923] PCIJ Rep Series A No 1 15 24.
152 *Reservations to the Convention on the Prevention and Punishment of the Crime of Genocide* (Advisory Opinion) [1951] ICJ Rep 15 23.

international obligations between States. The Court held that "[b]y their very nature the former are the concern of all States. In view of the importance of the rights involved, all States can be held to have a legal interest in their protection; they are obligations erga omnes".[153] The Court clarified that "'[s]uch obligations derive, for example, in contemporary international law, from the outlawing of acts of aggression, and of genocide, as also from the principles and rules concerning the basic rights of the human person, including protection from slavery and racial discrimination. Some of the corresponding rights of protection have entered into the body of *general international law* (...); others are *conferred by international instruments of a universal or quasi-universal character*." (emphasis added).[154]

Thus, it has been argued that the ICJ identified two categories of *erga omnes* obligations: 'proper'[155] *erga omnes* obligations (towards the international community as a whole) and *erga omnes partes* obligations (towards the parties to a multilateral treaty) distinguished on the basis of the 'importance' of the involved rights. There are thus obligations which are owed to the international community as a whole and obligations which protect a collective interest of parties to a multilateral treaty.

The distinction is supported also by the International Law Commission ('ILC') in its commentary to Article 48 of the Draft Articles on Responsibility of States for Internationally Wrongful Acts ('ARSIWA').[156] In the case of *erga omnes partes* obligations, this collective interest must be "over and above" individual States' interests and must extend to the interest of a group of States,[157] whereas

153 *Barcelona Traction, Light and Power Company, Limited (Belgium v Spain) (New Application: 1962)* [1970] ICJ Rep 3 para 33.

154 *Barcelona Traction, Light and Power Company, Limited (Belgium v Spain) (New Application: 1962)* [1970] ICJ Rep 3, para 34.

155 International Law Commission (ILC), 'Third Report on Peremptory Norms of General International Law (Jus Cogens) by Dire Tladi, Special Rapporteur' (12 February 2018) UN Doc A/CN.4/714 110 <http://legal.un.org/docs/?symbol=A/CN.4/714> accessed 04 July 2019.

156 ILC, 'Draft articles on Responsibility of States for Internationally Wrongful Acts, with commentaries – 2001' (2008) 114 97.

157 The ICJ provided further elaboration of the concept of '*erga omnes partes*' in its judgment in the Questions relating to the *Obligation to Prosecute or Extradite (Belgium v. Senegal)* case where it argued that the obligations assumed by States under the Convention Against Torture are obligations *erga omnes partes* because "[a]ll... States parties have a common interest in compliance with these obligations by the State in whose territory the alleged offender is present. That common interest implies that the obligations in question are owed by any State party to all the other States parties to the Convention. All the States parties "have a legal interest" in the protection of the rights involved and therefore 'each State party has an interest in compliance with them in any given case" (para 68). The Court further explained that the convention's object and purpose of making more effective the struggle against torture worldwide would be undermined if special interest were required. It therefore concluded that "any State party to the Convention may invoke the responsibility of another State party with a view to ascertaining the alleged failure to comply with its obligations *erga omnes partes*, such as those under Article 6, paragraph 2, and Article 7, paragraph 1, of the Convention, and to bring that failure to an end." (para 69). See *Questions relating to the Obligation to Prosecute or Extradite (Belgium v Senegal)* [2012] ICJ Rep 422 449, paras 68–69.

'proper' *erga omnes* obligations refer to an interest so significant that it is deemed every State[158] has an interest in protecting it.[159]

There are two main views regarding the effects of *erga omnes* obligations in international law. The first view argues that *erga omnes* obligations give rise to either individual rights of performance of all other parties to a multilateral treaty or all States in the cases of customary international law. The second view submits that there is a single right vested with the collective whereby individual States may act as agents thereof.[160] However, both views seems to be united in recognising a procedural focus of *erga omnes* obligations, a stance widely supported in scholarship.[161]

In light of the community interest of safety elaborated in the previous section, this brief and by no means exhaustive overview of the ICJ's case law suggests that States have *at the very least* an *erga omnes partes* obligation in the protection of the collective interest of safety of international air transport. Following the train of thought of safety as a community interest, the following additional arguments have been adduced to support the construction of safety oversight obligations as 'proper' *erga omnes* obligations.

First, as already mentioned, ICAO enjoys virtually universal membership which supports a finding that the matters of aviation safety, this being the primary objective of the organisation, are of concern for the international community. Furthermore, in Resolution 2309 (2016) the UNSC affirmed that "*all States have an interest to protect the safety* of their own citizens and nationals against terrorist attacks conducted against international civil aviation" (emphasis added),[162] asserting that this would be in compliance with (general) international law, incl. international human rights law and humanitarian law. The UNSC also observed that aviation's global nature implies a symbiotic relationship between States' aviation security systems and recognised this as the "the *common goal of the international community* (...) which means States are *dependent on each other* to provide a common secure aviation environment" (emphasis added).[163]

Second, as already highlighted, safety is inherent in the right to security and the right to life. One of the main rationales for safety's prominent place

158 Since all States are by definition members of the international community as a whole. See Draft articles on Responsibility of States for Internationally Wrongful Acts, with commentaries – 2001 (n 156) 98. The concept of 'international community as a whole' is deemed equivalent to the construction used by the Vienna Convention on the Law of Treaties (adopted 23 May 1969, entered into force 27 January 1980) 1155 UNTS 331 (Vienna Convention on the Law of Treaties) where the use of 'international community of States as a whole' in Article 53 highlights the importance of States in international law-making.

159 See, for example, the ruling in *United States Diplomatic and Consular Staff in Tehran (USA v Iran)* [1980] ICJ Rep 3 43–44 in which the Court held that the 'irreparable harm' caused by the violation of the rules on consular protection deserved the 'attention of the entire international community', para 92.

160 See more in Feichtner (n 144), para 45.

161 Malcolm N Shaw, *International Law* (Eighth Edition, Cambridge University Press 2017) 92.

162 UNSC Res 2309 (22 September 2016) (n 119) 3, para 2.

163 UNSC Res 2309 (22 September 2016) (n 119) 1, Preamble.

in civil aviation is the activity's inherently risky nature which may have grave consequences for the right to life. Commentators have further maintained the existence of an intrinsic link between safety obligations and the concept of 'elementary considerations of humanity'.[164] While the concept has its origins in international humanitarian law and human rights law, it gradually made its way into other branches of international law, such as the law of the sea.[165] In the *Corfu Channel* case, the ICJ recognised that the due diligence duty to warn is rooted in the 'elementary considerations of humanity'.[166] In the same vein, in the advisory opinion in the *Reservations to the Convention on the Prevention and Punishment of the Crime of Genocide* case, the Court also referred in this context to "the most elementary principles of morality".[167] The Court thus underscored the inextricable link between the two and reaffirmed their fundamental nature as an edifice of human values inherent in the very moral fabric of human society.[168] The Court further acknowledged in the advisory opinions in the *Legality of the Threat or Use of Nuclear Weapons*[169] and *Legal Consequences of the Construction of a Wall in the Occupied Palestinian Territory*[170] cases that the respect of 'elementary considerations of humanity' underpins many of the rules of humanitarian law which, in turn, reflect "intransgressible principles of international customary law".[171] Since all such references are inconspicuously followed by a pronouncement of *erga omnes* obligations, the argument goes, 'elementary considerations of humanity' are part and parcel of *erga omnes* obligations.[172] From this coign of vantage, commentators have read the 'elementary considerations of humanity' as inherent into the concept of safety. They have done so mainly by reference to the preamble of Protocol relating to an Amendment to the Convention on International Civil Aviation (Article 3*bis*). In the wake of the shooting down of Korean Air Lines Flight 007 by a Soviet fighter jet in 1983, the preamble's strong language comes as no surprise in highlighting

164 Huang (n 137) 162.

165 Matthew Zagor, 'Elementary Considerations of Humanity' in Karine Bannelier, Théodore Christakis and Sarah Heathcote (eds), *The ICJ and the Evolution of International Law: The Enduring Impact of the Corfu Channel Case* (Routledge 2012).

166 *Corfu Channel Case (UK v. Albania)* (n 66) 22.

167 Angela Del Vecchio and Roberto Virzo (eds), *Reservations to the Convention on the Prevention and Punishment of the Crime of Genocide* (Advisory Opinion) (n 152) 23.

168 Francesca Delfino, '"Considerations of Humanity" in the Jurisprudence of ITLOS and UNCLOS Arbitral Tribunals' Angela Del Vecchio and Roberto Virzo (eds), *Interpretations of the United Nations Convention on the Law of the Sea by International Courts and Tribunals* (Cham: Springer International Publishing, 2019) 425 <https://doi.org/10.1007/978-3-030-10773-4_21> accessed 4 May 2019.

169 *Legality of the Threat or Use of Nuclear Weapons* (Advisory Opinion) [1996] ICJ Rep 226 257, para 79.

170 *Legal Consequences of the Construction of a Wall in the Occupied Palestinian Territory* (Advisory Opinion) [2004] ICJ Rep 136 199, para 157.

171 *Legality of the Threat or Use of Nuclear Weapons* (Advisory Opinion) (n 169) 35, para 79.

172 Huang (n 137) 162 See critique in Matthew Zagor (n 165) 268–269.

that "in keeping with the elementary considerations of humanity the safety and the lives of persons on board civil aircraft must be assured".[173]

Finally, commentators have countered claims that *erga omnes* obligations are of generally prohibitive nature[174] by maintaining that the right to self-determination of peoples implies a positive obligation.[175] This line of argument has justified conclusions that the obligations of aviation safety oversight do not protect merely the collective interest of States to a multilateral treaty, but are elevated to *erga omnes* obligations towards the international community as a whole in that they protect a community interest.[176]

While the first and the second arguments may be convincing, the third argument countering the (solely) prohibitive nature of *erga omnes* is untenable. Admittedly, mentions to *erga omnes* in the case law of the ICJ have been notoriously confusing, with occasional references to both *erga omnes* 'rights' and 'obligations'.[177] However, the Court's recent advisory opinion in the *Legal Consequences of the Separation of the Chagos Archipelago from Mauritius in 1965* case seems to have brought some much-needed elucidation. In the context of the right to self-determination, the Court held that "[s]ince *respect for the right* to self-determination is an obligation *erga omnes*, all States have a legal interest in protecting that right" (emphasis added).[178] Thus, it could be argued that it is the obligation to respect this right, i.e. not to interfere with it, and not the right *itself* that is accorded *erga omnes* character. If this holds true as a matter of principle, the finding that safety oversight obligations have *erga omnes* character will suddenly find itself on a shaky ground since most of the safety oversight obligations are not prohibitive in nature; rather, they require active conduct on the part of States. This finding is even more important given some commentators' attempts to read into safety oversight obligations the origins of a peremptory (*ius cogens*) norm of international law.[179]

5.2. *IUS COGENS* OBLIGATIONS

While it is beyond the scope of this chapter to delve into discussions about the origin, nature, scope, means of identification or consequences of peremptory

173 Protocol Relating to an Amendment to the Convention on International Civil Aviation [Article 3*bis*] (1984) ICAO Doc 9436, incorp in Doc 7300.

174 Crawford (n 67) 578, 582–583.

175 Huang (n 137) 165.

176 Ibid 167.

177 *Armed Activities on the Territory of the Congo (New Application: 2002) (Democratic Republic of the Congo v Rwanda)* (Preliminary Objections) [2006] ICJ Rep 6 32, para 64. See also *East Timor (Portugal v Australia)* [1995] ICJ Rep 90 102, para 29.

178 *Legal Consequences of the Separation of the Chagos Archipelago from Mauritius in 1965* (Advisory Opinion) [2019] ICJ Rep 1 42, para 180.

179 Huang (n 137) 167–174.

norms of international law, the relationship between *ius cogens* and *erga omnes* obligations is worth considering since the two concepts are linked but different.[180] A proper understanding of the relationship between the two concepts will help to assess whether the obligations for protection of the allegedly community interest of safety have shown signs of 'peremptoriness'.

The concept of peremptory norms of international law was positively enshrined in Article 53 of the Vienna Convention on the Law of Treaties by reference to its derogatory effect vis-à-vis international treaties.[181] The provision reads the following: "A treaty is void if, at the time of its conclusion, it conflicts with a peremptory norm of general international law. For the purposes of the present Convention, a peremptory norm of general international law is a norm accepted and recognized by the international community of States as a whole as a norm from which no derogation is permitted and which can be modified only by a subsequent norm of general international law having the same character."[182] The importance of the concept was affirmed already by the PCIJ and was further endorsed also by the ICJ in multiple cases.[183]

There are perhaps as many doctrinal definitions of *ius cogens* as the 'legal operators' who have engaged with the concept.[184] Thus, for example, Prof James Crawford recognised *ius cogens* as rules of customary law whose distinct feature is their "relative indelibility",[185] whereas for Prof Malcolm Shaw *ius cogens* referred to a set of substantive norms bestowed with a "higher status", regardless of whether the source is custom or treaty.[186] Some commentators have defined

180 For an excellent and recent account of the debates surrounding *ius cogens*, see the four reports by ILC's Special Rapporteur Dire Tladi: ILC, 'First Report on Jus Cogens by Dire Tladi, Special Rapporteur' (8 March 2016) UN Doc A/CN.4/693 <http://legal.un.org/docs/?symbol=A/CN.4/693>; ILC, 'Second Report on Jus Cogens by Dire Tladi, Special Rapporteur' (16 March 2017) UN Doc A/CN.4/706 <http://legal.un.org/docs/?symbol=A/CN.4/706>; ILC, 'Third Report on Peremptory Norms of General International Law (Jus Cogens) by Dire Tladi, Special Rapporteur' (n 156); ILC, 'Fourth Report on Peremptory Norms of General International Law (Jus Cogens) by Dire Tladi, Special Rapporteur' (31 January 2019) UN Doc A/CN.4/727 <http://legal.un.org/docs/?symbol=A/CN.4/727>.

181 ILC, 'First Report on Jus Cogens by Dire Tladi, Special Rapporteur' (n 180) 52.

182 Vienna Convention on the Law of Treaties (adopted 23 May 1969, entered into force 27 January 1980) 1155 UNTS 331, Article 53 (Vienna Convention on the Law of Treaties).

183 *The Oscar Chinn case (Britain v. Belgium)* [1934] PCIJ Rep Series A/B no 63 65, Individual opinion of Judge Schücking. The ILC's Special Rapporteur counted impressive 11 explicit references to the concept in ICJ's jurisprudence and 78 express references in the individual opinions of the Court's members. See more in ILC, 'First Report on Jus Cogens by Dire Tladi, Special Rapporteur' (n 180) 71.

184 A risk that was highlighted most prominently in Robert Kolb, 'Effects of Jus Cogens' in *Peremptory International Law – Jus Cogens: A General Inventory* (Hart Publishing 2015) 115 <www.bloomsburycollections.com/book/peremptory-international-law-jus-cogens-a-general-inventory> accessed 10 May 2019, where he argued that deductive reasoning which neglects state practice should not be allowed as it opens the doors to activism on the part of the interpreting legal operator.

185 Crawford (n 67) 594.

186 Shaw (n 161) 92.

the concept by reference to its restrictive function towards States' treaty-making powers in light of their failures after the two world wars and its de-fragmentation and cohesion-building function in the international legal system.[187] Others have emphasised its protective function towards weaker States in that it guarantees a "minimum world legal order",[188] a "core treasury"[189] of international law.

The ILC's Special Rapporteur defined the core elements of *ius cogens* norms by reference to their (1) universal applicability[190]; (2) superiority[191]; and (3) protective function vis-à-vis the fundamental values of the international community.[192] He argued[193] that there are two cumulative criteria for the identification of *ius cogens* character of a norm which could be discerned from Article 53 Vienna Convention on the Law of Treaties. First, the norm must be one of general international law, which in turn entails a two-step process of (a) establishment of a 'normal' norm of general international law and (b) its subsequent endowment with a *ius cogens* status. Second, the norm must be accepted and recognised as having certain characteristics, e.g. impossibility of derogation, modification only by a subsequent norm of the same character etc.

The exceptional character of these norms is reflected in the legal consequences their breaching produces above and beyond the effects in the law of treaties. First of all, a breach of a peremptory norm leads to inapplicability of the circumstances precluding wrongfulness defined under Chapter V of ARSIWA, such as self-defence, force majeure, distress, necessity etc.[194] Second, a breach also creates rights for third States to invoke international responsibility.[195] Third, the breach entails a duty to cooperate to bring to an end through lawful means

---

187 Christian Tomuschat, 'The Security Council and *Jus Cogens*' in Enzo Cannizzaro (ed), *The present and future of jus cogens* (Sapienza università editrice 2015) 23, 35–26; Jean d'Aspremont, 'Jus Cogens as a Social Construct Without Pedigree' in Maarten den Heijer and Harmen van der Wilt (eds), *Netherlands Yearbook of International Law 2015: Jus Cogens: Quo Vadis?* (TMC Asser Press 2016) 91–92 <https://doi.org/10.1007/978-94-6265-114-2_4> accessed 19 May 2019.

188 Alain Pellet, 'Comments in Response to Christine Chinkin and in Defense of Jus Cogens as the Best Bastion against the Excesses of Fragmentation' [2006] Finnish Yearbook of International Law 83, 83, 90.

189 Christian Tomuschat (n 187) 36.

190 Meaning they do not operate on a bilateral basis. See ILC, 'First Report on Jus Cogens by Dire Tladi, Special Rapporteur' (n 180) 42, para 68.

191 Meaning they are hierarchically superior vis-à-vis other norms of international law and as a consequence trump any conflicting rules pursuant to Article 53 Vienna Convention on the Law of Treaties, which is widely accepted as having effect above and beyond the law of treaties as reflective of a norm of customary international law. See ibid 43, para 69.

192 Meaning they protect the 'core', fundamental values of the international community. See ibid, paras 70–71.

193 ILC, 'Second Report on Jus Cogens by Dire Tladi, Special Rapporteur' (n 180) 64.

194 Draft articles on Responsibility of States for Internationally Wrongful Acts, with commentaries – 2001 (n 156), Article 26.

195 Draft articles on Responsibility of States for Internationally Wrongful Acts, with commentaries – 2001 (n 156), Article 48(1)(b).

any such serious breach.[196] Finally, States have a duty not to recognise, aid or assist the maintenance of a situation created by a serious breach of a peremptory norm.[197]

It is these legal consequences that have usually been referred to as being indicative of the relationship between *ius cogens* and *erga omnes* obligations.[198] In his analysis, the Special Rapporteur, basing himself on ICJ's case law, seems to have adopted the view that that the only category of *erga omnes* obligations that do not 'derive' from ius cogens norms are the so-called '*erga omnes partes*' obligations. Thus, he suggests, the *erga omnes* status is an automatic consequence of the 'promotion' of a norm to *ius cogens* status.

The argument goes that since *erga omnes partes* obligations are owed to the contracting States to a multilateral treaty, they are not 'proper' *erga omnes* obligations.[199] In the Special Rapporteur's view, the 'essence of the link' between *erga omnes* and *ius cogens* is depicted by a textual argument in the *Barcelona Traction* case whereby the *erga omnes* effect is seen as deriving from *ius cogens* norms.[200] However, confining the *erga omnes* effect only to peremptory norms of international law creates difficulties in explaining the existence of norms of 'community interest' which have been accorded a 'doctrinal expression' as *erga omnes* obligations without necessarily having (yet) entered the 'exclusive club' of *ius cogens*.

The ICJ itself seems to make a distinction between *erga omnes* and *ius cogens* obligations. In its judgment on preliminary objections in the *Armed Activities on the Territory of the Congo* case, the Court noted that "[it] deems it necessary to recall that the mere fact that rights and obligations *erga omnes* or peremptory norms of general international law (*jus cogens*) are at issue in a dispute cannot in

196 Draft articles on Responsibility of States for Internationally Wrongful Acts, with commentaries - 2001 (n 156), Article 41(1). See also on the obligation of States to "co-operate with the United Nations to put [modalities required to ensure the completion of the decolonization of Mauritius] into effect" the somewhat controversial second part of para 180 of the court's advisory opinion in *Legal Consequences of the Separation of the Chagos Archipelago from Mauritius in 1965* (Advisory Opinion) (n 178).

197 Draft articles on Responsibility of States for Internationally Wrongful Acts, with commentaries - 2001 (n 156), Article 41(2).

198 International Law Commission, 'Third Report on Peremptory Norms of General International Law (Jus Cogens) by Dire Tladi, Special Rapporteur' (n 155) para 108.

199 Ibid para 110.

200 Thus, in para 33 the Court concludes by saying that "[i]n view of the importance of the rights involved, all States can be held to have a legal interest in their protection; they are obligations erga omnes" and then continues in para 34 that "[s]uch obligations derive, for example, in contemporary international law, from the outlawing of acts of aggression, and of genocide, as also from the principles and rules concerning the basic rights of the human person, including protection from slavery and racial discrimination. Some of the corresponding rights of protection have entered into the body of general international law". Since all of these obligations are almost unequivocally considered to form part of the edifice of *ius cogens*, the conclusion is made that *erga omnes* obligations "derive" their (procedural) legal effect from the normative force of material *ius cogens* norms.

itself constitute an exception to the principle that its jurisdiction always depends on the consent of the parties" (emphasis added).[201] Thus, in using the conjunction "or", the Court seems to have recognised that there are (at least some) 'proper' *erga omnes* obligations which are *not ius cogens.*

Various classifications of *ius cogens* and *erga omnes* obligations have been attempted.[202] Thus, for example, it has been suggested the international constitutional order, understood as a system of multilevel interactions, has a three-layer structure with (1) *ius cogens* norms with *erga omnes* effect on the top, followed by (2) customary *erga omnes* norms which do not have a *ius cogens* nature and, finally, (3) emerging norms linked to a community interest whose customary or *erga omnes* nature is still debatable.[203] It is submitted here, objections against the 'constitutional order' argument aside, that such a structure could help explain the existence of *erga omnes* obligations which are not *ius cogens.*

In light of these observations, it is maintained that *erga omnes* obligations are focused on the protection of a community interest and play a procedural role in depicting the generality of a rule vis-à-vis the international community as a whole.[204] Concomitantly, *ius cogens* could be seen as the culmination of a "long crystallisation process"[205] whereby norms essential to the very existence of international legal order emerge. They protect the very core of the world order by unconditionally prohibiting conduct which goes against it.

5.3. SAFETY OVERSIGHT AS A PEREMPTORY NORM OF INTERNATIONAL LAW

The finding that *ius cogens* norms are linked to the core of the world order has an important bearing on the qualification of aviation safety and, for that matter, safety-critical aspects of cyber(security) oversight obligations as having

201 *Armed Activities on the Territory of the Congo (New Application: 2002) (Democratic Republic of the Congo v. Rwanda)* (Preliminary Objections) (n 177) 51, para 125.

202 See generally ILC, 'Fourth Report on Peremptory Norms of General International Law (Jus Cogens) by Dire Tladi, Special Rapporteur' (n 180). See particularly for *ius cogens* their classification into three categories: (1) protecting individual human being, (2) States vis-a-vis the Security Council and (3) peoples, mainly through their right of self-determination in Christian Tomuschat (n 188) 35.

203 Erika De Wet, 'The International Constitutional Order' (2006) 55 International & Comparative Law Quarterly 51, 53, 62.

204 Shaw (n 161) 92. An example in the recent case law of the ICJ could be found in the Dissenting Opinion of Judge ad hoc Dugard in the case of *Certain Activities Carried Out by Nicaragua in the Border Area (Costa Rica v Nicaragua)* [2018] ICJ Rep 1, para 35, where he argued that "[t]he obligation not to engage in wrongful deforestation that results in the release of carbon into the atmosphere and the loss of gas sequestration services is certainly an obligation *erga omnes*", an obligation which certainly has not been recognised as having also a *ius cogens* character.

205 Pellet (n 188) 89.

ius cogens character. It is argued here that safety oversight obligations, while probably worthy of being endowed with *erga omnes* character, certainly do not qualify as peremptory norms of international law. Nevertheless, commentators have adduced the following arguments to maintain the view that at least some of the safety oversight obligations *may* have *ius cogens* character.

First, the argument that the principle of *aut dedere, aut iudicare* in international law, also enshrined in the Hague Convention for the Suppression of Unlawful Seizure of Aircraft,[206] belongs to the group of *ius cogens* norms is untenable.[207] It has been acknowledged by both the ILC and commentators that there is no sufficient evidence that the obligation to prosecute or extradite belongs to the edifice of customary international law.[208] *Per argumentum a fortiori*, it not being a norm of general international law,[209] the principle of *aut dedere, aut iudicare* cannot be said to have *ius cogens* nature.

Second, drawing parallels[210] between piracy at sea[211] and 'aerial' piracy, manifested in the prohibition of hijacking and sabotage, while compelling, is equally flawed. While it is not untenable that hijackers and saboteurs may be considered *hostis humanis generis*, there is no sufficient evidence or support of state practice and *opinio iuris*[212] to justify extending the *ius cogens* nature of piracy at sea to piracy in the air.

Third, the argument that the prohibition of use of weapons against civil aviation embodied in Article 3*bis* of the Convention on International Civil Aviation has *ius cogens* character[213] requires some clarification. Article 3*bis in fine* stipulates that it does not in any way modify the rights and obligations of States under the UN Charter. Consequently, the rule is subject to an exception at the very least in the cases of self-defence in response to an armed attack, e.g. when an aircraft no longer acts as a civil aircraft.[214] The prohibition of unlawful

206 Hague Convention, Article 7. See also footnote 101 above.

207 Huang (n 137) 170–171.

208 Crawford (n 67) 471.

209 The ILC Special Rapporteur argued that the generality of the norm refers to the scope of its applicability implying that while customary international law and general principles of law could meet this threshold, this is unlikely to hold true of treaties. See more in ILC, 'First Report on Jus Cogens by Dire Tladi, Special Rapporteur' (n 180), para 74.

210 Huang (n 137) 171.

211 The prohibition of piracy at sea allegedly has *ius cogens* status, as confirmed by the ILC. See International Law Commission, 'Fourth Report on Peremptory Norms of General International Law (Jus Cogens) by Dire Tladi, Special Rapporteur' (n 180), para 56.

212 Admittedly, the provision of Article 101(1)(a)(ii) United Nations Convention on the Law of the Sea (adopted 10 December 1982, entered into force 16 November 1994) 1833 UNTS 3 (UNCLOS) refers to aerial piracy. However, it should be kept in mind that the reference to aircraft is a novelty and likely to be considered progressive development rather than reflection of customary international law and, for that matter, *ius cogens*. See also Crawford (n 67) 303.

213 Huang (n 137) 172.

214 Charter of the United Nations (adopted 24 October 1945, entered into force 24 October 1945) 1 UNTS XVI, Article 51 (UN Charter).

use of force is undoubtedly part and parcel of the edifice of *ius cogens*.[215] However, the fact that this principle is part of customary international law and has its roots in the 'elementary considerations of humanity'[216] is insufficient in its own right to support a conclusion that it reflects a norm protecting safety in the air and that, as a result, this norm has a peremptory character.[217] It is the prohibition of unlawful use of force that has peremptory character and not safety of life as such.[218]

Finally, the Convention on International Civil Aviation stipulates that in time of war and emergency its provisions shall not affect the freedom of action of any of the Contracting States affected, whether as belligerents or as neutrals.[219] While such an invocation is unlikely to have impact on the rules which reflect customary international law,[220] the possibility for States to disregard their obligations under the convention additionally undermines any discussion about the *ius cogens* nature of safety oversight obligations. Therefore, the argument that (some) safety oversight obligations have made it into the stronghold of *ius cogens* is dubious and generally flawed.

5.4. COMMUNITY INTERESTS AND THE (CYBER) SECURITY OF THE GLOBAL AVIATION CRITICAL INFRASTRUCTURE

The analysis in the preceding sections has demonstrated that while the safety of aviation seems to meet the criteria of being a 'community interest', it is uncertain whether it entails *erga omnes* obligations, given most of the recognised

---

215 Crawford (n 67) 595.

216 It should be noted that the UNSC observed that the principle "concerning the non-use of weapons against such aircraft in flight" is "recognized under customary international law" and condemned the "use of weapons against civil aircraft in flight as being incompatible with elementary considerations of humanity". See UNSC Res 1067 (26 July 1996) 1996 UN Doc S/RES/1067, Preamble, para 6.

217 In the context of prohibition of unlawful use of force, an interesting question for future research is whether a State could lawfully use a non-kinetic 'cyber' weapon which does not inflict physical damage as a countermeasure in response to a violation of a State's airspace.

218 Furthermore, it is well-accepted that the right to life itself is not an absolute right and does not belong in the 'exclusive club' of *ius cogens*.

219 Convention on International Civil Aviation 1944 (adopted 07 December 1944, entered into force 04 April 1947) 15 UNTS 295, Article 89 (Convention on International Civil Aviation).

220 As a matter of principle, it has been argued that where a rule exists concomitantly in customary and treaty law, there is no presumption that the treaty rule 'swallows' the customary law; the two rules merely co-exist in the international legal system. See Shaw (n 161) 92. It seems that commentators have not accepted widely the view that principles other than the principle of complete and exclusive sovereignty reflected in Article 1 Convention on International Civil Aviation have become part of general customary international law. See Geert De Baere and Cedric Ryngaert, 'The ECJ's Judgment in Air Transport Association of America and the International Legal Context of the EU's Climate Change Policy' 26, 395.

obligations so far seem to have prohibitive content. Provided certain prohibitions form part of the safety oversight obligations, e.g. the obligation not to prohibit arbitrarily overflight of other States,[221] it could be maintained that at least these latter have *erga omnes* character. However, given these obligations do not reflect peremptory norms, one may wonder what the practical consequences of such recognition would be. For example, none of the material consequences under Part II, Chapter III of ARSIWA on the consequences of a serious breach of a peremptory norm would arise since the breach would not concern a *ius cogens* norm. Nevertheless, it is tenable that the responsibility of the breaching State could be invoked under Part III, Chapter I of ARSIWA by any other State to claim cessation of the internationally wrongful act, assurances and guarantees of non-repetition and performance of the obligation of reparation in the interest of the injured State.[222]

As argued in the preceding sections, the safety oversight obligations should encompass as a minimum also obligations concerning safety-critical aspects of (cyber)security. When these are construed as *erga omnes* obligations, one particular question comes to the fore, namely: can the community interest protected by these obligations justify a due diligence obligation on the international community to ensure the (cyber)security of global aviation critical infrastructure, such as shared cyber-physical, global cyber and supranational virtualised infrastructure?

The emergence of virtualised or otherwise cyber or cyber-physical infrastructure extending beyond the territory and control of a single State challenges how States discharge their due diligence obligations[223] to ensure the safety of airspace above their territory. This is precisely where the community interest of safety oversight comes into play. In order to protect this community interest, States can be argued to have an *erga omnes* due diligence obligation towards the international community to protect not only the infrastructure located on their territory, but equally so the 'commons' elements of this global infrastructure. This is essentially infrastructure that is not under the sovereign control of any particular State which is a fundamental departure from the customary principle of complete and exclusive sovereignty enshrined in Article 1 of the Convention on International Civil Aviation. Such an assertion seems to find support in the due diligence obligations arguably applicable to the cyberspace domain. The alleged shifting of focus more towards jurisdiction based on effects and community interests and less to such grounded in territorial

221 Convention on International Civil Aviation, Article 9.

222 Draft articles on Responsibility of States for Internationally Wrongful Acts, with commentaries – 2001 (n 157), Article 48(1)(b) *juncto* Article 48(2)(a) and (b).

223 Marieke de Hoon, 'Navigating the Legal Horizon: Lawyering the MH17 Disaster' (2017) 33 Utrecht Journal of International and European Law 90, 101.

control is yet another example of the diminishing role of the *Lotus* principle[224] in public international law.

In fact, similar arguments were raised during the 2017 Qatar Diplomatic Crisis regarding the status of Flight Information Regions. Soon after the implementation of the airspace closure by Egypt, Bahrain and UAE, the chief executive officer of Qatar Airways claimed that flight information regions ('FIR')[225] are "sovereign property of the international community (…) no country in the world has the right to ban".[226] The contention has raised a discussion as to whether the blocking of the FIR where Saudi Arabia exercises functional jurisdiction does indeed violate interests of the international community in light of what has become a conflict 'hot spot' arising out of the tensions between State sovereignty and the dictates of present-day commercial practices.[227] Ultimately, these assertions shed new light on the lively discussion of sovereignty and community interests in both international air law and cyber law, a debate that is critical for ensuring the "safe and orderly development" of international air transport.

6. CONCLUSION

The emergence of a global critical aviation infrastructure with distributed but interconnected elements has brought to light fundamental discussions about the nature and content of safety and security obligations of individual States and the international community as a whole. These discussions, however, are not new. They refer to almost the century-old question of the extent to which States are prohibited to act independently under international law. In 1927, the Permanent Court of International Justice elaborated a rather convenient, yet heavily disputed answer that States are limited only by explicit prohibitions. This principle, also known as the *Lotus* principle, is increasingly incompatible with the pursuit of interests so important that they require the concerted action of the international community as a whole. Such interests include, among others, the protection of the environment, global commons and safety of life at sea and in the air. This contribution argued that aviation safety oversight obligations have likely attained a status of community interest and thus require the parallel

---

224 An Hertogen, 'Letting Lotus Bloom' (2015) 26 European Journal of International Law 901, 902. See also *S.S. 'Lotus', France v Turkey, Judgment* (n 65).

225 Flight information regions are defined as "airspace of defined dimensions within which flight information service and alerting service are provided" where States allegedly exercise functional jurisdiction. See more in ICAO, 'Annex 2 to the Convention on International Civil Aviation – Rules of the Air', 10th edition (2005) 2 and Sreejith (n 49) 198.

226 Max Kingsley-Jones, 'Qatar Chief Outlines Impact of Ban and Its Network Plan' (*Flightglobal.com*, 19 June 2017) <https://www.flightglobal.com/news/articles/paris-qatar-chief-outlines-impact-of-ban-and-its-ne-438463/> accessed 28 May 2019.

227 Sreejith (n 49) 201–202.

efforts of all members of the international community. The same goes at least for the these aviation (cyber)security obligations which have a bearing on the safety. The effective protection of this community interest, however, requires endowing such obligations with *erga omnes* status. Such a finding which, while plausible, seems to encounter some methodological difficulties pertaining to the manner in which *erga omnes* obligations are construed in international law. This contribution also maintained that while the effective protection of the community interest of safety and safety-critical (cyber)security of civil aviation necessitates endowing the obligations with *erga omnes* status, the claims for *ius cogens* nature of these same obligations are untenable. *Ius cogens* is reflective of a minimum legal order defining the consensus around which the international legal system was built. It is also a tool for maintaining cohesion in this system; an exclusive club that does not and should not easily 'accept' new 'members'. Growing discussions about the *ius cogens* nature of safety oversight obligations, however, are indicative of the international community's need to reconcile the value of preserving this "core treasury" of the world legal order with the need for collective action against a growing number of existential risks. They are also symptomatic of the need to impose further restraint on nation-States' freedom to act to the benefit of community interests, especially in a world where critical and important, physical and cyber and individual and collective are increasingly conflating.

BIBLIOGRAPHY

— , 'Report on Civil Aviation and Cybersecurity' (ICAO 2015) C-WP/14266

Abeyratne R, 'Aviation Security Audits' in Ruwantissa Abeyratne (ed), *Aviation Security Law* (Springer Berlin Heidelberg 2010)

Baere GD and Ryngaert C, 'The ECJ's Judgment in Air Transport Association of America and the International Legal Context of the EU's Climate Change Policy' 26

Blumenkron J, 'International Safety Requirements' in Paul Stephen Dempsey and Ram S Jakhu (eds), *Routledge Handbook of Public Aviation Law* (Routledge 2016)

Boon KE, 'Are Control Tests Fit for the Future? The Slippage Problem in Attribution Doctrines' (2014) 15 Melbourne Journal of International Law 1

Brkan M, 'The Concept of Essence of Fundamental Rights in the EU Legal Order: Peeling the Onion to Its Core' (2018) 14 European Constitutional Law Review 332

Buchan R, 'Cyberspace, Non-State Actors and the Obligation to Prevent Transboundary Harm' (2016) 21 Journal of Conflict and Security Law 429

Chircop L, 'A Due Diligence Standard of Attribution in Cyberspace' (2018) 67 International & Comparative Law Quarterly 643

Cooper P, 'Aviation Cybersecurity: Finding Lift, Minimizing Drag' (Atlantic Council Brent Scowcroft Center on International Security 2017)

Crawford J, *Brownlie's Principles of Public International Law* (Oxford University Press 2012) d'Aspremont J, 'Jus Cogens as a Social Construct Without Pedigree' in Maarten den Heijer and Harmen van der Wilt (eds), *Netherlands Yearbook of International Law 2015: Jus Cogens: Quo Vadis?* (TMC Asser Press 2016) <https://doi.org/10.1007/978-94-6265-114-2_4> accessed 19 May 2019

Hoon MD, 'Navigating the Legal Horizon: Lawyering the MH17 Disaster' (2017) 33 Utrecht Journal of International and European Law 90

Delfino F, '"Considerations of Humanity" in the Jurisprudence of ITLOS and UNCLOS Arbitral Tribunals' in Angela Del Vecchio and Roberto Virzo (eds), *Interpretations of the United Nations Convention on the Law of the Sea by International Courts and Tribunals* (Cham: Springer International Publishing, 2019) https://doi.org/10.1007/978-3-030-10773-4_21

Dempsey PS, 'Introduction: Multilateral Conventions and Customary International Law' in Paul Stephen Dempsey and Ram S Jakhu (eds), *Routledge Handbook of Public Aviation Law* (Routledge 2016)

Enerstvedt OM, 'Introduction' in Olga Mironenko Enerstvedt (ed), *Aviation Security, Privacy, Data Protection and Other Human Rights: Technologies and Legal Principles* (Springer International Publishing 2017)

European Commission, 'Commission Staff Working Document on a New Approach to the European Programme for Critical Infrastructure Protection Making European Critical Infrastructures More Secure' SWD (2013) 318 Final <https://ec.europa.eu/energy/sites/ener/files/documents/20130828_epcip_commission_staff_working_document.pdf>, accessed 11 July 2019

Feichtner I, 'Community Interest', *Max Planck Encyclopedia of Public International Law* (Oxford University Press 2007) <https://opil.ouplaw.com/abstract/10.1093/law:epil/9780199231690/law-9780199231690-e1677> accessed 22 May 2019

French D and Stephens T, 'ILA Study Group on Due Diligence in International Law: Final Report' (2014) <https://ila.vettoreweb.com/Storage/Download.aspx?DbStorageId=1429&StorageFileGuid=fd770a95-9118-4a20-ac61-df12356f74d0> accessed 22 May 2019

Greer C and others, 'Cyber-Physical Systems and Internet of Things' (National Institute of Standards and Technology 2019) <https://nvlpubs.nist.gov/nistpubs/SpecialPublications/NIST.SP.1900-202.pdf> accessed 6 June 2019

Hertogen A, 'Letting Lotus Bloom' (2015) 26 European Journal of International Law 901

Hobe S, von Ruckteschell N and Heffernan D, *Cologne Compendium on Air Law in Europe* (Hardcover, Carl Heymanns Verlag 2013)

Hong J, 'Liability of Aviation Security Service Providers and Responsibility of States' (2010) 35 Air and Space Law 9

Huang J, 'Aviation Safety, ICAO and Obligations Erga Omnes' (2009) 8 Chinese Journal of International Law 63

Huang J, *Aviation Safety through the Rule of Law: ICAO's Mechanisms and Practices (Aviation Law and Policy Series)* (Kluwer Law International, BV 2009)

Huang Z and Mačák K, 'Towards the International Rule of Law in Cyberspace: Contrasting Chinese and Western Approaches' (2017) 16 Chinese Journal of International Law 271

International Commission on Intervention and State Sovereignty, 'The Responsibility to Protect' (*International Commission on Intervention and State Sovereignty,* 2001) <http://responsibilitytoprotect.org/ICISS%20Report.pdf> accessed 26 May 2019

International Law Commission, 'First Report on Jus Cogens by Dire Tladi, Special Rapporteur' (8 March 2016) <http://legal.un.org/docs/?symbol=A/CN.4/693> accessed 03 July 2019

International Law Commission, 'Second Report on Jus Cogens by Dire Tladi, Special Rapporteur' (16 March 2017) UN Doc A/CN.4/706 <http://legal.un.org/docs/?symbol=A/CN.4/706> accessed 04 July 2019

International Law Commission, 'Third Report on Peremptory Norms of General International Law (Jus Cogens) by Dire Tladi, Special Rapporteur' (12 February 2018) UN Doc A/CN.4/714 <http://legal.un.org/docs/?symbol=A/CN.4/714> accessed 04 July 2019 Kingsley-Jones M, 'Qatar Chief Outlines Impact of Ban and Its Network Plan' (*Flightglobal.com*, 19 June 2017) <https://www.flightglobal.com/news/articles/paris-qatar-chief-outlines-impact-of-ban-and-its-ne-438463/> accessed 28 May 2019

International Law Commission, 'Fourth Report on Peremptory Norms of General International Law (Jus Cogens) by Dire Tladi, Special Rapporteur' (31 January 2019) UN Doc A/CN.4/727 <http://legal.un.org/docs/?symbol=A/CN.4/727>

Masutti A, 'Single European Sky – a Possible Regulatory Framework for System Wide Information Management (SWIM)' (2011) 36 Air and Space Law 275

Masutti A and Tomasello F, 'The Challenge of Security' in *International regulation of non-military drones* (Edward Elgar 2018)

Meyer A and Radu C, 'Integrated Risk Management: A Holistic Approach to Managing Aviation Risk' (*Uniting Aviation*, 4 February 2019) <https://www.unitingaviation.com/strategic-objective/safety/integrated-risk-management/> accessed 25 May 2019

Mills E, 'Report: Hackers Broke into FAA Air Traffic Control Systems' (*CNET*) <https://www.cnet.com/news/report-hackers-broke-into-faa-air-traffic-control-systems/> accessed 8 May 2019

National Coordinator for Security and Counterterrorism, 'Resilient Critical Infrastructure' <https://english.nctv.nl/binaries/Factsheet%20Critical%20Infrastructure%20ENG%202018_tcm32-240750.pdf> accessed 10 July 2019

Newbery S and Dehghantanha A, 'Torture-Free Cyberspace – a Human Right' (2017) 2017 Computer Fraud & Security 14

Nuotio K, 'Security and Criminal Law: A Difficult Relationship' [2013] Law and Security in Europe: Reconsidering the Security Constitution 197

Pellet A, 'Comments in Response to Christine Chinkin and in Defense of Jus Cogens as the Best Bastion against the Excesses of Fragmentation' [2006] Finnish Yearbook of International Law 83

Ratajczyk MA, 'Regional Aviation Safety Organisations : Enhancing Air Transport Safety through Regional Cooperation' (Dissertatie, Leiden University 2014) <https://openaccess.leidenuniv.nl/handle/1887/29759> accessed 3 April 2019

Regional AVSEC Ministerial Conference, 'Dubai Declaration on Cyber Security in Civil Aviation: Reasons and Prospect' (GASeP: The Roadmap to Foster Aviation Security in Africa and the Middle East, Sharm El Sheikh Egypt, 22 August 2017) <https://

www.icao.int/Meetings/AVSEC-RMC-Egypt/Documents/PPTs/session3-6.pdf> accessed 18 April 2019

Robert Kolb, 'Effects of Jus Cogens' in *Peremptory International Law – Jus Cogens : A General Inventory* (Hart Publishing 2015)

Rose-Ackerman S and Billa B, 'Treaties and National Security' [2008] Faculty Scholarship Series <https://digitalcommons.law.yale.edu/fss_papers/595> accessed 03 July 2019

Schmitt MN (ed), *Tallinn Manual 2.0 on the International Law Applicable to Cyber Operations: Prepared by the International Groups of Experts at the Invitation of the NATO Cooperative Cyber Defence Centre of Excellence* (2nd edn, Cambridge University Press 2017)

Schubert F, 'The Technical Defragmentation of Air Navigation Services – The Legal Challenges of Virtualisation' [2013] From Lowlands to High Skies: A Multilevel Jurisdictional Approach Towards Air law 43

SESAR Joint Undertaking, 'A Proposal for the Future Architecture of the European Airspace' (Publications Office of the European Union 2019) <https://www.sesarju.eu/sites/default/files/documents/reports/Future%20Airspace%20Architecture%20Proposal.pdf> accessed 12 May 2019

Shackelford SJ, Russell S and Kuehn A, 'Unpacking the International Law on Cybersecurity Due Diligence: Lessons from the Public and Private Sectors' (2016) 17 Chicago Journal of International Law; Chicago 1

Shaw MN, *International Law* (Eighth Edition, Cambridge University Press 2017)

Simma B, 'From Bilateralism to Community Interest in International Law (Volume 250)' [1994] Collected Courses of the Hague Academy of International Law <https://referenceworks.brillonline.com/entries/the-hague-academy-collected-courses/from-bilateralism-to-community-interest-in-internationallaw-volume-250-ej.9789041104199.217_384> accessed 22 May 2019

Skyguide, 'The Virtual Centre Model' (2013) <https://www.skyguide.ch/wp-content/uploads/fileadmin/user_upload/publications/corporate/concept_paper_VCM_2013-04.pdf> accessed 6 June 2019

Sreejith SG, 'Legality of the Gulf Ban on Qatari Flights: State Sovereignty at Crossroads' (2018) 43 Air and Space Law 191

Takano A, 'Due Diligence Obligations and Transboundary Environmental Harm: Cybersecurity Applications' (2018) 7 Laws 36

Tomuschat C, 'The Security Council and Jus Cogens' in Enzo Cannizzaro (ed), *The present and future of jus cogens* (Sapienza università editrice 2015)

Tsagourias N, 'The Legal Status of Cyberspace' in *Research Handbook on International Law and Cyberspace* (Edward Elgar Publishing 2015)

UN, 'The Protection of Critical Infrastructures against Terrorist Attacks: Compendium of Good Practices' (*United Nations,* 2018) <https://www.un.org/sc/ctc/wp-content/uploads/2019/01/Compendium_of_Good_Practices_Compressed.pdf> accessed 7 May 2019

Wet ED, 'The International Constitutional Order' (2006) 55 International & Comparative Law Quarterly 51

Zagor M, 'Elementary Considerations of Humanity' in Karine Bannelier' in Christakis T and Heathcote S (eds), *The ICJ and the Evolution of International Law: The Enduring Impact of the Corfu Channel Case* (Routledge 2012)

CUMULATIVE BIBLIOGRAPHY

Abelson H and others, 'Keys Under Doormats' (2015) 58 Commun. ACM 24

Abelson H and others, 'The Risks of Key Recovery, Key Escrow, and Trusted Third-Party Encryption' (1997) 2 World Wide Web J. 241

Abeyratne R, 'Aviation Security Audits' in Ruwantissa Abeyratne (ed), *Aviation Security Law* (Springer Berlin Heidelberg 2010)

Accenture Security, 'The Cost of Cybercrime' (2019) <https://www.accenture.com/_acnmedia/PDF-96/Accenture-2019-Cost-of-Cybercrime-Study-Final.pdf#zoom=50>

Agarwal S and Sureka A, 'Applying Social Media Intelligence for Predicting and Identifying On-Line Radicalization and Civil Unrest Oriented Threats' (2015) ArXiv <http://arxiv.org/abs/1511.06858>

Alison L and others, 'Pragmatic Solutions to Offender Profiling and Behavioural Investigative Advice' (2010) Vol. 15 Legal and Criminological Psychology 115

Aljifri H and Sánchez Navarro D, 'International Legal Aspects of Cryptography: Understanding Cryptography' (2003) 22 Computers & Security 196

Allen TA, 'Guideline for Using Cryptographic Standards in the Federal Government - Cryptographic Mechanisms: NIST Releases Draft NIST SP 800-175B Rev. 1' (NIST, 3 July 2019) <https://www.nist.gov/news-events/news/2019/07/guideline-using-cryptographic-standards-federal-government-cryptographic>

Alpár G, Hoepman J-H and Siljee J, 'The Identity Crisis. Security, Privacy and Usability Issues in Identity Management' [2011] arXiv <http://arxiv.org/abs/1101.0427>

Amnesty International, 'Encryption: A Matter of Human Rights' (2016) <https://www.amnesty.nl/content/uploads/2016/03/160322_encryption_-_a_matter_of_human_rights_-_def.pdf?x68337>

Amundrud Ø, Aven T, Flage R, 'How the definition of security risk can be made compatible with safety definitions' (2017) 3, Proceedings of the Institution of Mechanical Engineers, Part O: Journal of Risk and Reliability <https://doi.org/10.1177/1748006X17699145>

Andress J, *The Basics of Information Security: Understanding the Fundamentals of InfoSec in Theory and Practice* (Elsevier 2011)

Aradau C, 'Security that matters: Critical infrastructure and objects of protection' (2010) 41 Security Dialogue <https://doi.org/10.1177/0967010610382687>

Arnardóttir OM, 'The Differences That Make a Difference: Recent Developments on the Discrimination Grounds and the Margin of Appreciation under Article 14 of the European Convention on Human Rights' (2014) Vol. 14 Human Rights Law Review 647

Arnardóttir OM, 'Vulnerability under Article 14 of the European Convention on Human Rights' (2017) Vol. 4 Oslo Law Review 150

Ayala-Rivera V and Pasquale L, 'The Grace Period Has Ended: An Approach to Operationalize GDPR Requirements' [2018] IEEE 26th International Requirements Engineering Conference 136

Azoulai L and Coutts S, 'Restricting Union citizens' residence rights on grounds of public security. Where Union citizenship and the AFSJ meet: P.I.' (2013) Vol. 50 Common Market Law Review 553

Baere GD and Ryngaert C, 'The ECJ's Judgment in Air Transport Association of America and the International Legal Context of the EU's Climate Change Policy' 26

Baker SA and Hurst PR, *The Limits of Trust : Cryptography, Governments, and Electronic Commerce* (Kluwer law international 1998)

Balzacq T, Léonard S, Ruzicka J, "Securitization' revisited: theory and cases' (2016) 30 International Relations <https: //doi 10.1177/0047117815596590>

Bamforth N, Malik M, O'Cinneide C, Discrimination Law: Theory and Context (Sweet & Maxwell 2008) 73

Barocas S and Selbst AD, 'Big Data's Disparate Impact Essay' (2016) 104 California Law Review 671

Barry B, *Political Argument* (Routledge and Kegan Paul 1965) 47–49

Bauer M and others, 'The Costs of Data Localisation: Friendly Fire on Economic Recovery' (European Centre for International Political Economy 2014) <http://hdl.handle.net/10419/174726>

Beaucill C, 'On opening up the horizon: the ECJ's new take on country sanctions' (2018) Vol. 55 Common Market Law Review 387–416

Bell E and La Padula L, *Secure Computer System: Unified Exposition and Multics Interpretation* (The MITRE Corporation 1976)

Bender J and others, 'Privacy-Friendly Revocation Management without Unique Chip Identifiers for the German National ID Card' (2010) 2010 Computer Fraud & Security 14

Benn SI and Peters RS, *Social principles and the democratic state.* (Allen and Unwin 1975) 142–147

Berendt B, 'Better Data Protection by Design through multicriteria decision making: On false tradeoffs between privacy and utility' in Erich Schweighofer and others (eds), *Privacy Technologies and Policy* (Springer 2017)

Berg H-P, 'Safety and Security of Critical Infrastructures with regard to nuclear facilities' in I Žutautaitė, M Eid, K Simola, V Kopustinskas (eds) *Critical Infrastructures: Enhancing Preparedness & Resilience for the Security of Citizens and Services Supply Continuity.* Proceedings of the 52nd ESReDA Seminar. Lithuanian Energy Institute & Vytautas Magnus University, 2017

Besson S, 'Sovereignty' Oxford Public International Law (2011) from Max Planck Encyclopedia of Public International Law [MPEPIL] <https://opil.ouplaw.com/view/10.1093/law:epil/9780199231690/law-9780199231690-e1472>

Beucher K and Utzerath J, ‚Cybersicherheit – Nationale Und Internationale Reguliserungsinitiativen – Folgen Für Die IT-Compliance Und Die Haftungsmaβstäbe' [2013] MultiaMedia und Recht 362

Bigo D, 'The European internal security field: stakes and rivalries in a newly developing area of police intervention' in Anderson M and Boer MD (eds), *Policing Across National Boundaries* (1994) 161

Blackwell C, 'A multi-layered security architecture for modelling complex systems' (2008) CSIIRW 35

Blind K, 'The Impact of Standardization and Standards on Innovation' (Manchester Institute of Innovation Research 2013) 13/15 <www.innovation-policy.org.uk/compendium/section/Default.aspx?topicid=30>

Blockmans S and others, *What Comes after the Last Chance Commission? Policy Priorities for 2019–2024* (Steven Blockmans ed, 2019)

Blumenkron J, 'International Safety Requirements' in Paul Stephen Dempsey and Ram S Jakhu (eds), *Routledge Handbook of Public Aviation Law* (Routledge 2016)

Boehm F, 'Data Processing and Law Enforcement Access to Information Systems at EU Level' (2012) 36 Datenschutz und Datensicherheit – DuD 339

Boholm M, Möller N, Ove Hansson S, 'The Concepts of Risk, Safety, and Security: Applications in Everyday Language' (2016) 36 Risk Analysis <https: //doi 10.1111/risa.12464>

Bolognini L and Bistolfi C, 'Pseudonymization and impacts of Big (personal/anonymous) data processing in the transition from the Directive 95/46/EC to the new EU General Data Protection Regulation' [2017] 33 Computer Law & Security Report 171

Boon KE, 'Are Control Tests Fit for the Future? The Slippage Problem in Attribution Doctrines' (2014) 15 Melbourne Journal of International Law 1

Boritz E, 'IS Practitioners' Views on Core Concepts of Information Integrity ' [2005] 6(4) International Journal of Accounting Information Systems 260

Bossong R and Wagner B, 'A Typology of Cybersecurity and Public-Private Partnerships in the Context of the EU' (2017) 67 Crime, Law and Social Change 265

Bourgeois DT and Bourgeois D, 'Information Systems Security' in David T. Bourgeois and Dave Bourgeois, *Information Systems for Business and Beyond* (Saylor Academy 2014)

Bourne M, *Understanding Security* (Macmillan International Higher Education 2013) 88

Braybrooke D, *Meeting Needs* (Princeton University Press 1987) 48

Brayne S, 'Big Data Surveillance: The Case of Policing' (2017) Vol. 82 American Sociological Review 977

Breaux T, *Introduction to IT privacy: A handbook for technologists* (International Association of Privacy Professionals 2014)

Brkan M, 'The Concept of Essence of Fundamental Rights in the EU Legal Order: Peeling the Onion to Its Core' (2018) 14 European Constitutional Law Review 332

Brown (ed.) G, *The Universal Declaration of Human Rights in the 21st Century* (Open Book Publishers 2016)

Brown H, 'U.S. National Security: The Next 50 Years' (2000) Centre for Naval Analyses <https://www.cna.org/CNA_files/PDF/D0001565.A1.pdf>

Buchan R, 'Cyberspace, Non-State Actors and the Obligation to Prevent Transboundary Harm' (2016) 21 Journal of Conflict and Security Law 429

Budish R, Burkert H and Gasser U, 'Encryption Policy and Its International Impacts: A Framework for Understanding Extraterritorial Ripple Effects' Stanford University 28

Bures O and Carrapico H (eds), 'Contributions of Private Business to the Provision of Security in the EU: Beyond Public-Private Partnership' in Bures O and Carrapico

H (eds), Security privatization: how non-security-related private businesses shape security governance (Springer Berlin Heidelberg 2017)
Burt A, 'Privacy and Security are converging. Here's why that matters for people and for companies' (2019) Harvard Business Review 1
Buzan B, 'Peace, Power, and Security: Contending Concepts in the Study of International Relations' (1984) 21 Journal of Peace Research 109
Bygrave LA, 'Data Privacy Law: An International Perspective' (2014) 25 King's Law Journal 497
Bygrave LA, *Data Privacy Law: An International Perspective* (Oxford University Press 2014)
Cameron I, *National Security and the European Convention on Human Rights* (Kluwer Law International 2000) 54
Cardwell PJ, 'The legalisation of European Union foreign policy and the use of sanctions' (2015) Vol. 17 Cambridge Yearbook of European Legal Studies 287–310
Carrapico H and Barrinha A, 'The EU as a Coherent (Cyber)Security Actor?: The EU as a Coherent (Cyber)Security Actor?' (2017) 55 Journal of Common Market Studies 1254
Carrapico H and Farrand B, '"Dialogue, Partnership and Empowerment for Network and Information Security": The Changing Role of the Private Sector from Objects of Regulation to Regulation Shapers' (2017) 67 Crime, Law and Social Change 245
Cavelty M and Søby Kristensen K, *Securing the homeland: critical infrastructure, risk and (in)security* (Routledge, 2008)
Cavelty M, 'Breaking the cyber-security dilemma: aligning security needs and removing vulnerabilities' 2014 20 Science and Engineering Ethics 701 <https://doi: 10.1007/s11948-014-9551-y>
Cavoukian A, 'Privacy by Design. The 7 Foundational Principles' <https://iapp.org/resources/article/privacy-by-design-the-7-foundational-principles/>
Cavoukian A, 'Privacy by Design and the Emerging Personal Data Ecosystem' in (*Information and privacy Commissioner of Ontario,* October 2012) <https://www.ipc.on.ca/wp-content/uploads/Resources/pbd-pde.pdf>
Ceccorulli M and Lucarelli S, 'Security governance: making the concept fit for the analysis of a multipolar, global and regionalized world' 2014 41 Global Governance Programme-98; European, Transnational and Global Governance <http://hdl.handle.net/1814/31282>
Chan H and Mubarak S, 'Significance of Information Security Awareness in the Higher Education Sector' (2012) 60 International Journal of Computer Applications 10
Charlton M, *A Handbook of Information Technology* (Global Media 2009)
Chattopadhyay A and Lam K-Y, 'Autonomous Vehicle: Security by Design' [2018] ArXiv <http://arxiv.org/abs/1810.00545>
Chaudhary T and others, 'Patchwork of Confusion: The Cybersecurity Coordination Problem' (2018) 4 Journal of Cybersecurity
Cherdantseva Y and Hilton J, 'A reference model of information assurance and security' (2013) IEEE Proceedings of the International Conference on Availability, Reliability and Security (ARES)
Chircop L, 'A Due Diligence Standard of Attribution in Cyberspace' (2018) 67 International & Comparative Law Quarterly 643

Choraś M, Kozik R, Flizikowski A, Hołubowicz W and Renk R, 'Cyber Threats Impacting Critical Infrastructures' in Roberto Setola and others (eds), *Managing the Complexity of Critical Infrastructures* (Vol 90, Springer Open 2016)

Christou G, 'Introduction' in Cybersecurity in the European Union: Resilience and Adaptability in Governance Policy (Palgrave Macmillan UK 2016)

Citron DK and Pasquale F, 'The Scored Society: Due Process for Automated Predictions' (2014) Vol. 89 Washington Law Review 33

Claes M, 'National Identity: Trump Card or Up for Negotiation?' in Alejandro Saiz Arnaiz and Carina Alcoberro Llivina, *National Constitutional Identity and European Integration* (Intersentia 2013) 109–140

Claes M, 'The Primacy of EU Law in European and National Law' in Arnull A and Chalmers D (eds), *The Oxford Handbook of European Union Law* (2015), 178–211

CNIL, 'Comment Permettre à l'Homme de Garder La Main ? Rapport Sur Les Enjeux Éthiques Des Algorithmes et de l'intelligence Artificielle' (2017) <https://www.cnil.fr/en/node/24008>

College of Policing, 'Intelligence Report' (2015) <https://www.app.college.police.uk/app-content/intelligence-management/intelligence-report/>

Collingwood L, 'Privacy Implications and Liability Issues of Autonomous Vehicles' (2017) 26 Information & Communications Technology Law 32

Cooper P, 'Aviation Cybersecurity: Finding Lift, Minimizing Drag' (Atlantic Council Brent Scowcroft Center on International Security 2017)

Coudert F, Dumortier J and Verbruggen F, 'Applying the Purpose Specification Principle in the Age of 'Big Data': The Example of Integrated Video Surveillance Platforms in France' [2012] ICRI Research Paper <http://dx.doi.org/10.2139/ssrn.2046123>

Council of Europe, 'National Security and Euopean Case-Law' (2013) <https://www.echr.coe.int/Documents/Research_report_national_security_ENG.pdf>

Council of Europe, Commissioner for Human Rights, 'Unboxing Artificial Intelligence: 10 steps to protect Human Rights' (May 2019) 11 <https://rm.coe.int/unboxing-artificial-intelligence-10-steps-to-protect-human-rights-reco/1680946e64>

Crane D, Logue K and Pilz B, 'A Survey of Legal Issues Arising from the Deployment of Autonomous and Connected Vehicles' (2017) 23 Michigan Technology Law Review 191

Crawford J, *Brownlie's Principles of Public International Law* (Oxford University Press 2012)

Cremona M, 'Coherence through Law: What difference will the Treaty of Lisbon make?', Hamburg Review of Social Sciences (2008) Vol. 3 11–36

d'Aspremont J, 'Jus Cogens as a Social Construct Without Pedigree' in Maarten den Heijer and Harmen van der Wilt (eds), *Netherlands Yearbook of International Law 2015: Jus Cogens: Quo Vadis?* (TMC Asser Press 2016) <https://doi.org/10.1007/978-94-6265-114-2_4>

Danezis G and others, 'Privacy and Data Protection by Design – from Policy to Engineering' (European Union Agency for Network and Information Security (ENISA) 2014) <http://bookshop.europa.eu/uri?target=EUB:NOTICE:TP0514111:EN:HTML>

Danezis G, Domingo-Ferrer J and Hansen M, 'Privacy and Data Protection by Design – from Policy to Engineering' (2014) European Union Agency for Network and

Information Security <https://www.enisa.europa.eu/publications/privacy-and-data-protection-by-design>

Danezis G, Domingo-Ferrer J and Hansen M, 'Privacy and Data Protection by Design – from Policy to Engineering' (ENISA 2014) <https://www.enisa.europa.eu/publications/privacy-and-data-protection-by-design>

Dashwood A and others, *Wyatt and Dashwood's European Union Law* (6th edition, Hart Publishing 2011) 482–485

Davis AM, *201 Principles of Software Development* (McGraw-Hill, Inc 1995)

De Bruyne J and Werbrouck J, 'Merging Self-Driving Cars with the Law' (2018) 34 Computer Law & Security Review 1150

De Cock D and others, 'The Belgian EID Approach' in Walter Fumy and Manfred Paeschke (eds), *Handbook of eID Security. Concepts, Practical Experiences, Technologies* (Publicis Publishing 2011)

De Geest G, 'Who Should Be Immune from Tort Liability?' (2012) 41 The Journal of Legal Studies 291

De Hert P and Papakonstantinou V, 'The Police and Criminal Justice Data Protection Directive: Comment and Analysis' (2012) 7 New Journal of European Criminal Law 7

De Pauw E and others (eds), *Technology-Led Policing* (Maklu 2011)

Death D, *Information Security Handbook: Develop a threat model and incident response strategy to build a strong information security network* (Packt Publishing 2017)

Deeks A, 'The International Legal Dynamics of Encryption' Stanford University 28

Delerue F, 'International Cooperation on the International Law Applicable to Cyber Operations' (2019) Vol. 24 European Foreign Affairs Review

Delfino F, '"Considerations of Humanity" in the Jurisprudence of ITLOS and UNCLOS Arbitral Tribunals' Angela Del Vecchio and Roberto Virzo (eds) Interpretations of the United Nations Convention on the Law of the Sea by International Courts and Tribunals (Cham: Springer International Publishing, 2019) https://doi.org/10.1007/978-3-030-10773-4_21

Dempsey PS, 'Introduction: Multilateral Conventions and Customary International Law' in Paul Stephen Dempsey and Ram S Jakhu (eds), *Routledge Handbook of Public Aviation Law* (Routledge 2016)

Dencik L, Hintz A, Carey Z, 'Prediction, Pre-Emption and Limits to Dissent: Social Media and Big Data Uses for Policing Protests in the United Kingdom' (2018) Vol. 20 New Media & Society 1433

Department for Digital, Culture, Media & Sport at UK Government, 'Secure by Design: Improving the cybersecurity of consumer Internet of things Report' (2018) < https://assets.publishing.service.gov.uk/government/uploads/system/uploads/attachment_data/file/775559/Secure_by_Design_Report_.pdf >

Derencinovic D and Getos AM, 'Cooperation of law enforcement and intelligence agencies in prevention and suppression of terrorism' (2007) Vol. 78 Revue internationale de droit penal 79

Dewitte P and others, 'A Comparison of System Description Models for Data Protection by Design' (2019) IEEE

Dhamija R and Dusseault L, 'The Seven Flaws of Identity Management: Usability and Security Challenges' (2008) 6 IEEE Security Privacy 24

Dimitrova A and Brkan M, 'Balancing National Security and Data Protection: The Role of EU and US Policy-Makers and Courts before and after the NSA Affair' (2017) Journal of Common Market Studies 751

Dobbs M, 'Sovereignty, article 4(2) TEU and the respect of national identities: Swinging the balance of power in favour of the member states?' (2014) Yearbook of European Law 33(1) 298

Douglass BP, *Agile Systems Engineering* (Elsevier 2016) <https://linkinghub.elsevier.com/retrieve/pii/C20140021028>

Drezner DW, 'Globalization, Harmonization, and Competition: The Different Pathways to Policy Convergence' (2005) 12 Journal of European Public Policy 841

Dutch Presidency, 'Non-paper: Developing a joint EU diplomatic response against coercive cyber operations 5797/6/16 of 19' (May 2016) <http://statewatch.org/news/2016/jul/eu-council-diplomatic-response-cyber-ops-5797-6-16.pdf>

EDPS, 'Preliminary Opinion of the European Data Protection Supervisor Privacy and Competitiveness in the Age of Big Data: The Interplay between Data Protection, Competition Law and Consumer Protection in the Digital Economy' <https://edps.europa.eu/sites/edp/files/publication/14-03-26_competitition_law_big_data_en.pdf>

Edwards I, 'GDPR the Security Angle' (2018) 60 ITNOW 42

Eeckhout P, *EU External Relations Law* (2nd edition, Oxford University Press, 2011) 502

Eisenhut D, 'Sovereignty, National Security and International Treaty Law. The Standard of Review of International Courts and Tribunals with Regard to "Security Exceptions"' (2010) 48 Archiv des Völkerrechts 431

Enerstvedt OM, 'Introduction' in Olga Mironenko Enerstvedt (ed), *Aviation Security, Privacy, Data Protection and Other Human Rights: Technologies and Legal Principles* (Springer International Publishing 2017)

Ensign D and others, 'Runaway Feedback Loops in Predictive Policing' (2017) ArXiv <http://arxiv.org/abs/1706.09847>

European Commission and others, *Feasibility Study on an Electronic Identification, Authentication and Signature Policy (IAS) Final Report* (Publications Office 2013) <http://dx.publications.europa.eu/10.2759/25928>

European Union Agency for Fundamental Rights (FRA) and the Council of Europe (eds), *Handbook on European Non-Discrimination Law* (2018 edition, Publications Office of the European Union 2018) 224–225

European Union Agency for Fundamental Rights (FRA) and the Council of Europe, *Handbook on European data protection law* (Publications Office of the European Union 2018)

European Commission, 'Commission Staff Working Document on a New Approach to the European Programme for Critical Infrastructure Protection Making European Critical Infrastructures More Secure' SWD (2013) 318 Final <https://ec.europa.eu/energy/sites/ener/files/documents/20130828_epcip_commission_staff_working_document.pdf>

European Commission, 'Modinis Study on Identity Management in EGovernment – Common Terminological Framework for Interoperable Electronic Identity Management' (2005) <https://ec.europa.eu/newsroom/dae/document.cfm?doc_id=2794>

European Union Agency for Fundamental Rights (FRA), 'Preventing Unlawful Profiling Today and in the Future: A Guide' (2018) 138 < https://fra.europa.eu/en/publication/2018/prevent-unlawful-profiling>

European Union Agency for Fundamental Rights (FRA), 'Towards More Effective Policing – Understanding and Preventing Discriminatory Ethnic Profiling: A Guide' (2010) < https://fra.europa.eu/sites/default/files/fra_uploads/1133-Guide-ethnic-profiling_EN.pdf>

European Union Agency for Network and Information Security (ENISA), 'Cyber Europe 2012' (*Key Findings and Recommendations*, December 2012) <https://www.enisa.europa.eu/publications/cyber-europe-2012-key-findings-report/at_download/fullReport>

European Union Agency for Network and Information Security (ENISA), 'Definition of Cybersecurity – Gaps and overlaps in standardization' (2016) <https://www.enisa.europa.eu/publications/definition-of-cybersecurity>

European Union Agency for Network and Information Security (ENISA), 'Critical Information Infrastructures Protection Approaches in EU' (2015) <https://resilience.enisa.europa.eu/enisas-ncss-project/CIIPApproachesNCSS.pdf>

European Union Agency for Network and Information Security (ENISA), IoT Security Standards gap Analysis. Mapping of existing standards against requirements on security and privacy in the area of IoT (V 1.0, 2018) <https://www.enisa.europa.eu/publications/iot-security-standards-gap-analysis>

European Union Agency for Network and Information Security (ENISA), 'Stocktaking, Analysis and Recommendations on the Protection of CIIs' (*ENISA*, January 2016) <https://www.enisa.europa.eu/publications/stocktaking-analysis-and-recommendations-on-the-protection-of-ciis>

European Union Agency for Network and Information Security (ENISA), 'Guidelines for SMEs on the Security of Personal Data Processing' (2016) <https://www.enisa.europa.eu/publications/guidelines-for-smes-on-the-security-of-personal-data-processing/at_download/fullReport>

Evas T and others, Study on a Common EU Approach to Liability Rules and Insurance for Connected and Autonomous Vehicles: European Added Value Assessment Accompanying the European Parliament's Legislative Own-Initiative Report (Rapporteur: Mady Delvaux) (European Parliament, 2018)

Everts P and Isernia P, *Public Opinion, Transatlantic Relations and the Use of Force* (Palgrave McMillan UK 2015) 236

Faden R and Shebaya S, 'Public Health Ethics' *The Stanford Encyclopedia of Philosophy* (Winter edn, 2016) <https://plato.stanford.edu/archives/win2016/entries/publichealth-ethics/>

Faure M, 'Private Liability and Critical Infrastructure' (2015) 6 European Journal of Risk Regulation 229

Feichtner I, 'Community Interest', *Max Planck Encyclopedia of Public International Law* (Oxford University Press 2007) <https://opil.ouplaw.com/abstract/10.1093/law:epil/9780199231690/law-9780199231690-e1677>

Fenwick M, Kaal WA and Vermeulen EPM, 'Regulation Tomorrow: Strategies for Regulating New Technologies' in Toshiyuki Kono, Mary Hiscock and Arie

Reich (eds), *Transnational Commercial and Consumer Law: Current Trends in International Business Law* (Springer Singapore 2018)

Feruza S and Kim T, 'IT Security Review: Privacy, Protection, Access Control, Assurance and System Security' (2007) 2 International Journal of Multimedia and Ubiquitous Engineering

Finnis J, 'Absolute Rights: Some Problems Illustrated' (2016) 61 American Journal of Jurisprudence 195

Fredman S, 'Emerging from the Shadows: Substantive Equality and Article 14 of the European Convention on Human Rights' (2016) Vol. 16 Human Rights Law Review 273, 277

Freedman L, 'The concept of security' *Encyclopedia of Government and Politics* (2nd edn, 2003)

Freeman P and Hart D, 'A Science of Design for Software Intensive Systems' (2004) 47 Commun. ACM 19.

French D and Stephens T, 'ILA Study Group on Due Diligence in International Law: Final Report' (2014) <https://ila.vettoreweb.com/Storage/Download.aspx?DbStorageId=1429&StorageFileGuid=fd770a95-9118-4a20-ac61-df12356f74d0>

Frisoni R and others, 'Research for TRAN Committee – Self-Piloted Cars: The Future of Road Transport?' (2016) (European Union, 2016), www.europarl.europa.eu/RegData/etudes/STUD/2016/573434/IPOL_STU(2016)573434_EN.pdf

Furnell S, 'The Usability of Security – Revisited' (2016) 2016 Computer Fraud & Security 5

Gallie WB, *Essentially Contested Concepts* vol 56 (Proceedings of the Aristotelian Society, 1956) 167

Gasser TM, 'Fundamental and Special Legal Questions for Autonomous Vehicles' in Markus Maurer and others (eds), *Autonomous Driving: Technical, Legal and Social Aspects* (Springer Berlin Heidelberg 2016)

Gauttier P, 'Horizontal Coherence and the External Competences of the European Union' (2004) 10 European Law Journal 23

Gebauer M, 'Unification and Harmonization of Laws', *Max Planck Encyclopedia of Public International Law* (Oxford University Press 2009) <http://opil.ouplaw.com/view/10.1093/law:epil/9780199231690/law-9780199231690-e1123>

Gellert R and others, 'A Comparative Analysis of Anti-Discrimination and Data Protection Legislations' in Bart Custers and others (eds), Discrimination and Privacy in the Information Society: Data Mining and Profiling in Large Databases (Springer Berlin Heidelberg 2013) <https://doi.org/10.1007/978-3-642-30487-3_4>Gerards J, 'Margin of Appreciation and Incrementalism in the Case Law of the European Court of Human Rights' (2018) Vol. 18 Human Rights Law Review 495

Gerards J, 'The Discrimination Grounds of Article 14 of the European Convention on Human Rights' (2013) Vol. 13 Human Rights Law Review 99

Gerards J, "Intensity of Judicial Review in Equal Treatment Cases" (2004) 51 Netherlands International Law Review 135

Gerber M, von Solms R and Overbeek P, 'Formalizing information security requirements' (2001) 9 Information Management & Computer Security 1

Glancy DJ, 'Sharing the Road: Smart Transportation Infrastructure Symposium: Smart Law for Smart Cities: Regulation, Technology, and the Future of Cities' (2013) 41 Fordham Urban Law Journal 1617

Gollman D, *Computer Security* (3rd edn, Wiley 2013)

Gong L and others, 'The application of data encryption technology in computer network communication security' (2017) AIP Conference Proceedings 1834

Google, 'Requests for User Information – Google Transparency Report' (*Google*) <https://transparencyreport.google.com/user-data/overview>

Gray C, 'A Crisis of Legitimacy for the UN Collective Security System?' (2007) 56 The International and Comparative Law Quarterly 157

Greenleaf G, 'The Influence of European Data Privacy Standards Outside Europe: Implications for Globalization of Convention 108' (2012) 2 International Data Privacy Law 68

Greenleaf G, 'A World Data Privacy Treaty? "Globalisation" and "Modernisation" of Council of Europe Convention 108', *Emerging Challenges in Privacy Law: Comparative Perspectives* (Cambridge University Press 2014)

Greenleaf G, 'APEC's Privacy Framework Sets a New Low Standard for the Asia-Pacific' in Andrew T Kenyon and Megan Richardson (eds), *New Dimensions in Privacy Law* (Cambridge University Press 2006) 91–120

Greer C and others, 'Cyber-Physical Systems and Internet of Things' (National Institute of Standards and Technology 2019) https://nvlpubs.nist.gov/nistpubs/SpecialPublications/NIST.SP.1900-202.pdf

Guastaferro B, 'Beyond the Exceptionalism of Constitutional Conflicts: The Ordinary Functions of the Identity Clause' (2012) Yearbook of European Law 263–318

Guretz D, Andress J and Leary M, *Building a Practical Information Security Program* (Elsevier Science & Technology Books 2016)

Gürses S and Hoboken J van, 'Privacy after the Agile Turn' [2017] SocArXiv <https://osf.io/preprints/socarxiv/9gy73/>

Gürses S, Kundnani A and Van Hoboken J, 'Crypto and Empire: The Contradictions of Counter-Surveillance Advocacy' (2016) 38 Media, Culture & Society 576

Gutmann P and Grigg I, 'Security Usability' (2005) 3 IEEE Security and Privacy Magazine 56

Hahn MJ, 'Vital Interests and the Law of GATT: An Analysis of GATT's Security Exception' (1991) 12 Michigan Journal of International Law 558

Hales TC, 'The NSA Back Door to NIST' (2014) 61 Notices of the American Mathematical Society

Harding L, *The Snowden Files: The Inside Story of the World's Most Wanted Man* (Vintage Books 2014)

Hertogen A, 'Letting Lotus Bloom' (2015) 26 European Journal of International Law 901

Heurix J and others, 'A taxonomy for privacy enhancing technologies' (2015) 53 Computers & Security

High-Level Expert Group on Artificial Intelligence, 'Ethics Guidelines for Trustworthy AI' (2019) <https://ec.europa.eu/digital-single-market/en/news/ethics-guidelines-trustworthy-ai>

Hildebrandt M, 'Balance or Trade-off? Online Security Technologies and Fundamental Rights' (2013) 26 Philosophy and Technology 357–379

Hobbes T, *Leviathan-Or the Matter, Form and Power of a Common-Wealth Ecclesiastical and Civil* (I Shapiro ed, first published 1651, Yale University Press 2010)
Hobe S, von Ruckteschell N and Heffernan D, *Cologne Compendium on Air Law in Europe* (Hardcover, Carl Heymanns Verlag 2013)
Hodeghatta Rao U and Nayak U, 'Introduction to Security' in Umesh Hodeghatta Rao and Umesha Nayak (eds), The InfoSec Handbook: An Introduction to Information Security (Apress 2014) 3–4
Hodgson G, 'Breaking Encryption and Gathering Data: International Law Applications' (2015) 20 Journal of Technology Law & Policy 39
Hofman D, Duranti L and How E, 'Trust in the Balance: Data Protection Laws as Tools for Privacy and Security in the Cloud' (2017) 10 Algorithms 2
Hong J, 'Liability of Aviation Security Service Providers and Responsibility of States' (2010) 35 Air and Space Law 9
Hong J, Kim J and Cho J, 'The Trend of the Security Research for the Insider Cyber Threat' in Dominik Ślęzak and others (eds), *Security Technology* (Springer Berlin Heidelberg 2009)
Hood C, Rothstein H and Baldwin R, *The Government of Risk: Understanding Risk Regulation Regimes* (Oxford University Press 2001)
Hoon MD, 'Navigating the Legal Horizon: Lawyering the MH17 Disaster' (2017) 33 Utrecht Journal of International and European Law 90
Hornung G, ‚Neue Pflichten Für Betreiber Kritischer Infrastrukturen: Das IT-Sicherheitsgesetz Des Bundes' [2015] Neue Juristische Wochenschrift 3334
Howells G, Twigg-Flesner C and Willett C, 'Product Liability and Digital Products', *EU Internet Law* (Springer, Cham 2017)
Huang J, *Aviation Safety through the Rule of Law: ICAO's Mechanisms and Practices* (Aviation Law and Policy Series) (Kluwer Law International, BV 2009)
Huang J, 'Aviation Safety, ICAO and Obligations Erga Omnes' (2009) 8 Chinese Journal of International Law 63
Huang Z and Mačák K, 'Towards the International Rule of Law in Cyberspace: Contrasting Chinese and Western Approaches' (2017) 16 Chinese Journal of International Law 271
Hurwitz JG, 'Encryption.Congress Mod (Apple + CALEA).(Communications Assistance for Law Enforcement Act of 1994)' (2017) 30 Harvard Journal of Law & Technology
Hussain Alqahtani F, 'Developing an Information Security Policy: A Case Study Approach' (2017) 124 Procedia Computer Science 691
Hussain W, 'The Common Good' *The Stanford Encyclopedia of Philosophy* (Spring edn, 2018) <https://plato.stanford.edu/archives/spr2018/entries/common-good/>
Information Commissioner's Office (ICO), *Anonymisation: managing data protection risk code of practice* (November 2012) <https://ico.org.uk/media/1061/anonymisation-code.pdf>
Information Commissioner's Office (ICO), *Guide to the General Data Protection Regulation (GDPR)* (2018) https://ico.org.uk/media/for-organisations/guide-to-the-general-data-protection-regulation-gdpr-1-0.pdf
International Association of Chiefs of Police (IACP), *Managing Cybersecurity Risk: A Law Enforcement Guide* (2017)

International Commission on Intervention and State Sovereignty, 'The Responsibility to Protect' (*International Commission on Intervention and State Sovereignty*, 2001) <http://responsibilitytoprotect.org/ICISS%20Report.pdf>

International Law Commission, 'First Report on Jus Cogens by Dire Tladi, Special Rapporteur' (8 March 2016) <http://legal.un.org/docs/?symbol=A/CN.4/693>

International Law Commission, 'Second Report on Jus Cogens by Dire Tladi, Special Rapporteur' (16 March 2017) UN Doc A/CN.4/706 <http://legal.un.org/docs/?symbol=A/CN.4/706>

International Law Commission, 'Third Report on Peremptory Norms of General International Law (Jus Cogens) by Dire Tladi, Special Rapporteur' (12 February 2018) UN Doc A/CN.4/714 <http://legal.un.org/docs/?symbol=A/CN.4/714>

International Law Commission, 'Fourth Report on Peremptory Norms of General International Law (Jus Cogens) by Dire Tladi, Special Rapporteur' (31 January 2019) UN Doc A/CN.4/727 <http://legal.un.org/docs/?symbol=A/CN.4/727>

International Organization for Standardization (ISO), *Standard ISO/IEC 27001:2013 – Information Security Management Systems – Requirements* (2013)

International Telecommunication Union (ITU), *The ITU National Cybersecurity Strategy Guide* (September 2011) <https://www.itu.int/ITU-D/cyb/cybersecurity/docs/ITUNationalCybersecurityStrategyGuide.pdf>

IT Governance Privacy Team, *EU General Data Protection Regulation (GDPR). An implementation and compliance guide* (2nd edn, IT Governance Publishing 2017) DOI: 10.2307/j.ctt1trkk7x

Ivan P, 'Responding to cyberattacks: Prospects for the EU Cyber Diplomacy Toolbox' (2019) European Policy Center <www.epc.eu/pub_details.php?cat_id=17&pub_id=9081>

Jacquemin H and Hubin J-B, 'Aspects contractuels et de responsabilité civile en matière d'intelligence artificielle' [2017] Intelligence artificielle et droit 73

Johnsen SO and others, *Risk Based Regulation and Certification of Autonomous Transport Systems* (2018)

Joinet L, 'Revised Version of the Guidelines for the Regulation of Computerized Personal Data Files' (United Nations Commission on Human Rights 1990) <http://digitallibrary.un.org/record/43365>

Jones ML, 'The Right to a Human in the Loop: Political Constructions of Computer Automation and Personhood' (2017) 47 Social Studies of Science 216

Jøsang A, 'Assurance Requirements for Mutual User and Service Provider Authentication' in Joaquin Garcia-Alfaro and others (eds), *Data Privacy Management, Autonomous Spontaneous Security, and Security Assurance* (vol 8872, Springer International Publishing 2015)

Jøsang A, 'Identity Management and Trusted Interaction in Internet and Mobile Computing' (2014) 8 IET Information Security 67

Kampouraki I, 'ENISA's Opinion Paper on Encryption' (2016) <https://www.enisa.europa.eu/publications/enisa-position-papers-and-opinions/enisas-opinion-paper-on-encryption>

Kaye D, 'Report of the Special Rapporteur on the Promotion and Protection of the Right to Freedom of Opinion and Expression' (United Nations Human Rights Council

2015) A/HRC/29/32 <www.ohchr.org/EN/HRBodies/HRC/RegularSessions/Session29/Documents/A.HRC.29.32_AEV.doc>

Kerr OS and Schneier B, 'Encryption Workarounds' (2018) 106 Georgetown Law Journal

Kestemont L, *Handbook on Legal Methodology. From Objective to Method* (Intersentia Ltd 2018)

Kim D and Solomon MG, *Fundamentals of Information Systems Security* (3rd edn, Jones & Bartlett 2018)

Kipker D-K, 'The EU NIS Directive Compared to the IT Security Act – Germany Is Well Positioned for the New European Cybersecurity Space' [2016] ZD-Aktuell 05363

Knieps G, 'Internet of Things, Big Data and the Economics of Networked Vehicles' (2019) 43 Telecommunications Policy 171

Knorr K, 'National Security Studies: Scope and Structure of the Field' in Frank N. Trager and Philip S. Kronenberg (eds), *National Security and American Society: Theory, Process and Policy* (Lawrence KS, 1973) 5

Kocsis RN and Palermo GB, 'Disentangling Criminal Profiling: Accuracy, Homology, and the Myth of Trait-Based Profiling' (2015) Vol. 59 International Journal of Offender Therapy and Comparative Criminology 313

Kocsis RN, Criminal Profiling: Principles and Practice (Humana Press 2006) 9

Korff D, 'European Commission Study on the implementation of Data Protection Directive: Comparative Summary of National Laws' (2002)

Kościelny C, Kurkowski M and Srebrny M, 'Public Key Infrastructure' in Czesław Kościelny, Mirosław Kurkowski and Marian Srebrny, Modern Cryptography Primer (Springer Berlin Heidelberg 2013) <http://link.springer.com/10.1007/978-3-642-41386-5_7>

Koutrakos P, 'Public Security Exceptions and EU Freed Movement Law' in P. Koutrakos, N. Nic Shuibhne & P. Syrpis (eds), *Exceptions from EU Free Movement Law: Derogation, Justification and Proportionality* (Hart Publishing 2016) 190

Kuner C and others, 'An Unstoppable Force and an Immoveable Object? EU Data Protection Law and National Security' 3

Kuner C and others, 'Risk management in data protection' (2015) 5 International Data Privacy Law 2

Kuwayama M, 'Pacific Alliance: A Latin American Version of"Open Regionalism"in Practice' [2019] IDEAS Working Paper Series from RePEc <http://search.proquest.com/docview/2188997245/>

Lammerant H and De Hert P, 'Predictive Profiling and Its Legal Limits: Effectiveness Gone Forever' (2016) Vol. 32 Exploring the boundaries of big data 145

Landau S and Diffie W, Privacy on the Line <https://mitpress.mit.edu/books/privacy-line>

Landau S, *Listening in: Cybersecurity in an Insecure Age* (Yale University press 2017)

Langer AM, *Guide to Software Development: Designing and Managing the Life Cycle* (2nd edn, Springer-Verlag 2016)

Lapowsky I, 'How the LAPD uses data to predict crime' (22 May 2018) <https://www.wired.com/story/los-angeles-police-department-predictive-policing/>

LaRose R, Rifon NJ and Enbody R, 'Promoting Personal Responsibility for Internet Safety' (2008) 51 Communications of the ACM 71

Leenes R and others, 'D2.2 – Report on Legal Interoperability' (2009) STORK project Deliverable D2.2

Leese M, Lidén K, Nikolova B, 'Putting critique to work: Ethics in EU security research' (2019) 50 Security Dialogue 59 <https://doi.org/10.1177/0967010618809554>

Lessig L, *Code and other laws of cyberspace* (New York, Basic Books 1999) 72–74

Lim HSM and Taeihagh A, 'Autonomous Vehicles for Smart and Sustainable Cities: An In-Depth Exploration of Privacy and Cybersecurity Implications' (2018) 11 Energies 1062

Lin H, 'Attribution of Malicious Cyber Incidents From Soup to Nuts' (*Hoover Institution*, 19 September 2016) <https://www.hoover.org/sites/default/files/research/docs/lin_webready.pdf>

Lin HS, 'Cryptography and Public Policy' (1998) 25 Journal of Government Information 135

Liu C and others 'The Security Risk Assessment Methodology' (2012) 43 Procedia Engineering

Lloyd IJ, *Information Technology Law* (Eighttth edn, Oxford University Press 2017)

Lloyd S and Adams C, 'Key Management' in Henk CA van Tilborg and Sushil Jajodia (eds), *Encyclopedia of Cryptography and Security* (Springer US 2011) <https://doi.org/10.1007/978-1-4419-5906-5_85>

Logan K, 'Access Controls' in Peltier TR (ed), *Information Security Fundamentals* (2nd edn, CRC Press 2014)

Lohmann MF, 'Liability Issues Concerning Self-Driving Vehicles' (2016) 7 European Journal of Risk Regulation 335

Long WRM, Scali G and Blythe F, 'European Union Overview' in Charles Paul A (ed), *The Privacy, Data Protection and Cybersecurity Law Review* (5th edn, Law Business Research London 2018)

Loutfi I and Jøsang A, '1,2, Pause: Lets Start by Meaningfully Navigating the Current Online Authentication Solutions Space' in Christian Damsgaard Jensen and others (eds), *Trust Management IX* (vol 454, Springer International Publishing 2015) <http://link.springer.com/10.1007/978-3-319-18491-3_12>

Ma Z and others, 'Towards a Multidisciplinary Framework to Include Privacy in the Design of Video Surveillance Systems' in Preneel B and Ikonomou D (eds), Privacy Technologies and Policy (Springer 2014)

Maass AS, *EU-Russia Relations, 1999–2015: From courtship to confrontation* (1st edn, Routledge, 2016) 46

Macken C, 'Preventive Detention and the Right of Personal Liberty and Security under the International Covenant on Civil and Political Rights, 1966' (2005) 26 Adelaide Law Review 1

Mantelero A, 'Personal Data for Decisional Purposes in the Age of Analytics: From an Individual to a Collective Dimension of Data Protection' (2016) Vol. 32 Computer Law & Security Review 238

Mantelero, A, 'From Group Privacy to Collective Privacy: Towards a New Dimension of Privacy and Data Protection in the Big Data Era' in Linnet Taylor, Luciano Floridi and Bart van der Sloot (eds), Group Privacy: New Challenges of Data Technologies (Springer International Publishing 2017) <https://doi.org/10.1007/978-3-319-46608-8_8>

Marquenie T and Coudert F, 'Roadmap for the Operationalization of Legal and Privacy Requirements in VALCRI Analysis' [2017] VALCRI White Papers Series

Marquenie T, 'The Police and Criminal Justice Authorities Directive: Data protection standards and impact on the legal framework' (2017) 33 Computer Law & Security Review 324

Martínez-Nadal A and Ferrer-Gomila JL, 'Comments to the UNCITRAL Model Law on Electronic Signatures' in Agnes Hui Chan and Virgil Gligor (eds), *Information Security* (Springer Berlin Heidelberg 2002)

Mason S, 'Digital Signatures', *Electronic Signatures in Law* (School of Advanced Study, University of London 2016)

Masutti A and Tomasello F, 'The Challenge of Security' in *International regulation of non-military drones* (Edward Elgar 2018)

Masutti A, 'Single European Sky – a Possible Regulatory Framework for System Wide Information Management (SWIM)' (2011) 36 Air and Space Law 275

Maurice P, 'Safety and safety promotion: definitions for operational developments' (2001) 8 Injury Control and Safety Promotion 238 <https://pdfs.semanticscholar.org/363d/81922697730c2ab49cca4f903d03ffe352b3.pdf>

Maxwell W and Bourreau M, 'Technology Neutrality in Internet, Telecoms and Data Protection Regulation' (2015) Computer and Telecommunications Law Review 1

McCarthy M and others, 'Access to In-Vehicle Data and Resources' (2017) Publications Office of the European Union

McCrudden C, Prechal S, 'The Concepts of Equality and Non-Discrimination in Europe: A Practical Approach' (2009) European Network of Legal Experts in the Field of Gender Equality 21

Meijer A and Wessels M, 'Predictive Policing: Review of Benefits and Drawbacks' [2019] International Journal of Public Administration 1

Midelieva L, 'The Elusive Cause and the Extensive Effect of the Principle of Supremacy of EU Law' (2017) 7 Southampton Student Law Review 21

Mijalkovic S and Blagojevic D, 'The Basis of National Security in International Law' [2014] Nauka, bezbednost, policija 49

Milakis D, Arem B van and Wee B van, 'Policy and Society Related Implications of Automated Driving: A Review of Literature and Directions for Future Research' (2017) 21 Journal of Intelligent Transportation Systems 324

Missiroli A, 'European Security Policy: The Challenge of Coherence' (2001) European Foreign Affairs Review 6(2)

Missiroli A, 'The Dark Side of the Web: Cyber as a Threat' (2019) 24(2) European Foreign Affairs Review 135

Mitrakas A, 'The Emerging EU Framework on Cybersecurity Certification' (2018) 42(7) Datenschutz und Datensicherheit – DuD 411

Mittelstadt B, 'From Individual to Group Privacy in Big Data Analytics' (2017) 30 Philosophy & Technology 475

Mourby M and others, 'Are 'pseudonymised' data always personal data? Implications of the GDPR for administrative data research in the UK' (2018) 34 Computer Law & Security Review 222

Murdoch J and Roche R, *The European Convention on Human Rights and Policing: A handbook for police officers and other law enforcement officials* (Council of Europe Publishing, 2013) 154

Murrill BJ, 'The "National Security Exception" and the World Trade Organization' (2018) <https://fas.org/sgp/crs/row/LSB10223.pdf>

National Institute of Standards and Technology (NIST), 'Security and Privacy Controls for Federal Information Systems and Organizations' (2013) NIST Special Publication 800–53

National Research Council, *Computers at Risk: Safe Computing in the Information Age* (The National Academic Press 1991)

Naudts L, 'How Machine Learning Generates Unfair Inequalities and How Data Protection Instruments May Help in Mitigating Them', in Ronald Leenes and others (eds) in, Data Protection and Privacy: The Internet of Bodies (Hart Publishing 2019) ch 3

Negreiro M, 'EU legislation in process – on ENISA and a new Cybersecurity Act' (3rd edition, 2019) <www.europarl.europa.eu/RegData/etudes/BRIE/2017/614643/EPRS_BRI(2017)614643_EN.pdf>

Newbery S and Dehghantanha A, 'Torture-Free Cyberspace – a Human Right' (2017) 2017 Computer Fraud & Security 14

Nicklas J, Mamrot M, Winzer P, Lichte D, Marchlewitz S, Wolf K, 'Use case based approach for an integrated consideration of safety and security aspects for smart home applications' (2016) 11th System of Systems Engineering Conference (SoSE) Kongsberg <https://ieeexplore.ieee.org/stamp/stamp.jsp?tp=&arnumber=7542908>

Nigam V, Pretschner A, Ruess H, 'Model-Based Safety and Security Engineering' (2019) ArXiv <https://arxiv.org/pdf/1810.04866.pdf>

Nuotio K, 'Security and Criminal Law: A Difficult Relationship' [2013] Law and Security in Europe: Reconsidering the Security Constitution 197

Nutall S, *European Foreign Policy* (2000), New York (N.Y.): Oxford UP 25

Nyman J, 'What is the value of security? Contextualising the negative/positive debate' (2016) 42 Review of International Studies <https://doi.org/10.1017/S0260210516000140>

O'Connell R, 'Cinderella Comes to the Ball: Art 14 and the Right to Non-Discrimination in the ECHR' (2009) 29 Legal Studies 211

Olsen M, Schneier B and Zittrain J, 'Don't Panic: Making Progress on the "Going Dark" Debate' (The Berkman Centre for Internet & Society 2016)

Olson M, *The Logic of Collective Action: Public Goods and the Theory of Groups* (revised edition, Harvard University Press 1971)

Organisation for Economic Cooperation and Development, 'OECD Guidelines for Cryptography Policy – OECD' (OECD.org) <https://www.oecd.org/sti/ieconomy/guidelinesforcryptographypolicy.htm>

Orji UJ, 'Regionalizing Data Protection Law: A Discourse on the Status and Implementation of the ECOWAS Data Protection Act' (2017) 7 International Data Privacy Law 179

Oscarson P, 'Information Security Fundamentals: Graphical Conceptualisations for Understanding' in Irvine C and Armstrong H (eds), *Security Education and*

Critical Infrastructures (IFIP – The International Federation for Information Processing, Springer 2003)
Palmerini E and others, 'RoboLaw: Towards a European Framework for Robotics Regulation' (2016) 86 Robotics and Autonomous Systems 78
Parliamentary Office of Science and Technology (Houses of Parliament), 'Cyber Security of UK Infrastructure (POSTNOTE)' <https://researchbriefings.parliament.uk/ResearchBriefing/Summary/POST-PN-0554>
Pellet A, 'Comments in Response to Christine Chinkin and in Defense of Jus Cogens as the Best Bastion against the Excesses of Fragmentation' [2006] Finnish Yearbook of International Law 83
Peltier J, 'Threats to Information Security' in Peltier TR (ed), *Information Security Fundamentals* (2nd edn, CRC Press 2014)
Peroni L and Timmer A, 'Vulnerable Groups: The Promise of an Emerging Concept in European Human Rights Convention Law' (2013) 11 International Journal of Constitutional Law 1056
Petit J, 'Automated Vehicles Cybersecurity: Summary AVS'17 and Stakeholder Analysis', *Road Vehicle Automation 5* (Springer, Cham 2019)
Porcedda MG, 'Patching the patchwork: appraising the EU regulatory framework on cyber security breaches' (2018) 34 Computer Law & Security Review 5
Prakken H, 'On the Problem of Making Autonomous Vehicles Conform to Traffic Law' (2017) 25 Artificial Intelligence and Law 341
Preneel B, 'Cryptographic Hash Functions: Theory and Practice' in Cong G and Gupta K (eds), *Progress in Cryptology – IndoCrypt 2010* (Springer Berlin 2010)
Pursiainen C, 'The Challenges for European Critical Infrastructure Protection' (2009) 31 Journal of European Integration 721
Purtova N, 'The law of everything. Broad concept of personal data and future of EU data protection law' (2018) 10 Law, Innovation and Technology 40
Qadir S and Quadri SMK, 'Information Availability: An Insight into the Most Important Attribute of Information Security' (2016) Journal of Information Security 7
Quintel T, 'European Union · Article 29 Data Protection Working Party Opinion on the Law Enforcement Directive' (2018) 4 European Data Protection Law Review 104
Raggad, B, *Information Security Management: Concepts and Practice* (1st edn, CRC Press 2010)
Ralph P and Wand Y, 'A Proposal for a Formal Definition of the Design Concept' in Kalle Lyytinen and others (eds), *Design Requirements Engineering: A Ten-Year Perspective* (Springer Berlin Heidelberg 2009)
Rao UH and Nayak U, 'Introduction to Security' in Umesh Hodeghatta Rao and Umesha Nayak (eds), *The InfoSec Handbook: An Introduction to Information Security* (Apress 2014) <https://doi.org/10.1007/978-1-4302-6383-8_1>
Ratajczyk MA, 'Regional Aviation Safety Organisations : Enhancing Air Transport Safety through Regional Cooperation' (Dissertatie, Leiden University 2014) <https://openaccess.leidenuniv.nl/handle/1887/29759> Ratcliffe J, *Intelligence-Led Policing* (2nd edition, Routledge 2016)
Regional AVSEC Ministerial Conference, 'Dubai Declaration on Cyber Security in Civil Aviation: Reasons and Prospect' (GASeP: The Roadmap to Foster Aviation Security

in Africa and the Middle East, Sharm El Sheikh Egypt, 22 August 2017) <https://www.icao.int/Meetings/AVSEC-RMC-Egypt/Documents/PPTs/session3-6.pdf>

Renaud K and others, 'Is the Responsibilization of the Cyber Security Risk Reasonable and Judicious?' ScienceDirect (2018) 78 Computer & Security 198

Republic of Estonia, 'Notification Form for Electronic Identity Scheme under Article 9 (5) of Regulation (EU) No. 910/2014' (2018)

Rid T, Buchanan B, 'Attributing Cyber Attacks' (2015) Vol. 3 Journal of Strategic Studies 1–2, 4–37 <https://ridt.co/d/rid-buchanan-attributing-cyber-attacks.pdf>

Ridgeway G, 'Policing in the Era of Big Data' (2018) 1 Annual Review of Criminology 401

Rigterink AS, 'Does Security Imply Safety? On The (Lack of) Correlation Between Different Aspects of Security' (2015) 4 Stability: International Journal of Security & Development 39 <http://doi.org/10.5334/sta.fw>

Robert Kolb, 'Effects of Jus Cogens' in *Peremptory International Law – Jus Cogens : A General Inventory* (Hart Publishing 2015)

Roe M, 'Who's Driving That Car?: An Analysis of Regulatory and Potential Liability Frameworks for Driverless Cars' (2019) 60 Boston College Law Review 317

Romm JJ, *Defining National Security: The Nonmilitary Aspects* (Council on Foreign Relations Press 1993)

Rose-Ackerman S and Billa B, 'Treaties and National Security' (2008) reprinted in Yale Law School Faculty Scholarship Series <https://digitalcommons.law.yale.edu/fss_papers/595/>

Rossi Copparoni & Partners, 'Approvato Il Decreto Di Attuazione Della Direttiva UE in Materia Di Trattamento Dei Dati Personali Da Parte Delle Autorità Competenti' (8 June 2018) <www.rpcstudiolegale.it/2018/06/08/approvato-il-decreto-di-attuazione-della-direttiva-ue-in-materia-di-trattamento-dei-dati-personali-da-parte-delle-autorita-competenti/>

Rotenberg M, Schwartz PM and Solove DJ, *Information Privacy Law* (2nd ed., Aspen 2006)

Russel M, 'EU sanctions: A key foreign and security policy instrument', (European Parliamentary Research, 2018) <www.europarl.europa.eu/thinktank/en/document.html?reference=EPRS_BRI%282018%29621870>

Sametinger J, Rozenblit J, Lysecky R, Ott P, 'Security Challenges for Medical Devices' 2015 58 Communications of the ACM <https://www.se.jku.at/wp-content/uploads/2015/03/TR-SE-15.03.pdf>

Schellekens M, 'Car Hacking: Navigating the Regulatory Landscape' (2016) 32 Computer Law & Security Review 307

Schellekens M, 'Self-Driving Cars and the Chilling Effect of Liability Law' (2015) 31 Computer Law & Security Review 506

Schmitt MN (ed), *Tallinn Manual 2.0 on the International Law Applicable to Cyber Operations: Prepared by the International Groups of Experts at the Invitation of the NATO Cooperative Cyber Defence Centre of Excellence* (2nd edn, Cambridge University Press 2017)

Schneier B, Seidel K and Vijayakumar S, 'A Worldwide Survey of Encryption Products' (Social Science Research Network 2016) SSRN Scholarly Paper <https://papers.ssrn.com/abstract=2731160>

Scholl M and others, 'An Introductory Resource Guide for Implementing the Health Insurance Portability and Accountability Act (HIPAA) Security Rule' (National institute of standards and technology 2008) <https://csrc.nist.gov/publications/detail/sp/800-66/rev-1/final>

Schreurs W and others, 'Cogitas, Ergo Sum. The Role of Data Protection Law and Non-Discrimination Law in Group Profiling in the Private Sector', in Mireille Hildebrandt and Serge Gutwirth (eds) *Profiling the European citizen* (Springer 2008) Ch 13

Schubert F, 'The Technical Defragmentation of Air Navigation Services – The Legal Challenges of Virtualisation' [2013] From Lowlands to High Skies: A Multilevel Jurisdictional Approach Towards Air law 43

Schutter OD, 'Three Models of Equality and European Anti-Discrimination Law' (2006) Vol.57 Northern Ireland Legal Quarterly 1

Seema S and others, 'A Review on Various Software Development Life Cycle (SDLC) Models' (2014) 3 International Journal of Research in Computer and Communication Technology 2320

Serpanos D and Wolf M, *Internet-of-Things (IoT) Systems – Architectures, Algorithms, Methodologies* (Springer 2018)

Servent AR, 'Protecting or Processing? Recasting EU Data Protection Norms' in Schünemann WJ and others (eds), *Privacy, Data Protection and Cybersecurity in Europe* (Springer 2017)

SESAR Joint Undertaking, 'A Proposal for the Future Architecture of the European Airspace' (Publications Office of the European Union 2019) <https://www.sesarju.eu/sites/default/files/documents/reports/Future%20Airspace%20Architecture%20Proposal.pdf>

Setola R, Luiijf E and Theocharidou M, 'Critical Infrastructure, Protection and Resilience', in Roberto Setola and others (eds), *Managing the Complexity of Critical Infrastructures* (Springer Open 2016)

Shackelford SJ, Proia AA, Martell B, Craig AN, 'Toward a Global Cybersecurity Standard of Care?: Exploring the Implications of the 2014 NIST Cybersecurity Framework on Shaping Reasonable National and International Cybersecurity Practices' (2015) 50 Texas International Law Journal

Shackelford SJ, Russell S and Kuehn A, 'Unpacking the International Law on Cybersecurity Due Diligence: Lessons from the Public and Private Sectors' (2016) 17 Chicago Journal of International Law; Chicago 1

Shahzad K, 'Cloud Robotics and Autonomous Vehicles' [2016] Autonomous Vehicle section 3.4

Shamir R, 'The age of responsibilization: on market-embedded morality' (2008) 37 Economy and Society 1

Shaw MN, *International Law* (Eighth Edition, Cambridge University Press 2017)

Simma B, 'From Bilateralism to Community Interest in International Law (Volume 250)' [1994] Collected Courses of the Hague Academy of International Law <https://referenceworks.brillonline.com/entries/the-hague-academy-collected-courses/from-bilateralism-to-community-interest-in-internationallaw-volume-250-ej.9789041104199.217_384>

Simmons GJ, *Contemporary Cryptology: The Science of Information Integrity* (IEEE Press 1994)
Sion L and others, 'An Architectural View for Data Protection by Design' (2019) IEEE
Skeete J-P, 'Level 5 Autonomy: The New Face of Disruption in Road Transport' (2018) 134 Technological Forecasting and Social Change 22
Sliwinski KF, 'Moving beyond the European Union's Weakness as a Cyber-Security Agent' (2014) 35 Contemporary Security Policy 468
Smedinghoff TJ, 'Solving the Legal Challenges of Trustworthy Online Identity' (2012) 28 Computer Law & Security Review 532
Smith B, 'Automated Driving and Product Liability' (2017) 2017 Michigan State Law Review 1
Smith BW, 'Regulation and the Risk of Inaction' in Markus Maurer and others (eds), *Autonomous Driving: Technical, Legal and Social Aspects* (Springer Berlin Heidelberg 2016)
Spindler G and Schmechel P, 'Personal Data and Encryption in the European General Data Protection Regulation' (2016) 7 Journal of Intellectual Property, Information Technology and Electronic Commerce Law [i]
Spindler G, ‚IT-Sicherheitsgesetz Und Zivilrechtliche Haftung – Auswirkungen Des IT-Sicherheitsgesetzes Im Zusammenspiel Mit Der Endgültigen EU-NIS-Richtlinie Auf Die Zivilrechtliche Haftung' (2016) 5 Computer und Recht 297
Sreejith SG, 'Legality of the Gulf Ban on Qatari Flights: State Sovereignty at Crossroads' (2018) 43 Air and Space Law 191
Stadler R, Brenner W and Hermann A, 'Evolutions and Revolutions in Mobility', *Autonomous Driving: How the Driverless Revolution will Change the World* (Emerald Publishing Limited 2018)
Stalla-Bourdillon S, 'Privacy Versus Security ... Are We Done Yet?' in Sophie Stalla-Bourdillon, Joshua Phillips, Mark D. Ryan (eds), *Privacy vs. Security* (Springer London, Springer Briefs in Cybersecurity 2014) 69
Stancel IN and Surugiu MC, 'Fleet Management System for Truck Platoons – Generating an Optimum Route in Terms of Fuel Consumption' (2017) 181 Procedia Engineering 861
Stilgoe J, 'Machine Learning, Social Learning and the Governance of Self-Driving Cars' (2018) 48 Social Studies of Science 25
Suominen K, 'Fueling Digital Trade in Mercosur: A Regulatory Roadmap' (Inter-American Development Bank 2018) <https://publications.iadb.org/handle/11319/9339>
Swire P and Ahmad K, 'Encryption and Globalization' (2011) 23 Columbia Science and Technology Law Review
Taeihagh A and Lim HSM, 'Governing Autonomous Vehicles: Emerging Responses for Safety, Liability, Privacy, Cybersecurity, and Industry Risks' (2019) 39 Transport Reviews 103
Takano A, 'Due Diligence Obligations and Transboundary Environmental Harm: Cybersecurity Applications' (2018) 7 Laws 36
Tene O and Polonetsky J, 'Privacy in the Age of Big Data, A Time for Big Decision' [2012] Stanford Law Review <https://www.stanfordlawreview.org/online/privacy-paradox-privacy-and-big-data/>

Thompson DF, 'Responsibility for Failures of Government: The Problem of Many Hands' (2014) 44 The American Review of Public Administration 259

Thomson G, *Needs* (Routledge and Kegan Paul 1988) 77–89, 98–107, 121–122, 125–128

Timmer A, 'Toward an Anti-Stereotyping Approach for the European Court of Human Rights' (2011) 11 Human Rights Law Review 707

Timmer A, Strengthening the Equality Analysis of the European Court of Human Rights: The Potential of the Concepts of Stereotyping and Vulnerability (2014)

Tipton H and Krause M, *Information Security Management Handbook* (vol 2, 6th edn, CRC Press 2009)

Tomuschat C, 'The Security Council and Jus Cogens' in Enzo Cannizzaro (ed), *The present and future of jus cogens* (Sapienza università editrice 2015)

Tostensen A, Bull B, 'Are Smart Sanctions Feasible?' (2002) Vol. 54 World Politics 375

Tran Dai C and Gomez MA, 'Challenges and Opportunities for Cyber Norms in ASEAN' (2018) 3 Journal of Cyber Policy 217

Trauner F, 'The Internal-External Security Nexus: More Coherence Under Lisbon?' [2011] SSRN Electronic Journal <www.ssrn.com/abstract=1885322>

Troncoso C and others, 'PRIPARE Deliverable 5.3 – Recommendations and Research Agenda' (2015) <http://pripareproject.eu/wp-content/uploads/2013/11/PRIPARE_Deliverable_D5.3_v1.0.pdf>

Trope RL and Smedinghoff TJ, 'Why Smart Car Safety Depends on Cybersecurity' (2018) 14 Scitech Lawyer 8

Tropina T and Callanan C, *Self- and Co-Regulation in Cybercrime, Cybersecurity and National Security* (Springer International Publishing 2015)

Tsagourias N, 'The Legal Status of Cyberspace' in *Research Handbook on International Law and Cyberspace* (Edward Elgar Publishing 2015)

Tsormpatzoudi P, Berendt B and Coudert F, 'Privacy by Design: From Research and Policy to Practice – the Challenge of Multi-Disciplinarity', in Preneel B and Ikonomou D (eds), *Privacy Technologies and Policy* (Springer 2016)

Turvey B, *Criminal Profiling: An Introduction to Behavioral Evidence Analysis* (4th edn, Oxford: Academic 2011)

United Nations (UN), 'The Protection of Critical Infrastructures against Terrorist Attacks: Compendium of Good Practices' (*United Nations*, 2018) <https://www.un.org/sc/ctc/wp-content/uploads/2019/01/Compendium_of_Good_Practices_Compressed.pdf>

United Nations Conference on Trade and Development, 'Building Confidence – Electronic Commerce and Development' (*UNCTAD* 2000) <https://unctad.org/en/pages/PublicationArchive.aspx?publicationid=1532>

United Nations, 'Promoting Confidence in Electronic Commerce: Legal Issues on International Use of Electronic Authentication and Signature Methods' (United Nations 2009) <www.uncitral.org/pdf/english/texts/electcom/08-55698_Ebook.pdf>

Van Aaken A and Wildhaber I, 'State Liability and Critical Infrastructure: A Comparative and Functional Analysis' (2015) 6 European Journal of Risk Regulation 244

Van Alsenoy B, 'Regulating Data Protection – The Allocation of Responsibility and Risk among Actors Involved in Personal Data Processing' (PhD dissertation, KU Leuven 2016)

Van Alsenoy B, *Data protection in the EU: roles, responsibilities and liability* (Cambridge: Intersentia, 2019).

Van Asselt MBA, Vos E and Wildhaber I, 'Some Reflections on EU Governance of Critical Infrastructure Risks' (2015) 6 European Journal of Risk Regulation 185

Van Hoboken J and Schulz W, 'Human Rights and Encryption – UNESCO Digital Library' (2016) <https://unesdoc.unesco.org/ark:/48223/pf0000246527>

Van Hoboken JVJ, 'Privacy and Security in the Cloud: Some Realism about Technical Solutions to Transnational Surveillance in the Post-Snowden Era Symposium: Who's Governing Privacy: Regulation and Protection in a Digital Era' (2013) 66 Maine Law Review 487

Vedder A and Naudts L, 'Accountability for the Use of Algorithms in a Big Data Environment' (2017) 31 International Review of Law, Computers & Technology 206

Vedder A, 'Inclusive Regulation, Inclusive Design and Technology Adoption' in E Palmerini and E Stradella (eds), *Law and Technology: The Challenge of Regulating Technological Development* (Pisa University Press 2013) 205

Vedder A, 'KDD: The Challenge to Individualism' (1999) 1 Ethics and Information Technology 275

Vellinga NE, 'From the Testing to the Deployment of Self-Driving Cars: Legal Challenges to Policymakers on the Road Ahead' (2017) 33 Computer Law & Security Review 847

Voigt P and von dem Bussche A, 'Organisational Requirements' in Paul Voigt and Axel von dem Bussche (eds), *The EU General Data Protection Regulation (GDPR): A Practical Guide* (Springer International Publishing 2017) <https://doi.org/10.1007/978-3-319-57959-7_3>

Voigt P and von dem Bussche A, *The EU General Data Protection Regulation (GDPR). A Practical Guide* (Springer International Publishing AG 2017)

Von Solms R and Van Niekerk J, 'From information security to cyber security' (2013) Computers & Security 38

Voulon M, 'Digitalisering En Het Nederlands Burgerlijk Wetboek' (2018) 3 Tijdschrift voor Privaatrecht 969

Wachter S, 'Affinity Profiling and Discrimination by Association in Online Behavioural Advertising' (SSRN Scholarly Paper ID 3388639, Social Science Research Network 2019) <https://papers.ssrn.com/abstract=3388639>

Waldron J, 'Safety and Security' (2006) 85 Nebraska Law Review 454

Walker Smith B, 'How Governments Can Promote Automated Driving' (2017) 47 New Mexico Law Review 99

Wall DS, 'Enemies within: Redefining the Insider Threat in Organizational Security Policy' (2013) 26 Security Journal 107

Walt SM, 'Realism and Security' *Oxford Research Encyclopedia of International Studies* (2010) <https://oxfordre.com/internationalstudies/view/10.1093/acrefore/9780190846626.001.0001/acrefore-9780190846626-e-286>

Weatherill S, 'Distinctive Identity Claims, Article 4(2) TEU (and a Fleetingly Sad Nod to Brexit) Editorial Note' (2016) 12 Croatian Yearbook of European Law and Policy VII

Wet ED, 'The International Constitutional Order' (2006) 55 International & Comparative Law Quarterly 51

Whitman ME and Mattord HJ, *Principles of Information Security* (4th edn, Course Technology Press 2011)

Whitson JR and Haggerty KD, 'Identity Theft and the Care of the Virtual Self' (2008) 37 Economy and Society 572

Wiater P, 'On the Notion of "Partnership" in Critical Infrastructure Protection' (2015) 6 European Journal of Risk Regulation 255

Widmer P, *Unification of Tort Law: Fault* (Kluwer 2015)

Wiggins D, *Needs, values, truth. Essays in the philosophy of value* (Aristotelian Society series vol. 6, Blackwell 1987) 48-

Wong R, 'The Data Protection Directive 95/46/EC: Idealisms and Realisms' (2012) 26 International Review of Law Computers & Technology 2

Zagor M, 'Elementary Considerations of Humanity' in Karine Bannelier' in Christakis T and Heathcote S (eds), *The ICJ and the Evolution of International Law: The Enduring Impact of the Corfu Channel Case* (Routledge 2012)

Zarsky TZ and Andrade NNG de, 'Regulating Electronic Identity Intermediaries: The Soft EID Conundrum' (2013) 74 Ohio St. LJ 1335

Zarsky TZ, 'Understanding Discrimination in the Scored Society' (2014) 89 Wash. L. Rev. 1375

Zerlang J, 'GDPR: A Milestone in Convergence for Cyber-security and Compliance' (2017) 6 Network Security 8

Zotos K and Litke A, 'Cryptography and Encryption' [2005] arXiv:math/0510057 <http://arxiv.org/abs/math/0510057>

Zuiderveen-Borgesius F, 'Discrimination, Artificial Intelligence, and Algorithmic Decision-Making' (Council of Europe, 2018) 51 <https://rm.coe.int/discrimination-artificial-intelligence-and-algorithmic-decision-making/1680925d73>

Zuiderveen-Borgesius FJ and Steenbruggen W, 'The Right to Communications Confidentiality in Europe: Protecting Privacy, Freedom of Expression, and Trust' (2019) 20 Theoretical Inquiries in Law 291

KU LEUVEN CENTRE FOR IT & IP LAW

The KU Leuven Centre for IT & IP Law Series brings together the results of research activities of the Centre for IT & IP Law. The central research themes of the series concern the legal and ethical aspects of information technology, innovation and intellectual property.

Each book in the series focuses on the essential developments in the current legal framework, necessitated by the rapid evolution of technology in various fields, such as government, media, health care, informatics, digital economy, banking, transport and culture. The research is characterised by an interdisciplinary approach, constantly cross-fertilising legal, technical, economic, ethical and socio-cultural perspectives.

Books are published in English, Dutch and/or French.

Recently published in this series:

1. Rán TRYGVADÓTTIR, *European Libraries and the Internet: Copyright and Extended Collective Licences*, 2018.
2. Niels VANDEZANDE, *Virtual Currencies*, 2018.
3. Aleksandra KUCZERAWY, *Intermediary Liability and Freedom of Expression in the EU: From Concepts to Safeguards*, 2018.
4. Letizia PAOLI, Jonas VISSCHERS Cedric VERSTRAETE, Elke VAN HELLEMONT, *The Impact of Cybercrime on Belgian Businesses*, 2019.
5. Niels VANDEZANDE, *When An Original Is Not Original. The Originality Requirement in Belgian Law*, 2019.
6. Brendan VAN ALSENOY, *Data Protection Law in the EU: Roles, Responsibilities and Liability*, 2019.
7. Anton VEDDER, Jessica SCHROERS, Charlotte DUCUING and Peggy VALCKE (eds.), *Security and Law. Legal and Ethical Aspects of Public Security, Cyber Security and Critical Infrastructure Security*, 2019.
8. Marie-Christine JANSSENS, *Handboek Merkenrecht*, 2019.
9. Centre for IT and IP Law, *Rethinking IT and IP Law. Celebrating 30 Years CiTiP*, 2019.

www.ingramcontent.com/pod-product-compliance
Ingram Content Group UK Ltd.
Pitfield, Milton Keynes, MK11 3LW, UK
UKHW051846100926
8556IPUK00005B/482